Acoustic Phonetics

Current Studies in Linguistics
Samuel Jay Keyser, general editor

Acoustic Phonetics

Kenneth N. Stevens

The MIT Press
Cambridge, Massachusetts
London, England

This book was set in Palatino on the Monotype "Prism Plus" PostScript Imagesetter by Asco Trade Typesetting Ltd., Hong Kong, and was printed and bound in the United States of America.

Library of Congress Cataloging-in-Publication Data

Stevens, Kenneth N., 1924–
    Acoustic phonetics / Kenneth N. Stevens
        p.   cm. — (Current studies in linguistics ; 30)
    Includes bibliographical references (p.) and index.
    ISBN 0-262-19404-X (hc : alk. paper)
    1. Phonetics, Acoustic. I. Title. II. Series: Current studies in linguistics series ; 30.
    P221.5.S74   1998
    414'.8—dc21   97-46999
                                                         CIP

Contents

Preface

The application of quantitative modeling methods to the acoustics of speech sound production underwent a major advance with the work of Gunnar Fant. His book, *Acoustic Theory of Speech Production*, together with his continuing work and that of his students and colleagues in the 1960s, 1970s, and 1980s, has been a major stimulus to raising the field of acoustic phonetics toward the level of a quantitative science. This book attempts to build on this earlier work of Fant and others over these decades.

The aim of the book is to present a theory of speech sound generation in the human vocal system. The acoustic aspects of this theory are grounded in a representation of speech sound production as the creation of sound sources in the vocal tract and the filtering of these sources by the vocal tract airways. The sources can be of various kinds, including the quasi-periodic laryngeal source, noise due to turbulent airflow, and transient sounds. Since the articulators move with time, the sound sources and the filtering also change with time. Examination of the time-varying sources and filtering leads to the observation that some aspects of the transformation from articulation to sound are categorial. That is, the types of sound sources and the filtering of these sources can be organized into classes. These classes are closely related to the discrete linguistic categories or features that describe how words appear to be stored in the memory of a speaker or listener. The theme of this book is to explore these relations between the discrete linguistic features and their articulatory and acoustic manifestations.

The book begins with a review of the anatomy of the speech production system, and a discussion of some principles relating airflows and pressures in the vocal tract. The next four chapters describe mechanisms of sound source generation in the vocal tract, present theories of the vocal tract as an acoustic resonator excited by these sources, review some principles of auditory psychophysics and auditory physiology as they may be relevant to auditory processing of speech, and present an introduction to phonological representations. With these five chapters as background, the remaining chapters are devoted to a detailed examination of the vowels (chapter 6), the consonants (chapters 7 to 9), and some examples of how speech sounds are influenced by context (chapter 10).

Little attention is given to the description and modeling of the production of sounds in languages other than English. The aim is not to be complete, even for the sounds of English, but rather to present an approach to modeling the production of speech sounds in general. An attempt is made to show that, when reasonable assumptions are made about the physiological parameters involved in producing a sound sequence, acoustic theory can make predictions about the sound pattern, and these predictions agree well with the measured pattern. A goal for the future is to extend this modeling effort to a wider variety of speech events across languages, and to examine not only the broad acoustic characteristics of different sounds but also their variability across speakers and across contexts.

The book is intended to be useful to speech scientists, speech pathologists, linguists with an interest in phonetics and phonology, psychologists who work in areas related to speech perception and speech production, and engineers who are concerned with speech processing applications. This book has evolved from notes for a graduate course in Speech Communication at the Massachusetts Institute of Technology. The course is taken by students in engineering and in a graduate program in Speech and Hearing Sciences. Some students in linguistics, cognitive sciences, and medical engineering also attend the course.

The writing of this book has benefited from the advice, guidance, and research collaboration of many people. One of these was the late Dennis Klatt, whose ideas have influenced a generation of speech researchers, particularly those concerned with speech synthesis and speech perception. Others were Sheila Blumstein, Gunnar Fant, Morris Halle, Arthur House, Jay Keyser, Peter Ladefoged, Sharon Manuel, and Joe Perkell. Interaction with these colleagues was always a pleasure and a learning experience. Special thanks go to Peter Ladefoged for his comments on the entire manuscript, and for his encouragement. This writing project was also helped significantly by comments and insights of many students over the past decade or two.

Several people were involved in the details of preparing the manuscript and the figures, and their contributions are acknowledged with thanks. I am especially grateful for the help of Arlene Wint in preparing many drafts of the class notes that evolved into this manuscript. I thank Marie Southwick for her role at an earlier stage of the writing. The help of Corine Bickley and Mark Hasegawa-Johnson in performing the calculations for some of the figures is gratefully acknowledged. Assistance in checking the manuscript was provided by Marilyn Chen, Jeung-Yoon Choi, Aaron Maldonado, and Arlene Wint. The figures were the expert work of Bob Priest and Rob Kassel. Many of the figures containing spectrograms and spectra were prepared using software developed by Dennis Klatt.

Much of the research described in the book was supported by grants from the National Institutes of Health and by funds from the C. J. LeBel Foundation.

Acoustic Phonetics

1 Anatomy and Physiology of Speech Production

1.1 COMPONENTS OF THE SPEECH PRODUCTION SYSTEM

For the purpose of discussing sound generation, it is convenient to divide the speech production system into three parts: (1) the system below the larynx, (2) the larynx and its surrounding structures, and (3) the structures and the airways above the larynx. These components of the speech production system are illustrated schematically in figure 1.1. During speech production, a constriction is usually formed in the airways at the level of the vocal folds, located within the larynx. This constricted region, which is just a few millimeters long, is called the glottis, and it forms the dividing line between the subglottal system and the supraglottal system. For the production of most speech sounds, the subglottal system provides the energy in the airflow, and the laryngeal and supraglottal structures are responsible for the modulation of the airflow to produce audible sound. As we shall see, the energy for some sounds is obtained by trapping air within an enclosed space above the larynx, and expanding or contracting the volume of this space.

In the following sections we review some of the main features of the structures that are used for speech production. A more comprehensive treatment of the anatomy and physiology of speech production can be found in a number of books, including Dickson and Maue-Dickson (1982), Zemlin (1988), and others.

1.1.1 The Subglottal System

Immediately below the glottis the airway consists of a single tube, the trachea, which has a cross-sectional area of about 2.5 cm^2 and a length in the range of 10 to 12 cm for an adult speaker. The trachea branches into two bronchi, each with about one-half the cross-sectional area of the trachea, and these bronchi in turn bifurcate into a series of successively smaller airways. These airways ultimately terminate in alveolar sacs which lie within the lungs. The lungs are contained within the chest cavity, and the lung volume can be caused to expand and contract by increasing or decreasing the volume of the chest cavity. The vital capacity is the maximum range of lung

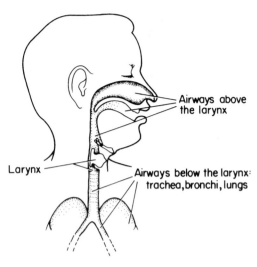

Figure 1.1 Schematic representation of the three components of the speech production system.

volumes available to an individual, from the inspiration of a deep breath to maximum expiration of air. The vital capacity is usually in the range of 3000 to 5000 cm³ in an adult. During normal breathing, the excursions in lung volume are much less than this—usually less than 1000 cm³.

The increases and decreases in lung volume are achieved by contracting several sets of muscles surrounding the chest cavity. The action of these muscles is shown schematically in figure 1.2. The principal muscles of inspiration are the diaphragm and the external intercostals, which fill the spaces between the ribs. Contraction of the muscles of the diaphragm causes a lowering of this domelike structure, whereas contraction of the external intercostal muscles causes the rib cage to be raised and expanded in diameter. When the lungs are expanded beyond their resting volume, expiratory forces are created in part by forces arising from elastic recoil of the lungs and surrounding structures. These expiratory forces can be augmented by contracting the internal intercostal muscles (which pull the ribs downward) or the abdominal muscles, either of which act to contract the lung volume. The manner in which chest wall movement and abdominal movement can contribute to changes in lung volume is illustrated in figure 1.2. During normal speech production, the lungs are expanded above their resting state (functional residual capacity), and the range of lung volumes that is used is in the range of 10 to 20 percent of vital capacity, or about 500 to 1000 cm³ in an adult (Hixon et al., 1973). Under these circumstances, the elastic recoil of the lungs always contributes an expiratory force, but this force may be augmented or reduced by the action of expiratory or inspiratory muscles. Situations can arise in speech in which a greater range of lung volume is used, and in which the lung volume decreases below functional residual capacity.

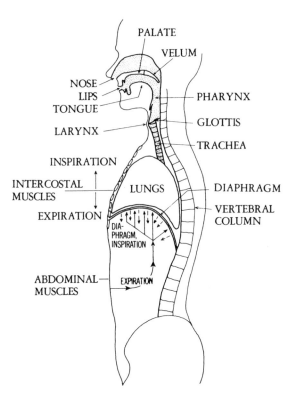

Figure 1.2 Schematic representation of the methods for controlling respiration. The principal inspiratory muscles are the external intercostals and the diaphragm. Expiratory muscles include the internal intercostals and the abdominal muscles. (From Pickett, 1980.)

The mechanical movements of the respiratory system are controlled, in effect, by forces that raise or lower the diaphragm, together with the abdominal mass below the diaphragm, and by forces that expand and contract the chest wall or thoracic cavity (Hixon et al., 1973, 1976; Hixon, 1987). These forces act to change the lung volume, and this change is reflected in an increase or decrease of pressure of the air within the lungs and, if there is not a complete closure in the airways above the lungs, a flow of air through the trachea and vocal tract. The decrease in lung volume during an utterance generally occurs through combined movement of the chest wall and the abdomen, although the relative contributions of these two components differ from one speaker to another (Hixon et al., 1973).

This mechanoaerodynamic system can be schematized as shown in figure 1.3. The two forces can be represented as pressure sources p_t for the thorax and p_d for the diaphragm. The thorax and the diaphragm (with abdominal contents) have their respective masses M_t and M_d, compliances C_t and C_d, and resistances R_t and R_d. The acoustic compliance of the lung volume is C_ℓ, and the effective acoustic resistance of the airways is R_a. The values of these physical properties vary greatly from one individual to another, but some

Anatomy and Physiology of Speech Production

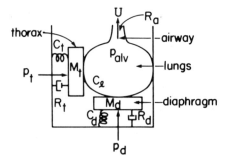

Figure 1.3 Schematization of the mechanoaerodynamic system for controlling respiratory pressure and flow. Two pressure sources are assumed: p_t for the thorax and p_d for the diaphragm. These forces give rise to an alveolar pressure p_{alv} and a flow U through the airways.

average values have been estimated (Van den Berg, 1960; Rothenberg, 1968). These estimates are as follows:

$C_t = 0.06 \, \text{cm}^5/\text{dyne}$

$M_t = 0.04 \, \text{gm/cm}^4$

$R_t = 4 \, \text{dyne-s/cm}^5$

$C_d = 0.09 \, \text{cm}^5/\text{dyne}$

$M_d = 0.2 \, \text{gm/cm}^4$

$R_d = 9 \, \text{dyne-s/cm}^5$

$C_\ell = 0.003 \, \text{cm}^5/\text{dyne}$

The resistance R_a is highly variable, depending on the configuration of the larynx and the structures above the glottis.

The units that are used refer to acoustic quantities of pressure, volume, and volume velocity. Thus, for example, a compliance of 0.06 cm^5/dyne for the thorax is interpreted to mean that a pressure of 1 dyne/cm^2 applied to the thorax surface causes a volume change of 0.06 cm^3. (If we use units that are more familiar to the respiratory physiologist, a pressure of about 1 cm H$_2$O causes a volume change of 0.06 liter.) An acoustic mass M_t of 0.04 gm/cm^4 implies that if a pressure of 1 dyne/cm^2 were applied to the mass of the thorax, the rate of change of volume velocity would be $1/0.04 = 25$ cm^3/s per second. The interaction of these various elements in terms of an equivalent circuit is discussed in section 1.4.

During the production of an utterance consisting of a few words, the pressure in the lungs is maintained at a value in the range of 5 to 10 cm H$_2$O for most persons speaking at a normal level. Within the utterance, the lung pressure may vary somewhat, depending on the emphasis to be placed on particular words in the utterance, but the variation in pressure is generally no more than about 30 percent from the maximum to the minimum (Ladefoged, 1968; Atkinson, 1973).

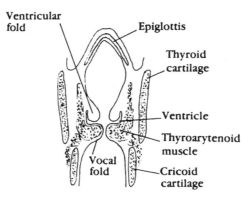

Figure 1.4 Coronal section through the larynx showing the vocal folds and the ventricular folds, together with the thyroarytenoid muscles and cartilages surrounding the folds. (From Dickson and Maue-Dickson, 1982.)

The surfaces of the structures that form the boundaries of the airways respond to low-frequency forces due to airflows and pressures in these airways and can influence the propagation of sound in the airways. The interaction between these surfaces and the time-varying aerodynamic and acoustic forces can be described conveniently in terms of the impedance of the surfaces. Direct measurements of the impedance of the various surfaces of the airways are difficult to make, but some approximate data have been reported. These data are described in section 1.1.3.7 and in chapter 3, where we discuss the acoustic behavior of the airways above and below the glottis.

1.1.2. The Larynx

1.1.2.1 Supporting Structures for the Vocal Folds The principal structures in the larynx that play a direct role in the production of speech are the vocal folds. These consist of two bands or cordlike segments of tissue of length 1.0 to 1.5 cm (for an adult) and of overall thickness of 2 to 3 mm. The vocal folds are arranged roughly parallel to each other in an anteroposterior direction. Immediately above and parallel to the vocal folds are paired secondary folds called the ventricular folds, as shown in coronal section in figure 1.4. The widening of the airway between the two sets of folds forms the laryngeal ventricle. The vocal and ventricular folds are supported at either end by a configuration of several cartilages. These supporting structures can be manipulated to adjust the positions of the vocal folds so that they are approximated (or adducted) or are separated (or abducted), leaving a space between the vocal folds. The supporting structures can also be displaced in a way that changes the vocal fold length, resulting in an increase or decrease in the tension of the folds, and a corresponding decrease or increase in the mass per unit length.

The supporting structures for the vocal folds are shown schematically in figure 1.5, as well as in the coronal section of figure 1.4. Immediately above

Anatomy and Physiology of Speech Production

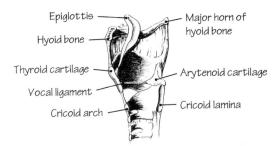

Epiglottis —
Hyoid bone —
Thyroid cartilage —
Vocal ligament
Cricoid arch —
Major horn of hyoid bone
Arytenoid cartilage
Cricoid lamina

Figure 1.5 Supporting structures surrounding the vocal folds. The vocal ligament is a part of the vocal fold which is connected anteriorly to the thyroid cartilage and posteriorly to the arytenoid cartilage. (From Dickson and Maue-Dickson, 1982.)

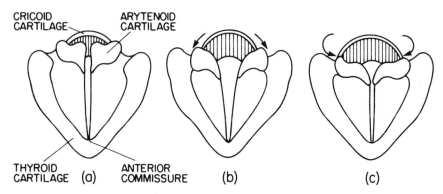

CRICOID CARTILAGE
ARYTENOID CARTILAGE
THYROID CARTILAGE (a)
ANTERIOR COMMISSURE (b)
(c)

Figure 1.6 Superior views illustrating (a) the approximate configuration of the arytenoid cartilages and vocal folds for phonation; and (b) the sliding motion and (c) rotary motion of the arytenoid cartilages on the cricoarytenoid joint. Configuration (b) leads to abduction of both the cartilaginous and membranous parts of the glottis, whereas only the cartilaginous part is abducted in (c).

the trachea there is a cartilaginous ring called the cricoid cartilage, with an internal diameter of about 1.9 cm for an adult female and 2.4 cm for an adult male, on average (Maue, 1971). The posterior portion of this ring (the cricoid lamina) has a greater vertical width than the anterior portion (the cricoid arch), as figure 1.5 indicates. Mounted on the upper edges of this cricoid cartilage on either side of the wider posterior end are two smaller cartilages shaped roughly like tetrahedrons, called the arytenoid cartilages. These cartilages articulate smoothly with the upper surfaces of the cricoid cartilage so that they can tilt from side to side and can also perform a sliding motion along these edges over a limited distance of about 2 mm. Some of the ways in which the arytenoid cartilages can rotate and translate are illustrated schematically in figure 1.6. The vocal folds are attached to the vocal processes at the front or anterior corners and medial margins of these arytenoid cartilages.

Lateral to the cricoid cartilage on either side is the thyroid cartilage, which consists of two winglike structures that are connected at the midsagittal plane at their anterior end, forming an angle of about 70 to 80 degrees, as

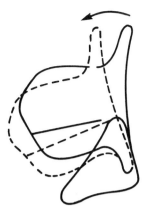

Figure 1.7 Midsagittal view showing the rocking motion of the thyroid cartilage in relation to the cricoid cartilage. The vocal folds are schematized by the solid and dashed straight lines.

shown in figures 1.5 and 1.6. This cartilage does not form a complete ring, but is open at the posterior end, and vertical projections extend upward and downward from the posterior end. The two lower projections near the inner posterior surfaces of the wings of the thyroid cartilage articulate with the cricoid cartilage to form the cricothyroid joint, as shown in figure 1.7, so that these two cartilages can rotate or rock relative to one another with these points forming the fulcrum. Figure 1.7 illustrates the rocking motion, but some horizontal translation of the thyroid cartilage in relation to the cricoid cartilage is also possible. The anterior ends of the vocal folds are attached to the anterior commissure at the inner surface of the angle of the thyroid cartilage. The rocking or translation motion of the thyroid cartilage in relation to the cricoid cartilage changes the length of the vocal folds. Downward movement of the anterior part of the thyroid cartilage in relation to the cricoid cartilage causes a stretching of the vocal folds. The relation between the relative movements of these cartilages and the length of the vocal folds can be estimated from the dimensions of the structures (cf. Fink, 1975; Fink and Demarest, 1978). The dimensions are such that a 1-mm downward movement of the anterior part of the thyroid cartilage causes the angle between the cricoid and thyroid cartilages to decrease by 2 to 3 degrees, given the dimensions of an adult larynx. This change in the tilt of the thyroid cartilage causes an increase in the length of the vocal folds of about 0.5 mm, or roughly a 3 percent increase in length. The variation in vocal fold length that occurs during speech production probably rarely exceeds 3 mm in an adult.

Several muscles are attached to the laryngeal cartilages, and perform the function of changing the positions of the vocal folds and their mechanical properties. These muscles are illustrated in figure 1.8. The cricothyroid muscle consists of a band of muscle fibers that connects the space between the cricoid and thyroid cartilages, as shown in the figure. Contraction of the anterior part of this muscle causes a rotation of the thyroid cartilage in relation to

Anatomy and Physiology of Speech Production

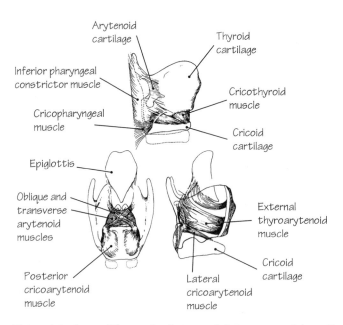

Figure 1.8 Some of the muscles that control the position and the stiffness of the vocal folds. (After Proctor, 1968.)

the cricoid cartilage, and, as noted above, gives rise to a lengthening and stretching of the vocal folds. Contraction of the posterior portion can also stretch the vocal folds, possibly through a translating motion of the thyroid cartilage in relation to the cricoid. It has been suggested (Fujisaki, 1992) that the translating motion in response to contraction of this more posterior muscle causes a change in vocal fold stiffness that is slower-acting than the change resulting from the anterior portion. (See section 1.3.2.) Two sets of muscles are connected to the lateral and posterior surfaces of the arytenoid cartilages, and perform the function of adducting and abducting the vocal folds at their posterior ends. One of these, the posterior cricoarytenoid muscle, forms a symmetrical pair of muscles, one on either side of the cricoid cartilage, and is connected between the posterior surface of the cricoid cartilage and the muscular process of the arytenoid cartilage at the lateral projection or corner of the cartilage. Contraction of this muscle pair causes an abduction of the vocal folds. It also tilts the arytenoid cartilages back and tends to lengthen the vocal folds and hence to increase their stiffness. The interarytenoid muscle is connected between the two arytenoid cartilages on their posterior surfaces. This muscle serves to bring the arytenoids and the posterior ends of the vocal folds together. The lateral cricoarytenoid muscle is attached between the muscular process of the arytenoid cartilage and the lateral surface of the cricoid cartilage. This muscle appears to serve as an additional adductor that complements the function of the interarytenoid muscle.

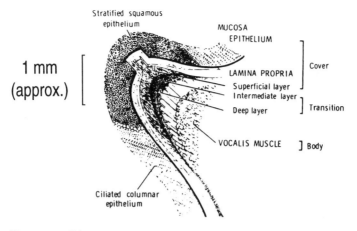

Figure 1.9 Schematic representation of a frontal section of a human vocal fold at the midpoint of the membranous portion. (From Hirano et al., 1981. The approximate scale at the left has been added.)

1.1.2.2 Properties of the Vocal Folds The vocal folds themselves form a rather complex layered structure. Lateral to the surfaces of each of the folds is the thyroarytenoid muscle, and this has a lateral component (the lateralis) and a medial component (the vocalis). Contraction of this muscle shortens and thickens the vocal folds. The lateralis also serves to adduct the vocal folds, including the ventricular folds.

Along the length of the vocal folds one can distinguish a membranous portion, with a length of about 1.5 cm for males and 1.0 cm for females, and a cartilaginous portion formed by the arytenoid cartilages at the posterior end, with a length of about 0.3 cm (Titze, 1989). A schematic representation of a lateral section through the membranous portion, shown in figure 1.9, gives the details of the layered structure of the vocal fold (Hirano, 1975). The thickness of the various layers varies with position along the vocal folds. The physical characteristics also vary from one layer to another, and these physical characteristics depend on the amount of stretching that is introduced by elongating the vocal folds.

The inner layer of the vocal fold consists of the vocalis muscle, which forms the main body of the fold. The diameter of this muscle is roughly 2 mm. The outer layers are mucosal, and the total thickness of these layers is about 1 mm, for both males and females (Hirano et al., 1983). The epithelium forms a thin outer surface, and the lamina propria constitutes an intermediate mucosal layer. The lamina propria in turn has a layered structure. The combination of the epithelium and the superficial layer of the lamina propria has been called the *cover* of the vocal fold. The inner layers of the lamina propria form a transition region between the cover and the muscle. The thickness of the cover is largest around the midpoint of the membranous vocal fold (average of about 0.4 mm for females and 0.5 mm for males), and is smallest at the two ends.

Anatomy and Physiology of Speech Production

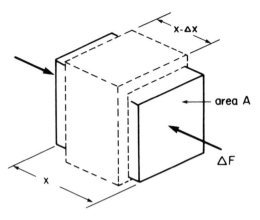

Figure 1.10 Illustrating how the Young's modulus $Y = (\Delta F/A)/(\Delta x/x)$ is defined in terms of the displacement Δx that occurs in response to a change in force ΔF.

The mechanical properties of the various layers have been measured for canine vocal folds (Kakita et al., 1981; Alipour-Haghighi and Titze, 1991). One property of interest from the point of view of the mechanism of vocal fold vibration is the Young's modulus of the tissue. Young's modulus provides an indication of the stiffness of the structure, since it is a measure of the static pressure over a surface of the material that is necessary to cause a specified displacement of that surface. A differential volume of the material is shown in figure 1.10, together with the modified shape of the volume when a change in force ΔF is applied to one surface, which has an area A. The dimension of the volume in the direction of the applied force is x, and the change in this dimension when the force is applied is Δx. Young's modulus is defined as

$$Y = \frac{\Delta F/A}{\Delta x/x} \tag{1.1}$$

and it has the dimensions of dynes per square centimeter if the force is in dynes and the area of the surface is in square centimeters. The Young's modulus for a portion of the vocal fold can be defined with the force applied longitudinally or with the force applied transversely to the length, and these values will be different. Equation (1.1) defines a *differential* Young's modulus, since the applied force is a differential force that may be superimposed on a static force.

Measurements of the differential Young's modulus for different layers of the tissue for a range of canine vocal folds are shown in figure 1.11. If these data are used to model the human vocal folds, they must be considered to be approximate only, since there are differences in structure between canine and human vocal folds (Kurita et al., 1983). As the vocal folds are elongated, all the Young's moduli increase, some more than others. In particular, the value for the lamina propria with a transverse applied force (LT in figure 1.11)

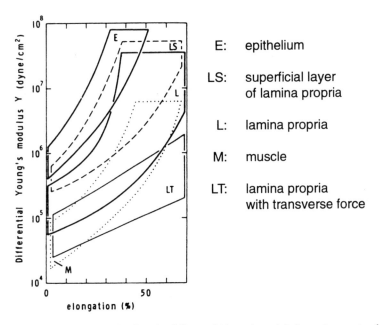

Figure 1.11 Range of values for differential Young's moduli for various parts of the tissue of the canine vocal fold. E, epithelium; LS, superficial layer of lamina propria; L, lamina propria; M, muscle; LT, lamina propria with transverse force. (From Kakita et al., 1981.)

increases less than the moduli based on a longitudinal applied force. As pointed out by Kakita et al. (1981), the (longitudinal) differential Young's moduli begin to increase rapidly when the elongation of the vocal folds exceeds 30 to 70 percent. Actual measurements of elongation of the human vocal folds over a range of fundamental frequencies during singing have been shown to be in this range (Hollein, 1983).

The cover of the vocal folds, and its outer surface, the epithelium, show a much greater differential Young's modulus than do the inner layers. When the vocal folds are relatively slack, the muscle is the layer with the smallest Young's modulus.

From these data one can make rough estimates of the effective mechanical mass and compliance of the human vocal folds in the relaxed condition, that is, with essentially no elongation. From figure 1.11 we estimate the Young's modulus of the muscle and the lamina propria for small values of elongation (up to about 10 percent) to be about 5×10^4 dynes/cm^2. This value is consistent with the differential Young's modulus for the canine vocal fold body reported by Alipour-Haghighi and Titze (1991). The total thickness of the cover and the muscle is about 2.5 mm for females and about 4 mm for males. For a female voice, we assume that the vertical height of the glottis is about 2 mm. The mechanical compliance (per unit horizontal length) for the female vocal fold is calculated from this value of Y and from these dimensions (from equation [1.1]) to be about 2.5×10^{-5} cm^2/dyne. The effective mass of the

Anatomy and Physiology of Speech Production

vibrating tissue can be assumed to be about one-half of the mass of the 2.5-mm depth of tissue. If we take the density of the tissue to be 1 gm/cm^3, then the effective mass of the vocal fold is about $0.125 \times 0.2 \cong 0.025$ gm/cm. For a male voice, the vertical length is about 0.3 cm and the depth is about 0.4 cm, so that the effective mass per unit length is about one-half of the total mass per unit length, that is, about 0.06 gm/cm. The mechanical compliance per unit length is about 3×10^{-5} cm^2/dyne. As figure 1.11 shows, these estimates of mechanical compliance can vary over a factor of 2 or more.

For a linear mass-spring system with mechanical compliance C and mass M, the natural frequency is given by $f = 1/(2\pi\sqrt{MC})$. The values of compliance and effective mass estimated here lead to natural frequencies of about 200 Hz for adult female vocal folds and about 120 Hz for adult male vocal folds. These values are in the expected ranges for adult speakers.

The vocal folds are also characterized by loss, and this loss can be described in terms of an effective acoustic resistance. Measurements of damping of the vocal folds when they are vibrating freely and are not under compression have been made by Kaneko et al. (1987). Their results show a Q of about 4 for a resonant frequency of 100 Hz, and about 7 at 200 Hz. These findings translate into an effective resistance per unit length of the vocal folds of about 8 dyne-s/cm^2 for male vocal folds and about 4 dyne-s/cm^2 for female vocal folds.

As the vocal folds are elongated by, say, 20 to 30 percent, the value of Y increases by about a factor of 2 for transverse displacements of the lamina propria, and increases much more for the inner muscle layer, probably by a factor of 4. These changes lead to a decrease in mechanical compliance by a factor of about 3 and a decrease in effective mass by about 30 percent, resulting in an increase in natural frequency by a factor of about 2. In effect, as the vocal folds are elongated, the mechanical compliance and mass are determined by a thinner portion of the vocal fold surface.

For some conditions that occur in speech production, the vocal folds are pressed together, so that the tissue is under compression. Application of a force to the tissue leads to a flow of the viscous fluid within the vocal fold through the porous and compliant solid material that forms the body of the fold. Mow et al. (1984) and Lee et al. (1981) discuss this process for articular cartilage, which is expected to have properties similar to the vocal folds. The consequence is that there is a viscous force that resists the applied force. This viscous force appears to be large compared with the inertial force associated with the mass of the structure. Thus when the vocal folds are under compression it is possible to neglect the inertial force, and to characterize the vocal fold by a mechanical compliance and a mechanical resistance. It is estimated that the effective mechanical resistance per unit length of the vocal folds when they are under compression is about 60 dyne-s/cm^2 for male vocal folds and about 30 dyne-s/cm^2 for female vocal folds. Much more research is needed to obtain more adequate data on the dynamic properties of the vocal folds when they are under compression.

A more detailed discussion of the physical properties of the vocal folds and their relation to the mechanism of sound generation at the larynx is given in chapter 2.

1.1.2.3 Laryngeal Structures Above the Vocal Folds   Immediately above the point on the thyroid cartilage where the anterior ends of the vocal folds terminate, a flat cartilage—the epiglottis—is attached, as shown in figure 1.5. This cartilage is about 3 cm long in a vertical direction, and about 2 cm wide at its widest point (for an adult), and it forms an anterior surface for the airways. The upper and lateral edges of the epiglottis are attached by ligaments to the apexes of the arytenoid cartilages (see figure 1.8). This ligament constitutes the upper edge of a sheet of tissue that, together with the epiglottis, forms a cylindrically shaped tube above the vocal folds. This tube has a length ranging from 2 to 4 cm and a diameter in the range of 1 to 2 cm for an adult, and opens into the pharynx at its upper end.

Figure 1.5 shows the position of the hyoid bone, which is located directly above the thyroid cartilage. This bone is open at the back, and forms a partial ring that surrounds the front and sides of the lower pharynx. Projections of this bone at the posterior ends of the two sides attach through ligaments to the upward-projecting prominences on the thyroid cartilage. A membrane connects the hyoid bone and the upper surface of the thyroid cartilage.

1.1.2.4 Extrinsic Laryngeal Muscles   Surrounding the entire larynx structure is the inferior pharyngeal constrictor muscle. Contraction of this muscle appears to narrow the larynx tube and the lower pharynx, and to contribute to narrowing the opening formed by the ventricular folds. Several other muscles connect between the larynx and structures external to the larynx, and these serve to stabilize the larynx and also can influence the configuration of the glottis and the state of the vocal folds. The sternohyoid and sternothyroid muscles, shown schematically in figure 1.12, attach to the sternum below the larynx, and contraction of these muscles draws the larynx downward. The figure also shows the thyrohyoid muscle, which is an extension of the sternothyroid muscle in the superior direction. Various muscles are attached between the hyoid bone and structures superior to the larynx, particularly the stylohyoid muscle and the anterior and posterior bellies of the digastric muscle, as described later in section 1.1.3. Contraction of these muscles can draw the larynx upward.

Downward displacement of the larynx causes the wide posterior surface of the cricoid cartilage to slide along the cervical spine. It has been pointed out by Honda et al. (1993) that the curvature of the cervical spine in this region causes the anterior surface of the cricoid cartilage to tilt forward as this downward movement occurs. The effect is shown schematically in figure 1.13. This tilting movement of the cricoid cartilage causes the angle between the thyroid and cricoid cartilages to increase, resulting in a decrease in vocal

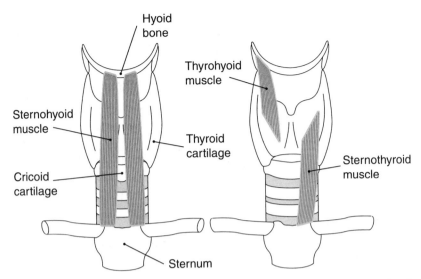

Figure 1.12 Schematic representations of the sternohyoid muscles (left) and the thyrohyoid and sternothyroid muscles (right).

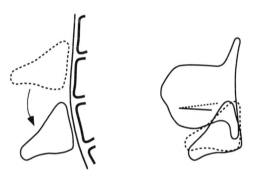

Figure 1.13 The drawing on the left shows how the cricoid cartilage can tilt forward as the larynx is lowered through the action of the sternohyoid and sternothyroid muscles. The drawing on the right illustrates how this tilting can rotate the cricoid cartilage relative to the thyroid cartilage, thereby shortening the vocal folds and decreasing their stiffness. (After Honda et al., 1993.)

fold length and consequently a decrease in the stiffness or tension in the vocal folds. It has also been suggested (Sonninen, 1968) that the location of the sternothyroid muscle on the thyroid cartilage is such that contraction of this muscle can cause an upward tilting of the thyroid cartilage in relation to the cricoid cartilage, again causing a decrease in vocal fold length. Thus there is potentially more than one mechanism whereby lowering of the larynx through contraction of the strap muscles such as the sternohyoid can cause a decrease in vocal fold tension (cf. Atkinson, 1973 and 1978; Erickson, 1993; Honda et al., 1993). Still another potential mechanism for increasing the angle between the thyroid and cricoid cartilage is contraction of the crico-

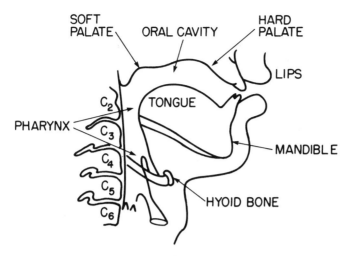

Figure 1.14 Midsagittal section of the vocal tract and surrounding structures, as obtained by tracing from a radiograph. The wings of the mandible and hyoid bone and the tips of the arytenoid cartilages are shown, although they are not in the midsagittal plane. The cervical vertebrae C1–6 are identified. (From Perkell, 1969.)

pharyngeus muscle (shown in figure 1.8), which tilts the cricoid cartilage downward (Honda and Fujimura, 1991; Honda et al., 1993).

1.1.3 The Vocal Tract Above the Larynx

The principal structures surrounding the vocal tract above the larynx are shown in the midsagittal section of figure 1.14. The pharynx forms the vertical portion of the vocal tract above the larynx. Above the pharynx, the airway for an adult turns approximately 90 degrees (for a normal head posture) into the oral cavity, with the lips forming the anterior end of the vocal tract.

1.1.3.1 Pharynx The pharynx is anterior to the cervical vertebrae, and is surrounded by a set of constrictor muscles. There are three components to the pharyngeal constrictor muscles (inferior, middle, and superior), extending from the laryngeal region up to the soft palate. Contraction of these muscles narrows the pharyngeal airway by decreasing both the sagittal and the lateral dimensions, as shown schematically in the left side of figure 1.15a. Widening of the pharynx is achieved by drawing the root of the tongue forward by contraction of the lower fibers of the genioglossus muscle, as illustrated in the right side of figure 1.15a, and in figure 1.15b. The genioglossus muscle attaches to the inner surface of the mandible near the midline.

Contraction of these sets of muscles can produce a wide range of shapes and cross-sectional areas of the airway in the pharyngeal region (Gauffin and Sundberg, 1978; U.G. Goldstein, 1980; Johansson et al., 1983; Baer et al., 1991; Perrier et al., 1992). Some examples of the cross-sectional shape of the

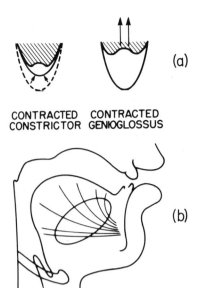

CONTRACTED   CONTRACTED
CONSTRICTOR GENIOGLOSSUS

Figure 1.15 Illustrating how the constrictor muscles and the lower fibers of the genioglossus muscle operate to change the shape of the airway in the pharyngeal region. (a) Schematic representation of the airway shape when the pharynx is narrowed (left) by the contraction of a constrictor muscle (the dashed line indicating the configuration in the absence of muscle contraction), and when the pharynx is widened (right) by contraction of the genioglossus muscle. (b) A sketch of the fibers of the genioglossus muscle in the lateral view.

airway at sections that are 1.0, 2.5, and 5.5 cm above the glottis are shown in figure 1.16 for the vowels /ɑ/ (left) and /i/ (right). At the lowest level, the shape is complex because there is a space lateral to the main airway in the laryngeal region at the level of the epiglottis. This space, called the piriform sinus, forms a side branch to the main airway. The shapes at the 5.5-cm level illustrate the wide range of cross-sectional areas that are used in the pharyngeal region to produce different vowels. For these two shapes, the areas are 0.60 cm² for /ɑ/ and 7.6 cm² for /i/. (See also Fant, 1960, and Chiba and Kajiyama, 1941.)

Knowledge of the cross-sectional area of the airway along its length is important for determining the aerodynamic and acoustic behavior of the vocal tract. It is, however, difficult to obtain direct measurements of the cross-sectional area, particularly when the shape of vocal tract is changing with time. Techniques are available for determining the cross-dimensions of the airway in the midsagittal plane from lateral radiographs or by tracking the locations of points on the midline of the tongue. There is some interest, therefore, in estimating the cross-sectional area at particular points along the vocal tract when the cross-dimensions at these points are known. In the pharyngeal region, the lateral dimension of the airway increases roughly in proportion to the midsagittal dimension, and consequently it is expected that the cross-sectional area is roughly proportional to the square of the

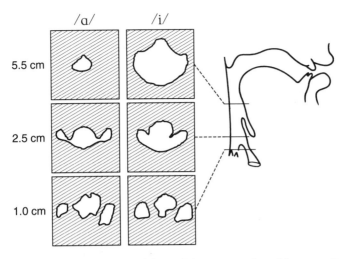

Figure 1.16 Cross-sectional shape of the airway at three different positions in the pharyngeal region when the vocal tract is configured to produce the vowels /ɑ/ (left) and /i/ (right). The distance of the section from the glottis is marked on each panel. The approximate locations of the sections are shown in the midsagittal tracing at the right. (The midsagittal tracing is not taken from the same vocal tract as the coronal sections.) The transverse sections were obtained by a magnetic resonance imaging technique. (Data from Baer et al., 1991.)

midsagittal cross-dimension. However, there appear to be substantial individual differences in this relation between area and cross-dimensions. It has been shown (cf. Heinz and Stevens, 1965; Baer et al., 1991) that a better fit to the data in the pharyngeal region is obtained from the equation

$$A = Kd^{\alpha}, \tag{1.2}$$

where A is the cross-sectional area, d is the cross-dimension in a direction normal to the airway, and K and α are constants that depend on the particular speaker and on where in the pharynx the cross-dimension is obtained. For example, at a level about 5 cm above the glottis, the values of K for two different speakers are 1.1 and 0.9, and the values of α are 1.5 and 1.9, when A is in square centimeters and d is in centimeters (Baer et al., 1991).

1.1.3.2 Soft Palate and Nasal Cavity

The upper end of the pharynx extends vertically into the nasal cavity. The opening of the airway into the nasal cavity, called the velopharyngeal opening, can be controlled by manipulating the position of the velum or soft palate together with the lateral walls of the upper pharynx. The manner in which these structures are maneuvered to close this opening is shown schematically in figure 1.17.

The soft palate or velum is a flap of tissue about 4 cm long, 2 cm wide, and 0.5 cm thick, extending back from the posterior end of the hard palate. These dimensions are approximate only, and show great variation with position along the soft palate and with the state of the musculature which positions the velum. In raised position, the posterior end of the soft palate

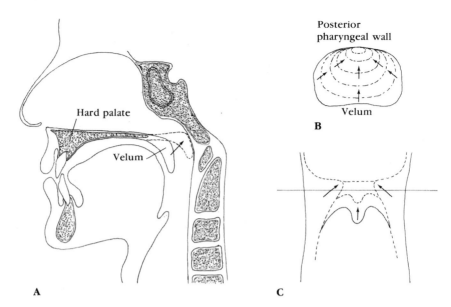

Figure 1.17 Showing how velopharyngeal closure is achieved. Solid lines represent the open position and dashed lines with arrows represent various positions toward closure. (a) Lateral view; (b) superior view; (c) anterior view. The figure shows that the closing maneuver involves raising of the velum in conjunction with an inward movement of the pharyngeal walls. (From Dickson and Maue-Dickson, 1982.)

makes contact with the rear wall of the pharynx, effectively closing the air passage between the oral and nasal cavities. When the velum is lowered, its lower surface can rest on the dorsum of the tongue (depending on the tongue position), and an opening is created between the pharynx and the nasal cavities.

Several muscles are inserted into the soft palate, and these perform the function of raising or lowering this structure, and thus of closing or opening the velopharyngeal port. The velum is raised by the levator veli palatini muscle, which inserts into either side of the velum near its upper surface, and connects to the bone forming the upper surface of the nasal cavity. The velum-lowering muscles consist of the palatopharyngus muscle, whose fibers insert into the walls of the pharynx, and the palatoglossus muscle, which inserts into the lateral edges of the tongue.

When the soft palate is raised, it forms the floor of the nasal cavity at its posterior end, as illustrated in figure 1.17. Lowering the soft palate creates an opening in the upper pharyngeal region between the vocal tract and the nasal cavity. The cross-sectional area of this velopharyngeal opening can be as large as 1.0 cm^2 or more when the soft palate is completely lowered, as it is during normal breathing. The opening is usually adjusted to be in the range of 0.2 to 0.8 cm^2 when a speaker is producing sounds that require the participation of the nasal cavity.

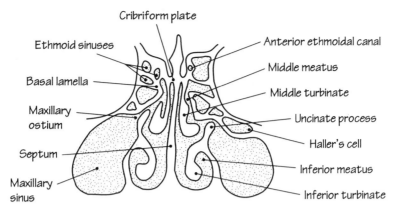

Figure 1.18 This coronal view of the nasal cavity was taken at about the middle of the nasal cavity so that some of the sinuses and undulations are not shown. The middle and inferior turbinates and the paranasal sinuses increase the total surface area of the nasal cavity. (Revised figure from Rice and Schaefer, 1993.)

Over much of its length, the nasal cavity is divided into two passages, and the passages are often asymmetrical. The septum that forms this division lies approximately in the midline, and begins about 3 cm from the posterior end of the nasal cavity. Along most of this divided portion of the nasal passage, the lateral walls of the cavity consist of a number of undulations or conchae. These conchae are illustrated in figure 1.18, which shows a coronal section of the nasal cavities. The undulations on the walls result in a surface area of the nasal cavity that is large compared with a cavity having the same cross-sectional area but with a circular cross-section.

The effective cross-sectional area of the nasal cavity of an adult male as a function of the distance along the midline has been estimated by Bjuggren and Fant (1964), and by Dang et al. (1994). Measurements of the cross-sectional area obtained by magnetic resonance imaging are given in the left side of figure 1.19 for four subjects. Substantial individual differences in this area function are apparent. The total length of the nasal passage from the posterior to the anterior end is about 11 cm and the total volume is about 25 cm^3. The narrowest portion of the nasal cavity is at the nostrils, where the total cross-sectional area is in the range of 1 to 2 cm^2. Also shown in figure 1.19 (right side) is the estimated perimeter of the cross section at each point along the length of the cavity. Because of the undulations in the walls of the nasal cavity, this circumference is three to five times greater than the perimeter that would exist if the cross section for a particular area were circular. This large surface area of the walls causes increased acoustic losses in the nasal cavities, as discussed in chapters 3 and 6.

Several pairs of sinuses are connected to the nasal cavity through small openings called ostia. The largest of these are two maxillary sinuses, located symmetrically on either side of the nasal cavities. These sinuses are shown in figure 1.18, as are the ostia that connect them to the main nasal passage.

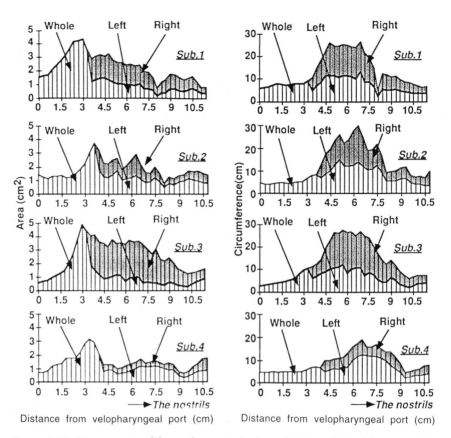

Figure 1.19 Measurements of the nasal passages for four subjects, as obtained from magnetic resonance imaging techniques. The left panels give the cross-sectional area as a function of distance along the nasal passage, and show differences between the passages to the left and right of the septum. The right panel gives the measured cross-sectional circumference. The abscissa is in units of 0.3 cm, indicating where sections were taken. (From Dang et al., 1994.)

Each of these has a volume ranging from 10 to 20 cm^3, on average (Dang et al., 1994), and a surface area estimated to be about 30 cm^2. The cross-sectional area and length of the ostia of these sinuses have been estimated (for one subject) to be about 0.06 cm^2 and 0.4 cm, respectively (Dang et al., 1994). The other principal sinuses are the frontal and sphenoidal sinuses whose volumes are, respectively, about 3 and 10 cm^3. All of the sinuses are frequently asymmetrical in size and shape, and their volumes can show large individual differences.

1.1.3.3 Oral Cavity, Tongue, and Mandible   The upper surface of the oral cavity consists of the hard palate, which covers roughly the anterior one-half to two-thirds of the length of the surface, and the soft palate, which covers the posterior one-half to one-third. A view of the hard palate is shown in figure 1.20a. The shape of the palate in coronal section at the level

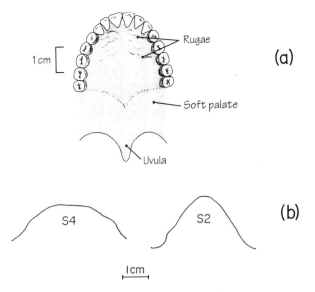

Figure 1.20 (a) Sketch of surfaces of hard and soft palate, showing arrangement of teeth around the palate. (From Dickson and Maue-Dickson, 1982.) The scale at the left is estimated. (b) Coronal section of hard palate in the vicinity of the molars for two adult males, showing individual differences in the vertical depth of the palate. (From Perkell et al., 1995.)

of the molar teeth is illustrated in figure 1.20b for two adult males. The figures indicate the teeth surrounding the hard palate, the alveolar ridge from which the teeth project, and the domed shape of the palate in lateral section. Over the anterior portion of the hard palate are some transverse ridges known as rugae. Adults show a range of values for the lateral distance between the molars and for the depth of the domed surface. At the molars, the average width for an adult is 3.5 cm, based on data summarized by U. G. Goldstein (1980). The height of the palate from a horizontal line drawn across the surface of the molars is about 2.0 cm (average for females and males) (Westbury et al., 1995; see also Broadbent et al., 1975). The shape of the palate varies considerably from one individual to another, as figure 1.20b shows.

If we regard the rear wall of the pharynx and the hard and soft palate as forming the outer walls of the vocal tract, then the dorsum of the tongue can be considered to form the inner wall, as shown in figure 1.14. The tongue is a mass of muscular tissue, and the dorsum of the tongue forms an arc of about 90 degrees that is roughly circular. It is supported by the mandible in the manner shown schematically in figure 1.21.

The mandible articulates with the skull on either side at the temporo-mandibular joint. The mandible can rotate about this joint, thus changing the vertical position of the tongue body, and can also perform some horizontal displacement. The lower teeth are inserted into the mandible, and the tongue occupies the space between the two lateral wings of the mandible. A

Anatomy and Physiology of Speech Production

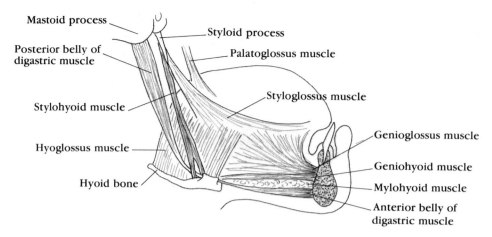

Figure 1.21 Extrinsic muscles of the tongue as viewed in lateral dissection. (From Dickson and Maue-Dickson, 1982.)

sheet of muscle—the mylohyoid—forms a surface between the lower edges of these wings of the mandible, thus forming a base for much of the tongue. This muscle inserts into the hyoid bone, which lies immediately above the thyroid cartilage. The lower teeth are located on the alveolar ridge that surrounds the upper edge of the curved anterior section of the mandible.

Figures 1.15b and 1.21 show that the connection between the tongue and the mandible is primarily through the genioglossus muscle. This muscle fans out from the inner surface of the front of the mandible and inserts into the tongue over a wide angle. As illustrated in figure 1.21, there are connections between the tongue and various other surrounding structures through a number of different muscles: to the hyoid bone through the geniohyoid muscle; to the styloid process through the styloglossus muscle; to the hyoid bone through the hyoglossus muscle; and to the soft palate through the palatoglossus muscle. The figure also shows the stylohyoid and the digastric muscle with two portions that insert into the hyoid bone. Contraction of these muscles can raise the larynx, in opposition to the sternohyoid and sternothyroid muscles. Several intrinsic muscles are located within the tongue, and serve to modify its shape and to stabilize its surface contour as the tongue body is displaced to make contact with surrounding structures. These intrinsic muscles include the superior and inferior longitudinal muscles, and the transverse and vertical lingual muscles. Contraction of some of these muscles (particularly the superior longitudinal muscles) can raise the tongue blade to make contact with the alveolar ridge, while maintaining a relatively fixed position for the tongue body. The inferior longitudinals, which form one of the larger intrinsic muscles, help to raise the center of the tongue by bunching it up in the front-back dimension.

As has been observed above, displacement of the tongue body forward and backward causes the width of the vocal tract in the midsagittal plane in

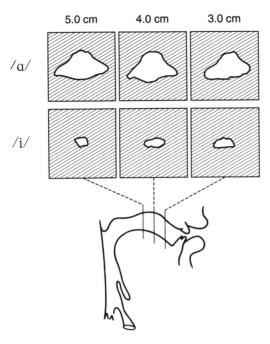

Figure 1.22 Cross-sectional shape of the airway at three different positions in the oral region when the vocal tract is configured to produce the vowels /ɑ/ and /i/. The distance of the section from the lips is marked on each panel. The approximate locations of the sections are shown in the midsagittal tracing at the bottom. (The midsagittal tracing is not taken from the same vocal tract as the coronal sections.) The coronal sections were obtained from a magnetic resonance imaging technique. (Data from Baer et al., 1991.)

the pharyngeal region to change. Raising or lowering of the tongue body is usually achieved in conjunction with raising or lowering of the mandible, although the tongue body can certainly be raised or lowered independently of the mandible. As the tongue body is manipulated in this way, the cross-sectional area of the airway that is surrounded by the surfaces of the hard palate and the tongue changes through a range of values. Coronal sections of the vocal tract at three different points in the oral region are shown in figure 1.22 when the tongue is positioned to produce two different vowels: a vowel with a low tongue body position (upper panels) and a high and a fronted tongue body (lower panels). In the case of the low tongue position, the contour of the hard palate can be seen, as well as the somewhat curved shape of the tongue blade. The cross-sectional areas for the low vowel are in the range of 4 to 5 cm², whereas those for the high vowel are in the range of 0.7 to 1.1 cm².

Empirical relations have been derived to permit the cross-sectional area of the vocal tract in the oral region to be estimated when the midsagittal cross-dimension d is known. A reasonable approximation to the area A is given by the same general equation (1.2) that was used for the pharyngeal region, that is

$$A = Kd^{\alpha}, \tag{1.3}$$

except that the constants K and α are different. For the oral region, Baer et al. (1991) have estimated the exponent α to be approximately 2.0 for their two speakers, whereas the constant K is generally in the range of 1.0 to 2.0, with the larger values being in the anterior region of the palate. (The area A and dimension d are in square centimeters and centimeters respectively.) Again, considerable variability in these constants is expected from one speaker to another.

1.1.3.4 Vocal Tract Volume With the mandible in a configuration for which the upper and lower teeth are in contact, it is possible to estimate the total volume of the space between the outer walls of the vocal tract (rear pharyngeal wall, soft palate, hard palate) and the inner surfaces of the mandible (including the floor of the mandible formed by the mylohyoid muscle). This volume is about 130 cm^3 for a female adult and 170 cm^3 for a male, on average. If the mandible is lowered by about 1 cm (a typical maximum opening that occurs in the production of speech), these values increase to about 150 and 190 cm^3, respectively. The volume of the tongue is estimated to be about 90 cm^3 for female adults and 110 cm^3 for males. Consequently, the volume of the airway that forms the vocal tract above the hyoid bone and behind the incisors for the closed and open mandible positions is about 40 and 60 cm^3, respectively, for females and 60 and 80 cm^3 for males. This is the volume, together with the lip region and the laryngeal region, that is manipulated to produce different sounds in speech. Needless to say, these volumes will show large variations from one individual to another. Even within a particular individual for a given mandible position, there will be some variation in vocal tract volume because the floor of the mandible is not rigid, and there can be some outward displacement of the surface of the neck when this slinglike structure is pushed downward.

1.1.3.5 Lips The anterior termination of the vocal tract is the opening formed by the lips. The lower lip is attached to the skin tissue that forms the outer surface of the mandible, and consequently moves up and down with the mandible. Several muscles are available to change the lip opening and shape of the lips independently of the mandible movement.

Various measures can be used to describe the shape of the lips and the dimensions of the lip orifice as the lips are manipulated to produce different vowels (Fromkin, 1964; Abry and Boë, 1986). Some of the dimensions that have been used are shown in figure 1.23. When different vowels are produced by adult speakers, the width of the lip opening (dimension A in figure 1.23) varies from about 45 mm to about 10 mm, whereas the height of the opening (dimension B) varies from about 20 to 5 mm. These two dimensions are only weakly correlated, although the correlation is greater when the same degree of protrusion is involved in changing these dimensions for vowels. Lowering of the jaw tends to increase the height of the lip opening, as expected. A spread configuration of the lips produces a wider opening, a

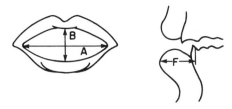

Figure 1.23 Some measures that are used to describe the shape of the lips and the dimensions of the lip orifice. (After Fromkin, 1964.)

Table 1.1 Estimates of vocal tract, pharynx, and oral cavity lengths (cm)

	Adult female	Adult male
Vocal tract length	14.1	16.9
Pharynx length	6.3	8.9
Oral cavity length	7.8	8.1

From Goldstein (1980).

decreased lip thickness in midsagittal section, and an effective acoustic termination of the vocal tract that is more posterior than with a nonspread configuration. In contrast, a pursed or rounded configuration decreases the size of the mouth opening, and the lips form the boundaries of a short acoustic tube anterior to the incisors. Protrusion of the lips can increase the dimension F (distance from the lower incisors to the outermost point of the lower lip) by about 5 mm, on average, although there are individual differences in the amount of this movement (Daniloff and Moll, 1968).

The cross-sectional area of the lip opening for different vowels is generally in the range of 0.3 to 7 cm². An acoustically relevant parameter is the ratio of the effective length of the lip opening to the effective area of the opening.[1] For different vowels, this ratio appears to vary over a range from about 0.2 cm^{-1} for a vowel with a lowered mandible or nonprotruded lips to about 6.0 cm^{-1} for a vowel with a raised mandible and protruded lips. As will be seen in chapters 3 and 6, the spread and rounding maneuvers have particular consequences for the properties of the sound that is radiated from the mouth opening.

1.1.3.6 Vocal Tract Length   The overall length of the vocal tract from the glottis to the lip opening depends, of course, on the position of the larynx and the configuration of the lips. Table 1.1 gives estimates of the average vocal tract length for adult females and adult males, assuming a neutral position of the larynx and the lips (U. G. Goldstein, 1980). The table also shows separately the pharynx length and the oral cavity length. The oral cavity length is almost the same for males and females, and the difference in overall length lies primarily in the pharyngeal region. The oral cavity length is greater than the pharynx length for adult females, whereas the pharynx length is greater for males. For children, the ratio of pharynx length to oral cavity length is much less than that indicated in table 1.1. For example, the average pharynx and oral cavity lengths for a 5-year-old are 4.4 cm and 6.4 cm, respectively (U. G. Goldstein, 1980).

1.1.3.7 Mechanical Properties of Vocal Tract Walls

The various structures that form the walls of the vocal tract have mechanical properties that influence the generation of sound in the vocal tract. These properties can be described in terms of mechanical impedance per unit area. If the pressure on the walls is represented as $p(t) = p_o \cos \omega t$, and the velocity in response to this pressure is $u(t) = u_o \cos (\omega t - \phi)$, then the mechanical impedance per unit area at the frequency $\omega/2\pi$ is $Z_s = (p_o/u_o)e^{j\phi}$.

Direct measurements of this impedance have not been made, but estimates can be made from impedance measurements on other body surfaces that are likely to have similar mechanical characteristics (Ishizaka et al., 1975; Wodicka et al., 1993). These measurements show that the impedance Z_s can be approximated by a compliance, a mass, and a resistance in series. That is, we can write

$$Z_s = 1/j\omega C_s + j\omega M_s + R_s \qquad (1.4)$$

This representation of the impedance by constant values of C_s, M_s, and R_s is approximate, and is valid only in a frequency range up to 100 to 200 Hz (Wodicka et al., 1993). Values of C_s, M_s, and R_s are, of course, different for different surfaces within the vocal tract. For example, the hard palate has a smaller C_s than the tongue surface or the soft palate. Furthermore, these quantities depend on the state of contraction of the intrinsic muscles within structures such as the tongue. For example, Svirsky et al. (1997) have measured C_s for the tongue surface by observing the displacement of a point on the tongue surface when intraoral pressure builds up during the closure interval for an intervocalic voiced and voiceless stop consonant. The wall compliance during the voiced stop consonant was found to be about three times that during the voiceless consonant. They concluded that there is a relaxation of the intrinsic tongue muscles during a voiced stop consonant and a possible stiffening of the muscles during a voiceless stop.

Estimates of the average values of these quantities over the vocal tract surfaces, together with their possible range of variation, are as follows:

C_s: 1.0×10^{-5} to 3.0×10^{-5} cm^3/dyne

M_s: 1.0 to 2.0 gm/cm^2

R_s: 800 to 2000 dyne-s/cm^3

These estimates indicate that the resonant frequency for the surface tissue is in the range of 30 to 40 Hz. The resistance, however, causes damping in excess of critical damping at this frequency. For an adult vocal tract, the total surface area of the walls of the vocal tract posterior to the incisors is estimated to be about 100 cm^2. Thus the total acoustic impedance (ratio of sound pressure to volume velocity) is obtained by multiplying C_s by 100 and dividing M_s and R_s by 100. This impedance is expected to be concentrated primarily in the pharyngeal region and over the tongue surface. The average compliance of the vocal tract walls would then be in the range of 1.0×10^{-3} to 3.0×10^{-3} cm^5/dyne, with the compliance being somewhat greater than this over the softer surfaces of the pharynx and tongue. These values are consistent with the estimates of Rothenberg (1968) and Svirsky et al. (1997).

1.2 BASIC AERODYNAMIC PROCESSES

1.2.1 Static Airflow in Tubes and Orifices

We have noted that the acoustic sources forming the excitation for the vocal cavities arise through modulation of the airflow at a constriction in the airways. This modulation may occur either at the glottal constriction or in the vicinity of a constriction or obstruction along the supraglottal pathways, or in both places simultaneously.

Air flows from the lungs as a consequence of a positive pressure that is maintained in the lungs. The alveolar pressure in the lungs is approximately equal to the subglottal pressure P_s, except when the volume flow of air from the lungs is large, giving rise to a pressure drop in the airways between the alveoli and the glottis. During production of an utterance on one expiration, P_s may fluctuate somewhat as a result of adjustment of the respiratory musculature and as a consequence of changes in the configurations of laryngeal and supralaryngeal structures.

The volume flow of air from the lungs under steady-state conditions depends on the alveolar pressure and on the resistance to airflow of the pathways above the lungs, the resistance being defined as the ratio of the pressure drop ΔP to the volume velocity U of the flow, that is, $R = \Delta P / U$. The resistance gives rise to energy loss in the airflow. It is determined by the dimensions of the pathways and by the flow velocity, and is greater when the pathways contain a narrow constriction or orifice.

1.2.1.1 Airflow in a Uniform Tube We consider first the flow of air through a tube of fixed cross-sectional dimensions. If the velocity of air through the tube is sufficiently slow, the flow in the tube is laminar, and the pressure drop ΔP across a given length L of the tube is proportional to the air velocity V or to the volume velocity of the airflow $U = AV$, where A is the cross-sectional area. For a tube with a circular cross-section of diameter D, the pressure drop per unit length is given by

$$\frac{\Delta P}{L} = \frac{128\mu U}{\pi D^4},$$ (1.5)

where μ is the viscosity. (See, e.g., Streeter, 1962.) For air at 37°C and 760 mm Hg, $\mu = 1.94 \times 10^{-4}$ dyne-s/cm^2. When the cross section is rectangular, of dimensions $a \times b$, where a is the narrower dimension and $a \ll b$, the pressure drop for laminar flow is (Streeter, 1962)

$$\frac{\Delta P}{L} = \frac{12\mu U}{ba^3}.$$

(1.6)

During speech production, the maximum volume velocity of air through the vocal tract when it is in a vowel-like configuration that is relatively unconstricted generally does not exceed about 1000 cm^3/s, and is usually less than 500 cm^3/s. The minimum dimension D for vowels (assuming a circular cross section) is about 0.6 cm, and this narrow opening extends over a length of 3 to 4 cm. Equation (1.5) shows that this laminar pressure drop in the vocal tract for the minimum opening and maximum flow is less than 10 percent of the subglottal pressure of 5 to 8 cm H_2O.

Experimental data indicate that when the flow velocity in a uniform tube exceeds a certain critical value, the flow is no longer laminar, but becomes turbulent. The air particles no longer flow in the direction of stream lines that are parallel to the walls, but there is mixing of the air in a direction perpendicular to the stream lines. This mixing takes the form of random fluctuations in air velocity both in the direction of the flow and at right angles to this direction. The conditions under which turbulence appears are determined by the Reynolds number of the flow, which is given by

$$Re = \frac{Vh\rho}{\mu},$$

(1.7)

where V is the velocity of the air particles, ρ is the air density, and h is a characteristic dimension that, in this case, is roughly equal to the diameter for a circular tube or the minimum cross-dimension for a rectangular tube. The critical Reynolds number above which laminar flow ceases to occur in tubes with rough surfaces is approximately 2000, although in some carefully controlled situations it is possible to achieve laminar flow for higher Reynolds numbers.

When the Reynolds number is higher than this critical value, the presence of turbulence has a drastic effect on the pressure drop in the tube. The value of $\Delta P/L$ is now proportional to V^2 instead of V, and becomes very much dependent on the roughness of the walls of the tube. Under these conditions we have a relation of the form

$$\frac{\Delta P}{L} = \frac{k}{D}\left(\frac{\rho V^2}{2}\right),$$

(1.8)

where k is a constant that depends on the roughness of the walls in relation to the cross-dimensions of the tube, and D is the diameter of the tube (Streeter, 1962). Empirically, it has been found that the constant k is in the range 0.02 to 0.08, the lower end of this range being for relatively smooth tubes and the upper end for rough tubes. The upper end of the range is obtained for cases in which the rough undulations of the wall surfaces are about 10 percent of the diameter.

For the vowel-like configuration with a constriction diameter of 0.6 cm^2 and a maximum flow of 1000 cm^3/s, the Reynolds number is about 12,000, that is, well above the critical value of 2000. The pressure drop for a 4-cm length, from equation (1.8), is about 2400 dynes/cm^2, assuming $k = 0.05$. This is an extreme case, however, and for normally produced vowels the average airflow is much less than 1000 cm^3/s and the minimum cross-sectional area is larger.

1.2.1.2 Airflow Through a Constriction in a Tube The vocal tract is rarely if ever shaped in the form of a long uniform tube, even over a few centimeters of its length, and hence the relations just discussed cannot be applied directly to determine the pressure drops and airflows that occur in speech. Usually the air passages between the trachea and the lips consist of a relatively wide pathway that contains one or more constrictions along its length. A constriction may be only a few millimeters long (such as the constriction formed by the glottis) or may be several centimeters long (such as a constriction formed by the tongue body). The conduit may contract and expand abruptly at the constriction, or the narrowing and widening may be gradual. When air flows through a constricted tube of the type formed by the vocal tract, the major contribution to the pressure drop is usually caused by losses at the contraction and expansion rather than in the constriction itself, except when the constriction is extremely narrow, or is relatively long.

Consider the flow of air in a tube with a constriction as shown in figure 1.24. Initially, we shall assume lossless flow in the tube, such that the fluid flows in stream lines. The pressure and velocity in the wide and narrow sections of the tube are P_1, V_1, and P_2, V_2, respectively. If we apply Newton's law to an element of fluid, and integrate the resulting equations, we obtain the relation

$$P_1 + \frac{\rho V_1^2}{2} = P_2 + \frac{\rho V_2^2}{2},\tag{1.9}$$

where ρ is the density of air. If the cross-sectional area A_2 of the constricted portion is small compared with the cross-sectional area A_1 of the wide portion, then $V_1 \ll V_2$, and we can write

$$P_2 - P_1 = -\frac{\rho V_2^2}{2}.\tag{1.10}$$

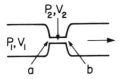

Figure 1.24 A simple constriction with airflow. The pressures and velocities upstream from the constriction and in the constriction are designated as P_1, V_1, and P_2, V_2, respectively. Points a and b are at the inlet and at the expansion, where energy losses are expected to occur.

The quantity $\rho V_2^2/2$ is sometimes called the dynamic pressure. It is the quantity that must be added to the static pressure P_2 in the constriction to obtain the upstream pressure P_1. We note, then, that, from equation (1.8), the pressure drop per unit length in a rough tube of uniform cross-dimensions is found experimentally to be proportional to the dynamic pressure.

Equation (1.10) also shows that the pressure P_2 in the constriction is always less than P_1, and, if P_1 is small (relative to atmospheric pressure), P_2 can in fact be negative. If P_1 is small (assuming the pressures are defined relative to atmospheric pressure), then $P_2 = -\rho V_2^2/2$. This is known as the Bernoulli pressure in the constriction, and it can play an important role in the mechanism of vocal fold vibration.

If there is viscosity, and the flow in the constricted portion of the tube is laminar, then the pressure drop, from equation (1.5) or (1.6), can become very large if the cross-sectional dimensions of the tube are very small. There are, however, additional energy losses in the flow at the transition from the wide tube into the narrow section (at point a in figure 1.24) and again at the expansion (at point b). These losses arise because eddies form in the flow in the vicinity of the contraction and expansion. The eddies can be thought of as volume elements of air that perform steady rotations immediately adjacent to either end of the constriction. Because of the viscosity of the air, the energy in the eddies is dissipated as heat, and this energy loss is manifested as an additional pressure drop or resistance in the flow.

At each end a and b of the transition, it is found experimentally that the pressure drop due to these losses is proportional to the dynamic pressure $\rho V_2^2/2$ in the constricted tube. It is convenient to represent the additional pressure drop ΔP at the contraction and at the expansion by

$$\Delta P = k_L \frac{\rho V_2^2}{2}. \tag{1.11}$$

It is again assumed that the velocity V_2 in the constriction is large compared with the velocity V_1 in the wider section.

At a contraction, the contribution to k_L depends to some extent on the area ratio A_1/A_2 and on the smoothness of the transition between these two areas. For a smooth transition from a large A_1 to a small A_2 it can be as low as 0.05, and for an abrupt transition it can be as large as 0.5 or greater. At an abrupt *expansion*, the contribution to k_L is often as high as 1.0, but may be much smaller (possibly as low as 0.2). Measurements of the total value of k_L, due to both contraction and expansion, have been made on models with several types of constrictions. Heinz (1956) found the total k_L to be in the range of 1.2 to 1.7 for constrictions with abrupt expansions and contractions. Van den Berg et al. (1957) measured the pressure drops in a model of the larynx, with a gradual transition to the glottal constriction and an abrupt expansion, and found the total k_L to be about 0.87. An even smaller value might be expected for a constriction with a gradual expansion and contraction. A value of about 1.0 is probably a reasonable average for the kinds of constrictions found in the vocal tract, including those formed by the tongue and lips as well as at the glottis, and is used in the calculations and charts shown later in this section. Depending on the constriction shape and location, this k_L value can probably be 20 percent larger or smaller in particular situations. Simple calculations show that the pressure drops due to laminar flow [equations (1.5) and (1.6)] and due to turbulent flow in the constriction [equation (1.8)] are small compared to the pressure drops due to a contraction and expansion, unless the vocal tract is very constricted in some region or unless the cross-sectional area is narrow over a relatively long region of the vocal tract.

When the air velocity in the constriction is sufficiently large, turbulence occurs in the flow. The turbulence is greatest in the region immediately downstream from the constriction, although there is also some turbulence near the constriction. The turbulence causes acoustic energy to be generated, and this acoustic source acts as excitation for the vocal tract. (The generation of turbulence noise is discussed in chapter 2.) The magnitude of the turbulent velocity fluctuations increases with the Reynolds number of the flow [equation (1.7)], where the velocity V and characteristic dimension h used to determine the Reynolds number are the velocity in the constriction and the diameter of the constriction (or a measure of the average cross-dimensional dimension if the constriction is not circular).

A chart giving the volume flow of air U for various orifice sizes A and for various values of pressure drop ΔP across the orifice is shown in figure 1.25. The relations between ΔP, U, and A are plotted in different ways in the two

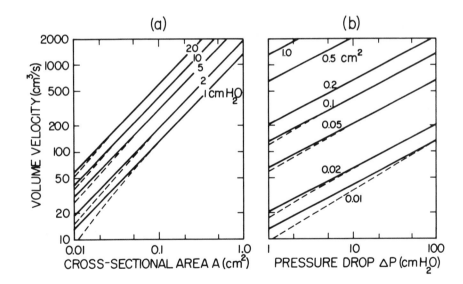

Figure 1.25 Relations between volume velocity, pressure drop, and cross-sectional area of a constriction like that in figure 1.24. The solid lines represent equation (1.12). The dashed lines show the effect of including viscous losses in the orifice, assuming a circular orifice of length 1 cm. The two charts show different ways of plotting the relations between the three parameters.

parts of the figure: with ΔP as the parameter in (a) and with A as the parameter in (b). The straight lines are representations of the equation

$$\Delta P = 1.0 \frac{\rho U^2}{2A^2},\tag{1.12}$$

which is derived from equation (1.11) simply by placing $V_2 = U/A$, where U is the volume velocity and A is the cross-sectional area, and by setting $k_L = 1.0$. On the chart, the pressure drop is expressed in cm H_2O rather than in dynes per square centimeter. (Note that 1 cm $H_2O = 980$ dynes/cm^2.)

For narrow orifices and small airflows, the flow conditions may be laminar, and hence the straight lines (on a log-log plot) for small values of A and for small airflows may not be accurate. The resistance of the orifice for laminar flow depends upon the orifice shape and on the length of the constricted region. Examples of the effect of laminar resistance are shown by the dashed lines in figure 1.25 for circular orifices of various cross-sectional areas and for an orifice length of 1 cm.

1.2.2 Airflow and Pressure in the Vocal Tract for Typical Static Configurations

When there is a single constriction in the airways during speech production, ΔP in figure 1.25 can be taken to represent the subglottal pressure P_s. For small and moderate airflows (up to 200 to 300 cm^3/s), the subglottal pressure is equal to the pressure in the alveoli of the lungs, since the pressure drop in the pathways from the lungs to the trachea is small. The resistance of these pathways is on the order of 2 cm H_2O/liter/s (about 2 dyne-s/cm^5), although it varies greatly from one individual to another, depending largely on the vital capacity. For a given individual, this resistance depends to some extent on the point in the respiratory cycle, that is, the volume of the lungs, at which it is measured (Briscoe and Dubois, 1958; Van den Berg, 1960; Dubois, 1964; Rothenberg, 1968). For large airflows, this resistance causes a pressure drop, and the subglottal pressure is lower than the alveolar pressure. When there is more than one constriction in the airways during expiratory airflow, such as a constriction at the larynx and in the vocal tract above the larynx, the pressure drop across each constriction is less than P_s. For steady flow, the total pressure drop P_s is equal to the sum of the pressure drops across the individual constrictions.

1.2.2.1 Configurations with a Supraglottal Constriction Particular

classes of speech sounds that are generated with a supraglottal constriction can be identified with different regions in figure 1.25. These regions are shown in figure 1.26. For voiced and voiceless fricative consonants produced at normal voice levels in prestressed position (i.e., preceding a vowel that is stressed), experimental data indicate that the volume flow is usually in the range of 200 to 500 cm^3/s and that the intraoral pressure is between 3 and

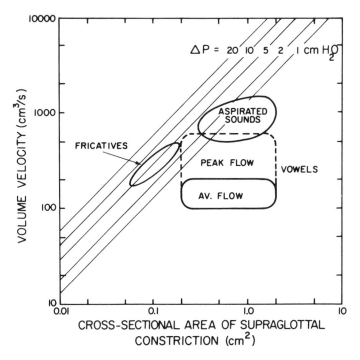

Figure 1.26 Sketch of approximate range of constriction sizes, airflows, and pressure drops at the supraglottal constriction for vocal tract configurations corresponding to various classes of speech sounds as indicated. (Adapted from K. N. Stevens, 1971.)

8 cm H_2O (Isshiki and Ringel, 1964; Hixon, 1966; Arkebauer et al., 1967; Klatt et al., 1968). Various values within these ranges are obtained depending on the speaker, the voice level, the place of articulation of the consonant, and the voicing of the consonant. The airflow and intraoral pressure are lower for voiced fricatives than for their voiceless cognates. Instances can certainly be found, however, where the airflow and the pressure drop across the constriction are outside these ranges. A contour is drawn in figure 1.26 to indicate the normal region of flows and pressure drops for fricative consonants. This contour shows that the constriction sizes for this class of consonants are normally between 0.05 cm^2 and 0.2 cm^2.

The articulatory configuration for a vowel sound usually has a constriction in some region along the vocal tract length, but the cross-sectional area at the constriction is, of course, greater than that for fricative consonants. The average airflow for voiced vowel sounds produced by adult male speakers is about 200 cm^3/s and for adult females is about 140 cm^3/s, although there are substantial individual differences (Holmberg et al., 1988). The minimum constriction size within the vocal tract for vowels is about 0.2 to 0.3 cm^2, and may be as large as 2 to 3 cm^2 (Chiba and Kajiyama, 1941; Fant, 1960; Heinz and Stevens, 1965; Baer et al., 1991; Perrier et al., 1992). From these data, a region can be delineated in the chart of figure 1.26 representing average airflow conditions at supraglottal constrictions for vowels. Throughout most of

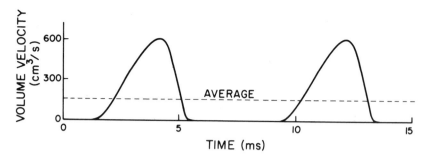

Figure 1.27 Sketch of the volume velocity of glottal airflow vs. time for normal adult male glottal vibration.

this region the Reynolds number is below 1800, and the average pressure drop across the constriction is negligible. During a cycle of glottal vibration, there are large variations in airflow, so that the peak airflow is considerably greater than the average flow. As we shall see in chapter 2, the peak airflow through the glottis for normal glottal vibration is in the range 200 to 700 cm^3/s (Flanagan, 1958; Holmberg et al., 1988). A typical waveform of the glottal airflow vs. time is shown in figure 1.27. In figure 1.26 a dashed line is drawn indicating the region that includes the peak airflow (taking a nominal value of 600 cm^3/s). For the vowels with the smallest cross-sectional area for the constriction, there can be a pressure drop across the constriction of a few cm H_2O when the flow reaches its peak value. This point is discussed in more detail when we consider the details of vocal fold vibration in chapter 2.

There are occasions during speech production when the vocal tract is in a vowel-like configuration but the glottis is spread and there may be no vocal fold vibration. The airflow under these conditions is considerably greater than it is during normally voiced vowel sounds, and is generally in the range of 500 to 1500 cm^3/s (Klatt et al., 1968; Rothenberg, 1968). These airflow conditions occur for voiceless or breathy-voiced vowels, for the sound /h/, and during the aspiration that follows the release of certain consonants, such as the stop consonants /p t k/ in prestressed position in English. A contour indicating the region in which these aspirated speech sounds occur is shown in figure 1.26. The exact shape of this contour for smaller constriction sizes is difficult to estimate, since measurements of the pressure drop across the constriction for speech sounds with these large airflows are not available. It is possible, however, to estimate the size of the glottal opening, and from this to calculate the flow through the two constrictions—one at the glottis and the other in the supraglottal tract. (See section 1.2.2.3.) The shape of the upper edge of the contour for voiceless or breathy vowel configurations was computed in this manner.

1.2.2.2 Constriction at the Glottis During normal vocal fold vibration, we have observed that the *peak* volume velocity through the glottis is usually

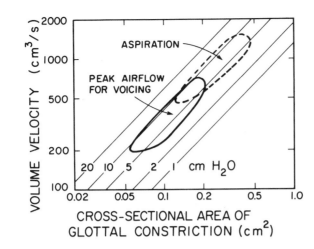

Figure 1.28 Approximate ranges of glottal areas, airflows, and pressure drops for the maximum glottal opening during normal glottal vibration, and a glottal configuration appropriate for speech sounds with aspiration noise. (Adapted from K. N. Stevens, 1971.)

in the range of 200 to 700 cm^3/s. The *average* volume flow is, of course, considerably less than the peak value, usually by a factor of 3 or more, as figure 1.27 shows. If there is no narrow supraglottal constriction, the pressure drop across the glottis is equal to the subglottal pressure, which, for speech levels that are normally employed, is in the range of 5 to 10 cm H_2O. A contour indicating the range of airflow conditions that occur at an instant of time when the glottis is maximally open during normal voicing is shown in figure 1.28. In this figure, the abscissa is the cross-sectional area of the glottal opening. The Reynolds number is below the critical value of 1800 over most of this range. Thus, except for the most extreme condition of high-amplitude vibration for modal voicing,[2] a minimal amount of turbulence noise is generated during the individual air puffs that emerge from the glottis. For modal voicing, the peak glottal area during the vibratory cycle is usually between 0.05 and 0.2 cm^2 for an adult, corresponding to a width of the glottal opening of about 0.5 to 2.0 mm, if the length of the glottis is taken to be 1.0 cm.

When the vocal folds are spread to give breathy voicing, or to produce whispered vowels or aspiration, the instantaneous airflow can be 1500 cm^3/s or higher, as noted above. The range of airflow conditions for these configurations of the glottis is indicated by the upper contour in figure 1.28. Reynolds numbers exceed 1800 for these kinds of speech sounds, and the glottal area is between 0.1 and 0.4 cm^2 (corresponding to an average glottal width of about 1.0 to 4.0 mm). If the airflow is large, the pressure drop in the airways below the glottis can become significant and, if a constant alveolar pressure is assumed, the subglottal pressure drops below the alveolar pressure.

1.2.2.3 Combined Effect of Glottal and Supraglottal Constrictions
Figures 1.26 and 1.28 give airflow regions for supraglottal and glottal

Anatomy and Physiology of Speech Production

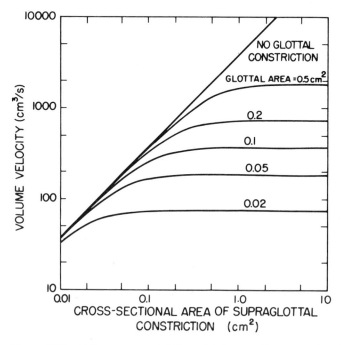

Figure 1.29 Airflow vs. supraglottal constriction size for various glottal openings, based on equation (1.12). A fixed subglottal pressure of 8 cm H$_2$O is assumed.

constrictions separately. For most speech events, just one of these constrictions accounts for the major part of the pressure drop between the trachea and the lips. Frequently, however, both constrictions play a role in determining the airflow in the vocal tract.

An example of the effect of two constrictions on the airflow is depicted in figure 1.29, which shows the airflow as a function of the area of the supraglottal constriction for several sizes of the glottal opening. A subglottal pressure of 8 cm H$_2$O is assumed for all of the curves, since this is representative of normal speech production. Different sets of curves would, of course, be obtained for other values of subglottal pressure. When the area of the supraglottal constriction is small compared with the glottal opening, the pressure across this constriction is equal to the subglottal pressure, and the curve simply follows the contour of figure 1.25a for $\Delta P = 8$ cm H$_2$O. At the other extreme, when the area of the supraglottal constriction is large, all of the pressure drop is across the glottis, and the airflow is independent of the size of the supraglottal constriction. There is, however, a wide range of cross-sectional areas between these two extremes, in which the airflow is determined by both constrictions.

The fricative consonants represent one class of speech sounds for which both the glottal and the supraglottal constrictions influence the airflow. These include the voiced and voiceless fricatives in English, as they are normally produced in prestressed position. It is estimated that glottal constrictions with cross-sectional areas in the range of 0.1 to 0.3 cm^2 (corresponding to a width of the glottal opening of about 1 to 3 mm for a speaker with a glottis length of 1.0 cm) are utilized in the production of *voiceless* fricative consonants by adult male speakers[3]. The cross-sectional area of the supraglottal constriction, calculated from simultaneous measurements of airflow and intraoral pressure, is in the range 0.05 to 0.15 cm^2 for the consonants /s/ and /š/ at normal speech levels (Hixon, 1966; Badin, 1989; Scully et al., 1992) and is probably close to this range for other voiceless fricatives. (See also figure 1.26.) These are average values for several speakers, and the range for individual speakers producing a variety of fricatives may exceed this. Thus for voiceless fricatives the area of the supraglottal constriction is usually somewhat less than that of the glottal constriction.

In the case of *voiced* fricative consonants, the picture is complicated by the fact that the vocal folds may be vibrating, and hence the airflow both in the glottis and at the supraglottal constriction varies periodically with time. It might be expected that, during the maximally open phase of the vocal fold vibration, the glottal opening is roughly 1.0 mm, and hence, for supraglottal constrictions like those for voiceless fricatives (0.05 to 0.15 cm^2), there is about the same pressure across the glottal and the supraglottal constrictions.

Estimates of the minimum cross-sectional area of the constriction for sustained fricatives based on magnetic resonance imaging techniques show values in excess of 0.15 cm^2 for some speakers and some fricatives (Narayanan et al., 1995a). In particular, the area for labiodental (/f v/) and dental (/θ ð/) fricatives tends to be greater than for /s z š ž/.

Another class of speech events for which both supraglottal and glottal constrictions can play a role in determining the airflow includes sounds produced with a relatively wide glottal opening. These are the /h/ sound, aspirated consonants, and whispered vowels. Figure 1.26 shows that the area of the glottal constriction is probably in the range of 0.1 to 0.4 cm^2 for these speech sounds, resulting in an airflow of 700 to 1500 cm^3/s if there is no significant supraglottal constriction. As noted earlier, however, the area of the supraglottal constriction for vowel-like configurations, particularly high vowels like /i/ and /u/, may be 0.3 cm^2 or even smaller, and hence there may be situations where this area is comparable to the area of the glottal constriction. (See section 8.3.)

Stop consonants are usually generated with the velum closed and with a complete closure at some point along the vocal tract, but for certain types of voiced stops two constrictions are utilized to control the airflow—one at the glottis and the other at the velopharyngeal opening (Rothenberg, 1968). The velopharyngeal opening is adjusted to be quite narrow, to permit a flow of air that is sufficient to maintain vocal fold vibration.

These questions of airflow and constriction adjustments for various classes of consonants, when these parameters change with time, are discussed further in section 1.4.

1.3 KINEMATICS OF ARTICULATORY MOVEMENTS

In section 1.2, the conditions of airflow and air pressure were examined when the glottal and supraglottal structures are fixed in specified positions and when the static pressures across the constrictions are known. During speech production, the structures rarely assume static positions for more than a few tens of milliseconds, and for much of the time there is motion from one configuration to another. We examine now some of the constraints on the timing of movements of individual articulatory structures and, in section 1.4, the time variations in the pressure and airflow in the vocal tract during appropriate sequences of movements. The acoustic consequences of these activities are considered in later chapters. We shall focus primarily on the events that occur in consonant-vowel and vowel-consonant syllables and in syllable sequences, as the articulatory structures move between a consonantal configuration and a vowel configuration, or as they perform cyclic movements.

These aspects of speech production relating to the constraints on the rates of movement of the various articulatory structures have not been well quantified. Consequently, only rough estimates can be made of the rates at which different kinds of articulatory movements can be made or the rates at which articulatory states can be changed. An understanding of these timing constraints in speech production (as well as the response of listeners to time-varying signals of the kind that occur in speech) is of basic importance to the study of language, since this knowledge may eventually provide some basis for explaining the constraints that exist in the sequential patterns of features that are allowed in various languages, and in some of the modifications that occur in utterances that are produced in a rapid or casual manner.

From the point of view of examining the kinematics of adjustment of the structures used in speech production, the control processes can be divided into three groups: (1) control of structures below the glottis that provide the source of pulmonic airflow, (2) adjustment of the stiffness of the vocal folds, and (3) movement of structures that form the walls of the airway above the trachea, including the glottis, the tongue root, the tongue body, the soft palate, the tongue blade, and the lips. Activity in the respiratory tract below the glottis gives rise to a subglottal pressure and potentially to an airflow through the glottis and the supraglottal tract. Sound sources are initiated or inhibited depending on the configuration of the glottis and of supraglottal structures, and the positioning of these structures also influences how these sound sources are filtered or modulated. Adjustment of vocal fold stiffness determines the fundamental frequency if the vocal folds are vibrating, and can also inhibit or facilitate continued vocal fold vibration.

The rates at which the muscles can move the structures and reverse their direction of movement are determined both by the physical properties of the structures and those of the airways (such as the mass and compliance of

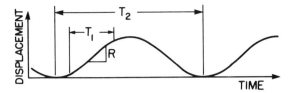

Figure 1.30 Illustrating various measures that can be used to specify rates of movement or response times of articulatory structures: the time T_1 to complete a unidirectional movement, the time T_2 to complete one cycle of movement, and the rate of movement R.

tissue, and the mass and compliance of the volume of air in the lungs) and by the properties of the response of muscles under various conditions of neural excitation. Under most circumstances, the principal timing limitation is that imposed by the neuromuscular processes, that is, the time constants of the response to the muscle contractions.

Several kinds of measures have been used to quantify the response times of the various articulatory structures. These measures are illustrated in the curve in figure 1.30, which shows the displacement of a hypothetical structure as a function of time during an articulatory movement. One set of measures attempts to quantify the time course of a *unidirectional* movement from one configuration to another, either in terms of the time T_1 to complete the movement (or to complete a specified portion of the movement, such as from the 10 percent point to the 90 percent point), or the maximum rate R of the movement. The time constant of a first-order or critically damped second-order dynamic system that produces an equivalent response to a step excitation could also be used. Another measure is the time T_2 taken for a structure or structures to perform a cyclic movement from one configuration to another and back again (or the time taken to complete a prescribed portion of the cyclic movement). As one might expect, T_2 is usually greater than $2T_1$, and is likely to be as much as $3T_1$. Several different kinds of estimates are presented in the following discussion, but frequently only limited types of data are available for a given class of movements.

To the extent that the idealized displacement of an articulatory structure in figure 1.30 is sinusoidal, the relation between the maximum velocity R and the peak-to-peak displacement D is given by

$$R = \frac{\pi}{T_2}D. \tag{1.13}$$

That is, the maximum velocity is linearly related to the peak-to-peak displacement D. Equation (1.13) would suggest that the rate R is proportional to the distance D, as long as the period T_2 remains the same for various amplitudes of alternating movement. There is, however, evidence that this relation between maximum velocity, displacement, and time to complete a movement is not invariant across rates of speaking, at least for the tongue tip with relatively slow rates (Adams et al., 1993).

Anatomy and Physiology of Speech Production

More directly relevant to the production of sound in the vocal tract are the changes in the dimensions of the airways in the vocal tract as the articulatory structures undergo these movements. Of particular importance acoustically are the rates of change of cross-sectional areas and of the impedances of constrictions that are formed in the vocal tract as consonant-vowel and vowel-consonant sequences are produced.

1.3.1 The Respiratory System Below the Larynx

The control of the muscles in the respiratory system has been reviewed by Rothenberg (1968). His estimates of the constraints on rates of change of the tensions produced in this musculature are based primarily on experiments with models of the subglottal system and larynx, the parameters of the models being determined from data in the literature on the physical properties of the structures, and on the properties of muscle response. His findings regarding time constraints of the subglottal system are derived also from measurements of rates of change of subglottal and supraglottal pressure that occur in normal speech. Rothenberg concluded that a unidirectional change in subglottal pressure of 5 to 10 cm H_2O (with an occluded vocal tract, i.e., with no airflow) can be achieved in 100 ms, although times in excess of this minimum value are more likely to occur under conditions of normal speech. Hixon (1987) notes that an abrupt change in pressure (of 1 to 3 cm H_2O) during speech production at normal loudness can be achieved in 75 to 150 ms. These data suggest that a cyclic change, consisting of an increase in subglottal pressure from some steady value to some other value, followed immediately by a decrease to the original pressure, requires 300 ms or more. This time is several times less than the duration of a respiratory cycle during normal breathing. The time constant of the physical system and airways that constitute the subglottal respiratory system is approximately 20 ms (as discussed below), and hence it can be concluded that the above times of about 100 ms and 300 ms are determined almost entirely by the properties of the muscle response.

Rothenberg also made estimates of the change of supraglottal pressure when there is a rapid change in the size of a constriction in the supraglottal tract—either a change from an open configuration to closure or a release from closure to an open position. The innervation of the respiratory muscles was held fixed when these changes were made in the model that was used to study these temporal phenomena. For an abrupt (step-function) change in the size of the supraglottal constriction, the response time of the subglottal pressure change is roughly 20 ms, that is, it takes about 20 ms for the subglottal pressure to make a transition to a new steady-state value appropriate for the changed supraglottal configuration. The response time of 20 ms is due to the physical properties of the system, including both the tissues surrounding the airways and the air volumes within the respiratory tract. The steady-state subglottal pressure when there is an occlusion is higher than the value with an open vocal tract, since in the latter case there is a pressure drop due to the rapid airflow in the flow resistance of the airways between the lungs and the mouth. (See section 1.2.) The difference in subglottal pressure for the more open configuration for vowels and for a closed configuration is usually only a small fraction of the total subglottal pressure, however.

1.3.2 Adjustments of Vocal Fold Tension

The tension or stiffness of the vocal folds is the principal determinant of the fundamental frequency of vocal fold vibration. Thus estimates of the rates of contraction of muscles controlling vocal cord tension (the vocalis muscle and the cricothyroid muscle) can be made from observations of changes in fundamental frequency during speech production. Informal studies of this kind indicate that a cyclic change in fundamental frequency within a vowel or across a vowel sequence (such as a rise in F_0 from a fixed value followed by a fall in F_0 back to approximately the original value) can be achieved in about 200 to 300 ms. A simple rise or fall in this case could be effected in about 100 ms. Somewhat related is the observation that when trained singers use vibrato, the frequency of the vibrato is in the range of 5 to 7 Hz (period of 140 to 200 ms) (Sundberg, 1994; Prame, 1994). It is recognized, however, that production of vibrato of a few hertz during singing is only indirectly related to production of the larger changes in F_0 that occur in speech.[4]

Fujisaki (1992) found that the accent components of F_0 contours in sentences could be approximated by the response of a critically damped second-order system to a brief pulse. The natural frequency of the system was 20 s^{-1}, and the minimum duration of the response to the pulse was in the range of 200 to 300 ms. The relaxation in vocal fold stiffness following the release of a voiceless consonant is marked by a fall in fundamental frequency. The time taken to complete this fall appears to be about 100 ms, measured from the time of the consonant release. It has been suggested (Fujisaki, 1992) that there is a mode of control of vocal fold tension with a much slower response time that has a time constant several times that of the faster mode of control just considered. As noted in section 1.1.2, this mode could involve changing vocal fold tension by a translation movement of the thyroid cartilage in relation to the cricoid cartilage. In any case, observation of fundamental frequency patterns in continuous speech indicates that at time intervals of 1 to 3 s or more, some resetting of the laryngeal posture occurs. The mechanism underlying this resetting is not fully understood. Thus there appears to be a mode of control of the larynx with a time cycle that is somewhat greater than the 200 to 300 ms required for a rapid cyclic change in F_0.

1.3.3 Movements of Glottal and Supraglottal Structures

For glottal adjustments and for most supraglottal structures involved in speech production, the minimum time taken to produce one period of a rapid

Anatomy and Physiology of Speech Production

repetitive movement is approximately 200 ms, on average, although there are some differences between articulators. This time can be as short as 150 ms for some structures, whereas for others it can be up to 250 or 300 ms. These times may be somewhat greater if the amplitudes of the movements are large, and may be shorter than 150 ms if the amplitudes are small. The structures and movements for which these measurements apply include glottal abductions and adductions, backward and forward movements of the tongue body, advancing and constricting of the tongue root, alternating vertical movements of the tongue body, raising and lowering of the tongue blade, opening and closing movements of the lips, and rounding of the lips. The similarity in the times required for cyclic movements of different articulators does not reflect the substantial differences in rate of unidirectional movement of the articulator or the rate of change of the area of the orifice in the vocal tract that results from movement of the articulator.

1.3.3.1 Adjustments of Glottal Opening Rough estimates of the response times for adducting and abducting maneuvers of the glottis can be made from measurements of mouth pressures and simultaneous acoustic records during the production of rapid sequences of appropriately selected speech sounds (Rothenberg, 1968), as well as from basic studies of the contraction of intrinsic larynx muscles in animals (Mårtensson and Skoglund, 1964; Mårtensson, 1968). These data suggest that cyclic closed-open-closed movements of the glottis require 80 to 150 ms to actualize. Unidirectional abducting or adducting movements would require less time, and it would appear (Mårtensson and Skoglund, 1964) that the adducting maneuver is faster than the abducting one. The time taken to perform a complete cycle of glottal abduction-adduction can also be estimated from acoustic measurements on a rapidly produced utterance such as haha.... Times as short as 200 ms are required to produce one complete cycle of such an utterance (Upshaw, 1992; see also data in Klatt and Klatt, 1990). The aspiration interval of about 50 ms for aspirated stop consonants before stressed vowels suggests that this time is required for the adducting maneuver from an open position (with a spacing between the folds at their posterior end of about 4 mm) appropriate for an aspirated consonant to a position that is sufficiently closed that vocal fold vibration can start. Maximum rates of change of glottal area, then, are estimated to be less than 5 cm^2/s. When the aspirated stop consonant occurs in intervocalic position, there is a minimum time interval of about 150 to 200 ms between the time that abduction can be detected in the first vowel (either through airflow measurements or from acoustic data) to the time when the glottis returns to its relatively adducted state in the second vowel.

1.3.3.2 Tongue Body and Tongue Root Cineradiographic data for a limited inventory of utterances (Perkell, 1969) suggest that a maneuver of the tongue root from one position to another requires a minimum of about

100 ms to complete. The timing of tongue body movements between vowel-like configurations has characteristics similar to that of the tongue root. A maneuver from one vowel configuration to another can be as short as 100 ms, whether or not a constricting consonantal gesture is superimposed on this maneuver by a structure like the lips or tongue tip (Ohman, 1967). These response times are obtained when the tongue body positions are associated with well-defined vowels that are not reduced. A reduced vowel can be actualized without specifying a target position for the tongue body, and hence response times for maneuvers involving reduced vowels may be shorter. Thus the cyclic tongue body maneuver between the two vowels /ɪ/ in the phrase "sit a bit" may be faster than the 200 to 300 ms indicated above. It may not, in fact, be appropriate to call this tongue body motion cyclic, since no target is specified for the middle vowel and the tongue body movement toward and away from this vowel is small. These times for cyclic tongue body movement are not inconsistent with the observation that a typical minimum duration of a stressed syllable in continuous speech is about 200 ms (Fant and Kruckenberg, 1989). This duration depends on the degree of openness of the vowel and increases with the number of consonants adjacent to the vowel. If the vowel is unstressed, this duration is considerably shorter.

1.3.3.3 Soft Palate The minimum duration of an alternating movement of the soft palate that produces a single complete cycle from a closed velopharyngeal port to an open port and back to a closed port is estimated to be in the range of 200 to 300 ms. This estimate is based on acoustic measurements in utterances like /imi/ or /ɑmɑ/ when they are preceded and followed by consonants that require a closed velopharyngeal port. The estimate is also consistent with measurements of velar movements from cineradiographic data (Moll and Daniloff, 1971). The acoustic data indicate the time from the first evidence of nasalization in the first vowel to termination of nasalization in the second vowel. Data on velum movements reported by Krakow (1993) also show a minimum duration of 200 to 300 ms for a complete closed-open-closed sequence when a nasal consonant is produced in rapid speech. This duration is similar to that for a comparable movement of other structures, such as the tongue body and mandible. When a nasal consonant or a nasal vowel is produced in an utterance in which an obstruent consonant precedes and follows the nasalized region of the utterance, the time interval in which there is an open velopharyngeal port may be somewhat less than 200 to 300 ms. It is probable that as the velopharyngeal opening decreases following the nasal segment, the creation of an oral constriction in the vocal tract causes a raised intraoral pressure. This increased pressure exerts a force on the soft palate that accelerates the closing movement.

The cineradiographic data reported by Moll and Daniloff (1971) indicate maximum rates of movement of the velum in the range of 7 to 10 cm/s. When the velopharyngeal port closes in anticipation of a following stop consonant, the velopharyngeal wall distance appears to decrease at a maximum rate of about 20 cm/s.

Acoustic data on vowel nasalization in utterances like /imi/ can be used to obtain indirect estimates of the rates of increase or decrease of the velopharyngeal area in such sequences. A rough estimate of the rate of increase of this area in a vowel preceding a nasal consonant is 10 cm^2/s (i.e., a time of about 50 ms is required to create a velopharyngeal area of about 0.5 cm^2). The rate of decrease of the velopharyngeal area following a nasal consonant may be somewhat greater than this. As noted above, this rate may be accelerated by the forces on the soft palate due to intraoral pressure following the nasal consonant in an utterance like *lumber*.

1.3.3.4 Lip Rounding The minimum time taken to maneuver the lips from an unrounded to a rounded configuration is estimated to be in the range of 50 to 100 ms (Perkell and Chiang, 1986; Perkell and Matthies, 1992). This estimate is based on direct measurements of the time course of lip opening and lip protrusion. The total time required from beginning of a protrusion movement to a nonprotruded configuration for a vowel like /u/ appears to be in the range of 200 to 300 ms (Perkell and Matthies, 1992).

1.3.3.5 Timing of Movements Toward and Away from Consonantal Constrictions A common event in speech production is one in which an articulator makes contact with an opposing structure or surface, and then this contact is released. Examples are the stop consonants /p/, /t/, and /k/. In the case of /p/, the two lips make contact and then are released; for /t/ the tongue blade is raised to touch the hard palate; and for /k/ the tongue body is raised to make contact in the palatal or velar region. Several measures can be used to describe the timing of these movements. One such measure is the time taken to perform a single reversal, in which the structure moves away from contact and then returns to make contact again (cf. Westbury and Dembowski, 1993). This time is expected to be somewhat more than about one-half of the time taken to make a complete cycle from one release to another release. A single movement of an oral articulator from a constricted position to a specified position for a vowel and back to the constricted position is generally not less than about 200 ms, as noted above. For some vowels, however, the required degree of opening during the vowel is not specified, and can be quite small. The duration of the opening-closing movement for such a reduced vowel can be considerably less than 200 ms.

Another kinematic measure is the rate of movement of the articulator as it moves toward or away from the opposing structure. Perhaps of more relevance acoustically is the rate of change of cross-sectional area of the constriction as the articulator performs these movements. When the cross-sectional area of a constriction is relatively small (up to about 0.3 cm^2), certain aerodynamic and acoustic parameters are especially sensitive to changes in area.

For all of the stop consonants /p/, /t/, and /k/, the articulators that form the constriction are linked to the mandible. Thus the movement of the mandible contributes to the motion of the lower lip, the tongue blade, or the tongue dorsum. Alternating movements of the mandible can be produced up to rates of about 7 Hz, that is, a period of about 150 ms. Peak velocities of mandible movement (as measured at the lower incisors) are in the range 10 to 20 cm/s (Nelson et al., 1984; Kent and Moll, 1972; Beckman and Edwards, 1993), but velocities of the jaw during normal syllable production are normally below 10 cm/s (Sussman et al., 1973; Folkins, 1981; Smith and McLean-Muse, 1986).

Alternating opening and closing movements of the lips require a minimum time of 150 to 200 ms for a complete cycle, as noted earlier. The duration of the lip opening or closing movement for a labial stop consonant is about 75 ms at fast speaking rates (Adams et al., 1993). Peak velocities of movement of the body of the lower lip immediately following the release of a labial stop consonant are estimated to be about 25 cm/s or less (Fujimura, 1961; Sussman et al., 1973; Smith and McLean-Muse, 1986; Westbury and Dembowski, 1993). These velocities are somewhat greater than the peak velocities of mandible movement noted above, since the downward displacement of the lower lip is a superposition of mandible movement and lip movement relative to the mandible.

The movements of the lip surfaces during the release of bilabial stop consonants have been studied in some detail by high-speed photographic techniques (Fujimura, 1961). Measurements of midline lip separation *versus* time during release of the stop consonant /p/ and the nasal consonant /m/ in English are shown in figure 1.31a. For the stop consonant, there is an initial

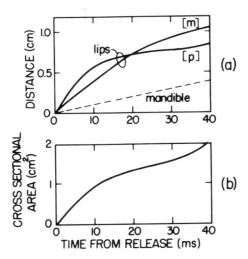

Figure 1.31 (a) Measurements of the distance between the lip surfaces vs. time at the release of the bilabial consonants /m/ and /p/ in the words *meat* and *peat*. The dashed line shows the displacement of the lower incisors relative to their position at the instant of lip release. (b) Estimate of cross-sectional area of lip opening at the release of the initial consonant /p/ in the word *pope*. (From Fujimura, 1961.)

Anatomy and Physiology of Speech Production

rapid separation in the first 5 to 10 ms after the release, due to the initial force from the pressure behind the closure. This initial rapid movement is followed by a slower approach to a position appropriate for the following vowel in the next 40-odd milliseconds. The trajectory for the nasal consonant is smoother. The initial rate of increase of lip separation is about 75 cm/s for the stop and about 30 cm/s for the nasal. The figure also shows an estimate of the displacement of the lower teeth during release of the stop consonant. The rate of change of lip separation is several times the downward velocity of the mandible as measured at the lower incisors.

Measurements of the velocity of a point on the lower lip by Kuehn and Moll (1976) for the consonant /p/ in an intervocalic environment give average values of about 21 cm/s for vowel-consonant movements and about 16 cm/s for consonant-vowel movements. As expected, these velocities are somewhat less than the rate of change of lip separation measured at the lip surface.

Figure 1.31b shows Fujimura's estimates of the cross-sectional area of the mouth opening, computed from measurements of the width of the lip opening as well as the lip separation. The time to achieve a cross-sectional area of 0.3 cm^2 (i.e., an area corresponding to a vowel-like configuration) for the stop consonant is very short—just a few milliseconds. The initial rate of increase of cross-sectional area is about 100 cm^2/s. Other estimates of this rate of increase by Poort (1994, 1995), based on observation of movements of points on the lips and on acoustic data, suggest a somewhat lower value of about 40 cm^2/s.

Data showing the tongue tip movement at the release of a consonant produced with the tongue blade have been obtained from cineradiographic studies of speech production (Perkell, 1969; Kent and Moll, 1972; Adams et al., 1993). These data are, perhaps, less precise than the results for bilabial consonants since the surface of the tongue tip is sometimes difficult to locate precisely on cineradiographic pictures, and the frame rate for the cineradiographic data is rather low. A plot of the tongue tip movement at the closure and release of the stop consonant /d/ before the vowel /ɑ/ is displayed in figure 1.32. This curve is adapted from data reported by Kent and Moll (1972) for the stop consonant /d/ in a vowel-consonant-vowel environment. The initial rate of movement of the tongue tip is in the range of 20 to 40 cm/s, with the faster rates for the implosion phase. These estimates are consistent with those of Kuehn and Moll (1976) and of Adams et al. (1993) for the consonant /t/. In the case of a release, there is again an initial interval of rapid movement, in this case 20 ms long, followed by an interval in which the speed of separation is slower. The rate of change of cross-sectional area for a release formed by the tongue tip will depend on the type of release. A release produced by the tongue tip against the alveolar ridge can be more rapid than a release of a laminal stop consonant, in which a larger area of the tongue blade is involved in forming the constriction. Acoustic and other

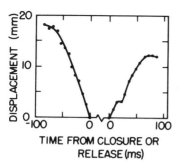

Figure 1.32 Displacement of the apex of the tongue vs. time during the utterance /ɑdɑ/ produced at a moderate speaking rate. The ordinate is the lingua-alveolar distance as estimated from cineradiographs. Data points are given at intervals of 6.7 ms. There is a break in the time axis during the consonantal constriction. (Adapted from Kent and Moll, 1972.)

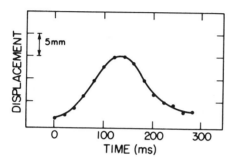

Figure 1.33 Vertical movement of a point on the dorsum of the tongue in the vicinity of closure during the production of an intervocalic consonant /g/. The data are plotted at intervals of 20 ms. (Adapted from Kent and Moll, 1972.)

data suggest that the rate of change of cross-sectional area for an apical stop or nasal consonant is in the range of 50 to 100 cm^2/s, and is somewhat slower for a laminal consonant.

The minimum time from one release to the next release for a sequence of two velar consonants is about the same as it is for a labial or alveolar consonant (Westbury and Dembowski, 1993). Observations of motions of points on the tongue dorsum for such alternating movements indicate that points on the tongue dorsum near where contact is made tend to perform a rotating movement rather than a simple linear movement toward and away from the palate (Mooshammer et al., 1995). An example of the vertical motion of a point on the tongue surface near the region of closure for a velar stop consonant in a vowel-consonant-vowel context is given in figure 1.33 (Kent and Moll, 1972). In the case of the movement of the tongue body toward or away from closure, the maximum velocity of the tongue surfaces in a direction normal to the palatal surface is about 20 cm/s, that is, somewhat greater than the maximum velocity of mandible movement at the lower incisors. Kuehn and Moll (1976) report a peak velocity of 10 to

Anatomy and Physiology of Speech Production

15 cm/s, averaged over several speakers. As a point of reference, a peak velocity of 20 cm/s would be obtained if the motion of the surface were sinusoidal with a period of 200 ms and an amplitude of 0.7 cm. The maximum rate of change of cross-sectional area of the constriction during this tongue body movement for a velar consonant is estimated to be about 25 cm^2/s. The width of the channel formed by the tongue surface probably increases more rapidly than the cross-dimensions, especially immediately following the release. As will be seen in chapter 7, this rate of change of area is consistent with observations of acoustic events at the implosion or release of a velar stop consonant.

The movement of the tongue body for a velar consonant is slower than that of the tongue tip and lip surfaces for alveolar and labial stops, and there is again a tendency for the speed to be greatest immediately following the release. This initial rate of movement appears to be faster than the rate that normally occurs for tongue body movements from one vowel configuration to another. It is probable that the velar consonant is produced with a local bunching or deformation of the tongue surface through contraction of intrinsic tongue muscles, superimposed on a gross tongue body movement. It might be expected that the initial rapid movement is primarily the result of fast intrinsic muscle activity. Aerodynamic forces may also be involved in the release of a stop consonant for which there is pressure buildup behind the constriction.

The rates of movement of the lips, tongue tip, and tongue dorsum depend to some extent on the following vowel. Available data suggest that the time taken to complete movement from the release to the configuration for the vowel for a given point of articulation is largely independent of the following vowel, whereas the average rate of movement depends on the distance that must be traversed by the structure to achieve a position appropriate for the vowel. The initial rate of movement (during the first few milliseconds) may, however, be relatively independent of the vowel.

1.3.3.6 Overall Speech Rates   The above survey has shown that one alternating movement of any given laryngeal or supralaryngeal structure requires a time interval that is in the range of 150 to 300 ms, depending somewhat on the structure and on the amplitude of the movement. This duration range can be compared with mean syllable durations in read script, which are in the range of 200 to 250 ms, with somewhat shorter durations for the fastest passages (Crystal and House, 1990). Each syllable has about 2.8 phones, on average, so that the median duration of a phone is in the range of 70 to 90 ms. It is clear that the articulatory movements to produce a given phone must be interleaved with the movements that are required to produce adjacent phones. The production of running speech requires intricate coordination of different articulators each of which has limitations on its rate of movement.

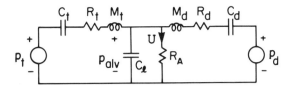

Figure 1.34 Equivalent circuit for the mechanoaerodynamic system for controlling respiratory pressure and flow, shown in figure 1.3.

1.4 TIME-VARYING AIRFLOWS AND PRESSURES

1.4.1 Model of the Respiratory System

For the production of most speech sounds the respiratory system below the larynx supplies the energy for moving air through the larynx and supraglottal structures, and this airflow is in turn modulated to generate sound. Some parameters of the mechanical aspects of this system have been described in section 1.1.1, and the aerodynamic aspects have been noted in section 1.2.

A model of the system in terms of an equivalent circuit that incorporates both aerodynamic and mechanical parameters is given in figure 1.34. In this equivalent circuit, the variable representing flow through the elements is volume velocity in cubic centimeters per second, and across the elements is a pressure drop, in dynes per square centimeter. The "charge" on a compliance element (such as C_ℓ) represents the volume increase or decrease associated with the path in which that element is located. This volume change ΔV is proportional to the pressure drop p_C across the compliance, and is given by $\Delta V = Cp_C$, where C is the value of the compliance. The appearance of a pressure drop p_C across C indicates that energy is stored in the compliance.

On each side of the circuit there is a path containing a pressure source. The flow in one of these paths is the flow due to contraction or expansion of the thorax. This path contains a pressure source p_t resulting from the contraction of muscles (primarily the intercostals) that cause motion of the walls of the thorax. In series with the source are mechanical elements representing the compliance of the thorax walls and the effective mass and resistance of the walls. The flow in the second parallel path arises from movement of the diaphragm. The values of the elements in this path are somewhat different from those in the thorax path. Approximate values for the elements have been given in section 1.1.1.

The compliance across both of these paths represents the acoustic compliance of the lung volume. This compliance is $C_\ell = V/P_o$, where P_o is the ambient pressure. A volume $V = 3000$ cm^3 is assumed, giving a compliance of $C_\ell = 0.003$ cm^5/dyne. At sufficiently low frequencies we can assume isothermal expansions and contractions, and this value of C_ℓ is based on this assumption. The element representing the impedance of the airways above the lungs depends on the state of these airways, particularly the configuration of the glottis and the supralaryngeal vocal tract. At low frequencies, this impedance is resistive, and is represented by a resistance R_A in figure 1.34. The airways can be completely closed, leading to an open circuit for R_A. For the production of vowels, a typical value of R_A for low frequencies is 52 acoustic ohms (dyne-s/cm^5), corresponding to an average airflow of about 150 cm^3/s for a subglottal pressure of 8 cm H_2O (cf. figure 1.26). For certain aspirated consonants, R_A can be as low as 10 acoustic ohms. A typical average value in normal speech production is $R_A = 40$ acoustic ohms. During normal breathing, when the airways are relatively unconstricted, R_A can be even smaller than 10 ohms.

During an inspiration, one or both of the sources in the circuit assume negative values (relative to the reference directions shown in figure 1.34), and, R_A is small. The expansion of the thorax or the lowering of the diaphragm causes a pressure drop across the compliance elements C_t and C_d. At the beginning of an expiration during speech production, a constriction is formed in the airways at the glottis or above the glottis, and the pressure in the lungs is typically about 8 cm H_2O, or about 8000 dynes/cm^2. If at the end of the inspiration the pressure drop across C_t and C_d achieves this value of 8000 dynes/cm^2, then the subglottal pressure necessary for the initiation of speech production can be generated without implementing the sources p_t and p_d. That is, speech production is initiated using the energy stored in the compliances C_t and C_d. If we assume an average airway resistance of 40 acoustic ohms during speech, or an average airflow of about 200 cm^3/s, then the pressure across the compliances C_t and C_d drops only slowly, with a net time constant of about 6 s. (For slow changes in the resistance R_A, the effect of the mass elements M_t and M_d can be neglected.) Thus if a constant subglottal pressure is to be maintained during an expiration, it is necessary to introduce the sources p_t or p_d only slowly. Rapid and precise control of these sources is not required to maintain a reasonably constant subglottal pressure. Most of the energy for producing the airflow during the initial few seconds of an utterance comes directly from the energy that has been stored in the expanded thorax or depressed diaphragm during the previous inspiration. Of course, if an inspiration is insufficient to provide the necessary pressure across the compliances C_t and C_d, then the sources must be invoked to provide the airflow needed for speech production.

During speech production, rapid changes often occur in the resistance R_A of the laryngeal and supralaryngeal systems. An extreme case is the release of a voiceless aspirated stop consonant, when there is an abrupt change from complete closure in the supraglottal airways to an airway resistance of about 10 acoustic ohms. In order to understand events immediately following the release, we shall simplify the circuit of figure 1.34 by including only the thorax branch. The main features of the response, shown in figure 1.35, will be the same independent of which branch (or both) is involved. The circuit has a response with a long time constant, given by

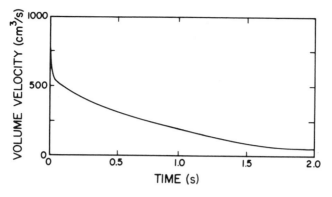

Figure 1.35 Calculation of volume velocity U in figure 1.34 when a sudden change is made from complete obstruction of the airway ($R_A = \infty$) to a value $R_A = 10$ acoustic ohms. The sources p_t and p_d are assumed to be zero, and an initial alveolar pressure of 8 cm H_2O is assumed.

$$\tau_1 = (R_A + R_t)C_t = 0.8\,s \tag{1.14}$$

and a faster initial component as shown in the figure. If the glottis were more adducted, as for normal vowel production, the rate of decay would be considerably slower than the rate shown in the figure.

1.4.2 Model of the Supraglottal System

During the production of most speech sounds, the average area of the glottal opening is relatively small, so that its impedance is large compared with the impedance of the subglottal system. Under these circumstances, the sub-glottal pressure throughout an utterance can often be assumed to be constant for purposes of calculating airflows and pressures in the vocal tract. Some changes in subglottal pressure may occur, however, on certain syllables that are stressed, and there may be some reduction of pressure toward the end of an utterance (Ladefoged, 1962; Atkinson, 1973).

Many consonants are produced with a narrow constriction in the vocal tract above the glottis, as in the configuration in figure 1.36a. A model that can be used for estimating the airflows and pressures in the vocal tract for such a configuration is shown in figure 1.36b. The impedances of the con-strictions at the glottis and at the supraglottal constriction are Z_g and Z_c. One or both of these impedances can be time-varying as the constriction sizes change during the production of particular speech sounds. The air volume between the two constrictions has an acoustic compliance C_v, and the elements R_w, M_w, and C_w represent the impedance of the walls, as noted in section 1.1.3.7. The constant subglottal pressure is represented by the source P_s.

As will be discussed in section 8.4, a speaker may actively expand or con-tract the volume of the vocal tract between the two constrictions during the production of some sounds. The effect of this expansion is represented by the

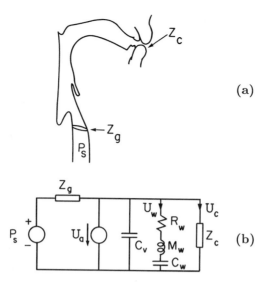

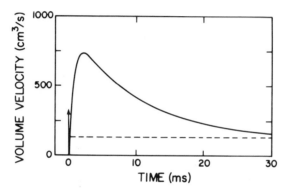

Figure 1.36 (a) Midsagittal shape of the vocal tract when there are constrictions at the glottis and at the lips. The acoustic impedances of these constrictions are Z_g and Z_c, respectively. (b) Equivalent circuit for the configuration in (a). See text.

Figure 1.37 Volume velocity response U_c for the circuit in figure 1.36b when the impedance Z_c of the labial constriction is abruptly changed at time $t = 0$ from an open circuit to a short circuit (i.e., from a complete closure to an open configuration). The subglottal pressure P_s is 8 cm H_2O, and there is no active expansion or contraction of the volume, that is, $U_a = 0$. The glottal impedance $Z_g = 60$ acoustic ohms, and other element values are given in the text. The vertical arrow at $t = 0$ indicates an initial pulse of volume velocity (volume = 0.3 cm^3) as the acoustic compliance C_v discharges through the short circuit. The horizontal dashed line shows the steady-state airflow that is reached when t is large.

volume velocity source U_a, which is positive if there is an active expansion and negative is there is a contraction of the volume. The volume velocity U_w through the wall impedance contributes a passive expansion of the vocal tract volume.

To illustrate how changes in flows and pressures can be estimated using the model of figure 1.36, we consider a configuration in which the glottis is in a relatively narrow or adducted state, so that Z_g is large. We assume that there is initially a complete closure at the supraglottal constriction, so that $Z_c = \infty$. Under these conditions, a steady pressure P_s equal to the subglottal pressure exists in the vocal tract, and this pressure appears across the compliances C_v and C_w. An abrupt opening movement is then created by the articulator forming the supraglottal constriction (the lips in the configuration of figure 1.36a), so that there is an abrupt reduction of Z_c. We shall assume here that the impedance Z_c changes to zero instantaneously. This sequence is a rough approximation to the articulatory movements following the release of an unaspirated stop consonant such as /b/. The airflow U_c through the lips following the release for this hypothetical situation for a subglottal pressure $P_s = 8$ cm H_2O is shown in figure 1.37. There is an initial brief pulse in the flow as the acoustic compliance C_v discharges through the opening (Massey, 1994). The volume of this pulse is equal to $P_s C_v$. For a vocal tract volume of about 60 cm^3, $C_v \cong 4 \times 10^{-5}$ cm^5/dyne, so that the initial volume pulse is $P_s C_v = 8 \times 980 \times 4 \times 10^{-5} = 0.3$ cm^3. The volume expansion due to the compliance of the walls is $P_s C_w = 8$ cm^3, taking C_w to be 10^{-3} cm^5/dyne. This volume discharges through R_w and M_w, as shown in figure 1.37. There is a relatively fast rise time, followed by a slower decay with a time constant equal to $R_w C_w = 10$ ms, for $R_w = 10$ dyne-s/cm^5. Following this rise and fall in the airflow, the flow reaches a steady value determined by the glottal resistance, which is taken here to be 60 dyne-s/cm^5.

The assumption of an infinite rate of increase of the area of the supraglottal constriction at the release of a stop consonant gives only a rough estimate of the airflow following the release. It indicates, however, that the time constant of the change in pressure in the supraglottal cavity when an abrupt change is made in the supraglottal constriction is on the order of 10 ms. More precise estimates on the changes in pressure and flow following the release of a stop consonant are given in chapter 7, and these show a duration of the volume velocity pulse to be a few milliseconds greater than the estimate from figure 1.37.

2 Source Mechanisms

As we have indicated in chapter 1, it is convenient to consider human speech sound production to be the consequence of the generation of one or more *sources* of sound, and the *filtering* of these sources by the vocal tract. To a large extent, the mechanism of source generation is independent of the filtering process. That is, the properties of the source tend not to be strongly influenced by the acoustic properties of the filters. Thus it is appropriate to discuss source mechanisms separately from the behavior of vocal tract resonators in response to the sources. We will, however, encounter situations in which there may be substantial interaction between source and vocal tract.

The generation of sound energy in the vocal tract always involves the modulation of airflow at or near a constriction in the tract. The sources can be the result of various kinds of modulation of the flow. One type of source is produced by varying the airflow through quasi-periodic lateral movements of the vocal folds, causing a periodic modulation of the glottal area. A source of sound can also be generated by creating turbulence or random fluctuations in the airflow, usually in the vicinity of a constriction or an obstacle. It is also possible to generate a source of sound by causing an abrupt stepwise change in the airflow in the vocal tract, through rapid release of air pressure within an enclosed volume in the vocal tract. We shall consider each of these source mechanisms in turn.

2.1 PERIODIC GLOTTAL SOURCE

The basic mechanism involved in producing a periodic source of sound due to vocal fold vibration can be described with reference to the sequence of glottal configurations shown in figure 2.1. Each panel of this figure shows a lateral section through the vocal folds sampled at one point in the cycle of vibration. Eight instants of time are shown throughout a typical cycle. These sections are reconstructed from observations of vibrations of an excised dog larynx (Baer, 1975). They are taken at a point about halfway between the thyroid and arytenoid cartilages. Also displayed in the figure are plots of the horizontal movement of the vocal fold surface throughout the cycle at the upper edge and at a point 1.3 mm below the upper edge. These trajectories

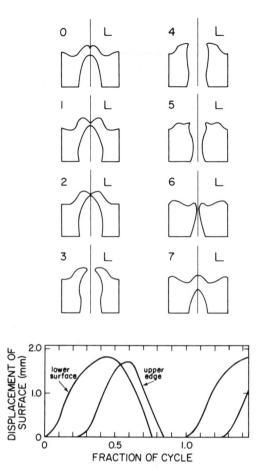

Figure 2.1 The upper part of the figure shows estimated lateral sections through the vibrating vocal folds at eight equally spaced times through the glottal vibration cycle. Data were obtained by Baer (1975) from an excised dog larynx. The scale of 1 mm is indicated by horizontal and vertical lines in the upper right of each panel. The curves in the lower panel show the lateral width of the glottal opening measured at the upper edge of the vocal folds and at a point 1.3 mm below the upper edge. These curves illustrate the time lag between the displacements of the lower and upper portions of the vocal folds. (From Baer, 1975.)

show phase differences in the motion of these two portions of the vocal folds, as will be discussed below. The picture in figure 2.1 will differ somewhat toward the anterior and posterior ends of the glottis, where the amplitude of vibration is usually less than it is in the middle. Although there are anatomical differences between a human larynx and a dog larynx, these pictures of the canine vocal folds illustrate the basic processes.

2.1.1 The Basic Process of Vocal Fold Vibration

Initially we describe qualitatively the process of vibration of the vocal folds, and then we will attempt to develop a more quantitative analysis. For a more

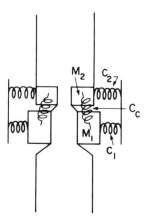

Figure 2.2 Two-mass model of the vocal folds, showing compliances coupling the two masses to the lateral walls and to each other.

detailed analysis of vocal fold vibration and of the acoustic source resulting from this vibration, reference may be made to the work of Fant (1982a), Ishizaka and Matsudaira (1968), Ishizaka and Flanagan (1972), Conrad (1980, 1983), Titze (1988, 1989), K. N. Stevens (1977), and Liljencrants (1991, 1994), among others.

The mechanism whereby vibration is maintained is dependent on the fact that the inferior and superior parts of the vocal folds do not move together as a rigid body, but that there is freedom for these parts to move relative to one another. To a first approximation, each of these parts of a vocal fold can be characterized by a mass and a mechanical compliance, with the two parts being connected by a coupling compliance. This situation is schematized by the mechanical model in figure 2.2. The mass of the superior part of the vocal fold is considerably smaller than that of the inferior part. This mechanical system has certain natural frequencies of vibration that are rather low—usually in the range of 100 to 300 Hz for adult speakers. (This model has, in fact, two natural frequencies or modes.) Thus the rate at which the positions of the parts of this system can change are limited to this frequency range, assuming that there are no abrupt changes in the system parameters. Given these limitations of the mechanical system, a mechanism is required for modulating the airflow to produce sound energy over a broad frequency range. The mechanism that is employed is to bring the folds together rapidly, thus causing an abrupt cessation of the airflow. This abrupt change in the flow produces acoustic energy over a wide band of frequencies. As we discuss the process of vocal fold vibration, then, it is useful to recognize that the principal aim of this process is to create this abrupt cessation of the flow (or at least a cessation or abrupt reduction of the flow through some part of the glottis) at a particular point in time in the cycle of vibration. The motion of the vocal folds at other points in the cycle serves to set up conditions that will result in this abrupt change in the flow.

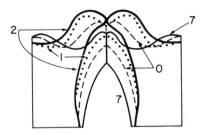

Figure 2.3 Tracings of vocal fold shapes at four instants of time during the closed phase, from figure 2.1. (From Baer, 1975.)

We begin with the vocal folds in a closed position, corresponding to panel 0 of figure 2.1. For the model in figure 2.2, this configuration corresponds to closure of the upper pair of masses, with some spacing between the lower pair. There is no airflow through the glottis, the pressure above the glottis is assumed to be atmospheric pressure, and there is a positive subglottal pressure. A typical value of the subglottal pressure is 8 cm H_2O, or about 8000 dynes/cm². This positive pressure exerts a lateral force on the surfaces of the vocal folds, causing these surfaces to move outward. The time course of this movement is determined by the subglottal pressure, the mass of the lower portion of each vocal fold, and the mechanical compliance of this part of the vocal fold. Figure 2.3 shows a superposition of the vocal fold shapes for several successive frames of figure 2.1 during the time interval when there is contact between the folds. As the lower portions of the folds are displaced laterally, the vertical length of the approximated portions of the folds decreases. This change in the vertical length can be seen in figure 2.1 in panels 7, 0, 1, and 2. In the model of figure 2.2, this initial part of the cycle corresponds to a closure of the upper mass and a gradual widening of the distance between the lower masses.

When the lateral displacement of the surfaces reaches a certain critical value, with a configuration indicated by the line labeled 2 in figure 2.3 or by panel 2 in figure 2.1, then airflow through the glottis begins. The upper edge of the vocal fold, which is represented by a small mass in the model of figure 2.2, accelerates rapidly in a lateral direction under the influence of the force arising from the mechanical compliance that couples the lower portion of the vocal fold to this upper section. As soon as airflow begins, there is a decrease in the outward pressure on the surfaces below the upper edges of the vocal folds. This pressure drops close to zero relative to atmospheric pressure (if the supraglottal pressure is zero) or could become negative as a consequence of the Bernoulli effect (Binh and Gauffin, 1983).

During the time the glottis is open and there is a flow of air through the glottis, then, the abducting force on the larger inferior portion of the vocal fold decreases, and can become negative. This part of the vocal fold (or the lower of the two masses in figure 2.2) then completes its outward excursion and begins an inward motion. This inward movement accelerates and the surfaces come together rapidly, as in panels 4 to 6 of figure 2.1. The flow through the glottis immediately ceases at the time the vocal folds touch. This medial displacement of the lower part of the vocal fold exerts an inward force on the upper edge of the fold, through the coupling compliance between the upper and lower parts, and this edge is also accelerated inward. The inward motion of the upper edge is, however, delayed relative to that of the lower part. After the vocal folds become approximated, the subglottal pressure again exerts a force on the lower surfaces of the folds, and the cycle begins again. Throughout the cycle of vibration, figures 2.1 and 2.3 show that there is a continuous change in the shape of the vocal folds, particularly during the time when the surfaces of the two folds are touching. Thus there is a continuous redistribution of the viscous material within the vocal folds, giving rise to energy loss within the folds.

This sequence of events during a cycle of vibration corresponds roughly to *modal voicing*. The glottis closes completely during some part of the cycle but the vocal folds are not pushed tightly together during the closed phase.

We will attempt now to be more analytical about the process. To simplify the analysis, we shall assume that the lateral motion of the folds is sufficiently small that the compliance elements in the model of figure 2.2 can be considered to be linear. As has been shown in section 1.1.2, this assumption of linearity is only an approximation.

During the initial phase of the vibratory cycle, when there is no airflow, there is an outward force on a spring-mass system. If we take the average vertical length of the lower, more massive, portion of the fold during this interval to be d_1, and if the subglottal pressure is P_s, then the average force per unit length on this lower part of the fold is $P_s d_1$. As figure 2.3 shows, the vertical length of the vocal fold over which the pressure is applied changes with time, so that d_1 must be considered as an average vertical length. We define the mass and effective mechanical compliance per unit length of the fold to be M_1 and C_1', respectively, and we neglect for the moment the losses in the fold.[1] The equation of motion for this part of the fold is

$$M_1 \ddot{x}_1 + \frac{1}{C_1'}(x_1 - x_0) = P_s d_1, \qquad (2.1)$$

where x_1 is the lateral displacement of the surface and x_0 is a resting position in the absence of any lateral force. It is possible for x_0 to be negative if the vocal folds are pushed together by adducting forces in the resting condition. If we assume that the fold is at rest before the outward displacement begins, then the solution to equation (2.1) is

$$x_1(t) = (P_s d_1 C_1' + x_0)(1 - \cos \omega_0 t), \qquad (2.2)$$

where $\omega_0 = 1/\sqrt{M_1 C_1'}$.

This curve has the form shown in the initial portion of the waveform in figure 2.4, labeled ABD. In order to plot this curve, we have selected some values for the parameters that are typical for adult male vocal folds:

$P_s = 8000$ dynes/cm^2, $x_0 = 0.01$ cm, $d_1 = 0.2$ cm, $M_1 = 0.1$ gm/cm, and $C_1' = 3 \times 10^{-5}$ cm^2/dyne. These values are in the range of estimates based on measurements of the properties of the vocal folds, as discussed in section 1.1.2.2 of chapter 1. For these conditions, the natural frequency is $f_0 = \omega_0/(2\pi) = 92$ Hz, and the peak amplitude of $x_1(t)$ in equation (2.2) is 1.2 mm. This peak is never reached, however, since before the displacement reaches this value, the upper edges of the vocal folds separate and the outward force $P_s d_1$ drops to zero or becomes negative. Experimentally it appears that the opening of the upper edges and the onset of airflow usually occurs for a value of x_1 less than 1 mm (i.e., an average separation for the lower portion of the vocal folds of less than 2 mm). We shall select a critical value of 0.6 mm for the purposes of illustration. This is the value of $x_1 = x_{10}$ in figure 2.4 indicating the end of the closed phase, labeled as point B, when the upper edge is about to open. Since conditions change at point B on the curve, the segment BD, which represents a continuation of the solution of equation (2.2), is not traversed by the lower portion of the vocal fold.

Following the opening of the upper edge, we shall assume for purposes of this analysis that the pressure within the glottis drops to zero, so that there is no longer an outward force on the lower surfaces of the vocal folds. This is an approximation only, but is roughly in accord with measurements on static models of the glottis, reported by Scherer and Titze (1983) and by Binh and Gauffin (1983). The motion of the lower mass during the subsequent interval is the unforced motion of the mass-spring combination, and it follows a sinusoidal trajectory. As noted above, we are assuming that the rest position of the lower portion of the vocal folds is $x_0 = 0.01$ cm, that is,

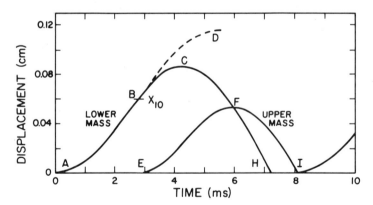

Figure 2.4 Schematic representation of the motion of lower and upper masses during a cycle of vibration of the two-mass model in figure 2.2. The displacement of the lower mass is given by ABCFH, whereas the trajectory of the upper mass is EFI. The upper mass begins its lateral motion at E, when the displacement of the upper mass is x_{10}. The dashed line to point D is the projected trajectory of the lower mass if the glottis did not open and if steady pressure on the lower mass were maintained. The glottis is open and airflow occurs in the region marked by the line EFH. The beginning of the second cycle is shown at the right. Assumed physical parameters of vocal folds are appropriate for an adult male, as described in the text.

the lower portions of the vocal folds are slightly separated in the absence of a subglottal pressure. The resulting movement of the lower part of the vocal folds is shown as segment BCFH in figure 2.4. There is no discontinuity in displacement or in velocity (i.e., the slope of the curve) at the point B where the two segments of the curve are joined at a time of 2.7 ms. For the assumptions we have made, it turns out that the peak value of x_1 is about 0.9 mm. At the point H of closure of this part of the vocal fold (which is also the point at which the glottal area drops to zero and the airflow stops) there is a discontinuity in the slope of the curve.

At the time the upper edges of the vocal folds separate, there is an outward force on these edges due to the coupling compliance C_c in figure 2.2. Neglecting, for the moment, the change in position of the lower parts of the vocal folds, the movement of the upper edge in relation to the lower portion will again follow a sinusoidal trajectory, at least during the initial part of its motion while the lower portion is passing through the maximum in its trajectory. The movement of the upper edge during this time is approximately of the form

$$x_2(t) = x_{20}(1 - \cos \omega_1 t), \tag{2.3}$$

where $\omega_1 = 1/\sqrt{M_2 C_c}$, M_2 is the mass per unit length of the upper edge, and time t is measured from the instant the upper edge begins to move. Typical values of M_2 and C_c are about 0.02 gm/cm and 5×10^{-5} cm²/dyne. (We shall assume that C_2 is large compared with C_c.) The amplitude x_{20} is approximately equal to the difference between the peak displacement of M_1 and the displacement x_{10} of the lower mass at the time the upper edge begins its motion. In our example, x_{10} is about 0.6 mm. The first part of the curve for x_2 in figure 2.4, labeled EF, is calculated for these conditions. Beyond $t = 5.0$ ms, the lower part of the fold begins to move inward more rapidly, and there is a corresponding additional inward force on the upper edge, which begins a larger inward acceleration at this point. Over this time interval, however, the upper edge is not playing a part in defining the glottal area or determining the glottal airflow, since the glottal area is determined by the lower edges. The movement of the upper edge during this time interval is sketched approximately as segment FI in the figure.

From this analysis, then, we observe that the upper and lower parts of the vocal folds vibrate with a difference in phase, as shown in the trajectories in figure 2.1. The displacement of the lower part precedes that of the upper part. The opening phase of the glottis (segment EF in figure 2.4) is determined by the outward movement of the upper edge of the vocal folds, and the closing phase (segment FH) is determined by the rapid inward movement of the lower part of the folds. The part of the cycle during which energy is supplied by aerodynamic forces is the interval AB in which the lower portions of the vocal folds move apart as a consequence of the subglottal pressure, before the upper edges begin to separate.

When the lower portions of the vocal folds come together, the horizontal velocity of the inner surface of each fold immediately drops to zero, whereas points within the fold lateral to the surface continue to move inward but with rapidly decreasing velocity. If one imagines the center of mass of the vocal fold as being located lateral to the surface, then the kinetic energy of this mass due to its inward movement just prior to contact becomes rapidly dissipated within the tissue. The lower portions of the vocal folds are under compression during this part of the cycle, and it is probable that the resistive component of the mechanical impedance of the fold becomes much greater than the inertial component. Thus the inward motion of the center of mass is probably strongly damped. (The behavior of the vocal folds under compression is discussed in more detail in section 2.1.6.) After the inward motion of the vocal folds ceases, the pressure on the lower surfaces of the folds again becomes equal to the subglottal pressure, and these surfaces begin their lateral movement as in the previous cycle. There is probably a delay in the initiation of this outward movement as the vocal folds regain their shape following the distortion in shape that arises from the rapid collision at point H in the figure. A brief delay is shown in the curve indicating the displacement of the lower mass in figure 2.4, at a time of about 8 ms. The length of time that some part of the glottis remains closed during the cycle is equal to the sum of this delay (HI in the figure) plus the time taken for the lower portion of the vocal folds to move apart until the upper edges separate (AE in the figure). In the example given in figure 2.4, the duration of this closed interval is about 4.0 ms and the time the glottis is open is also about 4.0 ms, so that the frequency F_0 is about 125 Hz. This frequency is somewhat higher than the natural frequency f_0 computed above for the lower, larger, portion of the vocal folds, that is,

$$f_0 = \frac{1}{2\pi\sqrt{M_1 C_1'}} \tag{2.4}$$

This frequency will be modified somewhat, however, depending on the degree of abduction or adduction of the folds, since this adjustment will influence events during the closed interval.

The lateral motion of the vocal folds is, of course, not the same at all points along the anteroposterior length. The width in the middle of the glottis is given by two times the displacement for the segment EFH in figure 2.4. In order to calculate the cross-sectional area of the glottal opening we shall assume initially that all points along the length of the vocal folds move in phase, but with a smaller amplitude at either end than in the middle. (The consequences of assuming a different waveform of lateral motion near the ends of the vocal folds relative to that at the middle is discussed later, in section 2.1.6.)

If we take the anteroposterior shape of the vocal folds to be roughly sinusoidal, with a length ℓ, then the area of the glottal opening is approximately equal to $(2/3)\ell$ times the maximum glottal width. For a glottal length

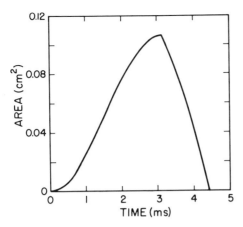

Figure 2.5 Area of glottal opening vs. time corresponding to figure 2.4, assuming an equivalent rectangular glottis of length 1.0 cm.

of 1.5 cm, then, we can calculate the area of the glottal opening by assuming an *effective* length of about 1.0 cm over which the lateral motion of the folds is uniform and equal to the values given in figure 2.4. Under this assumption, the glottal area for the conditions represented in figure 2.4 is given by the curve in figure 2.5. This curve has a discontinuity in slope at the point where the upper edge and the lower portion of the glottis have equal widths. The maximum glottal area during a cycle is 0.107 cm^2 in figure 2.5.

For a typical adult female voice, the dimensions and physical properties that have been assumed for purposes of analysis [using equations (2.1), (2.2), and (2.3)] are the following: $P_s = 8000$ dynes/cm^2, $x_0 = 0.005$ cm, $d_1 = 0.133$ cm, $M_1 = 0.04$ gm/cm, $C_1' = 1.9 \times 10^{-5}$ cm^2/dyne, $x_{01} = 0.03$ cm, $M_2 = 0.008$ gm/cm, and $C_c = 3.1 \times 10^{-5}$ cm^2/dyne. These values lead to a natural frequency for the lower mass of $\omega_0/2\pi = 183$ Hz, and for the upper mass of $\omega_1/2\pi = 294$ Hz. These values of the various parameters are roughly in accord with data given in chapter 1, except that the mass M_1 is somewhat greater than that estimated in chapter 1 (0.025 gm/cm). The total length of the female glottis is taken to be 1.0 cm, and the effective length (as defined above) is therefore about 0.7 cm.

Application of the analysis given above, based on equations (2.1), (2.2), and (2.3), and using these parameter values for the female voice, leads to the displacement and glottal area curves given in figure 2.6. As in figure 2.4, the displacement of the upper mass lags behind that of the lower mass. The period of vibration is about 4.3 ms, corresponding to a frequency of about 230 Hz, assuming that the lateral displacement of the lower edge begins at the time the upper edge closes. The time during which the glottis is open is about 2.4 ms. The maximum glottal area during a period is 0.037 cm^2, which is about one third of the maximum area estimated from the model for a male voice (see figure 2.5). Since the number of glottal pulses per second is about

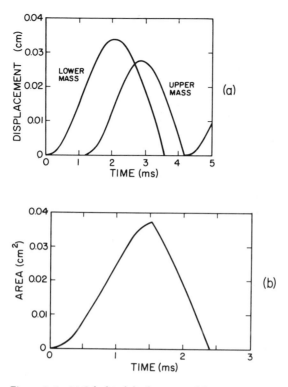

Figure 2.6 (a) Calculated displacement of the upper and lower masses for a two-mass model of the vocal folds (as in figure 2.4), with physical parameters adjusted for an adult female. Parameter values are given in the text. (b) Area of the glottal opening vs. time corresponding to the displacement curves above, assuming an equivalent rectangular glottis of length 0.7 cm.

twice that for a male voice, the average airflow is estimated to be about two-thirds of the flow for a male voice.

The glottal area curves in figures 2.5 and 2.6b show an asymmetry, with the rising phase occupying a longer time interval than the falling phase. This asymmetry occurs primarily because the upper mass is accelerated from essentially a rest position, whereas the lower mass achieves its maximum inward velocity just before it makes contact with the opposite mass. The asymmetry also rises in part from the particular selection of parameters for the model, especially the fact that the natural frequency of the lower mass is lower than that of the upper mass.

The details of the waveforms in figures 2.4, 2.5, and 2.6 are dependent on (1) the parameters specifying the stiffness and mass of the various elements of the model in figure 2.2; (2) the parameters indicating the adjustment of the spacing between the lower masses (x_0 in equation [2.1]) and the relative positions of the upper and lower masses (specified approximately by x_{10} in figures 2.4 and 2.6); and (3) the subglottal pressure. The influence of some of these parameters on the area waveform is considered in sections 2.1.3 to 2.1.7.

2.1.2   Waveform of Glottal Airflow

If a fixed subglottal pressure of 8 cm H_2O is assumed, then the airflow corresponding to the area variation in figures 2.5 or 2.6b can be calculated from standard aerodynamic equations. As we have seen in section 1.2, the equation relating the volume velocity U_g, the transglottal pressure drop ΔP_g, and the dimensions of the glottal slit, assuming quasi-static conditions, is

$$\Delta P_g = \frac{12\mu h}{\ell d^3} U_g + k \frac{\rho U_g^2}{2(\ell d)^2} = R_g U_g, \tag{2.5}$$

where μ = viscosity, h = thickness of glottal slit, ℓ = length of glottis, d = glottal width, ρ = density of air, and U_g is the volume flow. The constant k depends on the shape of the glottal slit, but is approximately equal to unity. The resistance R_g has two terms: the first accounts for viscous losses, and the second term represents the dynamic resistance. Except for the very smallest glottal widths, the first term can be neglected. The main features of the glottal flow can be calculated, then, if we approximate equation (2.5) by

$$\Delta P_g = \frac{\rho U_g^2}{2A_g^2}, \tag{2.6}$$

where A_g = glottal area.

If a constant transglottal pressure ΔP_g is assumed, then equation (2.6) shows that the airflow is proportional to the glottal area. This pressure can be taken to be the alveolar pressure if the pressure drop in the subglottal and supraglottal airways is small compared with the pressure drop across the glottis. If ΔP_g is 8 cm H_2O, and the area variation is that given in figure 2.5 or 2.6b, then the airflow determined from equation (2.5) is given by the dashed curves in figure 2.7. These airflow waveforms follow closely the waveforms of area vs. time, except when the area is small, in which case the viscous term in equation (2.5) becomes important.

A better approximation to the airflow can be obtained if equation (2.5) is modified to take into account the acoustic mass M_A of the air in the glottis and in the trachea and vocal tract below and above the glottis. Including a term to account for this additional component of the pressure drop gives the following equation:

$$\Delta P = R_g U_g + M_A \frac{dU_g}{dt}, \tag{2.7}$$

where ΔP is interpreted as the pulmonary or alveolar pressure. We are neglecting here any resistance that is introduced at a supraglottal constriction. This resistance will contribute to the pressure drop only for very narrow constrictions (less than about 0.3 cm^2). The effect of such narrow constrictions is discussed in section 2.1.7. (We are also neglecting the potential influences of tracheal or vocal tract resonances on the glottal flow. An analysis of these influences has been carried out by Ananthapadmanabha and Fant, 1982.)

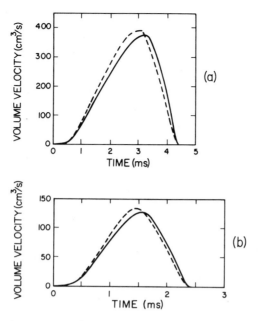

Figure 2.7 Volume velocity through the glottis corresponding to area functions in figures 2.5 and 2.6 under two conditions: no acoustic mass of airways (dashed lines); and a vocal tract with a modest constriction (area 1.0 cm², length 3.0 cm, as in figure 2.8) (solid lines). Top panel corresponds to model for male vocal folds and bottom panel for female.

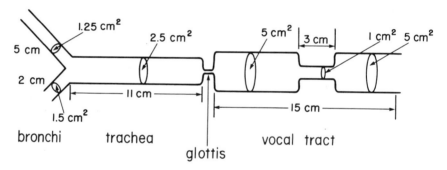

Figure 2.8 Configuration of trachea and vocal tract used to calculate airflows given by solid lines in figure 2.7.

The acoustic mass M_A of a tube of length ℓ and cross-sectional area A is given by $M_A = \rho\ell/A$. If the tube consists of a series of sections of different lengths ℓ_i and cross-sectional areas A_i, then we have $M_A = \rho\Sigma(\ell_i/A_i)$. It can be shown that the contribution of the glottal slit to M_A is usually small compared with the contribution of the subglottal and supraglottal airways. If we assume a moderately constricted vocal tract, with a minimum cross-sectional area of about 1 cm² and a constriction length of about 3 cm, then the sub- and supraglottal airways can be represented roughly as in figure 2.8. The total acoustic mass for this configuration is about 10ρ (gm/cm⁴ with ρ in gm/cm³), and is not strongly dependent on constriction size as long as the constriction area is not less than about 1 cm². Solution of equation (2.7) for the volume velocity U_g leads to the airflow waveforms shown by the solid lines in figure 2.7. As might be expected, these modified waveforms are more skewed than the waveforms that do not include the effect of the acoustic mass, and show a steeper slope during the glottal closing phase. The presence of the acoustic mass causes a delay in the increase in the volume velocity during the time when the area is increasing, and the more rapid decrease in volume velocity during the closing phase occurs because of the constraint that the velocity must become zero at the instant of closure. This effect of the acoustic mass of the airways in skewing the waveform has been discussed in detail by Rothenberg (1981) and by Fant (1982a). Increasing or decreasing the acoustic mass M_A, by forming a narrower or wider constriction in the vocal tract, causes a greater or smaller skewing of the waveform and modification in the slope during the closing phase.

This volume velocity waveform forms the excitation for the vocal tract when there is glottal vibration. Since the acoustic impedance of the glottis is usually large compared with the impedance of the supra- and subglottal cavities, at least over most of the glottal cycle and over most of the frequency range of interest for speech, the source of excitation of the vocal tract can be approximated by a volume velocity source. As is shown in detail in chapter 3, if the output of the vocal tract is taken as the volume velocity U_o at the lips, then the transfer function of the vocal tract with volume velocity excitation U_s at the glottis is given by $U_o(\omega)/U_s(\omega)$. This is an all-pole transfer function for nonnasalized vowels.

The output of ultimate interest is the sound pressure p_r at some distance r from the mouth. This sound pressure is given approximately by

$$p_r(t) = \frac{\rho}{4\pi r} \frac{\partial U_o(t - r/c)}{\partial t}, \tag{2.8}$$

or, in the frequency domain,

$$p_r(\omega) = \frac{j\omega\rho U_o(\omega)e^{-jkr}}{4\pi r}, \tag{2.9}$$

where ρ = density of air, c = speed of sound, and $k = \omega/c$. Equations (2.8) and (2.9) are based on the assumption that the volume velocity at the mouth opening can be approximated by a simple source. This assumption is valid at low frequencies, but may be in error by up to 5 dB for frequencies above about 2 kHz, as noted later in section 3.7. Of interest for our purposes is the fact that $p_r(t)$ is approximately proportional to the derivative of $U_o(t)$. Thus in order to interpret the essential features of the glottal waveform as it relates to the sound pressure ultimately reaching the ears of a listener, we should examine the time derivative of the glottal waveform (Fant, 1982b; Fant et al., 1985). The output sound pressure is the result of this differentiated waveform applied to the all-pole transfer function of the vocal tract. The derivatives of

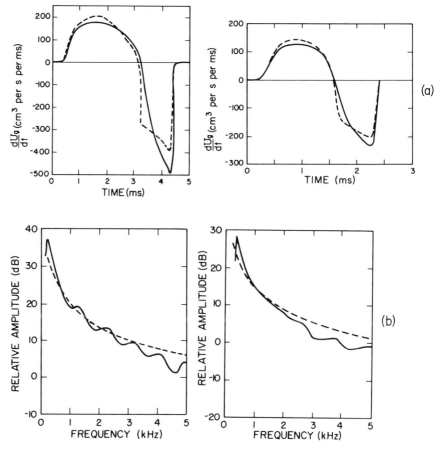

Figure 2.9 (a) Derivative of volume velocity waveforms in figure 2.7. Dashed lines correspond to no vocal tract loading, and solid lines are for vocal tract and trachea as in figure 2.8. Left and right panels are for male and female models, respectively. (b) Spectra of waveforms given by solid lines in the upper panels. The dashed lines indicate a downward spectrum slope of 6 dB per octave.

the modeled glottal volume velocity waveforms in figure 2.7 are given at the top of figure 2.9a. The solid lines are for the condition with the effect of acoustic loading and the dashed lines are without loading (as in figure 2.7).

The waveform of this effective glottal excitation has two main features. One is the negative pulse with a rapid (negative) rise and an abrupt fall to zero. The rapid decrease to zero is sometimes called the return phase. This pulse is a consequence of the rapid closing of the glottis, as the lower portions of the vocal folds come together at a relatively high velocity enhanced by the effect of the acoustic mass of the airways, as noted above. The other aspect of the waveform is the slowly varying positive portion prior to the negative pulse.

The spectra of the pulses (with loading by the airways) are shown as solid lines in figure 2.9b. The low-frequency part of the spectrum is determined by the gross shape of the waveform, particularly the slowly varying positive portion, whereas the high frequencies are determined by the negative pulse, particularly the discontinuity at the trailing edge. Superimposed on the spectra are dashed lines indicating a spectrum that decreases as $1/f$ (i.e., −6 dB per octave) at high frequencies. Comparison of the $1/f$ curves with the spectra derived from the model indicates that the spectra at high frequencies (above 2 to 3 kHz) decrease with frequency at a rate slightly greater than −6 dB per octave. This high-frequency behavior arises because the rise in the derivative curve from the negative peak is not exactly abrupt, but the change occurs over a brief interval of time. The fluctuations or bumps in the spectra arise in part because of the finite duration of the pulse. The frequency region where the slowly varying positive portion dominates is usually in the range of the first formant and below—probably 500 Hz or lower. The spectra in figure 2.9b show a slight bulge at low frequencies. When the pulses occur periodically, then the spectrum is a line spectrum, with the amplitudes of individual components being proportional to the Fourier transform of the single pulse. These components occur at multiples of the fundamental frequency F_0. The details of the spectrum and its relation to the waveform for different shapes of the waveform are discussed further in section 2.1.6.

The spectra for individual pulses for the male and female models in figure 2.9b are plotted to the same scale. At frequencies above about 1 kHz, the spectrum for the male is about 5 dB higher than that for the female. If one takes into account the higher fundamental frequency for the female speaker (by a factor of about 2), then the amplitude of a harmonic for the female model is comparable to that for the male model.

The analysis of vocal fold vibration and of the resulting volume velocity waveform, summarized in figures 2.4 to 2.9, has assumed that the vocal folds perform the same lateral motion at all points along their anteroposterior length, albeit with different amplitudes. The anterior ends of the vocal folds are supported in fixed positions so that there is negligible amplitude of vibration at this end of the glottis. Likewise, there is probably a reduced amplitude of vibration at the posterior end of the glottis where the vocal folds are attached to the arytenoid cartilages. There are, however, some differences in the physical properties of the vocal folds at different points along their length (Hirano et al., 1981). This nonuniformity in the vocal folds can cause a variation in the vibration pattern along their length. During a cycle of vibration the vocal folds come into contact slightly earlier near the anterior and posterior ends than in the middle.

The overall volume velocity waveform is a superposition of the waveforms at different points along the length. A consequence of the lack of synchrony of the closing time is that the waveforms of area vs. time and of volume velocity vs. time are less steep at their trailing edges than they would be if the entire vocal fold made contact at the same time (Fant et al., 1985). The differentiated volume velocity waveform does not show as marked a discontinuity at its trailing edge as does the waveform resulting from synchronous closing along the entire vocal fold length. The effect on the spectrum is to reduce by a few decibels the spectrum amplitude at high frequencies.

It is common for the arytenoid cartilages to be not completely adducted at their posterior ends during phonation, so that a fixed opening exists between the arytenoids while the vocal folds are vibrating in the manner described in figures 2.4 and 2.6. This fixed opening between the arytenoids results in a constant airflow that is superimposed on the sequence of pulses of the type shown in figure 2.7. The presence of the fixed opening also causes some modification of the shape of the pulses, particularly in the vicinity of the point of closure, as will be shown later in section 2.1.6.

The waveforms of the glottal volume velocity or its derivative derived from the two-mass model, shown in figures 2.7 and 2.9, are in general agreement with several aspects of the glottal waveform measured for a population of male and female speakers. One of the more comprehensive experimental studies of the volume velocity waveform for a large number of adult male and female speakers was carried out by Holmberg et al. (1988), with some newer results in Perkell et al. (1994). In these studies, an approximation to the glottal volume velocity waveform was obtained by inverse filtering the volume velocity waveform at the mouth, obtained with a low-resistance mask over the mouth, to remove the effect of the vocal tract transfer function (Rothenberg, 1973). For the condition of loud voice of Holmberg et al., the average subglottal pressure for the different speakers was 9.0 cm H_2O for males and 8.2 cm H_2O for females, that is, slightly greater than the subglottal pressure used for making calculations with the model.

The relevant data from Holmberg et al. are listed in table 2.1. Also given in the table are values of parameters derived from the calculations for the model. The subglottal pressure was obtained by Holmberg et al. by interspersing the stop consonant /p/ between the vowels being examined, and measuring the intraoral pressure during the stop closure. The calculated fundamental frequency and the maximum airflow declination rate are about the same as the average measured values. (However, in a later study with a different group of speakers and different processing methods, Perkell et al., 1994, reported somewhat higher declination rates.) The calculated maximum declination rates in table 2.1 and in figure 2.9a are also consistent with measurements for male and female nonsingers reported by Titze (1992), for a subglottal pressure of 8 cm H_2O. The peak flow for the model (equal to the ac flow) is about equal to the measured ac flow (i.e., difference between maximum and minimum flow) for the male speakers in table 2.1, but is somewhat less than the measured ac flow for female speakers. There is also a discrepancy between the calculated average flow for the female model (32 cm^3/s) and the average measured flow (after the dc component is removed). Some adjustment of the parameters of the female model may be necessary to bring the calculations for the model in line with average data for female speakers.

Table 2.1 Comparison of average values of measured parameters for the glottal wave for the condition of loud voice (from Holmberg et al., 1988) and values of the same parameters estimated from the waveforms derived from the vocal fold model (see figures 2.7 and 2.9)

	Males		Females	
	Measured	Model	Measured	Model
Subglottal pressure (cm H_2O)	9.0	8.0	8.2	8.0
Fundamental frequency (Hz)	126	123	223	238
Sound pressure level (dB re 0.0002 dyne/cm^2)	86.0	82	83.3	78
Maximum airflow declination rate (cm^3/s/ms)	481	490	249	230
dc component of flow (cm^3/s)	110		90	
ac flow (cm^3/s)	380	380	180	130
Average flow (cm^3/s)	200		150	
Average flow − dc flow (cm^3/s)	90	106	60	32
Open quotient	0.57	0.54	0.71	0.64

Note: Data for adult males and females are given. A dc component is not included in the model, but data from Holmberg et al. are listed for this parameter and for average flow. The data for sound pressure level assume a vocal tract configuration similar to the vowel /æ/, and a distance of 15 cm from the mouth opening.

However, the characteristics of the waveform from the model are well within the ranges observed for the twenty male and twenty female speakers in the study of Holmberg et al.

Details of the calculation of the sound pressure level at a distance of 15 cm are not given here, since they involve deriving the vocal tract transfer function, following principles discussed later in chapter 3. The calculated values of sound pressure level (SPL) in table 2.1 require that estimates of the vocal tract transfer function be made for the vowel /æ/ that was used in the experiments of Holmberg et al. The values of SPL calculated from the waveforms in figure 2.9 are several decibels below the average measured values, although a small part of the difference for male voices is due to the different subglottal pressures for the measured data and for the model. The remaining difference of 3 to 5 dB for both male and female voices must still be explained.

Based on the spectra in figure 2.9, we have constructed prototype spectra of $U_g'(t)$ for adult male and female voices with modal vibration. These spectra are shown in figure 2.10. The envelopes of these spectra are smoothed versions of the spectra in figure 2.9, and assume a fundamental frequency of 125 Hz for males and 230 Hz for females. These prototype spectra will be used in later chapters when calculations are made to compare the spectra of the sound pressure for sounds produced with vocal fold vibration and for sounds produced with turbulence noise or transients as the source. The spectra in figure 2.10 are intended to show the root-mean-square (rms) value of the volume velocity source for each component of the periodic waveform. As we have observed, the spectra at high frequencies (above about 3 kHz)

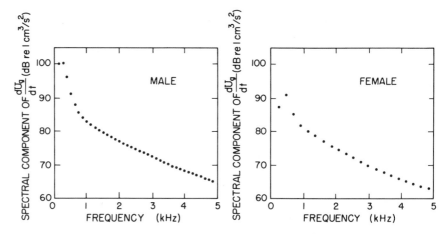

Figure 2.10 Spectra of derivative of periodic modal glottal source used as prototypes for the calculation of vowel spectra. The fundamental frequency is 125 Hz for the male voice and 230 Hz for the female voice. The ordinate is the root-mean-square level of each spectral component of $dU_g/(dt)$ in dB re 1 cm^3/s^2. A subglottal pressure of 8 cm H$_2$O is assumed.

lie a few decibels below a line with a slope of -6 dB per octave passing through the spectra in the frequency range of 1 to 2 kHz. This increased spectrum slope at high frequencies has also been proposed by Gobl (1989). Below 1 kHz, the spectrum amplitude rises to a broad peak that is a few decibels above this line. The spectrum amplitude of a component with frequency f in the range 1 to 2 kHz is determined by the maximum of $U_g'(t)$, designated as U_{gdmax}'. The rms amplitude of this component is $U_{gd}(f) = 2U_{gdmax}'/(\sqrt{2}T_o \cdot 2\pi f)$, where T_o is the fundamental period. The factor of 2 in the numerator accounts for the contribution of the positive and negative frequency components in the Fourier spectrum, and the $\sqrt{2}$ in the denominator gives the rms value.

As shown in the data of Holmberg et al. (1988), Klatt and Klatt (1990), Hanson (1995), and K. N. Stevens and Hanson (1995), there can be considerable differences in the spectrum of the glottal waveform from one speaker to another. For example, the amplitude of the harmonics near 2.5 kHz relative to the amplitude of the first harmonic can vary as much as 20 dB across speakers. The spectra in figure 2.10 represent speakers for whom the amplitude in the 2.5-kHz range is relatively high.

Given this rather simple picture of the individual glottal pulses for a particular rest configuration of the glottis, we turn now to examine the effects of manipulating some of the physical parameters of the vocal folds and the subglottal and supraglottal pressure.

2.1.3 Manipulation of Frequency of Vibration

The frequency of vocal fold vibration is determined primarily by the stiffness and mass of the vocal folds, as indicated by equation (2.4) above. The transglottal pressure can also influence the frequency, but this effect is relatively small, as is discussed in section 2.1.4. In this section we consider the changes in frequency resulting from manipulations that give rise to changes in mass and stiffness of the vocal folds.

We shall examine the consequences of changing the stiffness of the folds by stretching them from the ends. An increase in stiffness gives rise to an increased frequency, and is achieved through contraction of the cricothyroid muscle, and possibly through contraction of the posterior cricoarytenoid muscle, which causes a sliding of the arytenoid cartilages in a posterior direction (Hollein, 1983). At the lower end of the frequency range, a decreased stiffness and increased mass of the vocal fold is probably achieved by contraction of the vocalis muscle, which causes a shortening and thickening of the cover of the fold (Hirano, 1975). Shortening of the vocal folds, with consequent reduction in stiffness, can also be achieved by lowering the larynx through contraction of the strap muscles, as described in section 1.1.2. The changes in vocal fold length that have been observed by various investigators as fundamental frequency is manipulated during speech production are in the range of 20 to 30 percent. (See data cited in Hollein, 1983.) In terms of the simple model discussed in connection with figures 2.2 and 2.4, this increased length leads to a significant increase in the mechanical stiffness in figure 2.2, and also to small reductions in the vertical thickness of the vocal folds and in the mass per unit length of the folds. The principal effects of these changes are to increase the natural frequencies in equations (2.2) and (2.3), and hence to decrease the time taken for the vocal folds to undergo their abduction movement during the opening phase and their adduction movement during the closing phase. These opening and closing phases of movement of the lower portion of the vocal folds are approximately segments of sinusoids, and these segments will decrease in duration as the frequencies of the sinusoids increase. The result is a shortening of the glottal pulse and of the closure interval, and an increase in the frequency of vibration.

In sections 1.1.2 and 2.1.1 above, we have given estimates of the mass, stiffness, and dimensions of the vocal folds for conditions in which the folds are not stretched. Lengthening of the vocal folds by about 30 percent is estimated to increase the mechanical stiffness by a factor of about 3 (from figure 1.11) and to multiply the mass per unit length by a factor of about 0.7, leading to a frequency range that is about a factor of 2. This is approximately the range of fundamental frequency observed in the speech of female and male adults.

The adjustments in stiffness and mass that are carried out to effect a change in frequency lead to a modification of the waveform of the glottal area as a function of time. These changes are illustrated schematically in figure 2.11 for the model of the vocal folds for male speakers. The figure shows the displacement of the upper and lower portions of the vocal folds, in the manner previously discussed in connection with figure 2.4. The mechanical compliances used to calculate the displacement in figure 2.11 are taken

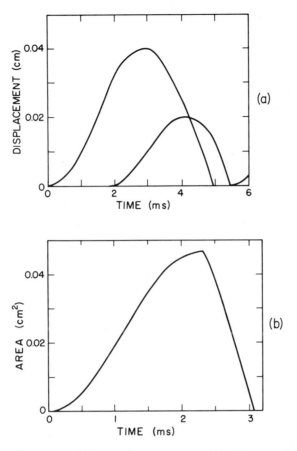

Figure 2.11   (a) Same as figure 2.4, except that stiffnesses in the two-mass model are increased by a factor of about 1.7, simulating a condition for which the vocal folds are adjusted to vibrate at a higher frequency. (b) Glottal area function corresponding to (a).

to be about 60 percent of those used for figure 2.4, and the masses are multiplied by a factor of 0.85, leading to an increase in frequency of about 40 percent relative to the condition for figure 2.4.

As before, the abducting phase of the lower portion occurs in response to the subglottal pressure acting over the surface. The trajectory of this portion of the cycle is determined by equation (2.2), but we now have a somewhat decreased thickness d_1, a decreased compliance C'_1, and an increased frequency ω_0. There is probably also an adjustment in the rest position of the lower portion, defined by x_0. This initial trajectory is a sinusoid with a more rapid rise but with a smaller final value. The average displacement of this lower portion for which the upper edge separates will probably be smaller than in the original case in figure 2.4, since the thickness of the vocal fold is decreased. The lateral movement of the upper edge, which determines the opening phase of the area function, is more rapid because of the increased stiffness, and the closing phase of the lower portion is also more rapid. The result is a shorter area waveform that has a somewhat reduced maximum amplitude, as shown in figure 2.11b. The figure shows a pulse with about 75 percent of the duration and a maximum opening that is about 40 percent of the maximum opening shown earlier in figure 2.4. The volume velocity waveform corresponding to this area function has been calculated, and is displayed in figure 2.12a. The volume velocity waveform is shown with and without the effect of the acoustic mass of the airways, the airways being defined by the configuration in figure 2.8. The differentiated waveform (for the condition of moderate acoustic loading) and its spectrum are displayed in figure 2.12b and c. Comparison of this waveform and its spectrum with the waveform and spectrum for normal vibration (shown previously in figure 2.9) indicates that the spectrum at high frequencies when the stiffness is increased is reduced by about 2 to 3 dB on average. This reduction is a consequence of a somewhat decreased maximum slope of the volume velocity pulse during the closing phase. The amplitudes of the harmonics for the periodic waveform for the higher-frequency pulses, however, show an increase in proportion to the frequency, so that the overall level of the harmonics for the low- and high-frequency pulses is about the same.

While the changes in the mechanical stiffness and mass of the vocal folds that result from adjustments in vocal fold length constitute the principal influence on the frequency of vibration, manipulation of the lateral position of the vocal folds can also have an effect on the frequency. Adduction of the folds leads to increased vertical thickness in the rest position, and the folds remain under compression during much of the cycle, leading to a different mode of vibration with a lower frequency. Manipulation of the vocal folds to a more abducted configuration can lead to only a limited degree of contact of the folds during a cycle, and this condition can result in a higher frequency of vibration. These effects of adduction and abduction of the vocal folds are considered in more detail in section 2.1.6.

2.1.4 Effects of Changes in Alveolar Pressure

Increasing or decreasing the alveolar pressure can change the form of some of the curves in figure 2.4 that depict the movements of the upper and lower portions of the vocal folds. The principal effect of a raised alveolar pressure is to increase the force on the lower portion of the vocal folds as they are being pushed apart before the upper edges separate. This increased force results in a more rapid acceleration, as indicated by equation (2.2). The movements of the lower and upper portions of the vocal folds for two values of alveolar pressure (8 and 16 H_2O) are compared in figure 2.13, assuming the same vocal fold parameters as in figure 2.4. The more rapid movement of the lower portion with the higher alveolar pressure is seen by comparing segments ABC (16 cm H_2O) and AB'C' (8 cm H_2O). When the upper edges separate at point B (assumed to be at about the same average displacement x_{10} of the lower portion of the folds as for the lower alveolar pressure), the

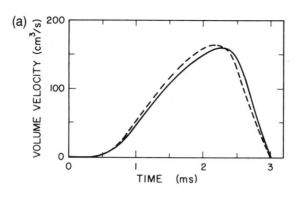

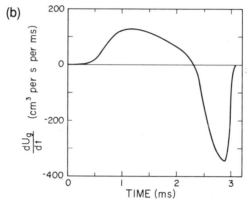

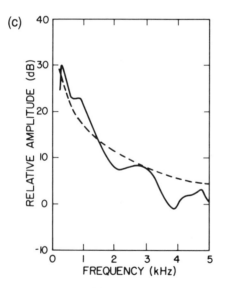

Figure 2.12 (a) The solid line is the volume velocity waveform corresponding to the model with increased stiffness, for which displacements of masses are as shown in figure 2.11, and supra- and subglottal configurations are as in figure 2.8. The dashed line corresponds to the waveform in the absence of the effect of supra- and subglottal acoustic masses. (b) Derivative of waveform given by solid line in (a). (c) Spectrum of dU_g/dt in (b). The dashed line has a -6 dB per octave slope.

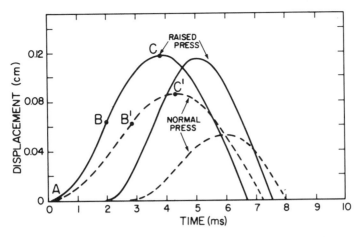

Figure 2.13 Comparing displacements of lower and upper masses of two-mass model for two different subglottal pressures: a raised pressure $P_s = 16$ cm H_2O (solid lines), and a more normal pressure $P_s = 8$ cm H_2O (dashed lines). Other parameters of the model are given in the text. Points B and B' identify times when the upper mass opens.

vocal folds are moving apart more rapidly, and consequently the maximum amplitude of movement following the opening time is greater. Since the upper edges of the vocal folds separate earlier in the cycle when the alveolar pressure is increased, the lower portion begins to accelerate toward closure earlier, and a small increase in the frequency is expected. In the example schematized in figure 2.13, the total duration of a cycle of vibration is decreased by about 8 percent when the subglottal pressure is increased by a factor of 2. This change in frequency with a change in alveolar pressure is, however, much smaller than the frequency shift that can be achieved by adjusting the tension of the vocal folds. Experimentally, the rate of change of frequency with alveolar pressure has been observed to be in the range 3 to 5 Hz/cm change in H_2O (Ladefoged, 1962; Ohala and Ladefoged, 1970).

The amplitude of movement of both the upper and lower portions of the vocal fold is expected to increase roughly in proportion to the alveolar pressure P_{alv}, since this pressure provides the force which initiates the outward vocal fold motion. Thus the maximum cross-sectional area of the glottis during the cycle of vibration is roughly proportional to P_{alv}. This variation of area (or of maximum opening) with P_{alv} is observed approximately in the example in figure 2.13, with the amplitude of the lower and upper masses showing an increase that is somewhat less than a factor of 2 for a twofold increase in pressure. The maximum area at the point where the displacements for the upper and lower masses intersect for the raised P_{alv} is about two times that for the lower P_{alv}. The volume velocity for a given area is proportional to $P_{alv}^{1/2}$ [from equation (2.6)], and for a given transglottal pressure is roughly proportional to the area. Consequently the peak volume velocity U_{peak} is expected to be proportional to $P_{alv}^{3/2}$.

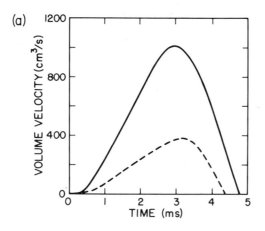

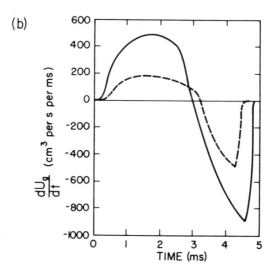

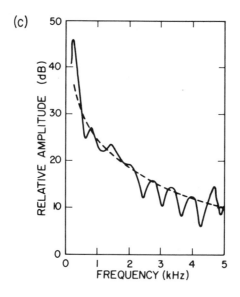

The effect of the alveolar pressure on the waveform of the volume velocity U_g at the glottis can be examined with reference to equation (2.7), which relates the alveolar pressure to the volume velocity. In figure 2.14 we compare calculations of the U_g waveform and its derivative for the two values of alveolar pressure of 8 cm H_2O (see figure 2.4) and 16 cm H_2O (see figure 2.13), again assuming the sub- and supraglottal configurations in figure 2.8. The figure shows that for a doubling of pressure the peak value of U_g increases by a factor of about 2.7, which is close to the expected value of $2^{3/2}$. It is expected, then, that the low-frequency amplitude of the glottal pulse should increase by about 9 dB for a doubling of alveolar pressure. This observation is verified in the spectrum in figure 2.14c, which is plotted with the same amplitude scale as figure 2.9. Comparison of the two spectra for a male model shows that the spectrum amplitude at low frequencies for the increased pressure is about 8 dB higher than the low-frequency amplitude in figure 2.9.

Experimental data also show that the overall sound pressure for vowel production increases approximately as $P_{alv}^{3/2}$ (Ladefoged, 1962; Isshiki, 1964; Bouhuys et al., 1968). Since the overall sound pressure of a vowel is determined primarily by the spectrum amplitude at low frequencies (below 1 kHz), these experimental data indicate that the spectrum amplitude of the glottal source at low frequencies must increase by about 9 dB per doubling of alveolar pressure. Thus the prediction of the amplitude change from the model is in general agreement with experimental observations.

Figure 2.14b shows a larger negative peak in the waveform of the derivative for the increased alveolar pressure, although in this example the amplitude of this peak does not change as much as the peak value of U_g. This difference is confirmed by comparing the spectra of the derivative waveforms at high frequencies. The high-frequency amplitude in figure 2.14c is just 5 to 6 dB greater than that in figure 2.9.

Measurements show that there is an increased spectrum amplitude at high frequencies relative to that at low frequencies for vowels produced with greater effort and hence with greater alveolar pressure (Holmberg et al., 1995; Tarnoczy, 1971). Thus we would expect a closing phase of the glottal area that is more rapid than that shown in figure 2.13 with increased alveolar pressure. It is probable that a speaker increases the activity of the adducting muscles of the larynx with increased alveolar pressure, leading to a more abrupt closure of the vocal folds, and hence to greater high-frequency energy in the airflow pulse. The effect of such an increased adducting force was not included in the calculations leading to figure 2.13.

Figure 2.14 (a) Calculated volume velocity waveforms for two values of subglottal pressure: 8 cm H_2O (dashed line) and 16 cm H_2O (solid line). (b) Derivatives of waveforms in (a). (c) Spectrum of dU_g/dt in (b) for a subglottal pressure of 16 cm H_2O. Dashed line has a -6 dB per octave slope.

A decrease in the alveolar pressure will produce the opposite effect on the airflow pulse. That is, there will be a reduction in the peak volume velocity in the pulse, and an even greater proportional reduction in the magnitude and abruptness of the pulse in the derivative waveform in the vicinity of closure.

2.1.5 Conditions for Glottal Vibration

From the simple analysis given in section 2.1.1, we can reason that there are several conditions that will prevent the vocal folds from vibrating. These conditions are expressed in terms of ranges of parameters that describe the pressure across the glottis, the configuration of the glottis, and the compliance of the vocal folds.

We consider first a range of conditions for which the vocal folds are adducted, so that in the rest position the vocal folds are pushed together. Vocal fold vibration will occur only if the transglottal pressure provides sufficient force to push the vocal folds apart. Otherwise, the glottis remains closed, and there is no flow of air. Reference to equation (2.2) indicates that this condition under which the vocal folds are pushed apart will occur when the quantity $P_s d_1 C_1' + x_0$ is positive, or

$$P_s d_1 C_1' > (-x_0). \tag{2.10}$$

Recall that P_s = subglottal pressure, d_1 = thickness of lower part of the vocal fold, C_1' = mechanical compliance of the vocal fold, and x_0 is a measure of the resting position of the vocal fold (with no pressure applied) if it were not prevented from moving inward by contact with the opposite fold. This resting displacement is negative if the vocal folds are exerting an inward force on each other in the absence of P_s. A number of combinations of these parameters will satisfy the inequality in equation (2.10). Vibration will be inhibited if the subglottal pressure is too small, if the vocal folds are too thin (i.e., d_1 is small), if the vocal folds are too stiff (i.e., C_1' is small), or if the vocal folds are pushed tightly together ($|x_0|$ is large).

Vocal fold vibration can also fail to occur when the glottis is sufficiently abducted. When the alveolar pressure is applied, the energy supplied by aerodynamic forces in a cycle of vibration is not sufficient to overcome energy losses in the vocal folds, and hence vibration is not maintained. This condition is more difficult to analyze quantitatively, although various attempts have been made to provide a comprehensive analysis (e.g., Ishizaka and Matsudaira, 1972; K. N. Stevens, 1977). The basic idea, however, is that for vibration to be initiated, the vocal folds must be in a configuration such that there is a pressure gradient across the vocal fold thickness from the lower to the upper edge. This gradient can be achieved only if the glottal width has a converging configuration. If the glottal width diverges, then the pressure in the lower section of the glottis remains approximately equal to the supraglottal pressure independent of the width of the lower section. Two con-

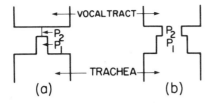

Figure 2.15 Schematization of two glottal configurations for which there is a fixed difference in width between the lower and upper sections. The difference between the pressures P_1 and P_2 in the two sections, for a given transglottal pressure, is much greater when the glottis is more adducted, as in (a), than for a more abducted configuration, as in (b).

verging configurations are schematized in figure 2.15. The requirement for vibration to be initiated is that $P_1 > P_2$, such that the outward motion of the lower edge leads that of the upper edge. In the case of the configuration in figure 2.15a, where the upper edge is adducted in the rest position, $P_1 - P_2$ at the beginning of a cycle is essentially equal to the subglottal pressure. For the abducted configuration of figure 2.15b, however, an approximate expression for the pressure difference in the two sections is

$$P_1 - P_2 = \Delta P \left[1 - \left(\frac{A_2}{A_1} \right)^2 \right] \tag{2.11}$$

where ΔP is the transglottal pressure, and A_1 and A_2 are the cross-sectional areas of the lower and upper portion of the glottis, respectively. If both A_1 and A_2 are increased by the same amount, corresponding to an abducting maneuver, the ratio A_2/A_1 becomes closer to unity, leading to a decreased pressure gradient $P_1 - P_2$. This decreased driving force will result in reduced energy supplied to the vibrating system. We will not go into a detailed analysis of this situation here, but we simply note that vocal fold vibration will be inhibited if the rest position is a relatively abducted vocal fold configuration (i.e., the parameter x_0 is large and positive). Observations of airflow and subglottal pressure for onsets and offsets of glottal vibration indicate that a glottal width of about 0.12 cm is needed for initiation of glottal vibration when the subglottal pressure is 8 cm H_2O, corresponding to an airflow of about 300 cm^3/s for adult females and 450 cm^3/s for males.

For a given subglottal pressure and vocal fold thickness, there would appear to be an optimal rest position x_0 for which vocal fold vibration can occur over a wide range of values of vocal fold stiffness (K. N. Stevens, 1977). When the vocal folds are adducted or abducted relative to this rest position, the above analysis suggests that the range of values of vocal fold stiffness, vocal fold thickness, and transglottal pressure over which vocal fold vibration can occur becomes more limited. We shall see in chapter 8 that some of these manipulations are used to inhibit or to facilitate vocal fold vibration for consonants where the formation of a constriction in the vocal tract results in an increased intraoral pressure.

Source Mechanisms

Experimentally, it has been determined that a transglottal pressure of at least 3 cm H_2O is needed to maintain vibration even when the other parameters are optimally adjusted (Finkelhor et al., 1987; Verdolini-Marston et al., 1990; Titze, 1992). A greater transglottal pressure is needed if these parameters deviate from these values. For example, when the vocal folds are adducted or abducted or stiffened, a greater transglottal pressure is required if vibration is to be maintained.

2.1.6 Factors Affecting the Glottal Waveform

In sections 2.1.1 and 2.1.2 we developed a semiquantitative analysis of the "normal" or "modal" process of vocal fold vibration, and we showed in figures 2.5, 2.7, and 2.9 some representations of the glottal waveform in terms of glottal area, glottal airflow, and time derivative of glottal airflow. We also examined the effect on the glottal waveforms of changing the stiffness of the vocal folds (in section 2.1.3) and the alveolar pressure (in section 2.1.4). In the model that was used to calculate these waveforms, we assumed a configuration in which the vocal folds were almost touching in the rest condition [i.e., x_0 was small in equation (2.2)] and other parameters were selected to be within the normal range. It was also assumed that the lateral movement of each vocal fold during a cycle of vibration was in phase at all points along the length of the vocal folds, albeit with different amplitudes. By appropriate manipulation of some of the parameters, particularly the resting position of the vocal folds as represented by x_0, while remaining within the range where vocal fold vibration is maintained, it is possible to generate glottal waveforms that have shapes and spectral characteristics that are significantly different from those in figures 2.7 and 2.9. Changes in the waveform will also occur if parameters such as the resting displacement and the vocal fold compliance and mass per unit length vary along the anteroposterior direction.

These different modes of vocal fold vibration correspond to configurations that lie between those assumed for modal vibration and those leading to cessation of vibration. On the one hand, the vocal folds can be rather tightly adducted, with the static value of x_0 being relatively large and negative. In the limit, if the adduction is sufficiently extreme, the vocal folds will cease to vibrate. On the other hand, the vocal folds can be abducted, with a static configuration for which the vocal folds are not touching. Again, if the abduction is sufficiently extreme, vocal fold vibration is inhibited. A related condition is one in which the vocal folds are in a modal configuration but the arytenoid cartilages are spread apart at their posterior end to form a triangular opening or a "glottal chink."

2.1.6.1 Pressed Voicing
We consider first the mode of vibration when the vocal folds are pushed rather tightly together in their static state. This mode of vibration is sometimes called creaky voicing or pressed voice. For

this condition it is probable that, except for their upper edges, the vocal folds remain under compression throughout the cycle of vibration. This state of the vocal folds is in contrast to the condition for modal vibration, where the folds are probably under tension, particularly during the open phase of the cycle of glottal vibration. Thus, as we have seen in equation (2.1) in section 2.1.1, portions of the glottal vibration cycle are estimated by approximating the vocal folds by a mass-spring system. In the case of pressed voicing, we assume that there is a resistive component R_1 that dominates the inertial component in the mechanical impedance of the lower section of the vocal folds. The upper edge of the vocal fold, however, is characterized as before by a combination of a simple mass and compliance.

Each vocal fold is represented then, by two sections, as in figure 2.2, except that the mass of the lower portion is neglected, and this section is coupled to the walls of the larynx through a compliance and a resistance. We consider a cycle of vibration as beginning with the vocal folds approximated. The subglottal pressure P_s gives rise to an abducting force equal to $P_s d_1$ per unit length of the vocal fold, where d_1 is the depth of the lower portion. Because the vocal folds are pressed together, this dimension d_1 is larger than it is for a more neutral vocal fold configuration. This portion of the fold undergoes a lateral movement $x_1(t)$ in response to this force, where $x_1(t)$ is a solution to the first-order equation

$$R_1 \dot{x}_1 + \frac{1}{C_1'}(x_1 - x_0) = P_s d_1. \tag{2.12}$$

In this equation, x_0 is the effective static position of the lower portion in the absence of an applied subglottal pressure, and is negative if the vocal folds are pressed together in the rest position. As in equation (2.1), C_1' is the effective mechanical compliance per unit length of the lower portion of the vocal fold.

The solution to equation (2.12) is given by

$$x_1(t) = (P_s d_1 C_1' + x_0)(1 - e^{-t/(R_1 C_1')}). \tag{2.13}$$

It is assumed that the depth d_1 and the compliance C_1' are adjusted to be sufficiently large that $P_s d_1 C_1'$ is greater than $-x_0$. This solution for $x_1(t)$ is shown as ABCD in figure 2.16. We have selected values of the parameters that are expected to be typical of male phonation in this mode: $C_1' = 8 \times 10^{-5}$ cm^2/dyne, $R_1 = 60$ dyne-s/cm^2, $d_1 = 0.4$ cm, $P_s = 8000$ dynes/cm^2, and $x_0 = -0.22$ cm.

When $x_1(t)$ exceeds some critical value x_{10}, the upper edges separate, and airflow through the glottis begins. In the example in figure 2.16, this separation occurs at point B, where $x_1 = x_{10} = 0.02$ cm. The movement $x_2(t)$ of the upper edges follows a trajectory that can be approximated over its initial portion EC by a sinusoid, as in figure 2.4 and equation (2.3). As airflow begins, the pressure within the lower portion of the glottis decreases, and consequently the abducting force decreases. This pressure drops to zero

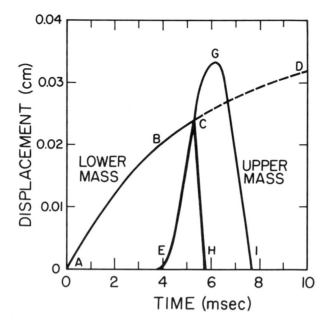

Figure 2.16 Same as figure 2.4, except that masses are pushed together in resting position, simulating a configuration appropriate for pressed phonation. Internal viscous forces in the vocal folds are assumed to dominate inertia forces for this condition.

when the displacement $x_2(t)$ exceeds $x_1(t)$. In constructing the trajectory for the lower mass, we have assumed that the curve in the region BC can continue to be approximated by the same rising exponential, even though the driving pressure has begun to decrease. At the time when x_1 and x_2 are equal, the restoring force due to the compliance C_1' causes the lower portion of the fold to return to the closed position, with a trajectory given by the solution to equation (2.12), with the right-hand side set to zero. The equation for this adducting motion of the lower portion of the fold under these conditions is

$$x_1(t) = x_0 + (x_{10} - x_0)e^{-t/(R_1 C_1')}. \tag{2.14}$$

This part of the trajectory for $x_1(t)$ is shown as CH in figure 2.16. It is essentially a linear trajectory with a slope of $-(x_{10} - x_0)/(R_1 C_1')$. At point H, $x_1(t)$ becomes zero, and the lower portions of the vocal folds collide. The upper portion of the vocal fold follows the trajectory CGI, and returns to a closed position I about 2 ms following the time when the lower portion closes.

Since $x_1(t)$ is a solution to a first-order differential equation (rather than the second-order equation [2.1]), there is not a requirement that the derivative of $x_1(t)$ be continuous in the region where $x_2(t)$ becomes non-zero. Thus there can be an abrupt change in the direction of the $x_1(t)$ trajectory, as figure 2.16 shows at point C. There can also be an abrupt change in slope as $x_1(t)$ increases from zero, at point A in the figure.

After the lower portions of the vocal folds come into contact, there is an interval in which the folds compress and the tissue redistributes itself as the folds change their shape under compression. Following this time interval, the lower portion again begins an abducting motion as a new cycle is initiated. In figure 2.16, the initiation of a new cycle would occur some time after the time at which the upper mass closes (at about 8 ms), so that a period in excess of 8 ms might be expected.

Displayed in figure 2.17 is the calculated airflow through the glottis, together with its derivative and the spectrum of the differentiated flow. A glottal length of 1.0 cm is assumed, as before. The airflow waveform and spectrum for a modal glottal configuration, shown previously in figures 2.7 and 2.9, are reproduced in figure 2.17 as dashed lines. The total area of the glottal pulse is much smaller for pressed phonation, whereas the rate of change of area during the closing phase is about the same in the two cases. The amplitude of the spectrum at high frequencies is slightly greater than that for modal phonation, and there is a bulge in the frequency range of 1 to 2 kHz, reflecting the reduced length of the pulse. The spectrum amplitude at low frequencies is considerably smaller than that for modal vibration.

When the vocal folds are vibrating in a modal configuration, the frequency of the glottal pulses is determined largely by the natural frequency of the vocal folds, which are under some tension. This frequency is given in equation (2.4). When the vocal folds are pressed together, however, the motion of the major portion of the folds is determined by the time constant R_1C_1, where R_1 is the resistance of the lower portion and C_1 is its compliance.

From figure 2.16, we observe that the time of opening of the upper edge of the folds occurs when the separation of the lower portion reaches a certain critical value. Since the trajectory ABC is relatively flat in this region, it is likely that this time of opening is subject to considerable variability, depending on the state of compression of the upper portion at this time. Furthermore, the trajectory ABC is quite sensitive to the degree of adduction of the folds, specified in the model by a negative value x_0, since the multiplying factor $P_s d_1 C_1' + x_0$ is the difference between two relatively large numbers. For these reasons, some variability might be expected in the period of vibration for this pressed mode of phonation.

2.1.6.2 Breathy Voicing The pattern of vibration is quite different when the glottis shows a fixed opening over some part of its length in the resting state. We examine first the situation in which the vocal folds themselves are in the modal configuration corresponding to figure 2.4, but there is a space through which air can flow between the posterior surfaces of the arytenoid cartilages. This configuration has been observed in the normal phonation of many speakers (cf. Södersten and Lindestad, 1990). We shall assume the area of this interarytenoid space to be about 0.03 cm^2, leading to a dc airflow of about 110 cm^3/s when the vocal folds are adducted and when the subglottal pressure is 8 cm H$_2$O. This minimum flow during the glottal cycle is in the

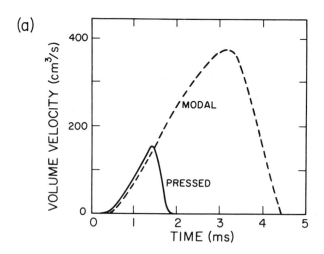

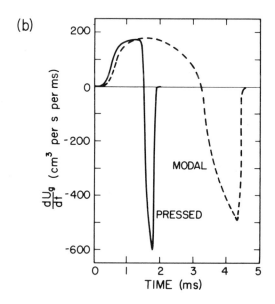

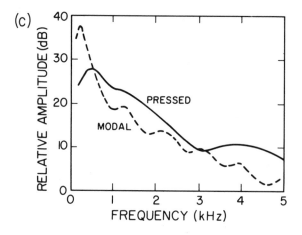

range that has been measured for both female and male speakers (Holmberg et al. 1988).

The calculated airflow (and its derivative) during a glottal cycle for this condition of an interarytenoid leak is shown in figure 2.18. For comparison, the calculations from figures 2.7 and 2.9 for modal voicing (male voice) are also displayed in the figure. The volume velocity waveform with the inter-arytenoid leak is, of course, raised relative to that with no leak, but there is also a difference in the waveforms near the instant of vocal fold closure. Because the leak provides a path for the airflow, an abrupt cessation of flow does not occur, and the inertia of the flow causes a smoother transition to steady flow during the time the vocal folds are approximated (Hanson, 1995). This difference can be seen more clearly in the derivative waveforms. The derivative for the leak condition has a smaller negative peak, and the return to zero derivative following this peak is more gradual. The consequence of these differences is that the spectrum for the leak condition is weaker at high frequencies. For the waveforms in figure 2.18, the spectrum above 2000 Hz is about 6 dB weaker, on average, for the leak condition in relation to the modal condition.

Phonation can also occur with the arytenoid cartilages separated at their anterior as well as their posterior ends. In a resting configuration, then, the vocal folds are somewhat abducted at their posterior ends where they insert into the arytenoids. The type of phonation for this state of the glottis is often called breathy voicing. A typical resting configuration might be as shown in figure 2.19, with the vocal folds adducted at the anterior commissure and gradually spreading toward the vocal processes of the arytenoid cartilages. The arytenoid cartilages are more abducted at their posterior than at their anterior edges. When a subglottal pressure is applied, the anterior portions of the vocal folds oscillate in much the same way as they do when the glottis is in a normal configuration, as described in connection with figure 2.4. The posterior portions of the vocal folds, near the vocal processes of the arytenoid cartilages, undergo lateral oscillation, but the vocal folds do not touch (or just barely touch) during a cycle of vibration. There may also be some mechanical coupling to the arytenoid cartilages, so that the cartilages themselves oscillate laterally with a low amplitude.

For purposes of analysis, we shall assume that the waveform of the glottal area vs. time is a superposition of three components, as schematized in figure 2.20: (1) The anterior 75 percent of the glottis vibrates in much the same way as for modal oscillation, except that this component is scaled to be three-fourths of the area in figure 2.5. (2) The posterior portion of the glottis fluctuates sinusoidally, with the vocal folds just touching at the time when

Figure 2.17 (a) Waveform of glottal airflow for vocal fold model under condition of pressed phonation (solid line) compared with corresponding waveform for modal phonation (dashed line). (b) Derivatives of waveforms in (a). (c) Spectra of waveforms in (b). Waveforms are calculated for conditions represented in figure 2.8.

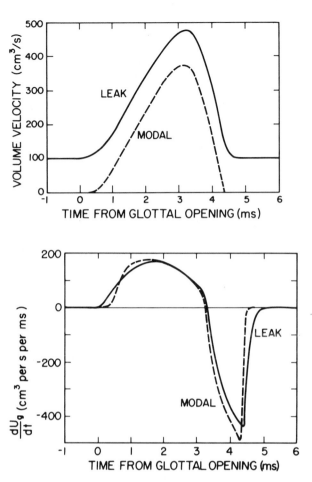

Figure 2.18 The solid lines give calculated airflow (top panel) and its derivative (bottom panel) for the two-mass model adjusted for modal vibration (as in figure 2.4) except that there is a fixed opening of area 0.03 cm² between the arytenoid cartilages. The dashed lines (labeled MODAL) show the calculated flows without a leak, from figures 2.7 and 2.9.

they are closest together. The peak-to-peak amplitude of the area variation is taken to be approximately equal to the amplitude of the first harmonic of the area variation in (1). (3) There is a fixed area of the space between the arytenoid cartilages equal to 0.05 cm², that is, somewhat greater than the example in figure 2.18. Figure 2.20 shows the overall area function as well as the individual components. As will be observed later, this particular selection of the components of the overall area function leads to a volume velocity waveform for which the first-harmonic amplitude is about equal to the first-harmonic amplitude for modal vibration. This is a condition that is approximated when a speaker makes a transition from modal to breathy voicing.

The airflow waveform and its derivative are shown in figure 2.21, together with the spectrum of the differentiated airflow. The airflow is calculated for the condition of a moderate vocalic constriction in the vocal tract, as in figure 2.8. For comparison, the waveform and spectrum for modal vibration

I cm

Figure 2.19 Idealized representation of vocal folds for a configuration simulating breathy voicing. There is a separation between the arytenoids that extends back from the vocal processes.

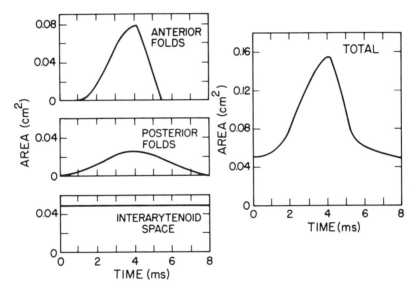

Figure 2.20 Showing method for constructing total area waveform (right panel) for two-mass model in a breathy configuration similar to that in figure 2.19. The left panels show the components that make up the area waveform: an anterior portion that vibrates in a modal fashion (*top*), a posterior portion with sinusoidal vibration (*middle*), and an interarytenoid portion with a fixed area (*bottom*).

are also plotted, as dashed lines. The spectrum for the breathy model is characterized by a high-frequency amplitude that is about 15 dB weaker than that for modal vibration, whereas the two spectra are approximately equal at low frequencies, in the vicinity of the first harmonic. Comparison of the spectra of vowels produced with modal and breathy voice by human speakers shows differences of up to 15 dB at high frequencies, whereas the amplitude of the first harmonic is about the same for the two modes produced with about the same effort.

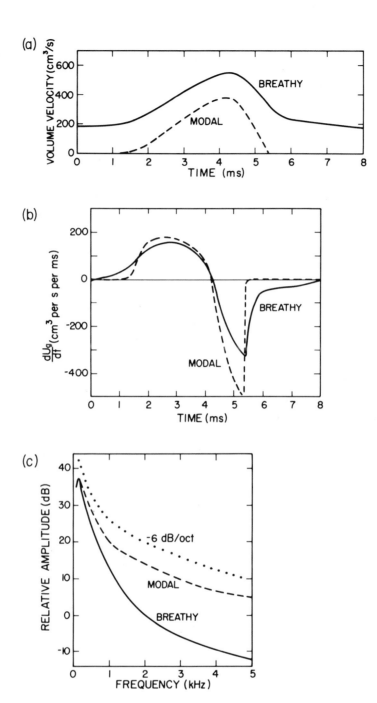

Figure 2.21 (a) Calculated airflow for breathy voicing configuration, as in figures 2.19 and 2.20. The airflow for the modal condition is shown for comparison. (b) Derivatives of airflow curves in (a). (c) Spectra of derivative waveforms. The dotted line shows a −6 dB per octave slope for comparison with the spectra.

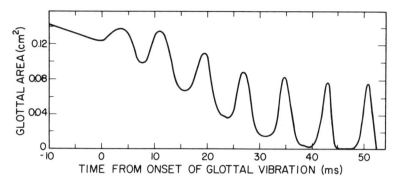

Figure 2.22 Representation of glottal area vs. time as the glottis undergoes an adducting maneuver from a spread configuration to a configuration appropriate for modal voicing.

The presence of a substantial glottal opening means that there can be a large continuous airflow through the glottis. This airflow can lead to the generation of turbulence noise, particularly if it impinges on surfaces in the region immediately above the glottis. This aspect of sound generation at the glottis is discussed in sections 2.2 and 8.3.

As has been noted in section 2.1.5, if the vocal folds are sufficiently abducted no vibration will occur. If the supraglottal vocal tract is not constricted, the glottal airflow will be limited by the cross-sectional area of the glottis. Turbulence noise may be generated in the vicinity of the glottis, as discussed in section 2.2. During speech production in some languages it often happens that the vocal folds are manipulated from an abducted configuration, for which the vocal folds do not vibrate, to a more adducted configuration, for which normal vocal fold vibration occurs. During this time interval, the vocal folds pass through a configuration for which breathy phonation occurs. The sequence of events is depicted schematically in figure 2.22. The first few cycles of vibration tend to be smooth pulses that have weak high-frequency energy but strong low-frequency energy, and there is a large average airflow during this time interval when breathy phonation is initiated. As the vocal folds become more adducted, the glottis becomes closed over a part of the cycle.

When the mode of vocal fold vibration is such that the glottis is closed or remains sufficiently narrow over a cycle of vibration, the acoustic source at the glottis can be approximated by a volume velocity source, as noted in section 2.1.2. During the closed phase, the impedance of this source is, of course, essentially infinite. During the open phase, the glottal impedance is usually large compared with the impedance of the vocal tract (although this may not always be true, as we shall see in the next section). Thus in this situation we can, as a first approximation, represent the acoustic excitation at the glottis by a volume velocity source with a relatively high acoustic impedance. The supraglottal system is essentially isolated from the subglottal system, and is excited by a monopole source.

When there is a fixed opening in the interarytenoid space that parallels the vibrating portion, as in the case of breathy voicing just discussed, then the

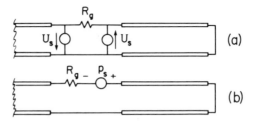

Figure 2.23 (a) Model of the supra- and subglottal cavities (represented as transmission lines) with volume velocity sources U_s exciting the two cavities. (b) Equivalent circuit for configuration in (a), where the sound pressure source $p_s = U_s R_g$.

glottal impedance may become comparable to the impedance of the sub- and supraglottal cavities, particularly at low frequencies (below about 1500 Hz). These cavities may no longer be considered to be acoustically isolated from each other in this frequency range. Under these circumstances, the volume velocity variation due to vocal fold vibration can be considered as a volume velocity $U_s(t)$ entering the supraglottal tract and a volume velocity $-U_s(t)$ entering the subglottal system. That is, we can approximate the source as a dipole, paralleled by the constant portion of the glottal impedance, as shown in figure 2.23a. If we represent this portion of the glottal impedance as a resistance R_g, then this dipole source can be modeled as a sound pressure source $p_s = U_s \cdot R_g$, as indicated in figure 2.23b. This representation of the glottal source will be useful when we discuss the influence of the subglottal cavities, in section 3.6.4.

2.1.7   Effect of a Vocal Tract Constriction on Glottal Vibration

The descriptions of the various modes of glottal vibration up to this point have been based on the assumption that the vocal tract is in a configuration that is relatively unconstricted. Under these conditions, changes in the configuration of the supraglottal cavities have only a minor influence on the waveform of the airflow pulses through the glottis. The principal effect is to introduce some additional skewness or asymmetry in the waveform of the glottal airflow, as illustrated in figure 2.7. During the production of certain vowel-like or consonant sounds, however, a narrow constriction or a complete closure may be formed at some point along the vocal tract above the glottis. If the vocal folds are in a normal configuration for voicing at the time the supraglottal constriction or closure is formed, then a change will occur in the waveform of the airflow and possibly in the configuration and in the vibration pattern of the vocal folds.

When there is a narrow constriction or a closure at some point along the length of the vocal tract, of the type that occurs with a voiced fricative or stop consonant, the effect on glottal vibration is substantial, and will be discussed separately in section 2.1.7.2. For a moderate constriction size that is not sufficient to produce a fricative consonant, there can be smaller but significant effects on the vibration pattern, and these are discussed first.

2.1.7.1 Moderate Constriction Sizes We showed in figure 2.7 that the acoustic mass of the sub- and supraglottal cavities causes some skewness and reduction in the peak amplitude of the volume velocity waveform for a given area function $A_g(t)$. This effect is about the same for any configuration of the supraglottal cavities as long as there is not too narrow a constriction in the vocal tract. For the configuration of figure 2.8, which has been assumed in the calculation of most of the airflow waveforms in section 2.1, there is a modest constriction with a cross-sectional area of 1 cm² and length of 3 cm. This constriction contributes less than one-third of the acoustic mass of the entire system, and hence is not a major factor in determining the airflow waveform at the glottis.

When the constriction becomes narrower, its acoustic mass can contribute significantly to the overall acoustic mass of the sub- and supraglottal cavities. For example, the total acoustic mass of the airways would be doubled if the cross-sectional area A_c of the constriction were decreased to about 0.23 cm², while maintaining a constriction length of 3 cm. When the constriction is as narrow as this, its kinetic resistance as well as its acoustic mass can contribute to the pressure drop in the airways. Consequently a term must be included in equation (2.7) to account for this resistance. Equation (2.7) then becomes

$$\Delta P = R_g U_g + M_A \frac{dU_g}{dt} + R_c U_g, \tag{2.15}$$

where the resistance of the constriction is given approximately by $R_c = \rho U_g/(2A_c^2)$. As before, we make the approximation that U_g is the same at the glottis and at the constriction.

The effect on the airflow of the decreased constriction size of 0.23 cm² has been calculated for the $A_g(t)$ function in figure 2.5, using equation (2.15). This waveform is shown in figure 2.24, and is compared with the waveform originally shown in figure 2.7 for the relatively unconstricted vocal tract. There is a decrease of about 1 to 2 dB in the peak amplitude of the pulse, and a comparable increase in the magnitude of the slope in the vicinity of closure. Modest effects of this kind can be expected for moderate constriction sizes in the range of 0.2 to 0.4 cm².

The calculated effects on the waveform in figure 2.24 are based on a model of the supraglottal airway consisting simply of an acoustic mass and a resistance. However, the impedance of the airway can be much higher than this at the frequency of the first formant. This high impedance can result in significant fluctuations of the pressure immediately above the glottis, so that at some parts of the glottal vibration cycle the supraglottal pressure may deviate appreciably from the reference (atmospheric) pressure. As a consequence, the transglottal pressure may fluctuate during the glottal cycle. The waveform of the volume velocity through the glottis, then, may deviate from the

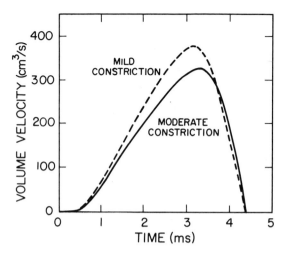

Figure 2.24 The solid line gives the calculated volume velocity waveform when the cross-sectional area of the constriction in figure 2.8 is reduced to 0.23 cm², while maintaining a constriction length of 3.0 cm. The dashed line gives the waveform for the less constricted configuration of figure 2.8, shown previously in figure 2.7a. A subglottal pressure of 8 cm H₂O is assumed.

waveform that is calculated on the assumption of a simple acoustic mass and resistance for the airway. This source-system interaction has been examined by Lin (1987, 1990) and by Fant and Lin (1987). Their analysis has shown that the interaction can introduce some irregularities in the glottal waveform and in its spectrum, but the main features of the spectrum, such as the low-frequency amplitude and the slope at high frequencies, are not significantly modified.

Another consequence of the fluctuation of the supraglottal pressure is a modification of the pressure within the glottis during the open phase of glottal vibration. This change in pressure influences the mechanical motion of the vocal folds. The net effect is to increase the length of time the glottis is open during the cycle and to cause the rate of closing of the glottis to be slower (Bickley and Stevens, 1986). The result is a reduction in the amplitude of the glottal source of a few decibels, with a somewhat greater reduction at high frequencies.

Thus for these moderate constriction sizes there are further modifications of the waveform of the glottal pulse beyond that shown in figure 2.24. These kinds of changes can be expected in the airflow waveform at the glottis for glides and liquids, and for vowels produced with a relatively narrow constriction. These modifications for glides and liquids are discussed further in sections 9.2 and 9.3.

2.1.7.2 Narrow Constrictions or Closure When the constriction is not too narrow, it has been reasonable to assume that the low-frequency features

Figure 2.25 Model of vocal tract with constrictions of area A_g at the glottis and A_c in the region above the glottis. P_s and P_m are the subglottal and intraoral pressures.

of the waveform of the airflow through the glottis and through the constriction are not influenced significantly by the constriction. When the constriction is sufficiently small, however, the resistance of the constriction increases to the point where the average airflow through the vocal tract causes a significant pressure drop across the constriction. The increased intraoral pressure creates abducting forces on the upper surfaces of the vocal folds, and these surfaces displace outward in response to these forces. As a consequence of the reduced transglottal pressure and the more abducted configuration, the peak-to-peak amplitude of the waveform of the glottal airflow decreases and the relative amplitude of the spectrum at high frequencies is reduced. The constriction area for which these effects come into play is in the range of 0.1 to 0.2 cm^2.

In order to estimate the effect of a narrow constriction on the glottal configuration, we consider the behavior of the model in figure 2.25. The cross-sectional area of the supraglottal constriction is A_c, and the area of the glottal constriction is A_g. If A_g is sufficiently small and if the pressure drop $P_s - P_m$ across the glottis is large enough, then the vocal folds will vibrate. For purposes of calculating average flow and intraoral pressure, A_g is taken to be the average area of the glottis. Based on the analysis in figures 2.4 and 2.6, we assume that this average area is determined largely by the maximum opening formed by the upper edges of the vocal folds.

When the intraoral pressure P_m is greater than zero, this pressure exerts an outward force on the upper edges of the vocal folds. The displacement of the upper edge in response to this force is given by $\Delta x = C_2 d_2 P_m$, where $d_2 =$ effective vertical depth of the edge, and $C_2 =$ mechanical compliance per unit length of this edge of the vocal fold. The average area of the glottis can be written

$$A_g = A_{go} + 2\Delta x \cdot \ell = A_{go} + 2\ell C_2 d_2 P_m, \tag{2.16}$$

where A_{go} is the average glottal area that would exist if there were no intraoral pressure, and $\ell =$ length of the glottis. An expression for the intraoral pressure can be derived from the equations $P_s - P_m = \rho U^2/(2A_g^2)$ and $P_m = \rho U^2/(2A_c^2)$, to obtain

$$P_m = P_s \cdot \frac{1}{1 + \left(\dfrac{A_c}{A_g}\right)^2}. \tag{2.17}$$

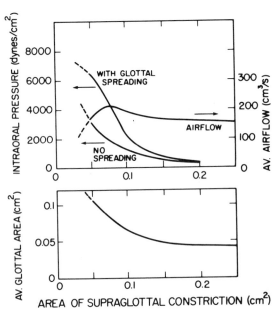

Figure 2.26 Calculations of intraoral pressure and airflow (top panel) and average glottal area (bottom panel) for different values of A_c in figure 2.25. The resting area of the glottis in the absence of a subglottal pressure is 0.04 cm^2, and subglottal pressure = 8 cm H$_2$O. As A_c decreases, the intraoral pressure increases and this pressure causes an increase in the glottal area. The intraoral pressure in the top panel is calculated for two conditions: (1) assuming no passive spreading of the glottis in response to the increased pressure, and (2) with glottal spreading.

Inserting equation (2.16) into (2.17) leads to an equation that can be solved for P_m, from which we can determine A_g and the airflow U.

Approximate values of parameters of the vocal folds for an adult male are: $\ell = 1.0$ cm, $C_2 = 5 \times 10^{-5}$ cm^2/dyne, and $d_2 = 0.1$ cm, so that $2\ell C_2 d_2 = 1.0 \times 10^{-5} P_m$. For modal vibration we assume $A_{go} = 0.04$ cm^2.

Figure 2.26 shows the results of calculations of P_m, A_g, and U as A_c is manipulated from 0.2 to 0.05 cm^2. The calculations for the model indicate that the glottis widens substantially due to the increased pressure on the upper surfaces of the vocal folds. As the supraglottal constriction narrows, the intraoral pressure rises more rapidly than it would if there had been no passive expansion of the glottis. There is an initial increase and then a decrease in the airflow as the supraglottal constriction becomes narrower. As the glottis widens with narrowing of the supraglottal constriction, the waveform of the glottal airflow will become more rounded, as in figure 2.21, with a consequent reduction in the spectrum amplitude at high frequencies. At some constriction size, possibly around 0.07 cm^2 in this example, the transglottal pressure becomes sufficiently small and the glottis becomes sufficiently spread that vocal fold vibration ceases. As will be seen in section 8.4, vocal fold vibration can be maintained by active expansion of the vocal tract

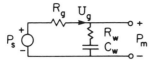

Figure 2.27 Low-frequency equivalent circuit for the configuration in figure 2.25 when $A_c = 0$, as for a stop consonant.

volume, thereby inhibiting the buildup of intraoral pressure as the supra-glottal constriction becomes narrow.

If a complete closure in the vocal tract is formed abruptly when the vocal folds are in a normal configuration with constant subglottal pressure, then a brief time interval of a few tens of milliseconds elapses before the intraoral pressure increases to a value equal to the subglottal pressure. The time course of the increase in intraoral pressure can be calculated approximately from the low-frequency equivalent circuit in figure 2.27. This equivalent circuit is a low-frequency modification of the circuit in figure 1.36b, with infinite impe-dance of the supraglottal constriction. In order to obtain a rough approxi-mation of the time course of the buildup of intraoral pressure following the closure, we estimate the average glottal airflow over the initial few tens of milliseconds following the closure to be about 150 cm^3/s, with an average glottal opening of about 0.07 cm^2 over this interval. The average value of $R_g = \rho U_g/(2A_g^2)$ [from equation (1.12)] is then about 20 dyne-s/cm^5. If R_w is taken to be 10 dyne-s/cm^5, and $C_w = 1.0 \times 10^{-3}$ cm^5/dyne (from section 1.1.3.7), then the time constant for the intraoral pressure increase following closure is roughly 30 ms. (Detailed calculations are given in chapter 7 where an analysis of stop-consonant production is given.) The vocal folds will con-tinue to vibrate for a few cycles after closure, with the amplitude of vibration gradually decreasing as the transglottal pressure decreases and as the vocal folds are displaced toward their steady abducted configuration during vocal tract closure. As noted above, the time interval over which the vocal folds continue to vibrate can be extended if the vocal tract volume is actively increased by raising the soft palate, by advancing the tongue root so that there is an outward movement of the neck surfaces, by lowering the larynx, or by a combination of these. On the other hand, this time interval can be shortened by making various laryngeal adjustments, as discussed in section 2.1.5, as well as by stiffening the walls of the vocal tract or by effecting a contraction of the supraglottal volume. Examples of these manipulations that are used to enhance or to eliminate vocal fold vibration during a consonant are discussed in chapter 8.

2.1.8 Models of the Glottal Source

It has been shown in the previous sections that the waveform of the glottal volume velocity is influenced by a number of factors, including the sex of the

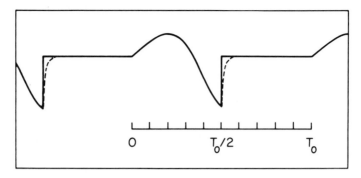

Figure 2.28 Waveform of derivative of glottal airflow U_g based on the LF model (Fant et al., 1985). The period is T_o and the open quotient $OQ = 50$ percent. The solid line is for an abrupt discontinuity in the derivative of U_g (i.e., parameter $T_2 = 0$) and the dashed line corresponds to $T_2 = 0.025 T_o$. See text.

speaker, the fundamental frequency, the subglottal pressure, and the resting position of the vocal folds. Several proposals have been made for modeling the volume velocity waveform (or its derivative) in terms of a small number of parameters, so that these parameters can then be used to describe the waveforms for different speakers and for varying states and configurations of the vocal folds.

One such model is that of Fant et al. (1985), called the LF model. In this model, the flow derivative $U'_g(t)$ is represented by a portion of a single cycle of an underdamped sinusoid

$$U'_g(t) = E_o e^{\alpha t} \sin 2\pi F_g t \tag{2.18}$$

for times t in the range $0 < t < T_1$, where $T_1 = OQ \cdot T_o$, $OQ =$ open quotient = fraction of the cycle in which the glottis is open, and $T_o =$ fundamental period. This waveform is displayed in figure 2.28. During the remainder of the cycle, an abrupt return to zero or a decaying exponential is appended to the end of the sinusoidal portion, as shown in the figure. This waveform up to $t = OQ \cdot T_o$ is defined by the three parameters E_o, α, and F_g. A fourth parameter of the LF model specifies the time constant T_2, beginning at the negative maximum of the underdamped sinusoidal portion, as the dashed line in figure 2.28 shows. For the periodic waveform in figure 2.28, the value of OQ is 0.5.

When the time constant $T_2 = 0$, that is, there is an abrupt return to zero at time T_1, then the limiting slope of the spectrum of the pulse at high frequencies is -6 dB per octave. For a non-zero value of T_2, the high-frequency slope of the spectrum increases to -12 dB per octave at a breakpoint frequency of $1/(2\pi T_2)$. Figure 2.29 shows the spectrum of the waveform constructed by repeating periodically the glottal pulse in figure 2.28, for $T_2 = 0$ and for $T_2 = 0.1$ ms, for a fundamental period of 8 ms, and for two values of the open quotient. The decreased high-frequency amplitude with the larger value of T_2 is apparent. Changing the open quotient by expanding or con-

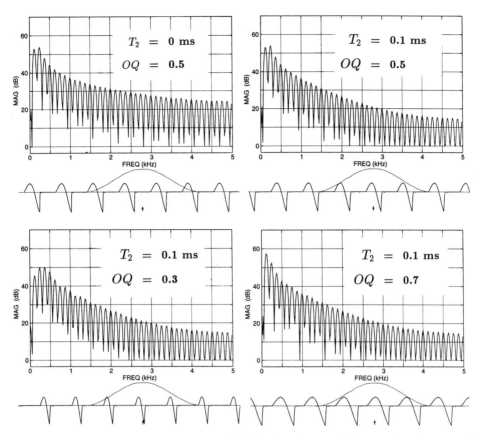

Figure 2.29 Spectrum of derivative of glottal airflow for LF model for several combinations of values of return time T_2 and open quotient OQ as indicated. Fundamental frequency $= 125$ Hz. These spectra were calculated from a version of the LF model developed by Dennis Klatt (Klatt and Klatt, 1990).

tracting the basic pulse (but keeping T_2 the same) has the effect of modifying the spectrum in the low-frequency range. For example, the difference between the amplitudes $H1$ and $H2$ of the first two harmonics changes from -5 dB to $+5$ dB as OQ changes from 30 to 70 percent. The spectrum given in figure 2.10 for a male voice, which is derived from the model described earlier, is similar to the spectrum in figure 2.29 with $OQ = 0.5$ and T_2 between 0 and 0.1 ms.

A model similar to the LF model was proposed earlier by Rosenberg (1971) and was modified and implemented by Klatt and Klatt (1990). This model specifies the derivative of the glottal volume velocity in the time interval $0 < t < OQ \cdot T_o$ by the equation

$$U_g'(t) = a\left(2t - \frac{3t^2}{OQ \cdot T_o}\right), \tag{2.19}$$

where a is a scaling constant. As with the LF model, this model also includes a parameter T_2 that accounts for the return time from the negative peak of the waveform in equation (2.19). The parameters of this model, then, are the amplitude a, the frequency $1/T_o$, the open quotient OQ, and the return time constant T_2. The spectrum of this waveform is similar to that of the LF model.

2.2 TURBULENCE NOISE SOURCES

2.2.1 Mechanisms of Turbulence Noise Generation at a Constriction in a Tube

The basic mechanism for the generation of sound in speech is to create one or more constrictions in the airways between the trachea and the lips, and to cause a rapid flow of air through this constriction. In the previous section we have seen one way in which sound can be produced when a constriction is formed at the glottis. In that case, the mechanism of sound generation involved mechanical vibration of the walls of the glottis, causing a modulation of the flow of air into the vocal tract. We examine now a method of generating sound at a constriction by creating turbulence in the flow of air. Turbulence will occur in the flow downstream from a constriction if the flow velocity at the exit is sufficiently large. The velocity fluctuations in this turbulent flow act as a source of sound.

Turbulence noise can be generated by three somewhat different mechanisms, as illustrated in figure 2.30. The figure shows a tube in which there is a rapid flow of air through a narrow constriction. In one case, the flow of air from the constriction forms a jet, as in figure 2.30a, and turbulent fluctuations in velocity are distributed over a region of space downstream from the exit of the constriction. These fluctuations in velocity occur in free space where there are no boundaries to exert a force on the medium. The second mechanism of turbulence noise generation involves the creation of turbu-

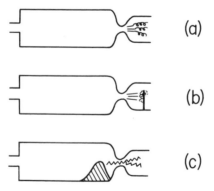

Figure 2.30 Schematic representation of three types of acoustic sources due to turbulence in the airstream near a constriction: (a) no obstacle; (b) obstacle in the airstream downstream from the constriction; (c) fluctuation in flow through the constriction.

lence by the rapid flow of air against an obstacle or a surface, as illustrated in figure 2.30b. The obstacle or surface generates a fluctuating force on the medium, and this fluctuating force constitutes a sound source. The third type of turbulence noise generation is a consequence of random velocity fluctuations in the airstream within the constriction. These fluctuations may arise due to irregularities in the configuration of the airways. One type of irregularity upstream from the constriction is schematized in figure 2.30c.

Experimental data have been collected with mechanical models similar to those shown in figure 2.30, to compare the sound pressures produced in the three situations (Shadle, 1985a; Pastel, 1987). The airflows and dimensions of the model were comparable to those found in the production of fricative consonants in speech. The SPL for the model with an obstacle was about 30 dB greater than that without an obstacle. This difference in level depends, of course, on the position and orientation of the obstacle in the flow, but is clearly a significant difference. It is evident that, for the flows and configurations of interest in speech, the sound energy generated by a mechanism involving an obstacle or surface interacting with the flow is significantly greater than that generated by turbulence in a free jet. For most if not all cases where turbulence noise is generated to signal a phonetic distinction in speech, the primary mechanism of sound generation involves turbulence at an obstacle or surface. Situations can occur, however, in which the fluctuating flow within the constriction can contribute significantly to the radiated sound.

2.2.2 Sound Pressure Source Due to Turbulence in the Flow

In figure 2.30 the obstacle is placed directly in the airstream at right angles to the flow. In this case there is a large fluctuating force that is almost perpendicular to the obstacle and in the direction of the flow, and this force is concentrated in a relatively small region defined by the dimensions of the obstacle and the jet. In another type of configuration, illustrated in figure 2.31, the flow passes over a surface or impinges on the surface at an angle. The fluctuating force in this case is a shear force in the direction of the flow or is oriented normal to the surface and perpendicular to the flow. For this configuration the turbulence may be distributed over a substantial area of the surface. The sound generated by the obstacle in figure 2.30b is considerably greater than that produced across the surface in figure 2.31, since the fluctu-

Figure 2.31 Airflow impinges on the wall of a tube downstream from a constriction, to generate turbulence noise at the wall.

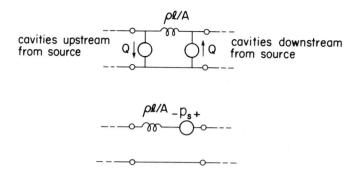

Figure 2.32 Equivalent circuit representation of a turbulence noise source as a one-dimensional dipole with two equal and opposite volume velocity sources Q (top) and as a sound pressure source (bottom).

ating forces on the medium are much greater when there is an obstacle against which the flow impinges almost perpendicularly.

In either case, the fluctuating force exerted by the obstacle or surface creates the equivalent of a distribution of dipole sources over the regions where these sources occur (cf. Landahl, 1975). If the source is concentrated over a narrow region of space within a tube, as it may be with an obstacle of the type shown in figure 2.30b, then the source of excitation of the principal mode of propagation in the tube can be represented as a single one-dimensional dipole, as schematized in the electric network analog in figure 2.32. That is, the source can be represented by two equal and opposite volume velocity sources (depicted by Q in figure 2.32) spaced a small distance apart (ℓ in the figure). This dipole source of strength $Q\ell$ is equivalent to a source of sound p_s in series with the acoustic tube, given by

$$p_s = j\omega\rho Q\ell / A, \tag{2.20}$$

where A is the cross-sectional area of the tube at the point where the source is located, and ρ is the density of air. The representation of a turbulence noise source as a series sound pressure source has been proposed by Fant (1960), based on experimental data from fricative consonants.

A turbulence noise source can be produced at any point along the vocal tract where a constriction can be formed, including the glottis. In some regions of the vocal tract it is possible to direct the airstream against an obstacle to generate a relatively strong source, or to produce a weaker source by preventing the airstream from impinging directly against an obstacle. The various alternatives that are available are considered in chapters 7 and 8. At the level of the larynx, when the vocal folds are vibrating, the peak velocity of airflow can be quite high, as shown above in section 2.1. Some noise can be generated when this flow impinges on the epiglottis or false vocal folds. The generation of turbulence noise at the glottis is discussed in sections 2.2.6 and 8.3.

The sound generated by turbulence at a surface or obstacle in the vocal tract may be concentrated primarily in a narrow region of the vocal tract (such as at the lower incisors), or may be distributed over a region of a centimeter or more downstream from the constriction. If the turbulence is distributed over a region, then a representation of the source as a single lumped sound pressure source as in figure 2.32 may be inappropriate. A distributed source may be needed to provide a better approximation to the sound generation. This distributed source may, in turn, be approximated by several lumped sources, and each source may have different amplitude and spectral characteristics.

It has been shown experimentally that the sound power generated in the middle- and high-frequency range by this kind of turbulent flow for a given constriction size is proportional to the sixth power of the velocity of the airflow (Shadle, 1985a). Since the velocity is proportional to $\sqrt{\Delta P}$, where ΔP is the pressure drop across the constriction, then the sound power generated by a turbulence noise source is proportional to ΔP^3. This relation between sound power and pressure drop has also been observed experimentally (but with slight variations) by Hixon et al. (1967), Badin (1989), and others. Suppose now that, for configurations of the type shown in figures 2.30b or 2.31, the cross-sectional area A of the constriction is changed, keeping other aspects of the configuration fixed. One would expect the area of the surface over which turbulence occurs to increase in proportion to the constriction area A, since this determines the cross-sectional area of the jet that impinges on the surface. The total sound power generated by the turbulence noise is proportional to the area of the region of turbulence on the surface, and therefore is proportional to the cross-sectional area A of the constriction. Consequently the sound power generated by the source is proportional to $\Delta P^3 \cdot A$. Since the radiated sound pressure is proportional to the square root of the sound power, then the magnitude of the sound pressure source in figure 2.32 is proportional to $\Delta P^{3/2} A^{1/2}$. Using equation (1.12) relating ΔP, A, and U, we note that

$$p_s = K U^3 A^{-2.5}, \tag{2.21}$$

where K is a constant. As we have observed earlier, the source strength is also influenced by the configuration of surfaces or obstacles in relation to the jet of air flowing through the constriction. Thus this configuration influences the value of the constant K in equation (2.21). Data from different fricative consonants, as well as experimental data from mechanical models, suggest that the value of K may differ by a factor of about 3 (or about 10 dB) depending on the configuration.

The spectrum of the sound pressure source that results from turbulence at an obstacle tends to have a broad peak at a frequency that is proportional to u/d, where u is the velocity of the airstream and d is the cross-dimension of the constriction (M. E. Goldstein, 1976). Experimentally it appears that the

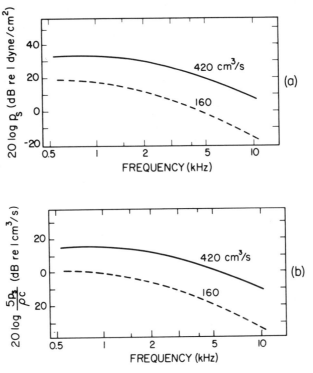

Figure 2.33 Spectrum of sound pressure source p_s for a configuration similar to that in figure 2.30b, for two values of airflow. Distance from the constriction to the obstacle is 3 cm, and the diameter of the (circular) constriction is 0.32 cm. The cross-sectional area of the tube is 5.0 cm^2. The spectra are in 300-Hz bands of frequency. (a) The ordinate is the absolute level of the sound pressure source, in decibels re 1 dyne/cm^2. (b) The same curves are given, but with an ordinate that is in units of volume velocity, to permit comparison with other volume velocity sources in the vocal tract. The sound pressure source p_s is normalized by dividing by the characteristic impedance $\rho c/5$. For 0 dB on the ordinate, $5p_s/(\rho c) = 1$ cm^3/s. When the area A_t of the tube downstream from the constriction is different from 5 cm^2, the curves in (b) should be scaled up by $20 \log (A_t/5)$ dB. For the upper curve in both panels, the value of $20 \log U^3 A^{-2.5} = 212$ dB, where U = volume velocity in cubic centimeters per second and A = area of constriction in square centimeters. When $20 \log U^3 A^{-2.5}$ is different from 212 dB, the upper curve should be scaled up by $20 \log U^3 A^{-2.5} - 212$ dB. Curves are based on experimental data of Shadle (1985a).

proportionality constant is in the range of 0.1 to 0.2 for the configurations of interest in speech production. The spectrum of the source drops off slowly above this frequency of 0.1 u/d to 0.2 u/d.

Measured spectra of the sound pressure source for a configuration like that in figure 2.30b are shown in figure 2.33a for two different flow velocities (Shadle, 1985a). These spectra were calculated from measurements of the sound radiated from the end of a cylindrical mechanical tube containing a narrow constriction with a diameter of 0.32 cm. Air flows through the tube and the airflow through the constriction impinges on an obstacle placed normal to the flow and 3 cm downstream from the constriction. The method of calculating the source amplitude and spectrum is based on principles to be described in chapter 3. In the spectra in figure 2.33, the frequency of the broad spectral peak is at the lower end of the frequency range of the measurements.

The spectra in figure 2.33a are expressed as the sound pressure in a frequency band of 300 Hz, in decibels relative to 1 dyne/cm^2. While the frequency band of 300 Hz may appear arbitrary, it is selected to match roughly the frequency resolution of the peripheral auditory filtering in the frequency range where turbulence noise tends to play the greatest role in the generation of consonant sounds. The frequency range is about 1500 to 4000 Hz, and the bandwidths of the peripheral auditory filters in this frequency range are 200 to 800 Hz, as observed later in section 4.2.6. Thus a spectrum based on an auditory representation of the noise can differ by up to 4 dB from a spectrum with a fixed bandwidth of 300 Hz.

For the two flows of 420 and 160 cm^3/s in figure 2.33, the expected difference in source level, from equation (2.21), is about $30 \log 420/160 = 13$ dB. The measured difference in this example is slightly more than this, especially at high frequencies, but the U^3 dependence in equation (2.21) provides a reasonable approximation to the variation with flow for most conditions. If the characteristic dimension d for the data in the figure is taken to be the diameter 0.32 cm, corresponding to a cross-sectional area of 0.08 cm^2, then the linear velocity u for the two flows is about 2000 and 5200 cm/s. The values of $0.1\, u/d$ are then 600 and 1600 Hz. The spectra in figure 2.33 exhibit the expected decrease above these frequencies, although the low-frequency spectrum does not show a decrease. There may be a monopole component that contributes to the low-frequency amplitude, as discussed in the next section.

In figure 2.33b we have normalized the sound pressure of the source for a configuration like that in figure 2.30b by dividing it by the characteristic impedance of the tube $pc/5$, since the cross-sectional area of the tube that is downstream from the constriction is 5 cm^2. This way of normalizing the source expresses the source strength in units of volume velocity, and thus permits comparison with the volume velocity source at the glottis.

As has been noted above, the magnitude of the sound pressure source depends on the cross-sectional area of the constriction, the airflow through the constriction (or, alternatively, the pressure drop across the constriction), and the configuration of nearby surfaces on which the airflow impinges. The spectra in figure 2.33 represent the source strength for the indicated values of volume velocity and for the constriction size of 0.08 cm^2, with an obstacle oriented normal to the flow and 3 cm downstream from the constriction, as already noted. Experimental data (to be described in chapter 8) suggest that the levels should be scaled down (possibly as much as 15 dB) for a less direct placement of the obstacle. The levels should be scaled up if an obstacle were placed directly in the airstream closer to the point at which the jet emerges from the constriction; this situation in which the levels are scaled up does not appear to occur in normal speech production. If the cross-sectional area of the constriction and the airflow are different from the values for which the spectra in figure 2.33 were obtained, then the curves should be scaled up or down according to equation (2.21). The value of $20 \log U^3 A^{-2.5}$ for the curves for $U = 420 \ \text{cm}^3/\text{s}$ in figure 2.33 is 212 dB, and this value can be used as a reference for scaling the spectrum up or down for different values of U and A. The conditions of volume velocity and constriction size for $U = 420 \ \text{cm}^3/\text{s}$ correspond roughly to the flows and dimensions usually found for fricative consonants in speech. Consequently the upper curve will usually be used as a standard source spectrum which is scaled up or down depending on the conditions for a particular speech sound. Finally, if the cross-sectional area A_t of the tube immediately downstream from the constriction is different from 5 cm^2, the spectrum in figure 2.33b should be scaled up or down by adding $20 \log A_t/5$ dB, where A_t is in square centimeters.

2.2.3 Monopole Source Due to Turbulent Flow

When air flows through a constriction in a tube with an abrupt termination, there can be fluctuations in the velocity of the flow emerging from the constriction. These fluctuations in velocity constitute a monopole sound source, and can be modeled as a volume velocity source. The magnitude and spectrum of this source is somewhat dependent on the configuration of the constriction, including its length, its smoothness, and the abruptness of its termination. The presence of obstacles or other impediments to smooth flow upstream or immediately downstream from the constriction can also influence the monopole source. Rough estimates of these source parameters can be made based on measurements with models. Such measurements have been made by Pastel (1987) for a simple configuration in which a jet of air is introduced in a direction perpendicular to the wall of a tube with a length of 17 cm, as shown in figure 2.34. For this configuration the wall of the tube is close to the outlet of the jet, and this wall is expected to cause a reaction on the flow through the orifice, resulting in a fluctuation of the flow and hence a monopole source. A dipole component of the turbulent noise source for this configuration is also to be expected, although this component will couple

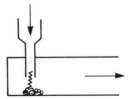

Figure 2.34 Airflow entering a tube normal to the axis, generating turbulence at the wall. At low frequencies the predominant source that couples to the modes of the tube is assumed to be a monopole source.

only weakly to the modes of the tube, especially at low frequencies. (The coupling of sources to the modes of the tube is discussed further in chapters 3 and 8.)

From measurements of the spectrum of the radiated sound pressure when air flows through the configuration in figure 2.34, it is possible to calculate the spectrum of the monopole component of the source. This calculated spectrum is given in figure 2.35. The absolute level of this source spectrum has been scaled (based on equation [2.21]) to correspond to the conditions of flow for which the sound pressure source for $U = 420$ cm^3/s in figure 2.33 is derived. The figure also shows the spectrum of the sound pressure source from figure 2.33, normalized, as in figure 2.33b, to have the units of volume velocity, with a tube having a cross-sectional area of 5 cm^2.

The figure shows that the monopole source has a spectrum that decreases with frequency more rapidly than that of the dipole source at the obstacle. At low frequencies, the level of the monopole source (after normalizing the sound pressure source by the characteristic impedance of the tube) is about 15 dB below that of the dipole source with a full obstacle. At these low frequencies, the monopole source usually couples more effectively to the modes of the vocal tract in front of the constriction than does the dipole source, as we shall observe later, and hence may contribute substantially to the spectrum of the radiated sound pressure. At middle and high frequencies, however, the spectrum of the sound output is usually dominated by the dipole component. (See chapter 8.)

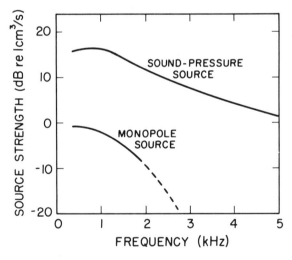

Figure 2.35 The upper curve is the (normalized) sound pressure source at an obstacle, and is the same as the upper curve in figure 2.33b (except for the linear frequency scale). The lower curve is the calculated amplitude of the volume velocity monopole source based on measurements with the model in figure 2.34 (after Pastel, 1987). Levels are in 300-Hz bands. For both curves the value of $20 \log U^3 A^{-2.5}$ is 212 dB, where U is in cubic centimeters per second and A is in square centimeters. The dashed portion of the monopole curve is an extrapolation from the experimental data.

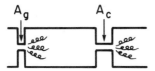

Figure 2.36 Tube with two constrictions, with turbulence noise generated at both constrictions. The cross-sectional areas of the constrictions are A_g and A_c, as indicated, representing the glottal and supraglottal constrictions.

2.2.4 Noise Generation for a Configuration with Two Constrictions

During the production of fricative and stop consonants, the upper airways can usually be considered to have two major constrictions—one at the glottis and one in some region of the vocal tract above the glottis. The configuration is shown schematically in figure 2.36. In general, turbulence noise can be generated at either of these constrictions. If we let A_g = cross-sectional area of the glottal constriction and A_c = cross-sectional area of the supraglottal constriction, then the volume velocity is given approximately by

$$U = \sqrt{\frac{2P_s}{\rho}} \frac{1}{\left(\dfrac{1}{A_g^2} + \dfrac{1}{A_c^2}\right)^{1/2}}, \tag{2.22}$$

where P_s = subglottal pressure. From equation (2.21), we can derive expressions for the relative magnitude of the sound pressure source in the vicinity of the supraglottal constriction and the source in the vicinity of the glottal constriction.

Figure 2.37 shows the relative sound pressure (in decibels) for each of these sources (assuming dipole or sound pressure sources) as a function of the cross-sectional area of the supraglottal constriction, for two values of the glottal constriction size. For a given glottal constriction, the level of the supraglottal source shows a broad maximum. It can be shown that, when U is given by equation (2.22), the value of A_c for which $U^3 A_c^{-2.5}$ is a maximum is $A_c = A_g/\sqrt{5}$. The level of the turbulence noise source at the glottis increases monotonically as the cross-sectional area of the supraglottal constriction increases. The curve showing the source level at the glottis assumes that the vocal folds maintain their configuration and that vocal fold vibration is not initiated.

The relative levels of the two curves in figure 2.37 representing the source levels at the two constrictions depend upon the configuration of the surfaces against which the airflow is directed in the vicinity of the constrictions. The curves in the figure assume that the constant K in equation (2.21) is the same for the two constrictions. For different configurations of surfaces or obstacles, one of the curves in the figures could be shifted up or down relative to the other.

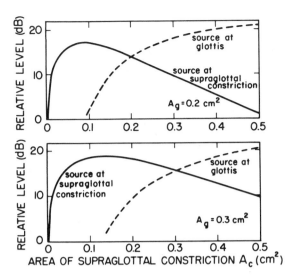

Figure 2.37 Relative level of noise source at each constriction of figure 2.36, as a function of the cross-sectional area of the supraglottal constriction. The cross-sectional area A_g is fixed at a different value for each panel. The constant K in equation (2.21) is assumed to be the same for the noise generated at each constriction.

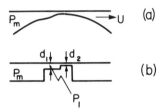

Figure 2.38 (a) A vocal tract constriction with pressure P_m applied behind the constriction. The curved line is intended to represent an articulator such as the tongue blade or tongue body. (b) Schematization of the constriction as a two-section configuration.

The curves in figure 2.37 assume that the adjustment of the cross-sectional area of the supraglottal constriction is made independently of the pressure across the constriction and the airflow through the constriction. However, the walls of the vocal tract in the vicinity of the constriction are not rigid, and there is some displacement of the walls in response to changes in pressure at the walls, in much the same way that the vocal folds undergo displacement in response to changes in the pressure at the vocal fold surfaces. This tendency for the area to increase with increased intraoral pressure has been noted by Badin (1989).

In order to gain some insight into the importance of this effect of yielding walls, we examine the forces on the walls for a typical constriction, as shown in figure 2.38. The configuration of the surface forming the constriction is sketched in (a), and (b) schematizes the configuration in the vicinity of the constriction by two uniform sections with cross dimensions d_1 and d_2. To simplify the analysis, we take the lateral widths of the two sections to be the same (w), and their lengths to be the same (ℓ). A pressure P_m (relative to atmospheric pressure) is applied behind the constriction, and a volume flow U occurs in response to this pressure. The average pressure in the upstream section is P_1, and the average pressure P_2 in the downstream section is taken to be zero. (We assume that $d_1 > d_2$ always.) The walls of the upstream section are assumed to have a linear mechanical compliance C_1. (We shall define C_1 as the compliance per unit area of surface, i.e., the ratio of surface displacement to pressure.) In the absence of an applied pressure, the two sections assume a static configuration. When the pressure P_m is applied, this static configuration is modified due to the pressure P_1 on the upstream section. If we assume that $d_2 > 0$ as a result of this applied pressure, then the pressure P_1 is $P_m - \rho U^2/(2(d_1 w)^2)$. Since the downstream section is the smaller one, then we have $P_m = \rho U^2/(2(d_2 w)^2)$, from which we can write

$$\frac{P_1}{P_m} = 1 - \left(\frac{d_2}{d_1}\right)^2.$$

(2.23)

The pressure P_1 in the upstream section causes an outward displacement of that section so that the width d_1 satisfies the equation

$$P_1 = \frac{1}{C_1}(d_1 - d_{10}),$$

(2.24)

where d_{10} is the static width in the absence of an applied pressure. Since the pressure P_2 on the downstream surface is zero, the difference $d_1 - d_2$ remains constant as d_1 increases in response to P_1. Setting $d_1 - d_2 = \Delta d$, we combine equations (2.23) and (2.24) to obtain

$$\frac{1}{P_m C_1}(d_2 - d_{20}) = 1 - \left(\frac{d_2}{d_2 + \Delta d}\right)^2,$$

(2.25)

where d_{20} is the static position assumed by the downstream section in the absence of an applied pressure. Solution of this equation leads to a relation between the minimum width d_2 of the constriction after the pressure is applied and the minimum width d_{20} that is assumed by the articulators in the absence of the applied pressure. We assume that $d_2 > 0$ after the pressure is applied, although the static position d_{20} could be negative, indicating complete closure in the absence of the applied pressure. The parameters of the equation are (1) the applied pressure P_m, which is often approximately the subglottal pressure; (2) the compliance C_1 of the wall of the constriction; and (3) the difference Δd which is an indication of the rate of decrease of area as one moves toward the constriction.

For purposes of illustration, we have picked values of these parameters that are estimated to correspond to a fricative configuration such as /s/ or /š/: $P_m = 8$ cm H_2O, and $C_1 = 3 \times 10^{-5}$ cm^3/dyne (somewhat greater than the average wall compliance assumed earlier for the entire surface of the vocal tract). Figure 2.39 shows the relation between d_2 and d_{20} for three

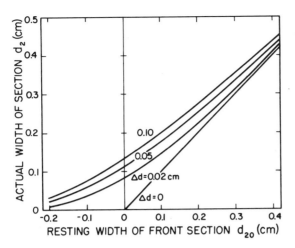

Figure 2.39 Actual width d_2 of the constriction for the configuration in figure 2.38b when pressure is applied, as a function of the "resting" width d_{20} that would occur in the absence of an applied pressure. A two-constriction model like that in figure 2.36 is assumed, with a constant subglottal pressure of 8 cm H_2O and a fixed area of 0.2 cm² for the glottal constriction. The parameter Δd is the difference between the minimum constriction width d_2 and the width d_1 immediately upstream, as in figure 2.38b. See text.

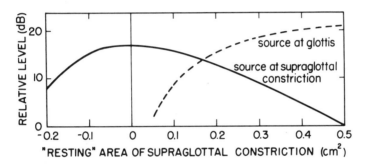

Figure 2.40 Relative level of noise source at each constriction of figure 2.36, as a function of the "resting" area of the supraglottal constriction. The supraglottal constriction is modeled as in figure 2.38, such that the applied pressure modifies the constriction size. Area of glottis is 0.2 cm² as in figure 2.37a, and $\Delta d = 0.02$ cm in figure 2.39.

values of Δd: 0.02 cm, 0.05 cm, and 0.10 cm. These calculated curves show that there can be an increase of 1 mm or more in the width of the constriction due to the applied pressure. More important, perhaps, we observe that in the range of d_{20} up to +0.1 cm, changing the width d_{20} by a given amount results in a smaller change in d_2. Since it is presumably d_{20} that is under the control of a speaker when producing a fricative, one can conclude that the aerodynamic forces make it easier for the speaker to adjust the constriction size to be within a certain critical range to maximize the amplitude of the turbulence noise source, as indicated in figure 2.37.

This observation is illustrated in figure 2.40, which shows the relative amplitude of the turbulence noise at the two constrictions as a function of

d_{20}, that is, as a function of the minimum constriction width that is set by the speaker in the absence of an applied pressure. This figure is derived from figure 2.37a with $A_g = 0.2$ cm^2, but with d_{20} rather than d_2 plotted on the abscissa. The amplitude of the noise at the supraglottal constriction shows a much broader maximum in figure 2.40 than in the corresponding curve in figure 2.37a. The maximum occurs in the vicinity of $d_{20} = 0$, that is, with a "resting" position for which the participating articulatory structures are just touching. A resting position with $d_{20} \leq 0$ for a fricative implies that, when the articulator is in the constricted configuration for the fricative, reduction of the intraoral pressure would cause the constriction to narrow and to form a complete closure.

If the subglottal pressure is P_s, then by appropriate abduction of the vocal folds to produce a relatively open glottis, the pressure drop across the supraglottal constriction becomes equal to P_s. The intraoral pressure between the glottis and the constriction can, however, be raised above the subglottal pressure by closing the glottis and contracting the volume of the space between the two constrictions. This contraction is achieved by raising the larynx or by manipulating the tongue root. Through this laryngeal adjustment and volume contraction, the pressure drop across the constriction can be increased to well above the subglottal pressure, and a greater amplitude of turbulence noise can be produced. This method is used to produce so-called ejective fricative or stop consonants.

As we have seen in section 2.1.7, it is possible to maintain vocal fold vibration when a supraglottal constriction is formed, leading to a voiced fricative consonant. Continued glottal vibration requires that the pressure drop across the glottis be greater than about 3 cm H$_2$O. A typical value of intraoral pressure during a voiced fricative is about one-half the subglottal pressure, whereas during a voiceless fricative the intraoral pressure might be 80 to 90 percent of the subglottal pressure. Consequently the pressure across the supraglottal constriction for a voiced fricative is about 60 percent of its value for a voiceless fricative. Thus the sound pressure resulting from the turbulence noise source for a voiced fricative is expected to be about 7 dB below that for a voiceless fricative if voicing is to be maintained (since $20 \log 0.6^{1.5} \cong 7$ dB). If the noise produced during a voiceless fricative is already quite weak (as with /θ/ or /f/ in English), then the level of the noise source for the voiced cognate will be even weaker, and may be inaudible.

2.2.5 Turbulence Noise at the Release of a Stop Consonant

In the previous section, we discussed how the level of the source of turbulence noise in the vicinity of a supraglottal constriction is dependent on the cross-sectional area of the constriction and on the size of the glottal opening. At the release of a stop consonant, the cross-sectional area of the supraglottal constriction increases from a complete closure, and there is a rapid flow of air through the constriction. This rapid flow can result in the generation of turbulence noise in the vicinity of the constriction. The pressure that is built up behind the constriction drops to atmospheric pressure during this time interval, while the subglottal pressure can be assumed to remain more or less fixed. The interval of turbulence noise generation near the supraglottal constriction is followed by a time interval in which the airflow is limited by the glottal constriction. As the pressure drop across the glottis becomes equal to the full subglottal pressure, several different events can occur depending on the configuration of the glottis: (1) there can be an interval of silence if the glottis remains closed; (2) there can be generation of turbulence noise at the glottis; or (3) vocal fold vibration can be initiated. Throughout this time following the release, the cross-sectional area of the glottal opening can undergo a change, either increasing from a narrow opening or closure, or decreasing from a relatively abducted configuration.

The situation can be examined more quantitatively with reference to the curves in figure 2.37, which show the amplitude of the noise source as a function of the constriction size, together with other parameters related to turbulence noise generation. The rate at which the cross-sectional area of a constriction increases with time has been discussed in section 1.3.3. We observed there that the initial rate of increase of area (averaged over the first few milliseconds) for a stop-consonant release is in the range of 25 to 100 cm^2/s, depending on the articulatory structures that form the constriction. In order to analyze the time course of turbulence noise generation following the release, we shall assume that the cross-sectional area follows a rising exponential time course, as in figure 2.41, and we shall examine two different initial rates of increase: $V_i = 25$ cm^2/s and $V_i = 100$ cm^2/s. In our initial analysis we shall assume that the glottal area remains fixed at 0.2 cm^2.

An equivalent circuit that can be used to estimate the airflow through the glottis (U_g) and through the supraglottal constriction (U_c) is shown in figure 2.42a. This is a modification of the equivalent circuit given previously in figure 1.36b, with U_a set to zero. The elements representing the constriction are time-varying. The parallel path containing the elements R_w, M_w, and

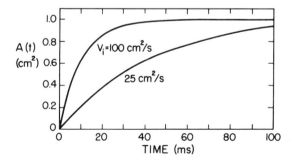

Figure 2.41 Cross-sectional area $A_c(t)$ of supraglottal constriction for two initial rates of opening V_i used in calculating the time course of the turbulence noise source at the release of a stop consonant.

Source Mechanisms

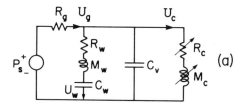

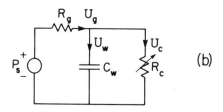

Figure 2.42 (a) Equivalent circuit of the vocal tract that can be used to estimate the time course of the turbulence noise source at the time-varying supraglottal constriction following the release of a stop consonant. (b) Equivalent circuit containing the principal elements that determine the turbulence noise source.

C_w represents the acoustic impedance of the walls of the vocal tract. Immediately prior to release of the consonant, R_c and M_c are infinite (i.e., they form an open circuit), and the pressure built up behind the constriction causes energy to be stored in the compliance C_w, as a consequence of an outward displacement of the walls. Following the release, the volume flow U_c through the constriction is a superposition of the airflow U_g through the glottis and the flow $-U_w$ resulting from an inward movement of the walls as the pressure behind the constriction decreases. (The acoustic compliance C_v of the air behind the constriction also appears in parallel with R_w, M_w, and C_w, but the airflow through this compliance is small in comparison with U_w in the time interval of interest here, as noted in section 1.4.2.)

The airflow U_c beginning from the instant of release ($t = 0$) can be obtained from the equations:

$$P_s = R_g U_g + R_c U_c + M_c \frac{dU_c}{dt} \tag{2.26}$$

$$P_s = R_g U_g + R_w U_w + M_w \frac{dU_w}{dt} + \frac{1}{C_w}\int_0^t U_w \, dt + \frac{P_0}{C_w} = 0 \tag{2.27}$$

$$U_w = U_g - U_c, \tag{2.28}$$

where P_0 is the pressure in the vocal tract at $t = 0$. Approximate solutions to these equations can be obtained if we recognize that, for the rates of change of the constriction for stop consonants (reflected in changes in R_c and M_c), the acoustic masses M_w and M_c have only a small effect on the airflows. Consequently we can use the equivalent circuit of figure 2.42b to solve for the airflows, particularly U_c.

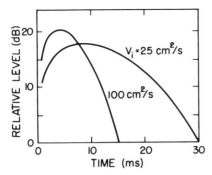

Figure 2.43 Calculated level of turbulence noise source vs. time at the release of a constriction for two rates of opening as in figure 2.41. Cross-sectional area of the glottal opening is fixed at 0.2 cm², and subglottal pressure is 8 cm H₂O. Other parameters are as discussed in text.

From this circuit we can find $U_c(t)$, and hence derive the relative sound pressure of the turbulence noise source, which is proportional to $U_c^3 A_c^{-2.5}$. This quantity is plotted in figure 2.43 for the two rates of opening noted above. The amplitude of the noise source shows a broad maximum in each case, the duration of the peak being somewhat greater for the slower rate of opening. If we arbitrarily define the length of the burst to be the time the noise is within 5 dB of its maximum value, then this length is about 9 ms and 19 ms for the two rates of opening. These curves will, of course, be different for different values of the glottal area. In general, the glottal area also varies with time over this interval, and consequently the amplitude of the envelope of the noise source will be modified still further. A wider range of conditions that occur at stop-consonant releases will be considered in chapters 7 and 8.

2.2.6 Simultaneous Glottal Vibration and Turbulence Noise

In section 2.1, the waveform of the glottal airflow was estimated for various configurations of the vocal folds. For a modal glottal configuration, there is airflow only during a part of the cycle, whereas for a more abducted configuration airflow continues throughout the cycle. As we have seen, the modulation of the flow by the vibrating vocal folds can be modeled as a volume velocity source at the glottis. The flow at the glottis can also give rise to turbulence noise both in the form of a sound pressure source as the flow impinges on laryngeal surfaces downstream from the glottis and in the form of an additional monopole source if there are random fluctuations in the flow through the glottis.

A rough estimate of the amplitudes of the turbulence noise sources during glottal vibration can be made from equation (2.21), using the airflow and glottal area waveforms described in section 2.1. For example, for modal vibration for a male voice, figures 2.7 and 2.5 show peak values of airflow and glottal area in a cycle of vibration to be about 380 cm³/s and 0.11 cm², respectively, resulting in $20 \log U_g^3 A_g^{-2.5} = 203$ dB. Similar calculations for

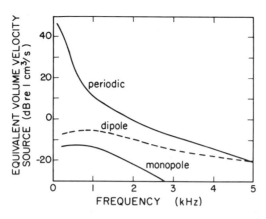

Figure 2.44 Comparison of calculated levels and spectra for periodic and turbulence noise sources at the glottis, for modal voicing. The calculations of the noise sources are averages based on average glottal area and flow. Levels are in 300-Hz bands. See text.

average values of U_g (150 cm^3/s), and A_g (0.04 cm^2) give 200 dB for this quantity. Consequently the source levels in figure 2.35 must be reduced by about 12 dB (on average) to account for the different area and flow relative to the values on which that figure is based. A further reduction of about 10 dB in the level of the dipole sound pressure source is made since the obstacles in the flow near the glottis are less effective in generating noise.

Figure 2.44 shows the levels of the various sources at the glottis after these corrections for the noise sources are made. The spectrum of the periodic glottal source is derived from the spectrum of $U_g'(t)$ in figure 2.10 by dividing the amplitudes of the components by $2\pi f$ (to obtain the spectrum of $U_g(t)$), and by correcting the spectrum upward by $10 \log 300/125$ to give a spectrum that would be obtained with an analyzing bandwidth of 300 Hz.

Figure 2.44 shows that the monopole component of the noise source is negligible in comparison with the periodic component, at least for this condition of modal voicing. The sound pressure source of turbulence noise is within a few decibels of the periodic component at high frequencies (3 kHz and above). As is shown later in section 8.3, however, the sound pressure source usually couples less effectively to the vocal tract modes than does the periodic source, so that the noise component in the radiated sound pressure is even less in relation to the periodic component than is indicated by figure 2.44, particularly at frequencies below about 3 kHz.

This is not the case for breathy voicing, however. As figure 2.21 shows, the periodic component at high frequencies can be 15 dB or more below that for modal voice. Furthermore, the value of $20 \log U_g^3 A_g^{-2.5}$ is about 3 dB higher than it is for modal voicing. For breathy voicing, then, the effective spectrum amplitude of the sound-pressure source can be well above that of the periodic source at high frequencies. Detailed discussion of these questions is given in section 8.3.

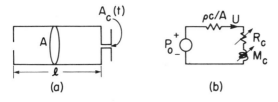

Figure 2.45 (a) Model for release of a stop consonant, in which the cross-sectional area $A_c(t)$ increases linearly with time over the initial few milliseconds following the release. (b) Equivalent circuit for determining the airflow U through the constriction in the model in (a), valid for times less than $2\ell/c$.

2.3 TRANSIENT SOURCES

In section 2.2.5 we examined the time course of the amplitude of the turbulence noise source in the vicinity of a supraglottal constriction following the release of a closure at the constriction. When the rate of change of area of the constriction is in the range normally observed for stop consonants, figure 2.43 shows that there is a rise in amplitude of the noise source within the initial few milliseconds, followed by a fall in amplitude as the constriction becomes larger than the glottal constriction. This burst of noise is not, however, the only source of acoustic energy at the release of a stop consonant. At the instant of release there is a rapid increase in the flow of air through the constriction. If the rate of change in cross-sectional area of the constriction is sufficiently rapid and if the length of the constriction is sufficiently short, the abrupt increase in airflow at the release can produce a transient source of sound that precedes the onset of the turbulence noise source. The abrupt increase in airflow that gives rise to this source occurs within the first 0.5 ms following the release. This brief transient source is generated before the noise source in figure 2.43 reaches its maximum amplitude. The presence of a transient in the airflow at the release of a stop consonant was noted in figure 1.37, and has been analyzed by Maeda (1987) and by Massey (1994).

In order to set the dimensions of the problem, we consider the configuration in figure 2.45a, consisting of a uniform tube of length ℓ and cross-sectional area A that is initially closed at the right-hand end (corresponding to a closure formed by the lips or tongue blade). We assume there is a pressure P_o within the tube, relative to atmospheric pressure. The constriction is then released, such that its cross-sectional area is $A_c(t)$ and its length is ℓ_c. We are interested in the airflow through the constriction in the time interval that is less than the roundtrip propagation time $2\ell/c$ in the tube behind the constriction. For example, if $\ell = 9$ cm, we consider the time interval up to 0.5 ms.

For times less than $2\ell/c$ following the release, the equivalent circuit of figure 2.45b can be used to estimate the airflow through the time-varying constriction. In this equivalent circuit we are representing only the forward wave in the uniform tube, for which the internal impedance is the characteristic impedance of the tube $\rho c/A$ and the Thevenin equivalent pressure source is P_o. The resistance of the constriction is given by a viscous part and a kinetic part, as we have seen in section 1.2, such that

$$R_c = \frac{12\mu\ell_c}{bd^3} + \frac{\rho U}{2A_c^2}.$$ (2.29)

The opening at the constriction is approximated as a narrow rectangle with larger dimension b and smaller cross-dimension d; μ is the viscosity. The acoustic mass of the constriction is given by $M_c = \rho\ell_c/A_c(t)$.

The relation between P_o and U in figure 2.45b can therefore be written

$$P_o = \frac{\rho c}{A}U + \frac{12\mu\ell_c}{bd^3}U + \frac{\rho U^2}{2A_c^2} + \frac{d}{dt}\left(\frac{\rho\ell_c U}{A_c(t)}\right).$$ (2.30)

As we shall verify later, for the constriction areas and lengths of interest for the release of the lips or the tongue tip in speech production, the major term in this equation over most of the 0.5-ms interval following release is the kinetic pressure drop across the constriction. Consequently an approximation to the flow can be derived from the equation

$$U(t) = \sqrt{\frac{2P_o}{\rho}}A_c(t).$$ (2.31)

A more detailed examination of the various terms in equation (2.30) has been made by Massey (1994).

At the release of a stop consonant, the initial rate of increase of the cross-sectional area of the constriction, dA_c/dt, is determined in part by the motion of the active articulator and in part by forces on the articulator due to the intraoral pressure. Because of the action of the pressure behind the closure, the surface of the active articulator at the posterior end of the constriction is pushed apart, as shown schematically in figure 2.46 for a labial

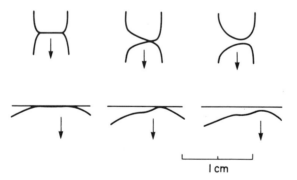

Figure 2.46 Schematic representation of the shape of the lips (top) and tongue surface (bottom) as a labial or a velar stop consonant is released. At the instant of release, the length of the constriction is relatively short, due to the distortion of the surfaces by the action of the intraoral pressure.

and a velar release. At the instant of release, only a short length of the active articulator surface is involved in forming the initial change in the area. As noted in section 1.3.3, measurements have shown that the initial rate of increase of area is in the range 40 to 100 cm^2/s for labials. The initial value of dA_c/dt is probably about the same for alveolar stop consonants. For velar stops, the initial rate of increase of area is slower; cineradiographic and acoustic data given in section 1.3.3 indicate that this rate is about 25 cm^2/s. Considerable variability can be expected in these rates of opening across subjects and across phonetic contexts.

As we have seen in connection with the study of the glottal source (equation [2.8]), the sound pressure at a distance from the tube is proportional to dU/dt, and hence, from equation (2.31), the parameter of interest for describing the effect of the transient source on the radiated sound pressure at the release is dA_c/dt. If we assume dA_c/dt at the initial part of the release of a labial stop consonant to be about 100 cm^2/s and the intraoral pressure to be 8 cm H_2O, then the rate of increase of the volume flow, from equation (2.31), is about 4×10^5 cm^3/s^2. This rate of change of airflow is comparable to the rate of change that occurs in the glottal flow in the vicinity of glottal closure during a cycle of vocal fold vibration, as we have seen in table 2.1. Thus the sound pressure resulting from this transient source can be of the same order of magnitude as that produced by a glottal pulse, at least over the high-frequency regions of the spectrum (above, say, 1000 Hz). This source is, of course, filtered by the vocal tract, and the transfer functions for the two types of sources will be quite different, as will be discussed in chapter 3.

Given this result that the rate of increase of volume flow is about 4×10^5 cm^3/s^2 during the initial few tenths of a millisecond after the release, we can determine whether we were justified in assuming that the kinetic term in equation (2.30) is the dominant term. At time $t = 0.2$ ms, for example, we would have $A_c = 0.02$ cm^2 and $U \cong 80$ cm^3/s, from equation (2.31). If the cross-sectional area A of the tube is taken to be 3 cm^2, then the first term for P_o in equation (2.30) is $(\rho c/A)U \cong 1000$ $dynes/cm^2$. If we take the constriction length ℓ_c at the moment of release to be 0.1 cm, and we select cross dimensions $d \times b$ for the opening to be 0.1×0.2 cm^2, then the viscous term is $U \cdot 12\mu\ell_c/(bd^3) \cong 100$ $dynes/cm^2$. For smaller values of A_c, and therefore smaller values of d, this term increases rapidly. If U increases in proportion to $A_c(t)$, then the last term in equation (2.30) is essentially zero. These calculations indicate that each of the terms on the right-hand side of equation (2.30) except the quadratic term is reasonably small compared with P_o, and hence it is valid to use equation (2.31) to determine at least an approximation to the initial value of dU/dt over the first few tenths of a millisecond. This conclusion may be somewhat less valid for the slower rate of increase of $A_c(t)$ assumed for velar releases.

The brief transient flow through the constriction at the release can be represented by a volume velocity source located at the constriction. An approximation to the spectrum of this source can be made by assuming that dU/dt

has a discontinuity at $t = 0$. The Fourier transform $U(f)$ at frequency f as a consequence of this discontinuity is given by

$$U(f) = \left| \frac{dU}{dt} \right|_o \cdot \frac{1}{(2\pi f)^2} \tag{2.32}$$

where $|dU/dt|_o$ represents the discontinuity in the slope of the volume velocity waveform. Thus, for example, within a frequency band of 300 Hz centered at a frequency of 1000 Hz, one would expect an amplitude[2] of about $[2 \times 4 \times 10^5/(2\pi \times 1000)^2] \times 300 = 6.1$ cm^3/s. The rms value is 0.707 times this amplitude. Consequently at 1 kHz the rms spectrum amplitude of the transient source in a 300-Hz band is about 13 dB re 1 cm^3/s. At higher frequencies, $U(f)$ decreases more rapidly than equation (2.32) indicates, since the rate of increase of $U(t)$ in the initial few tens of a millisecond is less rapid than that predicted in equation (2.31), due to the viscous term in equation (2.30). If we assume this time interval of slower rate of increase is about 0.2 ms (corresponding to a value of $A_c(t)$ of about 0.02 cm^2), then we would expect the spectrum $U(f)$ to decrease by $1/f^3$ above 2.5 kHz (taking 0.2 ms to be about three time constants). The initial transient of volume velocity will eventually decay and will reverse in amplitude, probably after 1 to 2 ms. This reversal will limit the spectrum amplitude of the transient below about 1000 Hz. Taking all of these factors into consideration, we settle on the curve in figure 2.47 as the spectrum amplitude (in 300-Hz bands) for the initial volume velocity transient at the instant of release of the labial or alveolar stop consonant, for a rate of area change of 100 cm^2/s and an intraoral pressure of 8 cm H$_2$O. At the release of a velar stop consonant, for which the initial rate of increase of area is assumed to be about 25 cm^2/s, the source strength in figure 2.47 should be reduced by 12 dB.

When the length of the constriction is greater than a few tenths of a centimeter, or when the rate of increase of the cross-sectional area is sufficiently small, the viscous term in equation (2.30) becomes important, and the value

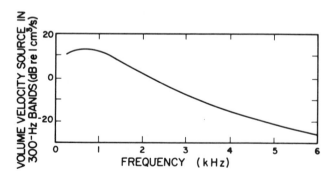

Figure 2.47 Estimated spectrum of volume velocity transient at the lips when a labial stop consonant is released. A point on this curve represents $1/\sqrt{2}$ times the Fourier transform of the transient, integrated over a 300-Hz band. The rate of increase of the cross-sectional area at the release is taken to be 100 cm^2/s, and the intraoral pressure prior to release is 8 cm H$_2$O.

of dU/dt following the release becomes much smaller. Thus there is a limited range of conditions for which the initial transient is a significant component of the sound at the release of a stop consonant. Comparison of the absolute level of the transient with that of the turbulence noise source at the constriction and of the periodic glottal source show, however, that there are configurations and frequency ranges for which the transient makes a significant contribution to the radiated sound (Massey, 1994). These questions are be discussed further in chapters 7 and 8.

When the constriction under static conditions is relatively long (e.g., 1 cm or more), as in the bottom portion of figure 2.46, it is possible that more than one transient release occurs as the moving articulator is displaced away from the fixed surface with which it makes contact during the consonant closure. Multiple transients are sometimes observed at the release of velar stop consonants or laminal stop consonants. The mechanism by which multiple transient releases occur is probably similar to the mechanism of vibration of the vocal folds. The pressure behind the constriction causes the walls immediately upstream from the constriction to be displaced outward, as shown in figure 2.46. The most anterior part of the closure then separates, and air flows through the opening. A consequence is that the pressure within the constriction falls, and the walls of the constriction are displaced back to the closed position, causing the airflow to be cut off. The process then repeats itself, and another pulse of air is generated. As these oscillations occur, the articulator is being displaced from the closed position. Depending on the rate of opening, two or more oscillations might occur before the separation becomes too great to permit further oscillation.

2.4 SOURCES PRODUCED BY SUCTION

The sources of sound that have been discussed up to this point are all produced by building up a positive pressure behind a constriction and modulating the outward flow resulting from this pressure. Another mechanism that is used in some languages for generating sound creates a negative pressure (relative to atmospheric pressure) behind a constriction, and the release of the constriction causes an inward flow of air through the constriction. The negative pressure is produced by forming a complete closure with the tongue body in the vicinity of the soft or hard palate and forming another constriction at a location anterior to the closure formed by the tongue body. For most clicks, the more anterior constriction is formed with the tongue blade, but clicks formed as a consequence of a lip closure are also possible. A typical vocal tract configuration with the two constrictions above the glottis is shown in figure 2.48. The volume V between the two constrictions is expanded from a shape labeled as 1 to shape 4, creating a negative pressure in this volume. Release of the configuration into a following more open configuration of the vocal tract occurs by first releasing the more anterior constriction and then later releasing the tongue body constriction.

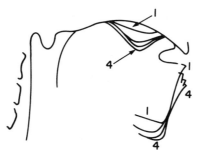

Figure 2.48 Midsagittal section of the vocal tract at four successive points in time as a negative pressure is created in the enclosed volume prior to release of the click /!/. (From Traill, 1985.)

The anterior constriction generally forms a complete closure during the expanding maneuver. The release can be either abrupt, with a rapid movement of the articulator and an abrupt onset of the sound, or more gradual, with a slower onset and decay of the sound.

The magnitude of the negative pressure in the volume V between the two constrictions can be large compared with the subglottal pressure. Suppose, for example, that the volume V has dimensions $2 \times 1 \times 0.5$ cm, giving a volume of 1 cm^3. If the narrow dimension is expanded by 0.05 cm, then there is a 10 percent change in volume, resulting in a decrease in pressure within V equal to 10 percent of atmospheric pressure, that is, about 100 cm H$_2$O. Apparently, then, it is relatively easy to achieve a pressure drop across the anterior constriction that is at least ten times the subglottal pressure. Cineradiographs, such as the one in figure 2.48 (Traill, 1985; Ladefoged and Traill, 1994), suggest that a volume increase greater than 10 percent can occur, with a correspondingly larger pressure difference.

In the course of the expansion, the negative pressure in the enclosed space creates an inward force on the walls of this space, particularly the tongue surface. If the mechanical compliance per unit area of the tongue surface is assumed to be linear, and has an average value in the range of 1.0×10^{-5} cm^3/dyne (i.e., a value at the lower end of the range given in section 1.1.3.7), then the average inward displacement of these walls in response to the negative pressure is substantial: the movement of the tongue surface is in the range of 1 cm or more. While the assumption of linearity may not be valid for such a large negative pressure, nevertheless it is apparent that, following the release of a click, there is a rather large outward movement of portions of the tongue surface. As we have seen earlier in section 1.4.2, the time constant of this movement in response to a sudden change in pressure is roughly 10 ms.

When the anterior constriction is released rapidly, the volume velocity through the constriction rises abruptly. This kind of release occurs only for clicks produced with the tongue tip or tongue blade as the active articulator. The initial discontinuity in dU/dt occurs because of the abrupt discharge of pressure within the enclosed space between the two constrictions. Within a millisecond or so following the release, the contribution of the outward-collapsing walls is probably small compared with the contribution due to the "charging" of the acoustic compliance of the air within the enclosed space. The inertia of the walls of the enclosed space limit the rate at which these walls can begin their outward movement.

If the initial (negative) pressure in the space between the constrictions is P_1, and if the initial rate of increase of the cross-sectional area A_c of the constriction is dA_c/dt, then the initial rate of increase of volume velocity through the constriction is given by

$$\frac{dU}{dt} = \sqrt{\frac{2P_1}{\rho}} \frac{dA_c}{dt}, \tag{2.33}$$

analogous to the result we have seen before in equation (2.31). In the case of these abruptly released clicks, we shall assume that dA_c/dt is about the same as it is for the releases discussed in section 1.3. If the magnitude of P_1 is about twelve times the subglottal pressure used in calculating the transient in section 2.3, then the discontinuity in dU/dt at the release for this two-constriction case is $\sqrt{12}$ times as great, that is, about 1.4×10^6 cm^3/s^2. That is, we can expect the high-frequency spectrum amplitude of the transient at the release to be about 11 dB greater than that for a normal stop-consonant release.

The total volume of ingressive air that occurs during this initial release is about $C \cdot P_1$, where C is the acoustic compliance of the volume. For a volume of 1 cm^3, and $P_1 = 100$ cm H$_2$O, the volume of the ingressive air is about 0.1 cm^3. In the case of a pulmonic stop consonant such as a labial or alveolar, the total volume of egressive air during the initial transient release is about 0.4 cm^2, assuming an initial intraoral pressure of about 8 cm H$_2$O. The low-frequency spectrum amplitude for the transient release should be roughly proportional to the total volume of air involved in forming the transient. Consequently the low-frequency spectrum amplitude of the transient for the click is expected to be about 12 dB weaker than that estimated for the pulmonic transient. At high frequencies, however, the spectrum amplitude of the click transient is about 11 dB greater, as noted above.

Figure 2.49 shows the estimated spectrum amplitude for the transient source for an abrupt click, compared with that for a transient that accompanies a pulmonic release of a labial or alveolar stop consonant, from figure 2.47. These transient sources are, of course, modified by the transfer function of the vocal tract. Preliminary acoustic data show general agreement with these estimates (Traill, 1994), although figure 2.49 may underestimate the amplitude of the transient, presumably due to underestimation of the magnitude of the negative pressure in the enclosed space prior to the release.

In contrast to the click with an abrupt release, a source that is more distributed in time can be generated by releasing the anterior constriction more slowly. The release is sufficiently slow that the ingressive air through the

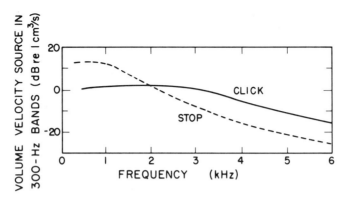

Figure 2.49 The solid line gives the estimated spectrum amplitude (in 300-Hz bands) of the transient source that occurs at the abrupt release of a click, as in figure 2.48. An enclosed volume of air equal to 1.0 cm^3 is assumed, with a negative pressure of 100 cm H_2O within this volume at the instant of release. The calculated transient for a release of a pulmonic alveolar or labial stop consonant is shown for comparison, from figure 2.47 (dashed line).

constriction can be largely a consequence of passive expansion of the walls surrounding the enclosed space. That is, the elastic properties of these walls cause them to return to their static configurations as the ingressive air reduces the magnitude of the negative pressure. We have observed above that, for a wall compliance of 1.0×10^{-5} cm^3/dyne, and assuming a wall area of 2 cm^2 that is susceptible to deformation, a negative pressure of 100 cm H_2O would cause a wall displacement of 1 cm, and a volume increase of 2 cm^3. Consequently there could be an ingressive volume flow of about 2 cm^3 due to the inward displacement of the tongue surface during the time of this more gradually released click.

Experimental data show that the duration of the release phase for these types of clicks is about 20 ms (Traill, 1994). During the release, it appears that a random series of brief pulses are created as narrow channels are formed and extinguished at the constriction. Thus the source consists of a random series of pulses of the type observed for an abrupt release, although the individual pulses may be somewhat weaker.

2.5 VIBRATION OF SUPRAGLOTTAL STRUCTURES

Any one of the transient sources described in section 2.3 usually consists of a single transient that is a consequence of the abrupt release of a closure at some point along the vocal tract. With appropriate adjustment of certain of the articulators, it is possible to produce vibration of the structure as a consequence of interaction between aerodynamic forces and mechanical forces within the structure. The mechanism of vibration involves principles similar to those involved in the vibration of the vocal folds (McGowan, 1992). Supraglottal structures that have the physical characteristics that favor this type of vibration are the tongue blade, the uvula, and possibly the lips.

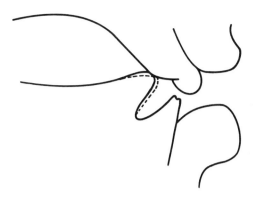

Figure 2.50 Schematic representation of the position of the tongue blade when a trill is occurring. The dashed line indicates the configuration of the midline just prior to release of the closure. The lowering of the surface of the tongue blade from the solid contour to the dashed contour occurs in response to the pressure behind the constriction.

We shall discuss the mechanisms of vibration with reference to the tongue blade, but the mechanism would be similar for the other structures. A more detailed analysis has been given by McGowan (1992). The configuration of the tongue against the hard palate is schematized in figure 2.50. There is a pressure in the space behind the closure that exceeds the atmospheric pressure, and this pressure exerts a downward (in the figure) force on the surface of the tongue blade. This part of the tongue responds by undergoing a downward displacement, much like the outward displacement of the vocal folds in the initial part of the glottal vibration cycle (figure 2.4 and equation [2.2]). The displacement of this part of the tongue surface is shown in the figure. The physical constants (the mass and compliance per unit area) of this part of the tongue blade are, of course, somewhat different from those of the vocal fold, with a larger compliance and a larger mass. Consequently the natural frequency is considerably lower than it is for the vocal folds. As this outward displacement behind the closure proceeds, the length of the closure (dashed line in the figure) decreases, and finally there is release of the closure. A rapid flow of air occurs, creating a source of sound that probably includes a turbulence noise component and a transient component defined by an abrupt rise in volume velocity. The tongue tip is displaced downward rapidly. As airflow is initiated, the pressure in the channel immediately behind the point of release decreases, and the restoring force due to the mechanical compliance of the tongue surface causes an upward or inward movement of this surface to begin. This movement eventually results in a closure with a configuration similar to the solid line, the airflow stops, the pressure behind the constriction increases, and the cycle begins again.

The frequency of vibration is determined by the natural frequency of the mechanical system. Very roughly, the tongue surface area involved in the vibration is estimated to be about 1 cm^2, and the mass M of the vibrating tongue tip is approximately 1 gm. If the mechanical compliance C per unit area is taken to be 3×10^{-5} cm^3/dyne, that is, at the upper end of the range of C_s given in section 1.1.3.7, then the natural frequency is given by $1/(2\pi\sqrt{MC}) = 30$ Hz. This is the range observed experimentally for tongue tip trills.

By this mechanism, then, a series of transient sources or noise bursts, or both, is generated, and these are spaced about 30 ms apart. If the vocal folds are in a configuration appropriate for vibration, there is a modulation of the amplitude of the glottal pulses as the intraoral pressure increases and decreases during the trill.

3 Basic Acoustics of Vocal Tract Resonators

3.1 SPEECH PRODUCTION IN TERMS OF SOURCE, TRANSFER FUNCTION, AND RADIATION CHARACTERISTIC

Chapter 2 was concerned with the properties of the sources that form the acoustic excitation for the vocal cavities during speech production. To a first approximation, these source properties are independent of the shapes of the cavities that are anterior and posterior to the source locations, and depend only on interaction between the airflow and the structures forming the constriction that accelerates the flow. The sound output of the acoustic cavities is usually taken as the volume velocity $U_o(t)$ at the lips, although for nasal sounds and for certain voiced consonants the volume velocity $U_n(t)$ at the nostrils and the volume velocity at the outer surfaces of the neck may also be components of the output. The sound pressure at a distance from the lips is usually the quantity that is of ultimate concern, since the human ear is sensitive to fluctuations in sound pressure, and most microphones respond to pressure variations.

The sound pressure $p_r(t)$ at distance r from the lips is linearly related to the volume velocity $U_o(t)$. The precise form of the relation depends on the shape of the mouth opening and on the head of the speaker. To a first approximation, for frequencies up to about 4000 Hz, the mouth opening can be regarded as a simple source of strength $U_o(t)$, radiating uniformly in all directions. The sound pressure produced at distance r (where r is greater than a few centimeters) from such a source is given by

$$p_r(t) = \frac{\rho}{4\pi r} \frac{\partial U_o\left(t - \frac{r}{c}\right)}{\partial t},$$

$$(3.1)$$

where c is the velocity of sound and ρ is the density of the air. Equation (3.1) states that the sound pressure at time t is proportional to the time derivative of the volume velocity at time r/c prior to t. If the time functions are represented in exponential form, that is, $p_r(t) = p_r(f)e^{j2\pi ft}$ and $U_o(t) = U_o(f)e^{j2\pi ft}$, where f = frequency, then we have the following relation between the complex amplitudes $p_r(f)$ and $U_o(f)$:

$$p_r(f) = \frac{j2\pi f \rho}{4\pi r} U_o(f) e^{-j(2\pi fr/c)}. \tag{3.2}$$

The quantity

$$R(f) = \frac{p_r(f)}{U_o(f)} = \frac{j2\pi f \rho}{4\pi r} e^{-j(2\pi fr/c)} \tag{3.3}$$

is called the radiation characteristic. We are usually concerned only with the magnitude

$$|R(f)| = \frac{f\rho}{2r}. \tag{3.4}$$

The radiation characteristic is proportional to frequency, that is, it rises with frequency with a slope of 6 dB per octave. Equation (3.4) is quite valid up to about 1000 Hz and is accurate to within a few decibels up to 4000 Hz, but above this frequency it is a poor approximation. The form of a more precise radiation characteristic is discussed in section 3.7.

If we denote the Fourier transform of the source as $S(f)$, and if we consider the vocal tract as a time-invariant linear system, then the filtering of the source by the vocal tract can be represented by a transfer function

$$T(f) = \frac{U_o(f)}{S(f)}, \tag{3.5}$$

where $U_o(f)$ is the Fourier transform of the output volume velocity. That is, any frequency component of the source of complex amplitude $S(f)$ and frequency f appears at the output as a volume velocity of complex amplitude

$$U_o(f) = T(f)S(f). \tag{3.6}$$

The Fourier transform of the sound pressure p_r at distance r is given, then, by

$$p_r(f) = S(f)T(f)R(f), \tag{3.7}$$

that is, the sound pressure is the product of a source function, a transfer function, and a radiation characteristic (Fant, 1960).

In general, the radiation characteristic $R(f)$ and the spectrum envelope of the source function $S(f)$ are smooth and monotonic functions of frequency. Typical spectra of $S(f)$ for the glottal source and for a turbulence noise source have been shown previously in figures 2.10 and 2.35. These spectra usually have no major peaks or other irregularities (although sometimes the glottal spectrum can show rather sharp minima). The transfer function $T(f)$, however, is usually characterized by several peaks corresponding to resonances of the acoustic cavities that form the vocal tract. Large changes in the positions and amplitudes of these peaks can be effected by manipulating the shapes of these cavities. Thus the character of the output sound for a given type of source is determined primarily by the transfer function.

The situation is depicted qualitatively in figure 3.1, which shows vocal tract configurations corresponding to a vowel, where the source is at the

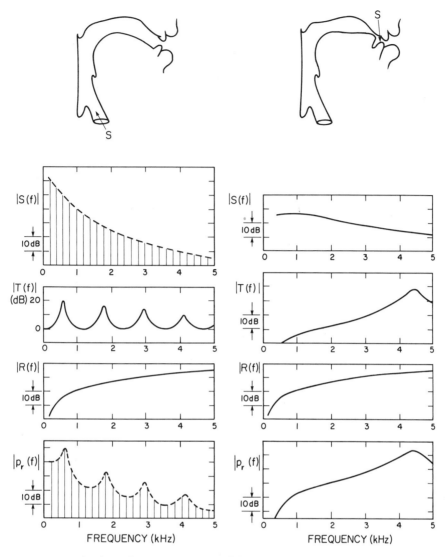

Figure 3.1 Sketches indicating components of the output spectrum $|p_r(f)|$ for a vowel and a fricative consonant. The output spectrum is the product of a source spectrum $S(f)$, a transfer function $T(f)$, and a radiation characteristic $R(f)$. The source spectra are similar to those derived in figures 2.10 and 2.33 in chapter 2. For the periodic source, $S(f)$ represents the amplitudes of spectral components; for the noise source, $S(f)$ is amplitude in a specified bandwidth. See text.

glottis, and a fricative consonant, for which the source is in the vicinity of a constriction. The approximate form of the source spectrum $S(f)$, the transfer function $T(f)$, the radiation characteristic $R(f)$, and the sound pressure $p_r(f)$ is shown in each case.

The determination of the transfer function for various vocal tract configurations and source locations involves application of the theory of sound propagation in tubes of arbitrary shape. Solutions of the acoustic wave equation must be found, given that appropriate boundary conditions are satisfied on the walls of the vocal tract and at either end of the tract. Except at low frequencies, the vocal tract walls are relatively hard surfaces acoustically, that is, the impedance of the walls (per unit area) is very large compared to the characteristic impedance of air. If we are interested only in the frequency range up to 5000 Hz, then the cross-dimensions of the vocal tract are substantially less than a wavelength of the sound, and the solutions that can exist in the tube depend only on the position along the midline of the tube, extending from the glottis to the lips. The sound pressure is approximately the same at all points in a plane that is perpendicular to the midline. In other words, the only mode of propagation that can exist in such a tube consists of plane waves parallel to the axis of the tube. The solution for these one-dimensional waves depends only on the cross-sectional area and not on the shape of the cross section at each point along the length of the tube, as long as the circumference of the cross section is less than a wavelength.[1]

The determination of the transfer function of the vocal tract reduces, therefore, to finding a solution to the one-dimensional wave equation in a tube whose cross-sectional area is a function of position x measured along the midline from the glottis, subject to appropriate boundary conditions at the ends of the tube and with a prescribed source. The cross-sectional area as a function of x, designated by $A(x)$, is called the area function.

3.2 GENERAL FORM OF THE VOCAL TRACT TRANSFER FUNCTION

If we express the transfer function in terms of the complex frequency variable s, that is, we replace $j2\pi f$ by s in $T(f)$, then $T(s)$ can be represented, up to a certain frequency, by the following quotient:

$$T(s) = K \frac{B(s)}{A(s)} = K \frac{(s - s_a)(s - s_b)(s - s_c) \ldots}{(s - s_1)(s - s_2)(s - s_3) \ldots},$$ (3.8)

where K is a constant, $s_a, s_b, \ldots$ are the zeros of $T(s)$, $s_1, s_2, \ldots$ are the poles of $T(s)$, and $B(s)$ and $A(s)$ are polynomials in s.

For most vocal tract configurations that are of interest, the poles and zeros occur in complex conjugate pairs, and the real parts of these complex frequencies are usually much less than the imaginary parts. Physically, this means that the peak acoustic energy stored in the vocal tract at the frequency of the pole or zero is much greater than the energy lost in one cycle of oscillation. (The validity of this statement will be demonstrated later.) It is possible, therefore, to express the poles of $T(s)$ as a product of terms of the form

$$\frac{1}{A(s)} = \frac{1}{K_p} \cdot \frac{s_1 s_1^*}{(s - s_1)(s - s_1^*)} \cdot \frac{s_2 s_2^*}{(s - s_2)(s - s_2^*)} \cdots,$$ (3.9)

where the stars indicate complex conjugates, and K_p is a constant. The numerators are selected so that each of the terms is normalized to unity at

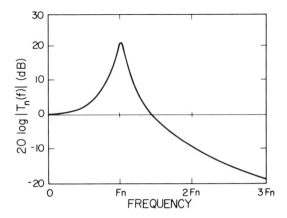

Figure 3.2 A plot of one of the terms of equation (3.9), that is, the component of the transfer function $T(s)$ associated with one conjugate pair of poles. The equation for this component is

$$T_n(s) = \frac{s_n s_n^*}{(s - s_n)(s - s_n^*)}$$

where $s = j2\pi f$, s_n is complex frequency of pole, and $s_n = \sigma_n + j2\pi F_n$. Ordinate represents magnitude of $T_n(s)$ on a decibel scale. Abscissa is frequency f. The bandwidth of the pole for this example is approximately $F_n/12$, so that $\sigma_n = F_n/12\pi$.

$s = 0$. The zeros of $T(s)$ can be expressed by similar terms but with the numerator and denominator interchanged.

The poles represent the complex natural frequencies of the vocal tract. The imaginary parts indicate the frequencies at which oscillations would occur in the absence of excitation, and are called the formant frequencies.[2] They are normally designated as $F1$, $F2$, ..., Fn, ..., in increasing order of frequency. The real parts give the rates of decay of these oscillations. Thus for a particular pole $s_n = \sigma_n + j2\pi f_n$, the sound pressure and the volume velocity at any point in the vocal tract, in the absence of excitation, would have the form $e^{\sigma_n t} \cos(2\pi f_n t + \phi)$, where ϕ is a constant. For a real system, of course, σ_n is negative, indicating source-free oscillations that decay with time. Since the vocal tract is a distributed system, the number of natural frequencies is, in principle, infinite. If the acoustic system is to be represented only up to a certain maximum frequency, then a finite number of poles and zeros provides an adequate description of the transfer function.

One of the terms in equation (3.9) is plotted in figure 3.2, with frequency f as the abscissa, and with the magnitude of the function expressed in decibels. The constant K_p is taken to be unity. It is assumed that the magnitude of the real part of the pole is much less than the imaginary part, that is, $|\sigma_n| \ll 2\pi f_n$. To this approximation, the height of the resonance peak is $|\pi f_n/\sigma_n|$, and the bandwidth B_n at the points 3 dB down from the peak is $|\sigma_n/\pi|$. The height of the peak is therefore approximately equal to f_n/B_n. For frequencies well above the peak, that is, for $f \gg f_n$, the amplitude of the curve falls with increasing frequency at a rate of 12 dB per doubling of frequency.

Basic Acoustics of Vocal Tract Resonators

The natural frequencies of the vocal tract are excited by a source or sources located either at the glottis or at some point along the length of the tract. When the spectrum of the source is relatively broad, then the spectrum of the sound pressure or volume velocity at any point in the vocal tract is characterized by a peak in the vicinity of each natural frequency or formant, similar to the peak shown in figure 3.2. For each natural frequency there is a distribution of spectral amplitudes of the sound pressures and volume velocities throughout the tract. The amplitude of the entire distribution of sound pressures and volume velocities throughout the tract for a given natural frequency depends on the degree of coupling of the source to that natural frequency. Thus the spectral amplitude of the output volume velocity at the lips in the vicinity of a natural frequency depends upon (1) the relative size of that volume velocity in comparison with other volume velocities distributed throughout the tract at the natural frequency, and (2) the amount of coupling of the source to the natural frequency.

The amount of coupling between the source and the output volume velocity at a given natural frequency s_n is given by the residue of $T(s)$ at $s = s_n$. In general, the coupling is small if there is a zero in $T(s)$ in the vicinity of $s = s_n$, is larger if there is no such zero, and is even larger if there is another pole close to $s = s_n$.

When the source is at the glottis and there is no acoustic coupling to the subglottal or nasal cavities, it can be shown that the transfer function has only poles and no zeros. (See section 3.5.) For this rather common situation in speech production, the magnitude of the transfer function, expressed in decibels, is the sum of a number of terms of the type shown in figure 3.2, with a different complex frequency for each conjugate pair of poles. The frequencies at which the poles occur depend, of course, on the configuration of the vocal tract, that is, on the area function $A(x)$.

Figure 3.3 shows four resonance curves corresponding to equally spaced formants at 500, 1500, 2500, and 3500 Hz, together with a fifth curve representing the contribution of poles higher than the fourth, assuming these poles to be equally spaced every 1000 Hz above 3500 Hz. [As will be shown later, this set of formant frequencies occurs when the length of the vocal tract is 17.7 cm and its cross-sectional area is uniform, i.e., $A(x)$ is constant. This configuration is roughly the area function for the schwa vowel /ə/ produced by an adult male speaker.] For purposes of illustration, all formants are assumed to have the same bandwidth of about 80 Hz (an assumption that is roughly valid only for the lowest two or three formants). The overall transfer function, obtained by adding the component curves in decibels, is also shown in the figure. For these particular formant locations, the amplitude of each resonant peak is the same, and the peaks are about 18 dB higher than the valleys. In order to obtain the spectrum of a vowel with these formant frequencies, it is necessary to add to this transfer-function curve the spectrum of the glottal source (in decibels), which has the form shown in figure 2.10, and the radiation characteristic (also in decibels).

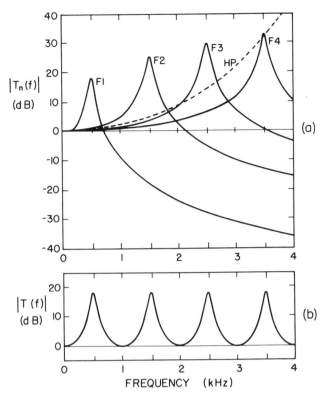

Figure 3.3 (a) The components of the vocal tract transfer function corresponding to four formants $F1$, $F2$, $F3$, and $F4$, together with the effect of higher formants (dashed curve, labeled HP). The sum of all these curves (in decibels), yielding the overall transfer function, is shown in (b).

Changing the vocal tract configuration, expressed by the area function $A(x)$, causes a shift in the formants to different frequencies. Shown in figure 3.4a are three curves representing the contribution of the first formant to the overall transfer function, for three different values of the first formant frequency $F1$. The peaks of the curves are, of course, at different frequencies but, in addition, the amplitude of the peak increases as the formant frequency increases, as shown in figure 3.3a, and the level of the curve at high frequencies also rises. The overall transfer functions corresponding to these three first formants are shown in figure 3.4b, assuming the higher formants remain fixed at the values used in figure 3.3. There is an appreciable shift in the relative amplitudes of the formant peaks as the frequency of the first formant is changed.

Examples of the all-pole transfer function for several other combinations of formant frequencies are shown in figure 3.5. The overall spectrum envelope of a vowel with a glottal source is the result of multiplying (or adding, in decibels) a transfer function of this type by the spectrum envelope of the source (as in section 2.1) and the radiation characteristic (equation [3.4]). The result is a spectrum envelope with a shape like that of the transfer function but with the high frequencies tilted downward, and with a downward tilt of the amplitude at the low frequencies (below $F1$). The examples in figure 3.5

Basic Acoustics of Vocal Tract Resonators

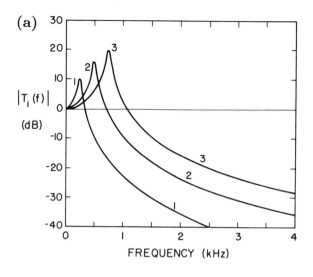

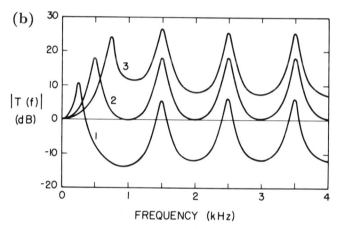

Figure 3.4 (a) The component of the vocal tract transfer function (in decibels) corresponding to the first formant for three different values of F1. Note the change in amplitude of the peak and the shift in level at higher frequencies. (b) The effect of a change in F1 on the overall transfer function, assuming formants above F1 remain fixed. The labels 1, 2, and 3 identify low, medium, and high values of F1.

further demonstrate that changes in the formant frequencies produce not only shifts in the positions of the spectral peaks but also modifications of the entire form or balance of the spectrum.[3] These modifications in the spectrum are governed by three general rules (Fant, 1956, 1960): (1) The overall the amplitude of the vowel for a given source spectrum, which is determined primarily by the amplitude of the first formant peak, increases as F1 rises in frequency. This attribute is illustrated by the curves in figure 3.4a. (2) Increasing a particular formant frequency raises the amplitude of the spectrum at frequencies above that formant, as illustrated in figure 3.4b. (3) When two or more formants come close together, there is an increase in the spectrum amplitude in the vicinity of these formants. Examples are shown in figure 3.5.

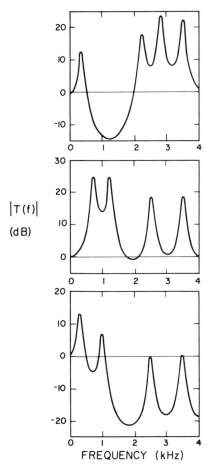

Figure 3.5 Computed transfer functions for three different configurations of formant frequencies, illustrating changes in relative amplitudes of peaks and valleys in the transfer function. Bandwidths of all resonances are fixed at 80 Hz.

The spectra of certain speech sounds can also be strongly influenced by the presence of zeros in the transfer functions. As will be shown in sections 3.5 and 3.6, zeros can occur in the transfer functions of a nasal sound and of a sound produced with a source at a vocal tract constriction above the glottis. Figure 3.6 shows the transfer function corresponding to a conjugate pole and zero pair, the different curves representing various amounts of separation between the pole and the zero. Again, for purposes of illustration, the same fixed bandwidth is assumed for both pole and zero. When the pole and the zero are close together, they almost cancel each other. There is a local perturbation in the transfer function, but the influence of the pair at more remote frequencies is small. The effect of the pole-zero pair on the overall shape of the spectrum increases, however, as the separation between them increases, illustrated by curves 1, 2, and 3 in the figure.

For certain source locations and vocal tract configurations, the transfer function from source to output is dominated in a particular frequency region

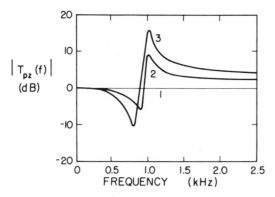

Figure 3.6 Effect of a pole-zero pair on the transfer function. The contribution of the pole-zero pair to the transfer function is

$$|T_{pz}(s)| = \frac{(s - s_0)(s - s_0^*)}{(s - s_p)(s - s_p^*)} \cdot \frac{s_p s_p^*}{s_0 s_0^*}$$

where $s = j2\pi f$, s_0 and s_0^* are a conjugate zero pair, and s_p and s_p^* are a conjugate pole pair. The three curves represent different spacings between s_0 and s_p, curve 1 corresponding to zero spacing. Ordinate is $20 \log |T_{pz}(f)|$ in decibels. The peak and valley become more pronounced as the pole and the zero become more separated.

by two poles and a zero. The magnitude of the transfer function for various locations of the zero with two fixed poles is sketched in figure 3.7. The relative amplitudes of the spectral peaks corresponding to the two poles are very much influenced by the location of the zero. For example, the peak corresponding to the lower of the two poles is obliterated when the frequency of the zero is equal to that of the pole (curve 2 in the figure). Also, the magnitude of the transfer function at high frequencies is affected by the zero locations, much as the frequency of a pole influences high-frequency amplitudes, as in figure 3.4.

3.3 NATURAL FREQUENCIES AND TRANSFER FUNCTIONS FOR VARIOUS RESONATOR SHAPES

In our initial discussion we shall be concerned with the natural frequencies corresponding to various vocal tract area functions in the absence of loss, so that the complex natural frequencies have no real parts. Later (in section 3.4) we shall include the effect of energy loss, both at the walls of the vocal tract and at the terminations. Since the losses are usually small, however, they do not greatly influence the imaginary parts of the complex natural frequencies, and consequently calculations of formant frequencies based on the assumption of zero acoustic loss are generally quite valid. Furthermore, measurements show that formant bandwidths, which are determined by losses in the vocal tract, are a more or less fixed function of frequency, at least for vowels. Hence knowledge of formant frequencies, combined with bandwidth estimates from this function, are sufficient to determine the approximate overall spectrum shape for a vowel. In our initial analysis we shall also assume that

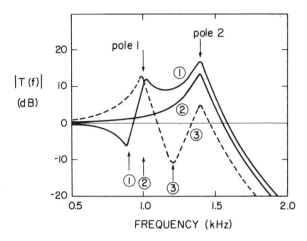

Figure 3.7 Shape of transfer function characterized by two poles and a zero, that is,

$$T(s) = \frac{(s - s_0)(s - s_0^*)}{(s - s_1)(s - s_1^*)(s - s_2)(s - s_2^*)} \cdot \frac{s_1 s_1^* s_2 s_2^*}{s_0 s_0^*}$$

for $s = j2\pi f$. The two poles remain fixed as shown at the top. Curves are shown for three zero locations, the frequencies of the zeros being indicated by the numbered arrows at the bottom. For case 2, the zero cancels one of the poles. The zero is below the two poles for case 1, and between the two poles for case 3.

the walls of the vocal tract are hard, the radiation impedance at the mouth opening is zero, and the impedance of the glottal opening is infinite. There is a reactive component to each of these impedances, and this reactance can cause shifts in the formant frequencies, but these shifts are usually small. These effects are also discussed later, in section 3.4.

The sound pressure $p(x, t)$ and the volume velocity $U(x, t)$ for one-dimensional wave propagation in an acoustic tube are related by equations derived from Newton's law and compressibility considerations (cf. Beranek, 1954). These equations are

$$\frac{\partial p}{\partial x} = -\frac{\rho}{A} \frac{\partial U}{\partial t} \tag{3.10}$$

and

$$\frac{\partial U}{\partial x} = -\frac{A}{\gamma P_o} \frac{\partial p}{\partial t}, \tag{3.11}$$

where A is the cross-sectional area of the tube at the point x, P_o is the ambient pressure, ρ is the ambient density of the air (0.00114 gm/cm^3 for air at body temperature), and γ is the ratio of specific heat at constant pressure to specific heat at constant volume ($\gamma = 1.4$ for air).

If we assume exponential time dependence, then we can write $p(x, t) = p(x)e^{j2\pi ft}$ and $U(x, t) = U(x)e^{j2\pi ft}$, where $p(x)$ and $U(x)$ represent complex amplitudes of sound pressure and volume velocity, respectively, and $f =$ frequency. In terms of these complex amplitude functions, equations (3.10) and (3.11) become

$$\frac{dp}{dx} = -\frac{j2\pi f \rho}{A} U \tag{3.12}$$

and

$$\frac{dU}{dx} = -\frac{j2\pi f A}{\gamma P_o} p. \tag{3.13}$$

Elimination of U from these equations leads to

$$\frac{d^2 p}{dx^2} + \frac{1}{A}\frac{dA}{dx}\frac{dp}{dx} + k^2 p = 0, \tag{3.14}$$

where $k = 2\pi f/c$, and $c = \sqrt{\gamma P_o/\rho}$, the velocity of sound. (For air at the temperature of the body, $c = 35{,}400$ cm/s.) Equation (3.14) is known as the Webster horn equation (Morse, 1948). Solutions to this equation can be found in closed form for just a few area functions $A(x)$.

The natural frequencies of an acoustic tube with area function $A(x)$ are values of the frequency f for which equation (3.14) has a solution, subject to the boundary conditions at either end of the tube. If we take $x = -\ell$ as the position of the glottis, and $x = 0$ as the mouth opening, then, as just noted, the boundary conditions we shall apply in our initial analysis are $p(0) = 0$ and $U(-\ell) = 0$, corresponding, respectively, to zero impedance at the mouth opening and infinite impedance at the glottis. In terms of the sound pressure, the latter boundary condition can be written [from equation (3.12)] $dp/dx = 0$ at $x = -\ell$.

3.3.1 Uniform Tubes

We consider first the natural frequencies for a tube of uniform cross-sectional area, closed at the end corresponding to the glottis and open at the other end. The configuration is shown in figure 3.8. For $A(x) = $ constant, equation (3.14) reduces to the one-dimensional wave equation

$$\frac{d^2 p}{dx^2} + k^2 p = 0. \tag{3.15}$$

Solutions of this equation, subject to the boundary condition at $x = 0$, are

$$p(x) = P_m \sin kx, \tag{3.16}$$

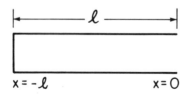

Figure 3.8   Uniform tube of length ℓ, closed at one end and open at the other.

where P_m is a constant whose magnitude represents the maximum value of the sound pressure. The volume velocity corresponding to this sound pressure, from equation (3.12), is given by

$$U(x) = jP_m \frac{A}{\rho c} \cos kx. \tag{3.17}$$

The boundary condition at $x = -\ell$ is satisfied only if $\cos k\ell = 0$, or if $2\pi f\ell/c = (2n - 1)\pi/2$, where n is an integer. The formant frequencies for the tube are, therefore,

$$Fn = \frac{2n - 1}{4} \frac{c}{\ell}, \tag{3.18}$$

where the formant number $n = 1, 2, 3, \ldots$. For a plane wave of frequency Fn, the wavelength is $\lambda_n = c/Fn$, and consequently the natural frequencies for the uniform tube correspond to $\ell = (2n - 1)\lambda_n/4$, that is, the length of the tube is an odd multiple of a quarter-wavelength.

For an average adult female speaker, the vocal tract length is estimated to be 14.1 cm, from table 1.1. When a speaker produces the schwa vowel /ə/, the cross-sectional area of the vocal tract is roughly uniform. Thus the formant frequencies are $Fn = [(2n - 1)/4] \cdot (35{,}400/14.1)$, or approximately 630, 1880, 3140, ... Hz. We will observe later that the effect of the radiation impedance at the mouth causes these frequencies to be about 5 percent lower. Table 1.1 gives an average vocal tract length for an adult male speaker as 16.9 cm, leading to formant frequencies for the schwa vowel of 520, 1570, 2620, ... Hz. Again there is a radiation correction, described in section 3.4.1, that lowers these frequencies, again by about 5 percent. This correction is equivalent to adding 5 percent to the length of the vocal tract. In the case of adult male speakers, addition of this correction to the vocal tract length leads to a corrected length of 17.7 cm. For a uniform vocal tract, this length gives formant frequencies of 500, 1500, 2500, ... Hz.

At the frequency of the nth formant, the distribution of pressure amplitude $p(x)$ along a uniform tube is

$$p(x) = P_m \sin \frac{2\pi Fnx}{c}. \tag{3.19}$$

The volume velocity corresponding to this sound pressure, from equation (3.12), is given by

$$U(x) = jP_m \frac{A}{\rho c} \cos \frac{2\pi Fnx}{c}. \tag{3.20}$$

These equations indicate the usual properties of a pure standing wave: the pressure and volume velocity at a particular point x are 90 degrees out of time phase, and the pressure and velocity distributions are 90 degrees out of phase in the x dimension, that is, the pressure amplitude is a maximum where the velocity amplitude is zero, and vice versa. The latter property of the standing waves is illustrated in figure 3.9, which shows the distribution of

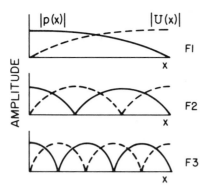

Figure 3.9 Distribution of sound pressure amplitude $|p(x)|$ and volume velocity amplitude $|U(x)|$ in a uniform tube for the first three natural frequencies F1, F2, and F3. Tube is closed at the left-hand end and open at the right-hand end.

Figure 3.10 (a) Uniform tube open at both ends. (b) Uniform tube closed at both ends.

sound pressure and volume velocity amplitude along a uniform tube for each of the first three natural frequencies.

For a tube that is open at both ends, as in figure 3.10a, the boundary conditions at both $x = 0$ and $x = -\ell$ are approximately $p(x) = 0$, and hence, from equation (3.16), we have $k\ell = 0, \pi, 2\pi, 3\pi, \ldots$. The natural frequencies for such a tube, therefore, are given by

$$F = 0, \frac{c}{2\ell}, \frac{c}{\ell}, \frac{3c}{2\ell}, \ldots. \tag{3.21}$$

In the case of a tube of length ℓ that is closed at both ends (figure 3.10b), the boundary conditions are $U(0) = U(-\ell) = 0$. Solution of equation (3.15) subject to these boundary conditions can be readily shown to lead to natural frequencies that are the same as those given in equation (3.21).

3.3.2 Lumped Acoustic Mass and Compliance

The acoustic impedance looking into one end of a uniform tube at $x = -\ell$, when the tube is open at the end $x = 0$, is the ratio of the complex amplitude of the sound pressure to the complex amplitude of the volume velocity at $x = -\ell$:

$$Z_A = j \frac{\rho c}{A} \tan \frac{2\pi f \ell}{c}. \tag{3.22}$$

This impedance has poles at the natural frequencies $f_n = [(2n - 1)/4]c/\ell$, and zeros at frequencies between these natural frequencies, that is, at $f = 0$, $c/2\ell, c/\ell, 3c/2\ell, \ldots$. If the length ℓ of the tube is small compared with a wavelength, such that $2\pi f \ell / c \ll 2\pi$, then we have the following approximation for the impedance of a short open tube:

$$Z_A \cong j2\pi f \frac{\rho \ell}{A}.$$ (3.23)

This impedance can be regarded as the ratio of the complex amplitude of the pressure across the ends of the tube to the volume velocity through the tube. From equation (3.17) it can be seen that the volume velocity is approximately uniform when $k\ell \ll 2\pi$. The quantity $\rho\ell/A$ is the acoustic mass M_A of the tube, and its acoustic impedance is analogous to that of an electrical inductance.

Since the volume velocity is the same throughout an acoustic mass, then there is no compression of the air in the tube, and hence only kinetic energy is stored in the tube. The average kinetic energy stored in an acoustic mass M_A in which there is a volume velocity of complex amplitude U can be shown to be

$$T = \frac{1}{4} M_A |U|^2.$$ (3.24)

The acoustic impedance looking into a tube of length ℓ that is closed at the other end is given by

$$Z_A = -j \frac{\rho c}{A} \cot \frac{2\pi f \ell}{c}.$$ (3.25)

If the length of the tube is short compared with a wavelength, that is, $2\pi f \ell / c \ll 2\pi$, then an approximate expression for the impedance is

$$Z_A = \frac{1}{j2\pi f \left(\dfrac{A\ell}{\rho c^2} \right)}.$$ (3.26)

The quantity $A\ell/\rho c^2$ is the acoustic compliance C_A of a short tube, and equation (3.26) is analogous to the expression for an electrical capacitance.

The sound pressure amplitude in a short tube that can be represented as an acoustic compliance is approximately uniform, and hence there is no pressure gradient within the tube. Consequently, only potential energy is stored. The average potential energy stored in an acoustic compliance C_A in which there is a sound pressure of complex amplitude p is

$$V = \frac{1}{4} C_A |p^2|.$$ (3.27)

3.3.3 Helmholtz Resonator
Another configuration that approximates a vocal tract shape encountered in speech production is a relatively wide tube terminated at one end by a complete closure (such as the glottis) and at the

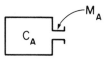

Figure 3.11   Helmholtz resonator.

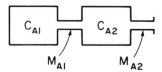

Figure 3.12   Configuration consisting of two Helmholtz resonators.

other end by a narrow constriction. Such a configuration, illustrated in figure 3.11, is sometimes called a Helmholtz resonator. At sufficiently low frequencies, the large volume can be regarded as an acoustic compliance C_A and the narrow constriction as an acoustic mass M_A. This combination of an acoustic compliance and an acoustic mass has a natural frequency

$$f_1 = \frac{1}{2\pi\sqrt{M_A C_A}}. \tag{3.28}$$

This expression for the natural frequency is valid provided that the dimensions of the volume and of the constriction are small compared with the wavelength $\lambda_1 = c/f_1$. If the cross-sectional area and length of the wide tube are A_1, ℓ_1 and of the narrow tube A_2, ℓ_2, then $C_A = A_1\ell_1/\rho c^2$, and $M_A = \rho\ell_2/A_2$, and the natural frequency is

$$f_1 = \frac{c}{2\pi}\sqrt{\frac{A_2}{A_1\ell_1\ell_2}}. \tag{3.29}$$

There are some vocal tract configurations that can be approximated by a resonator of the type shown in figure 3.12. The natural frequencies for this combination of two Helmholtz resonators is a rather complicated function of the two acoustic compliances C_{A_1} and C_{A_2} and the two acoustic masses M_{A_1} and M_{A_2}. There are two natural frequencies f_1 and f_2. In the case where M_{A_1} is large, the two natural frequencies are not greatly different from the natural frequencies of the individual resonators.

3.3.4   Natural Frequencies for Coupled Resonators

A number of vocal tract shapes, both for vowels and for consonants, can be approximated by two or more resonators or uniform tubes of different cross-sectional areas connected together. The natural frequencies for such a configuration are not simply the natural frequencies for each component separately, since the individual resonances are changed due to acoustic coupling between the components. There are, however, many situations of interest in which the coupling is small, and approximations to the natural frequencies of the

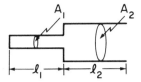

Figure 3.13 Two-tube configuration used to illustrate coupling of resonators.

entire configuration can be obtained by estimating the frequencies of the individual components, and then perturbing them slightly. We shall illustrate this procedure for two configurations, one of which approximates the area function for a vowel and the other for a consonant.

Consider first the two-tube configuration shown in figure 3.13. The vocal tract shape for a low vowel like the vowel /ɑ/ in *father* has an area function roughly similar to this configuration. A narrow tube of uniform cross-sectional area A_1 and length ℓ_1 is closed at one end and opens at the other end into a larger uniform tube of area A_2 and length ℓ_2. We shall assume the total length $\ell_1 + \ell_2$ remains constant, and we shall examine the natural frequencies of the configuration for different values of ℓ_1. If $A_1 \ll A_2$, then the narrow tube at the left end behaves almost like a tube that is open at one end, since for most frequencies the impedance looking to the right at the junction is very small,[4] being proportional to the reciprocal of A_2 [see equation (3.22)]. The natural frequencies of the narrow tube if it is open at the right-hand end are given by $c/4\ell_1, 3c/4\ell_1, 5c/4\ell_1, \ldots$. Likewise, the larger section of the configuration behaves like a tube that is open at one end and is almost closed at the other, since the impedance looking left at the junction is very large at most frequencies. The natural frequencies of the wide tube are $c/4\ell_2, 3c/4\ell_2, 5c/4\ell_2, \ldots$. The lowest natural frequencies of the individual tubes are plotted as a function of ℓ_1 as solid lines in figure 3.14, for a particular value of $\ell_1 + \ell_2$. The natural frequency of the narrow tube decreases as ℓ_1 becomes larger in relation to ℓ_2, while that of the wide tube increases.

The acoustic impedance looking to the right at the boundary between the two tubes is not zero, however, and hence this impedance has some effect on the natural frequencies of the narrow tube. Similarly, since the acoustic impedance looking to the left at the junction point is not infinite, it influences the natural frequencies of the wide tube. The natural frequencies of the combined system are the frequencies for which the sum of the reactances at the junction is zero, that is,

$$-\frac{\rho c}{A_1}\cot k\ell_1 + \frac{\rho c}{A_2}\tan k\ell_2 = 0. \tag{3.30}$$

When $A_1 \ll A_2$, the frequencies for which this equation is satisfied are shifted slightly from the frequencies of the individual tubes noted above.

The greatest shift occurs when the natural frequencies of the front and back tubes are equal. Under these conditions the natural frequencies of the

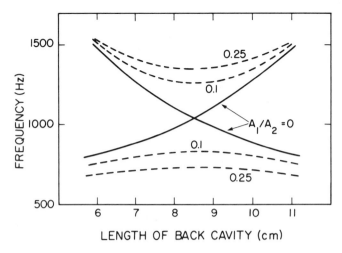

Figure 3.14 First two natural frequencies of the two-tube resonator in figure 3.13 as a function of the back-cavity length ℓ_1, for various area ratios A_1/A_2. Area ratio $A_1/A_2 = 0$ corresponds to no acoustic coupling between the tubes. The total length $\ell_1 + \ell_2$ is fixed at 17 cm.

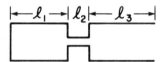

Figure 3.15 Uniform tube with a narrow constriction, used to approximate area functions for consonants.

combined system are not equal, but are split apart, one being higher than the natural frequency of each tube individually, and the other being lower. If the natural frequency of the uncoupled tubes is f_o, then the natural frequencies for the combined system turn out to be

$$f'_o \cong f_o \left(1 \pm \frac{2}{\pi} \sqrt{\frac{A_1}{A_2}} \right), \tag{3.31}$$

assuming that the ratio A_1/A_2 is much less than unity. When the natural frequencies of the two tubes are remote from one another, the influence of the coupling on the natural frequencies is small.

The actual natural frequencies for the coupled tube are represented by dashed lines in figure 3.14. Curves for two values of area ratio are shown, and indicate that as the coupling becomes greater, that is, as the ratio A_1/A_2 becomes closer to unity, the separation of the natural frequencies from the frequencies for the uncoupled tubes is greater and extends over a wider frequency range.

Another example of a system of coupled resonators is a tube having an area function with a single narrow constriction. An idealized form for such a configuration is shown in figure 3.15 and is a rough approximation to the vocal tract shape for a fricative consonant. The configuration consists of two

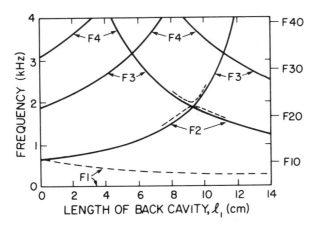

Figure 3.16 Relations between natural frequencies and the position of the constriction for the configuration shown in figure 3.15. The overall length of the tube is 16 cm and the length of the constriction is 2 cm. The lines sloping up to the right represent the resonances of the front cavity (anterior to the constriction); the lines sloping down to the right represent the resonances of the back cavity. The solid lines are the resonances if there is no coupling between front and back cavities. The dashed lines near the point of coincidence of two resonances at $\ell_1 = 9.3$ cm illustrate the shift in the resonant frequencies for the case where there is a small amount of coupling between front and back cavities. When the area of the constriction is very small, $F1 = 0$ as shown. When the constriction is larger, $F1$ increases as shown by the dashed line. The resonances of a 16-cm tube with no constriction are shown by the labeled marks at the right. The curves are labeled with the appropriate formant numbers.

uniform tubes of length ℓ_1 and ℓ_3 and cross-sectional area A_1 separated by a short narrow tube of length ℓ_2 and cross-sectional area A_2, where $A_1 \gg A_2$. The short constriction can be represented as an acoustic mass $M_A = \rho\ell_2/A_2$, and, if A_2 is sufficiently small, the impedance of this acoustic mass is large compared to the characteristic impedances of the front and back tubes.

The uncoupled natural frequencies of the back tube are $c/2\ell_1, c/\ell_1$, $3c/2\ell_1, \ldots$, and those of the front tube are $c/4\ell_3, 3c/4\ell_3, 5c/4\ell_3, \ldots$. There is also a low-frequency Helmholtz resonance between the acoustic compliance C_A of the back cavity and the acoustic mass M_A of the constriction. (We neglect here the acoustic mass of the front cavity, although it could contribute to the total acoustic mass under some circumstances.) The frequency of this resonance is $f_1 = 1/(2\pi\sqrt{M_A C_A})$, where $M_A = \rho\ell_2/A_2$ and $C_A = A_1\ell_1/\rho c^2$; this resonance theoretically approaches zero frequency as A_2 becomes very small compared with A_1. The lowest natural frequencies of the front and back cavities are plotted in figure 3.16 (solid lines) as a function of the back cavity length ℓ_1, assuming the overall length $\ell_1 + \ell_2 + \ell_3$ is constant. The constriction length ℓ_2 is held fixed, and hence ℓ_3 decreases as ℓ_1 increases. Thus the back-cavity natural frequencies fall as ℓ_1 increases, whereas the front-cavity resonances rise in frequency. When $\ell_1 = 2\ell_3$, two natural frequencies are equal. The lowest natural frequency of the back cavity is zero when $A_2 \ll A_1$. The curves in figure 3.16 are labeled with formant number, beginning with $F1$ at zero frequency.

At the right of figure 3.16, the lines labeled F10, F20, and so forth, indicate the frequencies of the first four formants if the constriction area $A2$ were increased to equal the area A_1 of the remainder of the tube in figure 3.15, that is, if the area of the tube were uniform. These frequencies for the uniform tube are higher than the natural frequencies when the constriction is near the front of the tube ($\ell_1 = 14$ cm), but the frequencies for the unconstricted configuration can be lower than the natural frequencies of the constricted tube for certain constriction locations.

If now there is a small amount of coupling between the two tubes as a consequence of a noninfinite acoustic mass of the constriction, then there is a shift in the natural frequencies of the coupled resonators relative to those of the tubes in isolation. This shift for the condition $A_2/A_1 = 0.067$ is shown by dashed lines in one region of figure 3.16 (near the point where $\ell_1 = 2\ell_3$). The effect of a small amount of coupling in this case is always to shift the natural frequencies upward, except when the individual natural frequencies are equal, in which case one of the frequencies remains unchanged and the other is shifted upward by a greater amount. The shift in the natural frequencies is proportional to the area ratio A_2/A_1. The low-frequency Helmholtz resonance is, of course, no longer zero, as shown by the dashed line near the bottom of figure 3.16.

At the point where the individual natural frequencies are equal, the distribution of pressure and volume velocity in the two tubes and in the constriction are quite different at the two natural frequencies. For the lower of the two, the sound pressure in the front and back tubes rises and falls in phase, and there is no velocity in the constriction. At the higher of the two natural frequencies the sound pressure variations in the two tubes are 180 degrees out of phase, and there is a large velocity in the constriction. These two modes are often called symmetrical and antisymmetrical modes of the system.

The two configurations shown in figures 3.13 and 3.15 illustrate a general property of coupled resonators. When the coupling is sufficiently small, the resonances of the coupled systems may be estimated by first finding the resonances of the individual components and then shifting these frequencies slightly to account for the coupling. In general the shift is greatest when the uncoupled natural frequencies are close together.

The production of a syllable consisting of a stop consonant (such as /b/, /d/, or /g/) followed by a vowel involves manipulating the cross-sectional area of a constriction from zero (complete closure) to a larger value appropriate for the vowel. During this manipulation, the formant frequencies follow trajectories beginning at values appropriate for the constricted configuration. In order to indicate how these trajectories depend on the change in cross-sectional area at the constriction, we have calculated the frequencies of the first four formants for the ideal case in which the constriction size in a tube like that in figure 3.15 is increased until it becomes equal to the size of the larger tube. The results are shown in figure 3.17. Two different constriction lengths (0.2 cm and 2.0 cm) are selected, and two different positions

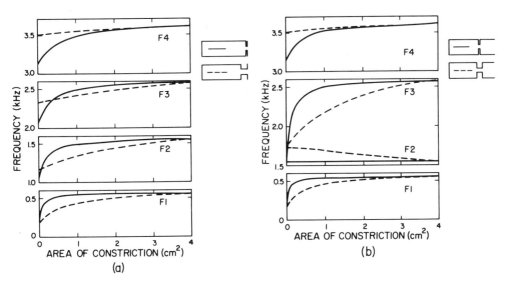

Figure 3.17 Plots of calculated values of first four formant frequencies vs. cross-sectional area of constriction for the configurations shown. Solid lines represent short constriction (length 0.2 cm) and dashed lines represent longer constriction (length 2.0 cm). (a) Constriction at end of tube. (b) Constriction located at a point one-third of the length posterior to the open end. Length of tube = 16 cm. See text.

of the constriction are illustrated. These are at the anterior end of the tube (figure 3.17a), as in the consonant /b/, and at a point about one-third of the distance along the tube from the anterior end (figure 3.17b), as in /g/. The frequency of the lowest resonance has been corrected to account for the mass of the walls, which in the human vocal tract has the effect of shifting this resonance up in frequency relative to the value it would assume if the walls were hard. (This effect is discussed in section 3.4.2, and a consequence is that the lowest resonance does not go below about 180 Hz when the area of the constriction is zero.)

For the configuration with the constriction at the front of the tube, we observe the expected rise of all of the natural frequencies as the cross-sectional area of the constriction is increased. The increase is much more pronounced for small cross-sectional areas when the length of the constriction is small. The lowest two natural frequencies are more sensitive to small increases in area than are the third and fourth.

When the constriction is centered one-third of the distance from the open end of the tube, we again observe that the frequencies tend to be more sensitive to constriction area changes (for small constriction sizes) for the shorter constriction. For a very narrow constriction, the natural frequencies of the front and back cavities (F2 and F3 in the figure) are equal. As the constriction size is increased, the lower of these two resonances changes very little, whereas the upper one (F3) increases rather rapidly. The lower resonance is characterized by symmetrical or in-phase variations in the sound pressure in the front and back cavities, and, since there is no volume velocity through the constriction for this mode, it is essentially independent of constriction size. The higher resonance, with antisymmetrical sound pressure variations and a large volume velocity through the constriction, is quite sensitive to constriction size.

These variations of the natural frequencies of a constricted tube with constriction area have implications for the interpretation of the acoustic properties of various classes of consonants (K. N. Stevens, 1972, 1989). These implications are discussed in chapters 7, 8, and 9.

3.3.5 Effects on the Formant Frequencies of Perturbations in the Area Function

Further insight into the relations between vocal tract configurations and formant frequencies can be gained if we examine the changes in the formant frequencies that occur as a result of small perturbations of the area function in some region along the length of the vocal tract (Chiba and Kajiyama, 1941; Schroeder, 1967; Fant, 1980). Data with regard to such perturbations can be used to determine the effects on the formant frequencies of movements of the vocal tract from one configuration to another during speech production. The data also indicate how a given vocal tract configuration should be manipulated to shift the formant frequencies in particular ways. Furthermore, the perturbation data can help to specify the vocal tract shapes for which one or more formant frequencies are minimally sensitive to changes in the configurations, as well as those for which the formants are maximally sensitive to perturbations in the configurations. Studies of this kind are relevant to the establishment of appropriate phonetic categories in language (K. N. Stevens, 1972, 1989).

Some data on the effects of perturbations in the area function can be obtained from graphs like those already shown for certain idealized configurations. It is possible, however, to formulate a general theory that predicts the changes in formant frequencies for small perturbations of an arbitrary area function. We will not develop this general theory here, but will give some results that apply to simple vocal tract shapes for which the pressure and velocity distributions for the various natural frequencies are known approximately.

In order to determine the effect of a perturbation in an area function on the formant frequencies, we make use of a theorem of electric network theory which states that, in a network containing inductances and capacitances, a perturbation in the inductance or capacitance values that causes an increase in the average stored energy at a given natural frequency results in a decrease in that natural frequency. For small changes, the shift in the natural frequency is proportional to the change in average stored energy (Staelin et al., 1994). The theorem applies to perturbations in the shape for any configuration of acoustic resonators.

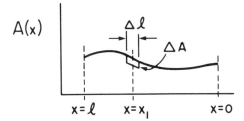

Figure 3.18 Illustrating a perturbation ΔA in the area of an acoustic tube at a short segment of length $\Delta \ell$ centered at point $x = x_1$.

Consider an acoustic tube with area function $A(x)$, in which a small change in area ΔA is made over a short length $\Delta \ell$, as shown in figure 3.18. Let us assume that the distributions of sound pressure and volume velocity amplitude along the unperturbed tube corresponding to a particular natural frequency Fn are given by $p_n(x)$ and $U_n(x)$. In general both $p_n(x)$ and $U_n(x)$ pass through zero n times, that is, there are n nodes, and $p_n(x)$ is a maximum where $U_n(x)$ is zero, and vice versa.[5] In a short section of length $\Delta \ell$ located at point x_1 in the tube, the average stored potential energy [from equation (3.27)] is

$$V_n = \frac{1}{4}|p_n(x_1)|^2 \frac{\Delta \ell A}{\rho c^2},\tag{3.32}$$

and the average stored kinetic energy [from equation (3.24)] is

$$T_n = \frac{1}{4}|U_n(x_1)|^2 \frac{\rho \Delta \ell}{A}.\tag{3.33}$$

We now change the cross-sectional area for this section $\Delta \ell$ by an amount ΔA, but assume that for this small perturbation the distributions of pressure and velocity amplitude for the formant frequency Fn remain unchanged. Under these conditions, the changes in average stored potential and kinetic energy are, respectively,

$$\Delta V_n = \frac{1}{4}|p_n(x_1)|^2 \frac{\Delta \ell \Delta A}{\rho c^2}\tag{3.34}$$

and

$$\Delta T_n = -\frac{1}{4}|U_n(x_1)|^2 \frac{\rho \Delta \ell \Delta A}{A^2}.\tag{3.35}$$

The increase in stored energy is, therefore,

$$\Delta W_n = \Delta V_n + \Delta T_n = \frac{1}{4}\frac{\Delta \ell \Delta A}{\rho c^2}\left[|p_n(x_1)^2 - \left(\frac{\rho c}{A}\right)^2 |U_n(x_1)|^2\right].\tag{3.36}$$

As noted earlier, the shift ΔFn in the natural frequency Fn is proportional to $-\Delta W_n$. (Note that ΔA is negative in figure 3.18.)

Equation (3.36) shows that the shift in a formant frequency due to a local-ized perturbation in the cross-sectional area of the vocal tract depends on the distribution of sound pressure and volume velocity amplitude along the tract. At a point x_1 where the sound pressure is close to a maximum (and the velocity is near zero), a reduction in cross-sectional area causes an increase in the formant frequency. If the cross-sectional area is reduced at a point where the volume velocity is a maximum, the formant frequency decreases. At an intermediate location, where the sound pressure amplitude and the volume velocity amplitude are between their maximum and minimum values, or, more precisely, where $|p_n(x_1)|^2 = (\rho c/A)^2 |U_n(x_1)|^2$, a perturbation in the cross-sectional area causes *no* shift in the formant frequency Fn. The shifts in for-mant frequencies due to a small *increase* in the cross-sectional area at point x_1 are, of course, also given by equation (3.36) but with a positive sign for ΔA.

When the acoustic tube representing the vocal tract has a uniform cross-sectional area A, we have seen that the distribution of sound pressure and volume velocity are sinusoidal and are given by

$$p(x) = P_m \sin \frac{2\pi Fnx}{c},\tag{3.37}$$

and

$$U(x) = jP_m \frac{A}{\rho c} \cos \frac{2\pi Fnx}{c},\tag{3.38}$$

where $Fn = [(2n-1)/4] \cdot c/\ell$ is the formant frequency and P_m is the maxi-mum sound pressure in the tube. A decrease in cross-sectional area of ΔA at point x_1 over a length $\Delta\ell$ causes a shift ΔFn in the formant frequency Fn proportional to the increase in stored energy, which is

$$\Delta W_n = \Delta V_n + \Delta T_n = -\frac{1}{4}|P_m|^2 \frac{\Delta\ell\Delta A}{\rho c^2} \cos \frac{4\pi Fnx}{c}.\tag{3.39}$$

The form of equation (3.39) for the first three formants of the uniform tube is shown in figure 3.19. At a particular point x for any one of these functions, the ordinate is proportional to the change in the formant frequency that results from a decrease in cross-sectional area over a small length located at this point. Conversely, an increase in cross-sectional area of the short section would give a ΔFn of sign opposite to that shown in the figure.

The curves show that a decrease in cross-sectional area at the open end, corresponding to the lip opening, causes a downward shift in all formants. This perturbation approximates the change in vocal tract configuration for a vowel when the lip opening is reduced, as for rounding. This general rule applies not only to the uniform tube but to an arbitrary configuration that is open at one end, since there is a minimum in sound pressure and a maximum in volume velocity at this point. Likewise, at the closed end, near the glottis, a decrease in cross-sectional area causes a rise in all the formant frequencies. Again, this rule applies generally to an arbitrary configuration that is closed

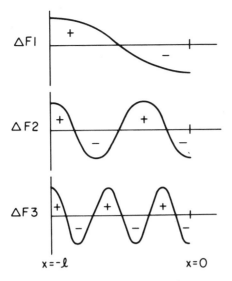

Figure 3.19 Curves showing the relative magnitude and direction of the shift ΔFn in formant frequency Fn for a uniform tube when the cross-sectional area is decreased at some point along the length of the tube. The abscissa represents the point at which the area perturbation is made. The minus sign represents a decrease in formant frequency and the plus sign an increase.

at one end. A reduction in area at any point in the anterior half of the uniform tube produces a drop in $F1$, the effect being greater when the perturbation is closer to the open end. Similarly a reduction in area in the posterior half of the uniform tube results in an increase in $F1$.

At a point where a curve for a given formant passes through zero, a perturbation in the cross-sectional area causes no shift in the formant frequency. The number of such points on a curve is always equal to $2n - 1$, where n is the formant number for that curve (Mrayati et al., 1988). This result applies to an arbitrary area function as well as to the uniform tube. In the case of the uniform tube, all curves have a zero at the midpoint, indicating that a perturbation in cross-sectional area at this point has no effect on any formant frequency.

The general result given in equation (3.36) can, of course, be applied to an arbitrary configuration if the distribution of sound pressure and volume velocity along the length of the vocal tract is known. Two examples of some interest in speech production are shown in figure 3.20.

Figure 3.20a (solid lines) is the approximate shape that was used in figure 3.13 to illustrate a vowel-like configuration that can be approximated by two uniform tubes. This shape is roughly appropriate for the vowel /æ/, except that this vowel tends to have a wider mouth opening than that indicted by the solid lines. The dashed lines represent a modified version of the original configuration. The resonances of the left-hand narrow tube all have a velocity maximum at the right-hand end of this tube, whereas the resonances of the right-hand wider tube all have a sound pressure maximum at the

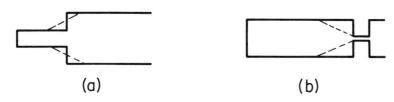

(a)   (b)

Figure 3.20 The configurations represented by the solid lines are idealized versions of the vocal tract shapes for (a) a low front vowel like /æ/ and (b) an alveolar consonant like /s/. The dashed lines represent a closer approximation to the vocal tract shape. The directions of the formant shifts from the solid to the dashed line configurations can be predicted from the perturbation principles given in the text.

left-hand end. The perturbation given by the dashed line represents a widening of the right end of the narrow tube and a narrowing of the left end of the wide tube. From the relations that have just been derived, this modification tends to increase all the formant frequencies, including $F1$, which in this case is a resonance of the front cavity.

The configuration in figure 3.20b is an idealized version of a consonant configuration with a constriction in the alveolar region. A better approximation to a true consonant configuration would be the shape represented by the dashed lines, which is formed by decreasing the cross-sectional area at the front end of the back cavity. Since the back cavity resonances are essentially those of a tube closed at both ends, this modification of the shape will increase the natural frequencies of the back cavity. (See discussion in connection with figure 7.22 in chapter 7.)

The techniques that have been used to estimate the effects of perturbations in cross-sectional area over a short length of the vocal tract can also be applied to small changes in the length of a section of the vocal tract. The calculation here is simple, since an increase in length of a short section always increases the energy stored in that section, assuming the distributions of sound pressure and volume velocity remain unchanged. Thus an increase in length of any portion of the vocal tract (and hence of the vocal tract as a whole) always tends to cause a downward shift in the formant frequencies. If two or more sections of the vocal tract are not closely coupled, then a length increase for a particular cavity clearly has the greatest influence on the resonant frequencies that are associated primarily with that cavity.

Two simple perturbations of the vocal tract that cause a change in length are rounding and protruding of the lips and lowering of the larynx. Both of these movements cause the formant frequencies to decrease. The opposite maneuvers—spreading of the lips and raising the larynx—tend to shorten the vocal tract and hence to raise the frequencies of the formants.

3.4 LOSSES AND EFFECTS OF WALLS OF RESONATORS

The major acoustic attributes that distinguish one class of speech sounds from another are determined primarily by the type and location of the acoustic excitation of the vocal tract and by the natural frequencies of the vocal tract. A first approximation to the natural frequencies can usually be obtained on the assumption that the vocal tract has no losses and is terminated by an infinite impedance at one end and zero impedance at the other. Generally, acoustic energy losses and finite terminating impedances are second-order effects that do not play a determining role in forming phonetic categories. These effects must, however, be considered if the detailed properties of the speech signal are to be understood. Furthermore, there are instances where losses and terminating impedances do indeed have an important influence on the primary attributes of certain speech sounds.

The effects of acoustic losses in the vocal tract will be expressed in terms of the contributions of these losses to the bandwidths of the resonances. The contribution B of a particular resistive component to the bandwidth of a resonance at frequency f (Adler et al., 1960) is given by

$$B = \frac{power\ dissipated\ at\ frequency\ f}{2\pi \times (total\ stored\ energy\ at\ frequency\ f)}. \tag{3.40}$$

If there are several resistive components in the resonator, each of these components contributes to the power dissipated, and each contributes an increment to the bandwidth. This method of determining the bandwidth is approximate, and is based on the assumption that the distribution of sound pressure and volume velocity in the resonator at frequency f in the presence of losses is not significantly different from the distribution for the lossless case.

3.4.1 Radiation Impedance

The radiation impedance of the mouth opening can be approximated by the radiation impedance of a circular piston in a sphere, the sphere representing the effect of the head surface. Analytical expressions have been derived for this impedance (Morse, 1948; Fant, 1960). Up to a frequency of about 6000 Hz, the acoustic radiation impedance can be written approximately as

$$Z_r = \frac{\rho c}{A_m}\left(\frac{\pi f^2}{c^2}A_m\right)K_s(f) + j2\pi f\frac{\rho(0.8a)}{A_m} \tag{3.41}$$

where A_m is the area of the mouth opening, a is the effective radius ($\pi a^2 = A_m$), and $K_s(f)$ is a dimensionless frequency-dependent factor that accounts for the baffling effect of the head. For a simple source, K_s is unity, and for a piston in an infinite baffle, $K_s = 2$. If the head is assumed to be a sphere of radius 9 cm, then K_s is unity at low frequencies, up to a few hundred hertz, and then rises to a maximum value of about 1.7 at about 2000 Hz. Above 2000 Hz, the behavior of K_s with frequency depends upon the size of the mouth opening, but for mouth areas of principal interest for most speech sounds, it is probably a reasonable approximation to take K_s as 1.5 in the frequency range of 2000 to 6000 Hz. Figure 3.21 shows the resistance R_r

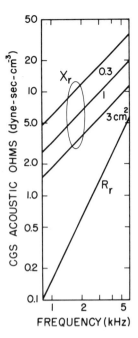

Figure 3.21 Approximate radiation resistance R_r and reactance X_r for a piston in a sphere of radius 9 cm, for three different cross-sectional areas of the piston, as shown. In equation (3.41), K_s is taken to be 1.5.

and reactance X_r of the radiation impedance for three different areas of the mouth opening. As equation (3.41) indicates, only the reactive part of the radiation impedance is influenced by the mouth opening.

The reactive term in Z_r is written in a form to show that the radiation reactance is that of an acoustic tube of area A_m and length $0.8a$. The reactance, therefore, increases the effective length of the vocal tract relative to the length that is assumed under conditions of no radiation loading. Thus, for example, for a uniform tube of length 14.1 cm and cross-sectional area 3 cm^2 (radius 1 cm) (corresponding to the average vocal tract length for an adult female speaker, as discussed in section 3.3.1), the end correction is 0.8 cm. This causes a decrease of all natural frequencies by 5 percent, with the result that the natural frequencies are in fact at 600, 1790, 2990, ... Hz rather than 630, 1880, 3140, ... Hz, as calculated in section 3.3.1. Similarly, as noted in section 3.3.1, for a uniform tube of length 16.9 cm (approximating an adult male vocal tract length) the end correction is also about 0.8 cm, leading to an effective length of 17.7 cm, and natural frequencies of 500, 1500, 2500 ... Hz. For most vocal tract configurations, the area of the mouth opening is less than 3 cm^2, and hence the shift in the natural frequencies due to radiation loading is generally less than 5 percent.

The resistive part of Z_r in equation (3.41) increases as f^2, but at all frequencies of interest is much smaller than $\rho c/A_m$, the characteristic impedance of a tube of area A_m. A perturbation calculation (Staelin et al., 1994) can be

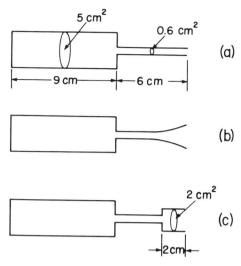

Figure 3.22 Examples of resonator shapes with a relatively narrow front cavity. The configuration of the front cavity at the right end influences the contribution of radiation to the bandwidth of the front cavity resonance. Three different terminations are illustrated.

made, therefore, to estimate the contribution of the radiation resistance to the real parts of the complex natural frequencies (or, equivalently, to the bandwidths of the formants). For a uniform tube of area A_m and length ℓ, the contribution of the radiation loss to the bandwidth of a formant turns out to be

$$B_r = \frac{f^2 A_m}{\ell c} K_s(f),\tag{3.42}$$

where f is the frequency of the formant. If the length of the tube is 17.7 cm, and the cross-sectional area is 3 cm^2, then for the formants at 500, 1500, 2500, and 3500 Hz, B_r is about 2, 16, 50, and 90 Hz, respectively.

The component of the total formant bandwidth that is due to the radiation impedance depends, of course, on the configuration of the acoustic tube that represents the vocal tract. For example, suppose the vocal tract configuration is such that it can be approximated by a two-tube resonator, as shown in figure 3.22a. Some of the natural frequencies of this configuration are associated primarily with the back cavity and others with the front cavity. For back-cavity resonances, the bandwidths are only weakly influenced by the resistive component of the radiation impedance. The contribution of the radiation resistance to the bandwidths of the front-cavity resonances can be calculated from equation (3.42), with A_m and ℓ taken to be the cross-sectional area and length of the front section of the configuration. In this example, $A_m/\ell = 0.1$ cm, and the lowest resonance of the front cavity has a frequency of 2950 Hz. The contribution of Z_r to the bandwidth of this resonance is 37 Hz. However, if the narrow portion of the configuration is terminated at the open end by a wider section, for example, as indicated in figure 3.22b,

Basic Acoustics of Vocal Tract Resonators

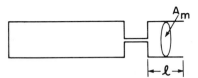

Figure 3.23 Resonator with a narrow constriction. Front-cavity resonances are influenced by radiation losses but back-cavity resonances are not.

then the contribution of the radiation resistance to the bandwidth of the resonance of the narrow portion may be increased significantly. For the configuration of figure 3.22c, which is an approximation to that in figure 3.22b, the contribution of Z_r to the bandwidth of the lowest resonance of the narrow section (at 2950 Hz) increases to about 200 Hz.[6] We will observe in section 6.6 that this ability to control the bandwidths of resonances in the frequency range of 2000 to 3500 Hz through modification of the shape of the vocal tract near the mouth opening is a contributing factor in producing a distinctive class of vowels.

As another example of the effect of the radiation resistance on the bandwidth of a resonant frequency, we consider the model of a consonant configuration of figure 3.23. Again, for this configuration the bandwidth of front-cavity resonances may be strongly influenced by radiation loss, whereas back-cavity resonances are unaffected by the radiation impedance. The frequency of the lowest front-cavity resonance is approximately $c/4\ell$, where ℓ is the length of the front cavity, and hence the bandwidth of this front-cavity resonance is

$$B_r = \frac{4f^3 A_m}{c^2} K_s(f). \qquad (3.43)$$

Figure 3.24 shows this bandwidth as a function of frequency (and of the front-cavity length) for such a resonance, for three values of mouth opening A_m. The bandwidth rises sharply with frequency, and if the front-cavity resonance is above 4000 to 6000 Hz, the bandwidth can be in excess of 500 Hz (compared with a 50- to 100-Hz bandwidth for the lower formants of a vowel).

3.4.2 Impedance of Vocal Tract Walls

Calculations of natural frequencies for various simple vocal tract shapes, discussed in section 3.3, have assumed that the walls of the conduit have infinite impedance. The fleshy surfaces of the tongue, cheeks, and pharynx are, however, not rigid; the acoustic effect of these surfaces can be represented by a specific acoustic impedance (acoustic impedance per unit area),

$$Z_{sw} = R_{sw} + jX_{sw}, \qquad (3.44)$$

where R_{sw} and X_{sw} are both large compared with ρc, the specific acoustic impedance of air.

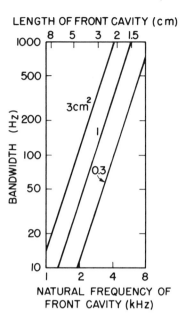

LENGTH OF FRONT CAVITY (cm)

NATURAL FREQUENCY OF
FRONT CAVITY (kHz)

Figure 3.24 Contribution of radiation loss to bandwidth of lowest front-cavity resonance for the configuration in figure 3.23. The abscissa is the natural frequency of the front cavity (bottom scale), which is inversely related to the length of the front cavity (top scale). The parameter is the cross-sectional area of the front cavity.

The resistive component of the wall impedance causes energy loss in the vocal tract and an increase in the bandwidths of the formants, particularly the first formant. For a uniform tube of cross-sectional area A and cross-sectional perimeter S, the contribution of this resistance to the bandwidth of a formant is

$$B_w = \frac{G_{sw}S\rho c^2}{2\pi A}, \tag{3.45}$$

where G_{sw} is the specific acoustic conductance (i.e., conductance per unit area) of the walls, given by $G_{sw} = R_{sw}/(R_{sw}^2 + X_{sw}^2)$. For this calculation it is assumed that the conductance is the same over all the surfaces of the vocal tract walls. The wall impedance is probably smaller over the surfaces in the pharyngeal region than in the oral region.

Estimates of the impedance of the inner surfaces of the vocal tract have been made from data on the impedance of the skin at other parts of the body, as discussed in section 1.1.3.7. In the frequency range of the first formant for vowels, this impedance (per unit area) is approximately $Z_{sw} = 1000 + j2\pi f \times 2.0$ dyne-s/cm^3. (At very low frequencies, below about 50 Hz, a series mechanical compliance must be added in series with Z_{sw} to give a good estimate of the wall impedance.) We observe that $X_{sw} > 3R_{sw}$ in this first-formant frequency range, and consequently $G_{sw} \cong R_{sw}/X_{sw}^2$. Calculation of the bandwidth contributions of the wall resistance for the first formant of a circular uniform tube of length 17.7 cm and diameter 2.0 cm gives $B_w \approx 11$

Basic Acoustics of Vocal Tract Resonators

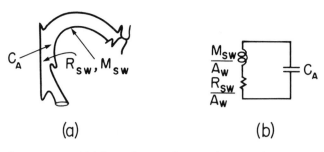

(a)   (b)

Figure 3.25 (a) Midsagittal section for a vocal tract configuration with closure at the lips. The resistance and mass of the walls are shown, together with the acoustic compliance of the vocal tract volume. (b) Low-frequency equivalent circuit for the configuration in (a) with closed glottis. A_w is the surface area of the vocal tract walls, and M_{sw} and R_{sw} are mass and resistance of walls per unit area.

Hz. This calculated bandwidth would be somewhat greater if account were taken of the fact that G_{sw} is larger in the pharyngeal region than in the oral region. For formants above the first, the reactive component of the wall impedance becomes even more significant in relation to the resistive component, with the result that G_{sw} decreases and B_w becomes smaller.

When the vocal tract configuration is a uniform tube, the reactive component of the wall impedance has a negligible effect on the frequencies of the formants. For a more constricted configuration, however, which gives a low first-formant frequency, the mass reactance of the walls can cause a significant shift in the first-formant frequency (Fant, 1972). The amount of this shift is greatest for a completely closed vocal tract, such as the configuration for a voiced stop consonant. Consider, for example, a configuration appropriate for a labial stop consonant, as illustrated in figure 3.25a. The vocal tract is closed at the lips and has an average cross-sectional area of, say, 3 cm², and a length of 15 cm. The total surface area is about 90 cm², and we shall assume that this surface has an average specific acoustic impedance of $Z_{sw} = R_{sw} + jX_{sw}$, where $X_{sw} = 2.0 \times 2\pi f$ dyne-s/cm³, that is, equivalent to a mass of 2 gm/cm² of surface area. The equivalent circuit for this configuration is shown in figure 3.25b. The natural frequency $F1_c$ is determined by the mass and the acoustic compliance C_A of the closed cavity and is given by

$$F1_c = \frac{\sqrt{A_w}}{2\pi\sqrt{M_{sw}C_A}}. \tag{3.46}$$

For a vocal tract volume of 45 cm³, $F1_c$ turns out to be about 190 Hz. If hard walls were assumed, this natural frequency would, of course, be zero. Consequently the vocal tract walls have a primary influence in this case. Actual measurements of the resonant frequency for a bilabial stop configuration give values of about 180 Hz for an adult male talker and about 190 Hz for a female talker (Fujimura and Lindqvist, 1971; Fant et al., 1976). The bandwidth of the resonance is fairly broad, but apparently the losses are not sufficient to cause critical damping. The calculated bandwidth for this case

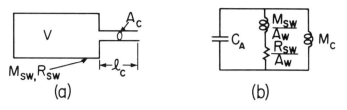

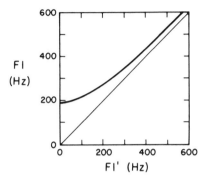

Figure 3.26 (a) Model for a constricted vocal tract configuration with yielding walls. (b) Low-frequency equivalent circuit for the model in (a).

Figure 3.27 Natural frequency $F1$ for configuration in figure 3.26, with yielding walls, as a function of natural frequency $F1'$ computed on the assumption of hard walls (i.e., $M_w = \infty$ in figure 3.26). Deviation of the curve from the diagonal line is a measure of the effect of the walls.

[from equation (3.45), which also can be shown to apply to this configuration] is about 90 Hz (Fant et al., 1976).

When the vocal tract configuration is constricted at some point, but not closed, as in the model in figure 3.26a, the equivalent circuit for low frequencies is as shown in figure 3.26b. The first-formant frequency assuming hard vocal tract walls (i.e., with $M_{sw} = \infty$ in the equivalent circuit) is [from equation (3.29)]

$$F1' = \frac{c}{2\pi\sqrt{\frac{V\ell_c}{A_c}}},$$

where V = volume behind the constriction, and ℓ_c and A_c are the length and cross-sectional area of the constriction. When the impedance of the walls of the vocal tract are included, the first-formant frequency becomes

$$F1 = \sqrt{(F1')^2 + F1_c^2}, \tag{3.47}$$

where $F1'$ is the first-formant frequency that would be obtained on the assumption of hard vocal tract walls, and where $F1_c$ is the resonant frequency for the closed configuration. Figure 3.27 is a graph of the corrected first-formant frequency $F1$, taking into account the effect of the walls, as a function of the first-formant frequency calculated from the configuration with the assumption of hard vocal tract surfaces. This curve shows that for

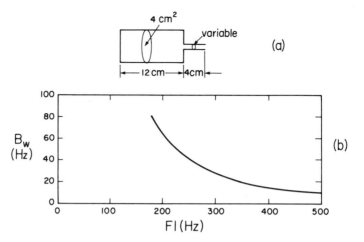

Figure 3.28 Contribution (B_w) to bandwidth of the first formant due to losses at the walls of the vocal tract. The vocal tract is modeled as a Helmholtz resonator with the dimensions shown in (a), in which the resonant frequency F1 is changed by manipulating the cross-sectional area of the opening. The bandwidth contribution B_w as a function of F1 is shown in (b).

large values of F1 the wall impedance has a negligible effect on the formant frequency, as noted earlier.[7] Another feature of this relation is that for low values of F1, the frequency becomes less sensitive to the configuration of the vocal tract. For example, for $F1 = 250$ Hz, the first formant is only one-half as sensitive to a change in some aspect of the vocal tract configuration (such as the cross-sectional area of the constriction) as it would be if the vocal tract walls were assumed to be hard. (Possible implications of this reduced sensitivity of F1 to perturbations in vocal tract shape are discussed further in chapter 6.)

Using equation (3.45) we can calculate the contribution to the F1 bandwidth of the resistive component of the wall impedance for the model of figure 3.28a. The bandwidth B_w is plotted in figure 3.28b as a function of the first-formant frequency. This frequency is manipulated by changing the size of the opening in the front part of the tube. The bandwidth component B_w decreases with increasing frequency, as expected.

3.4.3 Heat Conduction and Viscosity

The propagation of sound in a tube is accompanied by two kinds of losses at the walls of the tube, in addition to the losses due to the yielding walls (Fant, 1960; Flanagan, 1972). One type of loss is caused by viscous friction at the wall of the tube. This effect of viscous friction can be represented by an equivalent resistance R_v per unit length of the tube, given by

$$R_v = \frac{S}{A^2}\sqrt{\omega\rho\mu/2},\tag{3.48}$$

where $S =$ circumference of the tube, $A =$ cross-sectional area of the tube, $\omega = 2\pi f$, and $\mu =$ coefficient of viscosity $= 1.86 \times 10^{-4}$ poise (dyne-s/cm^2).

For small losses, the contribution of R_v to the bandwidth of one of the natural frequencies of a uniform tube that is closed at one end and open at the other is given by

$$B_v = \frac{R_v A}{2\pi\rho}. \tag{3.49}$$

Another source of loss arises because energy is drawn from the acoustic wave by heat conduction at the walls of the tube. The effect of heat conduction can be represented by an equivalent conductance per unit length along the transmission line representing the tube. This equivalent conductance is given by

$$G_h = S\frac{0.4}{\rho c^2}\sqrt{\frac{\lambda\omega}{2c_p\rho}}, \tag{3.50}$$

where λ = coefficient of heat conduction = 5.5×10^{-5} cal/cm-s-degree, c_p = specific heat of air at constant pressure = 0.24 cal/gm-degree.

The contribution of G_h to the bandwidths of the natural frequencies of a uniform tube of cross-sectional area A, closed at one end and open at the other, is given by

$$B_h = \frac{G_h\rho c^2}{2\pi A}, \tag{3.51}$$

that is, the equation is the same as equation (3.45). [Note that G_h is a conductance per unit length, whereas G_{sw} in equation (3.45) is a specific acoustic conductance, i.e., a conductance per unit area.]

Both B_v and B_h are proportional to the square root of frequency. When the lowest natural frequency is 500 Hz, and for a circular cylindrical tube of cross-sectional area 3 cm², we obtain $B_v = 5$ Hz and $B_h = 3$ Hz. As can be seen in the discussions in other parts of this section, there are other contributions to the formant bandwidths that are substantially greater than the contributions arising from viscosity and heat conduction.

Equations (3.48) to (3.51) indicate that the contributions of viscosity and of heat conduction to bandwidth are each proportional to S/A. Consequently both contributions become larger as the cross-sectional area of the tube decreases, assuming the shape of the cross section of the tube does not change as the cross-sectional area changes. These components also increase as the surface area of the tube increases, for example, if the surface contains undulations or irregularities. The nasal cavity has surfaces of this kind, as shown in figure 1.18.

3.4.4 Summary of Effects of Radiation and Wall Losses

We have observed that a number of different physical mechanisms can cause acoustic losses in a resonator like the vocal tract, and each of these contributes to increasing the bandwidths of the natural frequencies of the resonator.

Table 3.1 Calculation of contributions of radiation (B_r), vocal tract walls (B_w), viscosity (B_v), and heat conduction (B_h) to the formant bandwidths for two different vocal tract configurations

a. Uniform tube, length 15 cm, cross-sectional area 3 cm²

	Formant frequency (Hz)	B_r (Hz)	B_w (Hz)	B_v (Hz)	B_h (Hz)	Total B (Hz)
First formant	592	3	8	6	3	20
Second formant	1682	24	1	10	4	39
Third formant	2804	67	0	12	5	84
Fourth formant	3927	131	0	15	6	152

b. Resonator with dimensions in figure 3.28a, with area of opening equal to 0.32 cm²

	Formant frequency (Hz)	B_r (Hz)	B_w (Hz)	B_v (Hz)	B_h (Hz)	Total B (Hz)
First formant	300	0	28	12	2	42
Second formant	1475	0	1	8	3	12
Third formant	2950	0	0	11	5	16

Each of the bandwidth contributions has a different dependence on frequency and on the dimensions of the resonator.

The contributions of viscosity (B_v), heat conduction (B_h), radiation (B_r), and vocal tract walls (B_w) for two different resonator configurations are summarized in table 3.1. The formant frequencies given in the table have been corrected for the effects of the walls and the radiation impedance. The bandwidth estimates are approximate only, particularly in the case of B_w, since we do not have good data on the impedance of the vocal tract walls, or how this impedance varies over the wall surfaces. Furthermore, the surface area of the walls is greater than the area based on a circular cross section, and this increased surface area will add to the estimates of B_w, B_v, and B_h. The figures in the table serve to indicate roughly, however, what are the principal sources of loss in different frequency ranges. For the uniform tube (table 3.1a), radiation contributes the most to the formant bandwidths at high frequencies, whereas the other three components are more important at low frequencies. In the case of the resonator with a narrow opening (table 3.1b), radiation contributes little to the bandwidth for $F2$ and $F3$, since these are resonances of the back cavity. The walls contribute most to the bandwidth at the low frequency resonance of the Helmholtz configuration.

A more detailed analysis of the different sources of loss in the vocal tract is given in Fant (1972) and Liljencrants (1985). A comparison of these theoretical estimates of formant bandwidths with measurements of bandwidths of vocal tract resonances (with a closed glottis) is given in section 6.1.

3.4.5 Effect of Airflow at a Constriction

The sources of loss described in sections 3.4.1 to 3.4.4, and summarized in table 3.1 for particular configurations, arise from the configuration of the vocal tract independent of the shape of the glottal opening or of airflow through the glottis or the vocal tract. Airflow through a constriction can introduce acoustic loss in the form of a nonlinear resistance. This resistance can have a significant effect on the bandwidths of vocal tract resonances and hence on the overall shape of the spectrum of the sound produced by various sources and configurations. We turn now to examine acoustic losses arising from airflow at a vocal tract constriction or at the glottis.

We have noted in chapter 1 that when air flows through a constricted portion of a tube, there is a pressure drop across the constriction over and above the pressure drop due to viscous losses at the walls. For most constriction sizes and shapes of interest in speech production, this pressure drop is given approximately by

$$\Delta P = \frac{\rho U^2}{2A_c^2}, \tag{3.52}$$

where ρ is the density of air, U is the airflow, and A_c is the cross-sectional area of the constriction. As a consequence of this nonlinear relation between ΔP and U, there is an acoustic resistance for small fluctuations in ΔP and U, given by

$$R_c = \frac{\rho U}{A_c^2}. \tag{3.53}$$

This resistance can contribute acoustic losses and can therefore contribute to the bandwidths of the resonances.

As an example, we consider the lowest natural frequency of the Helmholtz resonator shown in figure 3.28a, in which the narrow opening has a cross-sectional area of $0.32\,\text{cm}^2$. This is the configuration for which the various contributions to the bandwidth were calculated in table 3.1b. If we consider a resistance R_c to be in series with the acoustic mass M_c of the narrow tube, then the contribution of R_c to the bandwidth of the lowest resonance is given by

$$B_c = \frac{R_c}{2\pi M_c}. \tag{3.54}$$

The acoustic mass $M_c = \rho \ell_c / A_c$, where ℓ_c and A_c are the length and cross-sectional area of the constriction. Substitution for R_c and M_c leads to the following expression for the bandwidth:

$$B_c = \frac{U}{2\pi \ell_c A_c}. \tag{3.55}$$

For the given dimensions of the resonator, and assuming a volume velocity $U = 200$ cm^3/s to represent the mean volume velocity during the glottal open phase for a male voice, we obtain $B_c = 25$ Hz. At the time of maximum flow during the cycle, the volume velocity can be about 400 cm^3/s, leading to a maximum bandwidth of 50 Hz, existing over at least part of the glottal cycle. Thus the contribution of the constriction resistance to the first-formant bandwidth is comparable to the contributions from other sources, indicated in table 3.1b. Equation (3.55) shows that the contribution of B_c to the total bandwidth increases as the cross-sectional area of the constriction decreases.

The resistance at a short and narrow constriction can have a significant effect on the bandwidths of resonances of cavities anterior or posterior to the constriction in addition to that of the low-frequency Helmholtz resonance. For example, for the configuration shown in figure 3.23, the acoustic resistance R_c of the constriction contributes a bandwidth increment to the front-cavity and back-cavity resonances equal to

$$B_c = \frac{\rho c^2}{\pi \ell A R_c \left(1 + \dfrac{4\pi^2 f^2 M_c^2}{R_c^2} \right)}, \tag{3.56}$$

where ℓ is the length of the front or back cavity that is being considered, A is its cross-sectional area, and M_c is the acoustic mass of the constriction. If the constriction has a length ℓ_c and cross-sectional area A_c, then $M_c = \rho \ell_c / A_c$.

Typical values of ℓ_c and A_c for a consonant configuration are 1.0 cm and 0.1 cm^2, respectively, and $R_c = \rho U / A_c^2$. If we select $U = 300$ cm^3/s and $A = 1$ cm^2, and we note that the frequency of the resonance of the front cavity (of length ℓ_f) is $c/(4\ell_f)$, then we calculate the contribution of the resistance to the bandwidth of the front-cavity resonance F to be the following:

F (Hz)	B_c (Hz)
1000	278
2000	170
3000	114
4000	84

Comparison with figure 3.24 shows that this effect on the bandwidth is greater than that of the radiation resistance at low frequencies and less at high frequencies. The reason for the decrease in B_c with increasing frequency is that the term containing f^2 in the denominator of equation (3.56) begins to dominate at high frequencies.

Similarly, the natural frequency of the lowest back-cavity resonance for the configuration of figure 3.23 (except for the Helmholtz resonance) is $c/(2\ell_b)$, where ℓ_b = length of back cavity. We shall assume a cross-sectional area of the back cavity to be 3 cm^2. Values of B_c for various values of ℓ_b (and of the lowest back-cavity resonance F_b) are as follows:

ℓ_b (cm)	F_b (Hz)	B_c (Hz)
15	1180	42
12	1480	35
9	1970	27
6	2950	19

These calculated values of B_c in the above two tables are shown to illustrate that the resistance due to airflow at a constriction can make an important contribution to vocal tract losses. These values are, however, strongly dependent on the dimensions of the resonator, particularly the cross-sectional area of the constriction, and on the airflow.

3.4.6 Impedance of Glottal Opening

The acoustic impedance of the glottis for small ac signals is of the form

$$Z_g = R_g + j2\pi f M_g, \tag{3.57}$$

where $R_g = 12\mu h/(\ell_g d^3) + K\rho U_g/(\ell_g d)^2$, $M_g = \rho h/\ell_g d$, μ = coefficient of viscosity, d = width of glottal slit, ℓ_g = length of glottal opening, h = thickness of glottis, U_g = volume flow through the glottis, and K = constant that we take to be close to unity. During vocal fold vibration, this impedance varies with time.

Estimates of the shifts in the real and imaginary parts of the complex natural frequencies of a vocal tract configuration can again be made using a perturbation procedure. The contribution B_g to the bandwidth of a formant due to losses at the glottis is given by an equation identical to equation (3.56) for B_c above, that is,

$$B_g = \frac{\rho c^2}{\pi \ell A R_g \left(1 + \dfrac{4\pi^2 f^2 M_g^2}{R_g^2}\right)}, \tag{3.58}$$

when the glottis forms the termination of a uniform tube of length ℓ and cross-sectional area A. At the frequency of the first formant, $2\pi f M_g < R_g$, whereas above about 1500 Hz the term $4\pi^2 f^2 M_g^2/R_g^2$ is greater than unity (assuming a subglottal pressure of about 8 cm H_2O). Thus the glottal impedance has the greatest influence on the bandwidth of the first formant.

Calculations of B_g for the first formant as a function of the glottal area $A_g = \ell_g d$, assuming a uniform tube of length 17.7 cm, a cross-sectional area of 3.0 cm^2, and a subglottal pressure of 8 cm H_2O, show that $B_g \cong 2.0 \times 10^3 A_g$, where A_g is in square centimeters, and B_g is in hertz.[8] The squared term in the denominator of equation (3.58) can be neglected for these conditions. During normal voicing a typical value for the average glottal opening during the open phase is about 0.06 cm^2, and this opening would contribute about 120 Hz to the average first-formant bandwidth in this part

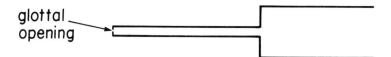

Figure 3.29 Two-tube resonator with narrow posterior portion, illustrating a configuration for which losses at the glottal opening make a large contribution to the bandwidth of the lowest natural frequency of the back cavity.

of the glottal cycle. When the average glottal opening is greater, as it might be during an aspirated consonant, the first-formant bandwidth is considerably greater. The bandwidth may be so great that the perturbation method used to calculate it is no longer valid. A glottal area in excess of 0.2 cm² would probably lead to a bandwidth that is comparable to the frequency of the first formant. A wide average bandwidth would also be expected during breathy voicing, when the average glottal area over the entire cycle of the glottal vibration may be 0.06 cm² or more.

The contribution to the bandwidth of the second formant for a uniform tube (length $\ell = 17.7$ cm), for the conditions described above ($A_g = 0.06$ cm², $A = 3.0$ cm²) from equation (3.58) is equal to about 80 Hz during the open phase of the glottal cycle. For higher formants, the value of B_g drops rapidly.

The effect of the glottal impedance on the bandwidth of a formant depends to some extent on the configuration of the vocal tract above the glottis. The effect can be particularly large when the vocal tract is constricted in the region immediately above the glottis (Fant, 1979). Consider, for example, the two-tube resonator shown in figure 3.29, with the glottis terminating the narrow portion at the left. A typical cross-sectional area for this narrow section is 0.5 cm², with a length of, say, 9.0 cm. The natural frequency of this section is about 980 Hz. With these reduced values of ℓ and A in equation (3.58), and assuming airflow and glottal dimensions as above, B_g for this resonance turns out to be very large. In fact, this resonance has a bandwidth that is wider than the frequency of the resonance during the open portion of the glottal cycle.

The reactive part of the impedance terminating the posterior end of the vocal tract causes an upward shift in the natural frequencies calculated on the assumption of infinite terminating impedance. This shift, expressed as a fraction of the formant frequency, is given by

$$\frac{\Delta F_g}{F} = \frac{\rho c^2}{A\ell} \frac{M_g}{R_g^2 + 4\pi^2 f^2 M_g^2}, \tag{3.59}$$

for a uniform tube of length ℓ and cross-sectional area A. The relative shift is greatest for the first formant, where R_g dominates the denominator of the expression in equation (3.59), and becomes progressively smaller for higher frequencies. The results of calculations of the shift ΔF_g for a uniform tube of length 17.7 cm and cross-sectional area 3.0 cm² show that when the maximum glottal area is, say, 0.11 cm² (figure 2.5), there is a modulation of the first-formant frequency of about 30 Hz.[9] For a relatively wide glottal opening of the type that would be used during an aspirated consonant like /h/, the glottal impedance could cause an upward shift in $F1$ of 50 to 100 Hz. A fall in $F1$ can in fact be observed in a syllable like /ha/, in which a relatively open glottis for /h/ is followed by a more constricted opening during the vowel.

3.5 EXCITATION OF ACOUSTIC RESONATORS

3.5.1 Some General Principles

We have seen that an acoustic tube or resonator of arbitrary shape, such as the vocal tract, can be characterized by a set of natural frequencies. For one-dimensional wave propagation, which applies as long as the cross-dimensions of the tube are small compared with a wavelength, these natural frequencies are dependent only on the area function, that is, the area as a function of distance along the tube. Corresponding to each natural frequency there is a distribution of sound pressure and velocity within the resonator, similar to that shown in figure 3.9 for a uniform tube. This distribution corresponding to a given natural frequency is called a normal mode. In the absence of sources, all of these normal modes can exist in the system with arbitrary relative amplitudes, depending on some previous excitation of the system. If there are small amounts of loss in the system, each of these natural frequencies is observable at all points in the system as a sound pressure or volume velocity waveform that is a decaying sinusoid. The decay rate depends on the amount of loss, and the frequency is almost equal to the natural frequency calculated on the assumption of a lossless system.

The normal modes must be excited by some configuration of acoustic sources. In chapter 2 we described the properties of several kinds of acoustic sources that can be produced in the vocal tract. These sources can be modeled either as volume velocity sources inserted in the vocal tract or as sources of sound pressure in series with the vocal tract. There are some general principles governing the acoustic excitation of the normal modes of a resonator by volume velocity sources or by sound pressure sources. Theoretical justification for these principles will not be given here, since they are in standard texts (e.g., Staelin et al., 1994), and we will simply state the principles without proof.

If a source is placed at some point in a system of acoustic resonators, it will excite the normal modes in different relative amounts depending on the location of the source relative to the pressure and volume velocity distributions for the modes. If the source is a volume velocity source, it will excite a normal mode in proportion to the relative amplitude of the *sound pressure* distribution at the point where the source is placed. On the other hand, if the source is a sound pressure source, it will excite a normal mode in proportion to the relative amplitude of the *volume velocity* distribution at the

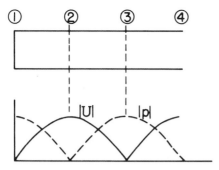

Figure 3.30 The lower panel shows the distribution of amplitude of sound pressure p and volume velocity U for the second natural frequency of a uniform tube, shown in the upper panel. At points 1 and 3 a volume velocity source gives maximum excitation of this mode, whereas at points 2 and 4 a sound pressure source gives maximum excitation.

point where the source is placed. In effect, the principle states that if a *volume velocity* source sees a high acoustic impedance (corresponding to a maximum of sound pressure across the source) at a particular natural frequency, then that frequency will be strongly excited. Likewise, if a sound pressure source sees a high acoustic admittance (corresponding to a maximum of volume velocity through the source) at a particular natural frequency, then that frequency will be strongly excited.

As an example, consider the distribution of sound pressure and volume velocity for the second normal mode of a uniform tube that is closed at one end and open at the other, as shown in figure 3.30. A volume velocity source inserted at the closed end (point 1) or at the two-thirds point (point 3) will maximally excite this mode. However, insertion of this source at points where the sound pressure distribution is a minimum (points 2 and 4) will not excite this mode. On the other hand, a sound pressure source in series with the tube at points 2 and 4 will maximally excite the mode, but will give no excitation at points 1 and 3. Both sources will produce some excitation of the mode at intermediate points.

3.5.2 Excitation from Glottal Vibration

In section 2.1 we showed that under most conditions of glottal vibration and for most vowel-like vocal tract configurations, the impedance of the glottal slit when it is maximally open during the cycle is large compared with the impedance looking into the vocal tract from the glottis. Consequently, to a first approximation the glottal source can be modeled as a volume velocity source, with a relatively high internal impedance.

We first calculate the transfer function for a lossless uniform acoustic tube of length ℓ that is open at one end, and a volume velocity source U_s is applied at the other end. The output of the tube is taken as the volume velocity U_o at the open end. We assume initially that there are no losses. In equation (3.17) we can write $U_s = U(-\ell)$, and $U_o = U(0)$, and we obtain

$$T(f) = \frac{U_o}{U_s} = \frac{1}{\cos k\ell}, \tag{3.60}$$

where $k = 2\pi f/c$. If we replace $j2\pi f$ by the complex frequency variable s, equation (3.60) becomes

$$T(s) = \frac{1}{\cosh \dfrac{s\ell}{c}}. \tag{3.61}$$

This function has poles at the natural frequencies $F_n = (2n - 1)c/(4\ell)$, as noted before, where n is a positive or negative integer. It can be shown that equation (3.61) can be written in the following form to identify explicitly the poles (cf. Morse and Feshbach, 1953):

$$T(s) = \frac{s_1 s_1^* s_2 s_2^* \cdots \cdots}{(s - s_1)(s - s_1^*)(s - s_2)(s - s_2^*) \cdots \cdots}. \tag{3.62}$$

The constant in the numerator guarantees that the transfer function is unity at zero frequency.

The magnitude of $T(s)$, with $s = j2\pi f$, is shown graphically in figure 3.31a. The transfer function goes to infinity at the natural frequencies. In terms of the principles of excitation of acoustic resonators just discussed, we note that the volume velocity source is applied at the closed end of the tube where the distribution of sound pressure is a maximum for every normal mode. Thus every normal mode is excited maximally by this volume velocity source, as figure 3.31a shows.

If we assume that there are small losses in the tube or at the ends of the tube, then the natural frequencies have bandwidths that are small in relation to the frequencies. Setting $\ell = 15$ cm, corresponding to an average vocal tract length for an adult female, then the magnitude of the transfer function has the form given in figure 3.31b if the bandwidths are assumed to be roughly those observed in vowels, corresponding to the calculations given in section 3.4. A transfer function similar to this has already been shown in figure 3.3. The ratio of the amplitudes of the spectral peaks to the amplitudes in the valleys is about 20 dB in the vicinity of the first two formants, and decreases to about 12 dB near $F3$ and $F4$. The ratio of the amplitude of the transfer function at the peak to the amplitude at the valley for uniformly spaced formants is dependent on both the bandwidth B of the formants and their spacing $S = c/(2\ell)$. If equation (3.62) is modified to include the effect of losses, it can be shown that the peak-to-valley ratio of the transfer function is $2S/(\pi B)$. Thus, for example, for a spacing of 1180 Hz (corresponding to a 15-cm vocal tract) and formant bandwidths of 80 Hz, the peak-to-valley ratio is about 19 dB.

Perturbing the shape of the tube so that it is no longer uniform has the effect of shifting the natural frequencies and hence the peaks in the transfer

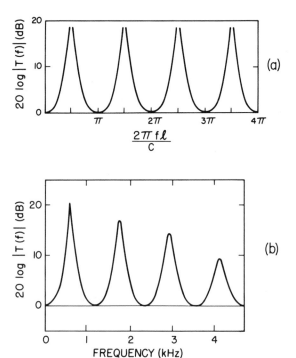

Figure 3.31 (a) Plot of magnitude of transfer function $T(f) = U_o/U_s$, expressed in decibels for an ideal uniform, lossless acoustic tube, shown in figure 3.8. (b) Magnitude of transfer function $T(f)$ for an ideal uniform tube of length 15 cm with losses similar to those occurring in the vocal tract.

function. The relative amplitudes of these peaks change as their frequencies change in accordance with the principles already discussed in section 3.2. Furthermore, the bandwidths of the different formants may change with frequency, as we have observed in section 3.4.

The overall spectrum of a vowel is obtained by multiplying the transfer function by the spectrum of the glottal source, discussed in section 2.1, and by the radiation characteristic, given in equation (3.4). The spectrum of the glottal source is taken to be the spectrum in figure 2.10 for a male speaker with a subglottal pressure of 8 cm H_2O. The radiation characteristic is calculated for a distance of 15 cm from the lips. In figure 3.32 we show the calculated spectrum envelope for three different vocal tract configurations, making reasonable assumptions about the bandwidths of the formants in accordance with the discussion in section 3.4 above. The ordinate in figure 3.32 is the calculated sound pressure level for the individual harmonics at a distance of 15 cm from the lips. Noted on each spectrum is the calculated overall sound pressure level for each vowel, as determined by adding the intensity of the individual harmonics in the output. The same method was used to calculate the overall sound pressure levels for the vowel /æ/, shown earlier in table 2.1.

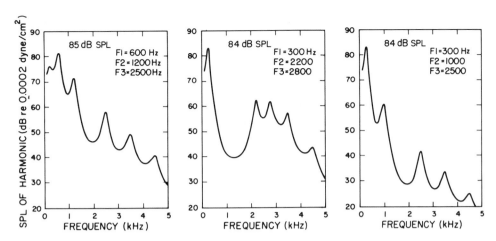

Figure 3.32 Computed spectrum envelopes approximating the vowels /ɑ/ (left), /i/ (middle), and /u/ (right). The formant frequencies are indicated in each panel, and formant bandwidths are selected to approximate those observed in natural utterances. The ordinate is the calculated sound pressure level for each harmonic at a distance of 15 cm from the lips, assuming a fundamental frequency of 125 Hz. A smooth curve is drawn through the amplitudes of the individual harmonics. The spectrum of the glottal source is that for a male voice, from figure 2.10. The calculated overall sound pressure levels are shown in each panel.

3.5.3 Excitation by Turbulence Noise in the Vicinity of the Glottis

A turbulence noise source can exist in the vicinity of the glottis as well as near a constriction above the glottis. If the principal source of turbulence noise is near the glottis, then the noise is called *aspiration* noise. The situation is represented schematically in figure 3.33a. The glottis is relatively open, and we shall assume it is not vibrating (although it is possible for vocal fold vibration and aspiration noise to occur at the same time). The noise source probably is located throughout a region above the glottis in the vicinity of the false vocal folds and the epiglottis. (A more detailed discussion of aspiration noise is given in section 8.3.) These structures form surfaces at which fluctuating forces occur, giving rise to sources of sound pressure, as discussed in section 2.2. In the model of figure 3.33b, a distributed sound pressure source is used to represent this turbulence noise. The section over which the source is distributed extends over a distance from the glottis. An equivalent circuit for this model for a particular location of the source at distance ℓ_s from the glottis is shown in figure 3.33c. There is a short section of transmission line of length ℓ_s between the source and the glottal impedance. The resistance R_g accounts for acoustic losses at the glottis. A typical glottal cross-sectional area is about 0.2 cm^2 when aspiration noise occurs, and, as we have seen, this area is sufficient to cause a large amount of acoustic loss at the first-formant frequency when there is airflow through the glottis. In fact, for most vocal tract configurations this glottal opening will give rise to critical damping of $F1$. The differential glottal resistance in figure 3.33c is given

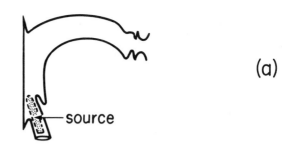

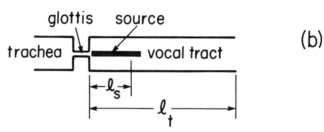

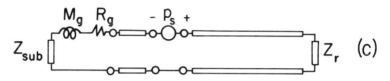

Figure 3.33 (a) Midsagittal section of vocal tract showing possible distribution of turbulence noise source during aspiration. (b) Idealized representation of vocal tract with distributed source. The dimension ℓ_s indicates the distance from the glottis to one component of the source. (c) Equivalent circuit for configuration in (b) for one location of source. Z_{sub} is the impedance of the subglottal cavities and Z_r is the radiation impedance.

approximately by $R_g = \rho U / A^2$, where $U =$ glottal airflow and $A =$ glottal-area. The model also shows a glottal acoustic mass M_g and a subglottal impedance Z_{sub}. In this analysis, the magnitude of Z_{sub} is assumed to be small compared with R_g.

The contribution of different portions of the distributed source in figure 3.33b to the excitation of the different normal modes of the vocal tract depends upon the distribution of volume velocity within each mode. As examples, we show in figure 3.34 the distribution of volume velocity for the first and third modes, assuming that the glottal impedance is large compared with the characteristic impedance of the tube. The portion of the source that contributes most to the excitation of the third mode is the section where the volume velocity distribution is a maximum. For any mode for which there is a maximum in the volume velocity distribution within the region of the source, we can expect that mode to be excited maximally by the sound pressure source. At low frequencies, however, when the length of the source is less than a quarter-wavelength (as for the lowest mode represented by the

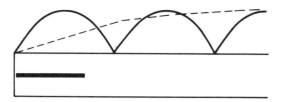

Figure 3.34 Model of figure 3.33b, showing idealized source distribution and distribution of volume velocity for first mode (dashed line) and third mode (solid line). Volume velocity distribution indicates strength of excitation of mode by the sound pressure source at different points along its length.

dashed line in figure 3.34), the maximum amplitude of the response of the mode to excitation by an element of the source will be reduced.

In figure 3.33c we define p_s to be the amplitude of the component of the sound pressure source located at distance ℓ_s from the constriction. The length of the cavity in front of the constriction is ℓ_t, and its (uniform) cross-sectional area is A_t. If we neglect losses, and if we assume the impedance of the glottis is large, then the transfer function from p_s to the output volume velocity U_o is

$$\left|\frac{U_o}{p_s}\right| = \left|\frac{A_t \sin k\ell_s}{\rho c \cos k\ell_t}\right|. \tag{3.63}$$

If we assume $k\ell_s \ll \pi/2$, that is, we assume that the distance ℓ_s from the constriction to the source is small compared with a wavelength, then equation (3.63) reduces to

$$\left|\frac{U_o}{p_s}\right| = \frac{2\pi f V}{\rho c^2} \cdot \left|\frac{1}{\cos k\ell_t}\right|, \tag{3.64}$$

where V is the volume of the space between the source and the constriction. The radiated sound pressure is calculated by multiplying this transfer function by the source spectrum, obtained from figure 2.33a, and the radiation characteristic. As discussed in section 2.2, it is necessary to adjust the amplitude of the source spectrum to take into account the airflow and the constriction area. An additional correction to the amplitude of the source spectrum may be needed to account for the fact that surfaces in the airstream immediately above the glottis may not be as effective in generating turbulence noise as the obstacle in the configuration on which figure 2.33 is based.

Calculations of the spectrum of the output sound pressure have been made for particular source locations in the model of figure 3.33b, based on the above assumptions and procedures. If the glottal cross-sectional area is taken to be 0.2 cm^2, and the subglottal pressure is 8 cm H$_2$O, then the airflow is about 750 cm^3/s, which is a typical airflow through the glottis for aspirated consonants. The acoustic resistance R_g is then 21 acoustic ohms. The factor $20 \log U^3 A^{-2.5}$ for the constriction is about 207 dB, that is, 5 dB less than the value of 212 dB on which figure 2.33a is based. The cross-sectional area of

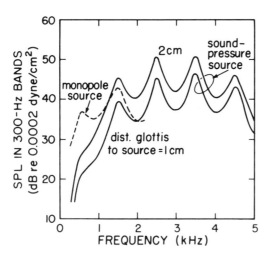

Figure 3.35 The solid lines show the calculated spectrum of the radiated sound pressure due to turbulence noise at surfaces downstream from the glottis for the model of figure 3.33b. Distance from mouth is 20 cm. Calculations are given for two values of the distance ℓ_s from glottis to source. The dashed line gives the estimated contribution from a monopole source of turbulence noise at the glottis. See text.

the portion of the tube where the turbulence noise is generated [A_t in equation (3.63)] is taken to be 2 cm^2, which is a typical value for the area of the larynx tube. An additional correction of -5 dB is applied since it is assumed that the surfaces downstream from the glottis are not as effective in generating turbulence as the obstacle in the model used to obtain figure 2.33. The total correction applied to the source spectrum of figure 2.33 to obtain the source spectrum p_s for the configuration in figure 3.33b is therefore -10 dB. Two values for the distance ℓ_s from constriction to source will be considered: 1 cm and 2 cm. In order to simplify the calculations we assume the formants to be equally spaced at 500, 1500, 2500, ... Hz, corresponding to a vocal tract length of about 17.7 cm. That is, we ignore any shifts in the formants resulting from the radiation impedance and the glottal impedance. The bandwidths of the formants are calculated following the procedures described in section 3.4. The bandwidths of the first five formants are approximately 400, 300, 250, 250, and 300 Hz, respectively.

The calculated spectra of the radiated sound pressure under these conditions are shown by the solid lines in figure 3.35. The most striking aspect of figure 3.35 when compared with the spectrum envelope for a vowel with a periodic glottal source is that the spectrum for the aspirated sound shows essentially no peak for the first formant and a greatly widened and attenuated peak for the second formant. These effects arise from acoustic losses at the glottal resistance and from the reduced amplitude of response of $F1$ to the noise source close to the glottis. At higher frequencies the loss at the glottis is smaller because the impedance $j2\pi f M_g$ dominates the resistance R_g. In the frequency range of the third formant and higher, the spectrum of the noise in figure 3.35 is roughly comparable to the spectrum amplitude for a vowel, shown in figure 3.32. (Note, however, that the noise spectrum in figure 3.35 is specified for 300-Hz bands, whereas the spectrum of the periodic sound in figure 3.32 is specified in terms of harmonic amplitudes, the harmonic spacing being 125 Hz in this case.) As expected, the output amplitude is greater for a 2-cm than for a 1-cm source distance.

The general shape of the spectrum of the radiated sound pressure for a noise source near the glottis may be modified further by the effects of subglottal resonances. These effects are discussed in section 3.6.4.

The airflow through the glottis shown in figure 3.33 may give rise to a monopole noise source as well as the sound pressure source just considered. We can use figure 2.35 to obtain an estimate of the amplitude and spectrum of this monopole source for the conditions of flow and constriction size for this model. We again multiply this source spectrum by the all-pole transfer function and the radiation characteristic to obtain the radiated sound pressure resulting from the monopole turbulence noise source. This component of the radiated sound pressure is given by the dashed line in figure 3.35. The figure shows that this source component contributes to the output only at low frequencies, primarily in the range of the first and second formants. The sound pressure or dipole source is dominant in the mid- and high-frequency ranges.

The relative amplitudes of the radiated sound from the periodic glottal source, the dipole turbulence noise source, and the monopole noise source cannot be compared directly with the relative amplitudes of the sources themselves, shown in figure 2.44. (The dipole source in figure 2.44 is converted to an equivalent volume velocity source.) The transfer functions for the sources are different. The transfer function for the dipole source contains a zero at zero frequency which, in effect, results in decreased coupling of the source to the lower-frequency modes. For both noise sources there are increased bandwidths for the lower formants (relative to those for modal glottal vibration) due to the greater glottal opening.

A more detailed analysis of the spectrum of the radiated sound due to turbulence noise at the glottis is given in section 8.3.

3.5.4 Sources Above the Glottis

In chapter 2 we found that several types of acoustic sources can be produced in the vicinity of a constriction that is formed at some point along the vocal tract when there is pressure buildup behind the constriction. The source can be a continuous noise if the constriction is narrow, or can be a brief noise or transient at the time of release of a closure. We examine now the form of the vocal tract transfer function when one or more of these sources is active.

3.5.4.1 Turbulence Noise Source at an Obstacle or Surface We consider first the type of source that is a consequence of turbulence when the

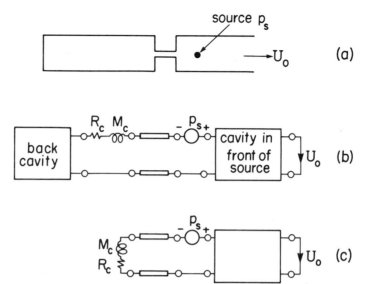

Figure 3.36 (a) Model of acoustic resonator with noise source in front of the constriction. (b) Equivalent circuit of configuration in (a). (c) Equivalent circuit neglecting the effect of the back cavity.

airstream is directed against an obstacle or past a surface. As we have seen, this source can be represented as a sound pressure source in series with the tube if the turbulence at the obstacle is concentrated in a narrow region of the vocal tract.

The source and acoustic resonator can be modeled as shown in figure 3.36a, with an equivalent circuit as in figure 3.36b. The source is located at some distance in front of the constriction, and we assume that the constriction can be represented as an acoustic mass M_c in series with a resistance R_c. The transfer function of the system is defined as the ratio of the volume velocity U_o at the mouth opening to the sound pressure p_s of the source. The sound pressure at a distance from the opening of the tube, at the right of figure 3.36a, is obtained by multiplying the spectrum of U_o by a radiation characteristic.

A first approximation to the transfer function can be obtained by assuming that the impedance of the constriction is large compared to the impedance looking into the back cavities behind the constriction. This approximation is equivalent to assuming that there is no acoustic coupling to the cavities behind the constriction. Under these circumstances, the equivalent circuit reduces to that shown in figure 3.36c. This is the same as the equivalent circuit for the situation in which the turbulence noise source is near the glottis, as in figure 3.33c, except that in figure 3.33c the length of the cavity in front of the constriction is the entire vocal tract length, whereas it is only a portion of the vocal tract in figure 3.36c. The surfaces of the resonator over which turbulence noise is generated may extend over a region downstream from the constriction.

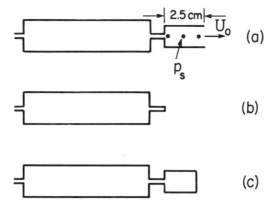

Figure 3.37 (a) Model for illustrating calculation of radiated sound pressure when a noise source is located in front of a constriction in the vocal tract. Three different source locations are indicated. (b) The natural frequencies of this configuration are the zeros of the transfer function U_o/p_s of the configuration of (a), with the leftmost source location. (c) Same as (b) but with the rightmost source location.

The spectrum of the sound output for the model of figure 3.36c (or for the equivalent model with a distributed source) can be calculated following procedures similar to those used to calculate the spectrum when there is a source of aspiration noise, in figure 3.35. The length of the cavity is shorter, so that the natural frequencies are higher, and there are differences in the bandwidths of the resonances. In order to determine the spectrum of the sound pressure at some distance from the opening of the model, we first calculate the transfer function U_o/p_s. This transfer function is then multiplied by the spectrum of the source (which can be estimated from figure 2.33), and by the radiation characteristic, which is assumed to be proportional to frequency, as in equation (3.4).

In figure 3.37a we show a model of the configuration in figure 3.36 with three different source locations. The source is a consequence of turbulence at the wall of the vocal tract, and, depending on the configuration of the constriction and the walls, it could be distributed over a region downstream from the constriction. The transfer function U_o/p_s for each of the source locations in the figure has poles at the natural frequencies of the front cavity. The lowest of these natural frequencies is approximately $c/(4\ell_f)$, where ℓ_f is the length of the front cavity. As noted above, a correction to ℓ_f should be made to account for the radiation reactance.

The transfer function also has zeros at frequencies for which the impedance looking back from the source is infinite. The frequencies of these zeros are, in effect, the natural frequencies of the configuration behind the source when a hard termination is placed at the location of the source. This configuration is shown in figure 3.37b and c for two of the source locations. In the case of the source at the more anterior positions (1 or 2 cm from the constriction), there is a zero at the frequency of the Helmholtz resonance between the acoustic compliance of the volume behind the source and the acoustic mass of the constriction (again neglecting the effect of the back cavity). Since there is airflow through the constriction, the constriction resistance will contribute substantially to the bandwidth of the zero (as in equations [3.54] and [3.55]). When the source is just 1 cm in front of the constriction, the zero is at a higher frequency than for the 2 cm location, since the volume of the cavity between the source and the constriction is smaller. For a source location immediately in front of the constriction the zero moves to a very high frequency.

We shall calculate the spectrum of the radiated sound pressure for the configuration in figure 3.37a for a particular selection of dimensions and for the three source locations. We take the front-cavity length to be 2.5 cm, and hence there is one major peak in the transfer function in the frequency range up to 5 kHz, corresponding to the front-cavity resonance at about 3.0 kHz. A constriction area $A_c = 0.1$ cm^2 and a constriction length $\ell_c = 1.0$ cm is assumed, and the cross-sectional area of the front cavity is taken to be $A = 1.0$ cm^2. The bandwidth of the resonance is calculated to be about 350 Hz based on acoustic losses at the constriction and due to radiation. The effect of the back cavity is neglected in calculating the spectra, that is, the impedance looking into the back cavity from the constriction is assumed to be small compared with the impedance of the constriction. (The effect of the back cavity is discussed later.)

To estimate the absolute levels for the spectra of the radiated sound pressure, we have assumed that the pressure drop across the constriction is 8 cm H$_2$O. The airflow for the 0.1-cm^2 constriction is thus 370 cm^3/s and the value of $20 \log U^3 A_c^{-2.5}$ is 204 dB, and hence we subtract 8 dB from the source spectrum in figure 2.33 (which is based on $20 \log U^3 A_c^{-2.5} = 212$ dB). In this example, we shall assume that there are obstacles or surfaces in the airstream that cause the generation of turbulence noise with an efficiency similar to that for the model used to obtain the spectrum in figure 2.33.[10]

Changing the position of the source in figure 3.37a does not change the frequency of the principal resonance, but it does modify the transfer function and the output spectrum in other ways. There is a zero in the transfer function at the Helmholtz resonance of the anterior part of figure 3.37b, which is at about 1780 Hz for the source location at 1 cm and at 1260 Hz for the source at 2 cm. The bandwidth of each of these zeros is calculated to be about 600 Hz.

If we neglect losses, the transfer function from the source sound pressure p_s to the output volume velocity U_o can be approximated at low frequencies (up to $f = c/(2\ell_p)$) as

$$\left| \frac{U_o}{p_s} \right| \cong \frac{1}{2\pi f M_g} \frac{1}{f_a^2} \left| \frac{f^2 - f_a^2}{\cos k\ell_f} \right|, \tag{3.65}$$

where f_a = frequency of the zero, which is assumed to be well below $c/(4\ell_f)$. The factor $1/(2\pi f M_g)$ is the limiting expression for the transfer function at low frequencies, neglecting losses. Equation (3.65) applies when the source location is downstream from the constriction. When the source is located at the outlet of the constriction, the lossless transfer function becomes

$$\left|\frac{U_o}{p_s}\right| = \frac{1}{2\pi f M_g} \left|\frac{1}{\cos k\ell_f}\right|. \tag{3.66}$$

Losses are incorporated into equations (3.65) and (3.66) by including bandwidths in the poles and zeros (including the pole at the origin).

Figure 3.38a shows the spectra of the radiated sound pressure based on the above assumptions. Each spectrum is calculated by multiplying the source spectrum by the appropriate transfer function—equation (3.65) or (3.66) (with losses)—and by the radiation characteristic (equation [3.4]) for a distance r of 20 cm. The figure shows that the level of the peak would increase by about 13 dB as the source is displaced downstream from the constriction if the spectrum and strength of the source were the same for the three source locations at 0, 1, and 2 cm from the constriction. This increase in amplitude is in accord with the earlier discussion (see section 3.5.1) which notes that the excitation of a resonator with a sound pressure source is proportional to the amplitude of the volume velocity in the standing-wave pattern. This volume velocity is small at the end of the constriction, but is relatively large at a point downstream from the constriction, as in figure 3.34. The assumption that the source strength would be the same at the end of the constriction as it would be at an obstacle (such as the teeth) downstream from the constriction may not be valid. A greater source strength is expected if the airstream impinges directly on an obstacle normal to the flow than if the turbulence is generated by the airstream incident on the vocal tract wall at an oblique angle immediately downstream from the constriction. Thus the difference in level for the two downstream source locations may be greater than the difference shown in figure 3.38a, as a result of differences in source strength at the two locations.

An approximation to the spectrum of the radiated sound for source locations downstream from the constriction in figure 3.37a can be obtained by assuming that the constriction has infinite impedance. The impedance looking back from the source is then a short tube terminated by a hard wall. The transfer function U_o/p_s for this configuration has a zero at zero frequency. The procedure for calculating the transfer function for this case is similar to that used in calculating the transfer function when the noise source is near the glottis (equation [3.63]). Figure 3.38b shows the calculated spectrum for the source location 2 cm downstream from the constriction for this case, compared with the spectrum given in figure 3.38a for this source location. The spectra are similar in the vicinity of the major peak and above, but there are differences at lower frequencies.

3.5.4.2 Effects of Back Cavity The effects of the acoustic cavity behind the constriction in figure 3.37a were neglected in calculating the spectra in

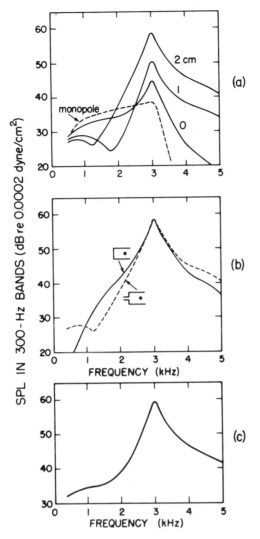

Figure 3.38 (a) Calculated spectrum of radiated sound pressure (at a distance of 20 cm) for the three source locations in the model in figure 3.37a. See text. (b) Comparison of calculated spectrum of radiated sound pressure for the source located 2 cm from the constriction when the constriction is modeled by an infinite impedance (solid line) and by an acoustic resistance and mass (dashed line). (c) Spectrum obtained by adding the contributions of the three source locations in (a), approximating the sound pressure for a distributed source.

figure 3.38a, since it was assumed that acoustic coupling to this cavity was small. We can, however, account for this coupling to the back cavity by introducing modifications in the spectra of figure 3.38a. The transfer function U_o/p_s has a set of poles that are the natural frequencies of the entire system, including both the front and back cavities. These natural frequencies for a constricted configuration have been discussed earlier in this chapter in connection with figure 3.16. The transfer function also has a set of zeros at frequencies for which the impedance looking back from the source (i.e., looking to the left of the source in figure 3.37a) is infinite. These zeros of the transfer function are the natural frequencies of the configurations in figure 3.37b or 3.37c. This way of interpreting the zeros is valid if the source is a point source.

We shall examine in detail the effect of the back cavity for the case in which the source location is at the anterior end of the constriction. When the constriction between front and back cavities is sufficiently narrow, the natural frequencies of the configuration in figure 3.37b are almost equal to the natural frequencies associated with the back cavity of the configuration in figure 3.37a. That is, the poles of the transfer function U_o/p_s corresponding to back-cavity resonances are almost equal to the zeros of the transfer function. These poles and zeros cancel, and we are left with a transfer function that is characterized only by front-cavity resonances, as we have seen in figure 3.38. For a small but finite cross-sectional area of the constriction, however, the natural frequencies of the back cavity in figure 3.37a are slightly different from the natural frequencies of the resonator in figure 3.37b, and consequently there is not complete cancellation of the poles and zeros of the transfer function. At each of these natural frequencies the pole-zero pair will introduce a perturbation in the transfer function of the type illustrated in figure 3.6. The amount of perturbation depends on the separation between the pole and the zero and on their bandwidths. This separation, in turn, is dependent on the cross-sectional area and length of the constriction that separates the front and back cavities. The fact that there is almost cancellation of these poles and zeros indicates that the natural frequencies associated with the back-cavity resonances are excited only weakly by a sound pressure source located anterior to the constriction. The distribution of volume velocity associated with these back-cavity resonances has a very small amplitude at the location of the source, and hence the source excites these natural frequencies with a very low amplitude.

If the constriction is small, and if the impedance of the constriction is dominated by its acoustic mass in the frequency range of interest, then the spacing between the pole and zero resulting from acoustic coupling to the back cavity can be calculated directly. We assume a back-cavity length of ℓ_b and of uniform cross-sectional area A_b. The admittance looking into the back cavity (from the posterior end of the constriction) is

$$Y_b = j \frac{A_b}{\rho c} \tan k\ell_b. \tag{3.67}$$

The natural frequencies of the configuration in figure 3.37b are the zeros of Y_b. These are at frequencies $nc/(2\ell_b)$, where $n = 1, 2, 3 \ldots$, and represent the zeros of the transfer function U_o/p_s. The frequencies of the poles that are associated with these zeros are the frequencies satisfying the equation

$$\frac{A_b}{\rho c} \tan k\ell_b - \frac{1}{2\pi f M_c} = 0, \tag{3.68}$$

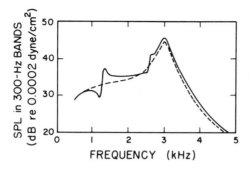

Figure 3.39 The solid line shows the calculated spectrum of the output of the model of figure 3.37a with a source location immediately anterior to the constriction, taking into account acoustic coupling to the back cavity. The dashed line is the spectrum given in figure 3.38a for the 0 cm location, neglecting the effect of the back cavity. See text.

where M_c is the acoustic mass of the constriction, given by $M_c = \rho \ell_c / A_c$. We neglect the impedance looking into the front cavity from the constriction. In the vicinity of $k\ell_b = n\pi$ ($n = 1, 2, 3 \ldots$), that is, in the vicinity of the zeros, we can make appropriate approximations for the tangent, leading to the following expression for the frequency difference Δf between the pole and the zero:

$$\Delta f = \frac{A_c}{A_b} \cdot \frac{c}{2\pi^2 n \ell_c}, \tag{3.69}$$

where n is an integer, defined above. For the model of figure 3.37a we shall assume the following dimensions for the back cavity: $A_b = 4 \text{ cm}^2$, $\ell_b = 14 \text{ cm}$. The constriction area $A_c = 0.1 \text{ cm}^2$ as before, and $\ell_c = 1.0 \text{ cm}$. The back-cavity resonances (zeros of the transfer function) are 1260 Hz and multiples of this frequency. The pole-zero separation is about 45 Hz for this lowest resonance, and is proportionately less for the higher resonances. The calculated spectrum is shown in figure 3.39, assuming nominal values of 100 Hz for the bandwidths of the poles and zeros. (The actual bandwidths will depend on factors such as the glottal opening and the airflow. Bandwidths of 100 Hz are within the expected range for vocal tract configurations of this type.) The gross features of the spectrum are the same as those in figure 3.38a for the 0 cm location (dashed line in figure 3.39), but superimposed on that spectrum we observe the perturbations resulting from coupling to the back cavity. The perturbations will, of course, be larger if the length of the constriction is less, or if its cross-sectional area is greater. The perturbations are also larger at lower frequencies.

When the natural frequencies of the front and back cavities are close together, the degree to which a natural frequency can be associated with one cavity or another becomes blurred, and both normal modes may be excited by a turbulence noise source located anterior to the constriction. In effect, there is a cluster of two poles and a zero in the transfer function U_o/p_s. As we have illustrated earlier in figure 3.7, this situation can lead to an output spectrum with two peaks that are close together. One or both of these peaks may be greater in amplitude than the single spectral peak that would occur as a consequence of just the front-cavity resonance, with no coupling to the back cavity.

3.5.4.3 Distributed Sources In the examples just discussed, we have assumed that the turbulence noise source is concentrated at one point along the length of the tube. In general, turbulence is distributed over a region of the vocal tract downstream from the constriction, and consequently the noise source may be distributed over a region. We can determine the output for this distributed source by calculating the output for each location within the region of turbulence and superposing these outputs in the manner discussed above when we considered turbulence noise sources near the glottis. This calculation has been done for the configuration in figure 3.37a, to give an approximation to the spectrum for a distributed source, in figure 3.38c. This spectrum is estimated by calculating separately the power spectra for the three source locations (assuming the total source strength is distributed uniformly among the individual sources) and then adding the power spectra assuming that the sources at the different locations are uncorrelated. The spectral prominence corresponding to the front-cavity resonance is evident in figure 3.38c, but there is no longer a sharp spectral minimum corresponding to a zero, as there was in some of the spectra in figure 3.38a. When there is a distributed source, it is expected that minima in the spectrum arising from zeros in the transfer function will be smoothed out.

In the examples in figures 3.38a and 3.38c we have represented the turbulence noise source either as being located at a point, corresponding to turbulence at an obstacle in the airstream, or as being distributed uniformly over a region, corresponding to turbulence over a surface parallel to the airstream. The situation that exists in practice is probably somewhere between these two extremes. For any source distribution, the peaks in the spectrum of the response are at the same frequencies, since these are the natural frequencies of the system. The magnitude of the excitation of these normal modes will be different for each source position, and hence the amplitudes of the spectral peaks will vary with source distribution.

In section 2.2, it was shown that, depending on the relative cross-sectional areas of the glottal and supraglottal constrictions, it is possible for turbulence noise to be generated primarily at the glottis, primarily at the supraglottal constriction, or in the vicinity of both constrictions, as noted in connection with figures 2.36 and 2.37. Thus it is not unusual to observe excitation of a cavity behind a constriction by a glottal source while there is also strong excitation of a front-cavity resonance by a source near the supraglottal constriction.

3.5.4.4 Monopole Turbulence Noise Source As has been noted in section 2.2, turbulence noise in the vocal tract can take the form of fluctuations in volume flow through a constriction. These fluctuations can be modeled as a monopole or volume velocity source U_{ms}, with a spectrum as shown in figure 2.35. The excitation of the vocal tract by a volume velocity source of this kind can be treated much like excitation by a quasi-periodic glottal source, except that it is the portion of the vocal tract downstream from the constriction that is being excited. The transfer function U_o/U_{ms} from the monopole source to the output volume velocity is all-pole (assuming no acoustic coupling to the back cavity), in contrast to the transfer function for a sound pressure source, which contains zeros as well as poles.

As an example, we consider the excitation of the configuration in figure 3.37a by a monopole turbulence noise source. The transfer function has poles corresponding to the natural frequencies of the front cavity, the lowest of which is about 3000 Hz in this case. If we take the source spectrum in figure 2.35, multiply by this transfer function, and include the radiation characteristic, we obtain the spectrum shown as the dashed line in figure 3.38a. As before, the source spectrum is scaled down by 8 dB to account for the different airflow and area compared to the values for which figure 2.35 is constructed. The spectrum for the monopole source has the expected peak at 3000 Hz, but the amplitude of this peak is considerably weaker than the amplitudes for the different locations of the dipole source. Thus the dipole source appears to dominate in this frequency range. On the other hand, at lower frequencies, below about 1.5 kHz, the contribution of the monopole source to the output spectrum is dominant. In spite of the weaker amplitude of the monopole source relative to the dipole source (see figure 3.35), the monopole source couples to the vocal tract more effectively at low frequencies than does the sound pressure source. A similar comparison of the radiated sound pressure due to dipole and monopole sources was made in section 3.5.3 for the case of turbulence noise in the vicinity of the glottis.

3.5.4.5 Transient Source

In section 2.3, methods were given for estimating the magnitude and spectrum of the initial transient of volume velocity that occurs when pressure behind a closure in the vocal tract is released. This transient source provides acoustic excitation for the vocal tract, and the radiated sound pressure is a consequence of the filtering of the source by the vocal cavities.

In order to examine this process further, we consider the model shown in figure 3.40a. The front- and back-cavity dimensions for this model are the same as those in figure 3.37a. We assume that a steady pressure P_m exists in the portion of the model behind the constriction. The cross-sectional area of the constriction is then abruptly increased, so that the pressure P_m decreases rapidly.

The radiated sound pressure that results from the transient release can be approximated as the sum of two components: (1) the result of the initial transient excitation of the acoustic cavity in front of the constriction, and (2) the result of excitation of the part of the vocal tract posterior to the con-

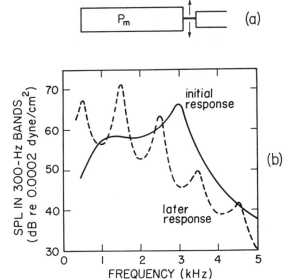

Figure 3.40 (a) Model for calculation of the transient that occurs at the release of the closure for a stop consonant, with a pressure P_m behind the closure. (b) Spectra of two components of the transient immediately following the release of the closure in (a). The initial response (solid line) represents the response of the front cavity, and the later response (dashed line) is the output resulting from excitation of the back cavity, assuming that the opening movement is essentially completed. See text.

striction. The initial component can be estimated by using the source spectrum in figure 2.47 (or a modified version of this spectrum depending on the pressure and on the rate of change of cross-sectional area at the release) as the volume velocity excitation for the front cavity, and filtering this source by the front-cavity transfer function and the radiation characteristic. The rate of increase of cross-sectional area for this source was assumed to be 100 cm²/s, with an initial pressure P_m of 8 cm H_2O. The front-cavity transfer function has a peak at about 3 kHz, but, in contrast to excitation by turbulence noise (as in figure 3.36), the transfer function is all-pole, and there is no zero at low frequencies. Adding (in decibels) the source spectrum, the all-pole transfer function, and the radiation characteristic yields a calculated spectrum shown as the solid line in figure 3.40b. The frequency of the spectral prominence depends, of course, on the length of the front cavity.

The transient also excites the cavity behind the constriction, so that acoustic energy oscillates at the natural frequencies of this cavity. These natural frequencies change rapidly as the area of the constriction increases following the release. For example, figure 3.17 shows that, for a short constriction, $F1$ has undergone most of its movement to the steady-state value after the area has increased to about 0.3 cm²—a movement that takes about 3 ms if the rate of increase of area is taken to be 100 cm²/s. A rough approximation to this component can be obtained by assuming that the same

Basic Acoustics of Vocal Tract Resonators

transient volume velocity is injected into the back cavity (with negative sign) but taking the natural frequencies to be those of a uniform tube (i.e., assuming for the present purposes that the model quickly takes the shape of a uniform tube). The spectrum of the radiated sound pressure under these conditions is the dashed line in figure 3.40b. This component would be observable in the signal only if minimal turbulence noise were generated at the glottis immediately following the release—a condition that might occur only if the glottis were narrow or closed, as, for example, for an ejective stop consonant. The formant bandwidths used for calculating the spectrum are relatively narrow, since it is assumed that the losses at the glottis and at the constriction are small.

The spectra in figure 3.40b have amplitudes that are comparable to or greater than those for turbulence noise sources, in figures 3.35 and 3.38. Thus the spectrum amplitude of sound from the transient at the release can, at least in some cases, be comparable to that from other sources. The total energy in the transient is, however, usually smaller than that in the burst of turbulence noise, which extends over a duration of several milliseconds. The role of the transient is discussed in greater detail in chapters 7 and 8.

3.5.4.6 Clicks with an Abrupt Release A somewhat different kind of transient is generated at the release of a click, as we have seen in section 2.4. The general approach to calculating the radiated sound pressure will be discussed in terms of the model in figure 3.41a. In this case the pressure P_o in the small cavity that is formed between the tongue body constriction (at the posterior end) and the tongue blade constriction (at the anterior end) is

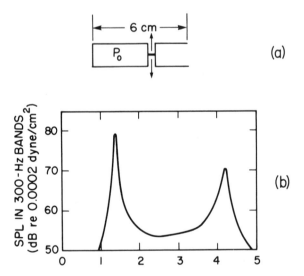

Figure 3.41 (a) Model for calculation of the transient that occurs at the release of a click, with a (negative) pressure P_o behind the closure. (b) Spectrum of transient response for the model in (a). See text.

negative relative to atmospheric pressure. The spectrum and amplitude of the initial inward transient in volume velocity has been estimated in figure 2.49. If we assume a very rapid opening at the constriction, then within a few milliseconds the cavity anterior to the tongue body constriction can be assumed to be uniform. We can, then, calculate the output assuming an initial unidirectional volume velocity pulse. The spectrum of the output volume velocity at the opening of the tube can be obtained by adding (in decibels) the spectrum of the source (from figure 2.49) and the all-pole transfer function for the tube. For the tube in figure 3.41a, with a length of 6 cm, the lowest two natural frequencies are about 1400 and 4200 Hz. There is no airflow in this resonator, and hence the bandwidths of these two resonances are rather narrow: about 50 Hz and 150 Hz, assuming a cross-sectional area of about 1 cm^2 for the front cavity. These bandwidths arise primarily from radiation losses and losses due to viscosity and heat conduction. (See section 3.4.)

The calculated spectrum of the radiated sound pressure at a distance of 20 cm for this idealized click is shown in figure 3.41b. Comparison with figure 3.32 indicates that the amplitudes of the spectral peaks for the click are usually considerably greater than the amplitudes of corresponding peaks for a following vowel, as has been shown in the data of Traill (1994).

3.6 NASAL COUPLING AND OTHER SIDE BRANCHES

We have observed in section 3.5.2 that when there is excitation of the vocal tract by a volume velocity source at the glottis, the transfer function from source volume velocity to volume velocity at the mouth opening contains only poles. This all-pole transfer function occurs when there is a single acoustic path from source to output, with no side branches. It is possible, however, to adjust the configuration of the articulatory structures to create a side branch or a parallel branch in this path. This additional branch can be produced either by forming an opening between the oral and nasal cavities at the velopharyngeal port, or by raising the tongue blade and placing it in a lateral position that creates more than one path for the sound to propagate through the vocal tract, or by forming a short side branch on the underside of the tongue blade. In each case, the result is to modify the all-pole transfer function to include zeros as well as poles.

The way in which the transfer function from glottal source to output is modified by the introduction of an additional branch can be illustrated with reference to the models in figure 3.42. In the case of the model in figure 3.42a, the cross-sectional area of the opening to a side branch is small compared with the cross-sectional area of the main acoustic tube, whereas for the models in figure 3.42b and c the cross-sectional area of the side branch is much larger. For these configurations in figure 3.42a, b, and c, the side branch is located near the midpoint of the main tube—a situation roughly analogous to nasal consonants and vowels—and its length is approximately one-half that of the main acoustic tube. In figure 3.42c, the main tube is

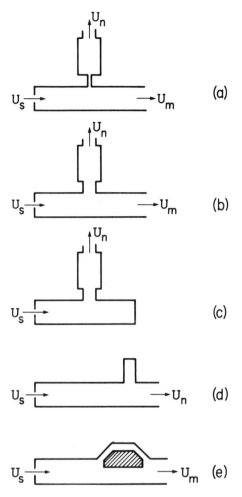

Figure 3.42 Five models for which there is a side branch in the acoustic path from source volume velocity U_s to output volume velocity (U_m, or U_n, or $U_m + U_n$). (a) and (b) Models for nasal vowels with different degrees of opening of the velopharyngeal port. (c) A model for a nasal consonant. (d) A model for a consonant for which a side branch is formed by the tongue blade. (e) A model for a configuration in which there are two acoustic paths from source to output over some portion of the length of the tube.

closed at a point anterior to the place where the side branch is coupled to it, and the output is the volume velocity U_n at the end of the side branch. This model is analogous to the configuration for a nasal consonant. The models in figure 3.42a and b are analogous to nasal vowels with two degrees of opening for the velopharyngeal port. For these nasal vowel configurations there are two volume velocity outputs: U_m from the main tube and U_n from the side branch.

In figure 3.42d, the side branch is located at a more anterior position, and is shorter than in the other models, simulating one aspect of the configuration for certain lateral and retroflex consonants. These lateral and retro-

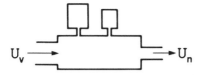

Figure 3.43 Schematization of nasal cavity with two sinuses. Volume velocity at velopharyngeal port is U_v, and output volume velocity at nostrils is U_n.

flex configurations are produced by shaping the tongue blade and tongue body in such a way that sound can propagate around the sides of the tongue body as well as along the midline. These two acoustic paths have different lengths, as schematized by the model in figure 3.42e. This split acoustic path can also introduce zeros into the transfer function from the glottal source to the output volume velocity.

For all of the configurations in figure 3.42 there is a general principle concerning the distribution of poles and zeros in the transfer function from the glottal source to the output. The total number of poles in the transfer function up to a certain frequency f (up to, say, 4 kHz) is given by $n_p = 2\ell_t f / c$ where ℓ_t is the total length of all of the tube components in the model, including side branches and parallel branches. If the distance from glottis to output by the most direct path is ℓ, then the number of zeros in the transfer function up to frequency f is given by $n_z = 2f(\ell_t - \ell)/c$. Another way of expressing this principle is that the *net* number of poles $n_t - n_z$ is given by $2f\ell/c$, that is, the average net spacing of the poles is $c/(2\ell)$. In addition to this set of poles there are a number n_z of pole-zero pairs, that is, every additional zero can be viewed as being paired with an additional pole. When the side branch or the parallel branch is obliterated through an appropriate articulatory movement, the pole and zero in a pair come together and are eliminated, leaving an all-pole transfer function with $2f\ell/c$ poles in the range below frequency f. For all of the configurations in figure 3.42, we are interested in the transfer function from the source volume velocity U_s to the output, whether it be U_m, U_n, or a combination of the two.

3.6.1 Acoustic Properties of the Nasal Tract

As described in section 1.1.3, the nasal tract begins at the velopharyngeal opening, for which the cross-sectional area can be adjusted. Over a part of its length, the nasal tract splits into two branches that are usually roughly symmetrical, and it ends at the two openings of the nostrils. Several sinuses connect to either side of the nasal cavity through narrow passages. Two such sinuses are shown in the schematic representation of the nasal tract in figure 3.43. Because of the sinuses, the acoustic properties of the nasal tract are complicated, and certain details show considerable variability from one individual to another. Furthermore, for some speakers, the two channels within

Basic Acoustics of Vocal Tract Resonators

the nasal cavity are not symmetrical, and this asymmetry has an effect on the acoustic output. We shall attempt, however, to summarize the main features.

Two system functions for the nasal tract are important for determining the response of a system like that in figure 3.42a, b, or c. One is the impedance looking into the nasal tract at the velopharyngeal port. This impedance has an influence on the transfer function U_m/U_s in figure 3.42a and b, since it acts as a shunt in the acoustic path from U_s to U_m. The other is the transfer function of the nasal cavity from the volume velocity U_v at the velopharyngeal port to the output U_n. This transfer function has an influence on the overall transfer function U_n/U_s.

Both the transfer function and the driving-point impedance have, of course, the same poles. Experimental data (Lindqvist and Sundberg, 1972) indicate that the lowest of these is probably in the range of 450 to 650 Hz. (See also Dang et al., 1994.) The volume of the sinuses appears to play an important role in determining the lowest natural frequency of the nasal tract. The sinuses also introduce additional pole-zero pairs in the driving-point impedance and in the transfer function. One of these is in the frequency range around 400 Hz and another is around 1300 Hz (Båvegård et al., 1993). Each sinus constitutes a resonator that is coupled through a narrow opening to the nasal tract proper, as schematized in figure 3.43. The spacing between the additional pole and zero depends in part on the cross-sectional area of this opening. The frequencies of the zeros in the driving-point impedance will be slightly different from those in the transfer impedance. One might expect the frequency and spacing of these pole-zero pairs to vary from one individual to another, since they depend on the volumes of the sinuses and the sizes of the openings to the sinuses. At higher frequencies, above about 1.3 kHz, the sinuses probably do not play a significant role in shaping the acoustic behavior of the nasal tract because the acoustic impedance of the narrow opening to a sinus becomes large. The second main resonance of the nasal tract (when it is closed at the posterior end) is in the vicinity of 2000 Hz. The first main minimum (i.e., zero not associated with a sinus) of the driving-point impedance is probably in the range of 1000 to 1500 Hz. The magnitude of the transfer function of the nasal tract as a function of frequency is schematized in figure 3.44. The two principal lowest resonances are shown (at 600 Hz and 2000 Hz), together with the effects of some pole-zero pairs in the frequency range above the lowest resonance. Considerable variability in this transfer function is expected from one individual to another, particularly in the pole-zero pairs corresponding to sinus resonances. Pole-zero pairs are also introduced if there is an asymmetry in the nasal passages on the two sides of the septum.

3.6.2 Transfer Function with Nasal Coupling

For the models in figure 3.42a to c, which contain a side branch in the path from source to output, the transfer function U_m/U_s or U_n/U_s can be calcu-

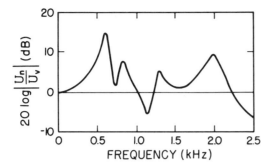

Figure 3.44 Estimate of transfer function of nasal cavity (output volume velocity U_n relative to volume velocity U_v at velopharyngeal port), based in part on measurements of Lindqvist and Sundberg (1972). Considerable interspeaker variability is expected in this transfer function.

lated by examining the susceptances looking into the parallel configuration of three tubes at the junction. In the model of a nasalized vowel in figure 3.45a, these susceptances are labeled B_p, B_m, and B_n, representing the susceptances looking into the pharynx, mouth, and nasal tubes, respectively. If there are no losses, the poles of the system function U_m/U_s or U_n/U_s are the frequencies for which $B_p + B_m + B_n = 0$. The zeros of U_m/U_s are the frequencies for which $B_n = \infty$, and the zeros of U_n/U_s are the frequencies for which $B_m = \infty$. The determination of the poles and zeros of either transfer function reduces, then, to estimation of these susceptances. If the losses are small, the poles and zeros calculated in this way will be modified to have small bandwidths.

The procedure will be illustrated for the system function U_m/U_s for the model of figure 3.45a. The sum $B_p + B_m$ has zeros at the natural frequencies of the uniform tube. For simplicity, the length of this tube is selected so that the natural frequencies are 500, 1500, 2500, ... Hz. The cross-sectional area is taken to be 3 cm². The negative of the susceptance $B_p + B_m$ is plotted as the solid line in figure 3.45b, assuming the junction point to be at the middle of the tube. We model the connection to the nasal cavity as a narrow tube with cross-sectional area A_n and length 1 cm. The remainder of the nasal cavity has acoustic characteristics similar to those given in figure 3.44. The susceptance B_n has zeros at 600 and 2000 Hz, and the pole intermediate between these two zeros is at a frequency that depends on the area A_n. This susceptance is plotted as a dashed line in figure 3.45b for $A_n = 0.2$ cm² and as a dotted line for $A_n = 0.1$ cm². The effects of the sinuses in causing additional pole-zero pairs are ignored here.

The points of intersection of the curve representing $-(B_p + B_m)$ and a curve B_n are the natural frequencies of the system, and hence are the poles of the transfer function U_m/U_s or U_n/U_s. A pole of B_n is the frequency of a zero of the transfer function U_m/U_s, that is, a frequency at which the transmission path from source to lips encounters a short circuit. The transfer function U_n/U_s has zeros at frequencies for which $B_m = \infty$ (2000 Hz in this

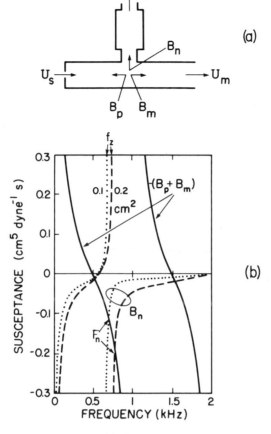

Figure 3.45 (a) Model of the vocal tract configuration for a nasal vowel, showing the susceptances looking into the three directions at the junction. (b) The solid line gives the calculated value of the susceptance $-(B_p + B_m)$ in (a), assuming a tube with uniformly spaced natural frequencies and with a cross-sectional area of 3 cm². The curves labeled B_n are estimated susceptances looking into the nasal cavity for two areas of the opening to the nasal cavity. See text.

example). We restrict the discussion here to U_m/U_s. We note that the frequencies of the original formants for no nasal coupling (at 500 Hz and 1500 Hz) are shifted upward slightly when there is an opening to the nasal cavity. An additional pole-zero pair (F_n and f_z) appears in the transfer function. For a coupling area of 0.1 cm², $F_n = 700$ Hz and $f_z = 680$ Hz, whereas with the larger coupling area, the pole-zero spacing is somewhat greater, with $F_n = 800$ Hz and $f_z = 750$ Hz. (If the output U_n from the nose were taken into account, the frequency of the zero for the combined output would be considerably higher. Nasalization of vowels is discussed in more detail in chapter 6.) The effect of the pole-zero pair on the transfer function U_m/U_s with a coupling area of 0.2 cm² is shown in figure 3.46. There is the expected perturbation of the transfer function in the vicinity of 700 Hz, as a consequence of the acoustic coupling to the nasal cavity.

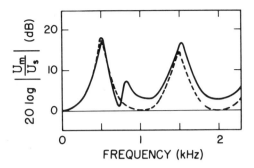

Figure 3.46 Calculated transfer function U_m/U_s for the configuration of figure 3.45a for no acoustic coupling to the nasal cavity (dashed line) and for a coupling area of 0.2 cm², as estimated from figure 3.45b.

As described in chapter 1, the nasal cavity has a large surface area, and is lined with soft tissue. These surface properties lead to losses at the walls that are greater than those for the vocal tract, particularly at low frequencies. Consequently the bandwidths of poles and zeros in the low-frequency range will be greater than the bandwidths normally observed or calculated for non-nasal vowels. No bandwidth adjustments were made, however, in calculating the transfer function in figure 3.46 for the nasal configuration.

When a complete closure is made at some point in the oral cavity, the mouth output U_m is zero, and the only output is the volume velocity U_n from the nasal cavity. A resonator configuration that models this situation has been shown in figure 3.42c.

For this configuration, the transfer function U_n/U_s again has a set of poles and zeros, which can be calculated in the manner shown in figure 3.45b. The zeros occur at frequencies for which the acoustic susceptance B_m looking into the mouth cavity is infinite. If this cavity is idealized as a uniform tube of length ℓ_m, then the frequency of the lowest zero is $c/(4\ell_m)$. In the case of a nasal consonant that is produced with a closure at the lips, the length ℓ for an adult is approximately 8 cm, and the frequency of this lowest zero is about 1100 Hz. The frequency of this zero increases as the position of the closure is displaced in a posterior direction from the lips.

The lowest natural frequency or pole of U_n/U_s when there is a closure at the lips can be computed to be approximately 250 to 300 Hz, after correction for the effective mass of the walls (Båvegård et al., 1993). The next highest natural frequency can be computed roughly from figure 3.45b if the curve for $-(B_p + B_m)$ is modified to correspond to a tube closed at both ends. For a velopharyngeal area in the range of 0.2 to 0.4 cm² (beyond the range given in the figure), this frequency is expected to be in the range of 750 to 1000 Hz.

A typical transfer function for a nasal consonant in the low-frequency range, then, would have the form shown in figure 3.47. There is a low-frequency peak at about 250 Hz, a second resonance in the range of 750 to

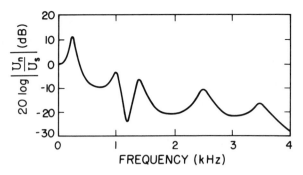

Figure 3.47 Transfer function U_n/U_s for a model of the type shown in figure 3.42c. The zero at 1200 Hz is the frequency at which the impedance looking to the right at the coupling point goes to zero. No attempt is made to represent accurately the poles and zeros above about 2 kHz.

1000 Hz, and a spectral minimum that occurs somewhat above it. A more detailed discussion of the acoustic attributes of nasal consonants is given in section 9.1.

3.6.3 Side Branch or Bifurcation Within the Vocal Tract: Lateral and Retroflex Consonants

Figure 3.42d and figure 3.42e are models for a class of vocal tract configurations that are produced by shaping the tongue body or tongue blade in a way that creates a bifurcation or a side branch, or both, in the acoustic path between the pharyngeal region and the incisors. This type of configuration is achieved by bunching the tongue, or by forming a lateral or a retroflex consonant. The tongue blade usually forms a significant narrowing of the airway in the anterior portion of the tract. Like the nasal configurations, these models also have transfer functions U_m/U_s that deviate from the all-pole pattern for non-nasal vowels. These transfer functions are also characterized by the presence of additional poles and zeros, but with a pattern that is different from that for nasal vowels and consonants.

The model in figure 3.42d shows a side branch that is considerably shorter than the main acoustic tube, and the side branch is located closer to the open end of the tube than in the models of figure 3.42a and b. The side branch introduces zeros into the transfer function U_m/U_s, and for the ideal model of figure 3.42d the frequency of the lowest zero is $c/(4\ell_s)$, where ℓ_s is the length of the side branch. The side branch also has an influence on the positions of the poles of the transfer function. When there is no side branch, the average spacing of the poles for the main acoustic tube (of length ℓ) is $c/(2\ell)$, whereas the average spacing with the side branch in place is $c/2(\ell + \ell_s)$. That is, the average distance between the poles is less when there is a side branch. The overall effect of the side branch for this case is schematized in figure 3.48. Comparison of the two cases (with and without side branch)

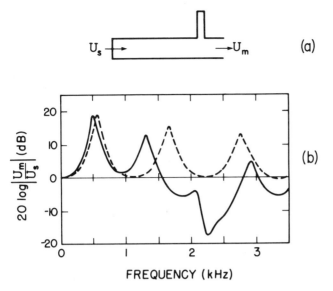

(a)

(b)

Figure 3.48 (a) Configuration with a side branch near the end of a tube, as in figure 3.42d. (b) The solid line shows the transfer function U_m/U_s for a configuration of the type in (a). Total length of tube $= 16$ cm; length of side branch $= 4$ cm; distance from end of tube $= 3.5$ cm. The dashed line is the transfer function of the tube without the side branch.

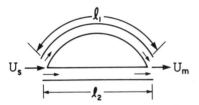

Figure 3.49 Simple configuration of tubes for which there are two unequal paths ℓ_1 and ℓ_2 from source U_s to output U_m.

shows that there are more spectral peaks when the side branch is present, and there is a significant minimum in the spectrum at the frequency $c/(4\ell_s)$. The position of the minimum and the frequencies of the poles can, of course, be manipulated by adjusting the configuration of the main acoustic tube and the configuration and length of the side branch.

Some insight into the behavior of the model of figure 3.42e can be obtained by considering the simpler configuration of figure 3.49. In this simpler model, there are two acoustic paths, each with the same uniform cross-sectional area: one with length ℓ_1 and the other with length ℓ_2. The volume velocity at the input is U_s, and we assume that the volume velocities at the two ouputs, U_{m1}, and U_{m2}, add, without significant interaction,[11] to give a combined output $U_m = U_{m1} + U_{m2}$. The overall transfer function (assuming no losses) can then be written

$$\frac{U_m}{U_s} = \frac{1}{2}\left(\frac{1}{\cos k\ell_1} + \frac{1}{\cos k\ell_2}\right)$$

$$= \frac{\frac{1}{2}(\cos k\ell_1 + \cos k\ell_2)}{\cos k\ell_1 \cos k\ell_2}$$

$$= \frac{\cos k \dfrac{(\ell_1 + \ell_2)}{2} \cos k \dfrac{(\ell_1 - \ell_2)}{2}}{\cos k\ell_1 \cos k\ell_2}. \tag{3.70}$$

This transfer function has poles at the natural frequencies of the component tubes. The numerator term $\cos k(\ell_1 + \ell_2)/2$ indicates zeros at odd multiples of frequencies $c/[2(\ell_1 + \ell_2)]$, which are intermediate between the frequencies of the poles. There are also zeros at odd multiples of the frequency $c/[2(\ell_1 - \ell_2)]$, which is at a much higher frequency than the other poles if ℓ_1 is not too different from ℓ_2.

The model of figure 3.42e is somewhat more complex than the configuration in figure 3.49, since the bifurcation is part of a larger concatenation of tubes, and since the two paths are not of equal cross-sectional area. We can, however, expect a similar interpretation of the transfer function relative to that for a simple tube with no bifurcations. That is, certain poles of the transfer function for the simpler tube are replaced by pole-zero-pole clusters, as illustrated earlier in figure 3.7. The lowest frequency at which this type of perturbation in the transfer function can be expected is the frequency for which the combined length $\ell_1 + \ell_2$ of the component tubes in the bifurcated section is equal to a half-wavelength, that is, in the vicinity of frequency $c/[2(\ell_1 + \ell_2)]$.

In section 9.3 we will see examples of these kinds of modifications of the transfer function for lateral and retroflex consonants. The sections ℓ_1 and ℓ_2 for these configurations probably extend over the oral cavity from the front of the hard palate back to the soft palate or upper pharyngeal region—a total length $\ell_1 + \ell_2$ of about 8 to 15 cm for an adult male. The most significant acoustic effects of these vocal tract adjustments, then, would be in the frequency range of 1200 to 2200 Hz. Much of this range is normally between the second and third formants for vowels.

3.6.4 Effects of Coupling to the Subglottal Cavities

As we have seen above, the acoustic properties of the main airway from the glottis to the mouth opening can be modified by opening the velopharyngeal port and providing acoustic coupling to this side branch of the vocal tract. Another acoustic system that is located adjacent to the vocal tract is the configuration of airways consisting of the trachea, bronchi, and lungs. The acoustic impedance looking into the trachea at a point just below the glottis is characterized by a series of poles and zeros much like the impedance looking upward into the vocal tract. One difference is that the config-

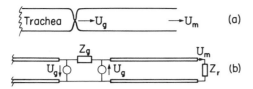

Figure 3.50 (a) Model of vocal tract with acoustic coupling to the trachea through the glottis. Volume velocity through the glottis is U_g. (b) Equivalent circuit showing volume velocity sources exciting supra- and subglottal tracts.

uration of the subglottal system is essentially fixed, and hence the poles and zeros of the impedance for a given individual are fixed. The lowest three poles have been observed to be about 600, 1550, and 2200 Hz for an adult male with bandwidths that are in the range of 200 to 400 Hz (Fant et al., 1972; Ishizaka et al., 1976; Cranen and Boves, 1987; Klatt and Klatt, 1990). These are the three lowest natural frequencies of the subglottal system with closed glottis. These frequencies are generally higher for female speakers, and can show individual differences from one speaker to another.

The subglottal system can influence the sound output from the mouth opening only when the glottis is open. When there is normal vocal fold vibration, acoustic coupling to the subglottal cavities can occur periodically during the open phase of the glottal cycle. The coupling is continuous when the glottis (or portions of the glottis) remains open, as it often does during the production of voiceless sounds or when there is breathy voicing.

In section 2.1 we showed that the glottal source during normal vocal fold vibration can be approximated by a volume velocity source. The impedance of this source is roughly equal to the impedance of the glottal opening, which for many glottal configurations is large compared with the impedance of the subglottal and the supraglottal cavities. The subglottal cavities are also excited by a volume velocity source that is equal and opposite to the source for the supraglottal cavities. The configuration is schematized in figure 3.50a, and an equivalent circuit is given in figure 3.50b.

If the impedance Z_g of the glottis is large compared with the impedance of the supraglottal and subglottal airways, then the excitation of the vocal tract above the glottis is essentially the right-hand volume velocity source. When there is a finite glottal opening, then at frequencies for which the subglottal impedance is infinite, no volume velocity will flow into the vocal tract. That is, there will be zeros in the transfer function U_m/U_g at these frequencies, which are the natural frequencies of the subglottal system when the glottis is closed. The poles of the configuration in figure 3.50a are at frequencies that are roughly equal to the natural frequencies of the separate subglottal and supraglottal configurations. These natural frequencies are shifted slightly from their values for the uncoupled system because there is some coupling between the two parts. The zeros in the transfer function will be close to the poles representing the natural frequencies of the subglottal airways. The

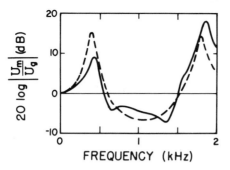

Figure 3.51 The solid line gives the magnitude of the transfer function of the vocal tract including the effect of acoustic coupling to the subglottal system. The dashed line shows the transfer function when there is no coupling to the subglottal cavities. See text.

spacing between the members of the pole-zero pair will depend in part on the cross-sectional area of the glottal opening.

In order to illustrate the effect of subglottal coupling on the transfer function U_m/U_g in figure 3.50, calculations have been made for a particular set of dimensions corresponding to an adult male vocal tract with a cross-sectional area of the glottal opening of 0.1 cm^2. The bandwidths of the zeros are taken to be 200 Hz, and calculations of the bandwidths for the poles take account of the losses due to airflow at the glottis. The calculated transfer function is shown in figure 3.51, together with the transfer function with no coupling to the subglottal cavities. A vocal ract shape with the first three natural frequencies equal to 400, 1800, and 2500 Hz is selected as the starting point with no subglottal coupling. In this example, there are perturbations in the transfer function of about ± 3 dB as a consequence of the subglottal coupling. The magnitude of these perturbations depends not only on the glottal opening but also on the supraglottal configuration. Further discussion of the influence of subglottal resonances on vowel spectra is given in section 6.8.

We have shown in figure 3.35 the calculated spectrum for an aspirated sound neglecting the effect of subglottal resonances. A more accurate estimate of the spectrum can be obtained by including the influence of the pole-zero pairs arising from coupling to the subglottal cavities. The principal modification of the spectrum is in the vicinity of the second and third subglottal resonances, since there is very little spectral energy in the vicinity of $F1$.

In summary, then, we observe that acoustic coupling to the subglottal cavities can modify the spectrum of the sound output from the vocal tract by introducing perturbations in the vicinity of the subglottal resonances. The amount of perturbation depends upon the size of the glottal opening. The overall effect of this coupling is to produce a sound in which the principal spectral peaks are less prominent, since additional peaks and valleys are superimposed on the spectrum.

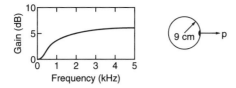

Figure 3.52 Ratio of the sound pressure (in the far field) for a point source located on the surface of a sphere (shown at right) to the sound pressure for the same source in the absence of the sphere. The radius of the sphere is 9 cm, approximating an adult human head. Sound pressure is measured on the axis through the center of the sphere and the source.

3.7 RADIATION OF SOUND FROM THE VOCAL TRACT

3.7.1 Radiation from the Mouth Opening

The principal opening from which sound is radiated during speech production is the mouth opening. Estimates of the sound pressure at a distance from the lips can be made by approximating the mouth opening by a small piston in a sphere. The radius of the sphere, representing the head, is about 9 cm for an adult, and the area of the piston depends, of course, on the size of the mouth opening, which is usually smaller than 4 cm². At low frequencies, for which the circumference of the sphere is smaller than, say, half of a wavelength (i.e., less than about 300 Hz), the radiation from the mouth opening is approximately the same as that from a simple source. If the volume velocity of the piston is U_o, the sound pressure p_r at a distance r from the piston in this low-frequency range is given by

$$p_r = \frac{j\omega\rho U_o}{4\pi r} e^{-jkr}, \tag{3.71}$$

as we have seen before in equation (3.2), where $k = \omega/c$ and $\omega = 2\pi f$. In this low-frequency range, p_r is independent of angle, and is dependent only on the distance r. In our calculations of the radiated sound pressure for various resonator configurations and sources up to this point, we have assumed that the radiation characteristic has this form. That is, we have assumed that p_r/U_o is proportional to ω.

At higher frequencies, the radiated sound pressure deviates somewhat from equation (3.71), and is dependent on the angle from the midline of the piston. The difference between the actual sound pressure on the midline and the sound pressure calculated on the assumption of a nondirectional simple source is shown as a function of frequency in figure 3.52. For these calculations the source on the sphere is assumed to be a point source (Morse, 1948). Above about 300 Hz, this function increases gradually to about 5 dB at 2 kHz and remains approximately fixed for higher frequencies. Typical plots of the sound pressure level vs. angle from the midline for two frequencies in this range are shown in figure 3.53. Measurements of this type for a more

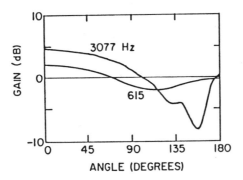

Figure 3.53 Sound pressure level at a distance from a point source in a sphere (radius 9 cm) as a function of angle from the midline, relative to level from a nondirectional source with the same strength. Calculations are given for two different frequencies.

realistic model of the human head and body show similar trends, but with some differences in the detailed shapes of the curves (Flanagan, 1972).

In addition to sound radiation from the mouth opening, there is radiation from the nose during the production of sounds for which the velopharyngeal port is open. The nostrils are sufficiently close to the mouth opening that radiation from the combination of nose and mouth can be approximated by radiation from a source for which the volume velocity is the sum of the volume velocities at the mouth opening and at the nostrils.

3.7.2 Radiation from the Walls of the Vocal Tract

In section 3.4 we observed that the vocal tract walls cannot be considered to be hard surfaces, particularly at low frequencies, and that the impedance of the walls can influence the acoustic behavior of the vocal tract. Another consequence of the yielding walls is that sound is transmitted through the tissue and is radiated from the outer surfaces of the head and neck.

Above about 100 Hz, the impedance of the walls can be represented by an acoustic mass in series with a resistance, as discussed earlier in section 3.4. When the vocal tract is somewhat constricted, so that it can be represented as a Helmholtz resonator at low frequencies (up to and including the frequency of the first formant), the equivalent circuit of the system with a glottal source can be represented as in figure 3.54. The volume velocity U_m is responsible for radiation from the mouth opening, and U_w represents the volume velocity of the surfaces of the vocal tract. Presumably some fraction of U_w gives rise to a volume velocity U_a on the outer surfaces of the head and neck, as a consequence of transmission through the tissue. It is estimated that $U_a \cong U_w/3$, based in part on measurement of the amplitude of the sound during a voiced stop consonant for which all of the sound output comes from U_a. In effect, we assume that the bony structures that partially surround the vocal tract block the transmission of vibrations to the outer surfaces of the head and neck. The relative contributions of U_m and U_a to

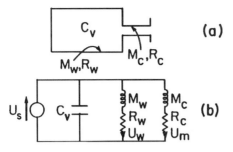

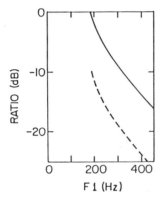

Figure 3.54 (a) Helmholtz resonator approximating vocal tract shape when there is a constriction in the anterior part of the tract. (b) Low-frequency equivalent circuit for resonator in (a), showing the two volume velocities U_m and U_w.

Figure 3.55 Solid line shows ratio of volume velocity U_w of vocal tract walls to total volume velocity $U_m + U_w$ (in figure 3.54b), in decibels, as the natural frequency $F1$ of the resonator is changed by manipulating the size of the constriction (i.e., by decreasing M_c in figure 3.54b). Dashed line is estimate of ratio of volume velocity U_a of the outer walls of the face and neck to total volume velocity $U_m + U_w$, in decibels, assuming $U_a \cong (1/3)U_w$.

the radiated sound pressure depend on the magnitude of M_c (the acoustic mass of the constriction) in relation to M_w (the effective acoustic mass of the vocal tract walls). (The resistances R_w and R_c are assumed to be small compared with the impedances of the acoustic masses.)

As we have seen in section 3.4, when M_c is infinite (i.e., when there is complete closure of the vocal tract), the natural frequency $F1$ of the combination of M_w and C_v is about 190 Hz for an adult. For this condition, if the vocal folds continue to vibrate and glottal pulses continue to be generated, all of the radiated sound is a consequence of U_a, that is, the sound is radiated from the surfaces of the head and neck. As the area of the mouth opening is increased, the natural frequency $F1$ of the system increases, the contribution of U_m to the radiated sound pressure increases, and the contribution of U_a decreases. The difference between the total output and the contribution from U_a (in decibels) increases at about 12 dB per doubling of the frequency $F1$ above 190 Hz. This difference is plotted in figure 3.55. Thus, for example, when $F1 = 300$ Hz, the value of U_w is about 8 dB below the total volume flow $U_w + U_m$, and, if we assume $U_a = U_w/3$, then the contribution of neck radiation is about 18 dB below the contribution from U_m. We assume that the shape of the glottal pulses does not change with constriction size. If there is a change in the glottal pulse as the constriction size decreases, as indicated in section 2.1.7, then there will be a further change in the amplitude of the spectrum envelope as the formant frequency decreases.

In any event, figure 3.55 shows that when $F1$ is below about 300 Hz, the sound radiated from the head and neck surfaces can make a significant contribution to the overall sound pressure at a distance from the mouth opening. The relative contribution of the sound radiated from the neck will be smaller if the sound pressure is observed close to the lips, such that the distance to the observation point from the lips is significantly less than the distance from the neck surfaces immediately above the larynx.

4 Auditory Processing of Speechlike Sounds

The processing of speech by a listener requires that the speech signal be interpreted in terms of a discrete linguistic representation consisting of sequences of words. As a first step in this processing, the speech waveform passes into the ear, where it is transformed first into mechanical movements of structures within the ear and then into electrical activity in the auditory nerve and in structures that are higher in the central nervous system. The manner in which speech or speechlike sounds are processed can be examined through physiological studies of neural signals at various levels in the auditory system, usually with animals, and through psychoacoustic studies of the responses of human listeners to sounds with speechlike properties.

In this chapter we review some findings in auditory physiology and psychoacoustics that have some relevance to the interpretation of the acoustic attributes of speech sounds. A discussion of the perception of vowel sounds, including potential auditory bases for vowel classification, is given in chapter 6.

4.1 AUDITORY PHYSIOLOGY

4.1.1 External and Middle Ear

Sound reaching a listener enters the ear canal and impinges on the eardrum, which forms the inner termination of the ear canal. A sketch of the ear canal and of the middle ear structures is given in figure 4.1. The length of the ear canal for an adult of average size is about 2.5 cm, and its diameter at the outer end is about 0.7 cm, with a cross-sectional area of 0.4 cm^2. The cross-sectional area becomes smaller toward the inner end, and the tympanic membrane at the inner end is oriented at a small angle relative to the midline, leading to a tapered termination over a length of about 0.8 cm.

The transfer function relating the sound pressure at the tympanic membrane to the free-field sound pressure that would exist at the head location is shown in figure 4.2 for several different angles of arrival of the sound (Shaw, 1974). The transfer function is close to unity (0 dB) at low frequencies, where the wavelength is large compared with the head size and the length of the ear canal. The head influences the transfer function at frequencies above about

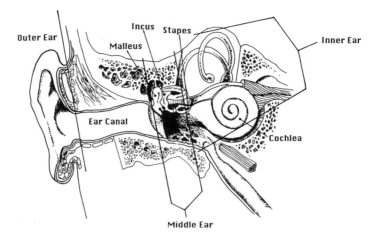

Figure 4.1 Sketch of the outer, middle, and inner ear. (From Berlin, 1994.)

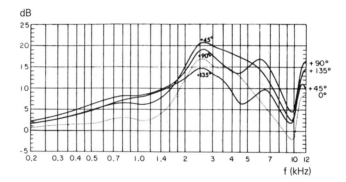

Figure 4.2 Ratio of the sound pressure at the tympanic membrane to the sound pressure that would exist (in the absence of the subject) at the point located at the center of the head, as a function of frequency for several values of azimuth of the source in the horizontal plane. Zero degrees azimuth is straight ahead, and 90 degrees azimuth is in line with the ears. (From Shaw 1974.)

500 Hz, and the detailed shape of the pinna has an effect at frequencies above about 4000 Hz. The first peak in the transfer function is at about 3000 Hz, representing the lowest resonance of the ear canal. The response at the peak is 15 to 20 dB greater than the response at low frequencies. The bandwidth of this peak is determined primarily by energy loss in the resistive component of the impedance of the tympanic membrane. There are additional peaks and valleys in the response at higher frequencies.

The sound pressure at the tympanic membrane provides the driving force that causes displacement of the membrane and, consequently, displacement of the malleus, which is the middle ear bone or ossicle that is attached to the tympanic membrane. The positions of the malleus and the other ossicles are shown in figure 4.1. The displacement of the malleus is transmitted through two additional small middle ear bones, the incus and the stapes, to provide

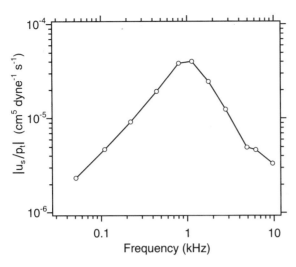

Figure 4.3 Transfer function of the middle ear, expressed as the ratio of the volume velocity at the stapes to the sound pressure at the tympanic membrane. (Data from Kringlebotn and Gundersen, 1985.)

mechanical excitation of the fluids within the inner ear. The transfer function relating the volume velocity U_s at the stapes to the sound pressure p_T at the tympanic membrane is displayed in figure 4.3. This transfer function has a broad peak at about 1 kHz (Kringlebotn and Gundersen, 1985). At 1 kHz, the volume velocity at the stapes for a sound pressure of 1 dyne/cm² at the tympanic membrane is about 4×10^{-5} cm³/s, which corresponds to a displacement amplitude of about 2×10^{-7} mm.

The middle ear structures contain small muscles which, when contracted, can modify the transfer function of the middle ear. There is a reflex mechanism whereby these muscles are contracted when the sound pressure at the ear exceeds about 90 dB re 0.0002 dyne/cm². The effect of this contraction of the middle ear muscles is to decrease the magnitude of the transfer function by about 10 dB over the frequency range below about 1 kHz when the sound pressure level (SPL) is about 110 dB re 0.0002 dyne/cm² (Rabinowitz, 1977). This reflex mechanism helps to protect the inner ear against the effects of high-intensity sound. When a listener is exposed to the speech of other talkers, the SPL is usually less than the level that brings into play the middle ear muscles. However, the level of one's own speech at the ear is often high enough to trigger this middle ear reflex.

4.1.2 Cochlear Mechanics

As shown in figure 4.1, the endplate of the stapes is coupled to the cochlea, which is a liquid-filled channel with a length of about 35 mm and an effective diameter in the range of 1.3 to 2.2 mm. The cochlear channel takes the form of a spiral, with about two and one-half turns. The representation of the

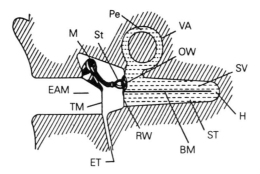

Figure 4.4 Schematic representation of the ear in a longitudinal section, with the cochlea "unrolled" to form a straight channel. OW, oval window; RW, round window; BM, basilar membrane; TM, tympanic membrane; ET, eustachian tube; SV, scala vestibuli; ST, scala tympani; H, helicotrema; EAM, external auditory meatus; M, malleus; St, stapes; VA, vestibular apparatus; Pe, perilymph. (Adapted from von Békésy and Rosenblith, 1951.)

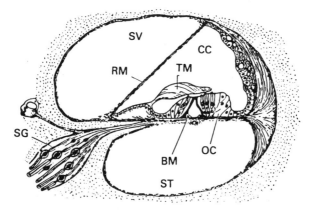

Figure 4.5 Section through the cochlear duct showing structures that form the cochlear partition. SV, scala vestibuli; ST, scala tympani; BM, basilar membrane; CC, cochlear channel (scala media); TM, tectorial membrane; RM, Reissner's membrane; OC, organ of Corti; SG, spiral ganglion. (Adapted from Davis, 1951.)

cochlea as a liquid-filled channel divided by a partition is shown schematically in figure 4.4, in which the cochlea is "unrolled" into a straight channel. The cochlea is divided into two main parts along its length by a flexible partition. The stapes is coupled to the end of one of these chambers (the scala vestibuli) through an opening called the oval window, and adjacent to this opening, at the end of the other chamber (the scala tympani), is an opening covered by a flexible membrane, called the round window. The round and oval windows are located at the base of the spiral, and there is a small opening between the two scalae at the apex of the spiral.

The partition that divides the cochlear channel, shown in figure 4.5, consists of two membranes: the basilar membrane on which an array of sensory cells is located, and Reissner's membrane, which is thinner and more delicate

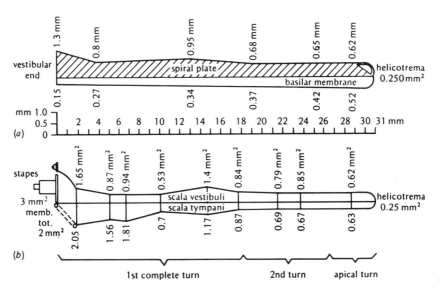

Figure 4.6 Schematic diagrams showing the dimensions of the basilar membrane (top) and of the scalae of the human cochlea (bottom). (Adapted from Fletcher, 1953, by Yost and Nielson, 1977.)

than the basilar membrane. These two membranes form a triangularly shaped liquid-filled enclosed space, called the scala media, and the sensory cells on the basilar membrane lie within this space. The physical properties of the basilar membrane vary with position along its length. A thin spiral plate of bone projects into the cochlear channel, and forms a portion of the partition dividing the channel. Some of the relevant dimensions of the scala, the basilar membrane, and the spiral plate are given in figure 4.6. The basilar membrane is wider and more compliant at its apical end, and is narrower and stiffer at the basal end.

When the cochlea is driven with a sinusoidal displacement at the oval window, the basilar membrane oscillates normal to its length, and the amplitude of these oscillations is greatest over one region along the length. Changing the frequency of the input signal changes the point on the basilar membrane at which the amplitude of motion is a maximum. For high frequencies, the point of maximum amplitude is near the base, and for low frequencies it is nearer to the apex. Examples of measurements of the amplitude of vibration as a function of position along the basilar membrane near the apical end for several different frequencies are given in figure 4.7. This figure shows that, for a given input frequency, there is some motion of the partition in the region between the base and the place where there is a peak in response, whereas the amplitude drops rapidly to essentially zero a short distance beyond the point of maximum excitation. Thus if one examines the amplitude of motion of the basilar membrane at a particular point as the frequency is changed, one observes a maximum at a particular frequency, a rapid drop in response above this frequency, and a more gradual decrease

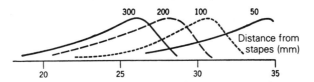

Figure 4.7 Relative amplitude of vibration along the cochlear partition for several frequencies of a sinusoidal stimulus (in hertz), as shown. (From von Békésy and Rosenblith, 1951.)

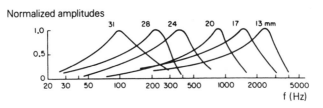

Figure 4.8 Frequency response for the amplitude measured at six places along the basilar membrane. The distance from the stapes is indicated on each frequency-response curve, and the amplitudes are normalized to have unity value at the peak. (From von Békésy and Rosenblith, 1951.)

in response for frequencies below the frequency at which the response is a maximum. Examples of the frequency response measured in this way are given in figure 4.8.

While the response patterns shown in figures 4.7 and 4.8 illustrate the gross patterns of basilar membrane motion as a function of frequency, more detailed studies of cochlear mechanics have demonstrated the presence of nonlinearities in the responses. Apparently some of the sensory cells on the cochlear partition change their mechanical properties with increased level of stimulation, and these changes are believed to cause a compression in the mechanical response at frequencies near resonance (Allen and Neely, 1992).

When a brief transient excitation is applied at the oval window, there is a time delay before the displacement of the basilar membrane at a particular point along its length occurs, depending on the distance along the cochlea. The maximum time delay, for a point close to the apical end, is about 3 ms. For points near the base, corresponding to high-frequency components of the signal above, say, 1000 Hz, the delay is less than 1.0 ms.

The mechanism whereby motion of the stapes at a given frequency is transferred into motion of a localized region of the basilar membrane is discussed in detail in a number of publications (von Békésy, 1960; Peterson and Bogert, 1950; Zwislocki, 1950). A few general comments will be made here, however, to indicate the main features of this mechanical process. In the frequency range of interest for hearing, the fluid in the cochlea can be considered to be incompressible. That is, wave motion in the fluid does not play a role in the mechanical process. As described above, the mechanical properties of the basilar membrane vary with position along its length. An element of length of the basilar membrane can be characterized by a stiffness, mass,

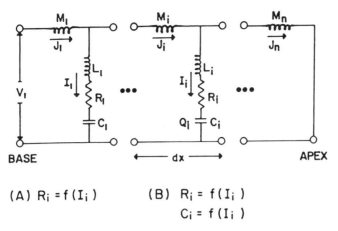

(A) $R_i = f(I_i)$ **(B)** $R_i = f(I_i)$
                                      $C_i = f(I_i)$

Figure 4.9 Equivalent circuit of an n-section transmission-line model of the cochlear partition. Some of the components of the model are nonlinear. The final section at the apex is at the right. (From Furst and Goldstein, 1982.)

and resistance, and an element of the cochlear fluid can be modeled as a mechanical mass. Thus the cochlea forms a nonuniform transmission line that can be approximated by a series of lumped elements, as shown in figure 4.9 (Peterson and Bogert, 1950; Schroeder, 1973; Hall, 1974; Furst and Goldstein, 1982). The resistance, inductance, and capacitance elements that form the parallel path are tuned to different frequencies, with the highest frequency (corresponding to the smallest mass and smallest compliance) at the basal end, and the lowest frequency (largest mass and compliance) at the apical end. As the figure shows, the resistance and compliance elements in the shunt branches are nonlinear.

For a given frequency at the input, one of the parallel paths will have a resistive impedance, and this path will have a large current (corresponding to a large velocity at this point along the basilar membrane). The parallel paths to the right of this point all have resonant frequencies that are below the driving frequency, and hence at this frequency they all have inductive impedances. Thus in this region of the model there is an inductive ladder network, and a rapid decrease in amplitude with increasing distance along the line. In effect, propagation to the right of the point of resonance is evanescent. To the left of the point of resonance, the parallel paths can be approximated by capacitances, C, with smaller values of C at the input end. Consequently in this region for this frequency we have a nonuniform transmission line terminated in a small resistance. The velocity of propagation of a disturbance gradually decreases as one proceeds along the line. There will be a standing wave on the line with a maximum velocity at the point of resonance and a gradually decreasing velocity for points to the left of this maximum. As the frequency of the input is increased or decreased, the point of resonance moves to the left or to the right on the line.

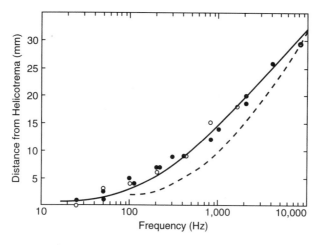

Figure 4.10 Relation between frequency and the point at which there is maximum response of the basilar membrane for the human cochlea. The dots are based on measurements made by von Békésy (1960) (solid dots) and on a study from which hearing loss and cochlear damage in pathological ears were correlated (Zwislocki, 1965) (open dots). The solid line is the mathematically calculated location of the vibration maximum, based on a cochlear model. The dashed line represents a pitch scale derived from psychophysical methods. (From Zwislocki, 1981.)

The relation between the frequency and the point at which there is maximum response of the basilar membrane for the human cochlea is shown in figure 4.10 (von Békésy, 1960; Zwislocki, 1981). This function indicates a roughly linear relation between frequency and position up to about 500 Hz, and then a gradual transition to a logarithmic relation. The midpoint along the cochlea corresponds to a frequency of about 1700 Hz.

This description gives a qualitative view of the behavior of the cochlea at different frequencies, at least over a substantial part of the frequency range. From this general description, one can conclude that when a sound impinges on the ear, the spectrum of the sound is translated into a distribution of amplitudes of motion along the basilar membrane.

When a narrow acoustic pulse or click is applied at the stapes, there is a transient displacement of the basilar membrane at all points along its length. As noted earlier, the initiation of this displacement is delayed by 2 to 3 ms toward the apex of the cochlea. At any one point along the basilar membrane, the response to the click is a damped oscillation with a frequency about equal to the frequency of a sinusoid that gives maximum displacement at that point. The time constant of the decay of the envelope of the oscillation is roughly proportional to the reciprocal of the bandwidth of the frequency response measured at this point, that is, the bandwidth of a response function like that shown in figure 4.8. Since the bandwidth of the response increases toward the basal end of the cochlea, the rate of decay of the response of the basilar membrane is more rapid.

The higher-frequency basal end of the cochlea provides the fine time resolution (but broader frequency resolution) necessary for the analysis of cer-

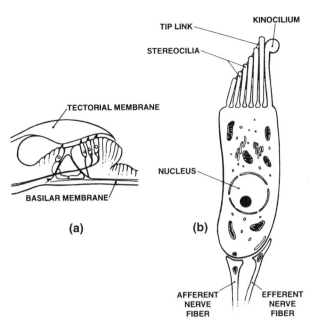

Figure 4.11 (a) The arrangement of inner and outer hair cells on the basilar membrane, and the configuration of the tectorial membrane. (b) A schematic representation of a hair cell. (From Hudspeth and Markin, 1994.)

tain consonants with rapidly time-varying properties. (These properties are discussed in chapters 7 to 9.) On the other hand, the finer frequency resolution at the low-frequency apical end is appropriate for extracting relevant acoustic properties for slowly varying signals such as vowels and glides, for which fine time resolution is not necessary.

A series of sensory cells are located within the organ of Corti, which lies on the surface of the basilar membrane within the scala media, as shown in figure 4.5. These cells consist of three or four closely spaced rows of outer hair cells and a nearby single row of inner hair cells. It is estimated that there are about 12,000 outer hair cells and about 3500 inner hair cells, spaced more or less uniformly along the length of the basilar membrane. The arrangement of these cells on the basilar membrane is shown in figure 4.11a. The hair cells, one of which is schematized in figure 4.11b, take the form of vertically oriented cylinders about 5 Å in diameter and 20 to 50 Å in length. A number of small hairs or stereocilia (about 100 per outer hair cell and about 50 per inner hair cell) project out of the upper surface of each cylinder, the length of each cilium being 2 to 6 Å. A soft ribbon-like structure called the tectorial membrane makes contact with the tallest row of cilia of the outer hair cells.

About 30,000 nerve fibers innervate the hair cells. The large majority of these are sensory nerves or afferent fibers that carry information from the sensory cells to the brain. Most of these fibers innervate the inner hair cells, with an average of about eight fibers for each hair cell. Some afferent fibers also innervate the outer hair cells, as shown in figure 4.11b.

The hair cells are polarized with a voltage of about −70 mV in their rest condition. Displacement of the basilar membrane causes deflection of the cilia on the hair cells through contact with the tectorial membrane. One direction of deflection causes a depolarization of the cells, whereas the other direction causes an increase in polarization. Depolarization of a hair cell favors the generation of a voltage spike on the nerve fiber that innervates the hair cell, whereas hyperpolarization inhibits the generation of a spike. Thus when there is mechanical displacement of some portion of the basilar membrane, there is an increased firing rate of the neurons that innervate the hair cells located in that region. The nerve fibers tend to fire at times when the basilar membrane is displaced in one direction.

There is a much smaller number of efferent fibers that carry information from higher levels of the auditory system primarily to the outer hair cells. The function of these efferent fibers is to inhibit auditory nerve responses over a wide range of sound levels. The role of efferent fibers in shaping the pattern of auditory nerve responses to complex stimuli is not yet well understood, but it is thought that they give rise to mechanical amplification and to sharpening of the frequency resolution (Hudspeth and Markin, 1994; see also Guinan, 1988). The existence of this sharpening process suggests that certain details in the response curves of the kind shown in figures 4.7 and 4.8 should be revised.

The connections in the auditory pathways above the level of the auditory nerve are displayed schematically in figure 4.12. As the figure shows, the signals in the auditory nerve undergo a complex series of processing steps via the cochlear nucleus, which has several components; the components of the superior olivary complex; the inferior colliculus; the medial geniculate body; and the cortex. Efferent pathways are not shown in this figure.

4.1.3 Basic Auditory Nerve Responses

The responses of an individual fiber of the auditory nerve to various kinds of acoustic stimulation can be described in terms of the discharge rate and the temporal pattern of discharges on the fiber in relation to the characteristics of the stimulus. The response of a particular fiber is stochastic in the sense that the pattern of discharges is related in a probabilistic fashion to the characteristics of the stimulus. When there is no acoustic stimulation, most fibers exhibit a spontaneous response, and different fibers may have different spontaneous rates. These spontaneous rates vary from 0 to more than 100 spikes per second for different fibers, although for most fibers the rates are in the narrower range of 40 to 80 spikes per second (Liberman, 1978). The distribution of the time intervals between spikes for the spontaneous activity in a typical auditory nerve fiber is approximately a Poisson distribution, except that there is a minimum interspike interval, indicating that after a nerve fiber fires there is a refractory period in which another firing cannot occur.

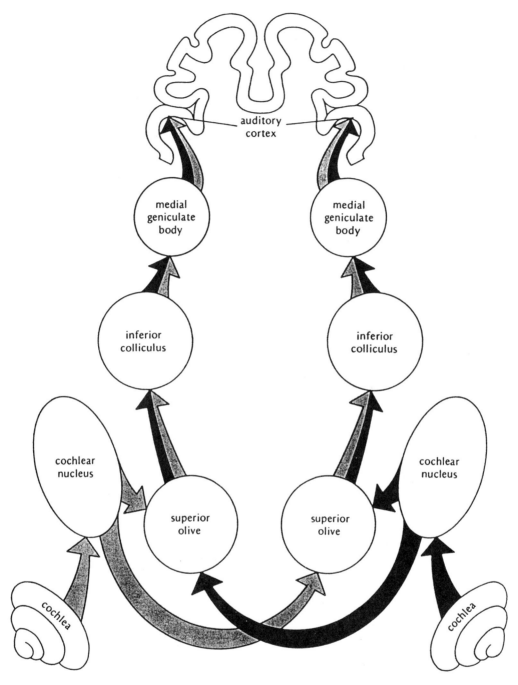

Figure 4.12 A schematic diagram of the bilateral central ascending afferent auditory pathways. (From Yost and Nielson, 1977, based on a similar diagram by Lindsay and Norman, 1972.)

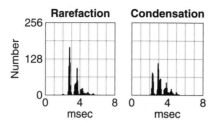

Figure 4.13 Example of a poststimulus time (PST) histogram of the spikes in response to a click. The PST histogram is obtained by observing the times of occurrence of spikes following many presentations of the click, and accumulating these occurrences in each of a number of time bins. Data are given for two polarities of the click, and show the shift in the time of the response. The characteristic frequency of the fiber is 1.65 kHz. (From Kiang et al., 1965.)

When an acoustic impulse or click is applied at the ear, we have seen that the displacement of the basilar membrane at a particular point has the form of a damped sinusoid. We have also observed that the depolarization of the hair cell that favors the initiation of a spike occurs for only one direction of the displacement of the basilar membrane. A consequence of this property is that, following presentation of a click, there are some time intervals when generation of a spike is enhanced and other time intervals when it is inhibited. The poststimulus time (PST) histograms in figure 4.13 illustrate this pattern of response. This display is obtained by presenting the click many times, and, for each repetition, measuring the time from the click onset to the spikes that occur subsequent to the click. These times are quantized into narrow intervals or bins, and the number of spikes occurring in each of these bins after a large number of repetitions of the click is accumulated. The ordinate in figure 4.13 gives this number and the abscissa is the time following presentation of the click.

The figure shows that the spikes tend to concentrate in particular time intervals following the click, and tend to be sparse in the intermediate times. The time interval between peaks in the histogram for a given auditory nerve fiber corresponds to the resonant frequency of the point on the basilar membrane where the hair cells are innervated by that nerve fiber. If the click is reversed in polarity, the spikes now concentrate in the regions that were sparse for the opposite polarity, as shown in figure 4.13. If recordings are obtained from another fiber, a different periodicity is obtained in the PST histogram, but otherwise the pattern of response is similar. This is the expected behavior, and supports the concepts that different points along the basilar membrane are tuned to different frequencies and that the generation of spikes is facilitated for one direction of motion of the hair cell and inhibited for the other.

When a pure tone is applied at the stapes, there is an increase in the discharge rate for fibers that have connections to regions of the cochlear partition that respond maximally to this frequency. For a given fiber, there is a frequency for which there is a maximum in the discharge rate. A "tuning

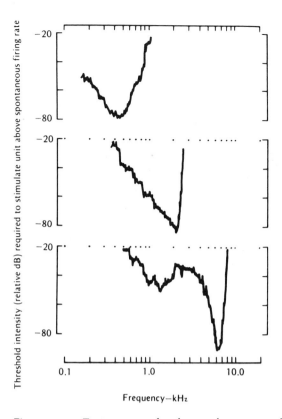

Figure 4.14 Tuning curves for three auditory nerve fibers with different characteristic frequencies. The level of the stimulus needed to reach the threshold of the unit is plotted as a function of the frequency of the stimulus. (After Kiang and Moxon, 1972.)

curve" can be specified, giving, for each frequency of a sinusoidal stimulus, the amplitude of the stimulus that gives rise to a given increase in response rate over the spontaneous rate. Examples of tuning curves for auditory nerve fibers in a cat are shown in figure 4.14. Associated with each fiber there is a *characteristic frequency*, which is the frequency to which the fiber is most sensitive, that is, the frequency with the lowest threshold on the tuning curve. The tuning curves have sharply increasing slopes at frequencies above the characteristic frequencies, particularly for the higher-frequency fibers. For low frequencies, the widths of the tuning curves (on a logarithmic frequency scale) are considerably greater than at high frequencies. The low-frequency sides of the tuning curves for higher characteristic frequencies have "tails," indicating that a fiber with a given characteristic frequency responds to sinusoids with lower frequencies if the levels of these tones are sufficiently high (Kiang and Moxon, 1974).

On a linear frequency scale, the widths of the tuning curves are relatively narrow at low frequencies, and become increasingly greater at high frequencies. This change in frequency resolution with increasing frequency is similar to the changes observed in the mechanical response of the basilar membrane.

The region above the tuning curve for a particular fiber is the response region for that fiber, that is, for stimuli with amplitudes and frequencies in this region, the firing rate of the auditory nerve fiber is above the spontaneous rate. When a second tone is presented simultaneously with the first (primary) tone, there can be an interaction such that the presence of the second tone inhibits the response to the primary tone (Sachs and Kiang, 1968). The frequency and amplitude of the second tone that causes this inhibition in a region is generally outside the V-shaped response region for the fiber. That is, the second tone is in a region that would not produce a response of the fiber if it were presented alone. This two-tone inhibition phenomenon shows that caution should be used in inferring the response of an auditory nerve fiber to a complex stimulus based on examination of the responses to single tones.

If the average discharge rate is measured for a pure tone stimulus at the characteristic frequency (CF) as the amplitude of the stimulus is increased, rate level curves of the type shown in figure 4.15 are obtained. These functions indicate that saturation occurs when the level is about 30 to 40 dB above the threshold for the fiber. For some fibers, saturation is not complete, and the rate level curve has a knee where the curve continues to rise but at a decreased slope (Sachs and Abbas, 1974). As the figure shows, fibers with different spontaneous rates (i.e., the rates for low stimulus levels) respond over different ranges of levels from threshold to saturation.

The data in figure 4.15 represent the average response rates for steady-state stimuli. When a stimulus is turned on abruptly, there is an increase in

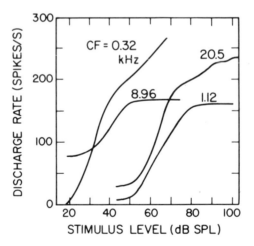

Figure 4.15 Discharge rate vs. stimulus level for four fibers from different cats. Stimulus frequency is the characteristic frequency (CF) for the fiber, and is shown (in kilohertz) beside each curve. The curves illustrate a variety of shapes, spontaneous rates, and stimulus ranges. (From Sachs and Abbas, 1974.)

the response rate above this average rate for a time interval immediately following the onset of the stimulus. When the stimulus is turned off abruptly, there is a decrease in the spontaneous rate immediately following cessation of the stimulus. This response pattern is illustrated in figure 4.16. This figure is a PST histogram for a particular fiber at its characteristic frequency, where the stimulus time is defined as the onset of the stimulus. The response rate immediately following stimulus onset is much greater than the steady response, and this onset effect is greater for higher levels of the stimulus. There is an immediate rapid adaptation within approximately the first 5 ms, followed by a continuing slower adaptation with a time constant of about 40 ms. Data for longer stimuli show that there continues to be a small amount of adaptation even beyond 100 ms after stimulus onset. Rate level functions measured in the few milliseconds following stimulus onset show a much greater dynamic range than do those observed for the steady-state response.

Figure 4.16 shows that there is a time interval of several tens of milliseconls after stimulus offset before the spontaneous rate returns to its average long-term rate in the absence of stimulation. Other experiments have shown that the response of auditory nerve fibers to a brief tone can be influenced by a preceding stimulus. An example is given in figure 4.17. An adapting tone of 200-ms duration is followed after 60 ms by a brief test tone with a duration of 20 ms. A PST histogram is obtained from responses to an auditory nerve for different intensities of the adapting tone. As the intensity of the adapting tone increases, the response to the test tone decreases significantly.

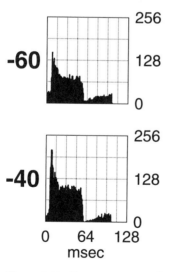

Figure 4.16 Response pattern of an auditory nerve unit to bursts of noise, for two levels of the stimulus, labeled as −60 and −40 dB. The burst duration is 50 ms, and the responses are displayed as poststimulus time histograms. Zero time of each histogram is 2.5 ms before the onset of the electrical input to the earphone. The spontaneous rate for the unit is about 50 on the vertical scale. (From Kiang et al., 1965.)

Auditory Processing of Speechlike Sounds

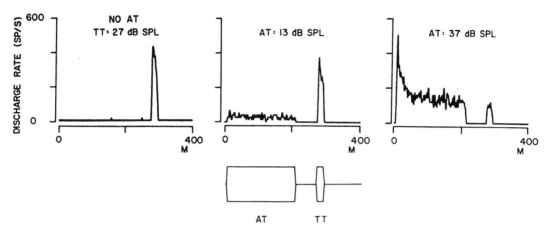

Figure 4.17 Poststimulus time histograms for an auditory nerve fiber in response to a test tone (TT) of duration 20 ms preceded by an adapting tone (AT) of duration 200 ms, with an interval between tones of 60 ms. The timing of AT and TT is shown at the bottom. The different panels show data for different levels of the adapting tone, with the test tone fixed at 27 dB SPL. (From Delgutte, 1980.)

When the response to a pure tone is above threshold, the individual spikes in the response are distributed in a way that shows a preference for firing at particular points in time in relation to individual cycles of the stimulus (Johnson, 1980). This synchrony can be represented by an interspike interval histogram which displays the probability that a particular interval occurs between responses of a fiber, as a function of the time interval. This synchrony with the period of the stimulus can be observed for low-frequency periodicities, but at higher stimulus frequencies, above about 3 kHz, there is a greatly reduced tendency for synchrony. When the stimulus is reversed in sign, the firings tend to occur at times that are displaced by half a period of the tone. This pattern of response is further evidence that nerve fibers tend to fire when the cochlear partition is displaced in one direction.

4.1.4 Auditory Nerve Responses to Speechlike Stimuli

We have reviewed some aspects of the pattern of responses of auditory nerve fibers to simple stimuli such as clicks and pure tones. These aspects include frequency selectivity, adaptation, dynamic range, and phase locking. These attributes can also be observed in the responses of auditory nerve fibers to more complex stimuli that have some of the characteristics of vowel and consonant sounds in speech.

The patterns of responses of auditory nerve fibers in cats to stimuli consisting of steady-state vowels have been examined by several investigators (Sachs and Young, 1979, 1980; Young and Sachs, 1979; Delgutte, 1980, 1984a,b; Delgutte and Kiang, 1984a). In a typical set of experiments, measurements of firing rate are obtained from a number of different fibers of the

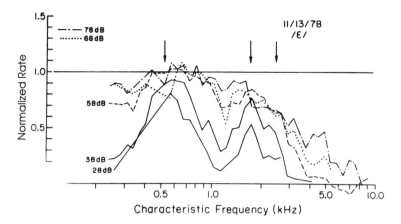

Figure 4.18 Illustrating the pattern of responses of auditory nerve fibers in cats to a steady-state vowel /ɛ/ presented at five different levels, as shown. The abscissa is the CF of the fiber. The ordinate is the rate of firing, normalized to the maximum rate for the fiber. Each curve is obtained by smoothing the data across fibers with different CFs. The arrows show the positions of the formant frequencies for the vowel. (From Sachs and Young, 1979.)

same animal when the stimulus is a steady-state vowel. For each fiber that is examined, the CF, the saturation rate, and the spontaneous rate are also measured. At relatively low levels of presentation for the vowel, fibers with CF near the first and second formant frequencies show greater response rates than other fibers. At higher SPL, however, there is saturation in the firing rate, and the formant pattern is less discernible in the firing rates of fibers with different CFs. An example of the results is shown in figure 4.18. The ordinate in this plot is a normalized firing rate, equal to the measured firing rate for the fiber expressed as a fraction of the range of firing rates (saturation rate minus spontaneous rate) for that fiber when tested with a sinusoidal stimulus at its CF. As the figure shows, there are peaks in the pattern when the CF is close to $F1$ and $F2$ (and sometimes $F3$) for low levels of the vowel stimulus, as indicated by the arrows. At higher levels, however, the formants no longer are evident as peaks in the pattern of responses.

Examination of the fine time patterns of discharge of the auditory nerve fibers reveals further detail about the spectral characteristics of vowel stimuli (Young and Sachs, 1979; Sachs and Young, 1980; Delgutte and Kiang, 1984a). Processing of the discharge patterns for a given auditory nerve fiber begins with the PST histogram of the response to a series of presentations of the vowel. This histogram shows a periodicity corresponding to the fundamental period of the vowel. Period histograms are then computed by adding together a series of periods of the PST histograms. The fine details of the period histograms reveal that some auditory nerve fibers tend to show synchrony not only with the fundamental period but also with the periods of $F1$ and $F2$. These details of the periodicities of firings become evident in the Fourier transform of the period histogram.

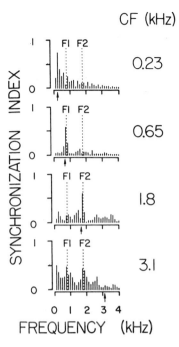

Figure 4.19 Harmonic spectra of period histograms illustrating how the auditory nerve fiber responses to vowels can show synchronization to the fundamental frequency and to the different formant frequencies for the vowel /æ/, as well as to the CF for the fiber. Data for nerve fibers with four different CFs are given. The frequencies F1 and F2 are marked above the harmonic spectra, and the arrows below these spectra indicate the CFs for the fibers. See text. (Adapted from Delgutte and Kiang, 1984a.)

Some examples, taken from Delgutte and Kiang (1984a), are given in figure 4.19. These are Fourier transforms of period histograms obtained from fibers with several different characteristic frequencies and for the two-formant steady-state vowel /æ/. The relative amplitude of a particular frequency component of this Fourier transform is a measure of the degree to which the firings of the auditory nerve fiber show synchrony with that frequency, and is called the synchronization index. The frequencies F1 and F2 of the vowels are indicated on the spectra. These transforms all have a fundamental frequency of 125 Hz, corresponding to the period of the vowel. Delgutte and Kiang pointed out several features of these spectra depending on the frequencies of the vowel formants and the characteristic frequencies of the fibers. For example, in figure 4.19 synchrony with F1 is evident for the vowel /æ/ for the fiber with a CF of 0.65 kHz. These and other data show that when the CF for a fiber is in the general vicinity of F1, synchrony with F1 occurs in the fiber. A similar statement can be made for F2: figure 4.19 shows synchrony with F2 for /æ/ at 1.8 kHz. On the other hand, the low-frequency (0.23 kHz) fiber shows synchrony with its own CF (as shown by the arrow at the bottom of each panel). For high CFs (3.1 kHz in this case),

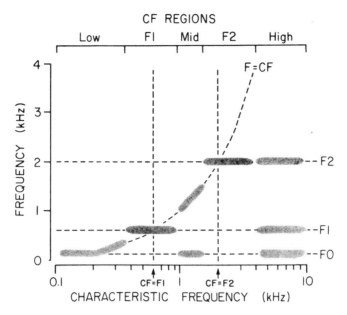

Figure 4.20 Schematic diagram showing five CF regions in which different synchronized response patterns of auditory nerve fibers are observed for vowels. The dashed lines show the positions of F0, F1, and F2 on the frequency axis, as well as the line $F = CF$. For purposes of exposition, the extents of different CF regions are greatly exaggerated, and not all regions are observed for any one vowel. (From Delgutte and Kiang, 1984a.)

synchrony with F0, F1, and F2 can be observed. In some cases, synchrony is observed with components that are products of nonlinearity, such as $2F1$ or $F2 - F1$. A similar general pattern of synchrony responses is observed over a range of stimulus amplitudes, in contrast to the response patterns based simply on average response rates.

Delgutte and Kiang summarize the synchronization responses with the schematic diagram in figure 4.20. This diagram shows the five CF regions that might exist for a hypothetical vowel with $F1 = 600$ Hz and $F2 = 2000$ Hz. In the low CF region, there is synchrony with F0 and some evidence for synchrony with CF. Synchrony with F1 and F2 occurs in the regions labeled as such. For CF between F1 and F2, there is synchrony with CF and F0. When the CF is in the high region, there is synchrony with F0, F1, and F2. Depending on the values of F1 and F2, some of these regions may be missing from the response pattern. As will be shown in chapter 6, these patterns of response provide some evidence for organizing vowels into different classes.

When the auditory input has a broadband spectrum with no major spectral prominences, it is expected that the dominant component of the PST histogram for each auditory nerve fiber response will be at the characteristic frequency for that fiber. That is, there is no spectral component of the PST histogram that is dominated by a peak in the spectrum of the stimulus. If the stimulus has only a broad spectral prominence at sufficiently high frequencies, above 3 to 4 kHz, there is again no dominant spectral component in the PST histogram, since there is greatly reduced synchrony of firing at these high frequencies. For this type of stimulus, then, different spectral shapes are represented by the pattern of average firing rates across fibers with different characteristic frequencies (Delgutte and Kiang, 1984b).

Figures 4.16 and 4.17 show that the pattern of response of auditory nerve fibers at a given time to an acoustic stimulus depends not only on the characteristics of the stimulus at that time but also on the context in which the stimulus occurs. During speech production, a particular acoustic pattern such as that corresponding to a vowel can be preceded by a variety of different patterns corresponding to different consonants. For example, the acoustic pattern following the initial burst in the syllable /da/ is similar to the acoustic pattern following the consonant release in syllables like /na/ and /ša/, and in a two-syllable utterance like /ada/.

Responses of auditory nerve fibers in cats to synthetic speechlike stimuli of this kind have been reported by Delgutte and Kiang (1984c). The stimuli were synthesized in such a way that the properties of the vowel and of the transitions of the formants after the consonant release were the same in all stimuli. Results showing the mean discharge rate during the time interval in which the formant transitions occurred are given in figure 4.21. Each point represents the discharge rate for one auditory nerve fiber, with the characteristic frequency of the fiber given on the abscissa. It is evident that the context that precedes the test interval has a significant influence on the response. For example, when the nasal consonant /n/ precedes the vowel, the responses of low-frequency fibers are depressed, because of adaptation by the low-frequency energy in this consonant. On the other hand, the consonant /š/ causes a decrease in responses of high-frequency fibers. When the responses of the fibers are analyzed in terms of synchronized response components (in a manner similar to that displayed in figure 4.19), the response pattern in the transition interval is not greatly affected by the preceding context.

Sinex and McDonald (1988) measured the discharge rate in chinchilla auditory nerve fibers in response to synthetic consonant-vowel stimuli containing stop consonants with different voice-onset times (such as /ga/ and /ka/). Their data showed that the patterns of average discharge rates for fibers with low CF were generally different depending on whether the voice-onset times were greater or less than 20 ms. For longer voice-onset times, there was an increase in average discharge rate at the onset of glottal vibration (as well as at consonant release), whereas for voice-onset times less than 20 ms changes in discharge rate were independent of voice-onset time.

The responses of auditory nerve fibers to consonant-vowel syllables were examined further in a series of studies carried out by Geisler and his colleagues (Carney and Geisler, 1986; Deng and Geisler, 1987; Silkes and Geisler, 1991;

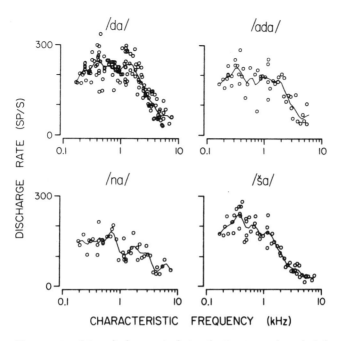

Figure 4.21 Mean discharge rate during the time interval in which formant transitions occurred in several consonant-vowel syllables (preceded in one case by an initial vowel), as indicated. The stimulus level is 75 dB SPL. The abscissa is the CF of the fiber, and each circle represents the average discharge rate for one fiber. The continuous lines represent band averages of the data. (From Delgutte and Kiang, 1984c.)

Geisler and Silkes, 1991). These investigators looked at differences in the response patterns of fibers with relatively high and relatively low spontaneous firing rates, and they observed the effects of noise on these patterns. The responses of the fibers were displayed as PST histograms and as Fourier transforms of PST histograms. In general, they observed robust synchrony of high-CF fibers to transitions in $F1$ and $F2$, particularly for fibers with high spontaneous rates. Fibers with low spontaneous rates appeared to preserve synchrony with formants more robustly when the syllables were mixed with noise (Silkes and Geisler, 1991). These fibers also showed strong synchronization with the fundamental period (Geisler and Silkes, 1991). These and other data suggest that both the high and the low spontaneous rate fibers have a role to play in the auditory representation of speech syllables depending on the noise conditions.

These few examples of auditory nerve responses to speechlike stimuli indicate that some acoustic attributes that help to signal a phonetic distinction are preserved and may be enhanced in the activity of auditory nerve fibers. However, special processing of the firings from groups of fibers are undoubtedly necessary at higher levels in the auditory pathways in order to extract the required distinctive properties.

4.2 BASIC AUDITORY PSYCHOPHYSICS

The study of audition through psychophysical methods has a long history, and a number of reviews of the field have been written (for example, Yost and Nielson, 1977; Green, 1976). We shall present here just a few of the results that are most directly related to an understanding of speech perception. The methods of auditory psychophysics will not be discussed in detail. We point out simply that there are standard experimental and analytical techniques for determining whether a listener can perceive that two stimuli are different, or, as a special case, can make a response that a stimulus is present in a particular time interval.

4.2.1 Absolute Thresholds for Tones

The minimum sound pressure of a tone that can be detected by a listener with normal hearing depends on the frequency of the tone. This absolute threshold of hearing for tones as a function of frequency is shown in figure 4.22. For this particular threshold curve, called minimum audible field (MAF), the ordinate is the sound pressure that would be measured at the position of the listener's head with the listener removed from the sound field, and with a plane wave incident from a direction in front of the listener. The threshold sound pressure increases as the frequency decreases below about 1 kHz. The minimum in the curve between 3 and 4 kHz is a consequence of the lowest resonance of the ear canal. The minimum is not as sharp as the resonance curve for an individual ear canal (see figure 4.2) because the threshold curve of figure 4.22 represents an average over a number of subjects, whose ear canals presumably have slightly different lengths and hence slightly different resonant frequencies. The threshold at very high frequencies rises very sharply, and the frequency at which this sharp rise occurs decreases with increasing age of the listener, on average. At 20 years of age, this cutoff frequency (which we define arbitrarily as the frequency at which the threshold

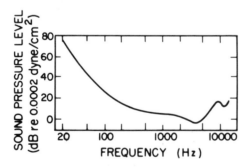

Figure 4.22 Absolute threshold for pure tones as a function of frequency for young listeners. The sound pressure level is the minimum audible field. See text.

SPL is 50 dB re 0.0002 dyne/cm²) is about 17 kHz, on average, whereas at 65 years it is about 8 kHz.

The threshold curve in figure 4.22 was obtained for tones with a duration of 500 ms or more. For durations in this range, the threshold is essentially independent of duration. When the duration is shorter, the threshold increases, but the duration at which this increase begins depends on frequency (about 400 ms at 500 Hz, and 200 ms for frequencies of 2 to 5 kHz). There are apparently substantial individual differences in the effect of duration in the range of 100 to 500 ms. When the duration is 100 ms or less, the threshold increases by about 3 dB for each halving of duration, that is, the threshold is determined by the total energy in the signal.

At the other end of the scale, the SPL of a sound can be increased to the point where it causes discomfort, tickle, or even pain to a listener. The levels at which listeners report discomfort is about 120 dB re 0.0002 dyne/cm², and tickle is reported at about 140 dB. These thresholds are relatively independent of frequency, at least in the range of 200 to 5000 Hz.

4.2.2 Loudness; Sensitivity to Changes in Amplitude or Spectrum

When the amplitude of a sound is increased, listeners judge the sound to be louder. It is possible for listeners to assign a numerical value or magnitude to the relative loudness of sounds presented at different intensities. The results from a series of experiments of this kind (S. S. Stevens, 1936) show that a power function is a good fit to the curve relating the assigned loudness value L and the intensity I of the sound, that is

$$L = KI^\alpha, \tag{4.1}$$

where K and α are constants. If the magnitude L is plotted on a log scale, then the relation between $\log L$ and the SPL is a straight line. The slope of this line is such that an increase in SPL of 10 dB corresponds to a doubling of loudness.

The loudness of a steady broadband noise is relatively independent of the duration of the sound when the duration exceeds about 60 to 70 ms, at least when the sound is heard at an SPL of 60 to 80 dB re 0.0002 dyne/cm². For shorter durations, the loudness is determined by the product of intensity and duration, that is, by the total energy in the signal (G. A. Miller, 1948).

Several studies have examined the sensitivity of listeners to change in the amplitude of a stimulus. In a typical experiment, a stimulus with root-mean-square (rms) sound pressure p is presented to a listener, immediately followed by a stimulus with rms sound pressure $p + \Delta p$. This pair of stimuli is preceded or followed by another pair in which both stimuli have a sound pressure of p. The task of the listener is to determine the pair in which the stimuli are different. The just noticeable difference (JND) is usually defined as the ratio $(p + \Delta p)/p$ for which a correct response is obtained 75 percent of the time. In decibels, the JND is $20 \log_{10}(p + \Delta p)/p$. Typical values of the JND in

Auditory Processing of Speechlike Sounds

amplitude for a pure tone or wide-band noise at amplitudes in the normal range for speech are in the range of 0.3 to 1.0 dB (Riesz, 1928; G. A. Miller, 1947). For tones the JND is slightly greater at low frequencies, and also increases somewhat at levels near threshold.

In the experiments summarized above, the stimuli were manipulated by changing the overall amplitude. For stimuli with more than one frequency component, or for broadband stimuli, experiments have been carried out to determine the sensitivity of listeners to changes in the amplitude of one part of the spectrum while leaving the amplitudes of the remaining spectral components unchanged. In general, the sensitivity to changes in spectrum amplitude over a limited portion of the frequency range is substantially poorer than the sensitivity to changes in the overall amplitude of the stimulus.

One experiment of this kind examined the sensitivity of listeners to changes in the amplitude of one spectral peak of a vowel while keeping all other spectral peaks fixed (Flanagan, 1957). A typical result, in which the discrimination of the amplitude of the second-formant peak was determined for a vowel having equally spaced formants, showed that the JND in $F2$ amplitude was about 3 dB—considerably greater than the JND for overall amplitude noted above.

The sensitivity of listeners has also been determined for changes in the bandwidth of a stimulus characterized by a single spectral prominence (K. N. Stevens, 1952). The stimulus was generated with white noise excitation or with periodic impulsive excitation of a single tuned circuit whose bandwidth was in the range of bandwidths of speech formants. With noise-excited formants, the JND in bandwidth is 15 to 20 Hz for relatively narrow formants (bandwidth of 50 Hz), and increases to 20 to 30 Hz for formants having a bandwidth of 100 Hz, for formant frequencies in the range 500 to 3000 Hz. For the wider formants, discrimination becomes poorer than this at lower formant frequencies. When the excitation is a periodic series of pulses, the JND is somewhat greater than it is with noise excitation (35 to 80 Hz), with the best discrimination occurring for formants in the frequency range of 1 to 2 kHz.

In another experiment, a flat-spectrum noise was used as the starting point, and this noise was modified by introducing a narrow peak or notch in the spectrum (Malme, 1959). Experiments were carried out to determine the height of the peak or the depth of the notch that was just detectable by listeners. The effective bandwidth of the peak or notch was about one-tenth of the center frequency of the peak or notch. In the case of peaks at 300, 1000, and 3000 Hz, the height of the peak that was just detectable was 9, 4, and 5 dB, respectively. The corresponding notch depths that were just detectable were 14, 7, and 9 dB. Thus listeners were less sensitive to the introduction of a notch in an otherwise flat noise spectrum than they were to the introduction of a peak. These JNDs are, of course, substantially greater than the JND in amplitude of a pure tone at the same frequency.

Still other experiments (e.g., Green et al., 1984) have examined the sensitivity of listeners to the amplitude of one component of a signal that consists of a sum of a number of sinusoidal components with different frequencies but the same amplitudes. Depending on the number of components in the sound (from 2 to 20 in different experiments), the JND in amplitude for one of the components is in the range of 1 to 4 dB. This JND is greater for durations less than 100 ms, but is approximately constant for longer durations.

4.2.3 Pitch Perception; Discrimination of Frequency of Tones and Other Spectral Prominences

When a sequence of two pure tones with the second higher in frequency than the first is played, a listener can report that the second tone has a higher pitch than the first if the frequency difference is sufficiently large. A listener can adjust the frequency of the second tone so that it sounds twice as high in pitch as the first. From a series of such judgments, a scale can be constructed such that frequencies that are spaced at equal distances along this scale are judged to be related by the same pitch ratio. This scale is shown in figure 4.23

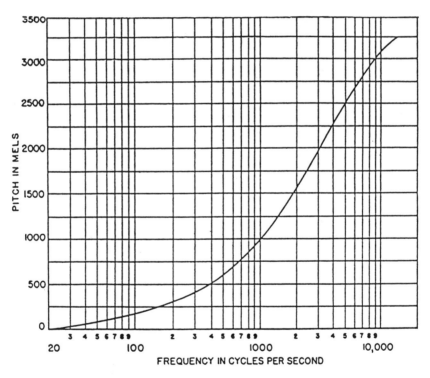

Figure 4.23 The pitch function. This curve shows how the perceived pitch of a tone (measured in mels) changes as a function of the frequency of the stimulus. This pitch function was determined at a loudness level of 60 phons. The mel scale was constructed by assigning arbitrarily the number 1000 to the pitch of a 1000-Hz tone. The number 500 is assigned to the pitch of a tone that sounds half as high, and so on. (After S. S. Stevens and Volkmann, 1940.)

(S. S. Stevens and Volkmann, 1940). The pitch scale is in mels, and is defined such that a pure tone with a frequency of 1000 Hz has a pitch of 1000 mels. At frequencies below about 500 Hz, equal changes of the frequency in hertz correspond approximately to equal changes in pitch. At higher frequencies, the relation is approximately logarithmic. That is, equal changes in log frequency correspond roughly to equal changes in pitch.

The JND in frequency for a pure tone depends on both the frequency and the amplitude of the tone. The dependence on amplitude is greatest for low amplitudes, within about 50 dB of threshold, but for normal listening levels (roughly 60 to 80 dB above the absolute threshold) the JND is relatively independent of amplitude. The JND under these conditions tends to be constant at about 1 Hz for frequencies up to about 1 kHz. At higher frequencies the JND increases to about 2 Hz at 2 kHz and to about 10 Hz at 4 kHz, and increases rapidly above 5 kHz. The JND for frequency turns out to be approximately equal to a fixed number of mels, independent of the frequency.

Of perhaps greater relevance to the study of speech perception are data on the discrimination of changes in frequency of a spectral prominence of the type associated with a formant of a vowel. When the stimulus contains a single spectral prominence, with a periodicity similar to that observed in a vowel, the JND in the frequency of the prominence is in the range of 10 to 20 Hz, for formant bandwidths and frequencies in the range normally observed for the first and second formants in naturally produced vowels (K. N. Stevens, 1952).

Discrimination of changes in formant frequency has also been determined for vowel-like stimuli containing several formants (Flanagan, 1955; Kewley-Port and Watson, 1994). As we have seen in section 3.2, when the frequency of a formant in a vowel is changed, it is accompanied by changes in the amplitudes of the spectral peaks associated with that formant and with other formants. The sensitivity of formant amplitude to a given change in formant frequency is especially great when two formants are close together in frequency. Results show that the JND in the second-formant frequency is in the range 20 to 100 Hz, depending on the relation of $F2$ to other formants. For the first formant, the JND is in the range of 10 to 30 Hz. For these multiformant stimuli, listeners are presumably basing their judgments both on the shift in the frequency of the spectral prominence and on the changes in amplitudes of the spectral peaks.

4.2.4 Discrimination of Duration and Temporal Order

The sensitivity of listeners to small changes in the duration of a stimulus depends upon the stimulus duration (Creelman, 1962). When the duration T of a burst of noise or a tonal stimulus is less than about 100 ms, the JND ΔT for changes in duration is approximately proportional to $\sqrt{T}$. For $T = 100$ ms, ΔT is about 10 ms, whereas for a 10-ms burst, ΔT is about 3 ms. Discrimination is poorer than this when the duration exceeds 100 ms, such that ΔT is roughly proportional to T in the range $100 < T < 500$ ms. Thus for $T = 200$ ms, ΔT is about 20 ms. One might speculate that two different mechanisms come into play in the discrimination of duration: one plays a predominant role for $T < 100$ ms and the other is dominant for larger T.

Another type of experiment related to the discrimination of temporal events examines the ability of listeners to identify the temporal order of two sounds that are presented with different onset times. Experiments of this kind have been done with several kinds of stimuli: two tones with different frequencies (Pisoni, 1977), a noise and a periodic "buzz" (J. D. Miller et al., 1976), and various combinations of tones, bands of noise, and clicks (Hirsh, 1959). The common finding for all of these experiments is that the time of separation between the onsets of the two stimuli needs to be 15 to 20 ms before listeners can reliably report which of the two sounds preceded the other.

4.2.5 Masking: Simultaneous and Nonsimultaneous

The acoustic patterns of speech can be represented in terms of short-time spectra that change with time. The information concerning the phonetic content of these patterns is determined by interpreting particular spectral components in relation to other spectral components that occur approximately simultaneously, and by evaluating the spectrum at one time in relation to the spectrum that occurs at an adjacent time. It is of some interest, then, to determine how a listener responds to a particular test stimulus when this stimulus is heard in the context of another stimulus that occurs either simultaneously with or immediately preceding or following the test stimulus. How is the listener response to the test stimulus changed as a result of the presence of the second stimulus? In a sense, one might regard the two stimuli as being different components of a single, more complex stimulus.

A special case of this interaction between two stimuli examines the conditions under which the test stimulus is rendered inaudible by the presence of the second stimulus. Under these circumstances, the test stimulus is said to be masked and the second stimulus is called the masker. The increase in the threshold of the test or probe stimulus due to the presence of the masker is called the amount of masking.

The amount of masking for a given test stimulus and a masker is usually greatest when both stimuli are presented simultaneously. For nonsimultaneous masking, the amount of masking depends on the time interval between the masker and the test stimulus. Figure 4.24 schematizes the kinds of results that are obtained with simultaneous and nonsimultaneous masking. In this example, the masker is a narrow band of noise centered at 5-kHz and the test stimulus is a brief 5-kHz tone. There is appreciable forward masking up to 50 ms after the end of the masker, with smaller amounts of masking beyond 50 ms. Backward masking, on the other hand, extends over a much shorter

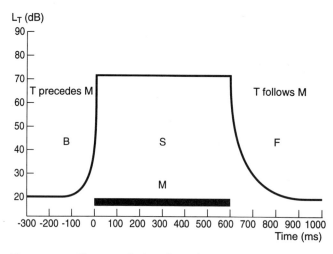

Figure 4.24 Illustrating backward, simultaneous, and forward masking. The time interval of the masking sound M (a narrow band of noise) is indicated by the black bar. The ordinate is the sound pressure level L_T of a brief 2-ms tone pip T that is just heard in the presence of M, and the abscissa is the location of the tone pip relative to the onset of M. B, regions of backward masking (T precedes M); S, simultaneous masking; F, forward masking (T follows M). (Adapted from Zwicker, 1975.)

time interval. Larger values of forward masking, extending over longer time intervals, are observed when the level of the masker is greater.

When the masking stimulus is white noise, the SPL of a pure tone that is just heard in the presence of this masker depends upon the frequency of the tone (Hawkins and Stevens, 1950). The amount of masking can be described by the ratio (in decibels) of the intensity of the tone at the masked threshold to the intensity of the noise in a 1-Hz band centered at the frequency of the tone. This ratio is independent of the amplitude of the masking noise as long as the masked threshold of the tone is well above its absolute threshold in the absence of the noise. This signal-to-noise ratio as a function of frequency is displayed in figure 4.25. The figure shows that this ratio remains approximately constant (at about 17 to 18 dB) in the frequency range up to 1 kHz, and increases at higher frequencies. This ratio can be interpreted as the bandwidth of the noise (in decibels) that has the same intensity as that of the tone at threshold. It has been called the critical ratio.

A more general case is a situation in which a test stimulus is presented in the context of a masking stimulus but the test stimulus is above the threshold. One approach to assessing the effect of the masking stimulus is to make a comparison between the loudness of the test stimulus under two situations: (1) in the absence of the masking stimulus, and (2) with the masking stimulus present. The level of the test stimulus under condition (1) is adjusted so that its loudness is the same as that of the test stimulus under condition (2). This matching is most conveniently done by presenting the test stimulus alone in one ear, and the masker plus test stimulus in the other.

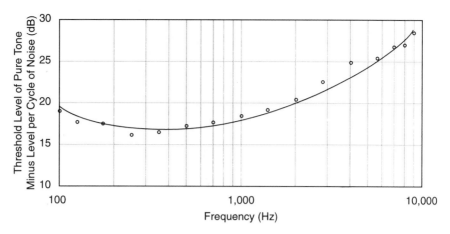

Figure 4.25 Ratio between the monaural masked threshold of a pure tone and the level per cycle of the masking noise measured at the frequency of the pure tone. The circles show experimental values. The smooth curve is from data obtained at Bell Telephone Laboratories. (Adapted from Hawkins and Stevens, 1950.)

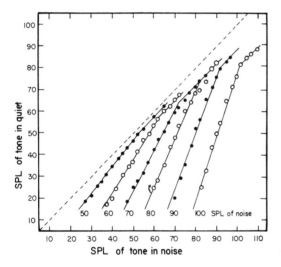

Figure 4.26 Sound pressure level at which a 1000-Hz tone in quiet is judged equal in loudness to a tone partially masked by white noise. The parameter on the curves is the level of the masking noise in decibels. (Adapted from S. S. Stevens and Guirao, 1967, by Scharf, 1978.)

A typical result is shown in figure 4.26, in which the masker is white noise and the test stimulus is a 1000-Hz tone (S. S. Stevens and Guirao, 1967). The data show that, for a given level of the masking noise, there is a wide range of levels for the tone where its loudness is reduced by the presence of the masker. For example, when a tone with an SPL of 70 dB is heard in the presence of noise with an SPL of 80 dB, it is judged to have the same loudness as a 50-dB tone in quiet. When the level of the tone is sufficiently high in relation to the masker, its loudness is almost the same as the loudness of the

Auditory Processing of Speechlike Sounds

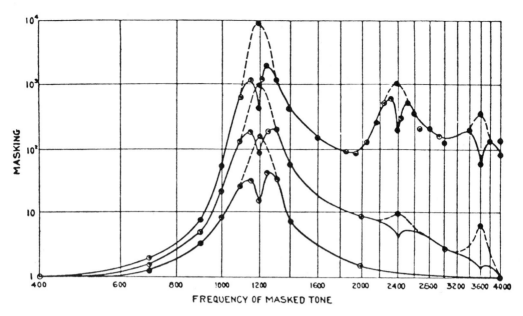

Figure 4.27 Example of masking of a tone by a tone. The frequency of the masking tone is 1200 Hz. Each curve corresponds to a different masker level, and gives the amount by which the threshold intensity of the masked tone is multiplied in the presence of the masker, relative to its threshold in quiet. The dashed lines near 1200 Hz and its harmonics are estimates of the masking functions in the absence of the effect of beats. (From Wegel and Lane, 1924.)

tone in quiet (except at very high levels of the masking noise). This example demonstrates that a masker can have an effect on the response of a listener to a probe tone not only at threshold but also at levels that are well above threshold.

4.2.6 Masking and Frequency Selectivity

When the masking stimulus is a pure tone, and a probe tone is presented in the presence of the masker, the threshold level for the probe tone depends on the difference in frequency between the two tones. The masking as a function of the frequency of the probe tone is displayed in figure 4.27 for a masker frequency of 1200 Hz (Wegel and Lane, 1924). Data for three levels of the masker are given. The ordinate for these curves is the amount by which the threshold intensity of the probe tone in quiet must be multiplied so that the tone is just heard in the presence of the masker. The greatest amount of masking occurs for frequencies in the vicinity of the masker. For the higher levels of the masker, the amount of masking at frequencies above the masker frequency is considerably greater than the masking at lower frequencies. There are some irregularities in the curves in the vicinity of the masker frequency and its harmonics because of some nonlinearities in the ear, and because of the presence of "beats" when the frequency difference between the probe tone and the masker (or its harmonics) is small.

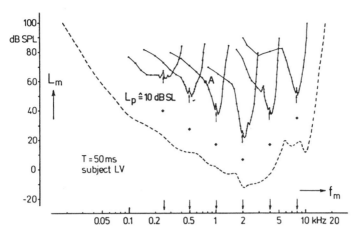

Figure 4.28 Psychophysical tuning curves illustrating masking of a tone by a tone. On any one of the curves the level of the probe tone is constant, and different points along the curve indicate the sound pressure level L_m of the masking tone (with frequency f_m) that is required to mask the probe tone. Different curves correspond to different frequencies of the probe tone. The level of the probe tone is always 10 dB above threshold and its duration is 50 ms. The dots give the levels of the probe tones and the arrows give their frequencies. The dotted line is the threshold of audibility for the masker. Point A is discussed in the text. (From Vogten, 1974.)

Another way of examining masking data when the test stimulus and the masker are pure tones is to fix the amplitude and frequency of the probe tone and to vary the frequency of the masking tone. At each frequency, the level of the masking tone is adjusted so that the probe tone is just masked. Data from a series of experiments on the masking of probe tones of different frequencies, with simultaneous presentation of masker and probe, are shown in figure 4.28 (Vogten, 1974, 1978b).

Several curves are displayed, each curve being associated with a probe tone of a different frequency. A point on one of these curves indicates the frequency and level of the masking tone that will just mask the probe tone. Thus, for example, the curve on which point A is marked represents data for a probe tone whose frequency is 1000 Hz, with a level of 10 dB above threshold. Point A indicates that, for a masking tone at a frequency of about 800 Hz, an SPL of about 60 dB (re 0.0002 dyne/cm^2) is needed to mask the probe tone.

Curves of the type shown in figure 4.28 have been called psychophysical tuning curves, and they provide one type of evidence with regard to the frequency resolution of the auditory filters. The ratio of the width of the curve (near the tip) to the center frequency appears to be roughly constant at high frequencies (above about 1 kHz), and to increase at lower frequencies. If the curves are plotted on a linear frequency scale, the widths are approximately constant at lower frequencies and increase in proportion to frequency above about 1 kHz.

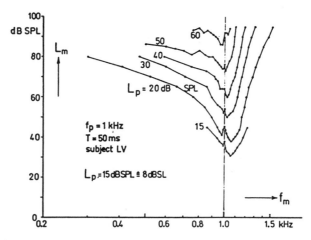

Figure 4.29 Sound pressure level L_m of a pure tone masker necessary to mask a 1-kHz probe tone (duration = 50 ms) as a function of the masker frequency f_m for various levels L_p of the probe tone. (From Vogten, 1974.)

For the higher-frequency probe tones, there is considerable asymmetry in the tuning curves. A probe tone is masked more effectively by a tone that is lower in frequency than by a higher-frequency tone. This observation can also be made from figure 4.27. The slope of the upper edge of the tuning curve is very sharp. There is an extended tail on the lower frequency end of the higher-frequency curves, indicating that a higher-frequency tone can be effectively masked by a tone that is several octaves lower, if it is of sufficient intensity.

The psychophysical tuning curves in figure 4.28 have shapes that are very similar to the physiological tuning curves, examples of which have been given in figure 4.14. Both sets of curves have the same asymmetrical form for the higher frequencies, with low-frequency "tails." The sharpness of the curves in the vicinity of the tips is approximately the same, except that there are anomalies in the psychophysical curves near the frequency of the probe tone because interaction of probe and masker give rise to beats.

The tuning curves of figure 4.28 were all obtained with a fixed level of the probe tone that is about 10 dB above threshold. Figure 4.29 shows a series of tuning curves corresponding to a number of different levels of a probe tone, all at the same frequency. The curves have similar overall shapes, with a sharp rise above the frequency of the probe tone, and a more gradual rise below that frequency. There are some differences as a function of level, however, particularly in the shapes of the curves at low frequencies.

Tuning curves of the type shown in figure 4.28 can be obtained using a forward-masking paradigm, in which the probe tone is presented a few milliseconds after termination of the masker (Vogten, 1978a; Moore, 1978). While these curves have a gross shape that is similar to the curves for simultaneous masking, there are some differences. The tips of the curves are deeper, presumably because there is not a problem with interaction between probe and masker as there is when the two tones are presented simultaneously. Another difference is that the forward-masking curves show a much more abrupt rise above the frequency of the probe tone.

The tuning curves in figure 4.28, as well as the curves in figure 4.27, obtained through experiments on masking of one tone by another, provide some insight into the frequency selectivity of the peripheral auditory system. Not unexpectedly, they show that a probe tone of a given frequency is masked most effectively by a masker whose frequency is centered within a narrow region in the vicinity of the probe tone. Another approach to examining this frequency selectivity is to measure the masking of tones centered in bands of noise with different bandwidths (Fletcher, 1940; Greenwood, 1961a). A series of experiments of this type has shown that when the noise bandwidth that is centered at a particular frequency is smaller than a certain critical value, then the masking of the tone is dependent on the overall level of the masking noise, and not on its bandwidth. In fact the level of the tone at the masked threshold is about 4 dB below the overall level of the noise. When the bandwidth of the noise exceeds the critical value, the frequency components of the noise that are outside of this critical range do not contribute to the masking of the tone. Another way of interpreting this result is to consider the masking noise to have a fixed sound pressure level per hertz, and to vary the bandwidth with this constraint. The threshold level of the probe tone centered in this band increases as the bandwidth increases until the critical width is reached. Increasing the bandwidth beyond this value does not change the threshold level of the tone.

The bandwidth within which the noise is effective in masking the tone is called the critical bandwidth. The critical bandwidth obtained through these kinds of masking experiments is plotted as a function of frequency in figure 4.30 (Zwicker et al., 1957; Greenwood, 1961a). The variation with frequency of this measure is similar to the frequency dependence of the bandwidths of the psychophysical tuning curves (see figure 4.28) or of the physiological tuning curves (see figure 4.14). The frequency dependence of the critical band is also similar to the frequency dependence based on pitch judgments and on frequency discrimination for tones. The width of a critical band is equal to about 140 mels, on average, where the mel scale is defined as in figure 4.23. The function relating position of maximum amplitude on the cochlear partition to frequency also has a similar shape (Greenwood, 1961b). Figure 4.30 shows for comparison the "critical ratio," from figure 4.25, that is, the ratio of the intensity of a tone at the masked threshold to the intensity of the masking noise in a 1-Hz band.

Another approach to examining the frequency selectivity of the peripheral auditory system is to determine how the loudness of a band of noise changes as the bandwidth is increased. Typical data are shown in figure 4.31 (Feldtkeller and Zwicker, 1956). On any one of the curves, the overall level of the

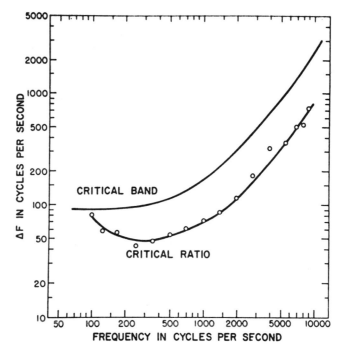

Figure 4.30 The upper curve plots the width ΔF of the critical band as a function of the center frequency of the band, as measured in masking experiments that manipulate the bandwidth of the masker. The lower curve gives the bandwidths calculated from the critical ratio, as in figure 4.25. (From Greenwood, 1961a.)

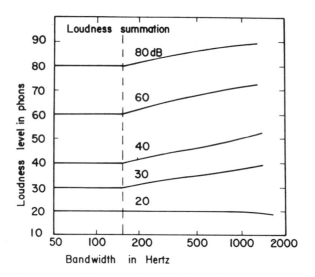

Figure 4.31 The loudness level of a band of noise centered at 1000 Hz, plotted as a function of the width of the band. The parameter labeling each curve is the sound pressure level of the noise. The vertical dashed line marks the bandwidth at which the loudness begins to increase. (Adapted from Feldtkeller and Zwicker, 1956, by Scharf, 1978.)

Table 4.1 Values of critical-band rate (in bark) and critical bandwidth as a function of frequency

Center frequency (bark)	Center frequency (Hz)	Critical bandwidth (Hz)	Center frequency (bark)	Center frequency (Hz)	Critical bandwidth (Hz)
1	50	100	13	1850	280
2	150	100	14	2150	320
3	250	100	15	2500	380
4	350	100	16	2900	450
5	450	110	17	3400	550
6	570	120	18	4000	700
7	700	140	19	4800	900
8	840	150	20	5800	1100
9	1000	160	21	7000	1300
10	1170	190	22	8500	1800
11	1370	210	23	10500	2500
12	1600	240	24	13500	3500

From Zwicker and Terhardt (1980).

noise is held constant while its bandwidth is increased, as indicated on the abscissa. The ordinate gives the loudness level of the noise band, obtained by determining the SPL of a 1000-Hz tone that is judged to be equal in loudness to the band of noise. The figure shows that, independent of the overall level of the noise, the loudness level is independent of the bandwidth below a certain critical value, and increases when the bandwidth exceeds this value. Within this critical bandwidth, the loudness level depends only on the overall level of the signal independently of how the spectral energy is distributed in the band. Bandwidths obtained from this kind of loudness matching experiment are similar to those derived from masking experiments of the type described above.

Data from these masking and loudness experiments, as well as other experimental evidence, have led to use of the critical band concept as a basis for designing filter banks for the analysis of auditory signals, including speech. When a series of critical-band filters is arranged in a nonoverlapping manner from low to high frequencies, there are twenty-four such filters (Zwicker and Terhardt, 1980). A scale on which critical bands are arranged in equal steps from 1 to 24 has been called a bark scale. The center frequencies and bandwidths of the critical-band filters, as proposed by Zwicker and Terhardt (1980), are listed in table 4.1. These authors have also proposed the following analytic formula for the critical band CB in hertz:

$$CB = 25 + 75[1 + 1.4 f^2]^{0.69},$$

where f is the frequency in kilohertz. This formula approximates the data in table 4.1 with an accuracy of ± 10 percent.

4.2.7   Perception of Sounds with Two or More Spectral Prominences

As we have seen in chapter 3, there is a class of sounds that are generated with quasi-periodic excitation of the vocal tract at the glottis. The spectrum of the sound is characterized by a series of harmonics, and the formants give rise to several narrow prominences in the spectrum envelope. As the larynx and the vocal tract assume various states, the fundamental frequency (i.e., the frequencies of the harmonics) and the frequencies of the spectral prominences shift up or down.

The mechanism of perception of these types of sounds has been examined in a number of different experiments where listeners are asked to respond to stimuli in which the fundamental frequency and the formant frequencies are manipulated in various ways. The listener response can be either an identification of the stimulus, a discrimination between two different stimuli, or a matching of one stimulus against another. The matching can be determined by a phonetic comparison or by an auditory comparison (Chistovich, 1985). In one type of manipulation, the spacing between two adjacent spectral prominences in the stimuli is adjusted. As discussed in chapter 3, manipulation of the vocal tract shape from that of a uniform tube has the effect of bringing some adjacent pairs of formants rather close together and increasing the separation between other pairs.

We examine first the effect of manipulating the relative amplitudes of the spectral prominences in a stimulus with two formants. The spectrum of a typical stimulus is schematized in figure 4.32. Chistovich and her colleagues (Chistovich and Lublinskaya, 1979; Chistovich et al., 1979; Chistovich, 1985) have investigated the auditory processing of these stimuli by a technique in which a stimulus with a single spectrum prominence (with frequency F') is adjusted so that it sounds similar in quality to the two-formant stimulus with prominences at frequencies F_a and F_b. The relative amplitudes of the two prominences are manipulated by the experimenter, and the subject adjusts the frequency F' to obtain a best match. The frequency spacing $F_b - F_a$ is set to different values in different experiments. Results reported by Chistovich and Lublinskaya for two subjects are shown in figure 4.33. When the spacing

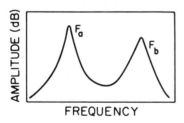

Figure 4.32   Schematization of the spectrum envelope of a two-formant sound used in the matching experiments of Chistovich and Lublinskaya (1979). The frequency spacing $F_b - F_a$ and the relative amplitudes of the spectral prominences were manipulated.

$F_b - F_a$ is less than a certain critical distance, the results on the left side of the figure are obtained. The matching frequency F' gradually changes through a set of intermediate values from F_a to F_b as the amplitude of the F_a peak is decreased in relation to the amplitude of the F_b peak (i.e., the ratio A_2/A_1 in the figure is increased). That is, F' is set at some measure of the "center of gravity" of the two-peaked spectral prominence. When $F_b - F_a$ is greater than a critical distance (right side of figure 4.33), the matching behavior is different: one subject tends to set F' equal either to F_a or to F_b depending on the relative amplitudes, and the other subject shows large variability in the setting when the relative amplitude is in the middle range. These experiments were repeated for various frequencies of $(F_a + F_b)/2$ in the normal range of the first and second formants in adult speech. The critical distance dividing these two types of matching adjustments was such that the $F_b - F_a$ was equal to about 3.5 bark.

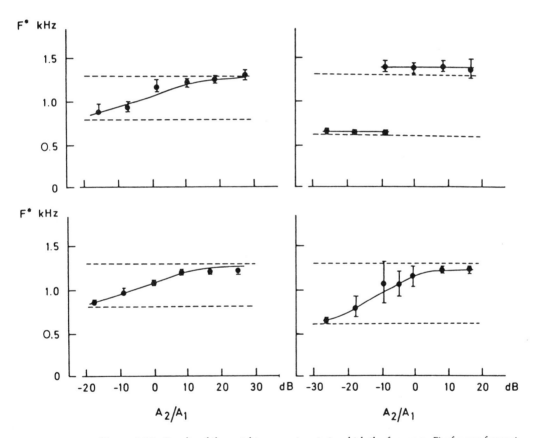

Figure 4.33 Results of the matching experiments in which the frequency F^* of a one-formant vowel is adjusted to match a two-formant vowel. The spacing between the two formant frequencies (shown by dashed lines) is less than 3.5 bark for the left column and more than 3.5 bark for the right column. The points give the mean and a measure of variability for the judgments as a function of the relative amplitude A_2/A_1 of the formant peaks for two subjects: L.C. (top) and V.L. (bottom). (From Chistovich and Lublinskaya, 1979.)

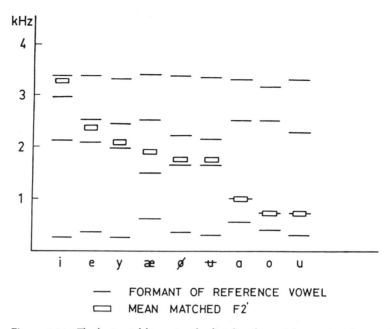

Figure 4.34 The horizontal lines give the first four formant frequencies of a set of Swedish vowels used in a matching experiment. The boxes show the mean frequency of the second formant ($F2'$) of a two-formant stimulus that gave a best match to the full vowel. $F1$ of the two-formant matching stimulus was set to $F1$ of the vowel. (From Carlson et al., 1970.)

The perceptual consequence of manipulating the spacing between two spectral prominences in a vowel-like sound has also been examined in an experiment in which a synthetic vowel with five formants was matched against a two-formant synthetic vowel (Carlson et al., 1970). The first-formant frequency was the same for both vowels, and the subjects adjusted the frequency $F2'$ of the two-formant vowel to give a best match in quality with the five-formant vowel. This matching task was carried out for a number of configurations of the five formants, corresponding to a variety of different vowels (in Swedish). The third formant for these vowels was always in the range of 2140 to 2960 Hz. The results of this experiment are shown in figure 4.34. The frequencies of the first four formants of the vowel are shown, together with the frequency $F2'$ of the two-formant matching vowel. When the spacing between $F2$ and $F3$ was less than about 3.0 bark, as it was for the front vowels (the first six vowels on the figure), subjects placed $F2'$ at a frequency that was usually between $F2$ and $F3$, and was sometimes between $F3$ and $F4$, depending on the values of $F2$ and $F3$ in relation to $F4$. Once again, then, there appears to be a critical spacing of $F2$ and $F3$ that leads to an interpretation of the two-peaked spectral prominence as a single broad prominence whose perceptual "center" is determined by its detailed shape. It should be noted, however, that adjustment of $F2'$ to give a best match does not lead to identical quality between the two-formant and the five-formant vowels. For vowels having $F1$ and $F2$ relatively close together (spacing of 300 to 400 Hz, corresponding roughly to 3.0 to 3.5 bark), we have seen (in section 3.2) that the third and higher formant peaks in the spectrum have amplitudes that are relatively low compared with the amplitudes of the $F1$ and $F2$ peaks. The best matches of two-formant vowels to these vowels occur when the two formants are adjusted to be equal to $F1$ and $F2$ of the five-formant vowel.

The implication of these matching experiments is that some aspect of the response of the auditory system undergoes a qualitative change when the spacing between two spectral prominences becomes less than a critical value of about 3.5 bark. Other experiments on vowel perception indicate that this concept of a critical distance between spectral prominences also applies to the distance between the fundamental frequency and the first-formant frequency of a vowel. These observations about critical spacing are relevant to the classification of vowels, as will be discussed in chapter 6.

5 Phonological Representation of Utterances

5.1 WORDS, SEGMENTS, FEATURES

At one level an utterance can be described as the sound that results from movements of various structures that surround the airways from the lungs to the lips. The adjustments of the sublaryngeal respiratory system and the articulatory structures that lie between the larynx and the lips cause sound sources to be generated, and these sound sources are filtered by the airways that are shaped by the articulatory structures.

These continuous articulatory and respiratory movements for an utterance are highly coordinated, and are the surface manifestation of units in a structured linguistic system whose elements are stored in memory in a discrete form. A basic unit in this system is the word. When we speak, we string together sequences of words in memory. The acoustic signal that results from a sequence of words may contain markers such as pauses indicating the grouping of words, but generally the boundaries between adjacent words are not marked by pauses. There may, however, be subtle cues in the sound for the beginnings of words, and these cues may be used by a listener to assist in the segmentation of the sound stream so that word sequences can be recovered. For example, when a stressed vowel occurs in the sound, there is a reasonable probability that the syllable containing this vowel is at the beginning of a word (Cutler and Carter, 1987). Also, there may be segmental cues to word beginnings; for example, a voiceless stop consonant is always aspirated when it is in word-initial position even if the following vowel is reduced, but is not aspirated before a reduced vowel in other positions in a word (e.g., /p/ is aspirated in *pit* or in *potato*, but not in *supper*).

There is also ample evidence that words are stored in memory as sequences of discrete segments. Part of this evidence comes from acoustic data showing that the implementation of most segments is signaled by landmarks in the speech stream. (This concept of acoustic landmarks is discussed in section 5.2.) A different kind of evidence comes from observations of the modifications of segments that occur when affixes and stems are joined to form words. For example, the prefix spelled *in-* in English takes on several different forms depending on the initial segment in the word, as in *in-fallible, im-possible, il-legal, im-moral, ir-regular*. In all of these examples, except the first, the last sound in the prefix is either deleted or undergoes assimilation depending on the following consonant. Evidence of this kind supports the view that words are stored in memory as sequences of discrete segments.

There is also evidence in support of the proposition that each segment is represented in memory in terms of a set of discrete classes or features (Jakobson et al., 1952; Chomsky and Halle, 1968; Halle, 1990). For example, a segment such as /m/ can be classified as being produced (1) with a complete closure in the oral tract, (2) with the closure made by the lips, and (3) with the velopharyngeal port open. Some of these classes are shared by other segments, so that, for example, item (2) is a feature of /p/ and /b/ as well as /m/, and item (3) is a feature of /n/ and /ŋ/ as well as /m/. Evidence for this discrete representation of segments comes both from articulatory and acoustic data (as in the examples just given) and from phonological observations. The phonological evidence is illustrated by the examples with the prefix *in-* given above. We observe that /n/ changes to /m/ just in case the word begins with the class of consonants that are produced with a complete closure of the lips (the consonants /m/ and /p/ in the examples). Furthermore, if the initial consonant is produced with no pressure buildup in the mouth (a so-called *sonorant* consonant, such as /r/ and /l/), then /n/ assimilates to the following consonant. Thus the rules governing the modification of /n/ apply to particular groups of segments that are characterized in terms of discrete classes or features.

We suppose, then, that words are stored in memory as sequences of segments, and each of these segments is represented as an array of distinctive features. The particular inventory of features that are used to make distinctions between words in languages is determined both by the properties of the articulatory system that generates speech and by the characteristics of the human auditory system that processes speech. The features have correlates both in the articulatory and in the acoustic and auditory domains. The features for each segment within an utterance that is stored in memory define which articulators are to be controlled, and provide a broad specification of how these articulators are to be manipulated. The features also specify the intended attributes of the sound that arises from the articulatory movements. These constraints on the articulation and on the sound pattern determine the detailed pattern of articulatory movements that are needed to implement the features within a segment.

There are two classes of features—articulator-free features and articulator-bound features (Halle and Stevens, 1991a). Articulator-free features are so named becaused they are defined without reference to any particular articulator. Articulator-bound features specify which articulators are active in producing the sound, and how these articulators are to be shaped or positioned. These features are binary in the sense that a given segment can either have the articulatory and acoustic attributes of the feature or not. The convention is to assign a value of + or − to a feature in a given segment.

Table 5.1 List of articulator-free features and their values for different classes of segments

Feature	Vowels	Glides	Conso-nants	n,l	t,b	s,z	θ,ð
Vocalic	+	−	−	−	−	−	−
Consonantal	−	−	+	+	+	+	+
Continuant				−	−	+	+
Sonorant				+	−	−	−
Strident						+	−

Note: The segment labels at the top of the last four columns are examples of the segments with the given feature values.

5.2 ARTICULATOR-FREE FEATURES AND LANDMARKS

An inventory of the articulator-free features is given in table 5.1. The features [vocalic] and [consonantal] are listed in columns 2 to 4 of the table, together with their values for the three broad classes of segments: vowels, glides, and true consonants. In the case of consonants, additional articulator-free features [continuant], [sonorant], and [strident] are defined, as shown by the feature listings in the last four columns of the table for particular groups of consonants. These additional features can only be relevant when a sufficiently narrow constriction is formed in the vocal tract, that is, for [+consonantal] segments, and are not required for vowels and glides.

A segment with the feature [+vocalic] forms the nucleus of a syllable. Such a segment is generally produced with a maximum in the vocal tract opening in the oral cavity. As has been shown in chapter 3, a maximum mouth opening generally causes a maximum in the first-formant frequency, and this maximum in $F1$ also gives rise to a maximum amplitude of the $F1$ spectral prominence. These attributes of vocalic nuclei are illustrated in figure 5.1, which shows a spectrogram of the sentence *Samantha came back on the plane*. Below the spectrogram is a contour of $F1$ vs. time during the voiced portions of the utterances. The points where there are maxima associated with the eight syllabic nuclei are marked by arrows below the spectrogram. The presence of such a maximum or landmark in the sound is acoustic evidence that a [+vocalic] segment has been implemented. Also shown below the spectrogram is a plot of the amplitude of the $F1$ spectral prominence vs. time. Peaks in this amplitude correspond roughly with peaks in the frequency of $F1$, except for influences of nasalization in some of the vowel nuclei.

For a segment classified as [+consonantal], a constriction or narrowing is formed in the oral cavity, and the cross-sectional area of the constriction is sufficiently small that an abrupt discontinuity occurs in the spectrum when such a segment is produced. Any one of three articulators can potentially be active in forming the constriction: the lips, the tongue blade, and the tongue body. The acoustic discontinuity arises either because of a rapid increase or

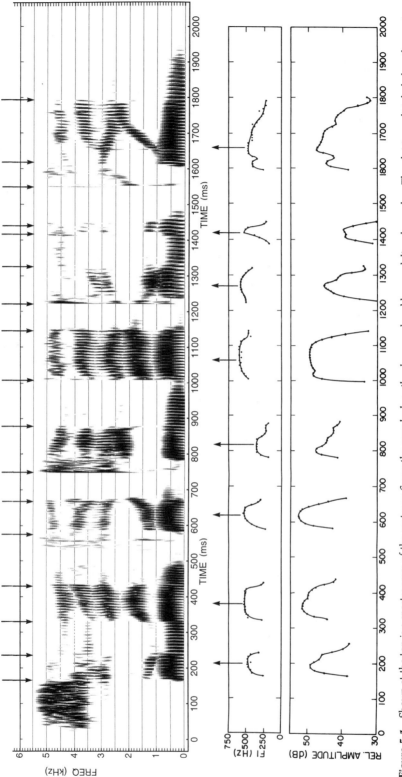

Figure 5.1 Shown at the top is a spectrogram of the sentence *Samantha came back on the plane,* produced by an adult male speaker. The plot immediately below the spectrogram gives the frequency of F1 vs. time during the vocalic regions, measured at 7.5-ms intervals. At the bottom is a plot of the relative amplitude of the first-formant prominence during the vocalic regions. Each point on this amplitude plot and on the plot of frequency of F1 is measured from a spectrum which is obtained by averaging a 10-ms sequence of spectra, each of which is calculated using a 6.4-ms Hamming window. The arrows below the spectrogram indicate vocalic landmarks and the arrows at the top identify consonantal landmarks. See text.

decrease in intraoral pressure or because of an abrupt change in the acoustic path in the vocal tract, such as the closure or release of nasal consonant. The formation or release of a constriction in the oral cavity always results in a rapid movement of the first-formant frequency $F1$—a downward movement of $F1$ when the constriction is formed and an upward movement when it is released. Some examples of these acoustic discontinuities are marked by arrows at the top of the spectrogram in figure 5.1. The movements of $F1$ in the vicinity of the discontinuities, shown below the spectrogram, illustrate the tendency for $F1$ to fall near a consonant closure and to rise following a release. These discontinuities constitute landmarks in the sound and are evidence for a segment with the feature [+consonantal]. The low-frequency amplitude contours at the bottom of the figure also show rather abrupt increases and decreases in the vicinity of most of the consonantal landmarks, although the rapid amplitude changes also occur at mid and high frequencies at these landmarks.

In principle, two acoustic discontinuities should occur when a [+consonantal] segment is produced—one when the oral articulator forms a constriction and one when the articulator is released. Although the paired closing-release articulatory movements are always present, it is possible that one of these components may not generate sound. An example occurs in the sentence in figure 5.1, where the time the tongue blade is raised to make contact with the palate for /l/ in the word *plane* occurs when the lips are closed for /p/. Consequently there is no sound to mark the time of contact for the tongue blade. Such an omission of an acoustic discontinuity is often observed when two or more consonants occur in sequence.

The feature values [−vocalic, −consonantal] identify glides. The special acoustic attributes of glides are a minimum in the low-frequency amplitude (relative to that in an adjacent vowel) and relatively slow movements of the formants. The principal cause for the minimum in low-frequency amplitude for a glide is a reduction of the amplitude of the glottal source. This reduction occurs either from an active abduction or adduction of the glottis, or as a consequence of a narrowing of the airway downstream from the glottis. (See section 9.2.) The segments that show these properties in the sound include /w/ and /j/, as well as sounds produced by forming a narrowing in the pharyngeal region (i.e., pharyngeal consonants) and the sounds /h/ and /ʔ/, which are formed with a widening or constricting of the glottis but with no major constriction in the vocal tract. There are no rapid movements of $F1$ toward or away from a low frequency for any of these segments.

The spectrogram in figure 5.2 gives examples of some glides. The sentence is *The yacht was a heavy one.* Displayed below the spectrogram are contours of the formant frequency movements and of the low-frequency amplitude changes in the regions of the glides. The measure of low-frequency amplitude is the spectrum amplitude of the first-formant prominence. Arrows indicate the approximate times where the low-frequency amplitude is a minimum. These arrows identify glide landmarks. In the case of the glides /j/ (in

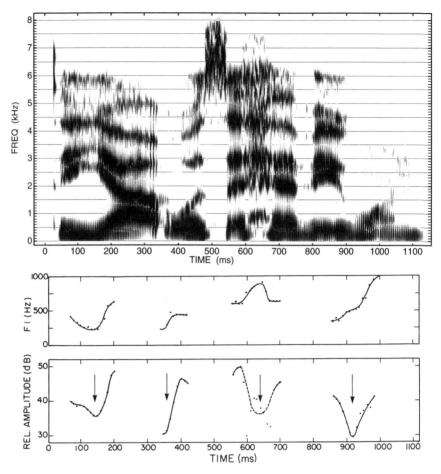

Figure 5.2 The spectrogram is the sentence *The yacht was a heavy one*, produced by a female speaker, illustrating acoustic attributes of glides. The first-formant frequency in the vicinity of the glides is shown immediately below the spectrogram. The plot at the bottom is the amplitude of the $F1$ prominence. The arrows at the amplitude minima for the glides identify the glide landmarks. The irregularities in the amplitude for /h/ are smoothed with the dashed line. Measurements are made at 10-ms intervals using the procedures described in the legend for figure 5.1.

yacht) and /w/ (in *was* and *one*) there are slow changes in amplitude, with a minimum in amplitude assumed to occur where the vocal tract is most constricted. For the segment /h/, there is a minimum in amplitude, and the lowest spectral prominence shows a rise in frequency during the aspiration, presumably because of the partially open glottis. (See section 3.4.6.) The low-frequency amplitude changes more slowly adjacent to glide landmarks than adjacent to consonantal landmarks.

In summary, then, we observe that implementation of the articulator-free features [vocalic] and [consonantal] provides a segmental structure to the speech stream. These features give rise to three types of landmarks in the sound: (1) vocalic landmarks at syllabic peaks, indicating the presence of a [+vocalic] segment in the utterance; (2) abrupt consonantal landmarks at acoustic discontinuities, signaling a [+consonantal] segment; and (3) landmarks defined by a particular type of minimum in low-frequency amplitude that is evidence for a glide with the features [−vocalic, −consonantal]. The presence of these landmarks provides acoustic evidence for the representation of words as sequences of discrete sounds or segments.

In the case of a [+consonantal] segment, it is necessary to specify whether the articulator that forms the constriction creates a complete closure (the feature [−continuant]) or a partial closure ([+continuant]). In the latter case, continuous turbulence noise is formed near the constriction. Examples are shown in table 5.1 and in figures 5.1 and 5.2 (/s/ and /θ/ in *Samantha*, /z/ in *was*, and /v/ in *heavy*). The feature [strident] can apply only to [+continuant] segments, and indicates whether an obstacle is placed in the airway downstream from the constriction, to enhance the acoustic excitation of the front cavity by turbulence noise. Thus the consonants /s,š/ are [+strident], whereas /θ,ð/ are [−strident]. Finally, the value attached to the feature [sonorant] specifies whether pressure builds up behind the constriction ([−sonorant]), or whether a bypass path for the airflow is provided to prevent the increase in pressure behind the constriction ([+sonorant]). Examples of [+sonorant] segments are the nasal consonants /m,n/ and the lateral /l/. Consonants produced with pressure buildup behind the constriction are sometimes called obstruent consonants.

A vocalic landmark signals a syllabic nucleus, as we have noted above. The syllable onset is indicated by one or more consonant or glide landmarks, with the constraint that a glide landmark must immediately precede a vocalic landmark. Another constraint on the sequencing of articulator-free features is that [+sonorant] consonants must occur immediately adjacent to [+vocalic] segments (or to glides). Thus sequences like *snail* or *mute* ([mjut]) are possible, but not sequences like [nsap], at least within a syllable.[1]

5.3 ARTICULATOR-BOUND FEATURES

The articulator-bound features specify which articulators are active in producing phonetic contrasts, and prescribe how these articulators are to be configured. There are six articulators that can be actively manipulated to produce sounds with distinctive acoustic attributes. These consist of the lips, the tongue blade, the tongue body, the soft palate, the pharynx, and the glottis. In addition, a seventh type of manipulation that can produce a distinctive acoustic output is the stiffening or slackening of the vocal folds.

These seven articulators or adjustments can be organized into three classes according to their anatomical location and to the acoustic pattern that results from manipulation of the articulators. One of these classes consists of the lips, the tongue blade, and the tongue body. As noted above, one of these articulators is always active in forming the constriction in the oral cavity for

[+consonantal] segments, and it is the movement of this articulator that creates the consonantal landmark. This articulator is sometimes called the major articulator (Sagey, 1986). As we have noted, the constricting movement for a consonant causes a decrease in the first-formant frequency. The surfaces of these articulators also have the common characteristic that they are rich in sensory receptors. These articulators can, of course, also be active in producing vowels and glides.

The activity of the lips can be either through lip rounding ([+round]) or through narrowing or closing the lip opening without rounding ([−round]). When the tongue blade is active in producing a segment, it can be positioned with the tongue tip making contact with the alveolar ridge or at a more forward location ([+anterior]) or with contact posterior to the alveolar ridge ([−anterior]). Each of these positions leads to a sound with distinctive characteristics, as will be seen for fricative consonants in section 8.1. For each of these tongue tip locations, the contact of the edges of the tongue blade with the palate can be adjusted to produce a relatively short narrow channel ([−distributed]) or a longer channel ([+distributed]). Each of these adjustments again gives rise to an acoustic output with distinctive properties. The shape of the tongue blade can also be modified to permit sound to propagate around the edges of the blade to form a lateral consonant ([+lateral]) or a type of retroflex consonant ([−lateral]). Manipulation of the tongue body is controlled by three features: [high], [low], and [back]. The articulatory and acoustic correlates of these features are discussed in detail in chapter 6 for vowels and in chapter 7 for velar consonants. The three articulators in this class, together with the features that describe the possible manipulations of these articulators in speech production, can be organized into a treelike structure[2] as in figure 5.3. When one or more of these articulators is active in producing a sound, the features arrayed under the articulators are assigned values of + or −.

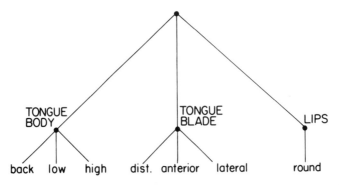

Figure 5.3 Showing the three oral articulators that are active in producing phonetic distinctions, together with the features specifying how these articulators are positioned or shaped. dist.: distributed. (Adapted from Keyser and Stevens, 1994.)

The second class of articulators includes the soft palate, the pharynx, and the glottis. For most segments, the soft palate is raised, creating a closure of the velopharyngeal port. The soft palate is lowered to produce nasal consonants and vowels. The value of the feature [nasal] indicates whether the soft palate should be raised or lowered. The pharynx is narrowed by implementing the feature [+constricted tongue root] and is widened if the feature is [+advanced tongue root]. The combination [+constricted tongue root, +advanced tongue root] is not possible. A similar pair of features is associated with narrowing and widening the glottis; the features are [spread glottis] and [constricted glottis]. Again it is not possible for a segment to have +values for these two features.

The third class of articulatory manipulations consists of two kinds of actions: (1) a raising or lowering of the larynx through contraction of the suprahyoid muscles or strap muscles, leading to a generalized stiffening or slackening of the vocal folds and of the soft tissue surfaces of the vocal tract above the glottis, and (2) independent adjustment of vocal fold tension by contraction of the cricothyroid muscle, causing a stretching of the vocal folds. These two methods of adjusting the larynx have been described in section 1.1.2. Thus there appear to be two features that underlie these adjustments of stiffness or slackness of the vocal tract walls and of the vocal folds. We call these features [stiff vocal folds] for direct adjustment of vocal fold tension, and [slack vocal folds] for adjustments of stiffness or slackness of the pharyngeal walls and the vocal folds by contraction of the strap muscles or the suprahyoid muscles. In contrast to the features specifying the movements of the articulators in the first two classes, that is, in the oral and in the pharyngeal and laryngeal regions, these features govern the stiffnesses of surfaces rather than the control of orifice positions and sizes within the vocal tract.

The feature [stiff vocal folds] gives rise to an increase in the fundamental frequency of vocal fold vibration relative to a lower "resting" frequency. For vowel segments, it is one of the features that specifies fundamental frequency contours in tone languages. The feature [slack vocal folds] is normally implemented for obstruent consonants. For an obstruent consonant with [−slack vocal folds], the stiffening of the vocal tract walls and of the vocal folds as the larynx is raised by suprahyoid muscles accelerates the buildup of pressure during the constricted interval for the consonant, and also inhibits vocal fold vibration during this interval. On the other hand [+slack vocal folds] assists in maintaining vocal fold vibration during the consonant. These issues relating to facilitation or inhibition of glottal vibration for obstruents are discussed in section 8.4. The feature [slack vocal folds] can also influence the frequency of glottal vibration during vocalic intervals. For vowels, these two features are thought to provide two modes for adjustment of the fundamental frequency: there are two "registers" defined by [−slack vocal folds] and by [+slack vocal folds], and within each of these registers the feature

Table 5.2 List of articulator-bound features, organized into three groups: oral region, pharyngeal and laryngeal region, and surface stiffness in laryngeal and pharyngeal region

Oral region
Round
Anterior
Distributed
Lateral
High
Low
Back

Pharyngeal-laryngeal region
Nasal
Advanced tongue root
Constricted tongue root
Spread glottis
Constricted glottis

Surface stiffness
Stiff vocal folds
Slack vocal folds

---

values [±stiff vocal folds] can be active, leading to four different levels of fundamental frequency.

The list of articulator-bound features is summarized in table 5.2. This list is organized into three groups corresponding to the three classes of articulators discussed above. A complete feature description of a segment consists of the values of these articulator-bound features together with the values of the features [vocalic] and [consonantal]. In the case of [+consonantal] segments, it is also necessary to specify the articulator-free features [continuant], [sonorant], and [strident], together with the articulator that produces the consonantal constriction (i.e., one of lips, tongue blade, or tongue body).

As noted above, the acoustic manifestation of the articulator-free features [vocalic] and [consonantal] in terms of landmarks provides evidence for the sequence of vowel, glide, and consonant segments. We will see in chapters 6 to 9 that acoustic evidence for the articulator-bound features for each segment resides in properties of the acoustic signal in the general vicinity of the landmark or landmarks for that segment.

We can regard a landmark as a point in time when specified articulators achieve approximations to particular intended positions or configurations, or, in the case of consonants, when they produce constricting or releasing movements. The articulator-bound features for the landmark describe these intended positions, configurations, or movements. However, more often than not the acoustic correlates of these features are dependent on the adjacent segments, and it is necessary to examine acoustic attributes of the sound

Table 5.3 Feature values for some vowels and glides in English

Feature	i	ɪ	e	ɛ	æ	ɑ	ɔ	o	ʌ	ʊ	u	ɝ	w	j	h	l̩
Vocalic	+	+	+	+	+	+	+	+	+	+	+	+	−	−	−	+
Consonantal	−	−	−	−	−	−	−	−	−	−	−	−	−	−	−	−
Round	−	−	−	−	−	−	+	+	−	+	+	−	+	−		−
Anterior													−			+
Distributed													−			−
Lateral													−			+
High	+	+	−	−	−	−	−	−	−	+	+	−	+	+		−
Low	−	−	−	−	+	+	+	−	−	−	−	−	−	−		−
Back	−	−	−	−	−	+	+	+	+	+	+	+	+	−		+
Nasal																
Advanced tongue root	+	−	+	−	−	−	−	+	−	−	+	−	+	+		
Constricted tongue root	−	−	−	−	−	+	+	−	−	−	−	−	−	−		
Spread glottis															+	
Constricted glottis															−	
Stiff vocal folds																
Slack vocal folds																

over time intervals preceding and following the landmark in order to make inferences about the intended articulatory states at the landmark. In chapter 1 it was observed that the time taken for an articulator to move toward a target configuration from a previous position or to move to a future position from a target is usually in the range of 70 to 100 ms or even greater. Therefore one may need to examine attributes of the signal over a time interval of 70 to 100 ms or more on either side of the landmark to be able to estimate the articulator-bound features for that landmark.

The feature values for a number of vowels and consonants in English are listed in tables 5.3 and 5.4, respectively. The glides are included in table 5.3. The syllablic /l̩/ (as in the word *apple*) is included in table 5.3 as an example of a syllabic consonant. For the affricate segments /č/ and /ǰ/ in table 5.4, the features [∓continuant] are assigned. As will be seen in section 8.2, this assignment of both [−continuant] and [+continuant] reflects the fact that these segments are produced with an initial complete closure of the airway with the tongue blade, followed by a release of just the anterior part of the constriction (the [−continuant] phase). An interval of continuous turbulence noise then occurs, followed by a second release of the entire tongue blade (the [+continuant] phase).

A number of entries are left blank in tables 5.3 and 5.4. There are several conventions for omitting feature values. In some cases it is not possible to implement a particular feature when other features are in the same segment.

Table 5.4 Feature values for some consonants in English

Feature	p	t	k	b	d	g	m	n	ŋ	f	θ	s	š	v	ð	z	ž	č	ǰ	l	r
Vocalic	−	−	−	−	−	−	−	−	−	−	−	−	−	−	−	−	−	−	−	−	−
Consonantal	+	+	+	+	+	+	+	+	+	+	+	+	+	+	+	+	+	+	+	+	+
Continuant	−	−	−	−	−	−	−	−	−	+	+	+	+	+	+	+	+	±	±	−	+
Sonorant	−	−	−	−	−	−	+	+	+	−	−	−	−	−	−	−	−	−	−	+	+
Strident										+	−	+	+	+	−	+	+	+	+		
Lips	+			+			+			+				+							
Tongue blade		+			+			+			+	+	+		+	+	+	+	+	+	+
Tongue body			+			+			+												
Round	−			−			−			−				−							
Anterior		+			+			+			+	+	−		+	+	−	−	−	+	−
Distributed		−			−			−			−	−	+		−	−	+	+	+	−	−
Lateral							−	−	−											+	−
High			+			+			+											−	−
Low			−			−			−											−	−
Back			+			+			+											+	+
Nasal							+	+	+											−	−
Advanced tongue root																					
Constricted tongue root																					
Spread glottis	+	+	+	−	−	−				+	+	+	+	−	−	−	−	+	−		
Constricted glottis	−	−	−	−	−	−				−	−	−	−	−	−	−	−	−	−		
Stiff vocal folds	+	+	+	−	−	−	−	−	−	+	+	+	+	−	−	−	−	+	−		
Slack vocal folds	−	−	−	+	+	+	+	+	+	−	−	−	−	+	+	+	+	−	+		

For example, the feature [strident] is only relevant when continuous turbulence noise is being generated at a constriction, and hence this feature is not specified for segments that are [+sonorant] or [−continuant]. If a particular feature in a segment is not distinctive in English, then it is usually omitted. A feature is distinctive if it can potentially be used to distinguish between words in a language, all other features in the segment being the same. Thus the feature [back] is distinctive for vowels in English. An example is the word pair *bet* and *but*. However, the feature [nasal] is not distinctive for vowels in English and therefore is not specified. For consonants, [nasal] and [lateral] are not specified for segments that are [−sonorant]. There are restrictions on which features for consonants (in English) are specified depending on whether the major articulator for the consonant is the lips, the tongue blade, or the tongue body.[3]

6 Vowels: Acoustic Events with a Relatively Open Vocal Tract

We turn now to an examination of the various acoustic properties that can result when the vocal tract is in a relatively open configuration. We have seen in chapter 2 (section 2.1.7) that there is a limiting cross-sectional area of the constriction in the vocal tract below which the acoustic resistance and acoustic mass of the constriction will show a significant effect on the spectrum of the sound output relative to the spectrum for a less constricted configuration. With a constriction that is too narrow there may be a modification in the amplitude and spectrum of the glottal source and a reduced amplitude and increased bandwidth of the first-formant spectral peak and possibly of other formants. (See discussion of glides and liquids in sections 9.2 and 9.3.) The constriction size for which this condition occurs is generally in the range of 0.2 to 0.4 cm^2. In our discussions in this chapter, we are concerned primarily with sounds produced when the narrowest point in the vocal tract is not sufficiently constricted to cause this effect on the sound output when the acoustic source is the volume velocity resulting from modal (or pressed) vocal fold vibration, that is, for modes of vibration for which the average airflow is not large enough to cause a significant pressure drop at the constriction. These configurations are normally associated with syllabic nuclei or vowels.

Since the pressure drop across the constriction is small, negligible noise is generated due to turbulent airflow in the vicinity of the constriction. Thus the principal source of sound is in the vicinity of the glottis. In this chapter we are concerned with situations in which the vocal folds are vibrating to yield a quasi-periodic source of volume velocity at the glottis. In section 8.3 we discuss the properties of the sound when there is a noise source near the glottis, as a result of turbulent airflow near the glottal constriction.

Several kinds of articulatory manipulations are available for producing distinctively different acoustic characteristics for vowels. The shape of the vocal tract between the glottis and the lips can be manipulated through adjustment of the position and configuration of the lips, the tongue blade, the tongue body, and the tongue root. Various adjustments can be made to the state of the laryngeal structures to produce different glottal source characteristics. And a velopharyngeal opening can be created to introduce acoustic coupling to the nasal cavity. These characteristics can also be present in the sound during the time intervals immediately preceding or following a constricted consonantal configuration. Acoustic properties in these time intervals can often indicate features of the consonant, as discussed in chapters 7, 8, and 9.

In the following sections we examine the kinds of acoustic distinctions that are produced by various manipulations of the articulatory and laryngeal structures. We review some data on the responses of listeners to sounds with these acoustic properties, and we comment on the physiological responses of the ear to these sounds.

6.1 FORMANT BANDWIDTHS FOR VOWELS

As has been shown in chapter 3, when the source of sound is a volume velocity source at the glottis, and when the vocal tract can be regarded as a tube with no side branches and no cross modes, the transfer function from the source volume velocity to the volume velocity at the mouth opening is an all-pole function. The transfer function is completely defined, then, by the frequencies and bandwidths of the poles. When the vocal tract shape is modified by adjusting the position of the tongue body and other structures, the frequencies of the poles, or formants, shift to new positions, and there may be changes in the bandwidths of the formants. Much of the discussion in this chapter is concerned with relations between vocal tract shapes and the formant frequencies. However, under some circumstances, the formant bandwidths can play a role in determining the spectrum shape that results from manipulation of the vocal tract configuration.

The formant bandwidths are determined by the acoustic losses in the vocal tract. As has been shown in section 3.4, these losses can arise from many sources, including the vocal tract walls, viscosity, heat conduction, and radiation. The contribution of each of these sources of loss to the formant bandwidths is roughly the same for different speakers, except for differences in scale. Each of these loss mechanisms has a different dependence on frequency, with the wall losses tending to dominate at low frequencies and radiation loss dominating at high frequencies. Some examples of the contribution of these losses to formant bandwidths have been given in section 3.4.

Measurements of the average formant bandwidth resulting from these four sources of acoustic energy loss, plotted as a function of frequency, are given in figure 6.1 (Fant, 1962, 1972; Fujimura and Lindqvist, 1971). The data in the figure were obtained from sweep-tone measurements, in which estimates of the transfer function were made by applying a transducer to the neck surface and measuring the sound pressure radiated from the mouth using a sinusoidal source. The glottis was closed when the measurements were made. Two figures are shown, one for the first-formant frequency (figure 6.1b), and the other for a wider range of formant frequencies (figure 6.1a). These bandwidth data are in reasonable agreement with data of House and

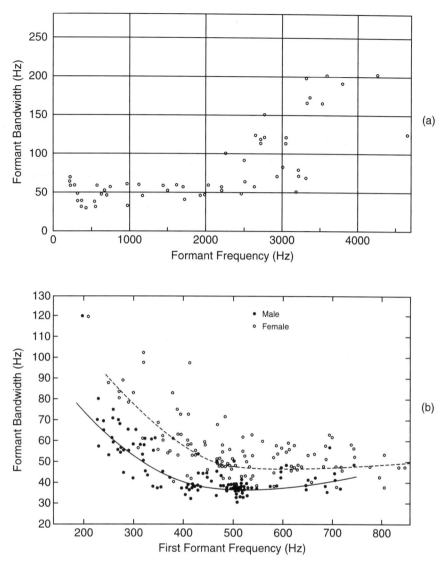

Figure 6.1 Measurements of formant bandwidths for a variety of vowels with a closed-glottis condition. The data in (a) were obtained using a sweep-tone method (Fant, 1962), and cover a range of vowel formants. The first-formant bandwidths in (b) were obtained by Fujimura and Lindqvist (1971), also using a sweep-tone method. Average curves are given for male and female speakers.

Stevens (1958), who obtained formant bandwidths for a closed glottis configuration by measuring the decay rate of the vocal tract transient response. Average values of the bandwidths of the first three formants for several vowel configurations were 54, 65, and 70 Hz, respectively, with the first-formant bandwidth varying from 39 to 73 Hz for different vowels. In the high-frequency range above about 2000 Hz, a major contributor to the bandwidth is acoustic loss due to radiation. Figure 6.1a shows that there is considerable variability in the formant bandwidths at these frequencies, depending

259   Vowels

primarily on the size of the mouth opening and on the cavity affiliation of $F2$, $F3$, and $F4$. In the first-formant range there is less variability, and some differences between male and female speakers can be observed. In the curves in figure 6.1b, there is a slight upturn at low frequencies, due to the effect of wall losses. There is a more abrupt upturn at high frequencies (in figure 6.1a) due to radiation losses. For certain vocal tract configurations, the bandwidth of a particular formant may deviate somewhat from the average curves in figure 6.1, as shown by scattering of points. For example, the bandwidth of the third formant for some vowels which have a relatively large mouth opening is relatively wide because of the increased losses due to radiation from the mouth (Fant, 1972).

The closed-glottis bandwidths in figure 6.1, as well as those reported by House and Stevens (1958), are somewhat greater than the bandwidths calculated for some simple resonator shapes, in table 3.1. Those shapes are a uniform cylindrical tube and a tube constricted near the open end. Actual vocal tract shapes are not cylindrical, and would have a greater surface area and hence greater acoustic losses at the walls.

In addition to losses arising from viscosity, heat conduction, wall impedance, and radiation, there may be losses at the glottis and at a narrow vocal tract constriction when there is flow through the constriction. These contributions to formant bandwidths (described in sections 3.4.5 and 3.4.6) depend on the glottal configuration used by the speaker and on the subglottal pressure, and may vary somewhat from speaker to speaker. Acoustic losses at the glottis can add substantially to the bandwidths of the first and possibly the second formant. Bandwidths estimated by fitting resonance curves to spectra of spoken vowels tend to be somewhat wider, on average, than the values given in figure 6.1 (Dunn, 1961). It is not unusual for the bandwidth at low frequencies to be two to three times the value given in figure 6.1 if the glottal configuration for the speaker is such that there is a glottal opening throughout the cycle of vibration (cf. K. N. Stevens and Hanson, 1995; Hanson, 1997).

Increases or decreases in the bandwidth of a formant can influence the prominence of the spectral peak corresponding to that formant. The peak-to-valley ratio for two adjacent formant peaks in the magnitude of the vocal tract transfer function when the formants are equally spaced is given by $2S/\pi B$, where S is the spacing (in hertz) between the formants and B is the bandwidth. (See also section 3.5.2.) Changes in the bandwidth of a formant can have a marked effect on this peak-to-valley ratio.

As we consider the effects of various articulatory manipulations on the formant frequencies for vowels, we will, in particular cases, comment on the possible influence of formant bandwidth changes on the spectrum shapes.

6.2 THE HIGH VOWELS

The principles underlying the relation between vocal tract shape and formant frequencies have been discussed in section 3.3 of chapter 3. If one begins

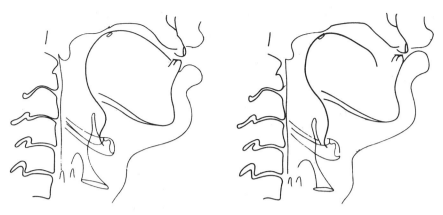

Figure 6.2 Midsagittal vocal tract configurations for the high vowels /i/ (left) and /u/ (right). Adult male speaker of English. (From Perkell, 1969.)

with a uniform tube that is closed at one end (the posterior end, or the glottis) and open at the other (the lips), then narrowing of the cross-sectional area in the front part of the tube, or widening of the cross-sectional area in the back half, results in a decrease of the first-formant frequency $F1$. The decrease of $F1$ is accentuated if both of these changes occur, that is, a narrowing of the front part of the tube (corresponding to the vocal tract anterior to the velo-pharyngeal region), and an increase in the volume of the back part of the tube (corresponding to the pharyngeal region). A narrowing in one part of the vocal tract will automatically be accompanied by a widening in other parts, since there is a constraint that the vocal tract volume is roughly constant, as observed in section 1.1.3.4. Since the anterior half of the vocal tract length is horizontal, the narrowing in this region is accomplished most effectively by raising the tongue body, so that the dorsum of the tongue on the midline approaches to within a few millimeters of the hard or soft palate.

Sketches of midsagittal vocal tract configurations for two vowels with a raised tongue body are shown in figure 6.2. These vowels are referred to as *high* vowels, since the tongue body is in a raised or high position. The high tongue body position is most readily achieved by adjusting the mandible to a raised position as well as by raising the tongue body in relation to the mandible. The combination of the acoustic compliance of the volume behind the narrowing and the acoustic mass of the narrow air passage between the dorsum of the tongue and the palate leads to a low-frequency first formant. The high vowels in figure 6.2 are produced with a fronted tongue body (the vowel /i/ on the left) or with a backed tongue body position (the vowel /u/ on the right).

6.2.1 First-Formant Frequency and Bandwidth for High Vowels

As the tongue body is raised to decrease the cross-sectional area of the constriction formed between the dorsum of the tongue and the palate, $F1$

decreases in frequency. If the vocal tract is assumed to have hard walls, the frequency of the first formant is approximately that of a Helmholtz resonator, as discussed in section 3.3.3. This frequency is given approximately by

$$F1' = \frac{c}{2\pi}\sqrt{\frac{A_c}{V\ell_c}}, \tag{6.1}$$

where c = velocity of sound, V = volume behind the constriction, and ℓ_c and A_c are the length and cross-sectional area of the constriction. As has been shown by Fant (1972), and as noted in section 3.4.2, an assumption of hard walls is not valid at low frequencies, and the mechanical mass of the vocal tract walls plays a role in determining the lowest natural frequency. A better approximation for the actual $F1$, for typical vocal tract wall characteristics, is given by

$$F1 = \sqrt{(F1')^2 + F_c^2}, \tag{6.2}$$

where F_c is the lowest natural frequency of the vocal tract when there is a complete closure. The value of F_c is in the range of 150 to 200 Hz for an adult, depending on the size of the vocal tract (Fant, 1972). We have seen in section 3.4.2 that the wall effects cause $F1$ to be less sensitive to constriction size than it would be if hard walls were assumed for the vocal tract.

The principal articulatory maneuver for producing a first formant that is in the required low-frequency range for a high vowel is to raise the tongue body to create a relatively narrow constriction of sufficient length (roughly 4 cm for an adult) in the oral cavity. Since the vocal tract volume remains about constant, this raised tongue body position leads to a large volume in the pharyngeal region relative to the pharyngeal volume when the vocal tract is in a neutral configuration with no major constriction. In terms of percentage change, this pharyngeal volume is rather insensitive to changes in the constriction size when the tongue body is high, and consequently it is the constriction size and length that are the principal determinants of $F1$. The high tongue body position is achieved in part through contraction of the posterior fibers of the genioglossus muscle, which widens the vocal tract in the pharyngeal region and causes an upward displacement of the tongue body (Baer et al., 1988).

With a raised mandible, we have seen (section 1.1.3.4) that the total vocal tract volume is about 50 cm^3 for an average adult female and about 70 cm^3 for a male. The volume of the cavity behind the constriction formed by the tongue body when a high vowel is produced forms a substantial fraction of this total volume, and is probably in the range of 40 to 60 cm^3 for a male, depending on whether the tongue body is in a fronted or a backed position (Baer et al., 1991). For example, if we select a value of V in equation (6.1) of 50 cm^3 and a constriction with a length of 4 cm and a cross-sectional area of 0.4 cm^2, $F1'$ is about 250 Hz from equation (6.1), and $F1$ from equation (6.2) (after correction for the wall impedance) is about 310 Hz. Reducing the constriction size to 0.2 cm^2 causes a lowering of $F1$ to about 250 Hz. Thus we observe considerable stability in $F1$ over this 2:1 range of constriction areas.

In the case of the vowel with the more backed tongue body position, the volume behind the tongue body constriction is somewhat less than it is for the more fronted vowel. Consequently the first-formant frequency from equations (6.1) and (6.2), assuming that the only constriction is the one formed by the tongue body, is somewhat higher than the values calculated above for the fronted vowel. However, by narrowing and lengthening the lip opening, an additional acoustic mass is created, and the actual $F1$ is decreased relative to this calculated value. (The effects of rounding of the lips are discussed in more detail in section 6.6.) Again, the influence of the acoustic mass of the vocal tract walls contributes to the stability of $F1$ to perturbations in the size of the constriction formed by the tongue body or the lips.

Another factor that contributes to the stability of $F1$ for vowels produced with a high tongue position arises from physiological considerations. For a high vowel, it is estimated that the position of the upper surface of the tongue body in the midline needs to be adjusted to within an accuracy of about 1 to 2 mm if the first-formant frequency is to lie within a range of 250 to 350 Hz. This estimate is based on calculation of $F1$ for Helmholtz reso-nators with different constriction sizes (making appropriate assumptions about the cross-dimensions of the vocal tract in the vicinity of the constric-tion). This degree of precision would be a difficult control task for a speaker if this adjustment were effected by raising the entire tongue body as a whole and positioning it at the desired point in space. A different strategy seems to be used by speakers when they produce a high vowel like /i/ (Fujimura and Kakita, 1978; Perkell and Nelson, 1982). In this view, the surface of the front part of the tongue is shaped and possibly stiffened in a local region near the midline by means of the intrinsic muscles, and by the upper more vertical fibers of the genioglossus muscle, so that in the lateral direction the surface is flat or slightly concave, with a depression in the midline. The tongue body is then displaced upward by contraction of the appropriate extrinsic muscles (particularly the lower fibers of the genioglossus muscle) so that the lateral and dorsal surfaces of the tongue are pressed against the contours of the hard palate. An open passage is preserved in the midline, however, as shown in figure 1.22 for the vowel /i/, because of the shaping of the tongue surface and because of the domed shape of the hard palate in lateral section, as in figure 1.20b. The shape of the tongue surface in relation to the hard palate is shown schematically in lateral section in figure 6.3. The cross-sectional area of the narrow part of the vocal tract is relatively insensitive to the amount of force exerted by the extrinsic tongue muscles to raise the tongue body. Some precision is required to shape the tongue surface locally so that it is flat or has a slight depression of 1 to 2 mm in the midline, but considerable vari-ability is possible in the degree of contraction of the muscles that cause an upward movement of the tongue body.

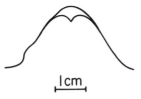

|1 cm|

Figure 6.3 Lateral section of hard palate, with a sketch of the estimated shape of the tongue surface when the tongue is in the position appropriate for the vowel /i/.

The bandwidth of the first formant for high vowels is primarily a consequence of acoustic losses at the vocal tract walls and at the glottis, with smaller contributions due to viscosity and heat conduction at the walls. Theoretical estimates, given in section 3.4, show an average $F1$ bandwidth for modal voicing that is approximately 80 Hz for high vowels. The bandwidth is somewhat greater during the open phase of glottal vibration, and somewhat less during the closed phase (as shown in figure 6.1). For some speakers, the glottis does not completely close during a cycle of vibration, and the average $F1$ bandwidth is greater for such individuals.

Spectra of two high vowels /i/ and /u/ (and, for contrast, a low vowel /ɑ/ having a high $F1$) are shown in figure 6.4. Spectra are given for configurations and fundamental frequencies appropriate for both adult female and adult male speakers. The waveforms for each of the vowels are displayed below the spectra. We concentrate here on the shape of the spectrum at low frequencies, in the range of the first formant. For the high vowels, the first formant is low and close to the fundamental frequency ($F0$), whereas for the low vowels the spacing between $F1$ and $F0$ is large, and there is a deeper spectral "valley" in the frequency range below $F1$. The periodicity at the fundamental frequency is evident in the waveforms. Within each period, the damped oscillation at the frequency of the first formant can be seen. There are just one or two such oscillations per fundamental period for the waveforms of high vowels, but several oscillations in the case of the low vowel.

High vowels, then, can be described acoustically as having spectra with only a narrow and shallow low-frequency dip in the spectrum below the first spectral peak. This property is evident in the examples of spectrograms in figure 6.5. The spectra for constructing the spectrogram are calculated with an effective filter bandwidth of about 300 Hz. For the high vowels, the lower edge of the first-formant prominence is close to the baseline, whereas for the low vowel there is a substantial gap between the baseline and the lower edge of the first-formant peak.

6.2.2 Perception and Auditory Response for High Vowels

With our present limited knowledge of the mechanisms of vowel perception, one can only speculate on possible ways in which the auditory system might respond to these vowels having a low $F1$. One possible explanation is based

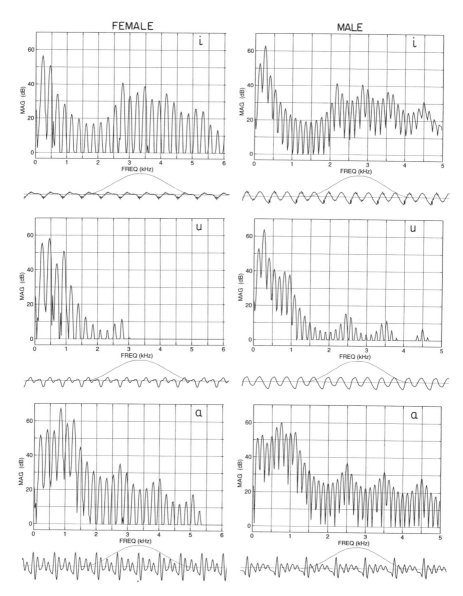

Figure 6.4 Spectra of the two high vowels /i/ and /u/ (top and middle panels) and the low vowel /ɑ/ (bottom panel), with formant frequencies and fundamental frequencies appropriate for an adult female speaker (left column) and an adult male speaker (right column). The waveform is shown below each panel. The window used to calculate the spectrum is shown on each waveform. The vowels were synthesized using a Klatt synthesizer (Klatt and Klatt, 1990).

on the concepts of auditory nerve synchrony to the stimulus, as developed by Srulovicz and Goldstein (1983), Sachs and Young (1979), Young and Sachs (1979), and Delgutte and Kiang (1984a). Another represents an extension of the ideas of Chistovich and her colleagues (Chistovich and Lublinskaya, 1979; Chistovich et al., 1979) concerning auditory perception of vowel-like stimuli with spectral prominences.

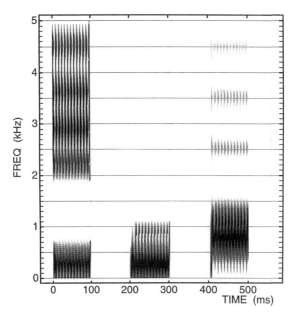

Figure 6.5 Spectrograms of 100-ms portions of the three vowels in figure 6.4 for the simulated male speaker.

A distinguishing characteristic of high vowels is that the first-formant frequency is generally within 100 to 200 Hz of the fundamental frequency. Since the auditory filters at low frequencies—at least as determined from physiological tuning curves—have gently sloping skirts (cf. figure 4.14), the synchrony in the waveforms at the outputs of these filters up to, say, 400 Hz, is expected to be dominated by a single frequency component, probably the harmonic of the fundamental that is closest with the first-formant spectral peak. Thus the synchrony of the responses of the low-frequency auditory nerve fibers is dominated in this low-frequency region by the first formant, and there is little or no synchrony with the fundamental frequency. That is, if the waveforms for high vowels shown in figure 6.4 were passed through the low-frequency auditory filters, a single dominant synchrony would be observed at the outputs of the different filters, and this frequency would be that of the harmonic closest to $F1$. This is, in effect, the dominant frequency of occurrence of the waveform peaks in the waveforms below the spectra for /i/ and /u/ in figure 6.4. A pattern of synchrony of this type for high vowels has been reported by Delgutte and Kiang (1984a), although their data on responses to low-frequency fibers are rather limited. This pattern of response is in contrast to the response for non-high vowels, for which the first formant is sufficiently displaced from the fundamental component that there are different populations of auditory nerve fibers that show primary synchrony with the fundamental frequency and the first-formant frequency. An example of such a response pattern for the vowel /æ/ has been shown in figure 4.19. Whether these different response patterns form a firm auditory basis for the high/non-high distinction for vowels must await the results of further research.

The frequency difference between the first formant and the fundamental frequency for high vowels is generally less than 3 bark for all speakers, whether they be adult males, adult females, or children (Syrdal and Gopal, 1986). (In the frequency range below 500 Hz, 1 bark is equal to 100 Hz, from table 4.1 and figure 4.30.) That is, the frequency range within which there is spectral energy below the first formant is less than 3 bark. For the spectra in figure 6.4, the differences $F1-F0$ in bark for the three vowels /i/, /u/, /ɑ/ are 0.9, 1.4, and 5.5 for the female examples, and 1.6, 1.7, and 5.2 for the male examples. As has been discussed in section 4.2.7, Chistovich and her colleagues have suggested that there is a mode of auditory analysis for vowels that estimates the center of gravity of a spectral prominence that spans 3.0 to 3.5 bark without regard to fluctuations of the spectrum within this band. That conclusion was based on experiments on the perception of vowel-like sounds with two formants. This concept has been extended to the low-frequency region for vowels, encompassing a group of the first few harmonics (Traunmüller, 1981; Hoemeke and Diehl, 1994). This mode of analysis would then interpret a cluster of harmonics that included both $F0$ and $F1$ as a single prominence, if the difference $F1 - F0$ were less than 3.0 to 3.5 bark. That is, when a high vowel is processed by such a mode of analysis, the peak that results from the first formant is the lowest peak. As we shall see later, the non-high vowels do not have this property.

It is noted that speakers tend to produce high vowels with a fundamental frequency that is 10 to 20 Hz higher than $F0$ for non-high vowels (Peterson and Barney, 1952; House and Fairbanks, 1953) for vowels in citation utterances. This intrinsic effect on $F0$ also occurs in running speech, although the amount of change depends on the position in the sentence (Shadle, 1985b). This adjustment of $F0$ would tend to reduce the difference $F1 - F0$ for a high vowel, and would therefore enhance the listener's identification of the vowel as a high vowel.

6.2.3 Summary: High Vowels

We observe, then, that a number of acoustic, physiological, and auditory factors combine to define a category of vowels that are produced with a high tongue body position and a low first-formant frequency. The impedance of the vocal tract walls contributes to stability of the first formant, the tongue surface in the lateral direction can be shaped to produce a stable acoustic output (at least for fronted tongue body positions) that is insensitive to the degree of contraction for the muscles controlling tongue height, and the auditory response to sounds with a low $F1$ appears to have distinctive properties. Two ways have been suggested of characterizing the auditory response to high vowels. One approach is based on the hypothesis that a sound with spectral peaks that are separated by less than 3.0 to 3.5 bark gives a response that is distinctively different from that for a sound with a wider spacing of the peaks. In the case of high vowels, the spacing between $F0$ and $F1$ is generally less than 3 bark, and this is a possible basis on which the class of high vowels can be specified. Another, possibly related, basis for defining the class of high vowels is in terms of the synchrony of discharges of low-frequency auditory nerve fibers. For high vowels, it appears that synchrony with $F1$ dominates the response of these fibers. The effect of these various factors is to produce a class of vowels that have a relatively stable acoustic property and that yield a relatively well-defined type of response in the auditory system.

Within the class of high vowels, there are a number of acoustic and articulatory properties that can define other categories, depending on the tongue body position in a front-back direction, the rounding of the lips, the position of the tongue blade, the maximum degree of constriction formed by the lips and tongue, the positioning of the tongue root, and the state of the laryngeal structures. Some of these categories are described later in this chapter.

6.3 THE NON-HIGH VOWELS: HIGH FIRST-FORMANT FREQUENCY

For non-high vowels, $F1$ is higher than for high vowels, and the spacing between $F0$ and $F1$ is usually greater than 3 bark. There is a significant fall in the spectrum amplitude below the first-formant peak, as the bottom panels of figure 6.4 show. The spacing between $F0$ and $F1$ is sufficient that auditory nerve fibers with characteristic frequencies near $F0$ show synchrony with $F0$, and their synchrony is not dominated by $F1$, as it is for high vowels. Fibers with characteristic frequencies in the vicinity of $F1$ show synchrony with $F1$, that is, with the high-frequency fluctuations in the waveforms shown in the lowest panels of figure 6.4. For non-high vowels there tends to be a fall in the amplitude of the broadband spectrum below the first-formant peak.

Within the class of non-high vowels there are two principal possibilities: *low* vowels that are characterized by a maximally high first formant, and *non-low* vowels for which the first-formant frequency is intermediate between that for a high vowel and that for a low vowel. We shall see that each of these two classes of non-high vowels has its distinguishing articulatory, acoustic, and perceptual attributes. We consider first the low vowels.

6.3.1 Articulatory and Acoustic Characteristics of Low Vowels

When a narrowing is made in the posterior one half of the vocal tract, the acoustic consequence is an increase in the frequency of the first formant relative to the value of $F1$ for a vocal tract of uniform cross-sectional area. This result comes directly from the perturbation theory outlined in section 3.3.5. This increase in $F1$ is enhanced if the cross-sectional area in the anterior one half of the vocal tract is increased. Both modifications of the vocal tract

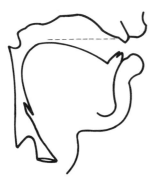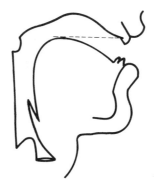

Figure 6.6 Midsagittal vocal tract configurations for the low vowels /ɑ/ (left) and /æ/ (right). The horizontal lines show the approximate location of the plane of the surfaces of the upper teeth. Adult male speaker of English. (From Perkell, 1969.)

shape—the narrowing in the posterior region and the widening in the anterior region—are achieved by constricting the vocal tract in the vicinity of the tongue root and by lowering the tongue body. Both of these maneuvers lower the superior dorsal surface of the tongue in the mouth cavity, and consequently these vowels are referred to as *low* vowels. Midsagittal configurations for two low vowels /ɑ/ and /æ/ are shown in figure 6.6. The narrowing in the pharyngeal region is especially apparent for /ɑ/. Both configurations show the low tongue body position and wide mouth opening, which are achieved by lowering the mandible. The place in the pharyngeal region where the maximum constriction occurs, or the extent of the region over which the narrowing occurs, can be adjusted by moving the tongue body in an anterior or posterior direction, as in /æ/ and /ɑ/, respectively.

There are several physiological constraints or landmarks that are available to help a speaker to achieve a stable and repeatable articulatory configuration and a sound output with stable properties for low vowels. The tongue surface is placed low in the front part of the vocal tract, and this low position can be guaranteed by ensuring that the lateral edges of the tongue are below the upper teeth, at least for the teeth anterior to the rearmost molars. That is, there is no contact between the tongue and the maxilla or these upper teeth. The lateral edges of the anterior portion of the tongue are usually in contact only with the lower teeth. Lowering the position of the jaw will help to achieve this goal. This property of the tongue position for a low vowel can be observed in figure 6.6, in which the plane of the upper teeth is shown.

The downward movement of the body of the tongue is achieved in part by lowering the mandible and in part through contraction of the hyoglossus muscle, at least for the vowel /ɑ/ (Baer et al., 1988). This muscle projects superiorly and anteriorly into the sides of the tongue from the superior surface of the hyoid bone, as seen in figure 1.21. Contraction of the hyoglossus muscle, therefore, displaces the tongue body downward and in a posterior direction. Additional narrowing in the pharyngeal region is presumably realized by contraction of the pharyngeal constrictor muscles.

Limitations on the minimum pharyngeal cross-sectional area that can be achieved for low vowels are determined by acoustic and aerodynamic factors. As in the case of high vowels, as the cross-sectional area at the constriction is reduced, a point is reached where airflow through the constriction during production of the vowel causes a pressure drop across the constriction, and can cause turbulence noise to be generated at the constriction. This buildup of pressure and possible generation of noise is not consistent with production of a vowel, and thus the reduction in constriction size for a low vowel should be limited to cross-sectional areas that are greater than this critical value. This value is probably in the vicinity of 0.2 to 0.4 cm^2 for adult vocal tracts, as noted earlier, and as illustrated in figure 1.26. The strategy for producing a low vowel, then, is to adjust the pharyngeal constriction to give an $F1$ that is as high as possible consistent with this limitation imposed by aerodynamic factors.

The acoustic consequences of narrowing the vocal tract in the pharyngeal region and widening it in the oral region can be estimated by referring to the discussion of two-tube resonator models in figures 3.13 and 3.14. The vocal tract shape for the low vowel /ɑ/ can be approximated by a configuration with a narrow tube at the glottis end and a wide tube at the mouth end. figure 3.14 shows that a maximum first-formant frequency is obtained when the narrow and wide tubes have approximately equal lengths. Depending on whether the back cavity is longer or shorter than the front cavity, $F1$ will be primarily associated with the back or the front cavity, respectively. When the lengths of the two component tubes are about equal, the first-formant frequency is higher when the ratio of areas of the back and front tubes decreases. For example, for a tube with an overall length of 17 cm and an area ratio of 0.1, $F1$ is about 50 percent higher than its value for a uniform tube with the same area. An area ratio of 0.1 is a not unreasonable average value for the vowel /ɑ/ (Fant, 1960; Baer et al., 1991), and a 50 percent increase in $F1$ for this vowel relative to a vowel with a uniform configuration is in rough agreement with acoustic data (Peterson and Barney, 1952). The minimum pharyngeal cross-sectional area reported for this vowel (for male speakers) is about 0.6 cm^2 (Fant, 1960; Baer et al., 1991). In the case of the vowel /æ/, articulatory data show that the narrowing at the glottal end of the vocal tract tends to be restricted to a length of about 6 cm, with a minimum area that is about 1.0 cm^2 (Baer et al., 1991). If this configuration is represented as a two-tube resonator with a 6-cm tube at the glottal end and an area ratio of 0.1, then figure 3.14 shows that $F1$ is about 40 percent higher than it would be for a uniform tube. Again this estimate is in rough agreement with acoustic data for this vowel. However, since the cross-sectional area of the vocal tract for this vowel shows a gradual widening beginning in the pharyngeal region, a two-tube model is only a rough approximation to the vocal tract shape.

The reduction in cross-sectional area in the pharyngeal region can have acoustic effects that influence the bandwidth or the degree of spectral prominence of particular formants. For example, for a low vowel with a backed tongue body, as in the left panel of figure 6.6, the first formant is often associated primarily with the back cavity, particularly for adult male speakers, who have a greater pharynx length than adult females. (See table 1.1.) That is, most of the acoustic energy at the frequency of the first formant is stored in this pharyngeal region. As has been discussed in section 3.4.6, the effects of the glottal opening on the bandwidth of the first formant can be substantial for this configuration. This increased bandwidth will occur during the open phase of the glottal vibration cycle, and the result will be an increase in the average or effective bandwidth of the formant (Fant and Liljencrants, 1979). Flattening of a first-formant peak will, in a sense, destroy the vowel-like non-nasal character of the sound (which requires narrow spectral peaks with valleys between the peaks). This condition, then, must be avoided by the speaker, and therefore places a limit on the degree of pharyngeal constriction that is allowable for low vowels, in addition to the limit determined by aerodynamic factors.

6.3.2 Vowels Intermediate Between High and Low Vowels

For vowels that are non-low and non-high, the height of the tongue body is intermediate between that for high vowels and that for low vowels. Examples of midsagittal sections for these vowels are shown in figure 6.7, both for a fronted and a backed tongue body position, represented by the vowels /e/ and /o/, respectively.

In the case of the fronted tongue body position, the lowering of the tongue body from the high to the intermediate position results in an increase in the cross-sectional area of the constricted region. This displacement causes a reduction in the acoustic mass of the constriction and consequently an

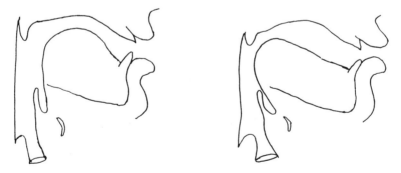

Figure 6.7 Midsagittal vocal tract configurations for the non-low, non-high vowels /e/ (left) and /o/ (right). Adult male speaker of French. (Adapted from Bothorel et al., 1986.)

increase in the frequency of the first formant. The first-formant frequency is intermediate between that for a high and that for a low vowel. This non-low, non-high configuration is normally achieved by placing the lateral edges of the tongue in contact with the upper teeth and the lateral surfaces of the hard or soft palate. On the other hand, the tongue body is not raised so much that it makes contact with the palate over a substantial part of its surface in a coronal plane, as it does for a high vowel. For the non-high vowel, then, only the lateral edges of the tongue are in contact with the rigid lateral boundaries of the palate.

What strategy does a speaker use to make this configuration repeatable and stable? It is probable that, at least for the vowels with a fronted tongue body position, the strategy is similar to that used to produce a high front vowel, as discussed in section 6.2. It is assumed that the front part of the tongue surface is stiffened to maintain a relatively flat contour in the lateral direction over an appreciable portion of its width. Activation of the muscles that raise the tongue body (particularly the posterior fibers of the genioglossus muscle) then pushes the tongue against the palate so that the lateral edges are in contact with the lateral surfaces of the palate. Because of the domed shape of the palate and the stiffened surface of the tongue, increasing the upward push on the tongue body does not result in additional upward displacement of the tongue surface toward the palate, and thus the cross-sectional area of the space between the tongue surface and the palate remains relatively stable. The tongue surface could be shaped so that the cross-sectional area near the anterior portion of the tongue would be less than that at a more posterior part of the upper tongue surface. Conditions could be adjusted to yield an $F1$ value in the appropriate midrange discussed above. This set of conditions is normally achieved with a jaw position intermediate between that for a low vowel and a high vowel; such a jaw position would be consistent with the tongue body configuration required for this class of vowels.

When the tongue body is backed, lowering of the tongue body from the high to the intermediate position permits the point of maximum constriction to be placed in the upper region of the pharynx. The volume behind the constriction is not as large as it is for a high vowel. On the other hand, raising of the tongue body from the low position can create a larger volume in the pharyngeal region below the constriction, as well as a point of constriction that is higher than that for a low vowel. These two adjustments contribute to a configuration with a first formant that is higher than that for a high vowel and lower than that for a low vowel.

In summary, then, we can define a class of vowels that contrasts with high vowels on the one hand and low vowels on the other. This contrast can be defined in terms of acoustic properties and in terms of articulatory strategies used to achieve these properties. As in the case of the high vowels, the non-high vowels can also be classified in terms of additional parameters such as front-back tongue position, lip rounding, velopharyngeal opening, and state and configuration of laryngeal structures. For each of these manipulations, however, the basic articulatory and acoustic attributes for the low and non-low vowels discussed above are maintained.

6.3.3 Auditory Response for Non-High Vowels

Partial evidence for a qualitative distinction between the classes of low and non-low vowels comes from studies of auditory nerve responses to these vowels. When a vowel has a high $F1$, it has been observed that low-frequency fibers with characteristic frequencies in the vicinity of $F1$ show responses that are synchronous with $F1$, whereas fibers with lower characteristic frequencies show synchrony with $F0$. If $F1$ is sufficiently high, however, there are fibers tuned to intermediate frequencies (between $F0$ and $F1$) whose responses are synchronous neither with $F0$ nor with $F1$. Rather, these fibers show synchrony with their own characteristic frequencies. That is, $F0$ and $F1$ are sufficiently well separated that neither frequency dominates the responses of the fibers. Fibers that respond in this way can be identified in the data of Delgutte and Kiang (1984a), as schematized in figure 4.20. This appears to be the pattern of response for a low vowel.

For a non-low, non-high vowel, the separation between $F0$ and $F1$ is not as great as it is for a low vowel. There are still some low-frequency fibers that show principal synchrony with $F0$, and others that are synchronized principally with $F1$. However, there is little or no intermediate frequency region where neither frequency dominates the response. To put it more positively, all the auditory nerve fibers with characteristic frequencies up to and above the first-formant frequency show principal synchrony either with $F0$ or $F1$. This pattern is in contrast to that for a low vowel, for which there are fibers in an intermediate range that show synchrony with neither $F0$ nor $F1$. As we learn more about the response of fibers with low characteristic frequencies, it will, we hope, be possible to specify more precisely the nature of the responses to low vowels, and how they differ qualitatively from the responses to non-low vowels and to other classes of speech sounds.

6.4 FRONT-BACK TONGUE BODY POSITION

Each of the classes of vowel configurations and low-frequency spectral shapes described above can be further subdivided into categories depending on the front-back position of the tongue body and on the spectrum shape above the frequency of the first formant. Midsagittal vocal tract shapes for both front and back tongue body positions are shown in figures 6.2, 6.6, and 6.7, and illustrate how the front-back movement is realized for the different tongue heights. The acoustic consequences of a front-back displacement of the tongue body are similar for different tongue body heights, but we will

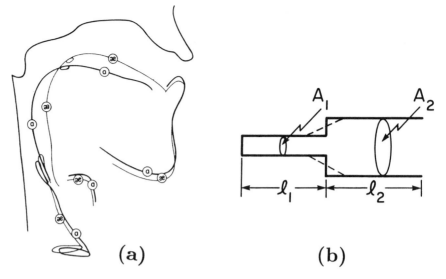

Figure 6.8 (a) Superimposed midsagittal configurations for the low vowels /æ/ and /ɑ/. (From Perkell, 1971.) (b) Model of low vowel vocal tract shape as a concatenation of two tubes. The dashed line indicates a tapered transition between the tubes.

discuss separately these acoustic correlates for low vowels, high vowels, and vowels with intermediate tongue body height.

6.4.1 Low Vowels

For the low vowels the tongue body is low in the mouth cavity, and there is a constriction or narrowing of the vocal tract in the pharyngeal region relative to its cross-sectional area in the oral region. A configuration with these characteristics is essential to achieving the high $F1$ appropriate for this class of vowels, as we have noted earlier. Within these constraints, however, there is some latitude in adjusting the tongue body position in a front-back direction. Figure 6.8a shows midsagittal sections of the low front and low back vowels /æ/ and /ɑ/ superimposed. The tongue body can be displaced back, producing a minimum constriction in the pharynx considerably above the larynx, with the tongue tip being displaced back from the inner surfaces of the lower incisors. Or the tongue body can be displaced forward, maintaining a narrowing in the lower pharynx but with the tongue tip in contact with the lower incisors or with the gum ridge immediately below these teeth. In order to estimate roughly the acoustic consequences of these displacements of the tongue body, we can approximate the vocal tract shape as a two-tube resonator with a narrow tube at the glottal (high-impedance) end and a wide tube at the open end, as shown in figure 6.8b. A slightly better approximation would include a tapered transition between the two component tubes. As the vocal tract is manipulated from the fronted position to the

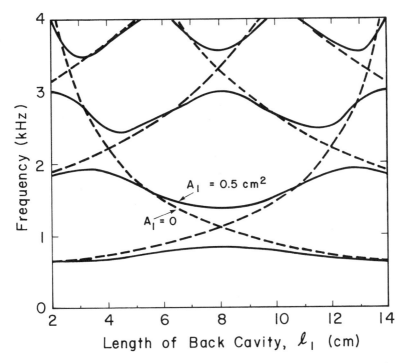

Figure 6.9 Frequencies of the first four natural frequencies for the nontapered configuration of figure 6.8, as the length ℓ_1 of the back cavity is manipulated. The total length $\ell_1 + \ell_2 = 16$ cm, and the cross-sectional area $A_2 = 3$ cm^2. The dashed line corresponds to the case where $A_1 \ll A_2$, and the solid line is for $A_1 = 0.5$ cm^2. The radiation impedance is assumed to be zero. (From K. N. Stevens, 1989.)

backed position in figure 6.8a, the length ℓ_1 of the back narrow section in the model is gradually increased, but with the total length of both tubes remaining the same.

The frequencies of the first four formants as a function of the length of the posterior tube in the model are plotted in figure 6.9. Two curves are shown: one gives the formant frequencies when the ratio of the areas of the two tubes is 6:1, and the other is for a theoretical situation where the area ratio is so large that there is no acoustic coupling between the two component tubes. (The effects of different amounts of coupling between the tubes has been discussed in section 3.3.4.) We observe that the frequency of the second formant undergoes significant fluctuations as the dimension ℓ_1 is manipulated, while $F1$ varies slowly with ℓ_1, with a broad maximum in the middle of the range. There are also fluctuations in $F3$ and $F4$, but these would be less significant than those of $F2$ if the frequencies were plotted on a bark scale, which compresses the frequency scale at high frequencies. The second-formant frequency has a minimum value for $\ell_1 = 8$ cm in the model, that is, at the point where the two sections of the model have about equal lengths.

For this configuration, the uncoupled natural frequencies of the two component tubes are about equal, and there is a spreading apart of the natural frequencies when the tubes are coupled together. The spacing between $F1$ and $F2$ depends upon the ratio of the cross-sectional areas of the two sections (cf. figure 3.14). We note, incidentally, that for this configuration ($\ell_1 = 8$ cm) where $F2$ is a minimum and is close to $F1$, $F3$ and $F4$ are also close together. This proximity of $F3$ and $F4$ will tend to enhance the spectrum amplitude for this vowel in the vicinity of these formants. A maximum value of the second formant frequency occurs for $\ell_1 \cong 4$ cm in the model. For this configuration, $F1$ is the lowest natural frequency of the anterior tube, and $F2$ and $F3$ are close together, one being the lowest natural frequency of the posterior, narrow tube, and the other being the second natural frequency of the wider, anterior tube. Again, these two formants are spread apart, relative to their values for the uncoupled resonators, as a consequence of acoustic coupling. Also, there may be some upward displacement of the formants for values of ℓ_1 in the vicinity of 4 cm if the model is modified to include a tapered transition between the two segments.

We observe, then, two qualitatively different configurations of natural frequencies depending on the value of ℓ_1 in the model. Either the second formant is maximally low and close to $F1$, or it is maximally high and close to $F3$. Both configurations have a relatively high $F1$ appropriate for a low vowel, although $F1$ is slightly higher for the configuration with $\ell_1 = 8$ cm in figure 6.8 than for the fronted configuration with $\ell_1 = 4$ cm.

Similar maximum and minimum values of $F2$ can be expected for fronted and backed positions of the tongue body in the actual vocal tract shown in figure 6.8a. As the tongue body is displaced forward while maintaining a narrowing in the lower pharynx, the frequency of the second formant will increase to a maximum value when the configuration is such that the natural frequency of the short section consisting of the larynx tube and the lower pharynx becomes roughly equal to the second natural frequency of the remainder of the vocal tract anterior to the constricted pharyngeal region. If necessary, the lips can be spread to decrease the effective length of the vocal tract and thus to maintain as high an $F1$ and $F2$ as possible. The widened mouth opening leads to an increased radiation resistance, and the increased acoustic losses result in greater bandwidths for higher-frequency formants (especially $F3$) relative to the bandwidths given in figure 6.1. An $F3$ bandwidth of 200 Hz or more is to be expected for /æ/. Displacement of the tongue body to the backed position in figure 6.8a will result in a constriction extending over an appreciable portion of the length of the pharynx. For an appropriate degree of backness, proper conditions are achieved to yield a maximally low value of $F2$, corresponding to the minimum in figure 6.9, while still maintaining a high $F1$ as required for a low vowel. For front-back perturbations of the tongue body when it is in one of the two positions just described, there is very little variation of $F2$, since we are operating in the vicinity of a maximum or a minimum on the curve of F2 vs. tongue body displacement. Thus there are not severe constraints on the accuracy with which the tongue body must be positioned along the front-back dimension (cf. K. N. Stevens, 1972, 1989).

6.4.2 High Vowels

We turn next to an examination of the acoustic consequence of front-back tongue body movements when the tongue body is in a raised or high position, that is, F1 is low. As in the case of low vowels, we will show that there is a fronted tongue body position for which F2 is high and close to F3 (and to F4), and a backed tongue body position which, if certain other conditions are satisfied, will give rise to a maximally low F2 that is close to F1.

We examine first the acoustic consequences of a fronted tongue body position. The vocal tract configuration is approximately as shown in the left side of figure 6.2. The constriction is smallest in the region to the front of the hard palate, and the cross-sectional area in the pharyngeal region is large. The configuration in figure 6.2 is achieved not only by moving the tongue body forward but also by raising the front part of the tongue or the tongue blade to create a relatively long and narrow constriction between the tongue surface and the hard palate. Perturbations of the position of the tongue body in the front-back direction cause an anterior-posterior displacement of the region where the constriction is smallest. The vocal tract shapes for these kinds of perturbations can be modeled with the idealized resonator shape shown in figure 6.10, with a large posterior cavity connected to a narrow anterior tube, with a slight widening at the front of this tube. Changes in front-back tongue body position correspond roughly to adjustments of the location of the point where the narrowing occurs. A more accurate model would have more gradual tapering of the area between the different sections. However, the general behavior of the natural frequencies of the model as the constriction position is manipulated would be about the same with or without this tapering.

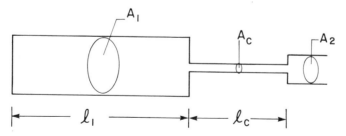

Figure 6.10 A resonator configuration approximating the vocal tract area function for a non-low front vowel. Approximations for different non-low front vowels can be obtained by manipulating l_1 and l_c. (From K. N. Stevens, 1989.)

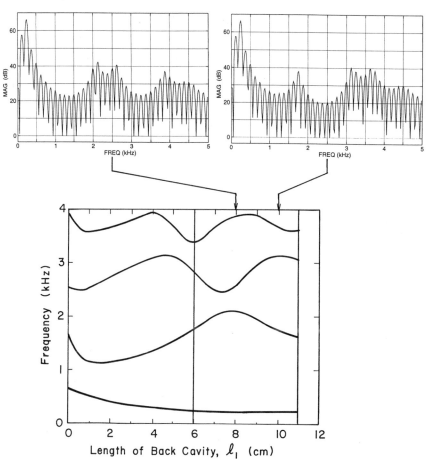

Figure 6.11 The bottom panel shows the natural frequencies of the configuration of figure 6.10, as the length ℓ_1 of the back cavity is manipulated. The fixed dimensions are $\ell_c = 5$ cm, $A_1 = 3.0$ cm^2, $A_c = 0.3$ cm^2, and $A_2 = 1.0$ cm^2, and the overall length of the tube is 16 cm. The portions of these curves between $\ell_1 = 6$ cm and $\ell_1 = 11$ cm are marked by vertical lines, and correspond approximately to the configurations for non-low front vowels. The upper two panels show spectrum shapes for vowels with formant frequencies corresponding to $\ell_1 = 8$ cm and $\ell_1 = 10$ cm, as indicated by the arrows.

Calculations of the frequencies of the first four formants as a function of the length ℓ_1 of the back cavity of the model in figure 6.10 are shown in figure 6.11 for a length ℓ_c of the constriction equal to 5 cm. The first-formant frequency remains low, in the range of 200 to 300 Hz, over the 5-cm range of back-cavity lengths that are of interest for the front vowel, shown in the figure. The second-formant frequency has a broad maximum in the middle of the range, and $F3$ and $F4$ each traverse maxima and minima within the range. Also shown in the figure are calculated spectra corresponding to two different configurations of formants. These spectra demonstrate that the amplitudes of the peaks corresponding to the formants are dependent on the formant frequencies. When two formants among $F2$, $F3$, and $F4$ are relatively close

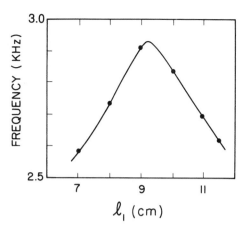

Figure 6.12 Estimates of center of gravity of the combined spectral prominences in the frequency range of $F2$, $F3$, and $F4$, for spectra corresponding to different values of ℓ_1, from figure 6.11. See text.

together (such as $F2$ and $F3$ for the left spectrum and $F3$ and $F4$ for the right spectrum), the corresponding peaks are of high amplitude and dominate the spectrum in this frequency region. There is evidence that the perceived vowel quality is determined more by the "center of gravity" of this multipeaked high-frequency spectrum than by the frequency of one of the formants (Carlson et al., 1970). In figure 6.12 we have plotted a measure of this center of gravity as a function of the length of the back cavity. The ordinate in this graph is the center of gravity of the high-frequency part of the pre-emphasized spectrum, with amplitudes of spectral peaks scaled in decibels and using a bark frequency scale. There is a broad maximum of this center of gravity in the vicinity of $\ell_1 = 9.3$ cm, in the region where $F3$ and $F4$ are rather close together. This appears to be an approximation to the configuration actually used by speakers of American English in producing a high front vowel, except that a more tapered back cavity in the model would lead to a higher $F2$. This configuration gives rise to a high-frequency spectral maximum that has a maximally high center of gravity. For this vocal tract shape, the second formant is associated primarily with the back cavity, consisting for the most part of the pharynx, while the closely spaced third and fourth formants are associated respectively with the lowest natural frequency of the anterior constricted region and the second natural frequency of the back cavity. Being associated with the front cavity, the third-formant bandwidth is strongly influenced by radiation loss, and tends to be wider than the average bandwidths in figure 6.1 in the $F3$ range.

We now examine the acoustic consequences of moving the tongue body back, while maintaining a high tongue body position. A simple model of this situation is shown in figure 6.13, where the constriction represents the narrowing formed by the raised hump of the tongue. As we shall see later, a stable acoustic characteristic for a high back vowel with a maximally low

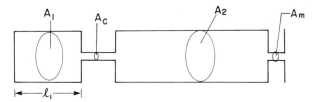

Figure 6.13 A resonator configuration approximating the vocal tract area function for a non-low back rounded vowel.

second-formant frequency can best be achieved by rounding the lips as well as displacing the tongue body backward, and consequently we have incorporated within the model the possibility for various amounts of constriction at the anterior end. The cross-sectional area of the constriction at the lips (A_m), as well as the size of the main constriction in the tube (A_c), is selected to be about 0.3 cm^2, which is about the smallest constriction size that will accommodate the airflow for a vowel without creating a pressure drop or without introducing turbulence noise. The right side of figure 6.2 shows a midsagittal section of a typical vocal tract configuration with a backed and high tongue body position.

The frequencies of the first three formants for the model in figure 6.13 are plotted as a function of the constriction position in figure 6.14a. The figure shows that, for this case in which there is a narrowing at the lips, the first-formant frequency remains at a low value (in the vicinity of 300 Hz) over a wide range of constriction positions. (The effect of wall impedance is not included in the calculations of $F1$, so that the $F1$ values in figure 6.14 are somewhat lower than they would be for a tube with the mass of the walls similar to that of the vocal tract surfaces.) A broad minimum of $F2$ occurs in the vicinity of a constriction position that is about 5 cm from the glottal end. At this minimum $F2$, the second formant becomes as close as possible to $F1$, consistent with the constraint that the constrictions cannot be narrowed beyond a certain limit if a vowel is to be produced. For the vowel /u/, the position of the tongue body constriction is probably around 7 to 8 cm from the glottis for this vocal tract length, but, as figure 6.14a shows, $F2$ remains low for this constriction position.

For this condition of minimum $F2$, there is a maximum acoustic and perceptual contrast between the high back vowel and the high front vowel discussed above. This contrast is illustrated in the upper two panels of figure 6.4, which show the spectra for these two vocal tract configurations. For the front vowel, there is a wide space between the low- and high-frequency peaks, whereas for the back vowel the combination of a low-frequency $F1$ and a low-frequency $F2$ results in a drastic reduction in the spectral amplitude at high frequencies.

In the case of the backed tongue body position, the condition of minimum $F2$ and the corresponding relative stability of $F2$ with perturbations in

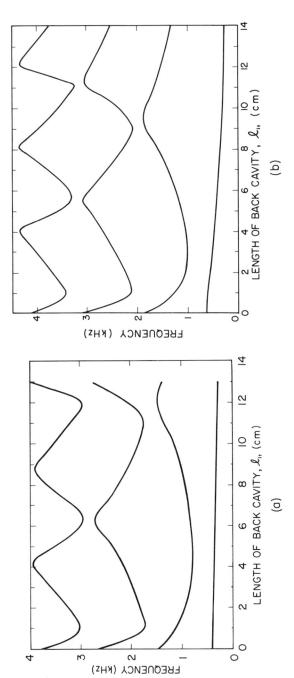

Figure 6.14 (a) Natural frequencies of configuration of figure 6.13, as the length ℓ_1 of the back cavity is manipulated. The cross-sectional areas of the different parts of the tube are $A_1 = A_2 = 3.0$ cm^2, $A_c = 0.3$ cm^2, and $A_m = 0.3$ cm^2. The constriction lengths are 2 cm for A_c and 1 cm for A_m, and the overall length is 16 cm. The portion of this chart for ℓ_1 in the range 2 to 6 cm corresponds approximately to the configuration for a non-low back rounded vowel. (b) Same as (a) except that $A_m = A_2 = 3.0$ cm^2 so that the model corresponds to an unrounded vowel.

tongue body position is achieved only if there is a constriction at the lips, that is, if the lips are rounded and a narrow opening is formed. The position of this minimum $F2$ would shift to the right (longer back cavity) if A_m were smaller in relation to A_c, and to the left if A_m were larger. If there were no lip rounding, that is, if $A_m = A_1 = A_2$ in figure 6.13, the formant frequencies as a function of ℓ_1 follow the pattern in figure 6.14b. There is again a minimum in $F2$, but it is shifted to even smaller values of ℓ_1. It is a common observation that lip rounding very often occurs with high back vowels in many different languages. Elimination of lip rounding for this tongue body configuration will result in an increase in $F2$ for values of ℓ_1 in the range 4 to 8 cm, so that there is a wider frequency separation between $F1$ and $F2$.

6.4.3 Vowels with Intermediate Height

The acoustic consequences of front-back tongue body displacements for vowels with intermediate tongue heights follow a pattern similar to that for high vowels. For the fronted tongue body position, the vocal tract constriction formed by the tongue surface against the hard palate is not as narrow as it is for the high front vowel. A midsagittal section for a typical front vowel that is non-high and non-low is displayed in the left side of figure 6.7. A model that approximates the vocal tract area function for a non-high fronted tongue position is similar to that in figure 6.10, except that the cross-sectional area A_c of the palatal constriction is greater. Displacement of the constricted part by changing the length of the back cavity gives rise to the patterns of formant frequencies similar to those in figure 6.11, but with higher values of $F1$ and a greater separation between $F2$ and $F3$ in the region where $F2$ is a maximum. Again, however, $F1$ is relatively stable over a few centimeters range of constriction positions, while $F2$ reaches a broad maximum. Because the constriction is not as narrow as for the high vowel, there is more acoustic coupling between the narrow and wide portions of the tube, and consequently $F2$ does not approach as close to $F3$ (nor $F3$ to $F4$), and thus the maximum $F2$ is not as high as it is for a high vowel. Nevertheless, $F2$ and $F3$ are close enough that their effects are combined auditorily, and there is an effective high-frequency center of gravity for the spectral prominence formed by these two formants. The frequency of this center of gravity is probably intermediate between $F2$ and $F3$. Whereas the tongue blade is raised to form the narrow constriction for the high front vowel /i/, it is less involved in forming the configuration for /e/.

An example of a vowel with a backed tongue body position for the intermediate tongue height is shown in the right side of figure 6.7. The model for this configuration is again similar to that for the high back vowel, but with two differences. One is that the tongue constriction can be displaced further back, because the tongue surface is not pushed as high against the palate. The other difference is that, because the jaw is usually slightly lowered to accommodate the somewhat lower tongue body, the maximum degree of narrowing for the lip opening does not have as small a cross-sectional area as does the model for high vowels. However, displacement of the tongue constriction for the rounded lip opening gives rise to formant patterns similar to those in figure 6.14a. The first formant for this non-high configuration remains in the mid-frequency range (400 to 500 Hz), whereas $F2$ shows a broad minimum when the constriction is in the pharyngeal region. That is, when the lips are rounded there is a range of positions of the tongue constriction for which $F2$ becomes close to $F1$ and is not very sensitive to perturbations in the position of the constriction. As in the case of high vowels, we observe that lip rounding is needed to achieve this condition which provides a maximal auditory and acoustic contrast between the front and back vowels with this intermediate tongue height. If the lips are not rounded, the minimum value of $F2$ that can be achieved for a non-high, non-low back vowel remains considerably separated from $F1$ (although still closer to $F1$ than to $F2$).

6.4.4   Summary of Front-Back Distinction

In summary, we find a common acoustic consequence of front-back displacements of the tongue body independent of the tongue height. Forward movement of the tongue body causes an increase of the second-formant frequency to a maximum value consistent with the types of constrictions that are possible for the different tongue heights. This maximum value is higher for the high vowels than for the low vowels. For the highest tongue body position, and, to some extent, for the intermediate position, the third and fourth formants combine with the second formant to produce a center of gravity of the high-frequency spectral prominence that is higher than $F2$. Front vowels, then, are always characterized by a broad minimum or "empty space" in the spectrum in the mid-frequency range between $F1$ and $F2$. For a backed tongue body, on the other hand, $F2$ is displaced to a value that is maximally low and close to $F1$ for a proper selection of the tongue body position. In the case of the non-low vowels, a value of $F2$ that is lowest and closest to $F1$ can be reached by rounding the lips. An acoustic consequence of an $F2$ value that is low and close to $F1$ is that the amplitudes of higher-frequency peaks in the spectrum are low relative to the amplitudes of the $F1$ and $F2$ peaks (as observed in section 3.2), and probably do not play a significant role in determining vowel quality.

Electromyographic data show a sharp distinction in the muscle activity involved in producing front and back vowels. Data reported by Baer et al. (1988) show that all back vowels exhibit activity of the styloglossus muscle, which is oriented to displace the tongue body back and upward. This muscle is especially active for non-low back vowels. Front vowels, on the other hand, show essentially no activity of the styloglossus muscle.

Table 6.1 Classification of a system of six vowels based on distinctive features

Feature	i	e	æ	ɑ	o	u
High	+	−	−	−	−	+
Low	−	−	+	+	−	−
Back	−	−	−	+	+	+

Another factor contributing to the contrast between front and back vowels is related to the resonances of the subglottal system. The influence of subglottal resonances on vowel spectra is considered in section 6.8.

6.5 SOME FURTHER ATTRIBUTES OF VOWELS IN A SYSTEM BASED ON HIGH-LOW AND FRONT-BACK DISTINCTIONS

In sections 6.2 and 6.3, we discussed possible articulatory, acoustic, and perceptual bases for a natural class of vowels with a high tongue body position and a class produced with a low tongue body position. Some arguments were also given for an intermediate class of vowels with a non-high, non-low tongue body. Analysis of the acoustic behavior of various shapes of tubes with constrictions, in section 6.4, led to the conclusion that, for each tongue body height, there are positions of the tongue body in the front-back dimension that lead to a second-formant frequency that is either maximally high and close to $F3$ or maximally low and close to $F1$. This observation provides some basis for postulating natural classes of front vowels and back vowels with well-defined acoustic and articulatory correlates.

This initial analysis, therefore, suggests a basic system of six vowels—three tongue body heights, each with a fronted and a backed position. These vowels are normally classified in terms of three binary features, [high], [low], and [back], as summarized in table 6.1. This table represents a subset of the vowels given in table 5.3. The feature combination [+high, +low] is not allowed. In many languages, there is a system of just five vowels, consisting of the four non-low vowels and a single low vowel. That is, in these languages, there is no front-back distinction for low vowels.

6.5.1 Derivation from Perturbation Theory

The articulatory and acoustic attributes of the various vowel distinctions discussed up to this point can be summarized by observing how these vowels can be derived from the so-called neutral or schwa vowel, that is, the vowel produced with a uniform vocal tract cross-sectional area. When the cross-sectional area is uniform, modeled by a tube of length ℓ, as in figure 6.15a, the formants are uniformly spaced at frequencies of $c/4\ell$, $3c/4\ell$, $5c/4\ell$, and so on, where c is the velocity of sound. The spectrum envelope of a vowel with these formant frequencies is shown in figure 6.15b. For this config-

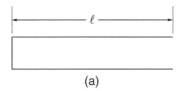

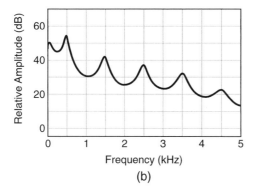

Figure 6.15 (a) Tube representing a vocal tract with a uniform cross-sectional area. (b) Spectrum envelope of vowel produced with a uniform vocal tract of length 17.7 cm. A hard-walled tube with zero acoustic impedance at the open end is assumed.

uration, the distribution of acoustic volume velocity for the first formant has a maximum in the front half of the tube, and the distribution of sound pressure has a maximum in the back half, as has been shown in figure 3.9. Consequently, perturbation of this uniform shape by narrowing the cross-sectional area in the front portion or widening the cross-sectional area in the back portion, or both, causes a lowering of the frequency of the first formant, following the principles discussed in section 3.3.5. Examination of the distributions of velocity and sound pressure for the second formant indicates that $F2$ will *increase* in frequency if the narrowing is made near the middle of the front half of the uniform tube, but will *decrease* if the narrowing is made at the front (cf. figure 3.19). These perturbations, then, shift the first two formants in the direction of a high front vowel and a vowel with a narrow lip opening. In the latter case, the lowering of $F2$ when there is a narrow opening at the lips can be further accentuated by forming a constriction at about the midpoint of the tube. A constriction at this point corresponds roughly to a constriction formed by a high back tongue body position. In figure 6.16 we represent the frequencies of $F1$ and $F2$ in a two-dimensional graph, with the point corresponding to the uniform tube plotted in the middle of the chart. Perturbation of the uniform tube to the high front configuration results in a shift in this point toward the upper left corner of the chart, that is, toward the point labeled /i/. Perturbation toward the high back rounded configuration shifts the point downward and to the left, toward the vowel /u/.

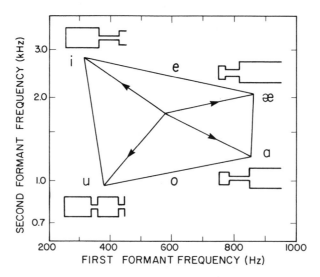

Figure 6.16 Plot of F2 vs. F1 showing how formants shift when the shape of an acoustic tube is perturbed in different ways. The midpoint represents equally spaced formants for a uniform tube of length 15.4 cm. The lines with arrows indicate how the formant frequencies change when the tube is modified as shown by the tube shapes. The corners of the diagram are labeled with vowel symbols corresponding roughly to the tube shapes. Approximate locations for the vowels /e/ and /o/ are also shown. Dimensions are selected to approximate the vocal tract size of an adult female speaker.

Similar arguments concerning perturbation of the uniform tube can give insight into the relations between articulatory configurations and formant frequencies for low vowels. The first formant is shifted up and the second formant is shifted down in frequency if the tube is constricted in a region somewhat behind the midpoint, and is widened in a region in front of the midpoint, as for /ɑ/. Both $F1$ and $F2$ are shifted up by constricting the tube near the back (i.e., near the closed end) and by widening it near the open end, as for /æ/. These shifts in the formant frequencies are in the direction of the points corresponding to low back and low front vowels, respectively, that is, to the vowels /ɑ/ and /æ/. The vowels /e/ and /o/ are also shown in figure 6.16, at points intermediate between /i/ and /æ/, and between /u/ and /ɑ/, respectively.

A detailed examination of the positions of the constrictions formed by the tongue body for vowels in several languages has been carried out by Wood (1979). He has shown that four such constriction locations are used to produce these vowels: a palatal constriction (as in /i/), a constriction in the vicinity of the soft palate (as in /u/), a constriction in the lower pharyngeal region (as in /ɑ/ and /æ/), and a constriction in the upper pharyngeal region (as in /o/). Wood points out that the muscles of the tongue are oriented in a way that favors the forming of constrictions in these four locations. He also notes that when a constriction is at one of these locations, $F1$ and $F2$ tend to be minimally sensitive to perturbations in the constriction position.

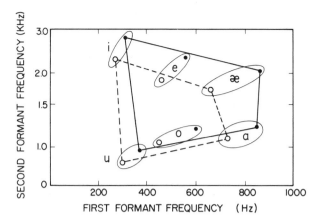

Figure 6.17 Plots of $F2$ vs. $F1$ for several vowels of American English. Open circles (joined by dashed lines) are data for adult male speakers and filled circles (solid lines) are for adult female speakers. The data for the vowels /i æ ɑ u/ are averages from Peterson and Barney (1952). Data for /e o/ are averages for two male and two female speakers.

6.5.2 Some Data from American English

Typical values of $F1$, $F2$, and $F3$ for the six basic vowels, as measured for American English, are given in table 6.2. The data for /i/, /æ/, /ɑ/, and /u/ are taken from Peterson and Barney (1952), who measured the formant frequencies of a set of nondiphthongized American English vowels in the context /hVd/, spoken by thirty-three adult males and twenty-eight adult females. We have added some data for the vowels /e/ and /o/ which are somewhat diphthongized. These data are sampled near the initial parts of these vowels in several different words, and are averages for two adult females and two adult males. The values of $F1$ and $F2$ for male and female speakers are plotted in the $F1$–$F2$ plane in figure 6.17. The vowels are in the expected relative positions based on the perturbation analysis in the previous section. The points for the four extreme vowels (from Peterson and Barney, 1952) have been joined by straight lines to form a quadilateral. Also shown in table 6.2 are the average fundamental frequencies for the vowels, as measured by Peterson and Barney, and the differences $B1$–$B0$, $B2 - B1$, and $B3 - B2$, expressed in bark. The spacing between $F2$ and $F1$ in bark is clearly less than $B3 - B2$ for the back vowels, whereas the opposite is true for the front vowels. For back vowels, the spacing between $F1$ and $F2$ is in the range of 2.1 to 4.7 bark and for front vowels, $B3 - B2$ is in the range of 1.1 to 2.3 bark. A distinguishing attribute of front vowels, then, is a spacing between $B2$ and $B3$ that is considerably less, on average, than the critical spacing of 3.0 to 3.5 bark proposed by Chistovich and her colleagues. (See discussion in section 4.2.7.) The difference $B1 - B0$ is in the range of 0.8 to 1.6 bark for high vowels and is greater than 3.0 bark for non-high vowels in table 6.2, suggesting that a critical spacing of about 3.0 bark between the first

Table 6.2 Average values of the first three formant frequencies and the fundamental frequency for six basic vowels of American English produced by adult male and female speakers

Vowel	F1 Hz	F2 Hz	F3 Hz	F0 Hz	B0 Bark	B1 Bark	B2 Bark	B3 Bark	B2 − B1 Bark	B3 − B2 Bark	B1 − B0 Bark
i (female)	310	2790	3310	235	2.8	3.6	15.7	16.8	12.1	1.1	0.8
i (male)	270	2290	3010	136	1.9	3.2	14.4	16.2	11.2	1.8	1.3
e (female)	560	2320	2950	223	2.7	5.9	14.5	16.1	8.6	1.6	3.2
e (male)	460	1890	2670	130	1.8	5.1	13.1	15.4	8.0	2.3	3.3
æ (female)	860	2050	2850	220	2.6	8.1	13.7	15.9	5.6	2.2	5.5
æ (male)	660	1720	2410	127	1.8	6.7	12.5	14.7	5.8	2.2	4.9
ɑ (female)	850	1220	2810	212	2.6	8.1	10.2	15.8	2.1	5.6	5.5
ɑ (male)	730	1090	2440	124	1.7	7.2	9.5	14.8	2.3	5.3	5.5
o (female)	600	1200	2540	220	2.7	6.2	10.2	15.1	4.0	4.9	3.5
o (male)	450	1050	2610	130	1.8	5.0	9.3	15.2	4.3	5.9	3.2
u (female)	370	950	2670	232	2.8	4.2	8.7	15.4	4.5	6.7	1.4
u (male)	300	870	2240	137	1.9	3.5	8.2	14.3	4.7	6.1	1.6

Note: Frequencies are given in hertz and in bark, and bark differences are also tabulated. Data for the vowels /i æ ɑ u/ are taken from Peterson and Barney (1952). Data for /e o/ are from a separate study with two female and two male speakers.

harmonic and the first formant provides a perceptual boundary between high and non-high vowels. This organization of the vowels according to the bark spacing between formants and between F1 and F0 has been discussed by Syrdal and Gopal (1986) for a wider range of American English vowels than those listed in table 6.2.

The data in table 6.2 show that, on average, the formant frequencies for female speakers in these studies are about 18 percent higher than those for male speakers. However, this scaling is not uniform across vowels and across formants, as can be observed in figure 6.17. For example, female/male formant ratios for F1 appear to be greater for low vowels than for high vowels (Fant, 1973a).

Another, more recent, study of the formant frequencies and fundamental frequencies of vowels with a large population of speakers has been reported by Hillenbrand et al. (1995). That study also measured vowel durations. Although the general pattern of formant and fundamental frequencies was similar to that of Peterson and Barney (1952), there were some significant differences. These differences underline the fact that groups of talkers with different regional dialects can show differences in their vowel patterns.

6.5.3 Spectrum Shapes and Equivalent F2′

As we have seen in chapter 3, the overall spectrum shape for a vowel is determined primarily by the frequencies of the formants and by the spectrum of the glottal source. The prominence of the spectral peak corresponding to

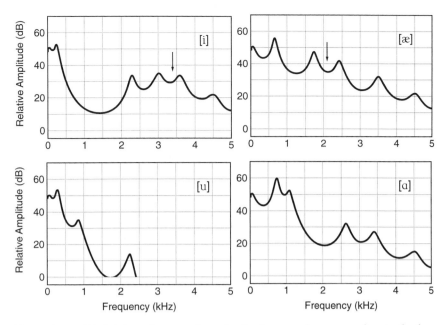

Figure 6.18 Calculated spectrum envelopes for the four vowels corresponding to the four corners of the quadilateral in figure 6.17, for an adult male speaker. The figure shows the relative amplitudes of the spectral prominences for the different vowels. The arrows in the two upper panels are estimates of where listeners would place an equivalent second-formant frequency $F2'$ for a two-formant matching vowel. The values of $F2'$ for front vowels are estimated from the data of Carlson et al. (1970), shown in figure 4.34.

a particular formant is also influenced, however, by the bandwidth of that formant. The formant frequencies given in table 6.2 for male speakers have been used to calculate idealized spectrum envelopes corresponding to the four extreme vowels in figure 6.17. Bandwidth values for the formants have been taken from figure 6.1, with some adjustments as noted above for certain formants of some vowels. These spectrum envelopes, displayed in figure 6.18, show the changes in the relative amplitudes of the spectral peaks and in the depths of the spectral valleys as the formants assume different positions. For example, for the back vowels, the first and second formants are close together, and the broad two-peaked prominence formed by these formants dominates the spectrum shape. In the case of /u/ especially, the third formant is relatively weak, and it is unlikely that it plays any role perceptually, since it would be masked by the dominant low-frequency energy. The spectrum envelopes for the two front vowels show that $F2$ and $F3$ (and, in the case of /i/, $F4$) together form a two- or three-peaked spectral prominence that is well separated from $F1$.

Perception experiments have shown that front vowels that are judged to have similar quality can be synthesized by replacing this complex of higher formants by a single formant that is located at some frequency in this $F2 - F3 - F4$ range (Carlson et al., 1970; see also figure 4.34). This "effective" higher formant frequency has been labeled as $F2'$. For the two front-vowel spectra in figure 6.18, the locations of $F2'$ (as determined by perception experiments) are indicated by arrows. In the case of the back vowels, perception experiments show that a two-formant synthetic vowel with the same quality as a multiformant vowel (that includes $F3$ and higher formants) is achieved by locating $F1$ and $F2$ at precisely the same frequencies as they occur in each vowel. That is, $F2' = F2$ for back vowels.

6.6 THE ROUNDING FEATURE: ENHANCING THE PROMINENCE OF A SPECTRAL PEAK

The four corner vowels depicted in figure 6.16 or 6.17 represent, in some sense, the most extreme vowels that can be produced with tongue body movements and with lip rounding. These vowels are extreme in the sense that it is not feasible to attempt to produce first- and second-formant frequencies outside the quadrilateral formed by joining the points corresponding to the extreme vowels. Attempts to go beyond these limits would require that the narrowest constriction in the vocal tract be too small to maintain a well-formed vowel. It is, however, possible to produce vowel categories by appropriate manipulation of the articulatory structures so as to yield points on or inside this quadrilateral. One such manipulation is modifying the rounding of the lips.

We have already seen in Figure 6.14 that rounding of the lips for the non-low back vowels helps to displace the second formant to a frequency that is lower than it would have been otherwise, and consequently to decrease the difference in frequency between $F2$ and $F1$. Spectrum envelopes for an unrounded and a rounded back vowel with $F1 = 500$ Hz are shown in figure 6.19. By bringing these two formants closer together, introduction of rounding for these vowels tends to accentuate the prominence formed by the formants and to weaken the prominences at higher frequencies. The center of gravity of the prominence formed by the two spectral peaks is at a lower frequency for the rounded than for the unrounded vowels.

Another potential advantage of using a rounded configuration for non-low back vowels is that $F2$ passes through a minimum value as the position of the tongue body constriction is displaced along the upper pharyngeal and velar region of the vocal tract (as demonstrated in figure 6.14a). When the tongue body is in this position that yields a minimum $F2$, both $F1$ and $F2$ are relatively insensitive to changes in the constriction position. Thus the precision with which the constriction must be located to give a stable and low value of $F2$ is relatively lax. Figure 6.14b shows that when there is no rounding, displacement of the position of the tongue body constriction within this upper pharyngeal and velar region does not yield a minimum in $F2$. The minimum in $F2$ for this unrounded configuration is lower in the pharyngeal region, where $F1$ is higher. This region is where the vocal tract is

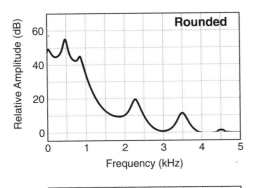

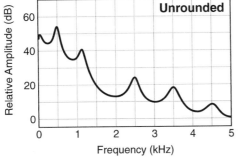

Figure 6.19 Calculated spectrum envelopes for two back vowels, illustrating the contrast between a rounded (top) and an unrounded (bottom) back vowel. The formants *F1* and *F2* are closer and higher-frequency peaks are weaker for the rounded vowel.

most constricted for a low back vowel, at least to the extent that such a vowel can be modeled as a tube with a single constriction.

Rounding of the lips can be superimposed on the other four of the basic set of vowels (i.e., the front vowels /i e æ/ and the low back vowel /ɑ/) to produce distinctively different vowel qualities. Lip rounding has the effect of decreasing the cross-sectional area at the anterior end of the vocal tract, and of lengthening the front part of the tract. As we have seen in chapter 3, the acoustic consequence of this movement is to lower the natural frequencies that are associated with the front cavity. Thus, for example, for a non-low front vowel such as /i/ or /e/, the effect of lip rounding is to narrow the anterior end of the narrow front cavity, and to lengthen this cavity. The acoustic consequence of this rounding movement is to lower the frequencies of the front-cavity resonances. This acoustic result can be seen if one takes the model of the resonator shape for /i/ in figure 6.10, with $\ell_1 = 9.5$ cm, and systematically narrows the cross-sectional area of the front cavity and lengthens this cavity. The effect of this front-cavity change on *F2*, *F3*, and *F4* is shown in figure 6.20. The abscissa in this figure is the ratio of the length ℓ_2 to the area A_2 of the front cavity. This ratio is proportional to the acoustic mass of the front cavity. Rounding leads to a closer proximity of *F2* and *F3*, and a lowering of the center of gravity of the spectral peak formed by *F2* and *F3*. Another consequence of narrowing the lip opening for these front

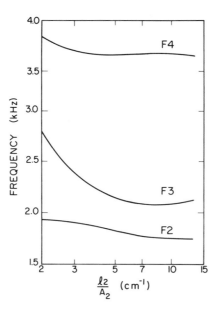

Figure 6.20 Calculated values of $F2$, $F3$, and $F4$ when the front cavity of the configuration in figure 6.10 is modified to approximate different degrees of lip rounding for a front vowel. The anterior portion of the front cavity is gradually narrowed and lengthened, and the abscissa represents the sum of the ratio of length to area of the sections making up this front cavity. The abscissa is proportional, then, to the acoustic mass of the front cavity.

vowels is to decrease the bandwidth of the third formant. This bandwidth is influenced strongly by the radiation resistance, which decreases when the area of the mouth opening decreases. This decreased bandwidth contributes to enhancing the prominence of the $F2$–$F3$ peak. Spectrum envelopes for the rounded and unrounded versions of the high front vowels are shown in figure 6.21. The downward shift in frequency of the high-frequency spectral prominence can clearly be seen. This spectral prominence also appears to be narrower and more salient for the rounded vowel.

Rounding of the low vowels (i.e., the vowels with a relatively high $F1$) has the effect of lowering $F1$ somewhat. For the low back vowel, $F2$ is also lowered, since both formants are influenced to some extent by the wide front cavity. In the case of the low front vowel, rounding causes a lowering of $F2$ and $F3$, and these two formants tend to be closer together. There is also reduction of the $F3$ bandwidth as noted above. These factors combine to produce a lower and more prominent $F2$–$F3$ spectral peak.

Figure 6.22 displays the frequencies of $F1$ and $F2$ for the adult male rounded and unrounded vowels. This figure has been schematized somewhat, in the sense that the shifts in $F1$ and $F2$ are estimated based on theoretical considerations with somewhat idealized models. It is assumed in estimating these frequencies that the rounding or unrounding for a given vowel is achieved without any adjustment of the tongue body position. The second-formant frequency $F2$ is always lower for the rounded member of each pair,

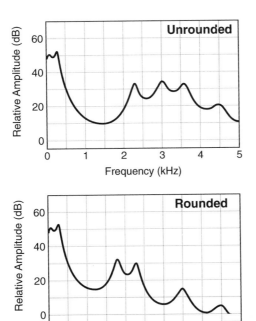

Figure 6.21 Calculated spectrum envelopes for an unrounded high front vowel (top) and a contrasting rounded front vowel (bottom).

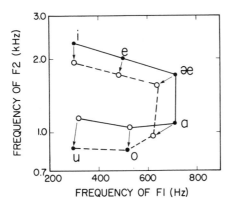

Figure 6.22 Comparison of the values of *F*1 and *F*2 for a set of six unrounded vowels (points joined by solid lines) and six rounded vowels (points joined by dashed lines). The labeled vowels (solid circles) are approximations to the six basic extreme vowels discussed in the text. The arrows indicate how the formants change when rounding occurs. The frequencies are in the range corresponding to adult male speakers.

and there is also a decrease in $F1$ for the low vowels. The two sets of vowels form two different quadrilaterals, with the figure for the rounded vowels being lower and not extending as far to the right. Not highlighted in the figure is the tendency for the major broad spectral peak for the vowel (formed by the $F1$-$F2$ pair for back vowels and the $F2 - F3 - F4$ combination for front vowels) to be more salient or more prominent for the rounded vowel than for its unrounded cognate. This increased prominence of the principal spectral peak, together with a lowered center of gravity of the peak, can be considered as primary acoustic correlates of the rounding feature.

In sections 6.2 and 6.3, arguments were made that the six outer vowels in figure 6.22 had the special attributes that (1) they represented extreme displacements from some neutral configuration, both in the articulatory and the acoustic domain, and (2) there were stable and reproducible articulatory and acoustic attributes for these vowels—attributes that could be realized without undue precision in positioning the tongue body. These attributes do not necessarily apply to the inner vowels in figure 6.22. For example, when rounding is used for a non-low back vowel, figure 6.14 has shown that the tongue body is in a position where $F2$ is minimum, and is relatively insensitive to movements of the point at which the constriction is narrowest. When rounding is removed and the tongue body remains in this position, $F2$ is more sensitive to perturbations in the tongue body position.

In the case of the vowel /ɑ/, rounding leads to a lower $F1$ and hence a less extreme vowel in the $F1$ dimension, but the vowel remains near the periphery of the quadilateral formed in the $F1$–$F2$ plane by the original six vowels. The high vowels have some degree of stability when they are rounded, at least in the sense that they are produced in a way that minimizes the spacing between $F2$ and $F3$.

6.7 THE CONSTRICTED-NONCONSTRICTED OR TENSE-LAX DISTINCTION

We have seen that the basic set of vowels in figures 6.16 and 6.17 can be derived starting with an ideal vocal tract of uniform shape and then perturbing the walls of this tube in particular ways. The vowels that reside on the periphery of the quadrilateral represent extreme perturbations from the uniform shape, and extreme displacements of the formants from their "neutral" values, consistent with maintaining a vowel-like configuration. It is possible, however, to produce vocal tract configurations and acoustic patterns intermediate between these extreme or peripheral vowels and the central or schwa vowel. These intermediate configurations are achieved by positions of the tongue body and lips that are less extreme. The narrowest part of the vocal tract is less constricted than that for peripheral vowels, and in parts of the vocal tract remote from the constriction the cross-sectional area is not as large. Vowels produced with these intermediate vocal tract positions are

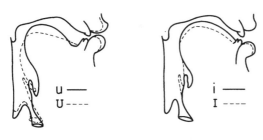

Figure 6.23 Comparing midsagittal vocal tract configurations for tense and lax high vowels for a speaker of American English. (Data from Perkell, 1969.)

sometimes called lax vowels, whereas the more extreme vowels are called tense vowels.

Examples of midsagittal vocal tract shapes for contrasting pairs of non-low tense and lax high vowels in English are shown in figure 6.23. Tense non-low vowels are produced with a widened pharynx, which is achieved by advancing the root of the tongue. The feature [advanced tongue root] (ATR) is sometimes used to describe these vowels (Halle and Stevens, 1969). (See also section 5.3.) Widening the pharynx causes the tongue dorsum to be pushed upward, resulting in a narrowing of the airway in the oral or upper pharyngeal region. For a lax vowel, this widening in the lower pharyngeal region is less extreme, and results in a lowering of the tongue dorsum in the oral part of the vocal tract relative to its position for the corresponding tense vowel. The increased opening in the oral region due to the reduced pharyngeal volume is usually also accompanied by a lowering of the mandible, leading to a wider mouth opening and a further lowering of the tongue dorsum.

Reducing the degree of constriction in the oral cavity and at the lips for a non-low vowel will increase the frequency of the first formant. This increased $F1$ can be predicted from the perturbation theory discussed in section 3.3.5, which shows that $F1$ increases when the anterior or oral part of the vocal tract is widened. Also, to the extent that the first-formant frequency can be considered to be a Helmholtz resonance between the acoustic compliance of the volume behind the constriction and the acoustic mass of the constriction, the frequency increase occurs both because the acoustic mass of the constriction is smaller (being proportional to the reciprocal of the area) and because the volume of the cavity in the pharyngeal region behind the constriction is smaller, leading to a reduced acoustic compliance. Because the movement toward a lax vowel configuration is in the direction of a vocal tract shape that is uniform, there is also a tendency for the formants to shift toward the center of the $F1–F2$ plot, especially for the high vowels. The formant frequencies in the $F1–F2$ plane for tense and lax non-low vowels in English are schematized in figure 6.24. The lax vowels /ɪ ɛ ɔ ʊ/ are paired, respectively, with the tense vowels /i e o u/. The figure shows that the net acoustic effect of moving from the tense to the lax cognate for the high

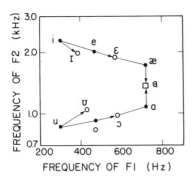

Figure 6.24 Comparison of the values of *F*1 and *F*2 for the basic set of six tense vowels (closed circles) and the four non-low lax vowels /ɪ ɛ ɔ ʊ/ (open circles). Arrows point from tense vowels to corresponding lax vowels. Data are appropriate for adult male speakers. For the high vowels, data are from American English (Peterson and Barney, 1952). For the vowels /e ɛ ɔ o/, data are estimates from measurements of vowels in English, Italian, and Korean, and for any one language the pair /e ɛ/ or /o ɔ/ may shift somewhat relative to the position shown in the figure. The point for the "lax" low vowel /a/ is arbitrarily placed between /ɑ/ and /æ/.

vowels is an upward shift in *F*1 and a tendency for an inward movement of *F*2 within the outer quadrilateral defined by the tense vowels. The movement for the non-low vowels from tense /e o/ to lax or open /ɛ ɔ/ is in a direction along the line forming the outer quadrilateral in figure 6.24.

The positions of these tense and lax vowels in the *F*1–*F*2 plane is expected to vary somewhat from language to language. For example, depending on the number of vowels in a given language, there appear to be some adjustments of vowel formant frequencies so as to maintain sufficient perceptual distance between vowels (Liljencrants and Lindblom, 1972).

In the case of the low back vowel, the production of a lax counterpart can be considered as adjustment of the tongue body to a less extreme back position to yield a low "mid" vowel. A similar definition could be made for the lax version of a low front vowel, and the result would be similar to the same low mid vowel. This vowel is labeled as /a/ in figure 6.24. The tense-lax opposition seems to occur most frequently for non-low vowels, and is rather rare in the low vowels. For example, among the West African languages that utilize this contrast, it is common to find it in the non-low vowels, but not in the low vowels.

When there is a contrast between the more extreme tense vowels and the less extreme lax vowels in a language, the acoustic difference between a particular contrasting pair is often accentuated or enhanced by acoustic and articulatory attributes other than the tongue body position or the formant frequencies. In English, for example, the lax vowels tend to be shorter than the tense vowels, and in many dialects the tense vowels have movements of the tongue body and other articulators during the course of the vowel. The tense front vowels /i/ and /e/ tend to be diphthongized toward a more extreme high front tongue body position, whereas /u/ and /o/ are diphthongized toward a more extreme high back tongue body position.

Examples of the tense-lax distinction are the vowels in the word pairs *beet-bit*, *bait-bet*, and *who'd-hood* in English, spectrograms of which are shown in figure 6.25. The figure also shows spectra sampled at points just before the middle of each vowel. In these pairs the differences in length and in diphthongization can be seen. From the spectra it is possible to observe the shifts in $F1$ and in $F2$ that occur between the tense and lax vowels. The spectrograms show that vowels /i/ and /e/ are diphthongized in the direction of a more extreme high front tongue body position, whereas /u/ shows movement toward a high back position. For the lax vowels, the formant movement is toward a more central position. One way of interpreting these kinds of formant movements is to say that implementation of the tense or lax feature of the vowel is somewhat delayed relative to implementation of the basic high-low and front-back features.

While the contrast between tense and lax vowels has been described in terms of modifications in vocal tract shape and consequent shifts in formant frequencies, there are other acoustic consequences of these vocal tract adjustments that appear to play a role in signaling this contrast. Furthermore, articulatory adjustments beyond those that produce a more or less constricted vocal tract shape may be implemented to augment or enhance the distinction between tense and lax vowels. Some of these articulatory adjustments and their acoustic correlates are not well understood, and will be discussed here only in general terms.

For example, since for non-low vowels, $F1$ is higher for lax than for tense vowels, the amplitudes of spectral prominences above $F1$ tend to be greater (relative, say, to the amplitude of the first harmonic) for lax vowels. These differences in spectrum shape can be seen in some of the spectra in figure 6.25. If this attribute plays a role in the perception of these vowels, then the acoustic contrast can be accentuated by modifying the glottal source for the two types of vowels. A more breathy or spread glottal configuration for tense vowels would reduce the spectrum amplitudes at high frequencies, whereas a pressed or constricted glottal configuration for lax vowels would enhance the high-frequency spectrum amplitude. This use of glottal adjustments to accompany the modifications in vocal tract shape for the tense-lax distinction has been reported (Stewart, 1967), although careful acoustic studies are needed to provide quantitative support for the observations.

A second, related acoustic consequence of the different vocal tract configurations for tense and lax vowels is concerned with the aerodynamic and acoustic effects of vocal tract constrictions. If tense vowels are regarded as being produced with a more constricted vocal tract, then this constriction can have two acoustic consequences. One is to create additional loading on the glottal source (as discussed in section 2.1.7) and hence to cause the length of the open phase of glottal vibration to be increased, resulting in a decreased spectrum amplitude of the source at high frequencies. This spectrum change would enhance the reduction in high-frequency amplitude caused by the lower $F1$ for tense vowels. A second consequence is to

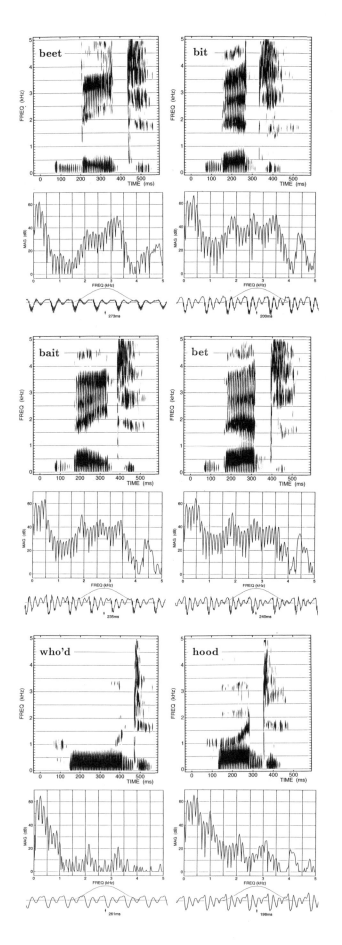

increase the acoustic losses in the vocal tract, particularly at low frequencies, leading to an increased bandwidth of the first formant. This increased $F1$ bandwidth would also occur for a breathy glottal configuration, as noted above.

In view of these potential multiple acoustic correlates of the tense-lax distinction (formant shifts, duration, diphthongization, glottal source characteristics, bandwidth changes) this vowel feature has been the subject of some controversy, and one can question whether a single feature provides an adequate description of this contrast. For example, in some languages the use of an advanced tongue root seems to be the primary mechanism for implementing the contrast (Painter, 1973; Lindau, 1979), whereas in a language like English other attributes play a role. One convention is simply to describe the contrast as open vs. closed, reflecting the difference in mandible position and mouth opening for the contrasting vowels. More research is clearly needed on this topic.

6.8 EFFECTS OF LARYNGEAL CONFIGURATION AND ACOUSTIC COUPLING TO THE SUBGLOTTAL SYSTEM

In some languages, a distinction is made between vowels produced with different glottal configurations and hence with different glottal vibration patterns (cf. Ladefoged and Maddieson, 1996). Thus, for example, two monosyllabic words may be identical in all respects except that in one case the vowel is produced with breathy voicing and in the other with modal voicing. Or, vowel distinctions may be realized by contrasting pressed voicing with modal or breathy voicing. Some of the acoustic consequences of these different laryngeal configurations have been discussed in chapter 2. In addition to the changes in source waveform and spectrum that result from adjustments in the laryngeal configuration, there can also be changes in the vocal tract resonances. For example, when the glottis is spread to produce breathy voicing, there can be a significant increase in the bandwidth of the first formant, as described in section 3.4.6. Acoustic coupling to the subglottal system can also cause modifications to vowel spectra by introducing extra prominences in the spectra. Some of the acoustic consequences of a spread glottal configuration can be observed when the aspirated consonant /h/ (or its voiced counterpart /ɦ/) is produced. These acoustic attributes are discussed in section 8.3.

Individual speakers may also exhibit different glottal vibration patterns. These differences arising from individual laryngeal characteristics often com-

Figure 6.25 Spectrograms and spectra of utterances illustrating the tense-lax pairs of vowels in American English produced by a male speaker. Tense vowels are on the left and lax vowels on the right. The spectrum under each spectrogram is sampled at a point about one-third of the vowel length from the onset. Waveforms are displayed below each spectrum. The spectra show the locations of the formant peaks and the different relative amplitudes of these peaks.

plicate the interpretation of the acoustic spectra of vowels. In this section we consider some of the acoustic consequences of these individual differences in laryngeal characteristics.

One of the consequences of a glottal opening is acoustic coupling to the subglottal airways. As described in section 3.6.4, the subglottal system has a series of resonances, which can be defined as the natural frequencies with a closed glottis. The average values of the first three of these natural frequencies have been estimated to be about 700, 1650, and 2350 Hz for an adult female and 600, 1550, and 2200 Hz for an adult male, but there are substantial individual differences in these frequencies (Ishizaka et al., 1976; Cranen and Boves, 1987; Klatt and Klatt, 1990). The analysis in section 3.6.4 has shown that the effect of these subglottal resonances is to introduce additional pole-zero pairs in the vocal tract transfer function from the glottal source to the mouth output. The most obvious acoustic manifestation of these pole-zero pairs is the appearance of additional peaks or prominences in the output spectrum. The influence of zeros can also be seen sometimes as minima in the spectrum. The theoretical analysis in section 3.6.4 suggests that the frequency of the zero is the closed-glottis natural frequency of the subglottal system, and this frequency is expected to remain unchanged for a particular speaker. The frequency of the nearby pole varies somewhat depending on the vowel, but is not expected to be displaced from the zero by more than about 200 Hz for most laryngeal configurations.

The effect on the vowel spectrum of the lowest subglottal resonance is generally not as pronounced as that of the second subglottal resonance since the partially open glottis introduces acoustic losses that reduce the degree of prominence of this lowest resonance. In effect, the glottal resistance tends to dominate the impedance looking down into the glottis and the trachea. Thus the principal effect of the glottis and the subglottal system for frequencies in the first-formant range is to widen the bandwidth of the first formant and to shift its frequency, usually in an upward direction. On the other hand, it is common to see in the spectrum an extra prominence in the vicinity of 1400 to 1800 Hz due to the second subglottal resonance. For example, if the second formant is well removed from this resonance, the amplitude of the additional prominence (relative to the spectrum amplitude if there were no subglottal coupling) would be in the range of 4 to 8 dB, if a pole-zero spacing of 100 to 200 Hz were assumed, with bandwidths of 200 Hz for the pole and zero. Sometimes there is also an extra prominence in the vicinity of the third subglottal resonance.

The presence of an extra spectral prominence arising from a subglottal resonance is illustrated in figure 6.26. This spectrum is sampled in the vowel /ɪ/ produced by a female speaker. The peak at 1600 Hz is assumed to be caused by the second subglottal resonance, and in this case this resonance is well separated from $F1$ and $F2$.

If the second-formant frequency is close to the frequency of the subglottal resonance, there can be a substantial perturbation in the spectrum in the

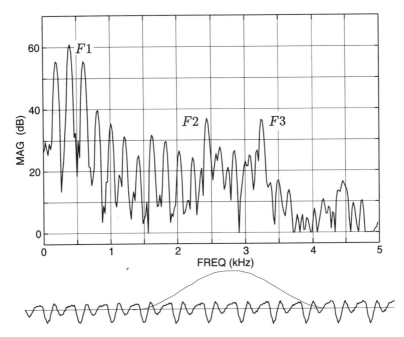

Figure 6.26 Spectrum of the vowel /ɪ/ sampled in the word *bit*, produced by an adult female speaker. The first three formant frequencies are labeled. The small prominence around 1600 Hz is assumed to be the effect of the second subglottal resonance. The waveform and the time window for calculating the spectrum are shown below the spectrum.

vicinity of *F2*. For example, the *F2* spectral peak can become less prominent when it is in the vicinity of the zero that is introduced by the second sub-glottal resonance, and there can be a marked shift in the frequency of the spectral prominence away from the frequency that would be expected for *F2* if there were no coupling to the subglottal system.

Some indication of the perturbation that can exist in the spectrum of a vowel when *F2* is in the vicinity of a subglottal resonance is given in figure 6.27. Figure 6.27a shows calculations of the frequencies of the relevant poles and zero in the transfer function as *F2* is displaced from 1000 to 1800 Hz. Here *F2* is taken to be the second natural frequency of the vocal tract for the closed-glottis condition, and *F2T* is the modified second-formant frequency as a consequence of subglottal coupling. For purposes of these calculations it is assumed that the second natural frequency of the subglottal system (with a closed glottis) is 1400 Hz, and this is taken to be the zero *FTZ* of the transfer function. Other assumptions are given in the figure legend. Shown in figure 6.27b are the calculated transfer functions for four values of *F2*. When *F2* is a few hundred hertz above or below the subglottal natural frequency, the subglottal coupling introduces a small extra peak or shoulder in the vicinity of the subglottal resonance. However, when *F2* is near the subglottal reso-nance, the formant appears to be represented by two closely spaced spectral prominences, and the relative amplitudes of these prominences change as *F2*

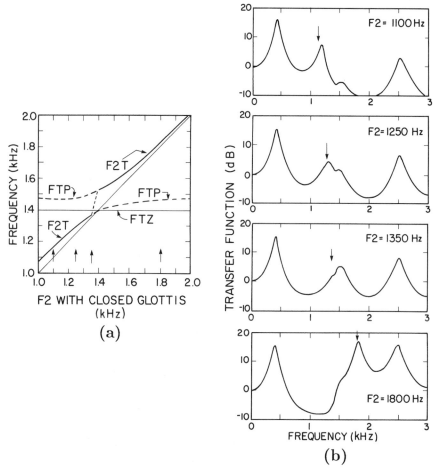

Figure 6.27 (a) Calculations of the frequencies of the two poles and zero in the vicinity of $F2$ when there is coupling to the trachea through a partially open glottis. The abscissa $F2$ is the formant frequency that would exist if the glottis were closed and there were no acoustic coupling to the trachea. $F1$ and $F3$ are held constant at 400 and 2500 Hz. The frequency of the tracheal zero (FTZ) is assumed to be fixed at 1400 Hz. $F2T$ represents the pole corresponding to $F2$, shifted by the influence of the tracheal system. FTP is the tracheal pole. The solid lines indicate the frequency of the most prominent spectral peak, which shows an abrupt jump in frequency (short-dashed) when $F2$ is just below 1400 Hz. The dashed lines represent the poles that are less prominent in the spectrum. (b) Calculated transfer function for four different values of $F2$, as indicated by the arrows in (a) and by the values of $F2$ given on each panel. The arrows on the transfer functions give the values of $F2$, and the deviation of the major spectral prominence from $F2$ can be seen. The cross-sectional area of the glottal opening is assumed to be 0.05 cm^2.

changes. As $F2$ passes near the zero (1400 Hz in this case), as in the panel with $F2 = 1350$ Hz, the most prominent peak jumps up in frequency, so that there is a discontinuity in the frequency of this peak. The solid heavy line labeled as $F2T$ in figure 6.27a indicates the frequency of the most prominent peak, and the short-dashed line shows how there is a jump in this frequency just below $F2 = 1400$ Hz.

In figure 6.28 we show spectra (and spectrograms) for the word *but* produced by two different female speakers. The utterance of one of the speakers (EL) illustrates several of the attributes discussed above, for vowels produced with a spread glottal configuration. In panel 1, the first-formant bandwidth is sufficiently wide that the spectral prominence for this formant is either weak or nonexistent. The amplitude of the first harmonic is greater than that of the second harmonic, indicating a breathy glottal configuration (cf. figure 2.21 and section 8.3). As the second formant increases in frequency through the vowel, it passes a point (around 200 ms in the spectrogram) where the second-formant prominence is diminished or even disappears, as shown in the spectrum in panel 2 of the figure. This reduction of the prominence occurs as $F2$ passes through the second subglottal resonance. In contrast to speaker EL is DE, who appears to have a glottal vibration pattern with little or no breathiness or effects of subglottal coupling. The formant peaks remain narrow and prominent throughout the vowel.

The second natural frequency of the subglottal system is in the vicinity of the dividing line between front vowels and back vowels. As can be seen in figure 6.17, for example, $F2$ values for front and back vowels are, respectively, above and below 1650 Hz for adult females or 1550 Hz for adult males. Given that this subglottal resonance can distort the $F2$ spectral peak if $F2$ is near that resonance, particularly if the glottis is partially open throughout the cycle of vibration, it is not unreasonable to expect that a speaker might avoid producing vowels having $F2$ in this frequency range. This effect of subglottal coupling, then, provides further evidence for a natural division between front and back vowels. In this regard, it is noted that the lowest subglottal resonance is at a frequency that tends to be lower than $F1$ for low vowels and higher than $F1$ for non-low vowels, and could, therefore, contribute to the division between these two classes of vowels.

6.9 NASALIZATION OF VOWELS

6.9.1 Theoretical Analysis of Vowel Nasalization

In sections 6.2 to 6.7 we examined how different positions of the articulators, particularly the tongue body, the pharynx, and the lips, can be manipulated to produce different shapes for the supraglottal airway and hence different filtering of the glottal source. This filtering can be described in terms of the frequencies and bandwidths of the formants, since the transfer function from the glottis to the lips is an all-pole function, provided that there are no side branches in this acoustic path and provided that sound propagation in the vocal tract is approximately one-dimensional, with no cross modes.

There are, however, situations for which additional acoustic systems are coupled to the main vocal tract airway, giving rise to zeros as well as poles in the transfer function. One example, discussed above in section 6.8, arises

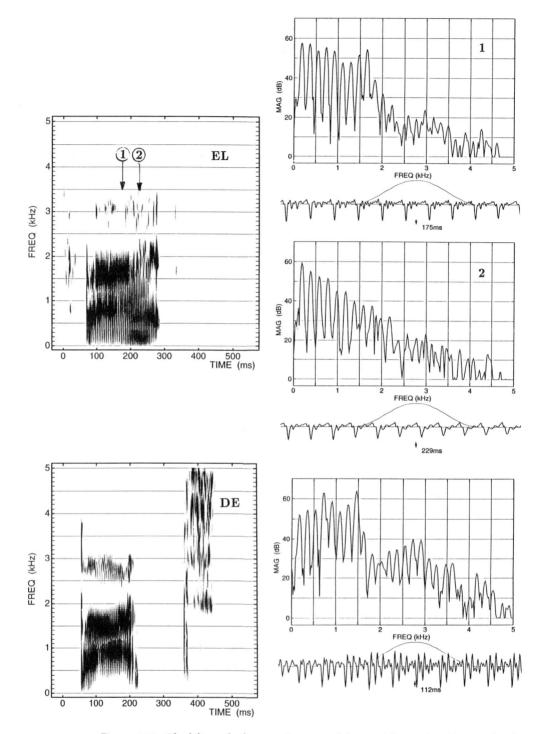

Figure 6.28 The left panels show spectrograms of the word *but* produced by two female speakers: EL (top) and DE (bottom). The spectra at the right are sampled at the times indicated: two spectra (arrows 1 and 2) for EL and one for DE. The data for EL illustrate various effects of a spread glottal configuration with subglottal coupling, whereas these effects are minimal for DE. See text.

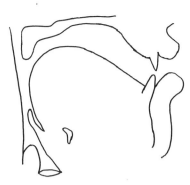

Figure 6.29 Midsagittal section of the vocal tract for the nasal vowel /ɑ̃/ produced by a speaker of French. (From Bothorel et al., 1986.)

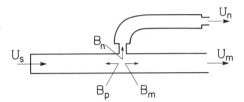

Figure 6.30 Schematization of the shapes of the vocal and nasal tracts for a nasal vowel. The volume velocities U_s, U_n, and U_m at the glottis, nostrils, and mouth are shown, as are the acoustic susceptances at the coupling point looking into the pharynx (B_p), the nasal cavity (B_n), and the mouth cavity (B_m).

from acoustic coupling to the subglottal system when there is a partial glottal opening. Another example is the acoustic coupling to the nasal cavity that occurs when the velopharyngeal opening creates a path between the main vocal tract and the nasal cavity. The presence of this velopharyngeal opening when the vocal tract is in a vowel-like configuration causes nasalization of the vowel.

A nasal consonant is produced with a velopharyngeal opening but with a complete closure of the main vocal tract at some point within the oral cavity. The acoustic properties for such a configuration are discussed in section 9.1. When a nasal consonant occurs adjacent to a vowel, there is usually some opening of the velopharyngeal port and hence some nasalization in at least part of the vowel adjacent to the consonant. In many languages, however, there is a contrast between nasal and non-nasal vowels, independent of the consonant that is adjacent to the vowel.

An example of the midsagittal configuration of the vocal tract for a vowel that is nasalized is given in figure 6.29. For purposes of analyzing the sound produced by such a nasalized configuration, we can model the vocal tract as a system of resonators, as in figure 6.30. (See also figure 3.45.) There are two outputs for this system: the volume velocity U_m at the mouth and the volume velocity U_n at the nose. The sound pressure at a distance is a result of the combined output $U_m + U_n$. The transfer function $(U_m + U_n)/U_s$ is the sum of the individual transfer functions U_m/U_s and U_n/U_s. These transfer functions have the same poles but different zeros. The general theory of vowel nasalization has been outlined in section 3.6. We develop that theory in more detail here.

In order to estimate the poles and zeros of these transfer functions, we examine the susceptances looking in different directions from the point at which the nasal cavity couples to the oral cavity:

B_n = susceptance looking into the nasal cavity

B_m = susceptance looking into the oral cavity

B_p = susceptance looking into the pharynx

The poles of the transfer functions are the frequencies for which $B_n + B_m + B_p = 0$. Zeros of U_m/U_s occur at frequencies for which $B_n = \infty$, and zeros of U_n/U_s are at frequencies where $B_m = \infty$.

As has been reviewed in section 3.6, the measurements of the natural frequencies of the nasal cavity with a closed velopharyngeal port for an adult speaker have been estimated to be approximately 500 Hz and 2000 Hz. The ranges of values of these natural frequencies for several male and female speakers are 450 to 650 Hz and 1800 to 2400 Hz, based on measurements of the transient response of the nasal cavity with a closed velopharyngeal port. Acoustic coupling between the sinuses and the main nasal cavity introduces additional resonances. One of these additional resonances that has been observed consistently is at a frequency of about 400 Hz or lower, and another is around 1300 Hz. In the initial part of the present analysis, we shall neglect these resonances that are due to the sinuses. Their influence on the sound output for nasal consonants and vowels is to introduce local fixed-frequency prominences in the spectrum as a consequence of additional pole-zero pairs in the transfer function of the combined vocal and nasal tract.

The impedance Z_n looking into the nasal tract is approximated as the sum of the impedance of the velopharyngeal port and the impedance of the nasal cavity, as depicted in figure 6.31. The velopharyngeal port is represented as a short acoustic tube of length l_{vp} and cross-sectional area A_{vp}, so that its acoustic mass is $M_{vp} = \rho l_{vp}/A_{vp}$. We have taken l_{vp} to be 2 cm in the following analysis. The impedance Z_{no} of the nasal cavity has poles at its natural frequencies, which are assumed to be 500 and 2000 Hz, and its impedance level is taken to be approximately that of a tube of cross-sectional area equal to 2 cm^2.

Figure 6.31 Representing the nasal cavity by an equivalent circuit consisting of the acoustic mass M_{vp} of the velopharyngeal opening and the acoustic impedance Z_{no} of the rest of the nasal cavity.

If we neglect losses, then the susceptance B_n looking into the velopharyngeal port is the reciprocal of the reactance X_n (the imaginary part of Z_n). Estimates of B_n for several values of the coupling area A_{vp} are shown in figure 6.32 for frequencies up to 1.8 kHz. The lowest zero of B_n is fixed at 500 Hz, that is, the lowest natural frequency of the nasal cavity. We do not consider here the high-frequency behavior of B_n. For different speakers we expect the curves in figure 6.32 to shift slightly to the right or the left.

The frequency of the lowest zero f_m of the transfer function U_m/U_s is the frequency at which $B_n = \infty$ in figure 6.32. It is usually in the range of 600 to 900 Hz, depending on the area of the velopharyngeal port. It is at the lower end of this range for a narrow velopharyngeal opening.

The frequency f_n of the lowest zero of U_n/U_s for a nasalized vowel is usually somewhat higher than f_m, and is generally between 1500 and 2500 Hz. It depends on the vocal tract configuration for the vowel, and is higher for front than for back vowels. The zero frequency f_n lies between F2 and F3 for the corresponding non-nasalized vowel configuration.

In order to estimate the frequency of the lowest zero of the overall transfer function $T(s) = (U_m + U_n)/U_s$, we write an expression for $T(s)$ for the lossless case as follows:

$$T(s) = a \frac{(s - s_m)(s - s_m^*)}{s_m s_m^*} \cdot P(s) + (1 - a) \frac{(s - s_n)(s - s_n^*)}{s_n s_n^*} \cdot P(s), \tag{6.3}$$

where $s_m = j2\pi f_m$, $s_n = j2\pi f_n$, and $P(s)$ is an all-pole component that is normalized so that $P(s) = 1$ for $s = 0$. Thus $T(s)$ is also unity at zero frequency. The constant a accounts for the division of the source volume velocity between the nasal and oral paths. This division (for the lossless case) is

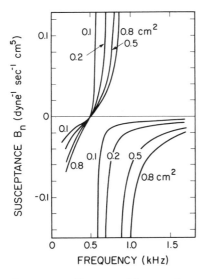

Figure 6.32 Estimates of the acoustic susceptance B_n looking into the nasal cavity for several values of the cross-sectional area of the velopharyngeal opening.

in inverse proportion to the acoustic masses of the two paths. Thus $a = M_n/(M_m + M_n)$, where M_m is the acoustic mass of the path in the oral cavity from the point of velopharyngeal coupling to the lips, and M_n is the acoustic mass of the path through the velopharyngeal port and nasal cavity to the nose output.

From equation (6.3) we can derive the following expression for the frequency of the lowest zero of the overall transfer function:

$$f_z = f_m \sqrt{\frac{1 + \dfrac{M_m}{M_n}}{1 + \left(\dfrac{f_m}{f_n}\right)^2 \dfrac{M_m}{M_n}}}, \tag{6.4}$$

The ratio f_z/f_m generally lies between 1.1 and 1.4 for nasalized vowels, as we shall observe. If the airway through the mouth has a large average cross-sectional area relative to that for the nasal passage, then most of the output is from the mouth, and $f_z \cong f_m$. On the other hand, if the two airways have comparable average areas, as they might for a high vowel, then f_z is intermediate between f_m and f_n. In the case of a nasal consonant, there is a complete closure of the oral cavity, and $M_m = \infty$. The frequency of the zero is then $f_z = f_n$.

As noted above, the poles of the system function can be determined by finding the frequencies for which $B_n + B_m + B_p = 0$. Some insight into the dependence of these poles on the vocal tract shape and on the velopharyngeal opening can be obtained by plotting curves of B_n vs. frequency and of $-(B_m + B_p)$ vs. frequency, and finding the frequencies of the points of intersection. Examples of such plots for vocal tract configurations for two different front vowels are given in figure 6.33. The frequencies f_m and f_n, where $B_n = \infty$ and $B_m = \infty$, respectively, are indicated on the figures, as are the frequencies F1 and F2 for the non-nasalized configurations. The configuration in figure 6.33a corresponds approximately to the vowel /i/ and the configuration in figure 6.33b corresponds to /æ/. The cross-sectional area of the velopharyngeal opening is 0.3 cm^2 for the high vowel in (a) and 0.5 cm^2 for the low vowel in (b). In the example in (a), the frequency of the first formant for the nasalized configuration is shifted upward to F1n and another resonance Fn is added at about 800 Hz. For the low vowel /æ/ the frequency F1n of the lowest resonance is lower than F1, and again there is an additional resonance Fn, which is about 930 Hz in this case.

The susceptance $B_m + B_p$ looking into the vocal tract at the point of intersection with the velopharyngeal opening is strongly influenced by the vocal tract configuration, and for some configurations it is also affected by the position of the velum. Lowering the velum to increase A_{vp} causes the vocal tract to be narrowed in the velar region and therefore changes the susceptance B_m and the acoustic mass M_m of the oral passage. This modification of the oral passage is schematized in figure 6.34, which shows midsagittal

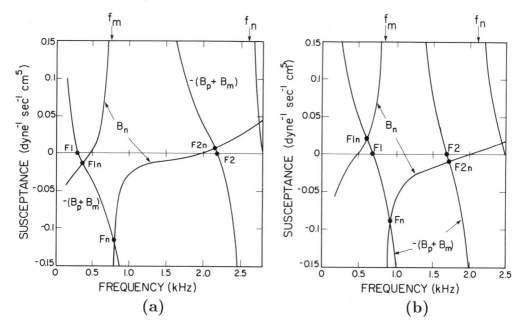

Figure 6.33 Estimated curves of susceptance vs. frequency for articulatory configurations corresponding to two nasalized front vowels: (a) the vowel /i/ with an area of the velopharyngeal opening equal to 0.3 cm^2; (b) the vowel /æ/ with a velopharyngeal area of 0.5 cm^2. The curves labeled B_n are estimates of the acoustic susceptance looking into the nasal cavity. The curves labeled $-(B_m + B_p)$ represent calculations of the (negative of the) sum of the susceptances looking into the pharyngeal and oral cavities. The arrows at the top indicate the frequencies of the zero in the mouth output (f_m, where $B_n = \infty$) and the zero in the nose output (f_n, where $B_m = \infty$). The formant frequencies $F1$ and $F2$ for the non-nasal configuration are labeled, as are the natural frequencies $F1n, Fn,$ and $F2n$ of the configuration with nasal coupling.

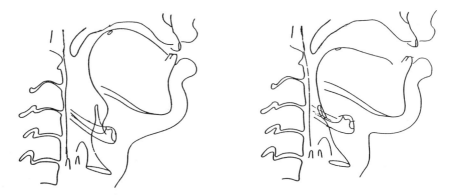

Figure 6.34 Midsagittal section of the vocal tract for two vowels of American English. The hypothetical position of the velum when it is lowered to produce a nasal vowel is shown. The lowered velum produces a significant constriction in the vocal tract, particularly for the vowel /ɑ/ at the right. (Adapted from Perkell, 1969.)

tongue positions for /i/ and /ɑ/ produced by a speaker of English, with a hypothetical configuration for a lowered velum. Figure 6.29 is a tracing from a cineradiograph for the nasal vowel /ɑ̃/ produced by a French speaker, and that picture also illustrates the modification of the oral passage.

As we have seen, the frequency f_z of the zero of the overall transfer function for the configuration is between f_m and f_n, and is usually closer to f_m. It is necessary to estimate M_m/M_n in order to determine f_z from equation (6.4). The acoustic mass M_n for the nasal passage or M_m for the oral passage is equal to the sum of the acoustic masses of individual sections within each passage. The acoustic mass of each section is proportional to the ratio of the length to the cross-sectional area of that section. In the case of the nasalized vowel /i/ in figure 6.33a, the ratio M_m/M_n is estimated to be about 1.0 for a velopharyngeal area of 0.3 cm². For the more open nasalized /æ/ configuration in figure 6.33b, with a velopharyngeal area of 0.5 cm², M_m is much smaller, and M_m/M_n is estimated to be about 0.5. The constriction in the oral passage due to the lowered velum contributes significantly to M_m for the vowel /æ/. From equation (6.4) we calculate f_z to be 1.36 f_m for the example in figure 6.33a and 1.18 f_m for the example in figure 6.33b. The values of f_m for the two cases are 750 and 840 Hz, respectively, leading to zero frequencies of 1020 Hz for /i/ and 990 Hz for /æ/.

The procedures just described illustrate the calculation of the frequencies of the two lowest poles and the lowest zero of the transfer function for a nasalized vowel. The bandwidths of these low-frequency poles and zero are influenced by the fact that the nasal cavity has a large surface area, as shown in figures 1.18 and 1.19. This mucosal surface introduces additional acoustic energy loss in the low-frequency range. The discussion of the various types of loss in section 3.4 shows that losses due to viscosity, heat conduction, and wall impedance in an acoustic tube are all proportional to the ratio of surface area to the cross-sectional area of the tube. Thus the bandwidths of the low-frequency poles and the zero for a nasal vowel are expected to be substantially greater than the bandwidths given in figure 6.1b. Acoustic measurements show considerable variation in these bandwidths. However, measured average bandwidths for the zero f_z and the additional pole F_n are about 200 Hz (Chen, 1995). The introduction of nasalization appears to add about 100 to 200 Hz to the bandwidth of the first formant.

The sinuses that couple to the nasal cavity can give rise to some fixed pole-zero pairs in the transfer function for a nasal vowel (Maeda, 1982b). These pole-zero pairs cause a perturbation of the transfer function consisting of an all-pole function augmented by the principal nasal pole Fn and zero f_z. The sinus pole-zero pair that probably has the greatest perceptual influence is due to acoustic coupling to the maxillary sinuses, which are the largest of the sinuses adjacent to the nasal cavity. This pole-zero pair is in the vicinity of the natural frequency of the resonator consisting of this sinus (volume approximately 20 cm³ on each side) together with the acoustic mass of the sinus walls and of the narrow opening to the nasal cavity. This natural fre-

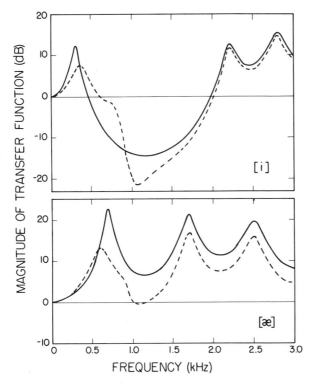

Figure 6.35 Calculated transfer functions for non-nasal front vowel configurations (solid lines) and the corresponding nasal configurations (dashed lines). The vowel configurations (/i/ and /æ/) and velopharyngeal openings (0.3 and 0.5 cm², respectively) are the same as those used in constructing figure 6.33. The bandwidths of the additional pole Fn and zero f_z are 200 Hz, and the bandwidth of $F1$ for the nasal vowel is also 200 Hz. The effects of a low-frequency pole-zero pair due to coupling to the maxillary sinuses is not shown.

quency is estimated to be in the frequency range of 200 to 400 Hz. The frequency of the zero of the pair is expected to be above the frequency of the pole. The influence of this pole-zero pair on the output spectrum for a nasal vowel will depend on the amount of low-frequency output from the nose relative to the mouth, that is, on the ratio M_n/M_m. The low-frequency pole will exhibit greater prominence in the spectrum for a heavily nasalized vowel.

The overall shape of the spectrum envelope for the nasalized vowel can be viewed as the sum (in decibels) of the spectrum that would be obtained if the transfer function were an all-pole function with the shifted and widened first formant, a function obtained from a pole-zero pair with frequencies Fn for the pole and f_z for the zero, and a function derived from pole-zero pairs due to coupling to the sinuses, particularly the maxillary sinus. Figure 6.35 shows the calculated all-pole transfer functions (at low frequencies) corresponding to the non-nasal /i/ and /æ/ configurations in figure 6.33, together with the transfer functions for the nasal vowel configurations, but without the effect of the acoustic coupling to the sinuses. The influence of the low-frequency sinus pole-zero pair is small in these examples for which the vowels are not

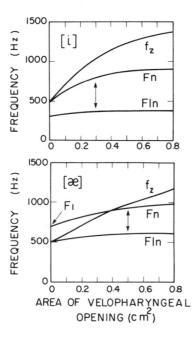

Figure 6.36 Calculated frequencies of the first formant (*F1n*) and the extra pole and zero (*Fn* and *f$_z$*) as a function of the area of the velopharyngeal opening for the vowel configurations /i/ (top) and /æ/ (bottom). The arrows indicate the values of velopharyngeal opening that were used in developing figures 6.33 and 6.35.

heavily nasalized. The bandwidth of *F1* is increased for the nasal vowel and *F1* is shifted in frequency. In this illustration the frequencies and bandwidths of the higher formants have not been changed, although in practice some modifications of these formants is expected.

The pole-zero pairs impose a perturbation on the all-pole spectrum. In particular, an additional peak is added to the upper shoulder of the first-formant prominence. A dip also appears in the spectrum, but this is expected to have less perceptual relevance than the additional spectral prominence.

The calculations based on the estimated susceptance functions in figure 6.33 show that introduction of acoustic coupling to the nasal cavity causes an upward shift in the first-formant frequency for the high vowel /i/ and a downward shift in *F1* for the low vowel /æ/. A pole-zero pair (*Fn* and *f$_z$*) is also added to the transfer function, and the values of *Fn* and *f$_z$* depend on the area of the velopharyngeal opening. Calculations of *F1n*, *Fn*, and *f$_z$* have been made for a range of areas of the velopharyngeal port for these two vowels, with the results given in figure 6.36. In making these calculations for the vowel /æ/, it was necessary to make some estimate of the narrowing that is introduced into the oral cavity when the soft palate is lowered, since this constriction influences the acoustic mass M_m of the oral passage and the frequency f_n at which the impedance looking into the oral cavity becomes zero. As figure 6.34 indicates, the relative effect on M_m of movement of the soft palate is small for the vowel /i/, since the major contribution to M_m is the constriction caused by the tongue body.

For the vowel /i/, increasing the area of the velopharyngeal port causes an increase in Fn and in f_z, with the separation becoming greater as the opening becomes larger. There is a small upward shift in $F1n$. The situation is somewhat different for the low vowel /æ/. For a small velopharyngeal opening, there is an increase in the natural frequency $F1$ of the original non-nasal vowel, and the pole-zero pair begins to separate in the vicinity of 500 Hz, the natural frequency of the nasal cavity with a closed velopharyngeal port. When the opening increases further, the frequency of the zero passes the original first formant frequency, and f_z can then be considered to be paired with that resonance. In figure 6.36 (botton), then, the resonance that was originally $F1$ becomes labeled as Fn for large values of the velopharyngeal area. The first formant of the nasal configuration is now called $F1n$, and this frequency is somewhat lower than the original $F1$. The values of velopharyngeal openings corresponding to the transfer functions in figure 6.35 are identified by arrows in figure 6.36. Comparison of the two parts of figure 6.36 shows that, for a given velopharyngeal opening, there is a greater separation of the pole-zero pair, and hence a more prominent nasal resonance, for the high vowel /i/ than for the low vowel /æ/. Partial support for this observation comes from articulatory data, which show that when vowels are produced in the environment of nasal consonants, the position of the soft palate is lower for the low vowel /ɑ/ than it is for the high vowel /i/ (Moll, 1960).

The pole-zero pattern for nasalized back vowels has an effect on the spectrum that is somewhat different from that for the front vowels in figures 6.33 and 6.35 since $F2$ for a back vowel is likely to be close to the nasal zero f_z. Because of this proximity to f_z, the $F2$ prominence may be modified significantly relative to that for a non-nasal back vowel.

In figure 6.37 we show estimates of $-(B_m + B_p)$ for two different back vowel configurations /ɔ/ and /ɑ/, superimposed on the B_n curves of figure 6.32. Only portions of the vocal tract susceptance curves are given, to indicate points of intersection with the B_n plots. Two different velopharyngeal openings are represented in the plots for /ɑ/, as shown by the dashed and solid lines. The curve for $-(B_m + B_p)$ is modified for the larger value of A_{vp} (cross-sectional area of the velopharyngeal port) to account for the narrowing formed by the lowered velum. Calculations of the frequencies of the zero, f_z, the nasal formant Fn, and the shifted first-formant $F1n$, are given in table 6.3. The vowels are identified at the top of the table, and the first- and second-formant frequencies for the corresponding non-nasal vowels are given in rows 1 and 2. The assumed area of the velopharyngeal opening is given in the third row of the table. We have taken this area to be 0.3 cm^2 for the vowels /ɔ/ and /ɑ/, and in the case of /ɑ/ we also calculate the poles and zero for an area of 0.8 cm^2. The frequency f_n of the zero of the nose output (identified by the arrows at the top of figure 6.37) is given in the next row. This frequency is taken to be between the second and third formant for the

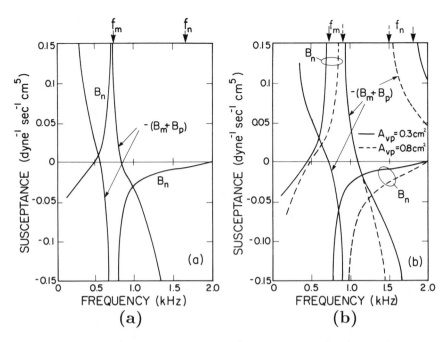

Figure 6.37 Estimated susceptance curves as in figure 6.33, except that the articulatory configurations correspond to the two nasalized back vowels /ɔ̃/ and /ɑ̃/. For the vowel /ɔ̃/ (a), the velopharyngeal area is 0.3 cm². For the vowel /ɑ̃/ (b), two sets of curves are shown, one for a velopharyngeal area A_{vp} of 0.3 cm² and the other for 0.8 cm². Details of calculations for these vowels are given in table 6.3.

Table 6.3 Calculation of critical frequencies in the transfer function for various nasalized vowels

	ɔ	ɑ	ɑ
1. F1 non-nasal (Hz)	550	720	720
2. F2 non-nasal (Hz)	840	1090	1090
3. Area of velopharyngeal port (cm²)	0.3	0.3	0.8
4. f_n (Hz)	1625	1745	1500
5. f_m (Hz)	750	750	910
6. M_m/M_n	0.28	0.21	1.4
7. f_z (Hz)	820	810	1145
8. Fn (Hz)	730	850	910
9. F1n (Hz)	540	600	640
10. F2n (Hz)	980	1150	1240

Note: See text for definitions of symbols.

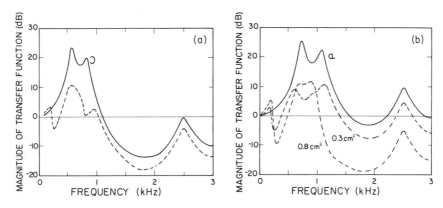

Figure 6.38 Calculated transfer functions for non-nasal back vowel configurations (solid lines) and the corresponding nasal configurations (dashed lines). The vowel configurations and velopharyngeal openings are the same as those used in constructing figure 6.37. For the vowel /ɔ/ in (a), the velopharyngeal opening is 0.3 cm². For the vowel /ã/ in (b), transfer functions for two areas of the velopharyngeal opening are shown: 0.3 cm² and 0.8 cm². See legend for figure 6.35. The estimated effect of coupling to the maxillary sinuses is shown at low frequencies.

vowel. The zero of the mouth output, f_m, from figure 6.32, is given in row 5. The calculated ratio M_m/M_n for each vowel is listed in row 6. The values of M_m and M_n are based on estimates of the acoustic mass (proportional to the overall ratio of length to area of the airway) of the oral and nasal passages, respectively. In the case of the nasal passage, the overall acoustic mass is equal to the acoustic mass of the velopharyngeal section (length of 2 cm, area given in row 3), the nasal cavity proper (length of 6 cm, area of 3 cm²), and the nostrils (length of 1 cm, area 0.5 cm²). The total length-to-area ratio is then 10.7 cm^{-1} for a coupling area of 0.3 cm² and 6.5 cm^{-1} for a coupling area of 0.8 cm². Estimates of the total length-to-area ratios for the different vowels are obtained from area functions of the type reported by Fant (1960). In the case of the last column, where the vowel is /ɑ/ and the coupling area is 0.8 cm², some reduction in the area of the vocal tract is assumed as a consequence of the lowered soft palate, as indicated in figure 6.34. This reduction gives rise to an increase in M_m and hence in the ratio M_m/M_n.

The values of f_z in row 7 of table 6.3 are calculated from equation (6.4). The frequencies Fn, $F1n$, and $F2n$ in rows 8, 9, and 10 are obtained from the appropriate points of intersection in the relevant curves in figure 6.37. As can be observed from figure 6.37, the value of $F1n$ is always between the natural frequency of the nasal cavity with a closed, velopharyngeal port (500 Hz in this case) and $F1$ in the absence of nasal coupling (given in row 1 of the table).

Figure 6.38 shows the calculated transfer function corresponding to the configurations for each of the columns in table 6.3. The influence of acoustic coupling to the maxillary sinus has been included by introducing a low-frequency pole-zero pair. Several observations can be made from these spectra and from the calculations in table 6.3. Introduction of a velopharyngeal opening for a back vowel results in three poles rather than two in the low-frequency region, although one of these poles may not be observed as a clear spectral prominence because of the influence of a nearby zero. The most prominent spectral peaks may be at frequencies that are somewhat displaced from the formant frequencies of the corresponding non-nasal vowel. Comparison of the spectra for /ɑ/ with two values of velopharyngeal opening shows that the larger opening has a more drastic influence on the spectrum, relative to the spectrum for the non-nasal vowel.

A general observation that applies to the calculated transfer functions for both front and back nasal vowels is that the spectrum shape at low frequencies (up to, say, 1200 Hz) is flatter and does not contain narrow or dominant spectral prominences. This spectral flattening is a consequence of several factors: (1) widening of the bandwidth of $F1$ (and, for back vowels, $F2$); (2) introduction of an additional resonance Fn that prevents any one low-frequency resonance from being dominant; and (3) introduction of a resonance below $F1$ due to acoustic coupling to a sinus, again preventing the dominance of one spectral peak.

The various acoustic correlates of nasalization are evident more strongly in nasal vowels that occur in languages that have a nasal-non-nasal contrast for vowels. In French, for example, it appears that a relatively wide velopharyngeal opening is used for producing nasal vowels, and the lowered soft palate introduces a constriction in the acoustic path in the posterior region of the oral cavity. A consequence is that the ratio M_m/M_n in equation (6.4) is small, and most of the acoustic output is from the nose. Evidence of acoustic coupling to the maxillary sinuses is strong, therefore, and enhancement of the spectrum amplitude below $F1$ is more evident. The existence of this low-frequency prominence was first observed by Hattori et al. (1958), and its significance as a cue to nasalization in French was noted by Delattre (1954, 1965). With the enhanced acoustic energy in the nasal cavity, a greater widening and weakening of the first-formant prominence is also expected.

6.9.2 Examples of Acoustic Data for Nasal Vowels

The acoustic effect of creating a velopharyngeal opening in a front vowel in English can be observed by examining the changes in the spectrum during the production of the vowel when it is followed by a nasal consonant. If the vowel is preceded by an obstruent consonant (a consonant for which there is pressure increase behind the consonant constriction), then the velopharyngeal port is closed at the time of release of the consonant. The port then opens during the vowel in preparation for the formation of the oral closure for the nasal consonant. A spectrogram of an utterance of this kind is shown in figure 6.39a. In this word *bender*, the release of the initial consonant /b/ occurs at 140 ms, and the closure for /n/ is at 260 ms. During the intervening vowel, the velopharyngeal port is expected to open.

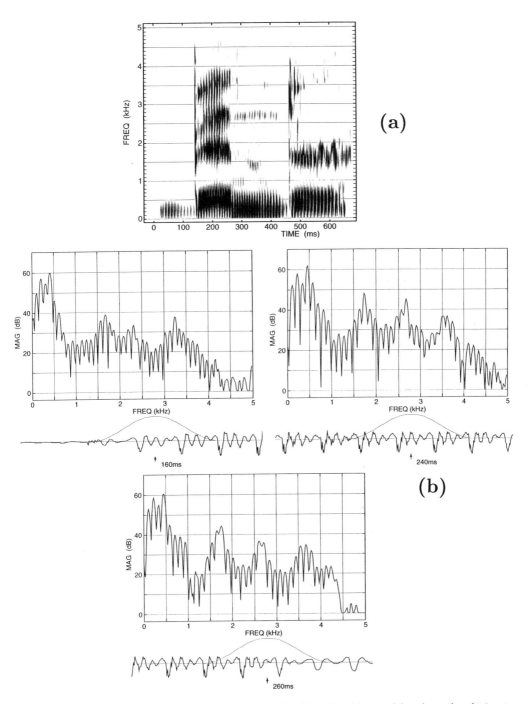

Figure 6.39 (a) Spectrogram of the word *bender* produced by an adult male speaker. (b) Spectra sampled at three points in the vowel /ɛ/. The spectra illustrate the influence of the increasing size of the velopharyngeal opening during the vowel. Waveforms are displayed below the spectra.

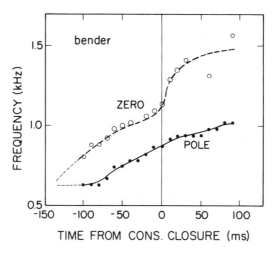

Figure 6.40 Frequencies of the extra pole Fn and zero f_z as a function of time during the vowel /ɛ/ in the word *bender* displayed in figure 6.39. The frequencies are estimated from spectra of the type shown in figure 6.39b. The time of consonant closure on the abscissa is at about 265 ms in figure 6.39.

Spectra and waveforms sampled at several times through the vowel are displayed in figure 6.39b. The extra nasal formant Fn can be observed as a shoulder on the upper edge of the first-formant prominence, and the effect of the zero f_z is a spectral minimum above the nasal formant. These perturbations in the spectrum are more evident later in the vowel. Estimates of the frequencies of the pole and zero can be made from these spectra, and plots of these estimated frequencies are shown in figure 6.40. There appears to be an initial rapid separation of the pole and zero, followed by a rise in both frequencies during the vowel, with a separation of about 200 Hz. (The behavior of the zero as the closure is formed for the nasal consonant is considered later, in section 9.1.) For this vowel /ɛ/, the non-nasal $F1$ is at about 500 Hz, and consequently the shift in $F1$ due to nasalization is small. The behavior of the pole and zero is consistent with the theory, although in the absence of data on the articulatory movements for the utterance, it is not possible to make quantitative evaluations of the adequacy of the theoretical predictions. The spectra in figure 6.39b also show evidence of a low-frequency resonance near the frequency of the second harmonic, presumably due to acoustic coupling to the maxillary sinuses. This enhanced amplitude of the second harmonic is not present when the vowel /ɛ/ is produced in a non-nasal context (cf. the spectrum for the vowel in *bet* in figure 6.25).

Shown in figure 6.41 are spectrograms and spectra for two utterances by a male French speaker. Each of these two-syllable utterances contains a nasal vowel and a non-nasal vowel: the French words are *combat* and *engage*. In the nasal vowel /ɔ̃/ in *combat*, the widened first formant is evident, together with an enhanced first harmonic, due presumably to the acoustic effect of the maxillary sinuses, as discussed above. In contrast, the non-nasal vowel shows

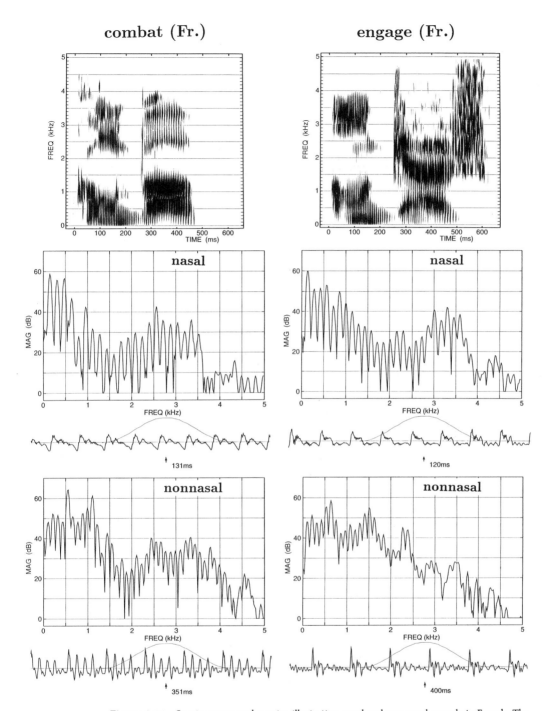

Figure 6.41 Spectrograms and spectra illustrating nasal and non-nasal vowels in French. The left column shows a spectrogram of the word *combat*, and the two spectra below are sampled in the nasal vowel and in the non-nasal vowel, respectively. Similar displays in the right column are for the word *engage*.

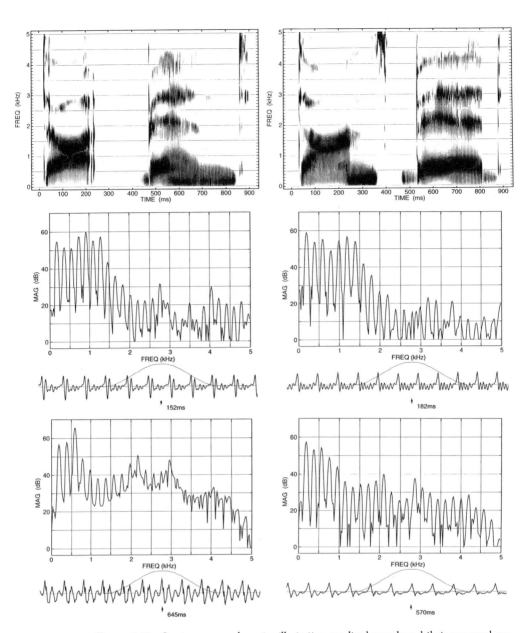

Figure 6.42 Spectrograms and spectra illustrating nasalized vowels and their non-nasal cognates in English for a female speaker. The spectrograms at the top are the utterances *dot bend* (left) and *don's bed* (right). The spectra immediately below the spectrograms are sampled in the non-nasal /ɑ/ in *dot* at the left and the nasalized /ɑ/ in *don* at the right. The spectra at the bottom are sampled in the non-nasal /ɛ/ in *bed* (left) and the nasalized /ɛ/ in *bend* (right).

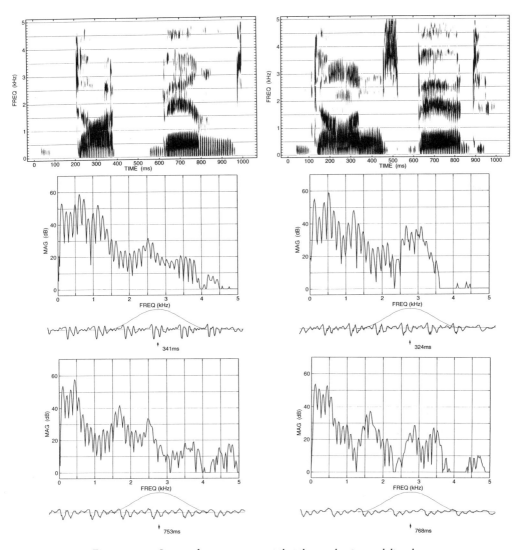

Figure 6.43 Same as figure 6.42, except that the speaker is an adult male.

prominent spectral peaks for the first two formants, with a relatively weak first harmonic. (The extra peak at 1500 Hz is presumably a subglottal resonance.) The nasal vowel /ɑ̃/ in *engage* also shows a greatly enhanced first harmonic, with a broadened first formant, whereas there are prominent formant peaks for the non-nasal vowel. The low and non-low nasal vowels are distinguished here by the frequency of the lowest broad spectral prominence. The overall effect of nasalization for these French vowels is a lack of prominent spectral peaks in the frequency range up to 1500 Hz. This general property of the spectra of nasal vowels has been noted by Maeda (1982a).

Comparison of nasalized and non-nasal vowels in English is illustrated in figures 6.42 and 6.43 for two different speakers—an adult female and an adult male. Spectrograms are shown for the two utterances *Don's bed* and *dot bend*. The utterances are selected to contrast the nasalized and non-nasal /ɔ/ in the first vowel and /ɛ/ in the second vowel. The female speaker (figure 6.42) has a somewhat enhanced first harmonic for non-nasal vowels, and her vowels are somewhat breathy. For the vowel /ɔ/, the effect of nasalization (upper right spectrum) is to produce additional enhancement of the first harmonic, and the spectrum up to 1500 Hz for the nasalized vowel is relatively flat and is lower in amplitude than the first harmonic. The widened bandwidth of $F1$ is even more evident in the nasalized /ɛ/ (lower right spectrum) when compared to its non-nasal counterpart.

For the male speaker's production of /ɔ/ (figure 6.43), the difference between the non-nasal and putatively nasal vowel is relatively small, with little evidence of a wider $F1$, but with an apparent low-frequency pole-zero pair (first two harmonics) and a nasal zero around 950 Hz. The vowel /ɛ/, however, shows the effect of nasalization more strongly, with a widened first-formant prominence, a nasal resonance at about 1000 Hz, and a zero at a higher frequency, as predicted from theory.

These examples provide some indication that there can be substantial differences in the spectra of nasal vowels in a language like French, where these vowels are heavily nasalized, and English, in which the nasalization that occurs in vowels before nasal consonants is apparently produced with a smaller velopharyngeal opening. There are, however, individual differences in the degree of nasalization of these vowels. These differences presumably arise both from anatomical differences (such as dimensions of the nasal cavity and the sinuses) and from variations in the control of the velopharyngeal opening.

7 The Basic Stop Consonants: Bursts and Formant Transitions

There are three classes of time intervals during which properties of the speech wave can contribute to the identity of phonetic features: (1) intervals when the vocal tract is constricted, (2) points in time when there is a release from a constriction or an implosion toward a constriction, and (3) time intervals when there is no narrow constriction in the vocal tract. We turn now to examine in detail the acoustic possibilities that are available to define phonetic categories during the first two of these classes—time intervals when the vocal tract has a narrow constriction, and the immediately adjacent points in time when there may be an implosion or a release of the articulatory structures from this constricted configuration. It is the combination of acoustic events that occur as the vocal tract moves toward or away from the constricted configuration that provides the principal perceptual correlates for particular consonant features.

In this chapter we limit the discussion to situations where one articulator is active in making a complete closure in the oral region of the vocal tract, pressure builds up behind this closure, and the glottis is not actively adjusted from its modal configuration. We examine first the articulatory and acoustic events for a basic stop consonant. The analysis will show the patterns of formant transitions that occur as consonantal closures and releases are formed, and will indicate the nature of the transients and noise bursts that are generated at the consonantal releases.

We will turn in chapter 8 to an examination of other consonants produced with pressure buildup behind the constriction. These include voiceless fricatives, voiceless aspirated stops, voiced stops and fricatives, and affricates. We also examine in more detail the voiceless unaspirated stops. The consonant /h/ is also considered in chapter 8. In chapter 9 we discuss the articulatory and acoustic attributes of sounds produced with similar types of articulatory closure or constriction in the oral cavity but with no buildup of pressure behind the constriction. These sounds include nasal consonants, glides, and liquids. For these configurations, the cross-sectional area of the airway throughout the nose or around the tongue blade is sufficiently large that turbulence noise is not produced in the vocal tract when the vocal folds are vibrating normally.

7.1 OVERVIEW OF BASIC STOP CONSONANTS

The production of a stop consonant in intervocalic position consists of a sequence of several articulatory and acoustic events. There is an initial phase in which a closure is made at a particular point along the vocal tract by manipulating the appropriate articulatory structure. This phase is followed by a time interval in which the vocal tract remains closed, and finally the closure is released. Over some period of time within and adjacent to the closure interval, the state of the vocal folds can be manipulated to generate particular characteristics in the sound. We assume at present that minimal active adjustments are made in the glottal configuration and in the stiffness of the vocal folds or the surfaces of the vocal tract during this sequence of maneuvers of the vocal tract structures.

The acoustic consequences of these movements of the articulatory structures are (1) to inhibit vocal fold vibration during the closure interval; (2) to produce in some frequency regions an abrupt decrease in amplitude at the implosion and an abrupt increase at the release; and (3) to generate appropriate distinctive spectral changes at the implosion and at the release of the closure, depending on the articulatory structure that is used to form the constriction.

7.2 AERODYNAMIC AND ARTICULATORY DESCRIPTION

The articulatory movements that are implemented to produce a stop consonant are shown schematically in figure 7.1. The cross-sectional area at the place in the vocal tract where the closure is made is plotted as a function of time in the upper panel. Midsagittal sections through the vocal tract during the closure interval for three different places of articulation are shown in figure 7.2. These configurations illustrate closures produced by bringing the lips together, by raising the apex of the tongue against the alveolar ridge, and by raising the tongue body so that the dorsum of the tongue makes contact with the palate.

In order to produce the closure effectively, it is frequently necessary to manipulate the tongue body or the mandible. For example, producing a closure with the tongue tip at the alveolar ridge is facilitated if the tongue body is placed in a somewhat fronted position and if the mandible is raised. A schematic representation of the motion of such a secondary structure is given in the lower panel of figure 7.1. This curve is shown to indicate that these secondary structures do not themselves form the constriction, and they move with relatively smooth trajectories. When the motion alternates between two extreme values, the time between two successive maxima or minima can be as short as 200 to 300 ms, as discussed in section 1.3.

The upper panel of figure 7.1 shows a discontinuity in the rate of change of cross-sectional area at the points of closure and release. The rate of change is a maximum just prior to the implosion and immediately following the

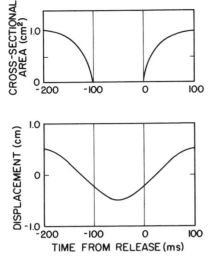

Figure 7.1 Schematic representation of articulatory movements when a stop consonant is produced in intervocalic position. Time from release of the closure is plotted on the abscissa. The upper panel is a representation of the cross-sectional area at a point in the vocal tract where the constriction is formed. The lower panel indicates the type of trajectory that might be followed by a secondary articulatory structure such as the mandible or the tongue body as the intervocalic stop consonant is produced. The durations, rates, and extents of movement are selected to be within the ranges observed in actual utterances, but do not necessarily correspond to a particular stop-consonant trajectory. The time course of the cross-sectional area may be modified somewhat from the smooth trajectory shown above as a consequence of forces due to the intraoral pressure.

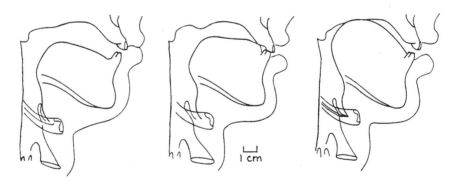

Figure 7.2 Midsagittal sections through the vocal tract during the production of stop consonants produced by closing the lips (left), raising the tongue tip to the alveolar ridge (middle), and raising the tongue body (right). Adult male speaker. (From Perkell, 1969.)

The Basic Stop Consonants

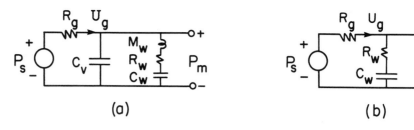

Figure 7.3 (a) Low-frequency equivalent circuit of the vocal tract when there is a complete closure in the oral cavity. (b) Approximate equivalent circuit that is used for calculating intraoral pressure P_m and glottal airflow U_g immediately following closure of a stop consonant. See text.

release. If the structure that forms the closure is the lips or the tongue tip, the rate of change of cross-sectional area immediately adjacent to the points of closure or release can be in the range of 40 to 100 cm^2/s, as we have seen in section 1.3.3.5 of chapter 1 (Fujimura, 1961), and the length of the constriction remains rather short (probably a few millimeters), as indicated in figure 7.2. If the closure is formed by manipulating the tongue body to make contact with the hard or soft palate, the rate of change of cross-sectional area is slower (probably about 25 cm^2/s), and the effective length of the constriction is greater (probably 1 to 2 cm). In the schematized representation in the top panel of figure 7.1, the rate of change of cross-sectional area at implosion and release is shown as about 50 cm^2/s, that is, it is intermediate between the faster and slower rates.

Up to the point in the closing gesture where the cross-sectional area of the supraglottal constriction remains above about 0.3 cm^2, the average pressure drop across the constriction due to the airflow from the glottis is negligible, and there is little effect of this constriction on the glottal vibration pattern. Thus prior to 3 to 10 ms preceding the implosion (depending on the rate of closure), the supraglottal movements have no major influence on the glottal vibration pattern and cause essentially no increase in intraoral pressure. The principal influences on intraoral pressure and on glottal activity occur after the instant of closure.

Immediately following closure there is a buildup of pressure behind the constriction, and this increased pressure can cause an outward displacement of the walls of the vocal tract and the glottis. The time course of this increased intraoral pressure can be estimated from the equivalent circuit in figure 7.3a. This equivalent circuit is the same as the circuit shown previously in figure 2.42, except that since there is a complete closure of the vocal tract, the impedance of the supraglottal constriction is infinite.

The resistance R_g of the glottis is, of course, time-varying as long as the vocal folds continue to vibrate. In order to estimate the change in intraoral pressure P_m, we shall assume an average value for R_g over each glottal period. The acoustic compliance C_v of the volume of air behind the closure is considerably smaller than the effective acoustic compliance C_w of the walls. Furthermore, for the rates of change of pressure and flow of interest here, the

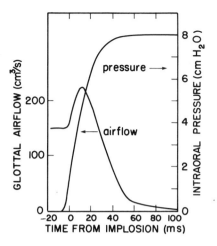

Figure 7.4 Calculations of intraoral pressure and glottal airflow immediately following closure for a stop consonant following a vowel. Subglottal pressure = 8 cm H_2O; average glottal area immediately prior to closure = 0.04 cm^2; acoustic resistance R_w of walls = 10 dyne-s/cm^5; acoustic compliance C_w of walls = 10^{-3} cm^5/dyne; mechanical compliance of vocal folds per unit length = 3×10^{-5} cm^2/dyne; depth of vocal folds = 0.3 cm; surface area of vocal tract walls = 100 cm^2. Calculations are based on equivalent circuit of figure 7.3b.

pressure drop across the acoustic mass M_w of the walls is small compared with the pressure drops across R_w and C_w. Consequently, a reasonable approximation to the time function $P_m(t)$ following the instant of closure can be obtained from analysis of the simplified equivalent circuit of figure 7.3b.

Just at the instant of closure, the intraoral pressure P_m is zero, and the pressure across the glottis is P_s. Air flows through the glottis and through the resistance R_w and the compliance C_w, resulting in an increased intraoral pressure P_m. The "charge" on the compliance is equal to the volume increase due to the outward displacement of the walls. As the intraoral pressure increases, it creates an abducting force on the vocal folds, and causes them to displace outward. As P_m approaches P_s, the transglottal pressure becomes small, and the glottal airflow decreases. Calculations of the smoothed airflow U_g and of the intraoral pressure P_m, assuming nominal values for P_s and for the compliances of the vocal tract walls and the vocal folds (as described in sections 1.1.3.7 and 2.1.1), lead to the trajectories shown in figure 7.4. The average glottal area immediately prior to closure is taken to be 0.04 cm^2, and $P_s = 8$ cm H_2O. Other values of the parameters are given in the figure legend.

The figure shows that the intraoral pressure increases to within 2 cm H_2O of P_s (i.e., $P_m \cong 6$ cm H_2O) in about 20 ms and that the average glottal airflow decreases rapidly after this time. The calculations show that the outward force on the vocal folds due to the increased intraoral pressure causes the average glottal area to increase from 0.04 cm^2 to about 0.14 cm^2 during the closure interval, assuming an effective glottal length of 1.0 cm. This passive widening of the glottis results in a small increase in glottal airflow

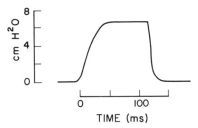

Figure 7.5 Tracing of intraoral pressure during the stop consonant /pʰ/ in the phonetic environment /ɑpʰɪ/. (Adapted from Subtelny et al., 1966.)

immediately following the implosion. The increase in the volume of the intraoral space as the vocal tract walls expand outward is about 8 cm³, that is, the area under the airflow curve. The dimensions and other parameters used to calculate the trajectories of figure 7.4 are based on a bilabial or alveolar point of closure. The rise in intraoral pressure would be more rapid for a velar or uvular point of closure, since the compliance C_w of the walls is smaller.

Experimental data on the increase in intraoral pressure following closure for voiceless stop consonants show trajectories similar to that in figure 7.4. An example is given in figure 7.5. In this example, the stop consonant is /pʰ/ as produced by a male talker in intervocalic position. There may be some differences in the glottal configuration at the beginning of closure for this aspirated consonant as opposed to a voiceless stop consonant for which there is no glottal abduction, and the increased glottal opening could cause the pressure to increase somewhat more rapidly than the increase shown in figure 7.4.

If the duration of the closure extends beyond 50 ms, the intraoral pressure reaches a steady value equal to the subglottal pressure, and the glottal airflow decreases essentially to zero. The walls of the vocal tract have been expanded as a consequence of the increased intraoral pressure (Rothenberg, 1968; Ishizaka et al., 1975; Westbury, 1983; Svirsky et al., 1997). The average outward displacement of the walls for an intraoral pressure of 8 cm H_2O is about 1 mm, but this displacement is presumably greater over some regions of the surface (such as the pharyngeal region or the dorsum of the tongue) and less over other regions (such as the hard palate).

At the release of the closure, we assume that the cross-sectional area of the constriction would follow a trajectory like that in figure 7.1, if there were no intraoral pressure. In the presence of an intraoral pressure, however, the trajectory is modified due to the interaction between the pressure and the mechanical compliance of the surfaces in the vicinity of the constriction. This modification will be greater when the release is slower and the constriction is longer, as it is when there is a release of a velar constriction like that in the right side of figure 7.2.

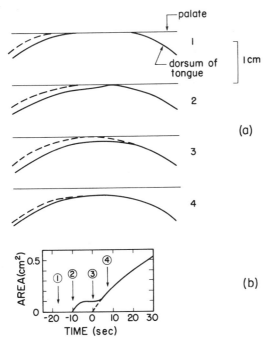

Figure 7.6 (a) Schematic representation of the surfaces of the tongue and the palate at several times during the release of a stop consonant produced by making a closure with the tongue body. The dashed lines indicate the tongue contour if there were no intraoral pressure, and the solid lines show the contour as modified by forces due to the intraoral pressure. (b) Estimated cross-sectional area vs. time at the constriction without the influence of intraoral pressure (dashed line) and with intraoral pressure (solid line). The labeled arrows indicate the points in time corresponding to the panels in (a).

An estimate of the true trajectory of area vs. time following the release can be made by examining the effect of the forces on the vocal tract surfaces in the vicinity of the constriction. The various parts of figure 7.6a illustrate schematically the sequence of events at the release of a closure similar to that for a velar consonant. In part 1 we show the tongue surface in contact with the palate as it might appear during closure, well before release occurs. The dashed line on the upstream or posterior side of the constriction indicates the shape of the tongue contour were there no intraoral pressure. As the tongue body is lowered during the initiation of the release maneuver (part 2), the length of the constriction decreases as the pressure causes a widening of the constriction immediately behind the point of closure. At the instant depicted in part 3, opening has occurred, although if there had been no intraoral pressure there would still be closure, as shown by the dashed line. After opening occurs in part 3, air flows through the constriction, and there is a decrease in pressure within the constriction. As a consequence, there is no longer an outward force on the wall of the constriction, and it begins to return to the position it would have in the absence of an intraoral pressure, that is, the solid line approaches the dashed line in the vicinity of the constriction.

The influence of these effects on the cross-sectional area of the constriction is shown in figure 7.6b. Here we display the trajectory as it would appear were there no intraoral presure (dashed line), together with the trajectory as modified by the influence of the intraoral pressure. The arrows indicate the approximate times at which the shapes in the numbered parts of figure 7.6a occur. In this example, the initial release occurs about 10 ms prior to the time of opening in the absence of intraoral pressure. If the release were slower, this time difference would be greater. In fact, a situation could occur in which, following the initial opening, the area returns to zero as the pressure drop within the constriction decreases (near part 3 in figure 7.6a), and there could be more than one release. Multiple releases are often observed for velar stop consonants. (See section 7.4.4 below.)

As noted above, this modification of the trajectory of area vs. time at the release of a stop consonant will be greatest when the constriction is relatively long and the rate of opening is slower, as it is for a velar consonant and for certain stop consonants produced with a flattened tongue blade. The modification is expected to be much smaller for consonants produced by making the closure and the release with the lips or with the tongue tip.

We turn now to the details of the airflow that occurs immediately following the release. At the release of the closure, there is an abrupt increase in airflow through the constriction and through the glottis, and a rapid decrease in intraoral pressure. Within the first millisecond or so, there is an initial airflow transient through the constriction, of the type discussed in section 2.3 (Massey, 1994). This initial transient occurs within the time interval of roundtrip propagation of sound from the point of release to the glottis. In terms of the equivalent circuit in figure 7.3a, this initial transient is caused by discharge of the air volume stored in C_v when a low resistance is connected across the output terminals. The rate of increase of flow in this initial pulse is dependent on the rate of increase of the cross-sectional area, and the transient is acoustically more significant in relation to the following burst when the release is rapid, as it is for a labial or alveolar stop consonant. As described in section 2.3, the initial transient of volume flow for these rapid releases is approximately

$$U(t) = \sqrt{\frac{2P_o}{\rho}} A_c(t), \tag{7.1}$$

where P_o is the intraoral pressure at the release and $A_c(t)$ is the cross-sectional area of the constriction. When $A_c(t)$ is very small (less than about 0.05 cm^2), the viscous resistance of the constriction dominates the dynamic resistance, and $U(t)$ increases less rapidly than equation (7.1) indicates.

Following the initial transient, the time course of events that influence the sources of sound in the vocal tract can be estimated from the equivalent circuit of figure 7.7. This circuit is similar to that in figure 7.3, except that now

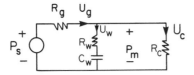

Figure 7.7 Equivalent circuit that is used to calculate airflows and intraoral pressure immediately following release of a stop consonant.

there is an element representing the time-varying impedance of the constriction. The airflow $U_c(t)$ at the constriction can be considered as the sum of two components: the airflow U_g through the glottis, and a component $-U_w$ that arises from the passive inward movement of the walls of the vocal tract as the intraoral pressure decreases. In terms of the equivalent circuit of figure 7.7, the latter component is the result of discharging the acoustic compliance C_w.

Calculations of the intraoral pressure and the various airflows (neglecting the initial transient) for two different rates of release are shown in figure 7.8. The rates are roughly comparable to the releases for labial stops on the one hand, and velar stops on the other. A rate intermediate between these two is expected for alveolar stops. In the case of the velar release, the effect of the intraoral pressure on the trajectory of area vs. time is included, as discussed in connection with figure 7.6. As the intraoral pressure decreases, there is a passive inward displacement of the vocal folds, thus decreasing the glottal area. In order to simplify the calculations, however, the glottal area is assumed to be constant. At some point, when there is sufficient transglottal pressure, vocal fold vibration will be initiated, as discussed below. The pressures and flows in figure 7.8 are, however, calculated on the assumption of no vocal fold vibration.

The airflow trajectories in figure 7.8 indicate that the inward movement of the vocal tract walls is a major contributor to the airflow at the constriction during the initial 10 to 20 ms, particularly for the more rapid rate of release. This contribution is responsible for an overshoot in the airflow at the constriction. The consequences of these results in the generation of sound are considered in the following sections.

7.3 LOW-FREQUENCY SOUND OUTPUT

The trajectories in figure 7.4 show estimates of the average or smoothed intraoral pressure and glottal airflow as a function of time immediately following the closure for a stop consonant. During the initial part of this closure interval the vocal folds continue to vibrate, and the instantaneous glottal area and airflow contain pulses that have a roughly triangular shape, as has been shown in chapter 2. As we have seen, the magnitude of the airflow pulses is roughly proportional to $P_{trans}^{1.5}$, where $P_{trans} = P_s - P_m = $ the transglottal pressure.

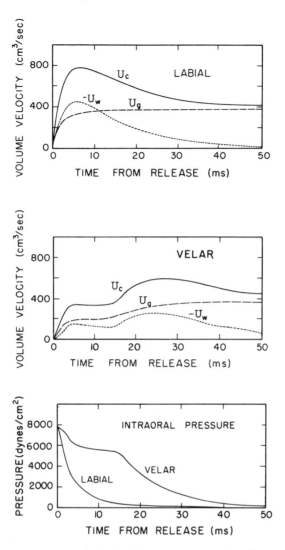

Figure 7.8 Calculated airflows (top two panels) and intraoral pressures (bottom panel) as a function of time following the release of voiceless unaspirated stop consonants. The constriction area follows a trajectory of the form $A_c = A_{max}(1 - e^{-t/\tau})$, where A_{max} is taken to be 1.0 cm^2, and $1/\tau = 100$ s^{-1} for labials releases and 25 s^{-1} for velars. The area for the velar release is further modified as in figure 7.6. The glottal area is assumed to be constant at 0.1 cm^2. Initial intraoral pressure is 8 cm H$_2$O, and other parameters are as given in figure 7.4. Negative U_w indicates that the walls of the vocal tract displace inward following the release. Note that $U_g = U_c + U_w$.

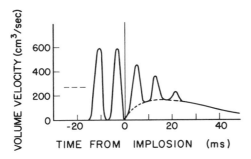

Figure 7.9 Estimate of instantaneous glottal airflow in the vicinity of the time of closure for a stop consonant. Closure occurs at $t = 0$ on the abscissa. The brief interval in which vocal fold vibration occurs after closure would be shortened if the supraglottal volume were prevented from increasing.

In figure 7.9 we show an estimate of the airflow as a function of time with the pulses included. We assume conditions for an adult male configuration, with the fundamental frequency at about 120 Hz during this brief interval. The magnitudes of the pulses and the average airflow have been adjusted to be consistent with the trajectories of pressure and airflow in figure 7.4. Glottal vibration terminates at a time when the transglottal pressure becomes less than about 2 cm H_2O. In figure 7.9 glottal vibration continues for about 25 ms following closure, although the amplitudes of the last two glottal pulses are less than -10 dB relative to the amplitude before closure. This time of voicing continuation as the vocal tract volume increases passively following closure is somewhat less than the experimental values of 50 to 100 ms reported by Ohala and Riordan (1980). However, their values were obtained with a subglottal pressure of 13 to 16 cm H_2O, whereas 8 cm H_2O is assumed for the present calculations. Thus, while the calculated value of 25 ms is on the low side, it is not inconsistent with the experimental data. Perception experiments have indicated that a brief interval of low-amplitude pulses such as this is not sufficient to cause listeners to hear the consonant as voiced, at least for fricative consonants (K. N. Stevens et al., 1992).

Following release of the closure, figure 7.8 shows that there is a rapid increase in the transglottal pressure. When this pressure reaches about 3 cm H_2O, vocal fold vibration is initiated. In the example shown in figure 7.8, the transglottal pressure reaches 3 cm H_2O after about 2 ms for the more rapid release, and after about 15 ms for the slower release. Again the magnitude of the glottal pulses is expected to be roughly proportional to $P_{trans}^{1.5}$. In figure 7.10 we estimate the time course of the first few glottal pulses following the release, corresponding to the more rapid release represented in figure 7.8. The figure shows that, after one or two pulses, the amplitude of the pulses achieves a steady value.

The glottal pulses shown in figures 7.9 and 7.10 form an excitation of the vocal tract in the vicinity of the times of implosion and release of the supraglottal closure. During the time intervals immediately preceding and

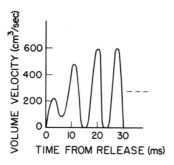

Figure 7.10 Estimate of instantaneous glottal airflow in the vicinity of the release for a voiceless unaspirated labial stop consonant.

following closure, the changing cross-sectional area of the constriction results in movements of the natural frequencies of the vocal tract. Examples of formant changes with changes in constriction size have been shown in figure 3.17 for some simple resonator shapes. In particular, when the constriction is formed at the labial, alveolar, and velar locations, the first-formant frequency decreases as the constriction size decreases. If we take the labial constrictions to be similar to the short constriction at the anterior end of a tube in figure 3.17a, and if we assume the rate of change of cross-sectional area to be about 100 cm^2/s, we can translate the calculations in figure 3.17 into estimated trajectories of $F1$ vs. time. Similar estimates can be made for the velar constriction, based on the calculations in figure 3.17b, and assuming a lower rate of change of area near closure of about 25 cm^2/s, modified by the effects of the intraoral pressure, as discussed above. The results of these manipulations are given in figure 7.11.

The first-formant trajectories show that most of the $F1$ movement for the more rapid change of cross-sectional area occurs within about 10 ms. (In addition to this rapid movement, there could be a slower component of the $F1$ trajectory as a consequence of the movement of the tongue body or mandible.) On the other hand, for the slower rate of change of area and the greater constriction length, $F1$ completes only about 50 percent of its movement away from closure in 40 ms. During the closure interval, the lowest natural frequency of the vocal tract is about 200 Hz. (The natural frequency of the vocal tract with a closure in the supraglottal tract is about 180 Hz when the glottis is closed, as has been seen in section 3.4.2. With a partially open glottis, this frequency is somewhat higher, because of the acoustic mass of the glottis and the subglottal system.)

Immediately prior to closure, then, there is a fall in $F1$ which occurs over a time interval of one to two glottal periods (depending on $F0$) for the fast closure, and a considerably longer time for the more slowly moving, longer constriction. A concomitant of this decreasing $F1$ is a reduction in the low-frequency amplitude of the radiated sound, as a consequence of the decreased amplitude of the $F1$ peak in the transfer function, as discussed in section 3.2,

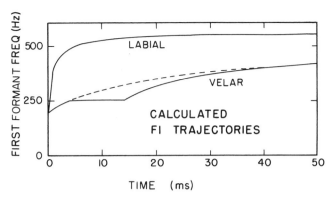

Figure 7.11 Calculated trajectories of movement of the lowest natural frequency of a vocal tract model for two different types of release of a stop consonant. The upper trajectory corresponds to a closure at the anterior end of the vocal tract, with a length of 2 mm and an initial rate of opening of 100 cm^2/s. The lower trajectory corresponds to a closure at the velar position, with a length of 2 cm and an initial rate of opening that would be 25 cm^2/s in the absence of the effects of intraoral pressure on the oral release. The actual area is modified as shown in figure 7.6, and results in the velar trajectory displayed as a solid line. The trajectory that would occur in the absence of the effects of intraoral pressure is indicated by the dashed line. Formant frequencies are taken from figure 3.17. The same trajectories reversed in time are assumed for the implosion of the consonant, except that the dashed line should be used for the velar implosion.

and of the tendency for an increased bandwidth in the lower frequency range of $F1$.

Immediately following the instant of closure, with the first-formant frequency at about 200 Hz, sound is radiated from the surfaces of the face and neck rather than from the mouth opening. The amplitude of the radiated sound is reduced relative to the low-frequency amplitude for the preceding vowel for two reasons: (1) the low first-formant frequency, and (2) the decreased amplitude of the glottal pulses, as shown in figure 7.8. Thus, for example, if there is an increase in intraoral pressure of about 3 cm H$_2$O during the time of the first glottal pulse following closure (corresponding to a decreased transglottal pressure from 8 cm H$_2$O to 5 cm H$_2$O), then the amplitude of this pulse is expected to be $(5/8)^{1.5}$ or about 6 dB below its amplitude with the full transglottal pressure.

Examples of the waveform of the radiated sound pressure in the vicinity of closure for a labial and a velar voiceless unaspirated stop consonant are given in the left panels of figure 7.12a and b, together with short-time spectra sampled at several points in the waveform. Also shown are measurements of $F1$ at each glottal pulse preceding the closure and a measure of amplitude change at low frequencies. The rather abrupt decrease in amplitude $A1$ and in frequency at the instant of closure for the labial is apparent, and two residual glottal pulses can be observed following closure (bottom left panel of figure 7.12a). The low-frequency amplitude decreases by more than 10 dB (relative to the amplitude in the vowel) for the first of these pulses, indicating a significant reduction in amplitude of the glottal pulses. The rapid fall in $F1$

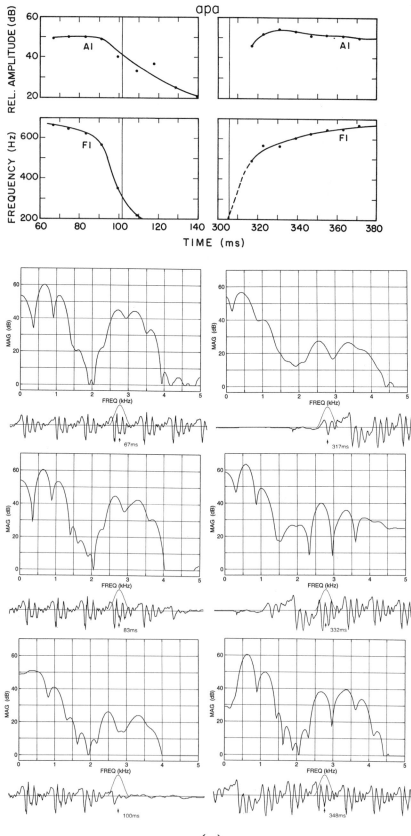

(a)

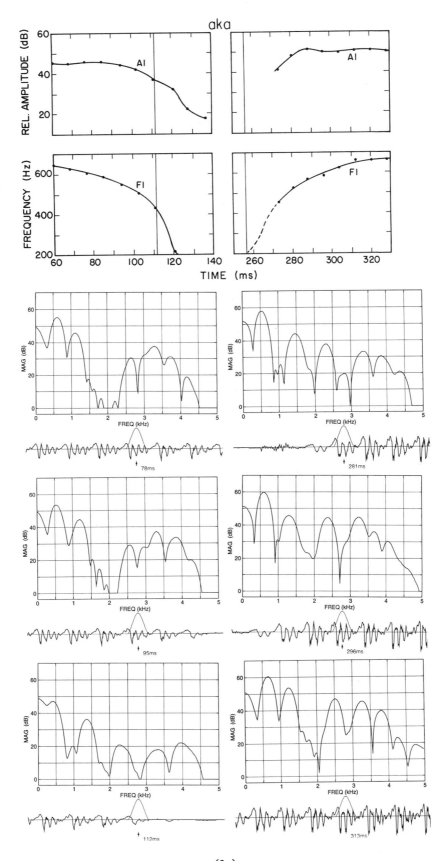

aka

(b)

immediately preceding closure (at time 102 ms) is manifested as a broadening of the $F1$ spectral peak, since the time window over which the spectrum is evaluated encompasses the rapid downward movement of $F1$ that is a consequence of the closing gesture. In the case of the velar, the fall in $F1$ is less abrupt, as expected. The first glottal pulse following closure shows about a 10-dB reduction in amplitude, and the second pulse is even weaker, presumably because of the smaller surface area that is available for expansion, compared with the labial closure. The time interval over which $F1$ is falling prior to closure for the velar consonant is about 50 ms. The formant trajectories prior to closure and the amplitude reduction immediately following closure for both the labial and the velar are consistent with the analysis given in figures 7.11 (assuming mirror-image trajectories, except for the pressure-related bump in the release for the velar) and 7.9.

At the release of a stop consonant of this type, figure 7.8 shows that there is a delay in the buildup of transglottal pressure. This delay is a consequence of the pressure drop across the supraglottal constriction as airflow from the glottis and from the inward-moving vocal tract walls passes through the constriction. As we have noted, vocal fold vibration is expected to begin at the time when the transglottal pressure reaches about 3 cm H_2O. In the case of the consonant with the rapid release (corresponding roughly to a labial stop consonant) conditions appropriate for this initiation of vocal fold vibration occur about 2 ms after the release. Another 2 to 3 ms might elapse before the vocal folds complete their initial adduction and make partial contact to form the first glottal pulse, as figure 7.10 shows. For the consonant with the slower release and the longer constriction, figure 7.8 predicts that the onset of vocal fold vibration is about 15 ms after the release. The first one or two glottal pulses after the onset of voicing are likely to be weaker than later pulses because the transglottal pressure is still increasing during this time, particularly for the slower release.

Examples of waveforms and measurements of $F1$ and $A1$ sampled in the vicinity of the release of a voiceless unaspirated labial and velar stop consonant are shown in the right panels of figure 7.12a and b. The greater delay in onset of glottal vibration for the velar is apparent in the waveforms. For the labial, much of the rising $F1$ trajectory is not visible in the spectra, since

Figure 7.12 Examples of waveforms, spectra, and low-frequency characteristics sampled at selected points near the implosion of voiceless unaspirated stop consonants in the utterances /ɑpɑ/ (a) and /ɑkɑ/ (b). In each part, several spectra are shown in the lower three panels, with the waveform and time window below each spectrum. The spectra at the left in each part are sampled at three points in time near the implosion, and the spectra at the right are sampled at times centered on three different glottal pulses following the release. The spectra are obtained by centering a 6.4-ms Hamming window over the initial part of the glottal period. In the top panels of each part, the measured $F1$ trajectories near the implosion and the release are shown, together with the amplitude $A1$ of the $F1$ prominence. The dashed portions of the curves are estimated extrapolations. The vertical lines are the estimated times of consonantal closure and release. The different rates of movement of $F1$ for the labial and velar consonants are apparent.

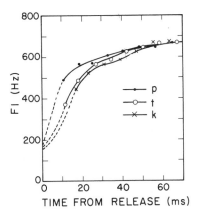

Figure 7.13 Measurements of the first-formant frequency following the release of the voiceless unaspirated stop consonants /p/, /t/, and /k/ with the following vowel /ɑ/. It is assumed that during closure (at $t = 0$) the lowest natural frequency is 180 Hz. The dashed lines are estimates of the formant movements from this point to the first time when a measurement can be made after the beginning of glottal vibration. Measurements are made at each glottal period. Data are for a male speaker.

most of the transition of $F1$ occurs before vocal fold vibration begins. The continuing rise of $F1$ after the initial 20-odd milliseconds is presumably a consequence of the fact that the labial area continues to increase as the jaw lowers for the vowel /ɑ/. This slower component of $F1$ increase is not shown in the calculation of the $F1$ trajectory in figure 7.11. In the case of the velar the slower rise in $F1$ is apparent. The initial glottal pulse in each case is weaker than later pulses, as indicated by the rise in $A1$.

Measurements of the $F1$ movement following the release are compared in figure 7.13 for the labial, alveolar, and velar stop consonants, with the following vowel /ɑ/, as produced by a male speaker. Data are plotted on a time scale beginning at the consonant release. Measurements of $F1$ cannot be made in the initial few milliseconds following the release, and the starting frequency for $F1$ at the instant of release is taken to be the theoretical value of 180 Hz, as noted in section 3.4.2. The comparison in figure 7.13 shows that the $F1$ transition is fastest for the labial and slowest for the velar, presumably reflecting the different rates of movement and different lengths of the constrictions.

In summary, then, we observe the following sequence of acoustic events at low frequencies when a labial, alveolar, or velar intervocalic stop consonant is produced with little or no active adjustment of the glottal configuration: (1) The amplitude of the glottal pulses decreases abruptly at the instant of closure. Glottal vibration may continue for 10 to 20 ms following closure but with a greatly reduced amplitude. (2) At the release of the closure, vocal fold vibration resumes 5 to 15 ms following the release, the amount of delay depending on the rate of opening of the constriction. (3) There is a downward movement of the first-formant frequency immediately prior to the implosion, and a rise in F1 following the release. The rate of movement of this transition depends on the rate of change of the area of the constriction and on its length; most of the F1 transition is completed in 10 to 20 ms for labials and is somewhat longer for velars and alveolars.

7.4 HIGH-FREQUENCY SOUND OUTPUT

7.4.1 General Description

The description of the characteristics of the sound in the low-frequency region for voiceless unaspirated stop consonants in intervocalic position has indicated several attributes that are the same independent of the place in the vocal tract where the constriction is formed. There is an abrupt decrease in amplitude of voicing at the instant of closure, with a few glottal pulses of decreasing amplitude after closure as the intraoral pressure increases to a value equal to the subglottal pressure. Following the release, the intraoral pressure decreases rapidly, and vocal fold vibration resumes within a few milliseconds. There are some differences in the timing of events depending on the length of the constriction and the rate at which the cross-sectional area changes before the closure and after the release. These differences are manifested in the rate of movement of the first formant and in the time taken for the intraoral pressure to decrease after the release, and hence in the delay between the release and the onset of voicing.

Additional acoustic attributes can be observed at frequencies above the first formant. These include the trajectories of the formant frequencies and changes in amplitudes of the spectral prominences immediately prior to closure, possible generation of a brief burst of noise at the instant of closure, generation of a transient and a burst of noise with particular spectral characteristics immediately following the release, and trajectories of formant frequencies following the release. The details of these various acoustic events depend on the place in the vocal tract where the constriction is made, and the rate of movement of the articulatory structure that forms the constriction. We examine in turn the acoustic events at higher frequencies in the vicinity of the closure and of the release for labial, alveolar, and velar stop consonants.

7.4.2 Labial Stop Consonants

7.4.2.1 Formant Transitions As a labial closure is formed and then released, the changing shape of the vocal tract gives rise to changes in the natural frequencies of the vocal tract. When the constriction is made at the lips, all of the vocal tract resonances are resonances of the cavities behind the constriction. When the cross-sectional area of the vocal tract behind the lips is relatively uniform, figure 3.17a has shown that all of the natural frequencies tend to decrease as the area of the constriction becomes smaller,

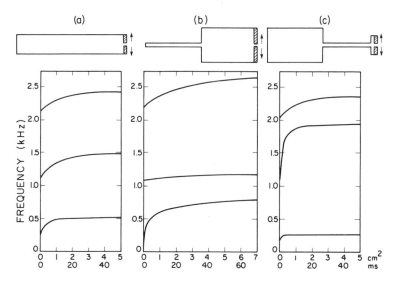

Figure 7.14 Showing the changes in the frequencies of the first three formants as the constriction area at the open end of a vocal tract model is increased to simulate the release of a labial closure. Three different vocal tract models are illustrated: (a) a uniform tube; (b) a concatenation of a narrow and a wide section simulating a back vowel like /ɑ/; (c) a concatenation of a wide and a narrow section simulating a front vowel like /i/. For all models, the overall length is 17 cm, and the length of the labial constriction is 0.5 cm. Two abscissas are shown: one gives the cross-sectional area of the constriction, and the other gives the time from the consonant release assuming a linear rate of increase in area of 100 cm²/s.

with the higher-frequency formants decreasing somewhat less rapidly than the lower frequencies. At the release of the consonant, the formant frequencies increase with trajectories that are roughly mirror images of the falling movements at closure. Figure 7.14a is similar to figure 3.17a, and shows calculations of the formant movements following the release for a uniform vocal tract shape, assuming a labial constriction length of 0.5 cm and an overall vocal tract length of 17 cm, as sketched at the top of the figure. A time scale has been placed on this figure assuming a linear increase in labial cross-sectional area of 100 cm²/s. Thus a time of 10 ms corresponds to an area of 1.0 cm². All of the formants show a rapid increase in frequency. Within about 6 ms, for example, $F2$ has traversed one-half of the total distance from its initial to its final value. As we will see, the formants may not be observable in the first few milliseconds after the release of a stop consonant because the major acoustic source is a noise burst rather than the glottal vibration source. (We distinguish here between the natural frequencies [or formants] of the vocal tract and spectral prominences that appear in the sound. Depending on the location of the source, not all formants are excited and hence not all formants are manifested in the sound as spectral prominences.)

The formant movements following the release of a labial consonant depend to some extent on the following vowel, since the tongue body position for the vowel can be largely in place at the time of consonant release. For example, if the following vowel is a back vowel, such as /ɑ/ or /u/, the articulatory configuration can be modeled by two coupled sections, with the closely spaced first two formants associated roughly with these two sections. In the case of the vowel /ɑ/, a two-tube resonator like that in figure 7.14b is a rough approximation to the vocal tract shape. To model the production of a labial stop consonant adjacent to such a vowel, a constriction is formed at the open end of this resonator, as shown in the figure. If the two components of the tube have equal lengths, as in the example in figures 3.13 and 3.14, then the natural frequency of each individual section is the same. With $A_1 = 0.7$ cm^2 and $A_2 = 7.0$ cm^2, and an overall length of 17 cm, the lowest two natural frequencies of the coupled resonators are 800 and 1180 Hz. The calculated frequencies of the first three formants as the labial constriction is increased from 0 to 7 cm^2 (again at the rate of 100 cm^2/s) are shown in figure 7.14b. There is a rapid rise of F1, but only a small upward movement of F2, since the back-cavity resonance is essentially unaffected by modifications of the front cavity. This relatively small transition of F2 is typical of labial consonants preceding back vowels, since the low-frequency back-cavity resonance remains almost unchanged as the labial constriction changes the front-cavity resonance.

The situation is somewhat different when a labial consonant precedes a front vowel. In this case, the second (or sometimes the third) natural frequency for the vowel configuration is associated primarily with the front cavity, or the anterior part of the vocal tract. The resonance of this part of the vocal tract is therefore quite sensitive to changes in the size of the labial opening. When the lip opening is narrow, the front-cavity resonance is always the second formant. Consequently the second-formant frequency shows a sharp rise as the labial area increases.

An example of modeling a labial release into a front vowel is given in figure 7.14c. An idealized vowel model, with a wide pharyngeal region and a narrow constriction in the anterior half, is shown at the top of the figure. The calculated time course of the formant movements is displayed on the graph, again assuming a rate of increase of the labial opening of 100 cm^2/s. This example shows a very rapid upward movement of F2 immediately following the release, and a slower, less extensive movement of F3. For this particular resonator shape, the natural frequency that is primarily associated with the large back cavity remains fixed at about 2000 Hz. At the beginning of the transition, this is F3, that is, the third natural frequency, whereas after the lips are more open, this resonance becomes F2, and the front-cavity resonance is F3. When a labial consonant is released into a more open front vowel, the F2 transition would not be as extensive or as rapid, and F2 would continue to rise slowly after the initial 40 ms following the release. As noted above, the rapid upward movement of F2 in the initial 5 to 10 ms would not be observed in the release of a labial stop consonant, in part because spectrum analysis could not resolve this rapid change and in part because this part of the transition would be obscured by the burst.

These observations illustrate several attributes of the transitions of the second and third formants into and out of a closure for a labial stop consonant. First, since the tongue body is more or less in position for the adjacent vowel at the time of release of the consonant, the major parts of the transitions of $F2$ and $F3$ following the consonantal release are due only to the lip motion and not to tongue body movements, with perhaps some contributions from jaw movement. Since the length of the lip constriction is small, and since the rate of area change for the lip opening is large, the motion of the formants is rapid. The major part of the formant movement is completed in 20 ms or less. Second, upward movement of $F2$ after a labial release into a front vowel is extensive and rapid, but the transition may continue slowly beyond 40 ms from the release, especially for a non-high front vowel, which has a larger labial opening than a high front vowel. There is also some upward movement of $F3$, but it is not as salient as the $F2$ movement. Third, before back vowels the upward movement of $F2$ is small.

Some examples of measurements of movements of $F1$, $F2$, and $F3$ for voiced labial stop consonants in intervocalic position, produced by a male speaker, are shown in figure 7.15. Data are given for the vowels /ɑ/ and /ɛ/. The rapid transitions of $F2$ when the consonant is in a front-vowel environment (/ɛ/ in this case) are evident, although the frequency at the release can-

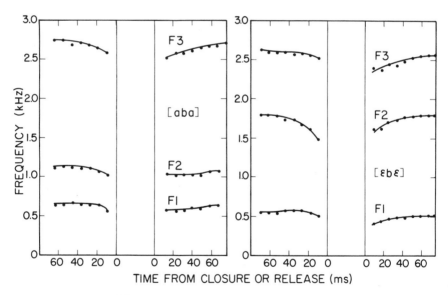

Figure 7.15 Measured frequencies of the first three formants for the utterances /ɑbɑ/ (left) and /ɛbɛ/ (right) produced by a male speaker. Measurements are made from discrete Fourier transforms by centering a 6.4-ms window on the initial part of each glottal period and recording the frequencies of the spectral prominences. The abscissa represents the time before closure and the time following release.

not be observed because the amplitude of the glottal source is not sufficient and because the burst obscures measurement of the formant. The $F2$ movements for the back vowel are relatively small, as expected based on the analysis given above. As noted earlier, the observed movements of $F1$ are relatively small since the rapid transitions adjacent to closure and release cannot be measured.

7.4.2.2 Changes in Source Amplitudes and Spectral Characteristics

The spectral characteristics in the vicinity of the closure and release of an intervocalic labial consonant are influenced both by the formant movements and by changes in the amplitudes of the glottal and frication sources at these times. If the source is at the glottis, all of the natural frequencies of the vocal tract are excited by the source, whereas a frication noise source in the vicinity of an oral constriction causes significant excitation of only a subset of the formants. We consider first the spectral changes that occur as the lips close in the first vowel, and then we examine the changing spectral characteristics following the release of the labial closure.

As $F1$ falls rapidly in the few milliseconds prior to closure, the spectrum amplitude at higher frequencies decreases as a consequence of the amplitude relations between the formants, as discussed in section 3.2. Thus, for example, a decrease in $F1$ from 500 to 250 Hz would result in a decrease in the amplitudes of higher-frequency spectral peaks of about 12 dB, everything else being equal. Once closure is achieved, any sound that is produced as a consequence of continued glottal vibration is radiated from the walls of the vocal tract rather than from the mouth opening. As noted in section 3.7.2, energy in the vicinity of the first formant can be radiated from the surfaces of the neck and face, but radiation of energy for higher formants is much weaker. Thus the decrease in spectrum amplitude at frequencies above $F1$ at the instant of closure tends to be even more abrupt than the decrease in amplitude at low frequencies. Other consequences of the closure movements at frequencies above $F1$ are related to the manner in which the higher formant frequencies change.

If the constriction is made with the lips, figure 7.14 has shown that all of the natural frequencies tend to decrease as the area of the constriction becomes smaller. When the cross-sectional area of the vocal tract behind the lips is relatively uniform, as in figure 7.14a, the higher-frequency formants decrease somewhat less rapidly than the lower frequencies. Starting from the formant movements for this configuration, shown previously in figures 3.17 and 7.14a, spectra have been calculated at several instants of time through this idealized closing gesture. These spectra are shown in figure 7.16a. A fixed glottal spectrum similar to that in figure 2.10 for a male voice was used to make these calculations. The figure also shows an estimate of the spectrum a few milliseconds after closure, before vocal fold vibration ceases. The overall pattern of spectrum change through this time interval can be de-

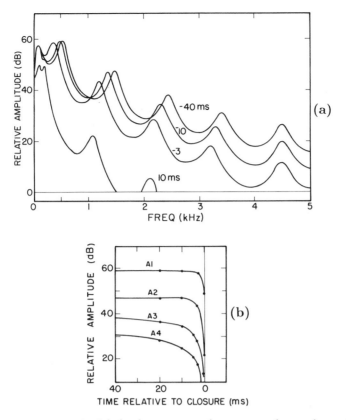

Figure 7.16 (a) Calculated spectrum envelopes at several times during the transition from a vowel model with uniformly spaced formants to a configuration with a labial closure, as in figure 7.14a (assuming that the formants follow the same trajectories during the closing movement into the consonant as during the release from the consonant closure). The parameter is the time relative to closure. (b) Time variation of the amplitudes of the spectral prominences for the different formants. A rate of change of area of 100 cm²/s is assumed.

scribed as an initial decrease in spectrum amplitude at high frequencies while the low-frequency amplitude remains essentially unchanged, followed by an abrupt decrease at low frequencies. The calculated amplitudes of individual formant peaks in the transfer function, shown in figure 7.16b, illustrate the trend of high-frequency amplitudes decreasing before low-frequency amplitudes. The details of this pattern will depend, of course, on the exact nature of the formant trajectories, which are determined in part by the preceding vowel. The overall tendency when all the formants move downward, however, is to obtain a pattern of spectrum change similar to that in figure 7.16a, even if the downward movement is synchronous for all formants. The pattern of high-frequency amplitudes decreasing before low-frequency amplitudes is accentuated if the initiation of the decrease of the frequencies of higher formants precedes that of the lower formants.

It should be noted that if there is no major narrowing of the vocal tract behind the labial constriction, then no two of the formants are in close proximity. That is, the formants at the time the constriction is formed are relatively equally spaced. The examples in figure 7.14 illustrate this fact if one examines the natural frequencies at the time of release. A consequence of this formant distribution is that there are no major spectral prominences formed by the proximity of two formants. The spectrum near the time the closure is formed shows an increasing downward tilt with a series of prominences no two of which are very close together.

Needless to say, the calculated spectrum envelopes in figure 7.16a will not be reflected in detail in the measured spectrum of the sound in the vicinity of closure. The change in the formant frequencies is often so rapid that a short-time spectrum represents an average over some portion of the interval. Thus, for example, the spectrum shape that would appear after processing by peripheral auditory filters in the frequency range of the second formant in figure 7.16a near time $t = 0$ would show a broad spectral prominence in the frequency range 1.1 to 1.4 kHz rather than the narrow peaks displayed in the individual quasi-static transfer functions. Furthermore, since the interval between glottal pulses is in the range 3 to 10 ms (for an adult speaker), a reasonable comparison of the short-time spectra at different times can only be obtained if the spectra are sampled at the same points in the successive glottal cycles. Nevertheless, the overall picture of the spectrum change at closure for a labial consonant is a decrease in amplitude that occurs first at high frequencies and then at lower frequencies, with no dominant peak in the spectrum during this time.

During the closure interval, the pressure behind the constriction builds up to a value equal to the subglottal pressure. As we have already seen, this intraoral pressure causes a displacement of the vocal tract walls, and the vocal folds move laterally in response to the increased pressure in the glottis. The volume increase resulting from the movement of the walls is about 8 cm^3 for an intraoral pressure of 8 cm H$_2$O, assuming that the closure is at the front part of the vocal tract. We have observed in figure 7.9 that vocal fold vibration at reduced amplitude continues for 10 to 20 ms following closure, assuming that no adjustment of the glottal configuration is made. An estimate of the spectrum of the radiated sound during this time is shown in figure 7.16a ($t = +10$ ms). For a simple stop consonant in intervocalic position in an utterance, the duration of the closure is approximately 80 ms, but this duration may increase or decrease somewhat depending upon a number of factors.

Immediately following the instant of release of a labial stop consonant, several events occur in sequence. Within the initial millisecond, the rate of increase of the cross-sectional area of the constriction can be very high as forces due to the pressure behind the constriction augment the forces resulting from contracting the muscles controlling the articulatory structures that form the constriction, in this case the lips. The lowering of the jaw also contributes to the rate at which the lip opening increases. With an initial rate of increase of 100 cm^2/s (Fujimura, 1961), a cross-sectional area of 0.1 cm^2 is achieved within 1 ms. As has been shown in section 2.3, and as noted above in section 7.2, the rapid increase in airflow resulting from this opening generates an initial transient that gives rise to the radiation of a brief pulse of sound energy. This transient occurs before there is significant inward movement of the vocal tract walls and before the effects of glottal airflow appear at the mouth opening. The magnitude of the rate of volume velocity change for this transient is comparable to the rate of change at closure for a normal glottal pulse.

Following this initial pulse of airflow there is a slower increase in the airflow through the constriction. As shown in figure 7.8, this airflow is a superposition of two components: one is a consequence of the inward movement of the walls of the vocal tract in response to the reduced intraoral pressure, and the other is the airflow from the lungs and trachea through the glottis into the vocal tract. For the glottal adjustments considered here, and for rates of release typical of labial stop consonants, the first of these components is the predominant one during the initial 10 ms following the release, as we have seen in section 7.2. The rapid airflow through the constriction causes the generation of turbulence noise in the vicinity of the constriction.

As the pressure above the glottis decreases, the abducting force that holds the vocal folds apart during the closure interval becomes smaller, and the vocal folds move inward. At some point in time the area of the supraglottal constriction becomes larger than that of the glottis, the airflow becomes limited by the glottal opening, and the noise at the supraglottal constriction decreases. Vocal fold vibration begins at about this time, although some turbulence noise might be generated at the glottis for a brief time interval before vibration is fully developed. The time interval from consonant release to onset of glottal vibration depends on the rate of opening of the supraglottal constriction. The analysis in figures 7.8 and 7.10 suggests that this time interval is roughly 5 ms for rates of area increase that are expected for labial consonant releases.

Following the onset of glottal vibration there may be additional movements of the articulatory structures toward a configuration appropriate for the following vowel. The changing lip opening leads to movements of the formants, as noted above in figure 7.14. There may also be slower components of the formant transitions as the tongue body and mandible move toward positions for the following vowel.

The sequence of acoustic events following the consonantal release has been described by Fant (1973a), and is summarized in schematic form in figure 7.17. The sequence consists of (1) an initial brief pulse of volume velocity; (2) a burst of turbulence or frication noise at the constriction as the expanded walls of the vocal tract return to their rest position; (3) a possible brief time interval in which turbulence or aspiration noise is generated at the glottis; (4) onset of vocal fold vibration as the supraglottal pressure decreases and the vocal folds move inward; and (5) further movement of the lips and tongue body (and possibly other gestures such as lip rounding)

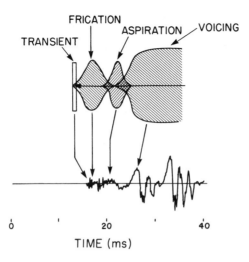

Figure 7.17 Schematic representation of sequence of events at the release of a voiceless unaspirated stop consonant. (From K. N. Stevens, 1993b.)

toward configurations appropriate for the following vowel. (Item [5] is not shown in the figure.) Not all of these events may be present for a given release, as we shall see later.

Each of these events will have somewhat different spectral and temporal characteristics depending on the articulatory structure that produces the closure and the place in the vocal tract where the closure is formed. Our concern initially is with the closure produced by the lips, corresponding to the unaspirated consonant /p/. We turn now to a more detailed examination of the various events at the consonant release.

When the closure is produced at the lips, there is no acoustic cavity in front of the closure, and the initial transient and the turbulence noise energy at the constriction are radiated directly from the lips. In section 2.3 we calculated the spectrum of the volume velocity for the initial transient, assuming that the rate of increase of cross-sectional area of the lip opening is 100 cm^2/s, with an intraoral pressure of 8 cm H_2O. The spectrum of the transient source under these conditions is given in figure 2.47. At a frequency of 1 kHz, for example, the volume velocity spectrum in a frequency band of 300 Hz is 13 dB re 1 cm^3/s, or about 4.5 cm^3/s.

Radiation of this transient volume velocity from the lip opening gives rise to a sound pressure $p_{rt}(f)$ at distance r of

$$p_{rt}(f) = \frac{f\rho U_t(f)}{2r} \tag{7.2}$$

from equation (3.4). At a frequency of 1 kHz and a distance of $r = 20$ cm, equation (7.2) gives a root-mean-square sound pressure level of about 56 dB re 0.0002 dyne/cm^2. A rough estimate of the spectrum of the radiated sound pressure (in 300-Hz bands) corresponding to the initial transient for $r = 20$ cm is given as curve T in figure 7.18.

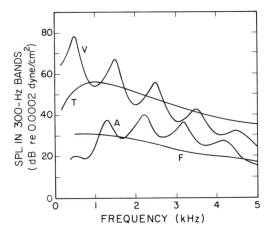

Figure 7.18 Calculated spectra of several components in the sequence of acoustic events following the release of a voiceless unaspirated labial stop consonant. The ordinate is the sound pressure level in 300-Hz bands at a distance of 20 cm from the mouth opening. (The radiation characteristic of a simple isotropic source is assumed.) The curves are labeled with letters indicating the different components as schematized in figure 7.17. T, initial transient at consonant release; F, sound due to frication noise generated at or near the labial constriction; A, sound due to aspiration noise generated near the glottis; V, vowel spectrum after onset of vocal fold vibration. The vowel has uniformly spaced formant frequencies.

For a few milliseconds immediately following the transient, a brief burst of turbulence noise is generated at the labial opening. The time course of the amplitude of this noise burst can be calculated from the trajectories of constriction area and volume velocity, given in figure 7.8. In chapter 2 (equation [2.21]) we estimated the amplitude of this noise source to be proportional to $U_c^3 A_c^{-2.5}$, where U_c is the volume velocity at the constriction and A_c is the cross-sectional area of the constriction. The solid line in figure 7.19 shows the time variation of $20 \log U_c^3 A_c^{-2.5}$ for the first few milliseconds following the release of the consonant. The amplitude of the turbulence noise source has a broad maximum 1 to 2 ms after the release, and then decreases by about 8 dB at 6 ms.

We can calculate the approximate absolute level and spectrum of the turbulence noise source using the source spectra in figure 2.33 as a starting point. As noted in that figure, the spectrum should be scaled up or down in amplitude depending on the value of $U_c^3 A_c^{-2.5}$. As a reference for calculating the absolute level of the source, we select a time 1.6 ms following the consonant release, that is, the time at which the amplitude of the source in figure 7.19 is a maximum. At this time, the volume velocity at the lips for a labial consonant is about 450 cm³/s (top panel of figure 7.8), and the cross-sectional area of the constriction is 0.16 cm², since we are assuming an average rate of increase of area of 100 cm²/s. As figure 7.19 shows, the value of $20 \log U^3 A^{-2.5}$ is then 199 dB, which is 13 dB below the reference value for the 420-cm³/s curve in figure 2.33. Thus the spectrum of the noise source

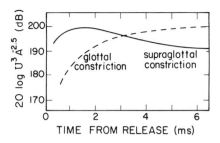

Figure 7.19 Calculation of relative levels of turbulence noise sources at the constriction (solid line) and at the glottal opening (dashed line) during release of a model of a voiceless unaspirated labial stop consonant. Levels are calculated from trajectories of airflow and area given in figure 7.8. The ordinate is $20 \log U^3 A^{-2.5}$, where U is the volume velocity at the constriction, in cubic centimeters per second, and A is the cross-sectional area of the constriction, in square centimeters. See text.

would be 13 dB below the reference spectrum in figure 2.33 if there were an obstactle in the airstream like the one for which the reference spectrum was measured. At the lips, however, there is no obstacle directly in the airstream, although the lips form surfaces against which the air jet grazes and creates turbulence. We arbitrarily subtract an additional 10 dB from the source level predicted from figure 2.33 to account for the reduced effectiveness of the lip surface in generating turbulence noise. Thus the sound pressure spectrum of the source at the 1.6-ms point is about 23 dB below the reference spectrum in figure 2.33a. For example, at 2500 Hz the source sound pressure in the reference spectrum is 28 dB re 1 dyne/cm^2 in a 300-Hz band, and consequently the sound pressure in the burst at the 1.6-ms point in the same band is 5 dB re 1 dyne/cm^2.

In order to calculate the spectrum of the radiated sound given the source spectrum, we first estimate the acoustic volume velocity at the lips due to the source. As a first approximation, we assume that the sound pressure source p_s is located on the lip surface, and that this source is in series with the acoustic mass of the labial constriction. The acoustic mass of the constriction is $M_c = \rho \ell_c / A_c$, where A_c is the cross-sectional area of the constriction and ℓ_c is its length. The magnitude of the acoustic volume velocity at the lips at frequency f is then

$$U_o = \frac{p_s}{2\pi f M_c} = \frac{p_s A_c}{2\pi f \rho \ell_c}. \tag{7.3}$$

At a distance r from the lips, the sound pressure amplitude p_r is given by

$$p_r = \frac{\rho f}{2r} \cdot U_o \tag{7.4}$$

from equation (3.4), assuming a simple source. The radiated sound pressure is then

$$p_r = \frac{A_c}{4\pi r \ell_c} \cdot p_s. \tag{7.5}$$

At a time of 1.6 ms, A_c is 0.16 cm^2, and we obtain $20 \log (p_r/p_s) = -58$ dB, taking $r = 20$ cm and $\ell_c = 0.5$ cm. Thus at a frequency of 2500 Hz, $20 \log p_r = -58 + 5 = -53$ dB re 1 dyne/cm^2. We note that p_r in equation (7.5) is proportional to $A_c p_s$, where p_s varies with time as in figure 7.19 and A_c is assumed to increase linearly with time over the first few milliseconds after the release. It turns out that p_r reaches a maximum when $A_c = 0.4$ cm^2, that is, at 4 ms following the release. At this time, $20 \log p_r = -49$ dB re 1 dyne/cm^2, or 25 dB re 0.0002 dyne/cm^2, again in a 300-Hz band centered at 2500 Hz. From equation (7.5) we observe that p_r has the same spectrum shape as p_s. The resulting spectrum of the peak radiated sound pressure due to the turbulence noise source is given as curve F in figure 7.18, and, as noted in figure 7.17, is called the frication noise. Calculation of the turbulence noise spectrum due to the monopole source (see figure 2.35) shows that this spectrum amplitude is small compared with the F spectrum in figure 7.18. The contribution to the spectrum from the turbulence noise source is small compared with the contribution from the transient source, according to these calculations. The relative amplitudes of these two components depends, however, on the rate of release of the lip opening, which is likely to vary from one speaker to another and from one utterance to another. Examples of the time variation of the frication noise source for two different rates of release have been shown in figure 2.43.

Also shown in figure 7.19 (as a dashed line) is the calculated value of $20 \log U_g^3 A_g^{-2.5}$, where $U_g =$ volume velocity at the glottis, and $A_g =$ cross-sectional area of the glottal opening. This quantity is a measure of the amplitude of the turbulence noise source in the vicinity of the glottis, during the same time interval of a few milliseconds following the release. This noise source is the aspiration noise in figure 7.17.

The glottal noise source amplitude, together with the spectrum shape given in figure 2.33, can be used as a starting point for calculating the spectrum of the radiated sound pressure when this turbulence noise source has its peak value (centered, say, at 4 ms in figure 7.19). At this time, the value of $20 \log U_g^3 A_g^{-2.5}$ is 199 dB. We shall assume the source to be located about 2 cm downstream from the glottis (although, strictly speaking, the source is distributed over a region above the glottis) and we take into account the acoustic losses at the glottis. The losses have an especially large influence on the bandwidth of the first formant. The end result is the spectrum labeled A in figure 7.18 at a distance of 20 cm from the lips. (The details of the procedures for calculating this spectrum are given in sections 3.5.3 and 8.3.) The formant locations used to calculate this spectrum are determined from the time 3 ms in figure 7.14a (or -3 ms in figure 7.16a).

We have not shown in curve A in figure 7.18 the effect of subglottal resonances. It is expected that the subglottal resonance in the frequency range of 1400 to 1600 Hz will be particularly evident as a perturbation in the spectrum, although it will not alter substantially the overall spectrum shape.

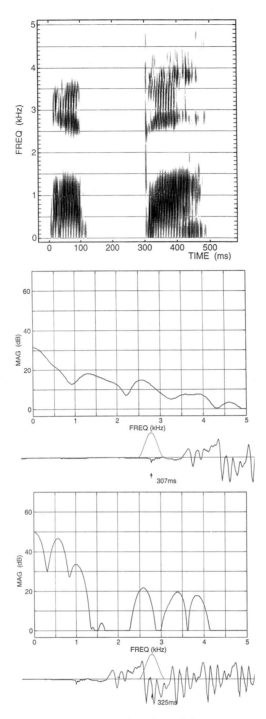

Figure 7.20 Acoustic data obtained from an utterance of a voiceless unaspirated stop consonant /p/ in the intervocalic environment /ɑpɑ/ (the same utterance as that displayed in figure 7.12a). A spectrogram of the utterance is shown at the top, and spectra and waveforms at the burst and 18 ms later are given below. The spectra are discrete Fourier transforms calculated with a Hamming window of 6.4-ms duration.

Finally we show in figure 7.18 the calculated spectrum of the vowel after steady state is reached, corresponding to the flat portions of the trajectories in figure 7.14a. Absolute levels in a 300-Hz band at a distance of 20 cm are given, assuming a glottal output similar to that in figure 2.10. This vowel spectrum is labeled V in figure 7.18. As shown in figure 7.16, this spectrum changes as the formant frequencies move in the time between the onset of glottal vibration and the achievement of steady state.

In summary, we identify the various spectra in figure 7.18 as follows: (1) the spectrum of the transient at the release of the consonant; (2) the spectrum of the sound resulting from turbulence noise at the labial constriction; (3) the spectrum of the sound resulting from turbulence noise at the glottis; and (4) the spectrum in the vowel after completion of the formant movements. These individual spectra cannot, of course, be directly observed at the release of a particular utterance, since they overlap in time. Each of these components contributes, however, to an overall pattern of spectrum change in a time interval of 0 to 20 ms following the consonantal release. At the instant of release the spectrum does not show a significant influence of the vocal tract resonances, which are resonances of the vocal tract behind the point where the source is generated. The brief noise source at the glottis contributes some spectral prominences at higher frequencies, but with amplitudes somewhat less than those from the periodic glottal source.

At the release of a particular labial stop consonant, considerable variability is expected in the shape of the individual spectral components in figure 7.18. This variability is a consequence of differences in the rate of release of the closure; particular anatomical details concerning the lips; the configuration of the glottis and structures immediately above the glottis; and the preceding and following vowels. In spite of this variability, however, a particular overall pattern of gross spectrum change is expected. There is an onset with no major spectral prominence, but with spectral amplitude having a broad peak in the frequency range of 1 to 2 kHz. During the following 5 to 10 ms, formant peaks appear in the spectrum, and the spectrum amplitude increases at all frequencies.

Acoustic data derived from a voiceless unaspirated labial stop consonant in intervocalic position in the utterance /ɑpɑ/ are illustrated in figures 7.20 and 7.21. A spectrogram of the utterance is shown in figure 7.20, together with spectra sampled at the burst and just after voicing onset. Spectra sampled at several points within this utterance after the onset of glottal vibration have been shown earlier in figure 7.12a. The frequencies $F2$ and $F3$ and the amplitudes of the spectral peaks corresponding to $F1$, $F2$, $F3$, and $F4$ are plotted in figure 7.21. Just before the implosion we observe the expected downward movements of the frequencies of the second and third formants. The earlier amplitude decrease for the higher formants ($F3$ and $F4$) relative to the amplitude of $F2$ can be observed as the implosion is approached.

The spectrum directly at the onset in figure 7.20 slopes downward at high frequencies more or less as expected. (The rise in the spectrum below 1000

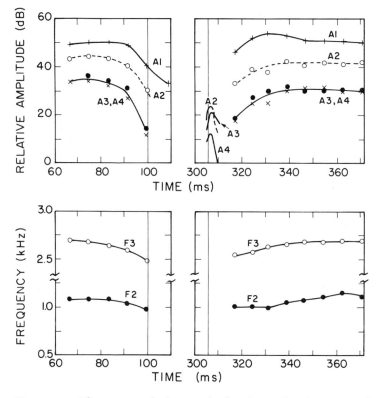

Figure 7.21 The upper panels show amplitudes of spectral peaks corresponding to the first four formants for the utterance /ɑpɑ/ in figure 7.20. Data near the implosion are given at the left, and data near the release are at the right. The amplitudes are obtained from spectra of the type given in figures 7.12 and 7.20, sampled pitch-synchronously. Within the burst, the spectrum amplitudes are obtained from short-time spectra sampled at 1-ms intervals, and these amplitudes are in the regions of the second, third, and fourth formants. Measured values of F2 and F3 near the implosion and the release are shown in the lower panels. Values of F1 have been given in figure 7.12a.

Hz is more than expected, and is presumably a consequence of the initial transient.) After a few milliseconds, the plots in figure 7.21 show evidence of aspiration noise, with the F2 and F3 peaks in this case being stronger than the peak corresponding to F4. (The calculated aspiration spectrum in figure 7.18 shows the amplitudes of the peaks corresponding to these three formants to be about equal.) Following voicing onset, increases can be observed in the frequencies of F2 and F3, with the F2 increase being relatively small, as suggested by the calculations from the model in figure 7.14b. As predicted by the theory, the spectrum amplitudes of the burst in the F2, F3, and F4 regions are less than the spectrum amplitudes of the corresponding peaks immediately following the onset of voicing. The somewhat later increase in A3 and A4 relative to A1 can also be seen in figure 7.21, as expected based on the calculations in figure 7.16.

7.4.3 Alveolar Stop Consonants

A somewhat different pattern of spectrum change emerges when the closure is formed with the tongue tip. (We shall limit the analysis here to consonant closures that have been described as apical. When a laminal rather than an apical closure is formed with the tongue blade, the formant transitions and the rate of release are expected to be slower.) In terms of the features listed in chapter 5, a consonant of this type would be classified as [+ anterior, − distributed].

There are no direct quantitative data that permit accurate estimates of the rate of change of cross-sectional area of the constriction at the implosion and the release of an alveolar stop consonant. Indirect estimates based on acoustic measurements of the time course of the burst and the transition of the first formant suggest that the initial rate of increase of cross-sectional area is somewhat slower than that for a labial consonant. We take the rate of increase to be about 50 cm^2/s in the present analysis.

7.4.3.1 Formant Transitions In the case of alveolar stop consonants, the closure is formed at a point about 1.5 to 2.5 cm posterior to the lip opening, as indicated in figure 7.2. The formation of a constriction at this point in an idealized vocal tract shape is schematized at the top of figure 7.22a. To produce an alveolar stop consonant, it is necessary to place the tongue body in a forward position so that the tongue tip can make contact with the alveolar ridge. This fronting of the tongue body is represented in the model of figure 7.22a by a modest narrowing of the tube in the anterior or oral region, and a widening in the posterior or pharyngeal region. The raising of the tongue tip to form a constriction causes a tapering of the area function behind the constriction point, as shown in the figure. When the constriction is released, there is an increase in the area formed by the tongue tip, and, at the same time, the tongue body moves to a position appropriate for the following vowel. If that vowel is a front vowel, there is little forward movement of the tongue body, and the calculated transitions of the formants for the model are primarily a result of a downward movement of the tongue blade, as shown by the curves below the model in figure 7.22a. There is a brief upward movement of $F1$ and $F2$, and a smaller rise in $F3$, but these transitions are essentially completed after about 10 ms. If the model were to include a burst of frication noise at the release, that burst would have a duration of about 10 ms, and the initial rapid formant transitions would not be observable in the sound.

When the following vowel is a back vowel, the tongue body moves back following the release, to form a narrowing in the pharyngeal region, as illustrated at the top of figure 7.22b. The result is a decrease in $F2$, as shown in the figure, and, in the case of this model of a low back vowel, a continuing rise in $F1$.

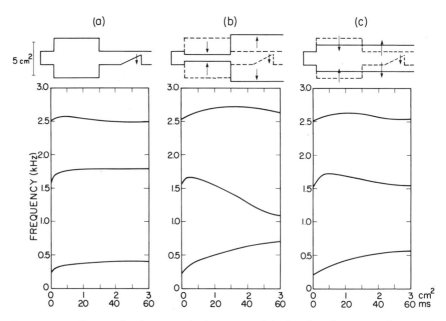

Figure 7.22 Showing the changes in the frequencies of the first three formants as the area of the constriction formed by a simulated alveolar stop consonant is increased in a model of the vocal tract. Movements to three different vowel models are illustrated. In each case, the shape of the model at the starting point of the movement is the same, with the constriction formed at a point 1.5 cm from the open end, and a tapering of the area behind the constriction, as shown at the top of (a) and as the dashed configurations in (b) and (c). In (a) the only movement is the simulated tongue blade, with the remainder of the model remaining fixed. In (b) and (c), there is concomitant movement of the model toward the configuration indicated by the solid lines and the arrows. This movement is a linear interpolation between the initial and final shapes, with a duration of 50 ms. The final shape in (b) simulates a low back vowel, and that in (c) simulates a uniform vocal tract shape. For all models, the overall length is 17 cm, and the vertical dimension is proportional to the area, as shown at the left of the model in (a). Two abscissas are shown at the bottom of each panel: one gives the cross-sectional area of the constriction, and the other gives the time from the consonant release, assuming a linear rate of increase of the constriction area of 50 cm²/s.

Figure 7.22c shows the calculated formant trajectories assuming that the following vowel has a uniform vocal tract shape, except for the narrowing near the glottis (illustrated at the top of this figure). The time taken for the tongue body to move from its fronted configuration following the release in figure 7.22b and c is taken to be 50 ms.

We observe, then, a two-component movement of the formants: a rapid upward movement of $F1$, $F2$, and $F3$ as the tongue tip is released and, for a following non–front vowel, a slow downward movement of $F2$ associated with the tongue body motion. Superposition of these two components in the case of a non–front vowel leads to a slow downward transition of $F2$. The formant movements after the initial 10 ms, which is occupied by the burst in the case of a stop consonant, are due almost entirely to the movement of the tongue body to the configuration appropriate for the vowel (Manuel and

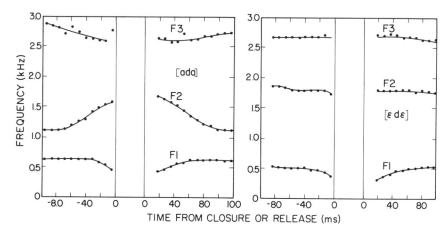

Figure 7.23 Measured frequencies of the first three formants for the utterances /ɑdɑ/ (left) and /ɛdɛ/ (right) produced by a male speaker. See legend for figure 7.15.

Stevens, 1995). Some variation of these general patterns is observed for the release of an alveolar stop consonant with different following vowels.

Measured formant frequencies in the region of the consonant closure for intervocalic alveolar stop consonants in a back- and a front-vowel environment, produced by a male speaker, are shown in figure 7.23. The points represent the frequencies of the spectral peaks for each glottal period, measured using a short time window of 6 ms. As predicted from the calculations based on the model, there is little movement of $F2$ and $F3$ for the front-vowel environment /ɛ/, whereas when the vowel is /ɑ/ there is a slow rise and fall of $F2$ as the tongue body moves forward to be in a position to make the alveolar closure and then returns to a backed position after the release. These formant movements for alveolar consonants contrast with transitions for labial consonants, shown earlier in figure 7.15, which exhibit little $F2$ movement for the back-vowel environment and a rise in $F2$ before a front vowel.

7.4.3.2 Changes in Source Amplitudes and Spectral Characteristics

Quasi-static spectra calculated at several points throughout a closing gesture with the model in figure 7.22b are shown in figure 7.24a. For this case, the following vowel has a backed tongue body configuration. The spectrum amplitude at high frequencies remains high until about 10 ms prior to closure (corresponding to 0.5 cm² area), and then decreases abruptly, in contrast to the more gradual change in high-frequency amplitude for the labial in figure 7.16. This more rapid change in high-frequency amplitude can be seen in figure 7.24b, which shows the calculated amplitudes of the spectral peaks corresponding to the different formants in the model. This pattern of amplitude change follows directly from the relations between formant amplitudes and formant frequencies, as discussed in section 3.2. The idealized spectra and amplitudes in figure 7.24 indicate tendencies that should be observable

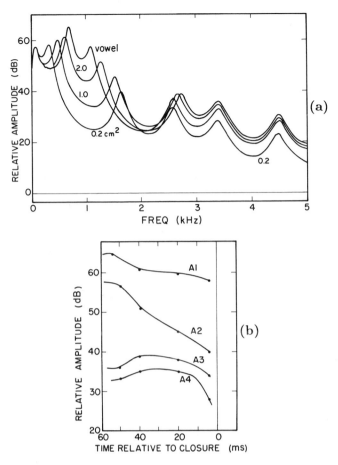

Figure 7.24 (a) Calculated spectrum envelopes at several times during the transition from a low back vowel to a configuration with an alveolar closure, as in figure 7.22b (assuming that the formants follow the same trajectories during the closing movement into the consonant as during the release from the consonant closure). Curves are labeled with cross-sectional area of constriction. (b) Time variation of the amplitudes of the spectral prominences for the different formants. A rate of change of area of 50 cm²/s is assumed.

in the measured short-term spectra in the vicinity of closure whenever a postvocalic closure is made for an alveolar stop consonant.

During the interval in which a complete closure is formed by the tongue blade, the acoustic events are similar to those for a labial stop consonant. There is an abrupt decrease in spectrum amplitude at the frequencies of formants above $F1$, and, as we have seen, the amplitude of vocal fold vibration decreases rapidly to zero over a time interval of two to three glottal periods.

The sequence of acoustic events immediately following the release of an alveolar stop consonant is similar to that for a labial consonant, although the details of the spectral changes and the relative amplitudes of the components are quite different. There is an initial transient at the instant of release, and this is followed by a brief interval of turbulence noise at the constriction.

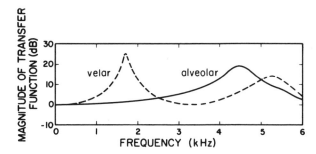

Figure 7.25 Transfer functions from volume velocity at constriction to volume velocity at mouth opening for a short front cavity of length 1.5 cm (solid line) and for a longer front cavity of length 5.5 cm (dashed line), representing, respectively, configurations for an alveolar and a velar consonant.

Aspiration noise may be generated at the glottis before vocal fold vibration begins. Following the onset of vocal fold vibration there may be some further movement of the tongue blade and tongue body, giving rise to movements of the formants, as has been noted above. The formant movements following the consonant release are assumed to be similar to those in figure 7.22. The principal difference between the details of these acoustic events for an alveolar and a labial stop consonant is a consequence of the fact that there is a short cavity anterior to the constriction in the case of the alveolar consonant, whereas there is essentially no such cavity for the labial. For an adult speaker (with a vocal tract like that illustrated in figure 7.2), the length of this cavity is probably in the range of 1.5 to 2.5 cm, as we have noted. For purposes of analysis, we shall assume a length of 1.5 cm for this cavity, but the effect of the radiation impedance increases somewhat the equivalent length of the front cavity.

The magnitude of the volume velocity for the initial transient at the alveolar release is somewhat less than that calculated for the release of the labial stop, since the rate of release is taken to be 50 cm^2/s rather than the 100 cm^2/s that was assumed for the labial release. The estimated spectrum of this transient for a release rate of 100 cm^2/s has been given in figure 2.47, based on an analysis bandwidth of 300 Hz. This spectrum amplitude is reduced by 6 dB to account for the slower release. In the case of an alveolar stop, however, the source is modified by the cavity anterior to the constriction, whereas for a labial stop this volume velocity acts as a source that is radiated directly from the lip opening. The transfer function from the volume velocity at the constriction to the volume velocity at the mouth opening is characterized by a pole at the frequency of the front-cavity resonance, which we take to be about 4.5 kHz. The bandwidth of this resonance is about 600 Hz, as estimated in figure 3.24. (See also Daniloff et al., 1980, who measured a bandwidth of 700 Hz for the spectral peak for alveolar fricatives.) This transfer function (for frequencies up to 6 kHz) is plotted as the solid line in figure 7.25. The product of the transient spectrum and the transfer function gives

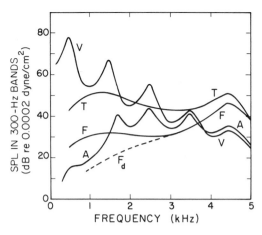

Figure 7.26 Calculated spectra of several components in the sequence of acoustic events following the release of a voiceless unaspirated alveolar stop consonant. See legend for figure 7.18. The calculated spectrum of the frication noise is labeled as F, as in figure 7.18. The dashed line F_d represents the component of the frication noise that would exist if the only frication source were a dipole source. At low frequencies the monopole component dominates the F spectrum.

the spectrum of the volume velocity at the lips. From this volume velocity one can calculate the radiated sound pressure at a distance from the lips, on an axis drawn normal to the mouth opening. The result of this calculation for a distance of 20 cm is shown as the spectrum labeled T in figure 7.26. The main feature of spectrum T is that it exceeds the spectrum of the vowel in the frequency range of the front-cavity resonance for the stop consonant. The increased spectrum amplitude at high frequencies relative to that for the labial consonant is a consequence of the peak of about 20 dB in the transfer function in figure 7.25. As we have indicated earlier, the magnitude of this transient can show considerable variability depending on the rate of release of the alveolar closure and on the detailed shape of the constriction immediately following the release.

Turning next to the turbulence noise source at the constriction, we calculate the source amplitude for the alveolar stop in a manner similar to that for the labial stop. The estimated time course of the amplitude of this source for a labial has been shown in figure 7.19. For an alveolar stop consonant, however, we assume a somewhat slower rate of release, and consequently the variation of the airflow and the source amplitude is somewhat different from that for a labial stop. The calculated source amplitude reaches a peak somewhat later than that for the labial consonant, in figure 7.19. The peak value of $20 \log U_c^3 A_c^{-2.5}$ turns out to be 201 dB, and occurs at a time about 2.3 ms from the release. The estimated spectrum of the dipole sound pressure source is similar to that shown as the upper curve in figure 2.33, adjusted downward by 11 dB because of the different values of U_c and A_c. A correction must also be made to account for the fact that there is not an obstacle directly in the path of the airflow. We estimate the correction to the spectrum to be about −5 dB. This is somewhat less than the correction for a labial consonant, since the lower teeth provide a partial obstacle to the flow.

We assume that the dipole sound pressure source that accounts for the turbulence noise is located at the lower incisors. This source, then, is about 1 cm anterior to the constriction, that is, just anterior to the midpoint of the front cavity. The transfer function from the source to the volume velocity at the mouth opening is characterized by a zero at zero frequency as well as by the pole indicated in figure 7.25. This transfer function is determined, then, by adding to the function in figure 7.25 (solid line) a correction of $20 \log[(A_f/\rho c) \sin(2\pi f \ell/c)]$ dB, where ℓ is the distance from the source to the posterior end of the front cavity (1 cm in this case) and A_f is the effective cross-sectional area of the front cavity, which we take to be 1 cm^2. We neglect any acoustic coupling to the cavity posterior to the constriction. Thus, for example, at a frequency of 4.5 kHz we compute the sound pressure level in a 300-Hz band due to the dipole noise source as follows:

1. From figure 2.33 the spectrum of the sound pressure source at 4.5 kHz (in a 300-Hz band) is 21 dB re 1 dyne/cm^2. We subtract 11 dB from this spectrum to account for the reduced value of $20 \log U_c^3 A_c^{-2.5}$, and an additional 5 dB to account for the less effective obstacle, giving a source level of 5 dB re 1 dyne/cm^2 at 4.5 kHz.

2. To obtain the transfer function from source to volume velocity U_m at the lips, we take the value at 4.5 kHz in figure 7.25 (19 dB), and add $20 \log(1/40) \sin(2\pi \times 4500 \times 1/35400) = -35$ dB, to obtain −16 dB.

3. The sound pressure at 20 cm is determined by multiplying U_m by $\rho f/2r = 0.13$, or −18 dB. The sound pressure level at 20 cm in a 300-Hz band at 4.5 kHz is thus $5 - 16 - 18 + 74 = 45$ dB re 0.0002 dyne/cm^2, with the term 74 dB accounting for the shift in the reference from 1 dyne/cm^2 to 0.0002 dyne/cm^2.

The spectrum of the dipole sound pressure source calculated in this way is given by the curve labeled as F_d at frequencies below 3 kHz in figure 7.26, and as F at frequencies above 3 kHz.

A similar set of calculations can be used to estimate the contribution of the monopole noise source to the spectrum of the burst. To determine the magnitude of the monopole source we again take the peak value of $20 \log U_c^3 A_c^{-2.5}$, which is 201 dB in this case, and subtract from the reference value of 212 dB for the monopole source spectrum in figure 2.35. This gives the spectrum of the monopole volume velocity source, which forms the excitation for the cavity anterior to the constriction. The transfer function for this cavity is given as the solid line in figure 7.25. The radiation characteristic is applied to the output volume velocity. The resulting monopole component dominates the frication spectrum at frequencies below 3 kHz, as shown by the curve labeled F in figure 7.26. At higher frequencies, the dipole component is dominant.

As figure 7.19 has shown, the amplitude of the noise source at the constriction decreases as the cross-sectional area of the constriction increases, and when the pressure drop across the glottis increases sufficiently, the amplitude of the source at the glottis increases and dominates the source at the constriction. If there is a delay in the onset of vocal fold vibration, there may be a brief interval of a few milliseconds in which turbulence noise is generated in the vicinity of the glottis, as has been seen in the case of the labial release. The spectral characteristics of this source and of the radiated sound pressure due to this source are similar to those for the labial stop consonant, discussed previously, except that the formant frequencies are slightly different. This sound pressure spectrum is shown as spectrum A in figure 7.26.

Finally, the onset of vocal fold vibration occurs about 10 ms following the release. Again we assume that the formant trajectories following the release are mirror images of the trajectories at the closure, shown in figure 7.22c when the following vowel has a uniform configuration. The estimated spectrum for the vowel after the transitions have been completed is identified as V in figure 7.26.

Once again we note that the individual spectra in figure 7.26 overlap in time, and these separate components cannot be isolated by direct measurement. The overall picture seems clear, however. At the release, the combination of the initial transient and the burst of turbulence noise at the constriction produces a spectrum in which the amplitude at high frequencies is greater than the spectrum of the following vowel at the same frequencies. The calculations show that the frication and transient spectra exceed the vowel spectrum in the $F5$ range by 15 to 20 dB. The principal reason for this high-frequency domination is the resonance of the short cavity in front of the alveolar constriction. This domination of the high-frequency amplitude can also occur following the onset of glottal vibration; that is, the spectrum amplitude at high frequencies soon after the onset of voicing can exceed the amplitude in the same frequency range later in the vowel, as has been shown in figure 7.24.

Figure 7.27 shows examples of acoustic data for the voiceless unaspirated alveolar stop consonant in the utterance /ata/. The figure displays a spectrogram of the utterance at the top and several spectra sampled in the regions close to the consonant closure and release, together with the waveforms. The amplitudes of the spectral peaks corresponding to individual formants, as well as the time course of $F2$ and $F3$ at the implosion and the release, are plotted in figure 7.28. Immediately prior to the implosion, there is an increase in $F2$, as expected, with a corresponding decrease in $F2$ following the release. The amplitudes $A3$ and $A4$ of the spectral peaks corresponding to the third and fourth formants remain high immediately prior to the implosion, and these amplitudes also are relatively high at the onset of voicing following the release. For this utterance, the amplitude of the burst in the region of $F4$ at the instant of release is approximately equal to the spectrum

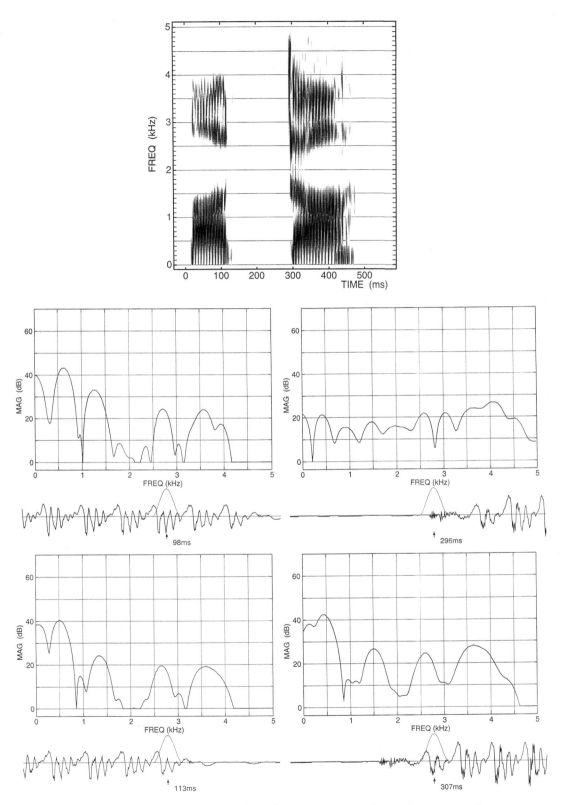

Figure 7.27 Acoustic data obtained from an utterance of a voiceless unaspirated stop consonant /t/ in the intervocalic environment /ɑtɑ/. The four spectra below the spectrogram are sampled at selected points before the consonant closure and after the release, as indicated by the waveforms and time windows below the spectra. See legend for figure 7.20.

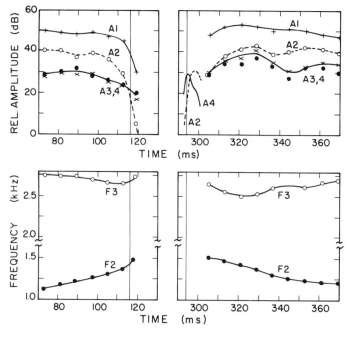

Figure 7.28 The upper panels show amplitudes of spectral peaks corresponding to the first four formants for the utterance /αtα/ in figure 7.27. The time course of the burst amplitude in the F2 and F4 ranges is also shown. The measured values of F2 and F3 near the implosion and the release are given in the lower panels. See legend for figure 7.21.

amplitude of this formant at the onset of the vowel, as predicted in figure 7.26, whereas the spectra in figure 7.27 show that the amplitude A5 at onset in the region of the fifth formant (about 4.5 kHz in this case) exceeds the spectrum amplitude in that frequency range at the vowel onset. The spectrum in the burst changes over the initial 10 ms, with A4 and A5 dominating at the onset, and A2 and A3 increasing as the aspiration component becomes evident.

Comparison of the formant movements and changes in formant amplitudes in figures 7.21 and 7.28 shows the contrast in the acoustic characteristics of the labial and alveolar stop consonants. The most striking differences are the high-frequency spectrum amplitude of the burst and the movement of F2 at the consonant implosion and release. The difference in the attributes of the burst for labial and alveolar stop consonants is further illustrated in figure 7.29. This figure shows the difference (in decibels) between the spectrum amplitude of the burst and the spectrum amplitude of the formant peaks in the following vowel (about 50 ms following the release) at the frequency of each of the peaks corresponding to F2 through F5. The data are averages of measurements from syllables consisting of /b/ or /d/ followed by each of eleven different vowels (three repetitions of each syllable), produced by a single male speaker of American English (not the speaker in the examples in figures 7.21 and 7.28). (The fact that the consonants are voiced rather than voiceless unaspirated might influence the amplitudes of the bursts somewhat, but

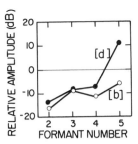

Figure 7.29 Average difference (in decibels) between the spectrum amplitude of the burst (for voiced alveolar and labial stops, as shown) and the spectrum amplitude of the formant peaks in the following vowel (about 50 ms following the release) at the frequency of each of the peaks corresponding to F2 through F5. Average data for one American English speaker over eleven different vowels.

should not affect the way in which the two consonants differ.) The measurements show that the burst spectra for the two consonants do not differ in the F2 and F3 range, and are 10 to 15 dB weaker than the vowel spectra at these frequencies, in rough agreement with predictions in figures 7.18 and 7.26. In the F4 and F5 regions, however, the two curves begin to diverge, and at F5 the amplitude of the /d/ burst is about 11 dB greater than the spectrum amplitude of the vowel and about 17 dB greater than that of the /b/ burst. Figures 7.18 and 7.26 predict the high-frequency burst amplitudes to be a few decibels greater than these values for a following vowel with neutral formant frequencies, but the predicted differences between the two consonants are in rough agreement with the measurements for this speaker.

7.4.4   Velar Stop Consonants

A velar stop is classified as [+ high] in the feature system in chapter 5. It differs from an alveolar or a labial stop in several ways that lead to a sound output with significantly different properties. The position of the constriction is, of course, much farther from the lips, such that the length of the cavity in front of the constriction is typically 5 to 6 cm, although this distance can increase or decrease depending on the vowel context in which the consonant is produced. Second, the length of the constriction is greater than that of an alveolar or a labial. And, finally, the rate of decrease or increase of cross-sectional area at the closure and at the release is less than that for an alveolar or labial, and is estimated to be about 25 cm²/s. A consequence of the tapered tongue shape behind the constriction is that the increased intraoral pressure during the closure interval can be an important factor in determining the trajectory of area vs. time, as we have seen in figure 7.6.

7.4.4.1   Formant Transitions   As the tongue body is raised to form a closure against the soft palate or the posterior portion of the hard palate, the lowest natural frequency of the cavity in front of the constriction will generally be associated with either *F2* or *F3*. Furthermore, one of the natural frequencies of the back cavity will be relatively close to the front-cavity resonance, compared with the average spacing of the formants for a uniform vocal tract. Thus we expect to see proximity of *F2* and *F3*, or possibly *F3* and *F4*, as the vocal tract makes a closure in this region. (The proximity of *F2* and *F3* for a particular constriction position can be seen in figure 3.16, for a back-cavity length equal to twice the front-cavity length.)

As has been noted above, the rate of change of cross-sectional area tends to be smaller and the length of the constriction is greater when the constriction is formed by the tongue body, rather than with the lips or tongue blade. As a consequence, the formants are not moving so rapidly in the vicinity of closure, leading to less flattening of the spectral peaks due to rapid formant movement.

Estimates of the formant movements in the vicinity of closure for a velar stop consonant can be made using the model in figure 3.17 in section 3.3.4, and shown in a somewhat revised form in figure 7.30a. In these models, the constriction length is 2 cm, and it is centered at about two-thirds of the dis-

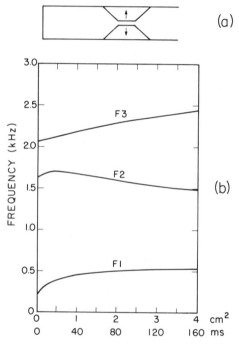

Figure 7.30 Showing the changes in the frequencies of the first three formants as the area of a constriction simulating a velar consonant is increased. (a) The model of a uniform vocal tract with a constriction. The overall length of the tube is 17 cm and the length of the narrow portion of the constriction is 2 cm. (b) Formant frequencies calculated from the model in (a) as the cross-sectional area of the constriction takes on increasing values, in square centimeters. The time scale on the abscissa in milliseconds is the time from release assuming a linear increase in area at a rate of 25 cm²/s.

tance from the glottis to the lips. The calculated changes in the first three formant frequencies as the constriction area of the model in figure 7.30a increases are shown in figure 7.30b. In this example, a uniform vocal tract shape is achieved after the movement from the constricted shape is completed. At the instant of release, the first formant frequency is low (at about 200 Hz), and F2 and F3 are close together. At this time, the natural frequencies of the back and front cavities are similar. As the cross-sectional area of the constriction increases, F1 rises, as expected, and F2 and F3 separate, with F2 decreasing and F3 increasing. The abscissa of figure 7.30b gives the cross-sectional area of the constriction, as well as a time scale assuming a linear increase of cross-sectional area at a rate of 25 cm^2/s. (In this figure, we neglect the modification of the area increase due to forces from the intraoral pressure, as illustrated in figure 7.6.)

When the vowel adjacent to a velar release is a front vowel, then in English and in many other languages, the constriction formed by raising the tongue body is in a more anterior position, so that the front cavity is shorter. There is still a convergence of F2 and F3, but at a higher frequency than shown by the model in figure 7.30. For an adjacent high front vowel, F3 may increase and become close to F4 as the constriction is formed to produce the vowel.

Examples of measurements of the first three formant frequencies in the utterances /ɑgɑ/ and /ɛgɛ/ are given in figure 7.31. The tendency for F2 and F3 to converge near the closure is evident in both utterances. The slower movements of the formants compared with the labial and alveolar consonants (figures 7.15 and 7.23) can also be seen, except that the duration of the F2 movement for /ɑdɑ/ is comparable to the durations of the formant movements for velars.

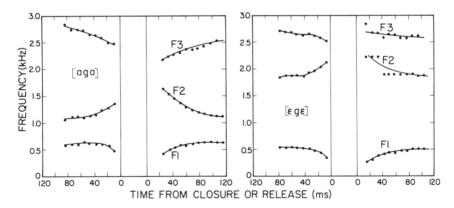

Figure 7.31 Measured frequencies of the first three formants for the utterances /ɑgɑ/ (left) and /ɛgɛ/ (right) produced by a male speaker. See legend for figure 7.15. The frequency of the major spectral peak in the vicinity of F2 for /ɛgɛ/ shows a discontinuity at about 40 ms. This discontinuity is presumably a result of interference by the third subglottal resonance for this utterance. The F2 curve is an estimate of the F2 movement if this interference were not present.

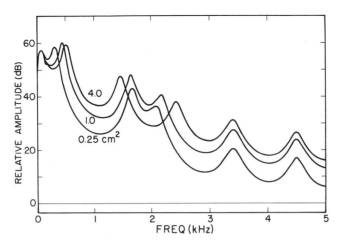

Figure 7.32 Calculated spectrum envelopes at several times during the transition from a vowel with uniformly spaced formants to a configuration with a velar closure, as in figure 7.30. The parameter is the cross-sectional area of the constriction.

7.4.4.2 Changes in Source Amplitudes and Spectral Characteristics
The calculated spectra at several points in time preceding the closure for a model of a velar stop consonant are shown in figure 7.32. The formants during the closing movement are assumed to follow the same trajectories as in figure 7.30, but in the reverse direction. As the second and third formants become closer, the spectral peak centered on this pair of formants becomes more prominent.

As the cross-sectional area of the constriction becomes small just before the instant of closure for a Vowel-Consonant-Vowel sequence containing a velar consonant, there can be a brief increase in the amplitude of noise due to turbulence at the constriction. This noise then decreases as the airflow drops to zero. Calculations show, however, that as long as there is not an appreciable abduction of the glottis immediately prior to closure, the amplitude of this turbulence noise source leads to an output spectrum amplitude that is about 15 dB below the amplitude of the spectral peak corresponding to F2 in the vowel. Thus the frication noise generated near the constriction immediately prior to closure for a voiceless unaspirated velar stop consonant is not expected to be perceptually important. (The situation may be different for an aspirated stop consonant.)

During the closure interval for a velar stop consonant, acoustic events will be similar to those for an alveolar or labial stop consonant. Vocal fold vibration is expected to continue for one or two periods, with a decreased amplitude of the glottal pulses. Since the surface area of the vocal tract walls posterior to the closure is less than that for a labial or alveolar consonant, there will be somewhat less expansion of the vocal tract volume, and consequently an even briefer interval of residual voicing immediately following the time of closure.

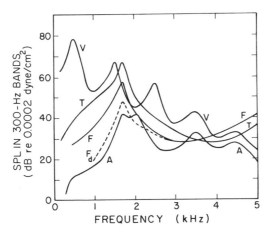

Figure 7.33 Calculated spectra of several components in the sequence of acoustic events following the release of a voiceless unaspirated velar stop consonant. The curves are labeled with letters, as in figure 7.18. In the case of the frication spectrum (labeled F) the solid line is the calculated overall spectrum, but this spectrum is dominated by different source types in different frequency ranges. At low frequencies, the dashed line F_d represents the spectrum calculated for a dipole source spectrum. In this low-frequency range the spectrum resulting from a monopole source dominates that from a dipole source, whereas at high frequencies the dipole source dominates. The vowel has uniformly spaced formant frequencies. See text.

Immediately following the release of a voiceless unaspirated velar stop consonant, the sequence of events is similar to that shown in figure 7.17, except that the timing, the spectral characteristics, and the relative amplitudes of these events are substantially different from those for labial and alveolar consonants.

We consider first the initial transient. If we take the rate of increase of cross-sectional area of the constriction to be about 25 cm²/s (i.e., about one-half to one-fourth of the rate assumed for labials and alveolars), then the amplitude of the initial transient will be about 12 dB below that of the labial consonant, as depicted in figure 2.47. This transient can be modeled as a volume velocity source, which forms the excitation for the acoustic cavity anterior to the constriction. For purposes of calculation, we shall assume that at the time of release this front cavity has an effective length of 5.5 cm, similar to the model in figure 7.30. The transfer function for this cavity (ratio of output to input volume velocity), assuming an ideal uniform tube, is shown as the dashed line in figure 7.25. This transfer function has two peaks in the frequency range up to 6 kHz, corresponding to the first two natural frequencies of the front cavity. The calculated spectrum at the release is displayed in figure 7.33 as curve T. Comparison of this spectrum with the calculated spectrum for the vowel (curve V) shows that the amplitude of the transient in the second-formant region is comparable to the spectrum amplitude of the vowel in the same frequency region.

Observation of acoustic events at the release of a velar stop consonant suggests that a series of transients of this kind may be generated. These

The Basic Stop Consonants

transients are presumably a consequence of vibration of the tongue surface that forms the constriction, as this surface is displaced downward from contact with the palate. We shall assume that the volume velocity associated with these transients is similar to the value used above, that is, about 12 dB lower in amplitude than that given in figure 2.47. The spacing between these transients is a few milliseconds, so that the curve T in figure 7.33 may be raised somewhat as a consequence of the contribution of more than one transient within the time window used to calculate the spectrum.

Immediately following the transient (or transients), turbulence noise is generated in the vicinity of the constriction. This turbulence or frication noise is in part a consequence of the airstream impinging on the surfaces of the vocal tract downstream from the constriction—a dipole noise source that can be modeled as a sound pressure source in the vocal tract. As observed in section 2.2.3 of chapter 2, there may also be turbulent fluctuations of the flow through the constriction, giving rise to a monopole source at the constriction. In calculating the frication noise for labials in section 7.4.2 above, the dipole noise appeared to dominate the monopole component, and was not considered. In the case of velars, calculations show that the monopole component makes a significant contribution to the radiated frication noise at low frequencies, as will be shown.

An estimate of the time couse of the amplitude of this noise source (both dipole and monopole) can be obtained from the calculations of airflow in figure 7.8. These calculations are based on an area change like that in figure 7.6 rather than the linear change in area that was used for calculating the formant movements in figure 7.30. The sound pressure amplitude of the source is proportional to $U_c^3 A_c^{-2.5}$, as we have seen in equation (2.21). The calculated value of this parameter as a function of time following the release, based on the data in figure 7.8, is given in figure 7.34. The figure also shows calculations of this parameter for the noise source at the glottis, assuming a fixed glottal opening during the release phase.

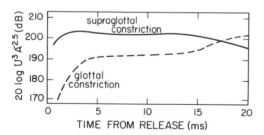

Figure 7.34 Calculation of relative levels of turbulence noise sources at the constriction (solid line) and at the glottal opening (dashed line) during release of a voiceless unaspirated velar stop consonant. Levels are calculated from trajectories of airflow and area given in figure 7.8. The ordinate is $20 \log U^3 A^{-2.5}$, where volume velocity U through the constriction is in cubic centimeters per second and the area A is in square centimeters.

The absolute amplitude of the dipole noise source in figure 2.33 is based on a configuration with an obstacle directly in the flow downstream from the constriction. This overall amplitude must be corrected by the value of $20 \log U^3 A_c^{-2.5}$ (as in figure 7.34) relative to the reference value of 212 dB in figure 2.33. In the case of noise generated at a velar constriction, there is no obstacle directly in the airstream, although the palate forms an obstacle against which the flow impinges at an oblique angle. We estimate that the amplitude of the dipole noise source at the constriction for a velar constriction should be reduced by about 10 dB to account for this lower efficiency of noise generation. We assume further that the noise source is located a distance of about 1 cm downstream from the constriction, so that the source is coupled only weakly to the lowest front-cavity resonance when this resonance is at low and mid frequencies (1 to 2 kHz). As for the alveolar consonant, the coupling factor is $20 \log[(A_f/\rho c) \sin(2\pi f \ell / c)]$ dB, where ℓ is the distance from the source to the constriction (1 cm in this case) and A_f is the effective cross-sectional area of the front cavity, which we take to be 2 cm^2 for this model of a velar consonant. This coupling factor is added to the all-pole transfer function for the velar in figure 7.25 to yield the overall transfer function from the sound pressure source to the volume velocity at the mouth. As before, application of the radiation characteristic (equation [7.4]) gives the sound pressure level at a distance from the mouth.

Calculation of the contribution of the monopole source uses the monopole reference spectrum in figure 2.35 as a starting point and scales this spectrum according to the value of $20 \log U^3 A_c^{-2.5}$, as before. The transfer function for this source has only poles, and is given in figure 7.25. Again, the radiation characteristic is applied to give the sound pressure level at a distance, due to the monopole source.

The calculated output spectrum arising from the combined dipole and monopole noise source is shown as curve F in figure 7.33. At high frequencies (above about 3 kHz), the contribution of the dipole source is dominant, and the effect of the monopole source is negligible. At low frequencies (below about 1.5 kHz) the monopole source is dominant, whereas both sources contribute to the overall frication curve F at intermediate frequencies. The dashed line indicates the contribution of the dipole source in the mid- and low-frequency regions. At the frequency of the major spectral peak (1700 Hz in this case), we observe that the frication noise spectrum is about 10 dB below the level of the F2 peak for the vowel, and is below the spectrum amplitude of the initial transient at this frequency. In effect, then, the transient source or sources at the consonant release dominate the source that results from turbulence in the airstream. This relative dominance of the transient component is in contrast to the alveolar consonant, for which the turbulence noise component is comparable to the transient.

A similar calculation can be made for the sound output resulting from the turbulence noise source in the vicinity of the glottis. This calculation follows procedures similar to those used in estimating the aspiration noise for the

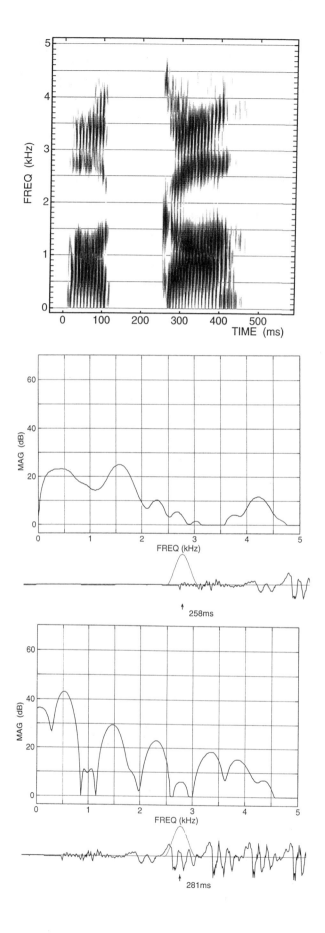

258ms

281ms

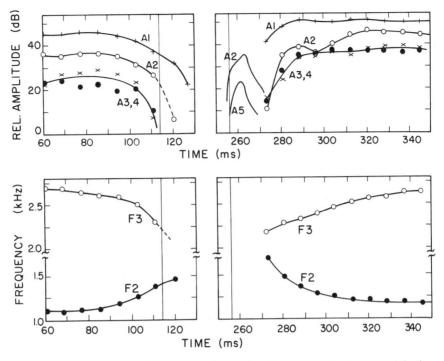

Figure 7.36 Amplitudes and frequencies of spectral peaks corresponding to some of the formants (as indicated) for the utterance /ɑkɑ/ in figure 7.35. See legend for figure 7.21. During the burst the F2 peak is evident in the spectrum, and the amplitude of this peak is plotted as A2. (See, e.g., the spectrum of the burst in figure 7.35.)

labial and alveolar consonants. The amplitude of the noise source at the glottis is taken from figure 7.34 in the time interval near 20 ms, that is, the time interval immediately preceding voicing onset. In this time interval following the release, we assume that the configuration of formant frequencies is similar to the configuration around $t = 20$ ms in figure 7.30b. The calculated aspiration noise spectrum is shown as curve A in figure 7.33. The aspiration noise is well below the spectrum of the vowel, except at higher frequencies.

In summary, then, the calculated spectra in figure 7.33 show that at the release of a velar stop consonant the transient component is dominant, and leads to a spectrum with a prominent peak in the mid-frequency range. The frequency of this peak is the lowest natural frequency of the portion of the vocal tract in front of the constriction. The spectrum amplitude of the peak is comparable to that of the F2 prominence in the following vowel. A second resonance of this front cavity results in another spectral peak at higher frequencies. The frication and aspiration components for the unaspirated velar stop consonant appear to be smaller than the transient component. Some

Figure 7.35 Acoustic data obtained from an utterance of a voiceless unaspirated stop consonant /k/ in the intervocalic environment /ɑkɑ/. See legend for figure 7.20.

variability is to be expected, however, in the relative importance of the transient and frication components if the velar consonant is released at a slower rate than the rate assumed for these calculations.

Acoustic measurements in the vicinity of the release for a velar stop consonant in intervocalic position are shown in figure 7.35. A spectrogram of the utterance /aka/ is displayed, and the short-time spectrum sampled at two times following the release is shown in relation to the waveform. Figure 7.36 shows the trajectories of the second- and third-formant frequencies, as measured from the peaks in spectra of the type given in figure 7.35. The amplitudes of some of the spectral peaks in the vowel and in the burst near the implosion and following the release are also shown in figure 7.36.

The time from the release to the onset of the first glottal pulse is about 22 ms—slightly longer than the estimated time of onset of vocal fold vibration for the conditions assumed above (in section 7.2) for a velar release. (The estimates of voice-onset time were based on the time taken for the transglottal pressure to reach 3 cm H_2O, in figure 7.8.) The spectrum during the burst shows the expected prominence in the second-formant range, at about 1500 Hz, with a lesser prominence at about three times this frequency. The amplitude of this higher-frequency prominence is shown as $A5$ in figure 7.36. There are some fluctuations in the bandwidth and amplitude of the spectral prominence at 1500 Hz. The amplitude of the $F2$ spectral prominence in the vowel immediately following voicing onset is within 1 to 2 dB of the amplitude of the prominence for the burst.

We observe in figure 7.36 that the two formants $F2$ and $F3$ come closer together as the closure is approached, and separate following the onset of voicing. During the burst, the movement of $F2$ is relatively small.

The theoretical analysis given above for velar stop consonants is based on a model of a velar stop for which the constriction is located at a point that is about two-thirds of the distance between the glottis and the lips. With a constriction at this point, the frequencies of the lowest resonance of the front cavity and the half-wavelength resonance of the back cavity are about equal, and $F2$ and $F3$ are close together at the time when the closure is formed or is released. While there is a tendency for this proximity of $F2$ and $F3$ for velar consonants in some vowel environments, particularly for some back vowels, there is in practice considerable variability in the position of the constriction depending on the front-back tongue position of the following vowel. This variability is especially apparent for languages like English, for which there is no distinction between back and front velars.

Before a front vowel, for example, the constriction is located further forward in the vocal tract than the position in figure 7.2 (right picture) or in figure 7.30a. In this case, the acoustic attributes depicted in figures 7.30 and 7.33 are changed somewhat, although some of the attributes in figure 7.33 remain the same. For example, when a velar consonant is before the vowel /i/, the tongue body is fronted, and the effective length of the cavity in front of the constriction may be as short as 2.5 cm for an adult speaker. The front-cavity resonance would then be in the range 3.0 to 3.5 kHz, and would correspond to $F3$ or $F4$. For this configuration, the release burst would have a spectral peak at this frequency, which is in the vicinity of $F2'$ for the vowel /i/. (See section 6.5.3 for a discussion of $F2'$.)

A spectrogram of the utterance /iki/ (where the /k/ is voiceless unaspirated) is shown at the top of figure 7.37. Following the release of the consonant, the rate of opening of the constriction is less than it is when the vowel is more open, and the burst persists for a longer time. Since there is some variability in the spectrum of the burst (presumably generated as a sequence of volume velocity pulses), we have calculated the average spectrum over the first 10 ms of the burst in order to smooth out irregularities. This average spectrum is shown in the middle panel below the spectrogram in figure 7.37, together with spectra sampled near the consonant implosion and just following onset of glottal vibration.

There is a relatively broad peak in the burst spectrum at about 3500 Hz, presumably a consequence of excitation of the front-cavity resonance by the source at the constriction. The bandwidth of this peak is large, because the cavity is small and the acoustic losses are great. The spectrum sampled soon after onset of glottal vibration shows a broad peak around 3.3 kHz, as a consequence of the proximity of $F3$ and $F4$ near the vowel onset. The amplitude of this peak is about 4 dB greater than that in the burst. A similar prominent peak is evident in the spectrum sampled near voicing offset in the first vowel (top spectrum in figure 7.37).

A common attribute of all velar consonants is that there is a prominent spectral peak in the range of the second major spectral prominence $F2'$ (as defined in chapter 6). This spectral peak is evident primarily in the burst, but contribution to the prominence is made by the proximity of $F2$ and $F3$, or of $F3$ and $F4$, in the vowel adjacent to the interval of velar closure.

7.5 SUMMARY OF ACOUSTIC CHARACTERISTICS OF VOICELESS UNASPIRATED STOP CONSONANTS

This chapter has described the acoustic properties of stop consonants that are produced with a glottal adjustment that does not differ significantly from a modal configuration. Consonants produced with closures with the lips, the tongue tip, and the tongue body are examined. These stop consonants as a class have several characteristics in common. At the stop-consonant release the following sequence of events occur: a transient, a burst of frication noise due to turbulence in the airflow near the constriction, aspiration noise due to turbulence in the vicinity of the glottis, and transitions of the formants into the vowel.

The generation of the sound sources for these events is modeled by calculating pressures across the time-varying constrictions and airflows through the constrictions, and by estimating the source characteristics from these pressures and flows. The filtering of the sources is modeled by estimating the

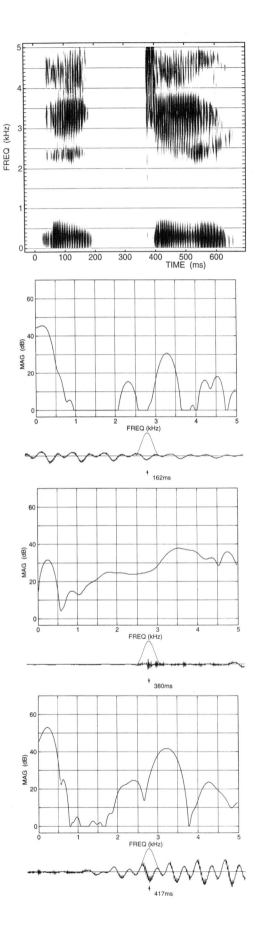

configurations and movements of the articulators and calculating formant movements and transfer functions. The filtering of the transients and the frication sources is determined primarily by the dimensions of the cavity anterior to the constriction. The spectrum shape of the frication noise for different consonants is reflected in the places in the vocal tract where the constrictions are formed for the consonants. The formant transitions are determined by the movements of the tongue body and mandible as these structures are displaced toward the vowel from configurations that they must assume to form the stop-consonant closure. Reasonable agreement is obtained between model predictions and acoustic data, although there is variability in the acoustic data that is not accounted for by the models.

Figure 7.37 Acoustic data obtained from an utterance of a voiceless unaspirated stop consonant /k/ in the intervocalic environment /iki/. The top and bottom spectra were sampled a few glottal periods before voicing offset and after voicing onset, respectively. The middle spectrum is obtained with a window centered on the burst, as shown in the waveform below the spectrum.

8 Obstruent Consonants

8.1 FRICATIVE CONSONANTS

Fricative consonants are produced by forming a narrow constriction at some point along the length of the vocal tract and generating turbulence noise in the vicinity of this supraglottal constriction. The glottal opening is usually adjusted to be greater than the cross-sectional area of the supraglottal constriction, at least for the most common types of fricative consonants. Two attributes distinguish the production of these fricative consonants from unaspirated stop consonants: (1) the supraglottal articulators form a narrow constriction rather than a complete closure, and (2) some adjustment of the glottal opening is made to maximize the amplitude of the turbulence noise that is generated near the supraglottal constriction.

In this section we discuss the articulatory and acoustic events associated with the basic voiceless fricative consonants, for which the glottal opening is adjusted to be greater than the area of the supraglottal constriction. We consider voiceless fricative consonants produced with a constriction in the oral region of the vocal tract, that is, at the lips and in the alveolar and palato-alveolar regions. In section 8.4 we examine voiced fricative consonants, which are produced with the glottis and vocal folds adjusted to facilitate continued glottal vibration.

Midsagittal sections of the vocal tract during the constricted interval for some typical fricative consonants in French are shown in figure 8.1. In each panel of the figure, two configurations are given, representing the tongue body shapes when the fricative is produced in syllables with two different following vowels. In the case of the labiodental fricative /f/, the tongue body shape is strongly influenced by the following vowel. (A similar influence of vowel environment has been noted for labial stop consonants in section 7.4.2.) For the dental consonant /s/ the influence of the adjacent vowel on the tongue body is smaller than for the labiodental, and for the palatoalveolar /š/ the contextual influence is even smaller.

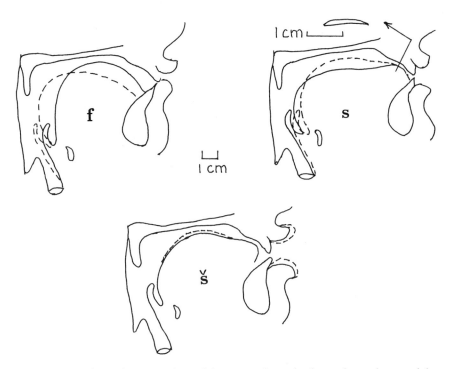

Figure 8.1 Midsagittal sections obtained from cineradiographs during the production of the three fricative consonants /f/, /s/, and /š/, as indicated. The subject is an adult female speaker of French. The approximate scale is given between the /f/ and /s/ configurations. In the case of the /s/ configuration, an estimate of the cross-sectional shape at the constriction is given. (This shape is drawn with an enlarged scale, as shown.) For each panel, two midsagittal sections for the tongue (and, in the case of /š/, for the lips) are shown, representing the fricative in two different phonetic environments. For /f/, the following vowel contexts are the high front rounded vowel /y/ (solid line) and /ɔ/ (dashed line); for /s/, /a/ (solid line) and /i/ (dashed line); and for /š/, /a/ (solid line) and /u/ (dashed line). (After Bothorel et al., 1986.)

8.1.1 Aerodynamic and Articulatory Description

We shall again consider the constriction to be formed in the context of a preceding and following vowel. The minimum cross-sectional area of the vocal tract in the adjacent vowel region is much greater than that for the consonant. We examine first the articulatory and aerodynamic attributes during the time interval in which the vocal tract is constricted and we then turn to events at the times when the constriction is being formed or is being released.

We assume first that the glottal opening A_g has been adjusted to be somewhat greater than the cross-sectional area A_c of the supraglottal constriction. It is assumed further that the pressure drop across A_g and A_c is given by the quadratic equation (1.12), that is, these areas are not so small that the viscosity term plays a significant role in determining the pressure drop across the constriction. If the subglottal pressure is P_s, then the pressure drop across the constriction (from equation [2.17]) is given by

$$\Delta P_c = \frac{1}{1 + \left(\dfrac{A_c}{A_g}\right)^2} P_s.$$

Thus if A_g is adjusted to be, say, twice the area A_c, then ΔP_c is about 80 percent of P_s. Measurements of intraoral pressure for voiceless fricatives indicate that ΔP_c is usually greater than this percentage of P_s (cf. Arkebauer et al., 1967).

The cross-sectional areas of the glottal and supraglottal constrictions during the constricted interval are determined in part by adjustments of the musculature that controls the relevant articulatory and laryngeal structures, and in part by forces on these structures due to the intraoral pressure. In the case of the glottis, since the pressure on the upper surfaces of the vocal folds is approximately equal to the subglottal pressure, the lateral displacement of the folds that occurs in response to this pressure is given by $\Delta x = P_s dC$, where C is the compliance per unit length of the folds and d is the effective thickness of the folds. If we take C to be about 3×10^{-5} cm^2/dyne, $d = 0.3$ cm, and $P_s = 8$ cm H$_2$O, we obtain $\Delta x = 0.07$ cm, corresponding to an increase in glottal width of 0.14 cm. For an effective glottal length of 1.0 cm, this increased width corresponds to an area increase of 0.14 cm^2. This passive increase in glottal opening arising from the increased intraoral pressure occurs over and above any adjustment in glottal configuration resulting from contraction of the adducting and abducting muscles of the larynx. The passive displacement of the vocal folds in response to an increased intraoral pressure also occurs for stop consonants, as we have seen in section 7.2. In the case of a voiceless fricative consonant, we shall assume that there is an active glottal abduction gesture in addition to the passive abduction that is a consequence of the increased intraoral pressure.[1] The contribution of the active abduction to the glottal area during the constricted interval is taken to be 0.18 cm^2, so that the maximum glottal area is $0.18 + 0.14 = 0.32$ cm^2.

In order to examine in detail the adjustment of the articulatory structures to form the constriction, we consider as an example the alveolar fricative consonant. A sketch of the tongue blade in midsagittal section for this fricative consonant is shown in figure 8.1. Also shown in the figure is a lateral section which estimates the cross-sectional shape of the constriction. Evidence for a section with this shape is derived from palatographic data and from imaging studies (Narayanan et al., 1995a). The cross-sectional area for this estimated section shape is about 0.1 cm^2.

In section 2.2.4 (see figures 2.38 and 2.39), we observed that the cross-sectional area of the constriction is determined in part by the adjustment of the structure that forms the constriction and in part by forces on this structure as a consequence of the intraoral pressure. Thus, during the time interval in which there is a narrow constriction in the vocal tract, the intraoral pressure causes some outward displacement of the articulatory structures behind

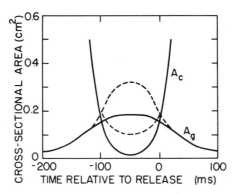

Figure 8.2 Estimates of the time course of the area of the glottal opening (A_g) and the area of the supraglottal constriction (A_c) when a fricative consonant is produced in intervocalic position. The solid lines indicate the area trajectories that would occur in the absence of a subglottal pressure, and the dashed lines indicate the modified areas that are calculated when forces on the structures due to the increased intraoral pressure are taken into account. The subglottal pressure is assumed to be 8 cm H_2O.

the constriction as well as production of an abducting force on the vocal folds, as we have just observed.

We show in figure 8.2 estimates of the time variation of the cross-sectional area A_c of the supraglottal constriction and the area A_g of the glottal constriction when a fricative consonant is produced in intervocalic position. Two curves are given for each of the areas: the solid curves represent the cross-sectional areas that would exist if there were no forces on the structures due to the increased intraoral pressure, and the dashed curves represent the modified cross-sectional areas when the intraoral pressure causes an additional displacement of the vocal folds (as noted above) and of the surface that forms the constriction. The displacement of the dashed curve relative to the solid curve for A_c depends to some extent on the articulatory structure that is used to produce the constriction. The estimates are based in part on observations of airflow and intraoral pressure for intervocalic fricative consonants, as we shall see below (cf. Hixon, 1966; Badin, 1989). The rate of change of cross-sectional area of the supraglottal constriction at the implosion and at the release is expected to be somewhat slower than the rates of change for stop consonants. Some variations in the trajectories in figure 8.2 are to be expected for different places of articulation of the fricative, but the general form of the curves is probably similar for all places of articulation.

From the trajectories of the glottal and supraglottal areas in figure 8.2 it is possible to calculate the airflow, the transglottal pressure, and the intraoral pressure as a function of time through the production of the intervocalic fricative consonant. The results of these calculations, which are based on equations developed in section 2.2.4, are given in figure 8.3, assuming a subglottal pressure of 8 cm H_2O. We observe a double-peaked airflow trajectory, which is commonly seen in measurements of airflow from fricatives

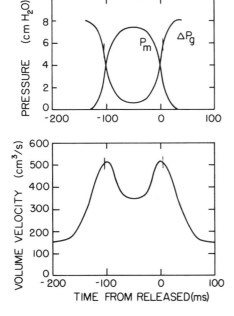

Figure 8.3 Top: Time course of intraoral pressure (P_m) and transglottal pressure (ΔP_g) corresponding to the area trajectories for an intervocalic fricative consonant, in figure 8.2. The vertical marks on the ΔP_g curve indicate times when vocal fold vibration is expected to stop and to start, that is, at about −105 ms and 5 ms. Bottom: Calculated airflow vs. time for the intervocalic fricative consonant. Only the average flow is shown in the figure. There are fluctuations in the flow when the vocal folds are vibrating. Offset and onset of vocal fold vibration are expected at times indicated by the vertical marks.

(Klatt et al., 1968). The peaks occur near the boundaries of the constricted interval where the areas of the glottal and supraglottal constrictions are about equal. The maximum intraoral pressure approaches the subglottal pressure during the consonant. With the abducted glottal configuration that exists in the vicinity of the times when the supraglottal constriction is formed, it is expected that the vocal fold vibration would cease when the transglottal pressure drops to about 3 cm H_2O (Titze, 1992). The calculated pressure curves indicate that this condition would occur at about −100 ms, and vocal fold vibration would begin again at about 0 ms for the idealized trajectories in figures 8.2 and 8.3.

An example of a measured airflow trace for the utterance /əfɑfə/ embedded in a carrier phrase is shown in figure 8.4. The airflow fluctuations due to individual glottal pulses can be seen on this tracing. The double-peaked airflow pattern is evident, and the times of termination and initiation of the glottal pulses coincide roughly with the airflow peaks.

If the vowel or other sonorant preceding or following the constricted interval for the fricative were produced with a more constricted vocal tract, the times of offset and onset of voicing would change somewhat. For example, if a fricative consonant were followed by a sonorant consonant, for

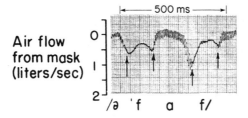

Figure 8.4 Trace of airflow vs. time for a male speaker producing the sequence /əfɑfə/, embedded in a carrier phrase. Airflow is plotted downward. The peaks in airflow at the edges of the fricatives are indicated by arrows. (Adapted from Klatt et al., 1968.)

which the vocal tract constriction is narrower than it is for a vowel, then there would be a greater delay before the onset of vocal fold vibration.

8.1.2 Low-Frequency Characteristics

There are several acoustic consequences in the low-frequency region when the glottal and supraglottal constrictions change in the manner shown in figure 8.2. These consist of modifications in the waveform of the glottal source and changes in the frequency and bandwidth of the first formant at the boundaries between the consonant and the vowel.

The increased glottal opening that begins a few tens of milliseconds prior to the onset of frication noise results in a gradual increase of breathiness in the glottal sound source. This increased breathiness is manifested in the sound as a decreased amplitude of the first formant in relation to the first harmonic, as has been shown in section 2.1.6. This attribute would also occur at the beginning of voicing following the frication noise if the different constriction areas followed the more or less symmetrical trajectories shown in figure 8.2.

The narrowing of the supraglottal constriction in the oral cavity causes a lowering of the frequency of the first formant. The decrease in $F1$ is dependent to some extent on the length of the constriction as well as its cross-sectional area. In the case of a labial or alveolar fricative, this length is estimated to be about 1 cm. When the glottis is partially abducted, the impedance looking down into the glottis and trachea also influences $F1$. An equivalent circuit that can be used to estimate $F1$ during the time interval spanning the boundary between the fricative and the vowel is given in figure 8.5. At one end of the vocal tract is the resistance and acoustic mass of the constriction and at the other end is the resistance and acoustic mass of the glottis, in series with the impedance Z_{tr} looking into the trachea. Changes in A_c and A_g as in figure 8.2 cause changes in R_c, M_c, R_g, and M_g, leading to changes in $F1$ and in the bandwidth of the first formant. Calculations based on the equivalent circuit in figure 8.5 lead to the estimated $F1$ trajectory shown in figure 8.6, over the time interval from the middle of the fricative through the first 50-odd milliseconds following onset of vocal fold vibration. The cross-

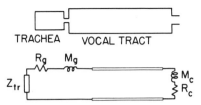

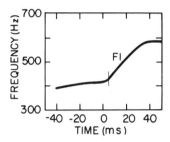

Figure 8.5 Top: Model used to calculate first-formant frequency and bandwidth in the vicinity of a fricative-vowel boundary. The vocal tract is idealized as a uniform tube of length 15.5 cm and cross-sectional area of 3.0 cm². The trachea is modeled as in figure 2.8. Bottom: Equivalent circuit for the model. The supraglottal constriction, represented by M_c and R_c, is assumed to have a length of 1 cm. The glottal impedance is represented by R_g and M_g, and the tracheal impedance by Z_{tr}.

Figure 8.6 Calculated movement of $F1$ vs. time corresponding to the changes in A_c and A_g given in figure 8.2 during the release phase of the fricative consonant. Calculations are based on the equivalent circuit of figure 8.5. The vertical mark indicates the point where vocal fold vibration is estimated to begin.

sectional area of the vocal tract is assumed to be uniform (area = 3 cm²) except at the point at the anterior end where the constriction is made, and the area of the constriction follows a path that is an extrapolation of the A_c curve in figure 8.2. During the constricted interval and up to the onset of vocal fold vibration, $F1$ is around 400 Hz for this model. It is not as low as the natural frequency of a closed configuration because of the partially open glottis and the lack of a complete supraglottal closure. Calculations based on figure 8.5 show that the bandwidth of $F1$ near the boundary (at about -100 ms and 0 ms in figure 8.2) can become very large (approaching critical damping), and approaches normal values about 20 to 30 ms preceding and following these boundaries.

The low-frequency characteristics of the sound in the vicinity of the implosion and the release for a voiceless fricative consonant in intervocalic position produced by a male speaker can be seen in the series of spectra in figure 8.7. The figure shows spectra sampled at two times (30 ms apart) preceding the implosion and at two times following the release, for a female and a male speaker. The utterance in both cases is /ɑfɑ/. The waveforms are displayed below the spectra, and the locations of the time windows for calculating the spectra are also shown. For both speakers, the frequency $F1$ falls

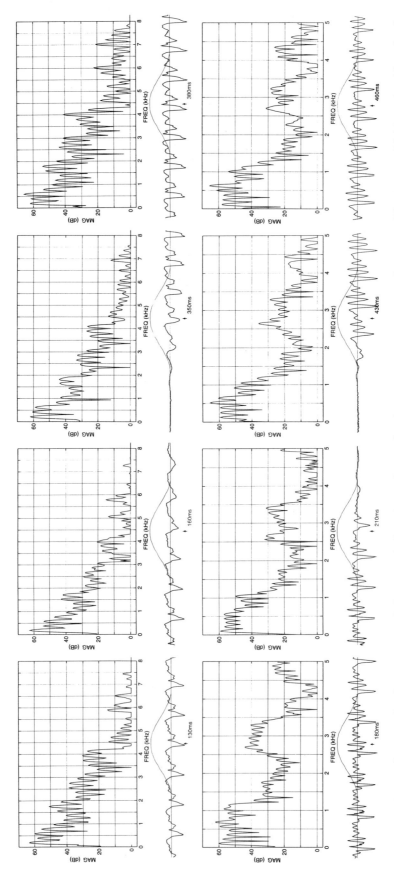

Figure 8.7 Spectra illustrating low-frequency spectral changes at the boundaries of a voiceless fricative consonant in intervocalic position. The utterance /ɑfɑ/ is produced by a female speaker (top panels) and a male speaker (bottom panels). The four spectra for each speaker are sampled, from left to right, about 40 ms prior to the vowel-consonant (VC) boundary, 10 ms prior to the VC boundary, 10 ms after the consonant-vowel (CV) boundary, and 40 ms after the CV boundary. The time window for the spectra is 30 ms, as indicated on the waveform below each panel. Of particular interest is the variation in the amplitudes of the first few harmonics and of the spectral peak corresponding to the first formant. Note the different frequency scales for the spectra from the female and male speakers.

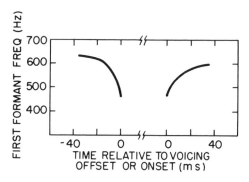

Figure 8.8 Movements of F1 immediately preceding voicing offset and immediately following voicing onset in /aCa/ utterances, where C is a voiceless fricative. Curves are averages from three utterances in which C is /f/, /θ/, and /s/.

slightly over the 30 ms prior to the end of the first vowel and rises after the beginning of the second vowel, as the consonantal constriction is formed. The first-formant peak becomes less prominent close to the offset and onset of glottal vibration as the glottis spreads, causing an increase in the bandwidth of F1. This spectral modification at low frequencies is more pronounced for the female than for the male speaker in these examples, and the effect is more pronounced at the vowel-consonant (VC) boundary than at the consonant-vowel (CV) boundary.

Similar asymmetries in the breathiness of the vowel at the vowel-fricative boundary and at the fricative-vowel boundary have been observed in a number of utterances of fricatives in intervocalic position. These data suggest that the symmetrical area trajectories in figure 8.2 should probably be modified to show a more gradual increase in A_g at vowel offset, and a more abrupt decrease in A_g at vowel onset.

The frequency of the first formant was measured at each glottal period near the VC and the CV boundaries for several fricatives. Average F1 trajectories for three vowel-consonant-vowel (VCV) utterances (/afa/, /aθa/, and /asa/) produced by one speaker are shown in figure 8.8. These formant movements are similar to those calculated for a simple model, as discussed above. That is, F1 values at vowel offset and onset are greater than 400 Hz, and the duration of the transition is 30 to 40 ms. The starting and ending frequencies for F1 will depend to some extent on F1 for the adjacent vowel.

8.1.3 Turbulence Noise Source

The turbulence noise that is generated in the vicinity of the constriction depends upon the volume velocity U of air through the constriction and the cross-sectional area A_c of the constriction, as we have seen in section 2.2. Figure 2.37 shows that the amplitude of this noise source, as a function of the cross-sectional area of the constriction, has a broad maximum centered at

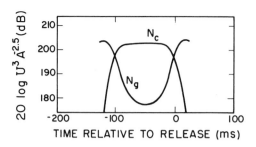

Figure 8.9 Calculated time course of amplitude of turbulence dipole source near the supraglottal constriction (N_c) and near the glottal constriction (N_g) for a fricative consonant in intervocalic position. The relative amplitude is represented by $20 \log U^3 A^{-2.5}$, where A is the cross-sectional area of the supraglottal or glottal constriction, in square centimeters, and U is the airflow, in cubic centimeters per second. Conditions are as specified in figure 8.2. A subglottal pressure of 8 cm H_2O is assumed.

an area that is in the range from about 25 to 75 percent of the area of the glottal opening. As noted in section 2.2.4, the ratio of constriction area to glottal area that maximizes the amplitude of noise at the constriction is calculated to be $1/\sqrt{5}$, or about 45 percent.

Calculations of the relative amplitude of the turbulence noise source at the constriction and at the glottis, corresponding to the variations in area and in airflow in figures 8.2 and 8.3, are given in figure 8.9. The amplitude of the noise source is taken to be proportional to $U^3 A_c^{-2.5}$ and $U^3 A_g^{-2.5}$ for the two sources. The absolute amplitudes and spectra of the sound pressure sources are determined by scaling the upper spectrum in figure 2.33 to account for differences in volume velocity and area, and for differences in the configuration of downstream obstacles to the flow. Since the value of $20 \log U^3 A^{-2.5}$ for the reference spectrum in figure 2.33 is 212 dB, that spectrum should be reduced in amplitude by an amount equal to the difference between 212 dB and the values given in figure 8.9. In the middle of the fricative, this correction is about 9 dB for the frication noise source N_c. Depending on the place of articulation of the fricative consonant in relation to possible obstacles in the airflow, the source amplitude at the constriction should be scaled down. In addition to the dipole or sound pressure source in the vicinity of the supraglottal constriction, there may also be a monopole or volume velocity noise source, for which the reference spectrum is given in figure 2.35. Again, this source should be scaled (relative to 212 dB) depending on the value of $20 \log U^3 A^{-2.5}$.

The noise amplitude at the constriction in figure 8.9 shows little variation throughout most of the constricted interval, in spite of changes in the constriction area and in the airflow. This relative stability of the noise amplitude with changes in constriction size has been discussed in section 2.2.4. Close to the boundaries of the constricted interval, the amplitude of the glottal noise source increases, and becomes comparable to the amplitude of the noise source in the vicinity of the constriction.

It is sometimes observed that there is a variation in noise amplitude throughout a fricative consonant in intervocalic position (Wilde, 1995). In such cases, the cross-sectional area of the supraglottal constriction may at times become sufficiently narrow that the linear term (proportional to viscosity) in the expression relating pressure drop and volume velocity becomes significant. This situation would arise when the cross-sectional area A_c becomes less than about 0.05 cm².

8.1.4 Labial Fricatives

The most common type of fricative consonant produced with a constriction at the lips is the labiodental fricative, for which the midsagittal section is illustrated in figure 8.1. The lower lip is placed close to the upper incisors to form the constriction, and the airstream from this narrow constriction is usually directed against the upper lip. The surface of the upper lip, then, forms an obstacle, and turbulence noise is expected to be generated on this surface, a few millimeters downstream from the constriction. This obstacle, however, is probably not as effective in generating turbulence noise as an obstacle placed directly in the airstream with normal incidence of the flow. We subtract 5 dB from the level determined from figures 8.9 and 2.33 to provide an estimate of the turbulence noise source for the labiodental configuration. The effective length of the acoustic cavity in front of the constriction is estimated to be about 0.9 cm (including a correction for the acoustic mass of the radiation impedance), leading to a lowest resonant frequency of this cavity of about 10 kHz.

These various dimensions and assumptions can be used as a basis for calculating the spectrum of the radiated sound resulting from this dipole noise source for a labiodental fricative consonant. The radiated spectrum is the product of (1) the spectrum of the sound pressure source located downstream from the constriction, given in figure 2.33, but modified to account for the different airflow, constriction area, and obstacle configuration; (2) the transfer function from this source to the volume velocity at the effective opening of the lips, assuming a front-cavity resonance of 10 kHz; and (3) the transfer function from this volume velocity to the sound pressure at a distance (in this case 20 cm) from the lip opening. We follow the same procedure for calculating the transfer function for item (2) as we did for the stop consonant burst in figure 7.18. The sound-pressure source is in series with the constriction, which is represented as an acoustic mass M_c. The acoustic volume velocity at the lips is given by equation (7.3), in which the length ℓ_c of the constriction is taken to be 0.5 cm² and, for the fricative, the cross-sectional area A_c of the constriction is assumed to be 0.1 cm². The results of these calculations for the dipole source assumed to be located on the surface of the upper lip are shown in figure 8.10 as the line labeled F_d at lower frequencies and F at the higher frequencies. The spectrum represents the level in 300-Hz bands. This calculated spectrum is only approximate, but it is

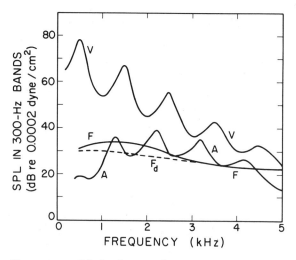

Figure 8.10 Calculated spectra that would occur at several points in time during the production of a labiodental fricative in a position between two neutral vowels. All spectra represent sound pressure levels (SPL) (in decibels re 0.0002 dyne/cm²) in a 300-Hz band at a distance of 20 cm in front of the mouth opening. Calculations are based on source models and assumptions about vocal tract configurations for an adult male speaker as discussed in the text. F_d, spectrum of dipole frication noise in middle of fricative; F, overall spectrum of frication noise in middle of fricative, including the effects of both monopole and dipole sources; A, spectrum of dipole aspiration noise near the fricative-vowel boundary (at times −100 and 0 ms in figure 8.2); V, spectrum of neutral vowel.

probably valid within a few decibels. One source of error is that the source location is distributed over the upper lip surface rather than being fixed at the constriction exit. In the frequency range up to 5 kHz, the assumed front-cavity resonance at 10 kHz has very little effect on the spectrum F.

When there is a constriction at the lips, a monopole noise source resulting from fluctuations in volume velocity at the lip opening can contribute to the frication noise, particularly in the lower-frequency range below about 2500 Hz. Calculation of the strength of this volume velocity source can be made based on the discussion given in section 2.2. First, a correction of 9 dB is applied to the monopole noise spectrum to account for the different values of volume velocity U and constriction area A_c relative to those for which the chart was derived. This volume velocity source is then modified by the transfer function of the short opening formed by the lips to yield the volume velocity of the radiating source. The radiation characteristic for a simple source is again used to determine the sound pressure level at a distance of 20 cm. All of these calculations are based on levels in 300-Hz bands. The results of these calculations of the contribution of the monopole source at the midpoint of the fricative give a small contribution to the radiated sound pressure in the low-frequency region, relative to the dipole component, as shown in figure 8.10. The curve labeled F is the combined effect of the monopole and dipole components.

At the midpoint in the fricative, there is a noise source in the vicinity of the glottis as well as at the lips. Figure 8.9 shows, however, that the amplitude of this glottal noise source is more than 20 dB below the amplitude of the noise source at the supraglottal constriction. Calculation of the spectrum of the radiated sound pressure for the noise source near the glottis at the midpoint in the fricative shows that this spectrum lies at least 20 dB below the spectrum of the frication noise. Consequently, we shall neglect the contribution of glottal noise to the spectrum near the middle of the fricative.

The overall spectrum of the frication noise within the fricative region decreases relatively gently at frequencies above 1.5 kHz; the spectrum amplitude at lower frequencies is determined by the monopole component of the frication noise and the amplitude at high frequencies is determined by the dipole component. If the calculations were extended to frequencies above 10 kHz, there would be a broad spectral prominence that is a consequence of the short front cavity.

In calculating the spectrum of the frication noise in figure 8.10, we have assumed that the transfer function from the source to the output volume velocity is determined only by the position of the source and by the short cavity anterior to the labiodental constriction. There will, in fact, be some acoustic coupling to the vocal tract behind the constriction, especially when the constriction is not too narrow, such as near the edges of the constricted interval. As has been shown in section 3.5.4, this acoustic coupling introduces pole-zero pairs into the transfer function, and peaks can appear in the spectrum, at least in the frequency range of $F3$ and $F4$ where the sound pressure (dipole) source is dominant. The effect of the pole-zero pairs is to superimpose peaks and valleys of 3 to 5 dB in the F spectrum in figure 8.10.

The transitions in the second and higher formants in the vowel adjacent to a labiodental fricative are expected to follow trends similar to those for a labial stop consonant, as discussed in section 7.4.2. However, since the constriction area for a fricative does not decrease to zero, as it does for a stop consonant, the extent of the downward movements of the formants at the VC boundary or upward movements at the CV boundary is not as great. In the case where the adjacent vowel has a uniform vocal tract shape, the ending (or starting) frequency for $F2$ at a boundary of a labial fricative, when the area of the constriction is about 0.25 cm^2, is expected to be about 200 Hz lower than the formant frequency for the vowel. $F1$ at the boundary is only slightly lower than $F1$ in an adjacent neutral vowel.

As the area of the glottal constriction decreases near the time of release, the amplitude of the source near the glottis increases, as figure 8.9 indicates, although there is not much change in the amplitude of the source at the constriction. For the hypothetical labial fricative we are considering, N_g is about equal to N_c at the times voicing ends and begins (at about $t = -100$ ms and $t = 0$ ms in figures 8.2 and 8.8). In this boundary region, then, the contribution of N_g to the overall spectrum can become significant.

From figure 8.9, the value of $20 \log U^3 A^{-2.5}$ for the source N_g at $t = -100$ ms and $t = 0$ ms is about 198 dB. This is close to the value calculated for the glottal noise source for unaspirated stop consonants in section 7.4. As in the calculations for the stop consonants, we shall assume this source to be located about 2 cm downstream from the glottis. (A more detailed discussion of aspiration noise, including the influence of a monopole component, is given in section 8.3.) The spectrum of the aspiration noise at these times near the edge of the labiodental fricative is similar, then, to the aspiration noise spectrum in figure 7.18.

We show as spectrum A in figure 8.10 the result of calculating the sound pressure due to the aspiration noise. This spectrum represents the maximum level that is achieved by the aspiration noise at the vowel-fricative and fricative-vowel boundaries, given the cross-sectional area variations in figure 8.2. Also plotted in figure 8.10 is the spectrum envelope of a neutral vowel, labeled V, assuming the same subglottal pressure as given in the analysis of stop consonants in chapter 7.

Near the vowel-fricative and fricative-vowel boundaries the amplitude of the frication noise decreases by 5 dB or more relative to its amplitude in the middle of the consonant. That is, the F_d and F curves become lower near the boundaries. Consequently, in the frequency range up to F4, the aspiration noise dominates over the frication noise even more than the difference shown in figure 8.10, and peaks corresponding to F2, F3, and F4 should be evident in the spectrum of the noise near the fricative boundaries.

Comparison of the calculated aspiration and frication spectra with the vowel spectrum in figure 8.10 shows that the spectrum amplitudes for both types of noise lie below the spectrum amplitude for the vowel, at least in the frequency range below 5 kHz. The amplitude of the frication spectrum is about 10 dB below the vowel spectrum in the region of F5, but is 20 to 25 dB weaker than the vowel prominences in the F3 and F4 regions. Likewise, the peaks in the aspiration spectrum near the boundary are 8 to 16 dB weaker than the F3 and F4 spectral peaks in the adjacent vowel.

Some modification of the spectra in figure 8.10 can be expected if changes in the areas A_c and A_g differ appreciably from the pattern assumed in figure 8.2. One possible deviation from the pattern is that the minimum value of the constriction area A_c becomes less than about 0.05 cm². When the constriction becomes as small as this, there is a significant drop in airflow as the viscous component of the constriction resistance becomes important, as noted above. The result is a reduction in the amplitude of the frication noise in the middle portion of the consonant relative to its amplitude closer to the edges of the noise interval. Such a dip in noise amplitude is sometimes observed in intervocalic fricative consonants.

Another type of modification of the pattern in figure 8.10 is an asymmetrical relation between the A_c and the A_g curves. An example is shown in figure 8.11a, where the supraglottal constriction for the fricative is released while the glottal opening is near its maximum value. Also shown (figure

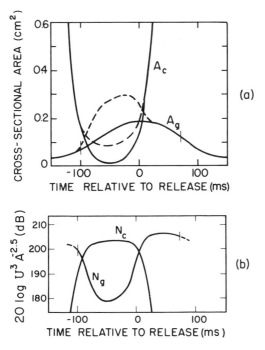

Figure 8.11 (a) Hypothetical time course of the area of the glottal opening (A_g) and the area of the supraglottal constriction (A_c) when the A_c movement is advanced 50 ms with respect to the A_g movement in figure 8.2. (See legend for figure 8.2.) (b) Calculated time course of amplitudes of turbulence noise sources near the supraglottal constriction (N_c) and near the glottal constriction (N_g). (See legend for figure 8.9.) The vertical marks on the A_g and N_g curves indicate estimated times of offset and onset of vocal fold vibration.

8.11b) are plots of the calculated values of the relative source amplitudes N_c (near the constriction) and N_g (near the glottis), determined in the same way as the curves in figure 8.9. During the time when the constriction area A_c is smaller than the glottal area A_g, the acoustic output is primarily frication noise, and the N_c curve is similar to that in figure 8.9. The spectrum of the radiated frication noise in this time interval is the same as in figure 8.10. Following the consonantal release, however, there is an interval of a few tens of milliseconds when the glottal area remains large, and before the glottis becomes sufficiently adducted that vocal fold vibration begins. In this time interval, the maximum amplitude of the aspiration source N_g (occurring at about 40 ms in figure 8.11b) is greater than that in figure 8.9 (occurring at about 0 ms) by about 7 dB. This aspiration noise occurs after the supraglottal constriction has been released, so that the formant frequencies have already reached values appropriate for the following vowel. When the aspiration source is filtered by the transfer function for this vowel configuration, the spectrum amplitude in the frequency range of $F3$ and higher is estimated to be about 12 dB greater than that shown by the A curve in figure 8.10 (7 dB for the increased source amplitude and 5 dB because of the modified transfer

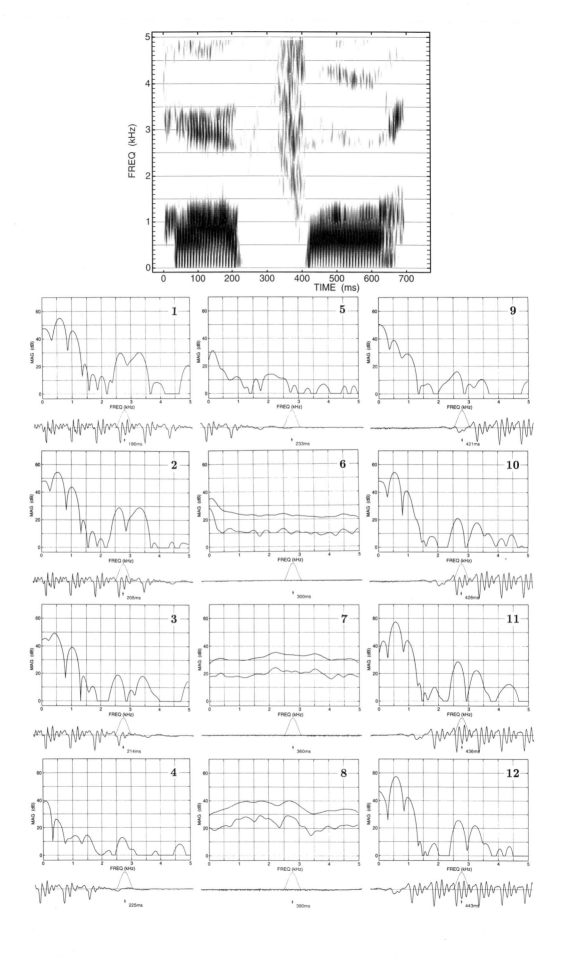

function with higher $F1$ and $F2$). This noise, occurring in a time interval of 30-odd milliseconds before the onset of voicing, will be of greater amplitude than the frication noise, particularly in the region below $F4$.

The departure from synchrony between A_c and A_g in figure 8.11 is extreme, and leads to a significant modification in the acoustic characteristics adjacent to the following vowel. For modest departures from symmetry, say 20 to 30 ms, the effect on the sound is considerably smaller.

Acoustic data derived from an example of a labiodental fricative in inter-vocalic position are given in figure 8.12. A spectrogram of the utterance /ɑfɑ/ is displayed at the top of the figure. Below this, spectra are sampled at selected points within the consonant and in the vowel immediately preceding and following the voiceless interval. These spectra in the vowel portions of the utterance are calculated with a time window of 6.4 ms, placed at the beginning of each glottal period. In the consonant interval, the spectra are again calculated with a window of 6.4 ms, but a series of spectra is averaged over a time interval of 20 ms.

The spectra in the lower panels of figure 8.7 were obtained in the same utterance /ɑfɑ/, but those spectra were calculated with a longer time window. The spectrogram and the spectra in figure 8.12 show a falling $F1$ and $F2$ preceding the VC boundary (frames 1 and 2) and a rise following the CV boundary (frames 10 to 12). The measured values of $F1$ and $F2$ are plotted in figure 8.13. As we observed in section 7.4.2 for labial stop consonants adjacent to back vowels, the transition of $F2$ is small, and a similar pattern can be seen for the labiodental fricative in figure 8.13. There is a rapid movement of $F1$ near the boundary, but $F1$ at the point of offset or onset of glottal vibration is not as low as one might expect for a configuration with a labial closure. For the voiceless fricative, $F1$ is prevented from decreasing too much because the labial constriction is not a complete closure and because there is some spreading of the glottis at the boundaries, as schematized in figure 8.2.

The spectra in figure 8.12 show a weakening of the spectrum amplitude in the $F3$–$F4$ range near the VC boundary—additional evidence for spreading of the glottis. The spectrum during the initial 100-odd milliseconds of the consonantal region (frames 5 to 7) is relatively flat, although there is some fluctuation in level. The spectrum amplitude of the noise in the $F2$ region is

Figure 8.12 A spectrogram of the utterance /ɑfɑ/ is shown at the top. The spectra in the three columns immediately below the spectrogram are sampled at several points in three regions of the utterance: in the vowel immediately preceding the consonant (left, panels 1 to 4); within the fricative region (middle, panels 5 to 8); and in the vowel immediately following the consonant (right, panels 9 to 12). These spectra are obtained with a 6.4-ms Hamming window. In the vowel regions, spectra are sampled at four adjacent glottal periods, whereas in the consonant the spectra are sampled more sparsely. In panels 6 to 8, where there is no evidence of glottal vibration, the lower spectra are averages of a series of spectra obtained with a 6.4-ms window over a 20-ms interval. The upper curves in these panels are smoothed versions of the average spectra. Waveforms and time windows, together with the times at which the spectra are sampled, are shown below each spectrum panel.

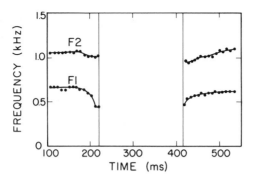

Figure 8.13 Frequencies of F1 and F2 measured from the utterance in figure 8.12. The points represent frequencies determined from peaks in spectra of the type shown in figure 8.12, with a 6.4-ms window placed on each glottal period.

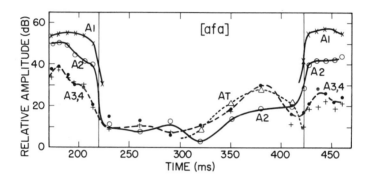

Figure 8.14 Spectrum amplitude in various frequency ranges in the utterance /ɑfɑ/, plotted as a function of time. The vowel-fricative and fricative-vowel boundaries are shown as vertical lines. In the vowel regions, A1, A2, A3 (dot symbols), and A4 (+ symbols) represent amplitudes of spectral peaks corresponding to the first four formants, obtained from spectra of the type given in figure 8.12 (6.4-ms window). Within the fricative, a given amplitude such as A3 represents the amplitude of the highest spectral peak in the F3 frequency range. The short-dashed curve labeled A_T represents the amplitude of a spectral prominence around 1800 Hz, presumed to be due to excitation of a tracheal resonance.

25 to 35 dB below that of the F2 prominences in the adjacent vowels, and is 10 to 25 dB weaker than the vowel in the F3–F4 region. These differences are roughly consistent with the theoretical differences in figure 8.10.

In the latter part of the consonantal interval (frame 8), the spectrum amplitude of the noise increases, and well-defined spectral prominences appear. Apparently in this utterance the cross-sectional area of the glottal constriction remains large after the supraglottal constriction is released, and noise is generated in the vicinity of the glottis to provide a relatively strong excitation of F3 and of a subglottal resonance (at about 1800 Hz). The pattern of change of the constriction sizes is, perhaps, similar to that given in figure 8.11.

Figure 8.14 shows data on the spectrum amplitude in various frequency regions, plotted as a function of time from a point near the edge of the first

Table 8.1 Differences (in decibels) between amplitudes of spectral peaks corresponding to F2, F3, F4, and F5 in the vowel adjacent to fricative /f/ and spectrum amplitude in the fricative region in the same four frequency ranges

	VCV speakers	Calculated difference (from figure 8.10)
$\Delta A2$	39(8)	33
$\Delta A3$	28(8)	26
$\Delta A4$	21(10)	18
$\Delta A5$	11(5)	10

Note: The middle column gives averages and standard deviations for two utterances produced by three speakers (two male, one female) with adjacent vowels /ʌ/ and /ɛ/, in a vowel-consonant-vowel context.

vowel to a point 40-odd milliseconds into the second vowel. Within the fricative, the amplitude $A2$ in the second-formant range fluctuates, but remains 25 to 40 dB below the level of the corresponding $F2$ spectral peak in the adjacent vowel. The spectrum amplitudes in the $F3$ and $F4$ range remain 10 to 20 dB below the spectrum amplitude in this frequency range in the vowel, except for a time interval near the end of the fricative. In this interval, $A3$ in the fricative is about equal to $A3$ in the vowel, and $A4$ in the fricative is only slightly below $A4$ in the vowel. The spectral peak at 1800 Hz in the noise, presumably due to a tracheal resonance, shows a rise in the final 75 ms of the fricative, as indicated by the curve labeled A_T. As noted above, it is probable that in this utterance, the glottis remains abducted after the area of the supraglottal constriction is increased, resulting in greater airflow and hence greater aspiration noise.

As a rough check on the theoretical basis for the calculated spectra for the frication noise in figure 8.10, measurements of the spectrum of the frication noise in /f/ and of the adjacent vowel have been made for several utterances of the form /VfV/ produced by three speakers (two male, one female). The spectrum was measured in the middle of the fricative using a 6.4-ms window and averaging a series of such spectra over a time interval of 32 ms. A similar spectrum was obtained in the second vowel, with the averaging centered over a time 50 ms after the fricative release. Utterances with two different vowels /ɛ/ and /ʌ/ were used to obtain a balance between a back and a front vowel that is neither high nor low. Measurements were made of the peak spectrum amplitudes of the fricative and the vowel in frequency ranges corresponding to $F2$, $F3$, $F4$, and $F5$. The differences in these amplitudes, $\Delta A2$ through $\Delta A5$, were obtained for each of the six utterances, and averages were taken. The results, together with standard deviations, are given in the middle column of table 8.1. Also listed, in the right column, are the calculated differences in spectrum amplitudes, from figure 8.10. Although there is some variability from speaker to speaker and from utterance to utterance, the average differences for the four frequency regions are in rough agreement with the differences expected on the basis of the calculations. Some lack of agreement is to be expected, since the measurements are for a limited number of utterances and speakers, and the calculations are based on a rather simplified model. Also, acoustic coupling to the back cavity could introduce peaks in the spectrum, particularly in the $F3-F4$ range, and these have been neglected in the calculations.

8.1.5   Alveolar Fricatives

An alveolar fricative is one of the class of fricatives produced by raising the tongue blade against the roof of the mouth to form a narrow constriction. For the alveolar fricative, the constriction is formed in the vicinity of the alveolar ridge, as shown in figure 8.1. The constriction is adjusted so that the airstream emerging from the constriction impinges on the lower incisors. The principal source of turbulence noise is at this obstacle, which is reasonably effective in generating a dipole source. We assume the relative level of this sound pressure source is given by the curve in figure 8.9. The absolute level is determined by scaling the values of $20 \log U^3 A^{-2.5}$ relative to the reference value of 212 dB (see figure 2.33), and applying a correction of -5 dB to account for the fact that the incisors are somewhat less effective in generating turbulence in the airstream than is a flat surface placed perpendicular to the airstream.

The effective length of the acoustic cavity in front of the constriction is similar to that for the alveolar stop consonants, discussed earlier in section 7.4.3—about 2.0 cm for a male speaker, and somewhat less for a female vocal tract. The natural frequency of the 2-cm front cavity is about 4500 Hz; the component of the transfer function from the noise source to the mouth output corresponding to this pole has been given in figure 7.25. The source is located somewhat downstream from the constriction formed by the tongue blade against the alveolar ridge. The distance from the source to the constriction is estimated to be about 1 cm, and consequently there are zeros in the transfer function near zero frequency and at a frequency of about 18 kHz. The calculated spectrum of the frication noise, therefore, is similar to the frication spectrum in the burst of an alveolar stop consonant, as shown previously in figure 7.26, except for an adjustment in level to account for the different airflow and constriction size. This spectrum includes the effect of the spectrum of the noise source (from figure 2.33) and the poles and zeros in the transfer function (the principal pole at 4500 Hz, and zeros at 0 and 18,000 Hz). From figure 8.9 we observe that the peak value of $20 \log U^3 A^{-2.5}$ is 203 dB, which is 2 dB higher than the peak value for the burst for the alveolar stop consonant (see section 7.4.3). We subtract 5 dB for the less effective obstacle, as we did for the stop consonant. Hence the frication spectrum for the alveolar fricative is 2 dB higher than the F spectrum in figure 7.26. We show this spectrum in figure 8.15, and label it F. This spectrum includes the contribution of a monopole component to frication noise

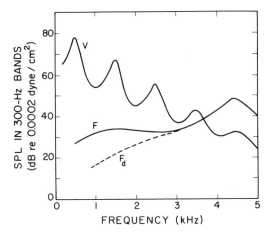

Figure 8.15 Calculated spectra that would occur at two points in time during the production of an alveolar fricative in a position between two neutral vowels. See legend for figure 8.10.

at low frequencies. As in figure 7.26, we represent the dipole component at low frequencies by F_d. As calculations in section 8.1.4 show, the contribution of aspiration noise to the spectrum in the middle of the fricative is negligible.

The formant transitions between the adjacent vowels and an alveolar fricative follow trajectories similar to those for an alveolar stop consonant, discussed earlier in connection with figures 7.22 and 7.23, but with some differences. As we have seen, $F1$ for the fricative at the onset of glottal vibration in the following vowel is not as low as it is for the stop. Furthermore, the higher formants do not reach the frequencies expected for a stop closure.

The aspiration noise immediately prior to voicing onset (at time 0 ms in the idealized plots of supraglottal and glottal areas in figure 8.2) or immediately following voicing offset has a spectrum similar to the A spectrum in figure 8.10. The frequency of $F2$ is different, however, and is about 1600 Hz at these points in time. The aspiration spectrum is not shown in figure 8.15.

Comparison of the frication noise spectrum with the vowel spectrum V in figure 8.15 indicates that the spectrum amplitude of the frication noise exceeds that of the adjacent vowel by about 16 dB in the frequency region of the front-cavity resonance—about 4.5 kHz in this case. This difference of 16 dB is expected to be quite variable, since it depends on the high-frequency spectrum amplitude of the vowel as well as the location of the lower incisors in relation to the position of the constriction. The high-frequency amplitude for the vowel varies with the vowel and with the speaker. The frequency of this spectral peak in the fricative spectrum is expected to be 15 to 20 percent higher for a female speaker. The lower-frequency peaks in the aspiration component at the boundary of the fricative (corresponding to $F2$ and $F3$) become evident in the noise spectrum near the edges of the fricative, but are considerably weaker than the corresponding peaks in the vowel spectrum.

Obstruent Consonants

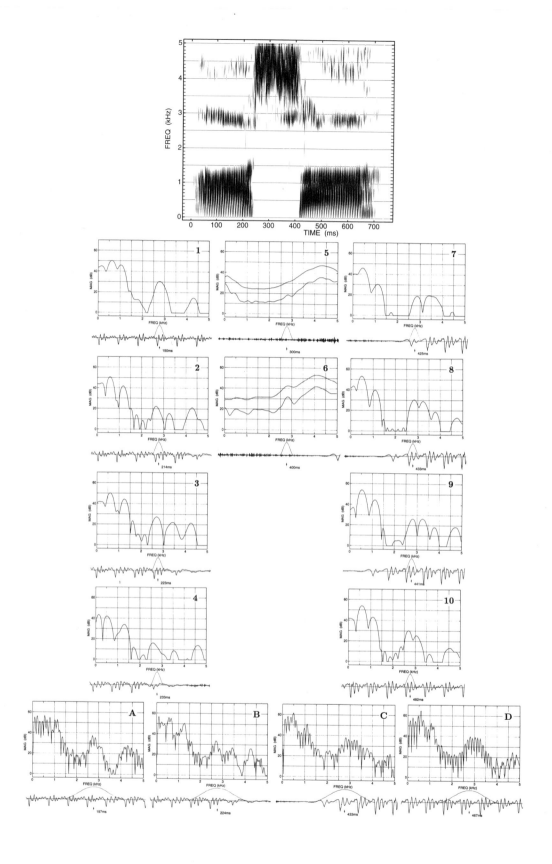

Acoustic data from an alveolar fricative consonant in the intervocalic environment /ɑsɑ/ are shown in figures 8.16, 8.17, and 8.18. A spectrogram is given at the top of figure 8.16, and the panels below the waveforms show short-time spectra (6.4-ms window) sampled at several times preceding the VC boundary (panels 1 to 4) and following the CV boundary (panels 7 to 10). In this sequence, the spectra in panels 1 and 10 are measured near the steady-state portions of the vowels, while the other spectra are for glottal periods close to the boundaries. Within the fricative itself, the two spectra that are displayed (panels 5 and 6) are average spectra over the initial half of the fricative region and over the final half. The spectra at the bottom of the figure are calculated with a longer time window of 30 ms, and are sampled at four points (panels A, B, C, and D): about 40 ms prior to voicing offset, near voicing offset, near voicing onset, and about 40 ms after voicing onset. These spectra near voicing offset and voicing onset show some evidence for glottal spreading, with a reduced amplitude of the second harmonic in relation to the first, a decreased amplitude of the $F1$ prominence, and with a subglottal resonance appearing around 1600 Hz.

The spectra in figure 8.16 indicate an increase in $F2$ of about 400 Hz in the vowel near the VC boundary, but a much smaller decrease in $F2$ (about 50 Hz) following the consonant release. The motion of $F1$ into the fricative and from the fricative into the vowel is likewise relatively small (150 to 200 Hz). These formant movements are shown in figure 8.17. The $F1$ movements are somewhat slower and longer than in the labiodental fricative (see figure 8.13), much like the differences between $F1$ movements for alveolar and labial stop consonants in figure 7.13. During the fricative interval, it was possible to observe an $F2$ prominence from time to time, and the points are plotted in figure 8.17 and joined by a dashed line. It appears that there was some posterior movement of the tongue body during the fricative for this VCV utterance, so that the $F2$ transition in the following vowel was negligible.

Figure 8.18 shows plots of the amplitude of the frication noise vs. time and of the amplitudes of the spectral peaks corresponding to several formants in the vicinity of the two boundaries. In the region of the fifth formant (4 to 5 kHz), the amplitude of the frication noise is 10 to 20 dB higher than the spectrum amplitude at this frequency for the adjacent vowels—in the same range as the difference calculated in figure 8.15. In the second half of the consonantal interval, there is an increased prominence of a spectral peak corresponding to $F3$ (at about 2750 Hz), as well as some increase in the amplitude of the high-frequency peak at about 4 kHz. The increased $F3$ prominence presumably arises from increased acoustic coupling to the vocal

Figure 8.16 Same as figure 8.12, except that the utterance is /ɑsɑ/. Panels 1 to 4 represent spectra (6.4-ms window) sampled at several times preceding the VC boundary, and panels 7 to 10 are sampled following the CV boundary. Panels 5 and 6 are average spectra calculated over the first and second halves of the frication region, respectively. The spectra in panels A, B, C, and D were obtained with a longer time window. See text.

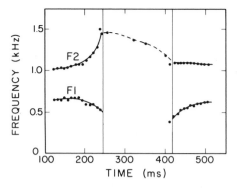

Figure 8.17 Frequencies of $F1$ and $F2$ measured from the utterance in figure 8.16. See legend for figure 8.13. The dashed line in the fricative interval is drawn for the few points where an $F2$ prominence was observed.

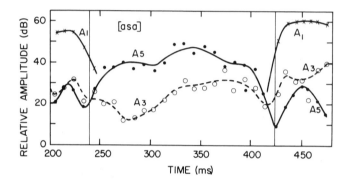

Figure 8.18 Same as figure 8.14, except that the utterance is /ɑsɑ/. Peaks corresponding to the third and fifth formant regions are labeled as $A3$ and $A5$.

tract behind the alveolar constriction as the area of that constriction becomes larger. The increased amplitude may also be due to excitation of $F3$ by aspiration noise. Presumably the cross-sectional area of the supraglottal constriction increases sufficiently in this portion of the consonant that the pressure drop across the glottal constriction, and hence the amplitude of the aspiration noise, increases significantly. This hypothesis is supported by the observation that the amplitude of the noise in the $F5$ region, which increases at about the midpoint of the fricative, then begins to decrease while the amplitude in the $F3$ region shows an increase (from time 340 to 380 ms in figure 8.18).

Measurements of the spectrum amplitude of the frication noise for /s/ relative to the spectrum amplitude in the corresponding frequency regions for an adjacent vowel have been made for three different speakers (two male, one female). The utterances were /VsV/, for two different vowels /ɛ/ and /ʌ/, as described above in connection with table 8.1. The measurements of the spectrum for the fricative were averages over the middle 32 ms of the consonant, whereas for the vowel average spectra were obtained over the same

Table 8.2 Differences (in decibels) between amplitudes of spectral peaks corresponding to $F2$, $F3$, $F4$, and $F5$ in the vowel adjacent to fricative /s/ and spectrum amplitude in the fricative region in the same four frequency ranges

	VCV	Calculated difference (from figure 8.15)
$\Delta A2$	30(3)	33
$\Delta A3$	19(6)	23
$\Delta A4$	9(7)	6
$\Delta A5$	−19(6)	−16

Note: The middle column gives averages and standard deviations for two utterances produced by three speakers (two male, one female) with adjacent vowels /ʌ/ and /ɛ/ in a vowel-consonant-vowel context.

time interval centered 50 ms after vowel onset. As in table 8.1 for the fricative /f/, differences (in decibels) between the peaks in the vowel spectrum and in the consonant spectrum were obtained in the frequency ranges of $F2$, $F3$, $F4$, and $F5$, and averages across speakers and vowels were calculated. These data are given in the middle column of table 8.2, together with standard deviations. The right column lists the differences calculated from the model, from figure 8.15. The measurements again show substantial variability across speakers and vowels, but the measured differences are consistent with the differences predicted from the model. The calculated differences in the $F2$ and $F3$ region are somewhat larger than the measured differences, presumably because coupling of the frication source to the resonances posterior to the constriction was not taken into account in the calculations. This coupling will introduce minor prominences in the fricative spectrum at these formant frequencies.

The observation that the spectrum amplitude of the frication noise for /s/ is significantly higher than the spectrum amplitude of the vowel in the frequency region of the fifth formant is in accord with the results of perceptual experiments with synthetic fricative-vowel syllables (K. N. Stevens, 1985). When the high-frequency spectrum amplitude of the noise in such syllables was manipulated, it was found that listeners identified the fricative as /θ/ if this amplitude was less than the high-frequency spectrum in the adjacent vowel, but identified it as /s/ when the amplitude of the fricative noise at high frequencies was greater than that of the vowel.

8.1.6 Palatoalveolar Fricatives

Figure 8.1 shows that, for the palatoalveolar fricative consonant, the point of maximum constriction is a few millimeters posterior to the alveolar ridge, and the tongue blade is shaped in such a way as to produce a relatively long and narrow channel behind the point of maximum constriction. This channel is formed between the surface of the tongue blade and the hard palate. The

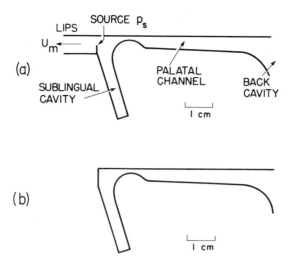

Figure 8.19 (a) Schematized representation of the detailed cavity shapes in the anterior portion of the vocal tract for /š/. The source of sound is assumed to be located at the lower incisors, as indicated. (From Halle and Stevens, 1991b.) (b) The zeros in the transfer function from source to mouth output in (a) are the natural frequencies of this configuration.

elevated tongue blade tends to create a space between the lower surface of the tongue blade and the floor of the oral cavity. As for the alveolar fricative consonant, the airstream emerging from the constriction is directed against the lower teeth, resulting in a turbulence noise source at this obstacle.

The vocal tract shape and source location in the front part of the oral cavity are shown in schematic form in figure 8.19a, where the dimensions are those expected for an adult male vocal tract (Halle and Stevens, 1991b). (The dimensions will be about 10 to 20 percent less for an adult female, on average.) The remainder of the vocal tract posterior to the palatal constriction (labeled BACK CAVITY in the figure) has a cross-sectional area that is large compared with the cross-sectional areas of the various components of the anterior part depicted in figure 8.19a, and consequently the posterior part is not expected to have a major effect on the natural frequencies of the front part. The average spacing of the natural frequencies for a configuration of this kind is about $c/2l$, where c is the velocity of sound and l is the overall length of the branches. (See section 3.6.) An initial approximation to these natural frequencies can be made by noting that the total length of all the branches in figure 8.19a is about 8.5 cm (1.2 cm for lip cavity, 2.6 cm for sublingual cavity, and 4.7 cm for palatal constriction). Thus the average spacing is about 2 kHz, and consequently two natural frequencies are expected in the frequency range up to 4 kHz.

The actual natural frequencies will depend on the details of the dimensions and cross-sectional areas of the system. If we assume that the system is divided roughly into two parts by the narrow constriction at the anterior end of the palatal channel, then we can estimate the frequencies of the two parts separately. The palatal channel, with a length of about 4 cm, would have a natural frequency of about 2200 Hz if it were closed at the constricted end. If we take into account the finite constriction at the anterior end and the gradual widening at the posterior end, we can estimate a natural frequency of about 2500 Hz for this portion. The length of the sublingual cavity of 2.6 cm would lead to a natural frequency of about 3500 Hz, or perhaps slightly lower if the effect of the lip cavity is taken into account.

Similar reasoning can be followed to determine the zeros of the transfer function from the sound pressure source at the lower incisors to the volume velocity at the mouth. These are the frequencies for which the impedance looking back into the configuration from the source is infinite, and they are the natural frequencies of the configuration in figure 8.19b. Again, there are expected to be two such frequencies up to about 4 kHz. The lower of these two zeros is roughly a resonance between the acoustic compliance of the sublingual cavity and the combined acoustic mass of the narrow constriction and the palatal channel. The volume of the space (including the sublingual cavity) between the source and the constriction is estimated to be about 3 cm^2, whereas the effective ratio of length to area of the constriction and palatal channel is roughly 0.5/0.1 cm^{-1} (for the constriction) +4/0.8 cm^{-1} (for the channel), for a total of 10 cm^{-1}. This lowest zero is thus about 1000 Hz. The second zero is expected to be between the two poles, and is estimated to be about 3000 Hz. In addition to the two poles and two zeros just described, the transfer function U_m/p_s for the system as depicted in figure 8.19 also has a pole at zero frequency, since at low frequencies the system can be approximated as a simple acoustic mass consisting primarily of the constriction and the palatal channel.

As noted below, the second formant for the overall configuration for /š/ (including the back cavity) is at about 1900 Hz (somewhat higher for a female vocal tract). Acoustic coupling of the frication source to this resonance can have a significant effect on the transfer function. This coupling will introduce an additional pole-zero pair, with the pole at 1900 Hz, and the frequency of the zero just below the pole. We take this pole-zero spacing to be 200 Hz, with bandwidths of 150 Hz for the pole and zero.

The overall transfer function from the sound pressure source at the lower incisors to the volume velocity at the mouth opening is shown in figure 8.20. The magnitude of this transfer function is adjusted to have the appropriate low-frequency behavior. We omit consideration of poles and zeros above 4 kHz.

As with the frication for the labiodental and alveolar consonants, we estimate the frication noise spectrum for the palatoalveolar fricative as the sum (in decibels) of the source spectrum, the transfer function in figure 8.20, and the radiation characteristic. The dipole source spectrum is the same as that used for the calculations for /f/ and /s/ in figures 8.10 and 8.15, with the same correction of −5 dB to account for the less effective obstacle relative to that for the reference spectrum in figure 2.33. The result is the spectrum

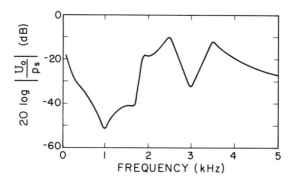

Figure 8.20 Estimated transfer function U_m/p_s for the configuration in figure 8.17. The estimated frequencies (bandwidths) of the poles and zeros (in hertz) are: poles—2500 (200), 3500(250); zeros—1000 (150), 3000 (250). A pole-zero pair just below 2 kHz is also inserted to account for acoustic coupling to the cavity behind the model of figure 8.19. The transfer function is normalized by multiplying by the characteristic impedance $\rho c/A$ of the cavity in front of the source, where $A = 1$ cm^2.

labeled F_d in figure 8.21. Also shown in this figure is the estimated spectrum of frication noise resulting from a possible monopole source at the constriction. The amplitude of this source is the same as for the labiodental and alveolar fricatives, and the transfer function from this source to the volume velocity at the lips is assumed to have a pole (at 3500 Hz) corresponding to the front-cavity resonance. The result of calculating the spectrum of the radiated sound pressure arising from this monopole frication source is identified as F_m in figure 8.21. (We neglect here the effect of the sublingual side branch, which introduces a zero in the transfer function from monopole source to lip output.) The contribution of the monopole source has the effect of obscuring spectral minima due to zeros in the spectrum of F_d. The overall spectrum of the frication noise that would be observed is given roughly by the maximum of the F_m and F_d spectra. At low frequencies, this spectrum is dominated by F_m and at high frequencies (above about 1800 Hz) by F_d.

The first formant for the palatoalveolar configuration is a Helmholtz resonance, and $F1$ is somewhat lower than the $F1$ contour given in figure 8.6 because of the longer constriction. The second-formant frequency for this consonant configuration is roughly the half-wavelength resonance of the back cavity. The length of the back cavity is about 10 cm (for a male vocal tract), which would have a natural frequency of 1770 Hz if the cross-sectional area were uniform. However, the tapered anterior end of this cavity would raise this frequency, leading to a value of $F2$ of about 1900 Hz (and proportionately higher for a female vocal tract), as noted above. Toward the edge of the fricative, $F2$ is expected to fall to about 1800 Hz.

Calculation of the spectrum of the aspiration noise at the vowel-fricative and fricative-vowel boundary is similar to the A spectrum in figure 8.10 but is based on the frequencies of the formants for the palatoalveolar configuration. This aspiration spectrum is not shown in figure 8.21. As before, the

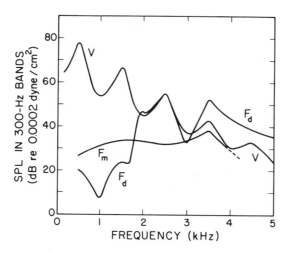

Figure 8.21 Calculated spectra that would occur at several points in time during the production of a palatoalveolar fricative in a position between two neutral vowels. See legend for figure 8.10.

spectrum of the adjacent vowel, with uniformly spaced formants, is given as V in the figure.

The calculated frication spectra in figure 8.21 indicate that the peaks at about 2.5 kHz and 3.5 kHz, which correspond to F3 and F4 in the vowel, have about the same spectrum amplitude. The F4 peak in the frication noise is about 10 dB above the corresponding peak in the vowel, whereas the calculated amplitude of the F3 peak is about equal to the amplitude of the corresponding peak in the vowel.

Acoustic data from an utterance of /aša/ produced by an adult male speaker are shown in figures 8.22, 8.23, and 8.24. As before, a spectrogram of the utterance is displayed at the top of figure 8.22, and a number of spectra sampled at different points in the utterance are arrayed below the spectrogram. For the most part, the spectra were obtained with a short time window (6.4 ms) that was centered on individual glottal periods near the edges of the preceding (panels 1 to 4) and following (panels 8 to 11) vowels. As in figure 8.16, the top panel in the VC sequence and the bottom panel in the CV sequence represent spectra sampled near the middle of the vowels. Three spectra within the fricative are shown: two spectra near the edges of the fricative (panels 5 and 7), where aspiration noise is expected to be evident, and an average spectrum for the major part of the fricative (panel 6). The spectra at the bottom were calculated with a longer time window (30 ms), and they show the individual harmonics in the vowel spectra near the edges of the vowels (panels A, B, C, and D).

The rising F2 transition near the offset of the first vowel is evident in the spectrogram and in the spectra (panels 1 to 4), and a similar but less extensive fall in F2 can be seen near the onset of the second vowel (panels 8 to 11). Plots of F1 and F2 vs. time near the VC and CV boundaries are given in

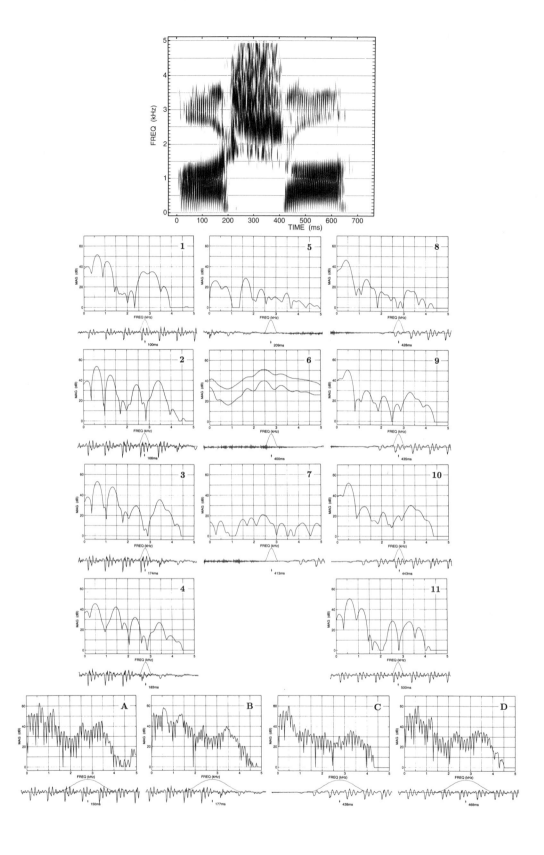

figure 8.23, together with measured frequencies of the $F2$ prominence within the fricative (dashed line). The $F2$ values at the boundaries and within the fricative for this utterance are somewhat lower than the values of 1800 and 1900 Hz estimated above. They are, however, higher than for /s/ (see figure 8.17), presumably because the tongue body is more fronted. This more fronted configuration can be seen by comparing the midsagittal sections for /s/ and /š/ in figure 8.1. The $F1$ movement is slow at the consonant release, similar to that for /s/, but the $F1$ fall at the VC boundary is rapid. This rapid fall of $F1$ is atypical.

Peaks corresponding to $F2$ and $F3$ appear in the noise spectrum near the edges of the fricative (panels 5 and 7 in figure 8.22), indicating the presence of aspiration noise, but these peaks are 10 to 20 dB weaker than the corresponding peaks in the vowel. During the frication interval, there are spectral prominences corresponding to $F3$ and $F4$, as expected from the theoretical discussion in connection with figure 8.21, with the $F4$ peak being about 4 dB weaker than the $F3$ peak. The frequencies of the $F3$ and $F4$ prominences for this utterance are about 2500 and 3250 Hz, with $F4$ being somewhat lower than the value estimated from the model in figure 8.19. In this utterance there is also a peak corresponding to $F2$, at about 1750 Hz, indicating some acoustic coupling from the source to the back cavity. The amplitude of the $F3$ peak in the consonant is about equal to that of the corresponding peak in the preceding vowel, and is about 10 dB stronger than the $F3$ peak for the following vowel. The amplitude of the $F4$ peak in the consonant is about equal to or a few decibels weaker than the $F4$ peaks in the adjacent vowels. These results differ by a few decibels from predictions based on the calculated spectra in figure 8.21. The movements of $F1$ and $F2$ can also be seen in the narrow-band spectra at the bottom of figure 8.22 (panels A and B, and C and D). There is some evidence of glottal spreading near the boundaries (especially panel B), with an increased bandwidth of $F2$ and an increase in the difference in amplitude of the first two harmonics ($H1$–$H2$) in panel B relative to A.

A plot of the amplitudes of the various spectral peaks as they change with time in the consonant and in the adjacent vowels is given in figure 8.24. There is some fluctuation in amplitudes, presumably as the vocal tract configuration changes during the consonantal interval. The frication noise shows a decrease in amplitude at the edges of the consonant.

Observations of the fricative /š/ produced by several speakers in different vowel environments, in both English and Polish,[2] show consistent evidence of $F3$ and $F4$ prominences in the frication spectrum, as expected from theory, but considerable variability in the relative amplitudes of these two prominences, and in their amplitudes in relation to the amplitudes of the corresponding prominences in the adjacent vowels. Amplitudes of spectral prominences in

Figure 8.22 Same as figures 8.12 and 8.16, except that the utterance is /ašɑ/. See text.

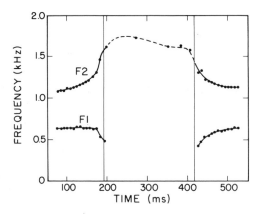

Figure 8.23 Frequencies of F1 and F2 measured for the utterance in figure 8.22. See legend for figure 8.13. The dashed line represents the frequency of the F2 prominence in the fricative interval.

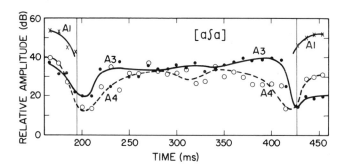

Figure 8.24 Same as figure 8.14, except that the utterance is /ašɑ/. Peaks corresponding to the third and fourth formants are plotted in the fricative region.

the $F2$, $F3$, and $F4$ ranges for vowels and fricatives in /VšV/ utterances have been measured for three American English speakers (two male, one female). Two different vowels (/ʌ/ and /ɛ/) were used. Average amplitude differences are given in table 8.3. Also tabulated are the calculated amplitude differences from figure 8.21. The average frequencies of the $F3$ and $F4$ prominences in the fricatives for the male speakers were about 2600 and 3200 Hz, in contrast to the values of 2500 and 3500 Hz used in calculating figure 8.21, and those for the female speaker were about 20 percent higher (except that there was no prominence corresponding to $F4$ for one utterance of the female speaker). The frequency of $F2$ in the fricative averaged about 1900 Hz for the male speakers and 2000 Hz for the female speaker. There are some discrepancies between the measurements and the calculations, especially for $\Delta A2$ and $\Delta A3$. Some adjustment of the frequencies of the poles and zeros could be made to correct the calculated $\Delta A3$.

The relative amplitudes of the peaks corresponding to $F2$, $F3$, and $F4$ in the spectrum for /š/ are rather sensitive to the frequencies of the poles and

Table 8.3 Differences (in decibels) between amplitudes of spectral peaks corresponding to $F2$, $F3$, and $F4$ in the vowel adjacent to the fricative /š/ and spectrum amplitude in the fricative region in the same three frequency ranges

	VCV	Calculated difference (from figure 8.21)
$\Delta A2$	15(4)	19
$\Delta A3$	−5(5)	0
$\Delta A4$	−6(7)	−10

Note: The middle column gives averages for two utterances produced by three speakers (two male, one female) with adjacent vowels /ʌ/ and /ɛ/ in a vowel-consonant-vowel context, together with standard deviations.

zeros in the transfer function. These in turn are sensitive to the detailed shape and position of the tongue blade, to the size of the constriction, and to the lip position. It is probable that a speaker uses an auditory criterion for adjusting the tongue blade and the amount of lip rounding to create a sound with the requisite spectrum and amplitude of the noise relative to that of the adjacent vowel in the $F3$–$F4$ region. Perceptual experiments with synthetic fricative-vowel syllables have shown that the spectrum amplitude of the noise in the $F3$ region should be at least equal to the spectrum amplitude of the $F3$ peak in the adjacent vowel if the fricative is to be identified as /š/ (K. N. Stevens, 1985).

8.1.7 Summary of Characteristics of Voiceless Fricative Consonants

Voiceless fricative consonants are produced with a narrowing of a supraglottal constriction that is formed by one of the supraglottal articulators. The cross-sectional area of this constriction is usually somewhat smaller than the area of the glottal opening, which is widened to form this type of fricative. At a fricative-vowel boundary, the glottis begins to close, and the area of the supraglottal constriction increases. This release phase tends to show an increased airflow relative to that in the fricative. Within the fricative, a turbulence noise source is generated, usually at some obstacle downstream from the constriction. The amplitude of this source is only weakly dependent (within a few decibels) on the cross-sectional area of the constriction or of the glottal opening over changes of 50-odd percent in these areas.

The amplitude and spectrum of the radiated sound for a fricative is strongly dependent on the location and shape of the constriction. In the case of a labiodental fricative, there is essentially no cavity in front of the constriction, the spectrum of the radiated sound has no major spectral peaks, and the spectrum amplitude of the noise is weak in relation to the vowel, at least below 5 kHz. For an alveolar fricative, the source is filtered by the front-cavity resonance, leading to a spectrum peak in the $F4$ or $F5$ range or higher.

The amplitude of that peak exceeds that of an adjacent vowel in this high-frequency range. The filtering for a palatoalveolar consonant gives rise to spectrum peaks in the $F3$ and $F4$ ranges that tend to have a greater amplitude than corresponding peaks in an adjacent vowel. Models of the noise source characteristics and of the filtering for the fricatives predict attributes of the radiated sound that are similar to those observed in naturally produced utterances. There is, however, considerable variability in the observed spectral characteristics of fricatives, and current models do not account for this variability.

8.2 AFFRICATES

In our discussion of stop consonants in chapter 7, we observed that the articulatory structure used to form the closure for the stop moves rapidly following the consonantal release, leaving a relatively unconstricted airway. The rapid increase of the cross-sectional area at the constriction gives rise to a transient, and there is a brief burst of turbulence noise following the transient. After the burst, the vocal folds begin vibration, assuming that they are in a configuration that permits glottal vibration.

A contrasting class of stop consonants is the affricate. An affricate is produced by shaping and positioning the articulatory structure in such a way that the rapid release is produced at the anterior end of the constriction formed by the articulator. Following this release, the constriction formed immediately posterior to the point of release is maintained for a few tens of milliseconds and is then released. This constriction is much like the constriction for a fricative consonant. The sequence of events characterizing an affricate is therefore an initial transient occurring at the release at the anterior end of the constriction followed by a few tens of milliseconds of frication noise prior to voicing onset for the vowel. The shaping of the constriction during the fricative portion must be adjusted so that the flow of air through the constriction is properly directed against an appropriate obstacle or surface. This shaping of the constriction must be effected before the release of the anterior closure.

The requirement for an affricate is that the constriction formed by the relevant articulator can be divided into two parts: an anterior part that executes the initial rapid release from closure, and a longer posterior part that is shaped to produce frication noise corresponding to the fricative portion of the sequence. The situation is schematized in figure 8.25 (K. N. Stevens, 1993a), where the vocal tract posterior to the constriction is represented as a uniform tube and the consonantal constriction is shown as a narrow section with cross-sectional area A_2 with a narrowing near its anterior end, with area A_1. The cross-sectional area of the glottal opening is A_g.

During the closure interval for the consonant there is a pressure buildup behind the constriction. We assume for purposes of analysis that the glottis

Figure 8.25 Schematized model of the vocal tract for an affricate consonant. Closure is formed by setting the area A_1 to zero at the front of the constriction. The channel behind the constriction, with area A_2, forms the fricative portion of the affricate after A_1 is released.

is somewhat abducted during this time, with a configuration similar to that for a voiceless fricative consonant. That is, we consider a voiceless affricate. A consequence of the increased pressure behind the constriction is that there is a force on the articulatory structure that forms the constriction, and the result of this force is a passive downward displacement of the surface, probably equal to about 0.1 cm, given the estimate of compliance of the vocal tract walls in section 1.1.3.7. At the initial release of the closure, the rate of movement of the articulatory structure that forms the anterior area A_1, and hence the rate of increase of A_1, is expected to be rapid, since the movement is enhanced by forces due to pressure behind the constriction. Following the initial release at the anterior end of the constriction, the force on the surface of the articulator behind the constriction A_1 is reduced, and there is an initial inward (upward) movement of the surface. Acoustic and articulatory events at the release of the fricative portion of an affricate consonant are similar to those for a fricative consonant.

The articulator used to produce an affricate can be the lower lip, the tongue blade, or the tongue body, although affricates such as /kx/ that are produced with the tongue body seem to be rare (Maddieson, 1984). The length of the constriction schematized in figure 8.25 is different for the different places of articulation for the affricate. For example, the constriction is much shorter for the labial affricate than for the palatal, although the general principles of an initial anterior release followed by an interval of frication noise apply to all of the affricates. The palatoalveolar affricate is the only one that occurs in English, and appears to be the most common affricate across languages (Maddieson, 1984). We shall restrict our consideration to this palatoalveolar affricate, represented either as /č/ or /tʃ/.

8.2.1 Articulatory Movements and Aerodynamic Parameters

For a palatoalveolar affricate, closure is made with the front part of the tongue blade at a point immediately posterior to the alveolar ridge. The configuration is similar to that for the palatoalveolar fricative, schematized in figure 8.19a, except that there is a complete closure near the anterior end of the palatal channel. Following the initial release of this closure, it is assumed that the tongue blade has a shape and position similar to that for a palatoalveolar fricative. The solid line in figure 8.26 shows a midsagittal section of the anterior part of the vocal tract for the palatoalveolar fricative (from

Figure 8.26 Conception of the midsagittal section of the anterior part of the vocal tract just prior to the initial release (dashed line) and 20 to 30 ms following the release (solid line) of a palatoalveolar affricate.

figure 8.1). Superimposed on this contour is a dashed line that gives an estimate of the configuration of the tongue blade just before the initial release of the closure formed by the anterior part of the tongue blade. The surface of the tongue blade behind the closure is shown to be depressed somewhat in relation to the position for the fricative. This downward displacement is due in part to the increased air pressure on the tongue surface during the closure. Immediately after the initial release, when flow begins through the palatal channel, this pressure decreases, and the tongue surface responds by moving upward. The figure also suggests that the volume of the space below the tongue blade is less immediately before release than it is some time after release.

When the initial release is made by lowering the tongue tip, there is a rapid increase in the cross-sectional area of the constriction at this point. The speed of the initial release is enhanced by forces due to the pressure behind the constriction. This initial rate of increase of cross-sectional area is taken to be 50 cm^2/s, intermediate to the initial rates of change of area assumed for the releases of labial and velar stop consonants and comparable to the rate for alveolar stops. This initial rapid release of the tongue tip occurs only in a fraction of a millisecond, and results in a discharge of the intraoral pressure, leading to an initial transient volume velocity source, as will be discussed later.

Following the initial release, which appears to be very brief (1 or 2 ms, as will be verified when we examine the acoustic events resulting from the release), the cross-sectional area of the constriction formed by the front part of the tongue blade continues to increase more slowly over the next 50-odd milliseconds. Direct evidence for the time course of this change in cross-sectional area is not available, but estimates can be made based on airflow data and on acoustic analyses of the changes in the amplitude and spectrum of the frication noise for affricates over this initial time interval. Figure 8.27 gives an estimate of the time course of the change in cross-sectional area for this front part of the affricate constriction, represented by A_1 in the schematized configuration in figure 8.25. We shall show later that the calculated sound pattern based on this area change is consistent with observed acoustic data. The rate of increase of the cross-sectional area over this part of the affricate is likely to be quite variable. Also shown in figure 8.27 is the estimated

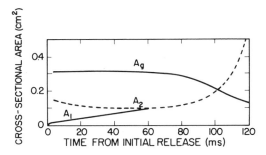

Figure 8.27 Estimated change in cross-sectional area for various constrictions in the vocal tract following the release of an affricate consonant. A_1, cross-sectional area of constriction formed with the front of the tongue blade (cf. A_1 in schematized model in figure 8.25); A_2, minimum cross-sectional area of palatal channel formed by the tongue blade (cf. A_2 in figure 8.25); A_g, cross-sectional area of glottal opening.

cross-sectional area of the palatal constriction following the initial release. This is the equivalent of the area A_2 in the schematized configuration in figure 8.25. The time course of this cross-sectional area over the time interval beyond 50 ms in figure 8.27, together with the change in cross-sectional area of the glottal opening A_g, are similar to the trajectories that have been assumed for the release of a fricative consonant, in figure 8.2. For the area changes in figure 8.27, vocal fold vibration is expected to begin at a time about 110 ms from the initial release. This duration for a voiceless affricate is consistent with average data for the duration from release to voicing onset of prestressed affricates. (Average duration for five speakers = 110 ms, with a range of 85 to 160 ms.)

The airflow through the supraglottal constriction corresponding to the area changes in figure 8.27 can be calculated based on the model in figure 7.7 that was used to estimate the airflow at the release of simple stop consonants. During the 10- to 20-ms interval following the release, the cross-sectional area of the constriction is small enough that the viscous component of the resistance must be included in the calculation of the airflow. The results of these calculations are displayed in figure 8.28. (The initial brief transient airflow is not shown in the figure.) Following the release, there is a gradual increase in the flow. In the later fricative part of the process, the airflow pattern is similar to that at the release of a fricative consonant, shown earlier in figure 8.3.

This calculated airflow can be compared with measurements of airflow at the release of a voiceless affricate. One such airflow trace for the utterance /ə'tʃɑ/ is displayed in figure 8.29. (A similar pattern is also reported in Fig. 4 of Klatt et al., 1968.) There is a steady increase in flow from the initial release to the later release of the fricative portion, similar to the calculated pattern based on the area changes assumed in figure 8.27. This comparison indicates that the area estimates in figure 8.27 are not unreasonable. The peak measured airflow in figure 8.29 is somewhat greater than the calculated flow, suggesting

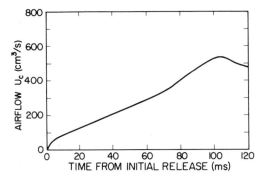

Figure 8.28 Calculated airflow U_c at the supraglottal constriction for a palatoalveolar affricate, based on the area changes in figure 8.27, and assuming a subglottal pressure of 8 cm H_2O. The initial transient is not shown.

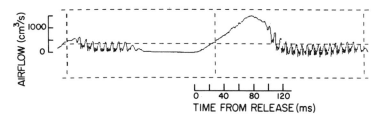

Figure 8.29 Measured airflow for a male speaker producing an affricate consonant in the nonsense utterance /əˈtʃɑ/.

that the subglottal pressure for the utterance was greater than the 8 cm H_2O assumed for the calculations, or that the area estimates in figure 8.27 should be scaled upward.

8.2.2 Acoustic Characteristics

At the instant of release of the affricate there is a transient source, similar to that for simple stop consonants. We shall assume that the amplitude and spectrum of this transient source is the same as the transient source calculated for an alveolar stop consonant in section 7.4.3, that is, 6 dB less than the spectrum given in figure 2.47. This volume velocity source excites the acoustic cavity in front of the constriction. As we have seen for the palatoalveolar fricative, the natural frequency of this cavity is approximately 3500 Hz for the dimensions given in figure 8.19. The sublingual cavity, however, forms a side branch in the path from the constriction to the mouth output, and consequently there is a zero in transfer function from the transient volume velocity source to the mouth output. For a side branch length of about 2 cm, the frequency of this zero is about 4500 Hz. The spectrum that results when the transient source is filtered by the front cavity with this pole-zero pair is given as T in figure 8.30. This is the spectrum of the sound pressure that would be obtained at a distance of 20 cm from the mouth

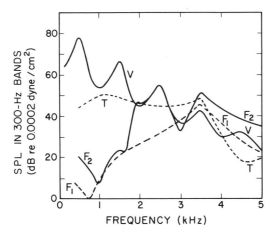

Figure 8.30 Spectra calculated at several times during the release of a palatoalveolar affricate consonant followed by a neutral vowel, using the model described in the text. All spectra represent sound pressure levels (SPL) (in decibels re 0.0002 dyne/cm²) in a 300-Hz band at a distance of 20 cm in front of the mouth opening, assuming a subglottal pressure of 8 cm H_2O. T, transient source at initial consonant release; F_1, spectrum of dipole frication noise about 10 ms following the initial release; F_2, spectrum of dipole frication noise about 50 ms following the release; V, spectrum of neutral vowel.

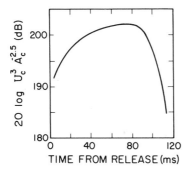

Figure 8.31 Estimated level of frication noise source for a palatoalveolar affricate as a function of time following the release. The ordinate is $20 \log U_c^3 A_c^{-2.5}$, where U_c is the airflow through the supraglottal constriction in cubic centimeters per second and A_c is the cross-sectional area of the constriction in square centimeters.

opening. The spectrum of the sound from this transient source can be compared with the theoretical spectrum V for a neutral vowel. The amplitude of the spectral peak at 3500 Hz for the transient is comparable to the amplitude of the $F4$ prominence for the vowel.

Following the initial transient, turbulence noise will be generated as a consequence of the airflow through the palatoalveolar constriction. The effective amplitude of the turbulence noise source is assumed to be proportional to $U_c^3 A_c^{-2.5}$, where U_c is the volume velocity through the constriction and A_c is the cross-sectional area of the constriction. A plot of this quantity, in decibels, is given in figure 8.31. During the 40- to 50-ms interval following the release, the amplitude of the noise source rises to a maximum value. After about 50 ms, the time course of the amplitude of the source is similar to that for a fricative, as shown earlier in figure 8.9.

During the initial phase of production of the affricate, the cross-sectional area of the constriction is small compared with the area of the palatal channel behind the constriction. Consequently there is little acoustic coupling to the palatal channel in this initial part of the affricate. In this interval, the turbulence noise source excites only the acoustic cavity anterior to the constriction. In the model we are considering here (cf. figure 8.19), the natural frequency of this front cavity is about 3500 Hz, and corresponds to the fourth formant of the entire vocal tract.

Calculation of the radiated sound pressure resulting from this noise source in the initial part of the affricate can be made considering the noise source to be located in the vicinity of the lower incisors, assumed to be about 1 cm anterior to the constriction. The model of figure 8.19, modified to have a narrower constriction in the postalveolar region and a somewhat reduced sublingual volume, can be used to calculate the zeros of the transfer function from the source to the mouth output. The lowest zero, and the one that is most relevant to determining the spectrum below 5 kHz, is a Helmholtz resonance between the volume behind the source (estimated to be 3 cm^3) and the constriction (with an area of about 0.025 cm^2 at 10 ms following the release, and an estimated length of about 0.5 cm). The zero is calculated to be at about 730 Hz for this model, although some variation is to be expected. Starting with the source spectrum in figure 2.33, shifting this spectrum down to account for the lower value of $U_c^3 A_c^{-2.5}$, applying a correction of 5 dB for the less effective obstacle, and multiplying by this transfer function and the appropriate radiation characteristic, we calculate the spectrum of the sound pressure at a distance of 20 cm from the mouth opening. This spectrum is shown as F_1 in figure 8.30, and is the spectrum resulting from the frication noise during the first phase of turbulence noise for the affricate release. Spectrum F_2 occurs later in the affricate, and is identical to the frication spectrum for the palatoalveolar fricative in figure 8.21. To simplify the figure, we show in figure 8.30 only the spectra resulting from the dipole components of the frication noise. The effect of the monopole components will be to raise somewhat the friction spectra at low frequencies, as shown in figure 8.21. During the latter part of the fricative, the constriction area has become sufficiently large that there is appreciable acoustic coupling to the palatal channel, leading to the appearance of a spectrum peak at about 2500 Hz, which is the natural frequency of the palatal channel.

This analysis has shown that there are three phases in the release of the palatoalveolar affricate. There is an initial brief transient with a spectral peak in the F4 region that can be comparable in amplitude to the amplitude of the corresponding spectral peak in the following vowel. Perception tests (Massey, 1994) have shown that this transient contributes signficantly to listeners' judgments of the naturalness of an affricate. Following the transient there is a brief interval of perhaps 40 to 50 ms in which the frication noise increases in amplitude. In this period after the release, the spectrum has a major peak in the $F4$ region (similar to the peak for the initial transient), indicating that the frication noise excites the acoustic cavity in front of the palatoalveolar constriction, but there is negligible coupling to the palatal channel. About 40 to 50 ms after the release the constriction has widened to the point where there is acoustic coupling from the frication source to the palatal channel, and the natural frequency associated roughly with that channel is manifested as a peak in the spectrum. That natural frequency corresponds to $F3$ for the entire vocal tract. Thus there is a change in the spectrum as the constriction widens during the initial part of the frication noise. After the palatal channel widens to produce a following vowel, the appearance of aspiration noise and the onset of glottal vibration with appropriate formant transitions follow a pattern similar to that for the palatoalveolar fricative. The timing of the initial frication phase (F_1 in figure 8.30) is likely to be quite variable, since there appear to be individual differences in the rate at which the area A_1 in figure 8.27 increases.

Acoustic data for a typical voiceless affricate produced by a female speaker and a male speaker are shown in figure 8.32. The utterance is /ə'tʃɑ/. A spectrogram of each utterance is displayed at the top of the figure. In order to illustrate the initial transient followed by weak but gradually rising frication noise, we show below the spectrogram a waveform of the initial 20-odd milliseconds following the release. The initial transient at the release is evident, and this is followed by a lower-amplitude frication noise that increases over the initial 20 ms. More detailed spectral data sampled at different times throughout the affricate and near the onset of the vowel are shown in the various panels below the spectrograms. The spectra represent average spectra over brief time intervals within the affricate.

For both speakers, the initial transient can be seen on the spectrogram at the release of the consonant closure. The spectrogram also shows the changing spectrum of the frication noise, with the fourth formant being excited by noise near the beginning of the frication, and excitation of $F3$ occurring later, as discussed in connection with figure 8.30. In the case of the female speaker (left side of figure 8.32), the transient onset (panel 1) has a peak at about 3100 Hz. The amplitude of the high-frequency peak in the spectrum T of the transient is about 13 dB less than the amplitude of the corresponding spectral peak in the following vowel (panel 4), and is considerably lower than predicted from the calculations in figure 8.30. Following the initial transient, there is an interval of weak frication noise (panel 2) with a broad peak in the range of 2900 to 3400 Hz and a minimum at lower frequencies. At a later time (panel 3), the frication noise increases, and there are peaks in the spectrum corresponding to both $F3$ (2200 Hz) and $F4$ (3100 Hz), with a minimum around 1000 Hz. There is general agreement with the calculations of frication noise spectra from the model, except that the amplitude of the $F4$ peak in panel 2 is weaker than expected.

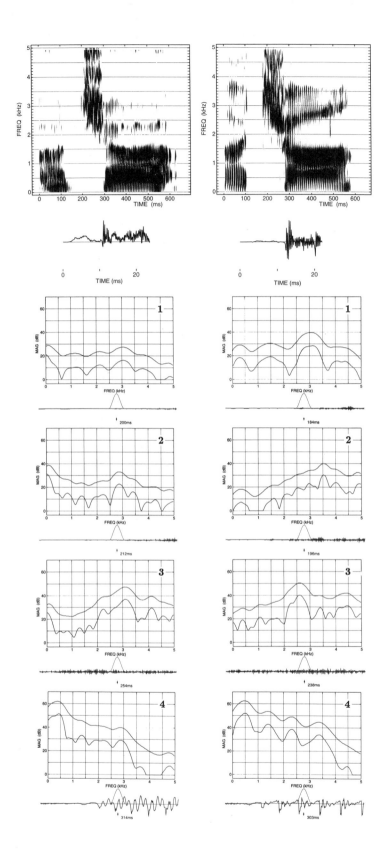

Table 8.4 Spectrum amplitude of the F4 peak at different times following the release of the affricate in syllables with initial /tʃ/ and with the vowels /ɛ ɑ ʌ/

	Measured amplitudes (dB)	Calculated amplitudes (dB)
Initial transient	−3(7)	+6
10 ms after release	−5(6)	+3
About 50 ms after release	+9(4)	+9

Note: Amplitudes are given in relation to the spectrum amplitude of the F4 peak near the beginning of the vowel. Measured values are averages for four speakers (two male, two female), and standard deviations (in parentheses) are across the 12 utterances. Calculated amplitudes are based on the model described in the text (see figure 8.30).

For the male speaker (right side of figure 8.32), the spectrum of the transient (panel 1) has a peak at about 3100 Hz, with a broad lower-frequency peak. The high-frequency peak in the F4 region has an amplitude that is a few decibels lower than the spectrum amplitude of the corresponding peak in the vowel (panel 4). The noise spectrum about 10 ms after the release (panel 2) has a peak at about 3.5 kHz with an amplitude about equal to that of the transient. At a later time in the frication noise (panel 3), a peak corresponding to F3 appears, as expected from the calculations in figure 8.30.

Measurements of the spectral properties at various points within the affricate for utterances by a number of speakers show trends similar to those in figure 8.32, but with some variation. Average values of the spectrum amplitude of the F4 peak at the times corresponding to the four panels in figure 8.32 have been obtained for four speakers (two male, two female). These data are summarized in table 8.4. The tabulated values represent the spectrum amplitude of the F4 peak in the affricate in relation to the spectrum amplitude of the corresponding peak about 20 ms after the onset of the following vowel. Average data for the affricate followed by three different vowels /ɛ ɑ ʌ/ are given, together with standard deviations. The table also shows the levels calculated from the model, as displayed in figure 8.30. There is good agreement between the predicted and measured relative amplitudes of the F4 peak later in the affricate, and the measured amplitude at this time shows relatively little variability across speakers and vowel contexts. The variability in the relative amplitude is much greater for the initial

Figure 8.32 Acoustic data for an affricate produced in the environment /ə'tʃɑ/ by a female speaker (left column) and a male speaker (right column). For each speaker, the spectrogram is shown at the top, and the acoustic waveform for the initial 20-odd milliseconds after the release is displayed below the spectrogram. The four spectra below the spectrograms are sampled at different times following the release: at the initial transient (panel 1); 10 ms following the release (panel 2); about 50 ms following the release (panel 3); and about 20 ms after the onset of the vowel (panel 4). The time window in all cases is 6.4 ms. Each spectrum (lower curve in each panel) is calculated by averaging three spectra sampled at 1-ms intervals. The upper curve is a smoothed version of the spectrum.

transient and for the frication noise 10 ms after release. Furthermore, the calculated amplitudes at these two times are too high. Some adjustment of the model is needed, probably by decreasing the rate of change of the cross-sectional area (A_1 in figure 8.27) immediately following the release.

8.2.3 Summary of Characteristics of Palatoalveolar Affricates

There is a sequence of three acoustic events following the release of a palatoalveolar affricate consonant. A transient at the instant of release is followed in the next 20-odd milliseconds by increasing turbulence noise. Both of these sources excite the cavity in front of the constriction, which usually corresponds to the fourth vocal tract resonance. As the tongue tip constriction widens, the turbulence noise also excites the vocal tract behind the constriction, leading to an additional spectral prominence corresponding to the third formant. Models have been developed to predict the relative amplitudes and spectra of these components. Some variability is expected in the articulatory and acoustic patterns for affricates produced by different speakers.

8.3 CONSONANTS WITH ASPIRATION

The production of consonants involves the formation of a constriction or obstruction in the vocal tract in some region above the glottis. The constriction or obstruction can be located at a number of different points along the vocal tract, ranging from the lips to the region of the ventricular folds or the epiglottis. In addition to the supraglottal constriction, some degree of constriction is also present at the glottis during the production of consonants (or, for that matter, of any speech sounds). The glottis can be adjusted to an abducted configuration, yielding a relatively large cross-sectional area of as much as 0.3 cm^2, it can be adjusted to an adducted configuration to produce a narrowing or closure in the glottal region, or it can assume a "modal" configuration such that there is essentially no active adjustment of the glottis relative to the state for modal glottal vibration for a vowel. These various glottal adjustments for consonants can have two kinds of consequences in the acoustic signal that is generated. Adjustment of the glottal configuration is one maneuver that influences the buildup of intraoral pressure during the time when there is a supraglottal constriction, and this pressure in turn is a factor in determining whether glottal vibration will occur and in determining some of the characteristics of turbulence noise at the supraglottal constriction. A second consequence of the glottal adjustment is evident in the sound during a sonorant interval that precedes or follows the consonantal interval.

Our aim in this section and the next is to investigate the acoustic consequences of various types of changes in the glottal configuration for consonants. We examine first (section 8.3.1) the acoustic and articulatory attributes of sounds that are produced with a spread or abducted glottal

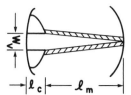

Figure 8.33 Schematization of glottal opening for an abducted glottal configuration. The glottal width at the level of the arytenoid cartilages is w_v; ℓ_m and ℓ_c are the lengths of the membranous and cartilaginous portions of the glottis.

configuration and with no significant constriction in the vocal tract above the region of the larynx. This initial study is concerned with the properties of the sound generated in the laryngeal region when there is no additional vocal tract constriction to create a pressure drop or to generate turbulence noise. Following this analysis, we turn to the effects of the various laryngeal adjustments for consonants for which there *is* a narrow constriction above the larynx. These include stop consonants produced with a spread glottal configuration (section 8.3.2). In section 8.4 we consider obstruent consonants for which the vocal folds are adjusted to give some vibration in the obstruent interval.

8.3.1 The Consonant /h/: The Transition Between Modal Voicing and Voiceless Aspiration

We consider first sounds produced with a spread glottal configuration with no significant constriction above the laryngeal region. We shall assume that the consonant is generated in intervocalic position, and that a modal glottal configuration is used to produce the vowels that precede and follow the consonant. From observation of airflow patterns and acoustic data (to be discussed later) we can estimate the approximate configuration of the glottis at the point where the glottal area is a maximum during the consonant. We have taken this maximum area to be about 0.25 cm^2.

As a starting point in estimating the properties of the sound, we shall approximate the glottal opening as shown in figure 8.33. We assume the length of the membranous part of the vocal folds to be l_m. The width of this portion gradually increases from a value close to zero at the anterior end to w_v at the vocal processes where the vocal folds attach to the arytenoid cartilages. The cartilaginous portion of the glottis is assumed to have a constant width w_v and a length of l_c. The cross-sectional area, therefore, is

$A_g = l_c w_v + \frac{1}{2} l_m w_v.$

For our analysis here, we shall take $l_m = 1.5$ cm and $l_c = 0.3$ cm, which are values typical of an adult male larynx (Hirano et al., 1981).

The assumed time course of the cross-sectional area of the glottis for an intervocalic consonant is shown in figure 8.34a. The total time taken for a

Obstruent Consonants

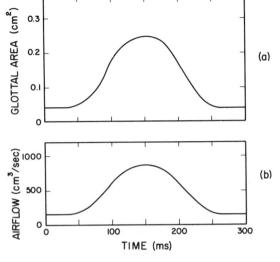

Figure 8.34 (a) Estimate of time course of glottal cross-sectional area during the production of /h/ in intervocalic position. (b) Calculated airflow corresponding to area variation in (a). A lung pressure of 8 cm H_2O is assumed. Resistance of subglottal airways is taken to be 1.5 acoustic ohms.

complete movement from modal to abducted to modal configuration is about 200 ms, and is consistent with the estimates given in section 1.3.3.1. The estimated airflow as a function of time corresponding to this opening is given in figure 8.34b, assuming a lung pressure of 8 cm H_2O. Calculation of the airflow U is based on the assumption of a linear resistance between lungs and glottis of 1.5 dyne-s-cm^{-5}, and a pressure drop across the glottis equal to

$$\Delta P = \frac{\rho U^2}{2A_g^2},$$

where A_g = glottal area. For the relatively large airflows with this glottal opening, the pressure drop in the bronchi and trachea can be significant. The airflow trace in figure 8.34b is roughly in agreement with reported airflows for /h/ in intervocalic position, that is, a peak flow of about 1000 cm^3/s and a duration of the flow peak in the range of 100 to 200 ms (Klatt et al., 1968). The duration is also in general agreement with acoustic data, as will be discussed later.

8.3.1.1 Low-Frequency Characteristics of /h/ During the time interval of modal vibration in the vowel (up to about 30 ms and beyond 260 ms in figure 8.34) the vocal folds will vibrate in such a way that the maximum glottal area during a cycle of vibration is about 0.11 cm^2 (from figure 2.5), or an average area of about 0.04 cm^2, as figure 8.34a shows. As the glottis spreads, beginning at 30 ms in figure 8.34, the anterior portion of the glottis widens less than the posterior portion, as shown in figure 8.33. The anterior portion, therefore, can be expected to continue to vibrate in more or less the same manner as it does for modal vibration. The posterior portion, however, will show quite a different vibration pattern. If the vocal processes are sufficiently abducted, the vocal folds at this posterior end of the glottis will vibrate without touching on the midline. As a consequence, the airflow through this portion of the glottis will never drop to zero, and the waveform will show no discontinuity in slope. The waveform of the volume velocity through this part of the glottis will be almost sinusoidal, that is, the first harmonic will dominate over higher harmonics. (See also discussion in section 2.1.6.2.) The process of abduction of the vocal folds at their posterior end is achieved primarily by contracting the posterior cricoarytenoid muscles. Contraction of these muscles displaces the arytenoids laterally and causes them to be tilted so that the lateral displacement of the apex is greater than that of the lower surface. This tilting results in a change in shape of the wall of the glottis, so that the glottal opening in the vertical direction tends to diverge rather than converge. As we have seen in section 2.1.5, energy from the subglottal pressure and flow cannot couple to the vocal folds to cause vibration if the glottis is diverging. Consequently it is hypothesized that there is no direct transfer of energy from the flow to aid in the maintenance of vocal fold vibration at the posterior end of the glottis. The anterior portion, however, continues to vibrate, and this vibratory movement is coupled mechanically to the posterior region to cause vibration to be maintained in that region. If there is sufficient abduction at the arytenoid cartilages, then the glottis will exhibit the diverging shape along an appreciable part of its length. Under these circumstances, vibration will cease.

In order to obtain an approximation to the pattern of airflow for these different glottal configurations, it is convenient to divide the membranous portion of the glottis in the anteroposterior dimension into two sections: an anterior section in which vibration follows a more or less modal pattern, and a posterior section in which the vocal folds do not touch during a cycle, and the airflow pattern is more or less sinusoidal. As the dimension w_v increases during the spreading maneuver, the proportion of the glottal length for which there is touching of opposite vocal folds during a cycle decreases.

Suppose, for example, that the arytenoid cartilages are abducted such that the vocal folds come together over only one-half of their length. We expect, then, that over the anterior half of the glottis we would observe modal glottal pulses of volume velocity with an amplitude equal to one-half of the amplitude that would be obtained for modal vibration along the entire length of the glottis. Vibration of the posterior half of the glottis would produce a sinusoidal waveform of volume velocity with an amplitude roughly equal to the amplitude of the first harmonic of the waveform for the anterior part. The net result is a volume velocity waveform like that shown in figure 8.35b. In the spectrum for the total waveform (figure 8.35d), the amplitude $H1$ of the first harmonic would be the same as that for modal vibration of the entire glottis, but the amplitude $H2$ of the second harmonic (and of higher

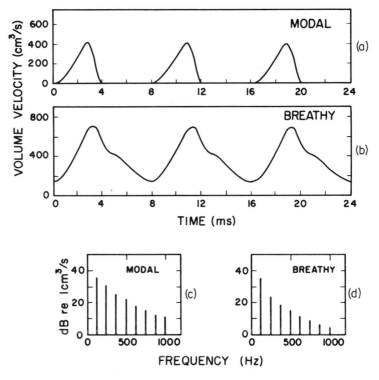

Figure 8.35 (a) and (b) Schematic representation of the waveforms and (c) and (d) spectra for modal voicing and for breathy voicing. For breathy voicing, the amplitude of the fundamental component is enhanced relative to the amplitudes of higher-frequency components. A fundamental frequency of 125 Hz is assumed. The amplitudes of the waveforms and of the spectral components are selected to be in the range observed for male voices.

harmonics) would be reduced by 6 dB relative to that for the modal condition. Figure 8.35 also displays for comparison the waveform (a) and spectrum (c) of the glottal airflow for modal vibration.

Measurements of the changes in the amplitudes of these first two harmonics at boundaries between /h/ and an adjacent vowel indicate that $H1 - H2$ changes by 8 dB or more. In terms of the simple model described here, this result would suggest that the vocal folds make contact only over about 40 percent of their length when maximum abduction is achieved during vocal fold vibration at an /h/-vowel or vowel-/h/ boundary. With respect to the plots in figure 8.34, these conditions would probably occur around 210 and 90 ms, respectively, when the average glottal area is about 0.14 cm² and the value of w_v in figure 8.33 is about 0.11 cm.

For an average glottal area of 0.14 cm², the analysis in section 3.4.6 shows an expected contribution to the $F1$ bandwidth due to the glottal opening to be about 280 Hz for a uniform vocal tract. This is three to four times the expected bandwidth for modal vibration.

Examples of waveforms and spectra in the low-frequency region in the vicinity of /h/ in intervocalic position are shown for two speakers in figure

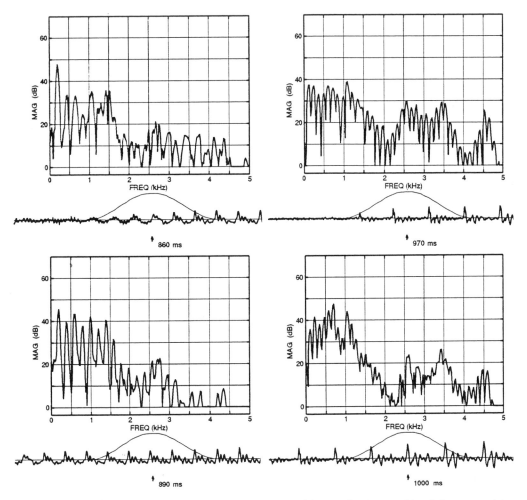

Figure 8.36 Spectra sampled near the onset of the vowel (upper panels) and about 30 ms later (lower panels) in the syllable /hɑ/ produced by two speakers: a female (left) and a male (right). Waveforms are shown below each spectrum, together with the time window over which the discrete Fourier transform is calculated.

8.36. The spectra are sampled near the onset of voicing and about 30 ms after voicing onset for the syllable /hɑ/. For present purposes, we focus on the spectral characteristics at low frequencies. For both speakers, $H1$ decreases slightly (by 1 to 2 dB) during this 30-ms time interval, whereas $H2$ increases. For the male speaker (but not apparent for the female speaker), it is evident that the bandwidth of the $F1$ peak is wider near voicing onset, where the abducted glottis gives rise to increased acoustic losses at low frequencies. The difference in the $F1$ prominence is about 10 dB for the two spectra. Displayed in figure 8.37 are plots of $H1$, $H2$, and $H1 - H2$ vs. time in the vicinity of the vowel-/h/ and /h/-vowel boundary for the utterance /ɑhɑ/ by the same two speakers. For these utterances, the time interval from first acoustic evidence of glottal abduction to the return to modal vibration is about 180 ms

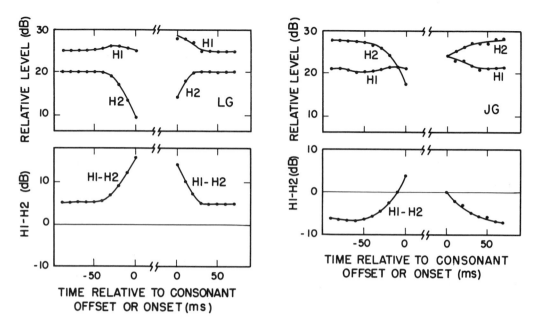

Figure 8.37 Plots of $H1, H2$, and $H1 - H2$ vs. time near the vowel offset and vowel onset for the utterance /ɑhɑ/. Data for a female speaker (left) and a male speaker (right).

for the female speaker and 260 ms for the male speaker. Examination of data of the kind given in figure 8.37 for a number of male and female speakers (Manuel and Stevens, 1989) shows that the magnitude of the change in $H1 - H2$ is 8 to 10 dB, on average, and the time over which this variation in $H1 - H2$ extends is in the range 40 to 50 ms. The difference $H1 - H2$ rarely changes by more than 15 dB without cessation of vocal fold vibration. Although the female and male speakers in figure 8.37 show similar changes in $H1 - H2$ near the boundaries, there are substantial differences in $H1 - H2$ during the vowels. For the most part, the change in $H1 - H2$ is a result of a change in $H2$, since $H1$ remains relatively constant near the boundaries.

8.3.1.2 Characteristics of Turbulence Noise at the Glottis   When the glottis is abducted or partially abducted, there is a rapid flow of air through the glottal constriction. This flow forms a jet, and the jet impinges on the walls of the vocal tract above the glottis. Figure 8.38 shows a sketch of the portion of the vocal tract over a distance of a few centimeters above the glottis. A possible shape of the jet is indicated both in midsagittal section and in lateral section, and the sketches show the jet impinging on the walls of the glottal airway. Turbulence noise generated at the walls is expected to be the dominant source of noise in the vocal tract, assuming that the supraglottal airway is not constricted in the pharyngeal or oral regions.

Figure 8.38 suggests that the noise source is located either along the surface of the epiglottis about 1.0 to 2.5 cm downstream from the glottis, or at the level of the ventricular folds, which are about 0.5 cm above the vocal

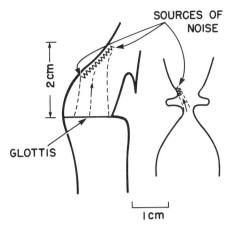

SOURCES OF NOISE

2 cm

GLOTTIS

1 cm

Figure 8.38 Schematized views of the laryngeal region in the sagittal plane (left) and in coronal section (right), indicating how airflow through the glottis might impinge on the surface of the epiglottis (left) or on the ventricular folds (right) to produce turbulence noise that is represented as a source of sound pressure.

folds. The noise source at each of these locations can be represented as a sound pressure source. As we have seen in section 2.2.3, for a configuration of this type there is also expected to be random fluctuation of the airflow through the glottis for a given fixed glottal area, and this random fluctuation constitutes a monopole source of volume velocity. The amplitudes and spectra of these noise sources can be estimated from the principles discussed in section 2.2.

As a starting point, we consider the noise generated by the airflow through the glottis during the time the vocal folds are not vibrating, say in the time interval from 100 to 200 ms in figure 8.34. We shall examine later the properties of the noise source when the vocal folds are more adducted, and vocal fold vibration occurs. From figure 8.34, the glottal opening during this time interval varies from 0.17 cm^2 to a maximum of 0.25 cm^2, and the airflow is in the range of 600 to 850 cm^3/s.

The analysis in section 2.2 shows that the amplitude of the noise source arising from turbulent airflow near a constriction is approximately proportional to $U^3 A^{-2.5}$, where U is the volume flow through the constriction and A is the cross-sectional area of the constriction. In this case, $20 \log U^3 A^{-2.5}$ is 206 dB at the midpoint in figure 8.34, and decreases by about 1 dB at 100 and 200 ms. We shall base our calculations on the maximum value, that is, a value of $20 \log U^3 A^{-2.5}$ that is 6 dB below the reference value on which figure 2.33 is based.

Since the effect of the noise source on the radiated sound is expected to be dominant in the frequency range of $F3$ or higher, we shall use as a reference the level of the noise in a frequency band centered at 2500 Hz. From figure 2.33 we determine that the average level of the sound pressure source is 28 dB re 1 dyne/cm^2 in a 300-Hz band at 2500 Hz, for the case of a maximally

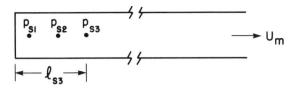

Figure 8.39 Schematic representation of dipole sources of turbulence noise at three locations in the laryngeal region downstream from the glottis. The distance ℓ_{s3} from the glottis to one of the sources is indicated. The output volume velocity U_m is shown at the right.

effective obstacle in the airstream. We subtract 6 dB to correct for the flow conditions for /h/, giving 22 dB re 1 dyne/cm^2. For the kinds of turbulence-generating surfaces in the laryngeal region, we estimate a reduction of the source level of 15 dB relative to this maximum condition, giving an effective average source level of 7 dB re 1 dyne/cm^2. A reduction of 15 dB in the level of the noise source relative to the level for a maximally effective obstacle is consistent with the data of Pastel (1987). She compared the source levels in a mechanical model in which a jet of air impinged obliquely on the smooth wall of a tube with and without an obstacle, and found that the obstacle caused an increase in the level of the noise source that ranged from 13 to 22 dB depending on the angle of the jet and on the frequency, with an average over all conditions of about 16 dB.

As we have noted above, this source of noise is probably distributed over a 2- to 3-cm region in the laryngeal area. We shall make a rough approximation of the equivalent noise source by assuming that one-third of the noise energy is located at the ventricular vocal folds (0.5 cm above the glottis), and the remaining two-thirds of the acoustic energy is generated on the epiglottis surface, distributed equally at 1.5 and 2.5 cm above the glottis. For each of these three sources, then, the effective sound pressure amplitude is $1/\sqrt{3}$ of the amplitude calculated above, that is, 2.2 dB re 1 dyne/cm^2 in a band centered at 2.5 kHz. (We assume the sources to be uncorrelated.)

For each of these three source locations, the coupling to the modes of the vocal tract is different. If we assume a uniform vocal tract, we can represent the situation schematically as in figure 8.39. In this model, the glottal end of the tube is assumed to have a high impedance—an assumption that is only an approximation, particularly at low frequencies. The frequencies of the zeros in the transfer function from source sound pressure p_s to mouth volume velocity U_m are different for each source location. If the distance from the glottis to one of the sources is ℓ_s, then the transfer function U_m/p_s has zeros at frequencies equal to $nc/2\ell_s$, where $n = 0, 1, 2, \ldots$. In figure 8.40 we show calculations of the contributions of each of these noise sources to the sound output from the vocal tract. The spectra in figure 8.40 are the spectra of the sound pressure (in 300-Hz bands) that would be obtained at a distance of 20 cm from the mouth opening except for the contribution of the poles of the system to the vocal tract transfer function. For example, the spectrum for

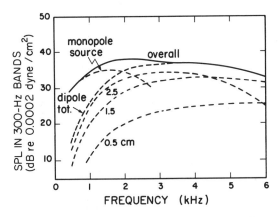

Figure 8.40 Calculated spectra (in 300-Hz bands) for various components of the turbulence noise source in the vicinity of the larynx during production of /h/. The ordinate is the sound pressure level (SPL) at a distance of 20 cm from the mouth opening, except that the all-pole component of the vocal tract transfer function is subtracted. Thus the spectra should be independent of the vocal tract configuration, assuming that the vocal tract shape does not influence the turbulence noise source or the periodic glottal source. In the case of the dipole noise sources, contributions from components at a distance of 0.5, 1.5, and 2.5 cm from the glottis are shown (dashed lines), as well as the overall spectrum obtained by adding the effects of these sources. The estimated monopole source of turbulence noise is the dominant noise source at low frequencies. The glottal airflow U (in cubic centimeters per second) and area A (in square centimeters) correspond to the values at a time of 150 ms in figure 8.34, such that $20 \log U^3 A^{-2.5} = 206$ dB.

the source p_{s2} at a distance of 1.5 cm from the glottis is obtained by the following steps:

1. The spectrum of the sound pressure source is that given in figure 2.33, adjusted in amplitude such that the level in the band centered at 2.5 kHz is 2.2 dB re 1 dyne/cm^2.

2. The transfer function from this source p_s to the volume velocity U_m at the mouth opening is the product of an all-zero transfer function $T_z(f)$ and an all-pole transfer function. The all-zero part of the transfer function is given approximately by

$$20 \log |T_z(f)| = 20 \log \left| \frac{A_m}{\rho c} \sin \left(\frac{1.5f}{c} \cdot 2\pi \right) \right| = -24.2 \, \text{dB at 2.5 kHz,}$$

where A_m is the cross-sectional area of the vocal tract, taken here to be 4 cm^2. This transfer function is added to the spectrum values in step 1.

3. To obtain the sound-pressure levels at a distance of 20 cm, we add the radiation characteristic $20 \log f \rho / (2 \times 20)$ dB, and add 74 dB so that the reference for sound pressure is 0.0002 dyne/cm^2. The result for the band centered at 2.5 kHz is 29.1 dB re 0.0002 dyne/cm^2.

To obtain the actual output spectrum from the spectra in figure 8.40 we must add an all-pole transfer function. This way of displaying the source spectra without including the all-pole part of the transfer function takes into account the locations and the spectra of the sources, and the effect of the detailed shape of the vocal tract must be superimposed on these spectra. These spectra can be compared directly with the spectrum of the periodic glottal source, as we shall see below.

In addition to showing the contribution of each of the sources, figure 8.40 gives the effective level of the combination of dipole sources. This effective overall level is obtained simply by calculating the sum of the intensities contributed by the three sources.

The monopole noise source at the glottis can be estimated from figure 2.35 in chapter 2. As shown in that figure, this source contributes acoustic energy primarily in the low- and mid-frequency regions. Making the correction for the reduced value of $U^3 A^{-2.5}$ relative to the value for the chart in figure 2.35, and adding the radiation characteristic for a distance of 20 cm, we obtain the contribution of the random monopole source shown in figure 8.40.

Finally, the total contribution of all the noise sources, before adding the effect of the all-pole component of the transfer function, is shown as the "overall" spectrum in figure 8.40. The calculations indicate that the noise sources at distances of 1.5 and 2.5 cm from the glottis (i.e., the sources on the surface of the epiglottis in figure 8.38) dominate the noise spectrum, at least in the frequency range of 3 to 5 kHz, and the source at the ventricular folds contributes little to the spectrum. It is, of course, possible that differences in anatomy in the laryngeal region could lead to a different distribution of sources.[3]

Figure 8.40 also shows that the monopole source can dominate the noise spectrum below about 2 kHz. This dominance of the contribution of the monopole source arises because the transfer function for this source has no zero at low frequencies, whereas there *is* a zero for the dipole source. In any event, the contribution of both sources to the output spectrum at low frequencies (below 2 kHz) is at least 15 dB below that of the periodic source due to glottal vibration, as we shall see.

For comparison with the overall spectrum of noise at the glottis, we plot in figure 8.41 the calculated spectrum of the sound pressure at 20 cm due to the periodic component of the glottal source. This spectrum is based on the prototype spectrum, for a male voice with a fundamental frequency of 125 Hz, given in figure 2.10. The prototype spectrum in figure 2.10 is the spectrum of the derivative of the glottal flow dU_g/dt. In order to translate this prototype spectrum into the spectrum of the radiated sound before adding the effect of an all-pole transfer function, it is necessary to add the radiation characteristic for a distance of 20 cm (in decibels), equal to $20 \log \rho/4\pi r$, and to add 74 dB to adjust for a reference sound pressure of 0.0002 dyne/cm². This correction is about -33 dB. The open circles in figure 8.41 give the amplitudes of the harmonics (every fourth harmonic is shown) with this correction. To make a direct comparison with the noise spectrum, which is based on a bandwidth of 300 Hz, we must add $10 \log 300/125 = 3.8$ dB

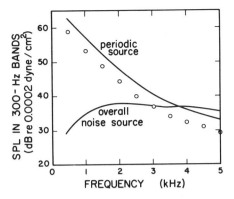

Figure 8.41 Calculated spectra of radiated sound (before adding the effect of an all-pole transfer function) due to sources of turbulence noise in the laryngeal region during /h/ and to the periodic glottal source at a time when the glottis is in a configuration for modal voicing in an adjacent vowel. For the periodic source, the solid line gives the levels in 300-Hz bands, whereas the open circles give the levels of every fourth harmonic, assuming a fundamental frequency of 125 Hz. The spectrum of the noise is in 300-Hz bands. The distance from the mouth is 20 cm. To obtain the spectra for a vowel, the all-pole component of the vocal tract transfer function must be added to these spectra. See text.

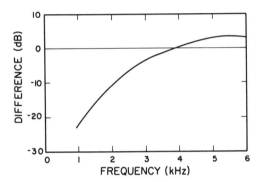

Figure 8.42 Difference (in decibels) between the calculated sound pressure level (SPL) of radiated sound resulting from turbulence noise sources in the laryngeal region for /h/ and the SPL of sound due to periodic source at the glottis during modal vibration, from figure 8.41. Both spectra are calculated in 300-Hz bands.

to the harmonic spectrum of the periodic source. This spectrum based on a 300-Hz bandwidth is also shown in figure 8.41.

At high frequencies above about 3 kHz, the contribution due to the noise sources near the glottis during /h/ can be equal to or greater than that of the periodic glottal source in the vowel, whereas at low frequencies the periodic glottal source is dominant. Plotted in figure 8.42 is the difference between the contribution to the output of (1) the noise sources (monopole and dipole) near the glottis during the consonant /h/, and (2) the periodic glottal source for modal vibration. This difference curve should be about the same independent of the vowel in an /hV/ syllable, if we assume that the vowel and

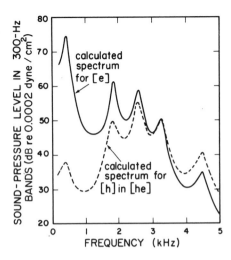

Figure 8.43 Calculated spectra when the vocal tract is in a configuration appropriate for the vowel /e/ for two source conditions: modal voicing (solid curve), and turbulence noise sources in the vicinity of the glottis with no vocal fold vibration (dashed curve). Spectra represent sound pressure levels in 300-Hz bands at a distance of 20 cm from the mouth opening. See text.

the /h/ are both produced with the same vocal tract configuration, and hence the transfer functions for both have the same poles.

In figure 8.43 we show the calculated spectrum for /h/ when the vocal tract is in a configuration appropriate for the vowel /e/. Also shown in the figure is the estimated spectrum for the vowel /e/ produced with modal glottal vibration. The spectra in figure 8.43 are calculated by adding (in decibels) an all-pole transfer function to the spectrum of the periodic source and to the "overall" spectrum in figure 8.41. (Recall that the "overall" noise spectrum in figure 8.41 already includes the effect of zeros in the transfer function from noise source to output.) The vocal tract shape is assumed to be the same for /h/ and for /e/, except that the transfer function for /h/ is given a somewhat wider bandwidth for the first formant to reflect the additional losses at the open glottis. (The upward shift in $F1$ that would be expected for /h/ as a consequence of the open glottis is not included.) The difference in level between the two spectra in figure 8.43 is the same as the difference curve in figure 8.42 since, except for the difference in bandwidth of $F1$, the formant frequencies and hence the all-pole transfer function are the same for both the vowel and the aspirated consonant.

Two examples of measured spectra for the consonant /h/ in intervocalic position are shown in figure 8.44, together with spectra sampled in the middle of the following vowel. These particular spectra are obtained by taking a discrete Fourier transform (time window = 30 ms) in the middle of the /h/ and in the vowel, and smoothing this spectrum with an effective bandwidth of about 400 Hz. Utterances from two speakers are shown: /he/ produced by a male speaker and /ho/ by a female speaker. The difference between the spectrum of /h/ and the spectrum of the vowel is large at low frequencies,

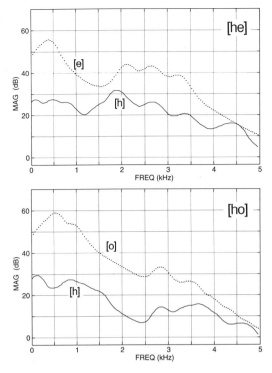

Figure 8.44 Examples of smoothed spectra sampled in /h/ (solid lines) and in the following vowel (dotted lines) for the utterances /he/ (male speaker) and /ho/ (female speaker) as indicated. Spectra were obtained by calculating a discrete Fourier transform (time window of 30 ms) and then smoothing this spectrum with a weighted frequency window of width about 400 Hz.

and is close to zero at high frequencies, as expected from the calculations in figures 8.41 and 8.42.

Another example of a comparison of the spectra of /h/ and an adjacent vowel, also for the syllable /ho/ for a different female speaker, is given in figure 8.45. The spectral peaks corresponding to $F2$, $F3$, and $F4$ on the vowel spectrum are labeled, and the corresponding peaks for the /h/ spectrum can be identified. For a number of such utterances, we have measured the difference $Ah - Av$ in the spectral amplitudes for each of the formants. One such difference—for the $F3$ peaks—is labeled in figure 8.45. Measurements were made for three different vowels /æ/, /ɑ/, and /o/, and averages (in both amplitude difference and formant frequency) were obtained separately for eight female speakers and six male speakers. The differences are plotted in figure 8.46, together with the calculated difference curve from figure 8.42.

Considerable scatter in the data points is evident, but the points generally follow the expected trend. One can have some confidence, then, in the various assumptions that were made in computing the spectra in figures 8.40 and 8.41. A number of possible reasons for the scatter of the data points can be

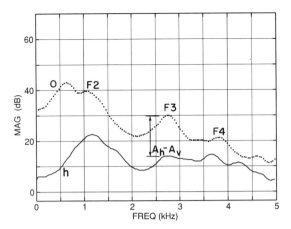

Figure 8.45 Smoothed spectra (as in figure 8.44) for an utterance /ho/ produced by a female speaker. Spectral prominences corresponding to $F2$, $F3$, and $F4$ are labeled, and the method of measuring the amplitude difference $Ah - Av$ for the $F3$ prominence is shown.

given. These include (1) different orientation of laryngeal structures, such as the epiglottis or the ventricular folds, for different vowels and speakers, leading to a turbulence noise source of different amplitude or with a location different from that assumed for the calculations; (2) possible turbulence noise sources at obstacles or constrictions in the supraglottal airways other than immediately above the glottal opening (see section 8.3.1.4 below); (3) the influence of subglottal resonances on the spectrum, as noted below; (4) variations in the spectrum of the glottal volume velocity source from one vowel to another and from one speaker to another; (5) variability as a consequence of the fact that the noise spectra are sampled over a limited region of the /h/ sound; and (6) increased losses and hence a greater bandwidth for $F2$ for /h/ than for the adjacent vowel.

8.3.1.3 Tracheal Coupling During /h/ The aspiration spectrum in figure 8.43 is calculated based on the assumption that there is a high impedance looking down into the glottis at high frequencies. At lower frequencies this impedance is simply an acoustic mass in series with a resistance. The resistance introduces additional losses, particularly for $F1$, and causes a substantial increase in the bandwidth of $F1$ relative to its bandwidth for a vowel produced with modal phonation. The acoustic mass causes a small shift upward in the frequencies of the lower formants, particularly $F1$, although this shift is not included in the calculation for figure 8.43. This assumption of a simple resistance and acoustic mass looking down into the glottis is only an approximation, but it permits an estimate to be made of the broad features of the spectrum for /h/ and for the breathy-voiced interval in a vowel adjacent to /h/.

A closer approximation to the estimated spectra for sounds with aspiration noise can be made by taking into account the impedance of the sub-

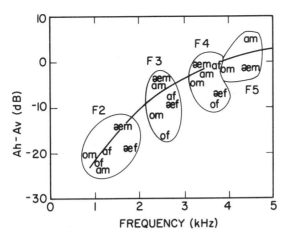

Figure 8.46 The points represent measured differences (in decibels) between the spectrum amplitude Ah of a formant peak during /h/ and the amplitude Av of the corresponding peak in the adjacent vowel in syllables consisting of /h/ plus vowel. Data are for syllables with three different vowels /o ɑ æ/ as indicated by the points. Average data are given separately for eight female speakers (f) and for six male speakers (m). The points are grouped according to formant number. Thus, for example, point om within the $F4$ contour represents the average $Ah - Av$ and the average fourth-formant frequency for the male speakers in the context of the vowel /o/. The solid line is the predicted relation between $Ah - Av$ and frequency, from figure 8.42.

glottal system. The general effect of acoustic coupling to the subglottal airways has been discussed in sections 3.6.4 and 6.8. A model for estimating the influence of the subglottal airways on the sound output when there is an aspiration noise source is given in figure 8.47. This acoustic model shows both a sound pressure source p_s and a monopole noise source U_s. The effect of the subglottal airways on the transfer function from the sound pressure noise source or from the monopole noise source to the volume velocity U_m at the mouth opening is to introduce pole-zero pairs in addition to the poles and zeros due to the vocal tract proper (Klatt and Klatt, 1990). The additional poles are the natural frequencies of the subglottal system in figure 8.47 (as modified by acoustic coupling through the glottis to the vocal tract), and the additional zeros (in the case of the sound pressure source p_s) are the frequencies for which the impedance looking upstream from the source becomes infinite.

The pole-zero pair that has the greatest effect on the spectrum for /h/ and for breathy voicing is often the one in the vicinity of the second subglottal resonance, which is in the range of 1400 to 1800 Hz for an adult. At the frequency of the lowest subglottal resonance, the losses can be large, since the resistance of the glottal opening tends to have a dominant effect on the spectrum, and the subglottal resonance may not be evident in the spectrum. For natural frequencies above the second, the greater impedance of the acoustic mass of the glottal opening diminishes the coupling to the subglottal airways, and hence causes a reduced spacing of the corresponding pole-zero

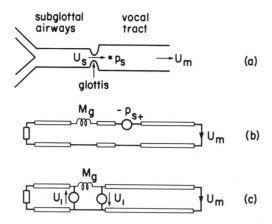

Figure 8.47 (a) Model of the airway configuration used to estimate the effect of the subglottal airways on the transfer function from a noise source near the glottis to the output volume velocity U_m. Two noise sources are shown: a monopole source U_s at the glottis and a sound pressure source p_s above the glottis. Parts (b) and (c) show equivalent circuits corresponding to two types of turbulence noise sources: (b) a sound pressure source p_s located immediately above the glottis, and (c) a volume velocity source at the glottis, represented by two sources U_1. The acoustic mass of the glottis is M_g. The glottal resistance is not shown. The vocal tract and the subglottal airways are represented as transmission lines.

pair in the transfer function and a relatively small effect on the spectrum. These effects depend, however, on the cross-sectional area of the glottal opening and on the subglottal pressure.

The frequencies and spacing of the pole and the zero depend to some extent on the natural frequencies of the vocal tract. Consider, for example, a vowel for which there is not a formant close to this second resonance of the subglottal airways, and $F2$ lies above this frequency. If we take the subglottal natural frequency to be 1400 Hz with a closed glottis, then the frequency with an open glottis will be somewhat above this frequency. (See Fant et al., 1972.) The bandwidth is estimated to be about 300 Hz for a glottal opening of 0.25 cm². From figure 8.40 we note that the monopole noise source at the glottis is dominant in the frequency range around 1400 Hz. For this source, the zero is at a frequency for which the impedance looking upstream from the glottis is infinite, that is, at the natural frequency of the subglottal system when the glottis is closed. In this case, then, the frequency of the zero is 1400 Hz. The glottal resistance does not contribute to the bandwidth of this zero, which is taken to be 200 Hz (Ishizaka et al., 1976).

The contribution of the subglottal coupling to the transfer function in the vicinity of 1400 Hz, then, is as shown in figure 8.48a. The modified spectrum for /h/ (relative to that in figure 8.43) with this pole-zero pair included is displayed in figure 8.48b. In this example, the tracheal coupling perturbs the spectrum by adding an extra resonance at about 1600 Hz, with an adjacent dip in the spectrum about 300 Hz below this frequency, as shown in figure 8.48a. The extra resonance due to tracheal coupling does not show up as an

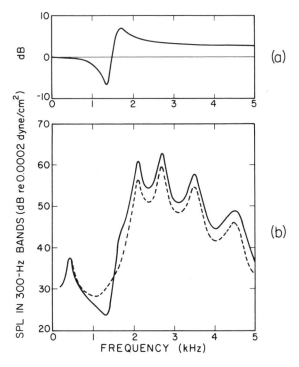

Figure 8.48 (a) Contribution to the vocal tract transfer function (ratio, in decibels, of volume velocity at the mouth to glottal volume velocity, as defined in figure 8.47c) due to acoustic coupling to the subglottal system at the second resonance of this system. See text. (b) The spectrum of /h/ in figure 8.43 is modified to take into account the acoustic coupling in the vicinity of the second tracheal resonance. Both the original spectrum (dashed line) and the modified spectrum (solid line) are shown. Other subglottal resonances would show perturbations in the spectrum at different frequencies.

additional prominence, but simply modifies the shape of the F2 prominence by adding a "shoulder" below the prominence. As noted above, considerable variability is expected in the amount by which tracheal coupling perturbs the spectrum. For example, if F2 is below the frequency of the second subglottal resonance, the pole-zero spacing is expected to be much smaller, and the pole is likely to be below the zero.

Pole-zero pairs corresponding to other subglottal resonances can sometimes be observed in spectra of /h/. Klatt and Klatt (1990) observed these effects, and have catalogued the frequencies at which the effects of the additional poles and zeros are evident. Some of their findings are summarized in table 8.5, which shows average values of the frequencies of the additional poles for a group of male and female speakers. These additional peaks were not observed clearly in all cases, however.

Examples of spectra sampled in /h/ in some /hV/ syllables are given in figure 8.49. In order to show more clearly the major spectral peaks or valleys, and to minimize fluctuations due to the noise, these are spectra averaged over a time interval of 50 to 80 ms, representing the main portion of the

Table 8.5 Estimates of median values of the frequencies (in hertz) of extra (tracheal) poles in aspiration spectra for ten female and six male talkers

	Female	Male
P1	750	—
P2	1650	1550
P3	2350	2200

Note: The lowest pole for male speakers could not be observed consistently.
From Klatt and Klatt, 1990.

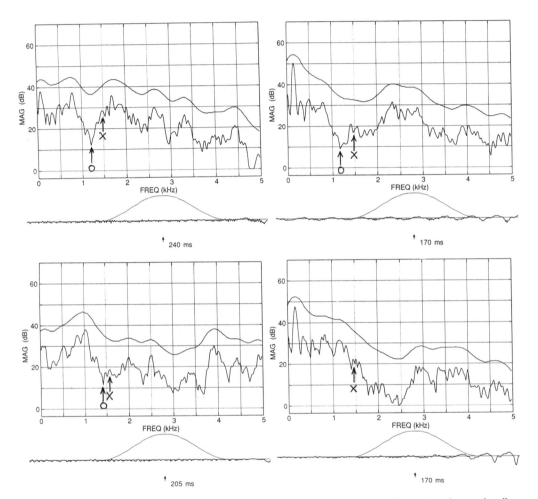

Figure 8.49 Spectra sampled in the vicinity of an /h/ in intervocalic position for a male talker (two left panels) and a female talker (right panels). The utterances represented are /ə'he/ (upper panels) and /ə'ho/ (lower panels). Each spectrum represents an average (root-mean-square) over the steady-state part of the /h/, which ranged in duration from 50 to 85 ms. The window for calculating the spectra is 30 ms. The arrows show estimated locations of zeros and poles arising from tracheal resonances.

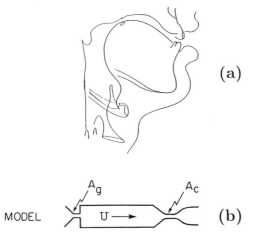

MODEL

A_g A_c

U →

(b)

Figure 8.50 (a) Midsagittal section of vocal tract for vowel /i/, showing constriction in the palatal region. (From Perkell, 1969.) (b) Schematization of the airway with two constrictions—one at the glottis, with cross-sectional area A_g, and the other in the supraglottal airway, with cross-sectional area A_c.

consonant. Arrows on the spectra mark estimates of the locations of the poles and zeros (when it is possible to make such estimates) resulting from the second subglottal resonance. In the case of the female speaker, there was some weak glottal vibration during the /h/'s, which were in intervocalic position.

8.3.1.4 Consequences of a Constriction in the Supraglottal Airway
In the above discussion of the acoustic consequences of abducting the glottis, we assumed that the vocal tract was in a relatively open vowel-like configuration. More specifically, it was assumed that the cross-sectional area of the narrowest part of the vocal tract above the glottis was significantly larger than the glottal area, so that the pressure drop across any supraglottal constriction was small compared with the pressure drop across the glottis. Negligible turbulence noise is generated at the supraglottal constriction in this situation.

For some vowel-like vocal tract configurations, the constriction formed by the tongue body or the lips is comparable to the cross-sectional area of the glottis during the production of /h/. In this case, a pressure drop appears across the supraglottal constriction, and turbulence noise is generated in the vicinity of the constriction.

We consider a configuration for which the cross-sectional area of the supraglottal constriction is A_c, the area of the glottal opening is A_g, and A_c and A_g are comparable. A typical vocal tract shape of this kind is that for the vowel /i/, shown in figure 8.50a, for which the cross-sectional area in the palatal region is about 0.3 cm^2 (Fant, 1960). This vocal tract shape with a supraglottal constriction is schematized in figure 8.50b. We will calculate the

Obstruent Consonants

relative amplitudes of the sources of turbulence noise near the glottal and supraglottal constrictions as the area A_c of the supraglottal constriction is manipulated through a range of values corresponding to the constriction sizes normally observed for vowels. We assume a fixed value of A_g of 0.25 cm^2, corresponding to the maximum glottal area in figure 8.34.

From equation (2.22), the volume velocity U is calculated from the equation

$$P_s = \frac{\rho U^2}{2}\left(\frac{1}{A_g^2} + \frac{1}{A_c^2}\right) = KU^2,$$

where P_s is the subglottal pressure, and

$$K = \frac{\rho}{2}\left(\frac{1}{A_g^2} + \frac{1}{A_c^2}\right).$$

When the volume velocity is large, it is necessary to take into account the resistance R of the airways between the lungs and the glottis. Thus the total pressure drop P_ℓ from the lung pressure to the mouth can be written

$$P_\ell = RU + KU^2,$$

where $R \cong 1.5$ dyne-s-cm^{-5}. Solution of this equation for U gives

$$U = \sqrt{\left(\frac{R}{2K}\right)^2 + \frac{P_\ell}{K}} - \frac{R}{2K}. \tag{8.1}$$

If we assume that the pressure drop in the subglottal airways is small compared with the pressure drops at the constrictions A_g and A_c, then equation (8.1) reduces to

$$U \cong \sqrt{\frac{P_\ell}{K}}\left(1 - \frac{R}{2\sqrt{KP_\ell}}\right).$$

The relative amplitudes of the turbulence noise sources near the glottis and near the supraglottal constriction are given, respectively, by $U^3 A_g^{-2.5}$ and $U^3 A_c^{-2.5}$, assuming that, for each source, the configuration of surfaces against which the air impinges is about equally effective in generating turbulence noise at the two locations. These relative amplitudes (in decibels) are plotted as a function of A_c in figure 8.51. As the supraglottal airway is narrowed, the noise generated near the supraglottal constriction increases and the noise near the glottis decreases. The amplitudes of the sources are equal when $A_c = A_g$, again assuming similar efficiency of noise generation at the two locations.

The transfer function from the sound pressure source to the mouth output is, of course, different for the two sources. As an example, we consider the high front tongue body configuration in figure 8.50a. The portion of the vocal tract anterior to the most constricted region can be modeled as in figure 8.52, and the source is assumed to be concentrated primarily in the region where the palatal contour is curved, where turbulence on the palatal

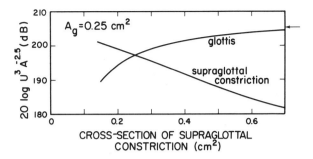

Figure 8.51 Calculation of relative levels of turbulence noise sources near the glottal and supraglottal constrictions as a function of the cross-sectional area of the supraglottal constriction. A lung pressure of 8 cm H₂O is assumed. Area of glottal opening is $A_g = 0.25$ cm². The arrow at the right gives the relative level of the source near the glottis when there is no pressure drop at the supraglottal constriction, that is, when the supraglottal airway is unconstricted.

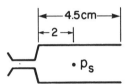

Figure 8.52 Model of the anterior part of the vocal tract when it is in the configuration for /i/ but with frication noise generated in the vicinity of the palatal constriction. The figure shows estimates of a typical location of the frication noise source p_s and the relevant dimensions.

surface is expected to be a maximum. The source is thus about 2 cm anterior to the constriction. The length of the cavity in front of the constriction is about 4.5 cm, leading to a front-cavity resonance of about 3000 Hz after correcting for the effect of the tapering and the constriction at the posterior end of the cavity. The bandwidth of this resonance is calculated to be about 300 Hz. The transfer function from the source sound pressure to the volume velocity at the mouth has a zero close to zero frequency, and a pole at the front-cavity natural frequency of 3000 Hz. (The zero is actually somewhat higher in frequency, and there will be some effect of coupling to the back cavity, but these factors will be neglected in this approximate calculation.) The effect of the zero (and of higher-frequency zeros) on the transfer function at frequency f is approximately $20 \log |(A/\rho c) \sin (2\pi df/c)|$ dB, where d is the distance from the constriction to the source location, and A is the cross-sectional area of the front cavity, estimated to be 2 cm² in this case. This approximation to the contribution of the zeros is valid for values of f that are not too close to $c/2d$, where the effect of the bandwidth of the zero must be taken into account. In the configuration considered here, $d = 2$ cm, and $c/2d = 8.8$ kHz. We are interested here in frequencies that are well below 8.8 kHz.

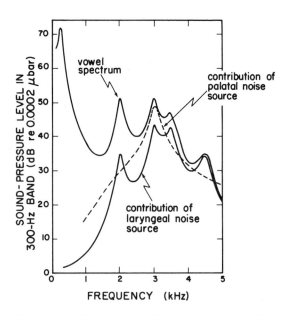

Figure 8.53 Example of calculation of contribution of frication noise to spectrum of /h/ when there is a supraglottal constriction, as in the syllable /hi/. The upper solid line curve is the estimated spectrum for an /i/-like vowel with modal vocal fold vibration. The other two spectra show the contribution to the output spectrum from (1) a source of turbulence noise (aspiration) near the glottis, and (2) a source of turbulence noise (frication) generated in the palatal region near the supraglottal constriction. See text.

We show in figure 8.53 the calculated spectra of the sound pressure at a distance of 20 cm from the mouth opening, resulting from the two sources: the aspiration source near the glottis and the frication source near the supraglottal constriction. From figure 8.51 we note that, for a supraglottal constriction of 0.3 cm², the amplitude of the source near the glottis is about 6 dB lower than it would be if there were no supraglottal constriction. The sound pressure contributed by the aspiration source, therefore, is obtained by applying an all-pole transfer function for the /i/ configuration to the "overall" noise spectrum in figure 8.41, adjusted downward by 6 dB. The sound pressure contributed by the frication source is calculated by starting with the standard turbulence noise spectrum, in figure 2.33, and adjusting it in level as indicated in figure 8.51. In this case, the value of $20 \log U^3 A_c^{-2.5}$ is 196 dB, leading to an adjustment of -16 dB relative to the reference of 212 dB for figure 2.33. An additional correction of -10 dB is made to account for the less efficient generation of noise at the palatal surface. We then apply a transfer function with the appropriate zeros and poles, as noted above, together with the radiation characteristic.

The spectra in figure 8.53 show that, at the frequency of the front-cavity resonance, which corresponds to $F3$ in this case, the contribution from noise near the supraglottal constriction dominates the spectrum. The amplitude of the spectral peak that contributed by the frication source is about 6 dB higher than that contributed by the aspiration source, and is slightly lower than the amplitude of the $F3$ prominence in the adjacent vowel. At the frequencies of $F2$ and $F5$, the effect of the aspiration noise is dominant, although the frication source does have an influence. The reason for the dominance of the contribution of the frication over the aspiration source at $F3$ is not that the amplitude of the frication source is greater than that of the aspiration source (it is actually somewhat less, as figure 8.51 shows), but rather that the magnitude of the transfer function from frication source to mouth output at the frequency of the front-cavity resonance is greater.

This example serves to illustrate that, when the cross-sectional area of the supraglottal constriction becomes comparable to the area of the glottal opening, significant turbulence noise can be generated in the vicinity of the supraglottal constriction. The contribution of this frication noise to the sound output can dominate the spectrum at frequencies corresponding to front-cavity resonances. The supraglottal constriction also causes a reduction in airflow and consequently a reduction in the amplitude of the aspiration noise source. This effect of supraglottal turbulence noise during a spread glottal configuration will be especially evident for high vowels, for which there is a narrowing in the oral cavity, and sometimes for low back vowels, for which there is a narrow constriction in the pharyngeal region.

Some examples of spectra of /h/ occurring in intervocalic position are given in figure 8.54, for the high vowel context /i/ and /u/, for which there is a narrow constriction in the oral cavity. Data are shown for a male and a female speaker, and the spectra are smoothed, as discussed earlier in connection with figure 8.44. In the case of /hi/, the amplitude of the $F3$ peak during /h/ is comparable to the corresponding peak amplitude in the following vowel, similar to the relative amplitude in the calculation of figure 8.53, indicating that turbulence noise was probably generated in the vicinity of the palatal constriction. For /hu/ it is the $F2$ peak that is dominant in the consonant, since turbulence noise near the velar constriction provides acoustic excitation for the front-cavity resonance, which corresponds to $F2$. The amplitude of the $F2$ peak for /h/ in the context of /u/ is much greater in relation to the $F2$ peak for the vowel than would be predicted from figure 8.42.

8.3.1.5 Turbulence Noise at the Glottis During Breathy and Modal Voicing The transition from the condition of maximum glottal opening for /h/ to a following vowel involves a gradual adduction of the glottis, as schematized in figure 8.34. When the vocal folds come sufficiently close together, vibration begins. During the initial few periods, the mode of vibration is breathy, with a waveform similar to that in figure 8.35b. After a few tens of milliseconds, the transition to modal vibration is probably complete, as suggested by the measurements of $H1$ and $H2$ in figure 8.37. When the vocal folds are vibrating, there is, of course, airflow through the glottis for all or part of the cycle of vibration. This airflow can result in turbulence, and con-

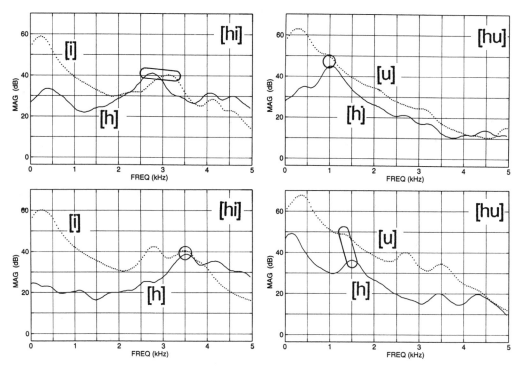

Figure 8.54 Some smoothed spectra sampled in the syllables /hi/ and /hu/. For each utterance, two spectra are shown: a spectrum sampled within /h/ (solid line) and a spectrum sampled in the following vowel (dotted line). The prominence of the $F2$ or $F3$ peak in the noise spectrum is indicated in each panel. The upper row represents a male speaker, and the lower row a female speaker.

sequently some noise will be generated; this source of sound is superimposed on the periodic volume velocity source. We turn now to an examination of the noise component of the glottal flow for modal and breathy phonation.

We consider first the turbulence noise that is generated at the glottis during modal vibration. The noise component of the flow will vary with time during the glottal cycle since the airflow U and A vary with time. The amplitude of the noise source is roughly proportional to $U^3 A^{-2.5}$, as we have seen. Since the pressure drop ΔP across the glottis is approximately constant (equal to the subglottal pressure), it is convenient to write the expression for the amplitude of the sound pressure source as

$$U^3 A^{-2.5} = \left(\frac{2}{\rho}\right)^{3/2} \Delta P^{3/2} A^{1/2}, \tag{8.2}$$

using the standard approximate relation $\Delta P = \rho U^2 / (2A^2)$, where ρ = density of air. For modal vibration, the average value of $A^{1/2}$ from the area curve in figure 2.5 (from which figure 8.35a is derived) is about 0.12 cm$^{1/2}$. Hence the mean value of $U^3 A^{-2.5}$, in decibels, is 196 dB for a subglottal pressure of

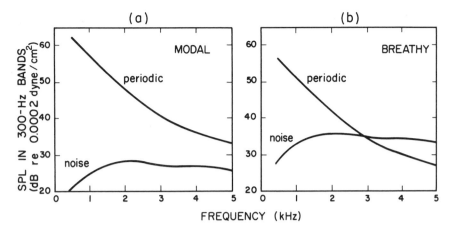

Figure 8.55 The curves in this figure represent calculated spectra of the effective periodic and noise components of the glottal source with the effect of the poles of the vocal tract transfer function subtracted out, as in figure 8.41. Noise spectra are calculated by the method shown in figure 8.40. (a) Periodic and noise components during modal glottal vibration. (b) Periodic and noise components during breathy voicing. Waveforms and periodic spectra of glottal flow are assumed to be as shown in figure 8.35. Sound pressure levels (SPL) are in 300-Hz bands at a distance of 20 cm.

8 cm H_2O. The corresponding value for mid-/h/ is 206 dB. Thus the average effective level of the noise source over a cycle of modal glottal vibration is about 10 dB below the level already calculated for /h/, and shown in figure 8.40.

Figure 8.55a shows a comparison of the calculated average noise spectrum (in 300-Hz bands) at a distance of 20 cm (excluding the all-pole transfer function from glottis to lips) and the spectrum of the periodic volume velocity source due to modal glottal vibration. The noise component is at least 10 dB below the periodic component at all frequencies up to 4 kHz, and the difference reduces to about 6 dB at 5 kHz. Substantial variation in this difference is expected from one individual to another because of differences in the anatomy and physiology of the laryngeal structures (cf. Hanson, 1995). For most speakers, however, the noise component is well below the periodic component of the glottal source.

When there is breathy voicing during the transition from /h/ to modal voicing, the waveform of the glottal volume velocity is like that in figure 8.35b. The average airflow and the average glottal area are greater than they are for modal glottal vibration, and the spectrum amplitude of the periodic volume velocity source is less than for modal vibration, at least above the frequency of the fundamental, as the spectra in figure 8.35 show. The average value of $A^{1/2}$ for the volume velocity curve in figure 8.35b is about 0.30 $cm^{1/2}$, leading to an average value of $U^3 A^{-2.5}$ (in decibels) of about 204 dB, again assuming a subglottal pressure of 8 cm H_2O. The spectrum of the noise in this transition interval, therefore, is about 2 dB less than the estimated spectrum at the midpoint of /h/. The spectrum of the periodic component for breathy voicing above the first harmonic is, however, taken to be 6 dB weaker than that for modal voicing.

The comparison of the noise spectrum and the periodic component for breathy voicing based on these calculations is shown in figure 8.55b. As before, these are spectra that would be obtained at 20 cm from the lips, before adding the all-pole component of the transfer function for the vocal tract. The figure shows that the periodic component is dominant below about 3 kHz, whereas at higher frequencies the noise component exceeds the periodic component. During this kind of breathy voicing, then, one expects to see a lack of clear harmonic components in the spectrum above the frequency of the third formant. Again, considerable variation in the periodic and the average noise components of the spectra is expected from one speaker to another (Hanson, 1995; 1997).

For both modal and breathy voicing, we have estimated the contribution of turbulence noise near the glottis, averaged over a period of glottal vibration. There will be some variation in the noise over a period as the flow and the glottal area increase and decrease. For both modes of vibration, the maximum noise during a cycle will occur about when the glottal opening is widest,[4] and this time is just before the volume velocity undergoes its maximum negative rate of change. This time of maximum negative rate of change is when the vocal tract receives maximum excitation from the periodic monopole source. The maximum amplitude of the noise source will be a few decibels above the mean amplitude as estimated in figures 8.55a and b.

The interplay of the periodic and noise components of the source is schematized in figure 8.56. This figure shows the estimated mid-frequency amplitudes (in the third-formant range) of these two source components as a function of time for /h/ in intervocalic position. During the modal-voiced regions of the vowels, the noise component is well below the periodic component. At the edges of the vowel, the noise increases and the spectrum amplitude of the periodic source decreases, so that the two amplitudes become comparable. During the /h/ the noise component dominates, and there tends to be no vocal fold vibration. Sometimes vocal fold vibration continues through the consonant, as indicated by the dashed line in the figure.

Evidence for turbulence noise at high frequencies for breathy voicing can be seen in the displays of portions of the utterance /he/ produced by a female and a male speaker, in figure 8.57. The spectra in the figure are sampled in the initial breathy-voiced part of the vowel and 30 to 40 ms later. The female speaker's data are displayed at the top and the male speaker's data at the bottom. In each case, there is a well-defined harmonic structure in the spectrum sampled later in the vowel, up to frequencies well above 3 kHz. The periodic component of the glottal source dominates the noise component in these spectra, as expected from the calculations in figure 8.55a. The

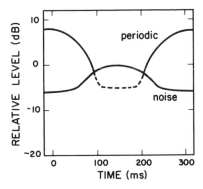

Figure 8.56 Estimates of changes in the relative amplitudes of the periodic and noise components of the spectrum in the F3 range during an utterance of /h/ in intervocalic position. The dashed line indicates an estimated amplitude of the periodic component if glottal vibration continues through the /h/.

spectrum in the initial breathy-voiced portion of the vowel shows a clear harmonic structure at low frequencies, suggesting that the periodic laryngeal source is dominant. The spectrum amplitude in the range of F3 or higher for the breathy-voiced portion is weaker by 10 dB or more than it is for the modal-voiced region. Consequently it appears that the degree of abduction for the breathy-voiced samples is greater than that on which the estimated waveforms and spectra in figures 8.35 and 8.55b are based.

Below each pair of spectra in figure 8.57, two waveforms are shown. One is the original sound pressure waveform over a 100-ms interval spanning the end of the /h/ and the first part of the vowel. The other is obtained by filtering the waveform through a bandpass filter centered on the third formant, with a bandwidth of 600 Hz. (This method of highlighting the presence of noise at higher frequencies during glottal vibration was proposed by Klatt and Klatt, 1990.) The wideband waveform shows the gradual onset of periodicity with increasing amplitude. The female speaker shows some periodicity within the /h/ (which was in intervocalic position), whereas the male speaker does not. For both speakers, there is a reasonably well-defined periodicity in the waveform for the F3 component toward the right-hand side of the display, where the glottal vibration is assumed to approximate the modal form. These are times when the right-hand spectra are sampled. Earlier in time, however, the wide-band waveform shows a well-defined periodicity, albeit with a lack of sharp discontinuities at each period, whereas the fluctuations in the F3 waveform are more random and do not show a clear synchrony with the individual periods that are evident in the full waveform. It can be concluded that turbulence noise, probably generated near the glottis, dominates the F3 waveform during this breathy-voicing portion of the sound.

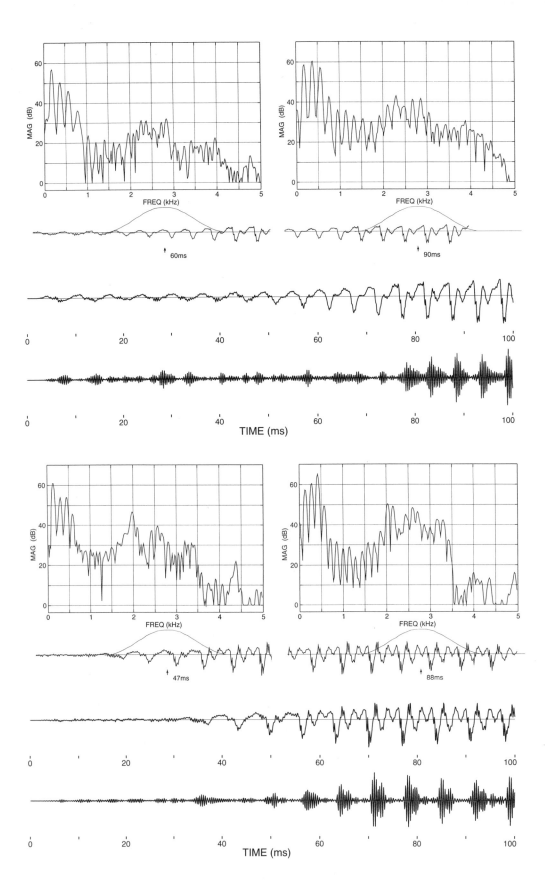

8.3.2 Voiceless Aspirated Stop Consonants

8.3.2.1 Laryngeal Movements, Airflow, and Voicing Onset In the preceding section, we examined the attributes of the sound that is generated during an /hV/ syllable. Initially the glottis is abducted, and then the vocal folds are brought together to produce modal voicing, while a relatively fixed and open vocal tract configuration is maintained. There is an initial time interval in which turbulence noise is generated near the glottis (and possibly near a supraglottal constriction), followed by an interval in which there is breathy voicing, followed in turn by modal voicing.

A similar sequence of events at the glottis can be implemented following the release of the closure for a stop consonant, to produce a voiceless aspirated stop consonant. The time course of the cross-sectional areas at the glottis and at the supraglottal constriction take the form shown in figure 8.58. The rate of change of the cross-sectional area at the supraglottal constriction is different for a labial stop consonant and for a velar stop consonant, with the rate for an alveolar consonant release expected to be in between. The rate is somewhat slower for a velar consonant, as we have seen in figure 7.6 for the unaspirated stop consonant, and there is a "bump" in the curve at the release. We have assumed that the curve representing the control of glottal area vs. time is similar for /h/ and for a voiceless unaspirated stop consonant. The actual glottal area for the stop consonant is modified somewhat from that for /h/ since the increase in intraoral pressure for the stop causes a passive abducting force on the vocal folds. Figure 8.58 shows two trajectories for the glottal opening during the closure interval: one similar to that for /h/ in figure 8.34, and the other taking into account the abducting forces due to the increased intraoral pressure (assumed to be 8 cm H_2O). The glottal area following the release will actually fall less rapidly for the velar than for the labial or alveolar, since the intraoral pressure decreases more slowly for the velar. For the present analysis, we will neglect this difference, and we will approximate the change in glottal area following the release by the dashed straight line.

There is evidence that the abducting force due to the increased intraoral pressure is counteracted by an increased stiffness of the walls of the glottis (Halle and Stevens, 1971). This increased stiffness is apparently realized by

Figure 8.57 Displays of several aspects of the acoustic signal in the vicinity of voicing onset in the syllable /he/ produced by a female speaker (top) and a male speaker (bottom). The upper panel of each section gives the spectrum (30-ms window) sampled near the onset of glottal vibration (left) and 30 to 40 ms later (right), as indicated by the waveforms immediately below the spectra. Below these waveforms is the complete waveform for about 100 ms near voicing onset. The bottom waveform in each section was obtained by passing the signal through a bandpass filter (bandwidth = 600 Hz) centered on the third formant. This waveform is less regular near voicing onset than it is later, indicating the dominance of the noise component in the glottal source.

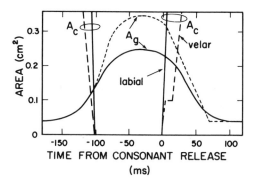

Figure 8.58 The various curves represent the assumed time variation of the cross-sectional area of the glottal opening A_g and the supraglottal constriction A_c when a voiceless aspirated stop consonant is produced in intervocalic position. In the case of the curves for A_g, the solid curve represents the trajectory A_g would have if there were no pressure increase in the mouth; it is the same A_g that was assumed for /h/, in figure 8.34. The short-dashed curve represents the actual A_g that would occur as a consequence of the abducting forces due to the increased intra-oral pressure for the stop consonant. The sloping straight line following the consonant release (from $t = 0$ to $t = 70$ ms) is an approximation to $A_g(t)$ during this time interval, and was used to determine the calculated curves in figure 8.60. The supraglottal curves $A_c(t)$ are intended to approximate the changes in cross-sectional area for a velar consonant (dashed lines) and for a labial consonant (solid lines).

contraction of the cricothyroid and vocalis muscles, but contraction of the posterior cricoarytenoid muscle, which tilts the arytenoids back, could also contribute to the increased stiffness. As a consequence of this stiffening of the vocal fold surfaces, the abducting movements of the vocal folds due to the increased intraoral pressure are somewhat smaller than they would be if there were no active stiffening in response to the pressure. Following the release of the supraglottal constriction, there is expected to be a relaxation of the increased stiffness. As will be noted in section 8.4, there is also indirect evidence for an active increase in the stiffness of the vocal tract walls as the intraoral pressure increases during the closure interval. This greater stiffness limits the expansion of the vocal tract volume in response to the increased intraoral pressure. These changes in stiffness of the vocal folds and of the vocal tract walls both have the effect of inhibiting vocal fold vibration immediately following the implosion of the consonant. At the onset of glottal vibration in the vowel immediately following the consonant release, the enhanced vocal fold stiffness results in a raised frequency of glottal vibration, which then decreases as the stiffness is relaxed.

The aerodynamic events and low-frequency acoustic characteristics at the implosion and at the release can be calculated following principles discussed in chapters 1, 2, 3, and 7. The airflows and pressures in the vocal tract can be estimated from the equivalent circuit in figure 8.59. We assume that the rates of change of the flows are sufficiently small that we can neglect the storage of kinetic energy in the flow or in the mass of the vocal tract walls. The time-varying resistances R_g and R_c are given approximately by $R_g = \rho U_g/(2A_g^2)$

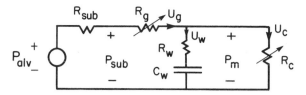

Figure 8.59 Equivalent circuit used to calculate the flows and pressures at the release of a voiceless aspirated stop consonant. Values of the elements are discussed in the text and in the legend to figure 7.4. $R_{sub} = 1.5$ acoustic ohms.

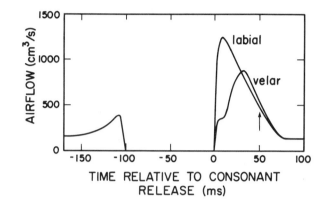

Figure 8.60 Calculated values of airflow versus time for intervocalic voiceless aspirated stop consonants, corresponding to the time variation of glottal and supraglottal areas given in figure 8.58. Calculations are based on the equivalent circuit in figure 8.59, with a subglottal pressure of 8 cm H_2O. Element values for C_w and R_w are given in the legend for figure 7.4. The estimated time of onset of vocal fold vibration is indicated by the arrow at 50 ms.

and $R_c = \rho U_c/(2A_c^2)$, where A_g and A_c are the cross-sectional areas of the glottal and supraglottal constrictions, respectively, and U_g and U_c are the corresponding airflows. During the implosion and at the release, the resistance R_c is changing rapidly, whereas R_g changes relatively slowly, in accordance with the changing glottal area in figure 8.58. Since the flows can be large, a linear resistance R_{sub} should be included in the subglottal airways between the lungs and the glottis. In the calculations to be shown below, however, we have neglected this relatively small resistance. The elements R_w and C_w represent the resistance and compliance of the vocal tract walls, as given in the legend for figure 7.4. The compliance C_w is expected to decrease somewhat during the closure interval if there is an increased stiffening of the walls.

Calculations of the average flow at the supraglottal constriction in the time intervals preceding and following the consonantal closure have been made for the two time functions representing the change in cross-sectional area for the supraglottal constriction—one corresponding roughly to labial stop consonants and the other corresponding to velars. These calculated flows $U_c(t)$ are shown in figure 8.60. The assumed time course of the change

Obstruent Consonants

in glottal area $A_g(t)$ for making these calculations is the idealized version, shown as the downward sloping straight line in figure 8.58. A subglottal pressure of 8 cm H_2O is assumed.

The calculated flow at the constriction shows a slight rise just prior to the implosion, as the glottis begins to spread in preparation for the generation of aspiration noise following the release. During the closure interval, there is, of course, no airflow at the constriction, and the intraoral pressure (not shown in figure 8.60) increases rapidly to become equal to the subglottal pressure. This increase will be more rapid than the increase in intraoral pressure estimated for the voiceless unaspirated stop consonant, in figure 7.4, since the glottis is more open and since there may be an increased stiffness of the vocal tract walls (reflected in a decreased value of C_w in figure 8.59).

Immediately following the release, the airflow increases very rapidly, particularly for the labial consonant. The peak airflow is in the range of 1000 cm^3/s, and this peak is smaller and occurs later for the velar consonant. As the airflow decreases following this peak, it is determined primarily by the area of the glottal opening. At some point during this time (indicated by the arrow), glottal vibration will begin (as discussed below), and the average flow eventually levels out at a value corresponding to modal vocal fold vibration. In the time intervals when there is glottal vibration and where there is increased flow due to an abducted glottis, we can expect a breathy mode of vocal fold vibration, of the type we have seen in a vowel adjacent to /h/ in the previous section.

Calculations of aerodynamic events immediately following the release of the stop consonants are shown in greater detail in figure 8.61. Airflow estimates are given for both the supraglottal constriction and the glottal constriction. The difference between U_c and U_g is the flow contributed by the walls of the vocal tract, which are displaced inward when the intraoral pressure decreases. In terms of the equivalent circuit in figure 8.59, this flow from the walls is the negative of the flow U_w into the acoustic compliance C_w. Because of the slower release of the constriction, the intraoral pressure drops more gradually for the velar model than for the labial model. The curves in figure 8.61 are similar in form to those in figure 7.8 for unaspirated voiceless stop consonants, except that the flows are larger and the pressure drops more slowly for the aspirated stops because of the larger glottal opening.

The time at which vocal fold vibration begins occurs when the glottal opening reaches a critical value that will permit vocal fold vibration. This critical value is estimated to be about 0.12 cm^2, as has been noted earlier (see section 2.1.5). For the assumed time course of $A_g(t)$ in figure 8.58, this critical point is reached about 50 ms after the release. A more careful analysis would show that $A_g(t)$ decreases somewhat more slowly following the release for the velar than for the labial or alveolar, since the decrease in intraoral pressure is more gradual (as figure 8.61 indicates). Thus the time at which onset of vocal fold vibration occurs is somewhat later for a velar than it is for a labial (or alveolar) voiceless aspirated stop.

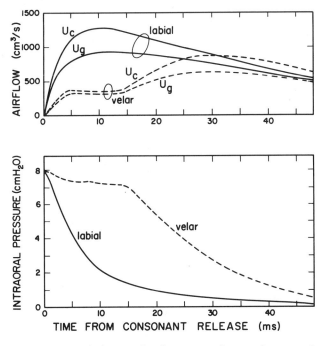

Figure 8.61 Calculations of airflow (top) and intraoral pressure (bottom) at the release of a voiceless aspirated stop consonant. Curves are shown for airflow through the supraglottal constriction (U_c) and through the glottis (U_g). Dashed lines represent estimates for velar release, and solid lines for labial release. See text.

We turn now to some examples of acoustic, aerodynamic, and physiological data that provide evidence for the time course of laryngeal and supralaryngeal movements during voiceless aspirated stop consonants. Figure 8.62 shows airflow data from utterances of the form "say /ə'CɑC/ again," where the consonant C is one of voiceless aspirated /p, t, k/ in English (Klatt et al., 1968). The peak airflow for the prestressed aspirated stop consonants is in the range of 1500 to 2000 cm³/s, that is, somewhat higher than the calculated airflow in figure 8.60. (The subglottal pressure for the experimental data may have been somewhat higher than the assumed value of 8 cm H_2O for the calculations, or the glottis may have been more abducted than the estimate of figure 8.58.) Onset of vocal fold vibration occurs 50 to 60 ms following the release of the prestressed consonant, and the airflow continues to decrease after voicing onset, indicating an interval of breathy voicing. When the consonant precedes an unstressed vowel, the airflow peak is smaller, reflecting a less abducted glottis, and there is a shorter interval of aspiration. Nevertheless, the small increase in airflow toward the end of the vowel provides evidence for an abducting glottal maneuver in anticipation of the partially aspirated consonant.

Other evidence for the time course of the glottal opening during a voiceless aspirated consonant comes from direct observations of the opening.

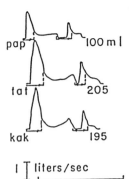

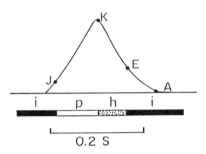

Figure 8.62 Airflow traces for portions of utterances of the form "say /hə′CɑC/ again," where C = /p, t, k/ as indicated. The traces begin during the closure interval for the initial consonant C, and end in the /g/ of the final word. The vertical dashed lines mark the times of onset of glottal vibration. The numbers to the right of each trace give the total volume of air that is expelled during the syllable, in milliliters. (From Klatt et al., 1968.)

Figure 8.63 The curve gives a measure of the glottal opening (as sensed using a photoelectric glottograph device) during the voiceless aspirated stop consonant /pʰ/ in the context /ipʰi/. The lower horizontal bar shows the regions of voicing (solid), consonant closure (open), and frication and aspiration (stippled). The labeled points are discussed in the text. (Adapted from Dixit, 1975.)

One way of making such observations is through the use of a photoelectric glottograph. The tracheal region is illuminated from a light source placed on the neck below the thyroid cartilage, and the light passing upward through the glottis is sensed with a photodiode placed into the pharyngeal region through the nose. The amount of light at the photodiode is assumed to be a measure of the glottal opening. An example of a photoelectric glottograph trace for an intervocalic voiceless aspirated stop consonant for a speaker of Hindi, taken from Dixit (1975), is shown in figure 8.63, together with markers indicating the times of voicing onset, consonant release, and voicing offset. The trace does not give an absolute measure of glottal area, but the timing of the glottal maneuver in relation to other events is in general agreement with the assumed glottal area function for the model in figure 8.58. In particular, the abducting maneuver precedes the time of voicing offset (point J), the measured function shows an abrupt change in slope at the instant of release (point K), and voicing onset (point E) occurs before the time when the adducting movement is complete (point A).

Acoustic data also provide evidence for the changes in glottal opening and state of the vocal folds. For example, figure 8.64 shows the acoustic data in the vicinity of the implosion and the release for the utterance *a pill*. Spectra sampled with a time window centered at several points along the waveform are displayed in the figure 8.64a. These spectra show a decrease in the amplitude of the second harmonic during the 30 ms prior to the offset of glottal vibration (spectra 1 to 4 in the left column of figure 8.64a), as well as a decreased prominence of the first formant peak—evidence that the glottal opening is increasing. Similar changes in the reverse order are evident in the right column of spectra (spectra 5 to 8), as the glottis closes during the first few cycles of vibration.

A plot of $H1 - H2$, the difference in amplitude of the first two harmonics, in figure 8.64c, shows a rise near the implosion and a fall after voicing onset, suggesting that, in this example, the glottal abducting movement begins 20 to 30 ms prior to the implosion, and the abducting movement toward modal vibration is complete about 20 ms after voicing onset. These times are somewhat shorter in this example than the corresponding times at voicing offset and onset for an intervocalic /h/. We note that in the 30-ms time interval from voicing onset, the amplitude of the first harmonic remains about constant, whereas the amplitudes of the second harmonic and of the peaks corresponding to $F2$, $F3$, and $F4$ all increase by 5 to 10 dB. This type of spectrum change is roughly in accord with the changes assumed for breathy voicing in figure 8.35. Figure 8.64b shows the time course of the fundamental frequency of glottal vibration immediately before voicing offset and after voicing onset for the utterance *a pill*. There is a fall in fundamental frequency of about 18 Hz in the 20 to 30 ms after onset of glottal vibration, presumably reflecting an increased vocal fold stiffness that occurs during the closure interval and carries over for a few tens of milliseconds after the consonant release. The raised fundamental frequency in a vowel immediately following a voiceless consonant has been well documented (cf. House and Fairbanks, 1953; Ohde, 1984).

8.3.2.2 Frication and Aspiration Noise

Estimates of the relative levels of turbulence noise sources at the glottal and supraglottal constrictions can be made by calculating from figures 8.58, 8.60, and 8.61 the quantity $U^3 A^{-2.5}$ as a function of time for each constriction (U = airflow and A = cross-sectional area of the constriction). The actual amplitude of the noise source in each case may need be corrected by a scale factor, depending on the configuration of the constriction and nearby obstacles or surfaces at which turbulence may be generated. Figure 8.65 shows plots of the quantity $U^3 A^{-2.5}$ in decibels for each of the release conditions (velar or labial) and constrictions (glottal and supraglottal). The sound radiated from the lips is,

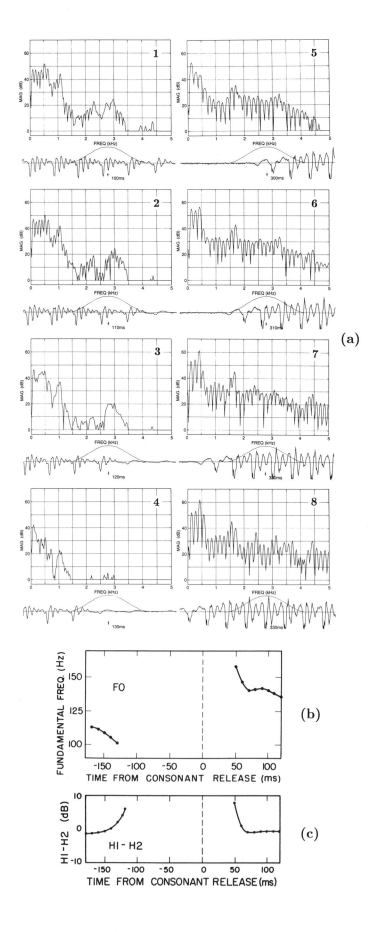

of course, the result of these noise sources filtered by appropriate transfer functions, so that the amplitudes in figure 8.65 do not necessarily reflect the relative amplitudes of the radiated sound pressure for the different places of articulation.

For both the labial and the velar cases, the noise at the supraglottal constriction increases abruptly within 1 or 2 ms after the release. For the labial consonant model, the calculations show that the noise source at the supraglottal constriction is the dominant source in the initial 6 ms, and then the noise source at the glottis becomes dominant. After about 10 ms from the release, the amplitude of the aspiration noise source remains relatively constant until the onset of vocal fold vibration (at about 50 ms, as noted above). Comparison with a similar plot for the voiceless unaspirated stop consonant in figure 7.19 shows that the peak amplitude of the frication noise source N_c is about 5 dB greater for the aspirated consonant, and the time over which this source is the dominant one is about twice as long for the aspirated stop (6 ms as opposed to 3 ms).

For the voiceless aspirated velar, the level of the source at the supraglottal constriction remains larger than the glottal noise source for the initial 25 ms. The aspiration noise then becomes dominant until voicing onset. This result can be contrasted with calculations for the voiceless unaspirated velar (see figure 7.34), for which the amplitude of the frication noise source is about 5 dB less and the frication source dominates the aspiration source for about 18 ms.

In addition to these sources of turbulence noise, an initial transient source is generated at the instant of release of the consonant. As we have seen in the analysis of voiceless unaspirated stops, this transient is a consequence of the rapid increase in airflow during the initial millisecond or so as the intraoral pressure drops but before the onset of the flow U_c resulting from U_g and U_w in figure 8.59. The amplitude of this transient depends on the initial intraoral pressure and on the rate of increase of cross-sectional area at the constriction. The method of calculating the amplitude of this transient source has been developed in sections 2.3 and 7.2.

These three types of sources that occur in sequence—transient, frication, and aspiration—form the excitation of the time-varying vocal tract, as has been schematized in figure 7.17 for a voiceless unaspirated stop consonant. The difference for the aspirated consonant is that the frication noise source is

Figure 8.64 The spectra in the upper panels (a) were sampled at several times preceding the offset (panels 1 to 4 in the left column) and following the onset of voicing (panels 5 to 8 in the right column) for the utterance a pill. Below each spectrum is the waveform and the time window (26 ms) used for obtaining the spectrum. (b) A plot of the fundamental frequency vs. time for the utterance. The vertical dashed line is the point of consonant release. (c) A plot of $H1 - H2$ vs. time for the utterance. $H1 - H2$ is the difference in amplitude (in decibels) of the first and second harmonics in the vowel spectrum. The time from -120 to 0 ms is the closure interval for the consonant.

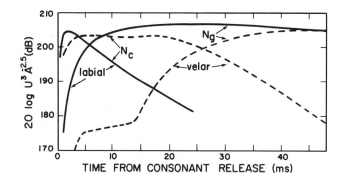

Figure 8.65 Calculations of the relative amplitudes of the turbulence noise sources following a labial release (solid lines) and a velar release (dashed lines), for voiceless aspirated stop consonants. The ordinate is $20 \log U^3 A^{-2.5}$, where U is the volume velocity through the constriction in cubic centimeters per second and A is the cross-sectional area of the constriction in square centimeters. Calculations are based on the area and airflow curves in figures 8.58 and 8.61. In each case, the amplitude of the noise source at the supraglottal constriction is labeled N_c, and at the glottal constriction is labeled N_g.

stronger, the interval of aspiration is substantially greater, and there is a slight increase in the duration of frication, relative to the values for the unaspirated consonant, for which the aspiration interval is very brief. The spectra of the radiated sound pressure for these sources for the various places of articulation for a voiceless aspirated stop consonant are, for the most part, similar to the spectra for the unaspirated stop, calculated in figure 7.18 for the labial, in figure 7.26 for the alveolar, and in figure 7.33 for the velar. There are, however, some differences. The interval of aspiration for the aspirated stop consonant extends into the time when the formants have essentially reached their steady-state values for the vowel, so that there is little further movement of the formant frequencies from the aspiration interval into the voiced interval. Furthermore, as we have seen, in the initial part of the vowel after voicing onset, the vocal folds are somewhat abducted, leading to an interval of breathy voicing. The spectral changes that occur during the latter part of the aspiration and the initial part of the voicing are similar to those for /h/, as discussed in section 8.3.1.

Figure 8.66 shows calculated spectra sampled at several phases of the CV syllable with an initial /pʰ/ followed by a neutral vowel with equally spaced formants. The figure is organized in the same way as figures 7.18, 7.26, and 7.33. The spectrum labeled V represents the calculated spectrum of a neutral vowel with formants equally spaced at 500, 1500, 2500, ... Hz, at a distance of 20 cm from the mouth opening. The spectrum T represents the initial transient, and is the same as that given earlier (see figure 7.18) for the unaspirated labial stop consonant. The frication spectrum F is also the same as that for the corresponding unaspirated stop consonant, except that it has been scaled up by 5 dB because of the greater peak airflow and hence the greater turbulence noise for the aspirated consonant (cf. figures 7.19 and 8.65

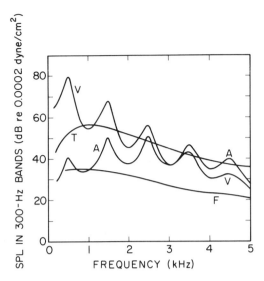

Figure 8.66 Calculated spectra of several components in the sequence of acoustic events following the release of the voiceless aspirated stop consonant /pʰ/. The ordinate is the sound pressure level (SPL) in 300-Hz bands at a distance of 20 cm from the mouth opening. The curves are labeled with letters indicating the different components following the release. T, initial transient at consonant release; F, sound due to frication noise generated at or near the consonantal constriction; A, sound due to aspiration noise generated near the glottis immediately before onset of glottal vibration; V, vowel spectrum for modal voicing. The vowel has uniformly spaced formant frequencies. See text.

for the estimated source amplitudes). The aspiration spectrum A for the aspirated consonant is different from that for the unaspirated stop in two respects: (1) the source amplitude is greater because of the different airflow and glottal area, and (2) the aspiration spectrum is calculated after the vowel formants have reached frequencies equal to those for the following neutral vowel. As we have noted, the time course of the change from spectrum T through spectra F, A, and V for the aspirated stop consonant is quite different from that for the voiceless unaspirated stop consonant.

Similar patterns of spectra could also be drawn for the voiceless aspirated stop consonants /tʰ/ and /kʰ/. The vowel spectrum and the aspiration spectrum (sampled close to the onset of glottal vibration) are essentially the same as those given in figure 8.66. The transient spectrum is the same as that shown in figures 7.26 and 7.33, and the frication spectra are also the same, except that these spectra are scaled up about 5 dB, reflecting the slightly higher airflow through the constriction because of the more open glottis.

We show in figure 8.67 detailed acoustic analyses of some examples of voiceless aspirated stop consonants in prestressed position. For each utterance, spectra are sampled at several points throughout the release, the aspiration, and the onset of vocal fold vibration.

The five spectra in the left column were obtained from an utterance of /əˈpʰɛt/. The spectrum at the top was averaged over about the first 4 ms

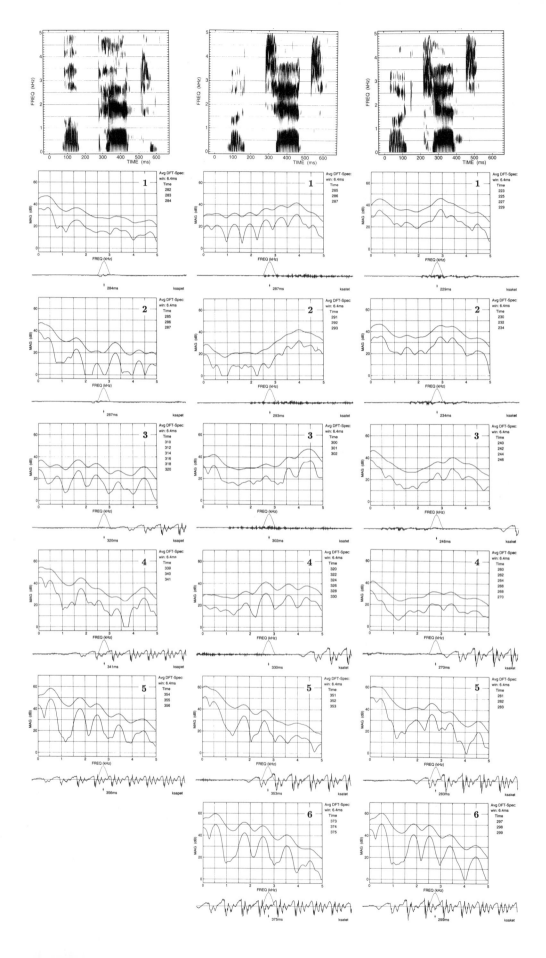

following the release, and shows the flat or falling shape that is expected for the initial transient. Relative to the amplitudes of the spectral peaks corresponding to F4 and F5 in the vowel (spectrum 5) the broad high-frequency peak in spectrum 1 is 5 to 10 dB weaker. The spectrum of the transient based on the theoretical analysis in figure 8.66 is 2 to 5 dB weaker than the F4 and F5 prominences in the vowel, whereas the predicted level of the frication burst is somewhat lower. The next spectrum (spectrum 2), averaged over about a 4-ms interval that is centered 4 ms following the release, already shows significant peaks corresponding to F2, F3, and F4, suggesting that there is some contribution from aspiration noise near the glottis. This onset of aspiration noise that dominates the spectrum after about 4 ms is roughly in agreement with the theoretical predictions in figures 8.65 and 8.66. The third spectrum was obtained by averaging over a 10-ms interval in the aspiration immediately prior to the onset of glottal vibration. Well-defined formant peaks corresponding to F2, F3, and F4 are observed, confirming that, in this region of the sound, the source is almost entirely aspiration noise near the glottis. The low-frequency peak at about 800 Hz is evidence for acoustic coupling to the subglottal system.

The fourth spectrum is centered on the first reasonably strong glottal period following the release. Well-defined formant peaks, including a peak for F1, appear in this spectrum. There is some evidence of acoustic coupling to the trachea through the partially open glottis, with spectral peaks at about 1400 and 2200 Hz. The final spectrum in this set is centered two glottal periods later, and shows the spectrum when there is modal glottal excitation. We note in this example that the amplitudes of the spectral peaks for the aspiration noise relative to those in the vowel for F2, F3, F4, and F5 are, respectively, -13, -12, -9, and 0 dB. These differences are in the range found in figure 8.46 for aspiration noise measured in /h/, although there are deviations of a few decibels from theoretical predictions.

In the case of the alveolar example (in the utterance /ə'tʰɛt/ in figure 8.67), six spectra are shown to illustrate the various acoustic events during the release. The first spectrum, covering the initial 4 ms, has a gentle peak at high frequencies, with a shape similar to the one calculated for the initial transient in figure 7.26. The next spectrum, centered 7 ms following the release, shows the shape expected for alveolar frication noise, with little evidence of midfrequency formant peaks that would indicate aspiration noise. These peaks begin to appear about 15 ms after the release (third spectrum),

Figure 8.67 Spectrograms and spectra for the utterances /ə'pʰɛt/ (left), /ə'tʰɛt/ (middle), and /ə'kʰɛt/ (right). In each case, the spectrogram is shown at the top, and spectra (time window of 6.4 ms) sampled at several times following the release are given below the spectrogram. The spectra are obtained by averaging spectra sampled at several adjacent times in the burst, aspiration, or vowel onset. The times at which these spectra were sampled are shown at the right of the displays. Two curves are shown on each spectrum display: the lower curve is the discrete Fourier transform (DFT) and the upper curve is a smoothed version of the DFT, with a smoothing window of about 400 Hz. Waveforms are shown below each spectrum. See text.

and are strongly evident 40 ms after the release (fourth spectrum). Evidently the rate of increase of cross-sectional area of the constriction for this alveolar stop is somewhat slower than the rate assumed for a labial stop in figure 8.58, so that the frication noise dominates over the aspiration noise for a longer time than would be predicted for a labial, from figure 8.65. The final two spectra for /t/ are sampled after voicing onset. The differences in the transitions of $F2$ and $F3$ for /p/ and /t/ are apparent in the aspiration noise, with $F2$ being higher after /t/ than after /p/. Comparison of spectrum 6 with spectra 1, 2, or 3 shows that the spectrum amplitude near the release of the stop consonant /t/ at high frequencies (4 kHz and above) is greater than that of the vowel in the same frequency range. This difference is in agreement with the theoretical predictions. The amplitudes of the spectral peaks in the aspiration noise in relation to those in the vowel can be determined by comparing spectra 4 and 6. The differences in the amplitudes of the peaks corresponding to $F2$, $F3$, $F4$, and $F5$ are -20, -9, -1, and $+10$ dB respectively. Except for the $F5$ peak, these are in the range observed for the aspiration noise in relation to an adjacent vowel for /h/, in figure 8.46.

Finally, spectra sampled following the release of /kʰ/ in the utterance /əˈkʰɛt/ are shown at the right of figure 8.67. The first spectrum is averaged over the initial 6 ms, and shows the prominent peak that corresponds to $F3$—the natural frequency of the cavity in front of the constriction. In spectra 2 and 3 (about 10 and 20 ms after the consonant release, respectively) we see evidence of acoustic excitation by frication noise of both $F3$ and $F4$, which are close together, and little evidence for significant aspiration noise in the form of noise excitation of $F2$ (which in this case is probably around 2 kHz). Aspiration noise appears to dominate in spectrum 4, which is sampled close to the onset of glottal vibration. The two spectra (5 and 6) sampled after voicing onset show $F2$ moving down, with some evidence of tracheal coupling in spectrum 5. The spectrum amplitude of the $F3$ peak immediately after voicing onset is comparable to that in the burst (about 36 dB in spectra 1 and 5). The amplitudes of the spectral peaks in the aspiration noise (spectrum 4) in relation to those in the vowel are slightly below the expected range, based on the theoretical and experimental analysis for velars given in figure 7.33.

When a voiceless aspirated stop consonant is followed by a high vowel, for which the cross-sectional area of the narrowest vocal tract constriction is relatively small, it is expected that the frication noise immediately following the consonant release will be followed by an interval in which turbulence noise is generated near the vocalic constriction in addition to the laryngeal region. That is, the aspiration noise is mixed with frication noise that is a consequence of turbulent airflow at the vocalic constriction, as discussed in section 8.3.1.4.

8.3.2.3 Summary of Characteristics of Voiceless Aspirated Stop Consonants
The acoustic attributes of the transient and the frication burst

that occur at the release of a voiceless aspirated stop consonant are similar to those for a voiceless unaspirated stop consonant. Measurements of these spectral properties are in agreement with theoretical predictions. The spectrum at the release of a labial stop tends to slope downward, and its high-frequency amplitude is weaker than that of the following vowel in the same frequency range. At the release of an alveolar stop, the spectrum amplitude in the $F4$ or $F5$ range is greater than that of the following vowel, due to enhancement of the transient or frication source by the resonance of the short front cavity. For a velar stop there is a midfrequency spectrum peak in the burst that is comparable in amplitude to the $F2$ or $F3$ prominence in the following vowel. The spectrum of the aspiration noise following the frication burst contains peaks corresponding to $F2$ and higher formants, which show place-dependent transitions in frequency similar to those described in chapter 7 for unaspirated stops.

Just prior to the onset of glottal vibration following an aspirated stop, the formant transitions are almost completed, and the spectrum amplitude of the aspiration noise in the high-frequency range ($F4$ and $F5$) is roughly comparable to the spectrum amplitude after the onset of glottal vibration. The first few periods of glottal vibration show breathy voicing, as illustrated by a decreased amplitude of harmonics above $H1$. There is also an increased fundamental frequency of glottal vibration in this time interval, presumably a result of increased stiffness of the vocal folds that is an attribute of these voiceless consonants.

These various attributes of the transient and burst spectrum, together with the formant transitions (particularly $F2$) in the aspiration, provide cues that identify whether the consonant is produced with the lips, the tongue blade, or the tongue body. The characteristics of the spectrum of the aspiration near the onset of glottal vibration, together with the spectrum after this onset, are cues indicating that the glottis is in a spread configuration at the time the consonant is released. While these attributes of voiceless aspirated stop consonants are observed in most tokens of these consonants, it should be emphasized that there may be considerable variability in individual tokens depending on the vowel context and on the speaker.

8.4 VOICING FOR OBSTRUENTS

For some classes of stop and fricative consonants, the transglottal pressure and the state and configuration of the vocal folds are manipulated in such a way that vocal fold vibration occurs over at least part of the interval when the vocal tract is constricted. Vocal fold vibration is, of course, possible only if a transglottal pressure is maintained, so that a positive airflow occurs through the glottis from the lungs. We examine now the articulatory and acoustic events associated with consonants of this type.

In the discussion of voiceless unaspirated stop consonants in intervocalic position, we noted that, if no active adjustments are made in the laryngeal

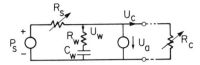

Figure 8.68 Low-frequency equivalent circuit for estimating flows and pressures in the vocal tract for voiced obstruent consonants. The volume velocity source U_a accounts for the increase in vocal tract volume due to active expansion of this volume. The resistance R_c is connected to the circuit during fricatives and after release of the consonants.

configuration or the supraglottal volume, vocal fold vibration continues for just two or three cycles following closure, with rapidly decreasing amplitude. (See figure 7.9.) During this brief interval of a few tens of milliseconds after closure, pressure in the vocal tract builds up rapidly as the vocal tract walls expand passively and the transglottal pressure decreases. If vocal fold vibration is to continue during at least a portion of the closure interval, as required for a voiced stop consonant, the volume of the vocal tract must expand so that the transglottal pressure is sufficient to maintain vibration. (Expansion of the vocal tract volume can also assist in the maintenance of vocal fold vibration during the production of a voiced fricative consonant.) A part of the expansion is achieved by an active increase in the vocal tract volume, and this increase can be represented as a source of volume velocity U_a in the equivalent circuit of figure 8.68. (This is a simplification of the circuit given in figure 1.36b.) The maximum increase in vocal tract volume that can be achieved by active expansion of the volume for an adult is probably about 10 cm³, that is, about 20 percent of the total vocal tract volume. Some of this volume expansion is obtained by lowering the larynx. This component is generated by contraction of the strap muscles that extend from the hyoid bone and the thyroid cartilage to the sternum. Another component is expansion of the pharyngeal volume, and still another contribution to the volume increase can come from raising the soft palate.

Lowering of the larynx can cause a downward tilt of the cricoid cartilage as it slides over the convex surface of the spine. As described in section 1.1.2, and as discussed by Honda et al. (1993), this tilting of the cricoid cartilage causes a shortening and hence a slackening and thickening of the vocal folds. From the data of Honda and colleagues, it appears that a downward movement of the larynx of 1 cm can increase the tilt of the cricoid cartilage by roughly 3 degrees. If this change in tilt is a consequence of curvature of the spine, then the radius of curvature of the spine necessary to cause this change would be $180/3\pi \cong 20$ cm.

Ewan and Krones (1974) have measured the position of the larynx during the production of voiced and voiceless stop consonants in intervocalic position. They showed that the larynx position is 4 to 6 mm lower for voiced than for voiceless stops. This larynx lowering should lead, then, to a shortening of the vocal folds by 2 to 3 percent. (See section 1.2.1.1.) Based on the data presented in figure 1.11 (with Young's modulus in the range for muscle

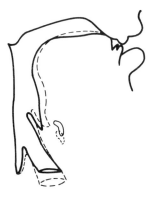

Figure 8.69 Schematic representation of midsagittal section of the vocal tract at two points in time during production of the voiced stop consonant /d/ in intervocalic position: at the time the closure for the consonant is produced (solid contour), and immediately before the consonant is released (dashed contour). The changing midsagittal contour is intended to illustrate the expansion of the vocal tract volume during the closure interval for the consonant.

and for the lamina propria with transverse force), this reduction in vocal fold length should lead to a decrease in stiffness in the range of 9 to 15 percent. If this reduced stiffness carried over into a vowel adjacent to the voiced consonant, the fundamental frequency in the vowel would be lowered by 5 to 7 percent, assuming a square root dependence on stiffness. The measured lowering in $F0$ in a vowel adjacent to a voiced stop consonant relative to $F0$ in a vowel adjacent to a voiceless stop consonant is usually somewhat greater than this, in the range of 10 to 15 percent (Ohde, 1984; Kingston and Diehl, 1994). The difference could arise because of active stiffening of the vocal folds that occurs for a voiceless stop consonant, resulting in a somewhat increased $F0$ in the adjacent vowel. A consequence of the slackened vocal fold state is that vocal fold vibration can be maintained at a reduced transglottal pressure (K. N. Stevens, 1977; Halle and Stevens, 1971), and hence vibration is likely to continue for a longer time during the consonantal interval as the intraoral pressure builds up.

In addition to the active vocal tract expansion and vocal fold slackening that occurs during a voiced consonant, there is evidence that there is a slackening of the muscles that lie near the surface of the tongue, so that there is an increased passive displacement of the surface due to the raised intraoral pressure (Svirsky et al., 1997). This passive wall displacement contributes an additional volume increase that helps to maintain glottal vibration during the consonant.

When a voiced stop or fricative consonant is in intervocalic position, then, expansion of the vocal tract volume is one method whereby vocal fold vibration is maintained in the obstruent interval following the first vowel. We shall assume that a principal mechanism for achieving this expansion is a lowering of the larynx, coupled with an advancing of the tongue root and epiglottis, as illustrated in figure 8.69. A typical forward displacement of the tongue root and of the tip of the epiglottis might be in the range of 3 to 5 mm (Perkell, 1969).

8.4.1 Voiced Unaspirated Stop Consonants

Some of the articulatory and aerodynamic consequences of these maneuvers for stop consonants are summarized in figure 8.70. Similar changes are expected for fricative consonants, although there will be some differences since airflow continues through the constricted interval for fricatives. Although the curves in figure 8.70 are somewhat schematized, they are consistent with various articulatory, aerodynamic, and acoustic data, and they are consistent with each other. In the figure, we compare parameters for a voiced unaspirated stop consonant (left side of figure) with estimated parameters for a voiceless unaspirated stop consonant (right side of figure). The curves show changes in the parameters, relative to their values for an adjacent vowel, except for the glottal flow, where the actual average flow is given in both vowel and consonant intervals. In estimating parameters for the voiceless unaspirated stop consonant, we assume some active changes are made in the stiffness of the vocal tract walls and the vocal folds, in contrast to the baseline condition in chapter 7 where no such changes were assumed.

The forward displacement of the tongue root (upper panels of figure 8.70) and epiglottis is greater for the voiced consonant than for the voiceless cognate. These data are approximations based on cineradiographic observations (Perkell, 1969). The curves are also consistent with measurements of the displacement of the tongue surface during intervocalic voiced and voiceless stop consonants (Svirsky et al., 1997), which is assumed to be similar to the displacement of the pharyngeal wall. This displacement includes both the passive response due to increased intraoral pressure and the movement resulting from active contraction of muscles inserting into the tongue root (the lower fibers of the genioglossus muscle). In the case of the voiceless consonant, the pharyngeal displacement is due entirely to a passive movement in response to the pressure increase, and it is assumed that, in addition, there is an active tensing of the pharyngeal muscles to inhibit this movement. For the voiced stop, there is an active component of pharyngeal widening in addition to the passive displacement. Following release of the consonant, it is assumed that the tongue root and epiglottis return to their preconsonantal position within a time interval of 40 to 60 ms (cf. Perkell, 1969; Svirsky et al., 1997), although the actual motion of these structures will depend on the configuration required for the following vowel.

The change in the vocal tract volume during the closure interval (second panels from the top in figure 8.70) has two components: a component due to passive expansion of the pharyngeal and oral region as the intraoral pressure increases (U_w in figure 8.68) and an active component (U_a in figure 8.68). The passive expansion is given by the product of the intraoral pressure (schematized in the third panel) and the effective acoustic compliance of the

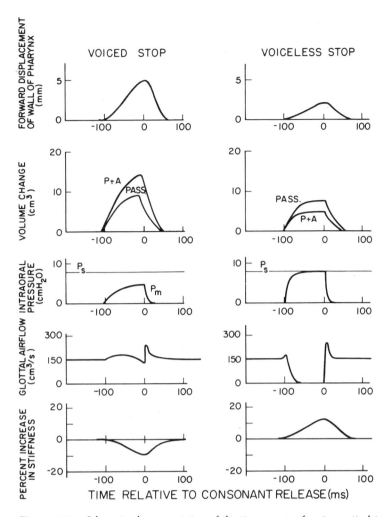

Figure 8.70 Schematized representation of the time course of various articulatory and aerodynamic parameters during the production of an intervocalic voiced stop consonant (left) and voiceless stop consonant (right), both consonants being unaspirated. The implosion of the consonant occurs at time −100 ms on the abscissa and the consonant release occurs at time zero. An intraoral pressure of 8 cm H_2O is assumed. The top panel in each column gives the forward displacement of the pharyngeal wall (data estimated from Perkell, 1969). The next panel shows the estimated change in volume of the vocal tract during the closure interval. The curves labeled PASS. give the estimated passive volume change as a consequence of the increased intraoral pressure; the curves P + A are the estimated combined volume increase due to active volume change as well as passive change. The third panel gives the intraoral pressure P_m, with the subglottal pressure indicated by the horizontal line. The fourth panel shows the estimated glottal airflow. The bottom panel gives estimates of the percent change in vocal fold stiffness, relative to the stiffness in the vowels, that occurs during the closure interval and immediately following the release.

vocal tract walls, assumed to be about 1.0×10^{-3} cm^5/dyne for a voiceless stop and about 3.0×10^{-3} cm^5/dyne for a voiced stop (from section 1.1.3). The curves in figure 8.70 show the integral of U_w and of $U_w + U_a$. For the voiced stop, the total active increase in volume during the closure is taken to be about 5 cm^3, which, when added to a passive volume increase of about 10 cm^3, leads to a total volume change of 15 cm^3. (These estimates are comparable to or slightly greater than those of Rothenberg, 1968.) In the case of the voiceless stop, we have taken the active volume increase to be negative; that is, there is an active *reduction* in volume relative to the volume increase that would occur as a consequence of passive outward displacement of the vocal tract walls. Thus the net increase in volume is somewhat less than that due to passive effects alone, and is less than that assumed in the analysis of the unaspirated stop consonant in chapter 7, where no active adjustment was considered.

The third and fourth panels in figure 8.70 show the estimated intraoral pressure and the average airflow through the glottis, assuming a subglottal pressure of 8 cm H$_2$O. The pressure builds up more slowly for the voiced stop than for the voiceless stop, and the transglottal pressure remains sufficiently large that vocal fold vibration is maintained. Airflow through the glottis continues through the closure interval of the voiced stop as the intraoral volume increases monotonically. As the intraoral pressure increases, an abducting force is created on the walls of the vocal folds, causing a passive widening of the glottis. As the closure is released, there is a peak in the glottal flow as the full subglottal pressure appears across this widened glottis. In the case of the voiceless stop there is a rapid increase in intraoral pressure following consonantal closure, and the glottal flow and glottal vibration cease quickly.

In the bottom panel of figure 8.70, we give estimates of the changes in stiffness of the vocal folds during and immediately following the consonantal release. For the voiced stop, the stiffness decreases during the closure, possibly as a consequence of the downward displacement of the larynx, as noted above. This vocal fold slackening carries over into the following vowel, causing a decreased fundamental frequency of vocal fold vibration during the initial 50 to 100 ms of the vowel. If the lowering of the larynx is about 5 mm, then, as indicated above, the decrease in lateral stiffness of the vocal folds corresponding to this change in length is roughly 12 percent, and the decrease in the frequency corresponding to this stiffness change is about 6 percent, taking into account the square-root relation between frequency and stiffness. The frequency change is expected, then, to be about 7 Hz for a male voice and about twice this for a female voice, and this lowering of the fundamental frequency would be observed in a vowel immediately following a voiced unaspirated stop consonant.

In the case of the voiceless stop consonant, an increase in stiffness is postulated, as discussed in section 8.3.2 in the analysis of the voiceless aspirated stop. This increased stiffness accounts for the increased fundamental frequency observed at the beginning of the following vowel. As noted earlier, the mechanism for achieving this increased stiffness is presumably associated with the general increased stiffness in the pharyngeal-laryngeal region that is implemented as part of the active inhibition of volume increase in response to the increased intraoral pressure. It is possible that contraction of the posterior cricoarytenoid muscle creates an arytenoid movement that contributes to this increase in stiffness, together with causing some glottal abduction (Benguerel et al., 1976). Increased stiffness could also be achieved by contraction of the cricothyroid muscle (Löfqvist et al., 1989). An increase of fundamental frequency of 5 to 10 percent at the beginning of a vowel following a voiceless obstruent consonant is not uncommon, suggesting an increased stiffness of 10 to 20 percent.

All of these changes in airflow, pressure, vocal tract volume, and vocal fold stiffness have consequences for the acoustic pattern that is observed near the implosion, during the closure interval, and near the release of a voiced intervocalic stop consonant in English. Since the glottis remains in a relatively adducted position (except for passive abducting forces), the vocal folds are slackened, and the pressure across the glottis remains in the range where vocal fold vibration is possible, the vocal folds will continue to vibrate into the interval in which the closure occurs. Glottal vibration can continue throughout the closure interval if the vocal tract volume undergoes a steady increase, and the frequency will decrease because of the reduced transglottal pressure. The amplitude of the glottal pulses during the closure interval will be weaker than it is in the vowel before and after the closure. As we have seen in chapter 3, the amplitude of the glottal pulses is roughly proportional to $\Delta P^{1.5}$, where ΔP is the transglottal pressure. The estimated intraoral pressure change for the voiced stop in figure 8.70 implies a gradually decreasing transglottal pressure and hence a gradually decreasing amplitude of the glottal pulses within the closure interval for the consonant. We note, however, that if the transglottal pressure decreases below a threshold of about 3 cm H_2O, there will be a cessation of vocal fold vibration. Since the intraoral pressure at the time of release of the consonant is somewhat less for the voiced stop than it is for the voiceless stop, the amplitude of the burst at the consonant release is expected to be somewhat weaker.

Spectrograms and spectra sampled at several points in time are shown in figure 8.71 for the consonants /b/ and /d/ in intervocalic position. The figure also gives plots of the amplitude $H1$ of the first harmonic vs. time (measured with a time window of 30 ms), the frequencies of the first two formants ($F1$ and $F2$) in the vicinity of the implosion and the release, and the fundamental frequency $F0$. During much of the closure interval, the amplitude of the first harmonic is 5 to 10 dB below the amplitude in the following vowel. If we take the amplitude of the first harmonic to be a rough measure of the amplitude of the glottal pulses, then one might expect that the ratio of the transglottal pressure during the closure interval to that in the vowel is in the range of 0.5 to 0.7 ($20 \log 0.5^{1.5} = -9$ dB and $20 \log 0.7^{1.5} = -5$ dB). In these

(a)

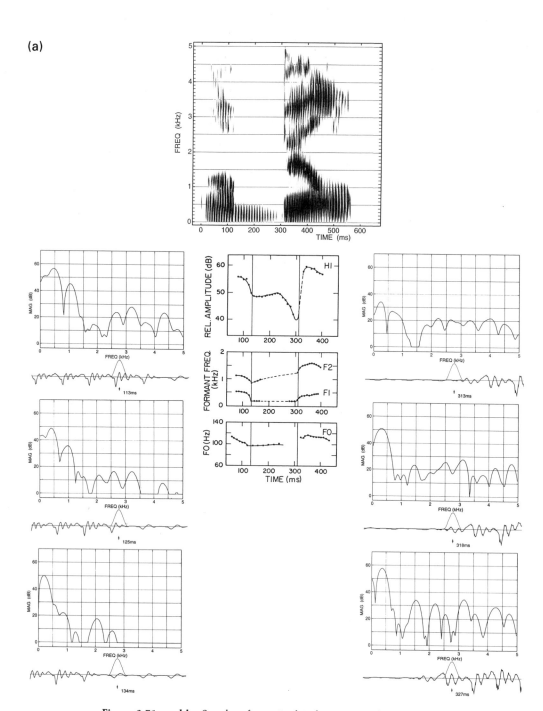

Figure 8.71a and b Samples of acoustic data for two voiced stop consonants in intervocalic position. The utterances are *a bill* (a) and *a dill* (b). The spectrogram of the utterance is displayed at the top. In the center below the spectrogram are plots of the time course of several parameters: the amplitude of the first harmonic, obtained from a discrete Fourier transform at 10-ms intervals; the frequencies of the first and second formants measured from the peaks in a 6.4-ms discrete Fourier transform centered on the initial part of each glottal period, with interpolations in the closure interval shown as dashed lines; and the fundamental frequency. The vertical lines

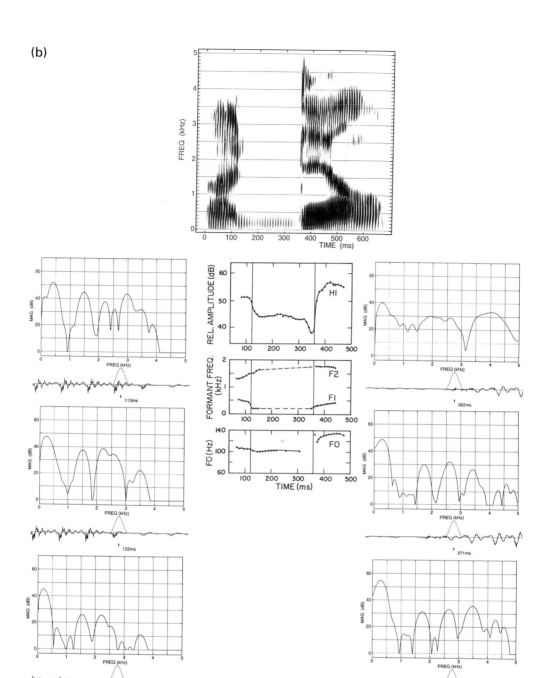

(b)

Figure 8.71 (continued)

indicate the instants of consonant closure and release, as estimated from the acoustic signal. The spectra at the left and right are sampled at times near the implosion and release respectively; they are discrete Fourier transforms with a 6.4-ms Hamming window. The waveform and the time window are shown below each spectrum.

utterances the glottal pulses decrease in amplitude still further in a 20- to 40-ms interval preceding the release, so that immediately prior to the release it is possible that the intraoral pressure becomes sufficiently small that glottal vibration is not maintained.

The first-formant frequency decreases to about 200 Hz at the implosion in a time interval of 10 to 20 ms, and increases from 200 Hz in a similar time interval at the release. The contrasting trajectories of $F2$ for the labial and alveolar are evident in the formant plots, as described in chapter 7. The spectrum of the burst in relation to the spectrum of the vowel after the initial glottal pulse shows the expected pattern for the labial and the alveolar, as discussed in chapter 7 for the voiceless unaspirated stop. That is, the burst for the alveolar consonant (upper right spectrum in figure 8.71b) has a high-frequency amplitude (around 4 kHz) that is well in excess of the high-frequency amplitude in the following vowel (lower right spectrum). The burst for the labial is much weaker at high frequencies. Just after the release, the fundamental frequency for these two utterances shows an increase of 5 to 10 percent, which is in the range predicted from the analysis in figure 8.70, and this increase occurs over a time interval of 20 to 40 ms. In both utterances, the initial glottal period following the burst is shorter than the subsequent periods, presumably as a consequence of some irregularity as the pressure drop across the glottis suddenly increases (cf. Ohde, 1984). The lowered $F0$ immediately following the release is indirect evidence that there is a decrease in vocal fold stiffness at the end of the closure interval for the consonant.

8.4.2 Voiced Aspirated Stop Consonants

The class of voiced stop consonants just described is produced with no active abduction or adduction of the vocal folds, and consequently modal vibration of the vocal folds begins very soon after the consonant release, when a pressure drop appears across the glottis. It is possible to adjust the glottal configuration so that when vibration occurs after the consonantal release it is in a breathy mode. In order to maintain vocal fold vibration during the closure interval for this type of consonant, it is necessary to expand the vocal tract volume in a manner similar to that illustrated in the top two panels in figure 8.70 for the voiced stops, although some differences are expected. At some time during the closure interval the vocal folds are abducted so that after release occurs, vibration in a breathy mode can take place. A possible pattern of change of average glottal area for this type of stop consonant in intervocalic position is displayed in the second panel of figure 8.72. A pattern similar to this, with an increase in glottal area during the latter part of the closure interval and a peak in area some time after the release, has been observed for voiced aspirated stop consonants in Hindi (Dixit, 1975; Benguerel and Bhatia, 1980). An example of a photoelectric glottograph for a Hindi speaker producing a voiced aspirated stop consonant

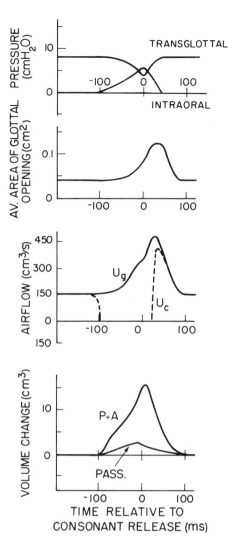

Figure 8.72 Schematized representation of the time course of various articulatory and aerodynamic parameters during the production of an intervocalic voiced aspirated stop consonant. The implosion of the consonant occurs at time −100 ms on the abscissa and the consonant release occurs at time zero. An intraoral pressure of 8 cm H$_2$O is assumed. The top panel gives the estimated intraoral and transglottal pressures. The second panel shows the estimated area of the glottal opening, and the third gives the airflows U_g and U_c at the glottis and the supraglottal constriction. The bottom panel displays the passive (PASS.) and combined passive and active (P + A) change in vocal tract volume during and immediately following the closure interval.

Obstruent Consonants

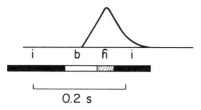

0.2 s

Figure 8.73 The curve gives a measure of the glottal opening (as sensed using a photoelectric glottograph device) during the voiced aspirated stop consonant /bh/ in the context /ibhi/, produced by a Hindi speaker. The lower horizontal bar shows the regions of voicing (solid), consonant closure (open), and frication and aspiration (stippled). (Adapted from Dixit, 1975.)

in the syllable /bhi/ is shown in figure 8.73. This glottal trace, taken from Dixit (1975), can be compared with the trace for a voiceless aspirated stop consonant, shown in figure 8.63. The onset of significant glottal abduction for the voiced aspirated consonant is later in the closure interval, and the peak occurs in the aspirated interval, after the release of the consonant.

The estimated intraoral pressure during the production of this voiced aspirated stop consonant is given in the top panel of figure 8.72, together with the transglottal pressure, assuming a subglottal pressure of 8 cm H_2O. Also shown in figure 8.72 are plots of the estimated glottal airflow U_g, the airflow U_c through the supraglottal constriction, and the volume change of the vocal tract. Since the volume expansion is relatively vigorous and the glottal configuration remains adducted during the early part of the closure interval, the intraoral pressure rises only slowly. This relatively low intraoral pressure plays a role in maintaining an adducted configuration of the glottis and in maintaining a relatively strong glottal vibration. The glottal airflow in the third panel is consistent with the transglottal pressure and the glottal area in the top two panels, through the usual relation between pressure drop, airflow, and area [equation (1.12)]. Since the intraoral pressure remains small, the passive change in volume due to this pressure is small. Consequently, the active increase in volume that must be implemented to maintain vocal fold vibration is greater than it is for the unaspirated voiced stop. The airflow U_c through the supraglottal constriction is zero during the closure interval, but the glottal airflow U_g continues as the transglottal pressure drop is maintained and as the glottis opens.

After the consonant is released, the intraoral pressure rapidly returns to zero (atmospheric pressure), although for the conditions given in figure 8.72 the change in intraoral pressure at the release is relatively small. The glottal opening is increasing rapidly at the instant of release. It is possible that, in view of this abducted glottal state, vocal fold vibration ceases for an interval of time after the release. Resumption of vocal fold vibration occurs when the glottal opening reduces to a value that will support vibration—possibly an area of 0.1 cm^2 or less.

Shown in figure 8.74 is a spectrogram of the syllable /dhɑ/ produced by a Gujarati speaker. Displayed at the right are spectra sampled at several points throughout the utterance, including the prevoicing (panel 1), the release (panel 2), the aspiration (panel 3), near the time of resumption of vocal fold vibration (panel 4), and a few tens of milliseconds after onset of voicing (panel 5). During the times when there is glottal vibration (panels 1, 4, and 5), narrow-band spectra are shown, and during the noise portions (panels 2 and 3), average spectra using a shorter time window are displayed. Also shown in the figure below the spectrogram are plots of the measured frequencies of the first and second formants during the aspiration and the initial part of glottal vibration in the vowel, and the amplitudes $A2$ and $A3$ of the spectral peaks corresponding to $F2$ and $F3$ during this same time interval.

The data for this utterance show that vocal fold vibration is maintained throughout the closure interval, and that this vibration ceases immediately following the release. A transient is observable at the release. The $F1$ trajectory shows an initial rise as the consonant is released, presumably due to glottal abduction as well as the increase in cross-sectional area of the constriction formed by the tongue blade, and both $F1$ and $F2$ decrease as the glottis is adducted near the onset of glottal vibration. Evidence for continuing adduction after onset of glottal vibration comes from a comparison of spectra at times 205 and 235 ms (panels 4 and 5) in which a decrease in the difference $H1 - H2$ can be seen. The amplitudes $A2$ and $A3$ drop immediately following the initial transient and burst of frication noise, and then increase again as the aspiration noise builds up. Glottal vibration resumes about 80 ms following the release for this utterance. The amplitude of the aspiration is unusually high for this utterance, particularly at low frequencies, and it is probable that some turbulence noise is being generated near the constriction formed by the tongue in the lower pharynx. Some variability in the acoustic pattern following the release is expected.

8.4.3   Voiced Fricative Consonants

To produce a voiced fricative consonant in intervocalic position, adjustments are made in the glottal state, the supraglottal volume, and the supraglottal constriction so that vocal fold vibration occurs over at least some portion of the constricted interval adjacent to the preceding or following vowel. That is, vocal fold vibration in the preceding vowel continues at least until the consonantal constriction is formed, and glottal vibration also occurs as the constriction is being released into the following vowel.

The series of plots in figure 8.75 gives a schematic representation of how these conditions are achieved. Panel 1 shows a typical plot of the intraoral pressure P_m during an intervocalic voiced fricative. The variation of intraoral pressure with time is similar to that shown in figure 8.70 for a voiced stop consonant. The intraoral pressure increases to a value that is somewhat less than the subglottal pressure P_s (assumed to be 8 cm H_2O), so that a pressure drop is maintained across both the glottal and the supraglottal constriction during the constricted interval. Estimates of the average cross-sectional area

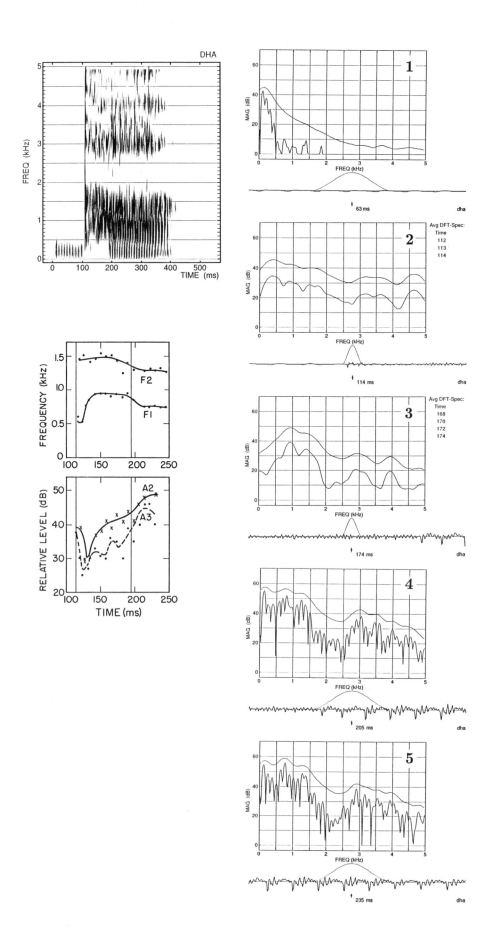

A_g of the glottal constriction and the area A_c of the supraglottal constriction are given in panels 2 and 3. Some abduction of the glottis is assumed to occur before the supraglottal constriction is formed (beginnning at about -140 ms) in order to provide sufficient airflow to generate frication noise at the supraglottal constriction. The glottis continues to abduct during the constricted interval. Part of this abduction is due to lateral forces on the vocal fold surfaces arising from the increasing intraoral pressure.

The airflow plots in panel 4 of figure 8.75 are calculated from the values of pressure and area in the first three panels. There is some difference between the glottal flow U_g and the flow U_c at the supraglottal constriction, since U_g includes the effect of the passive wall expansion. We have assumed here that there is no active expansion or contraction of the vocal tract volume. The calculated airflow U_c at the supraglottal constriction has peaks at the edges of the fricative, as has been observed in measured airflows for voiced fricatives (Klatt et al., 1968).

In panel 5 of figure 8.75 we show the estimated time variation of the amplitude of the turbulence noise at the supraglottal constriction. The estimate is based on the model given in section 2.2, indicating that the amplitude of turbulence noise at a constriction is proportional to $\Delta P^{1.5} A_c^{0.5}$, where ΔP is the pressure drop and A_c is the cross-sectional area of the constriction. The noise amplitude shows an asymmetry, with the noise being weaker near the beginning of the constricted interval, and then reaching a steady value in the last half of the interval. Below this panel is a plot of the estimated amplitude of the glottal pulses. This amplitude is assumed to be proportional to the three-halves power of the pressure drop $\Delta P = P_s - P_m$, and it is plotted in decibels.

The shapes of the various plots in figure 8.75 are, of course, dependent on many factors, and the trajectories in the figure are intended to show trends and to indicate the relations between the various pressures, flows, noise sources, and cross-sectional areas. Panel 6 of the figure shows glottal vibration continuing throughout the constriction, with a decrease in amplitude of about 10 dB toward the end of the consonantal interval. For a small modification of the conditions depicted in figure 8.75, such as a slightly smaller A_c during the constriction, it is possible that after the first half of the fricative the transglottal pressure would drop below the value for which vibration

Figure 8.74 Acoustic data from the syllable /dha/ produced by an adult male Bengali speaker. The spectrogram is displayed at the top left. To the right of the spectrogram are spectra sampled at five points throughout the utterance: (1) in the prevoicing, (2) at the consonant release, (3) during the aspiration, (4) near the onset of glottal vibration, and (5) 30 ms after spectrum 4. Different time windows were used to calculate the spectra, as shown on the waveforms, and in the case of (2) and (3) the spectra are averages over the times indicated beside the spectra. Also shown (below the spectrogram) are plots of the first- and second-formant frequencies vs. time and the amplitudes of the peaks in the F2 and F3 regions, for the time interval following the consonant release. The vertical lines indicate the times of release and of onset of glottal vibration.

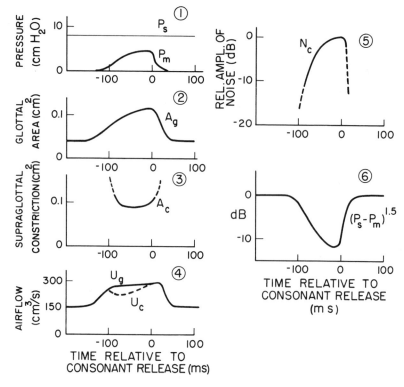

Figure 8.75 Schematized representation of the time course of various articulatory, aerodynamic, and acoustic parameters during the production of an intervocalic voiced fricative consonant. Panel 1 is the estimated intraoral pressure P_m, and shows the (constant) subglottal pressure P_s. The estimated average glottal area and the area of the supraglottal constriction are given in panels 2 and 3. The glottal area is an average over the vibration cycle during times the vocal folds are vibrating. The fourth panel gives the estimated airflow at the glottis (U_g) and at the supraglottal constriction (U_c). The difference is due to the changing volume of the vocal tract. Panel 5 is the estimated time course of the amplitude of the noise source at the supraglottal constriction, calculated from $20 \log (\Delta P^{1.5} A_c^{0.5})$, where ΔP is the intraoral pressure and A_c is the cross-sectional area of the constriction. Panel 6 gives an estimate of the amplitude of glottal vibration, assumed to be proportional to $(P_s - P_m)^{1.5}$.

could be sustained with the somewhat abducted configuration indicated in panel 2. Measurements of a number of intervocalic voiced fricatives in English have shown that glottal vibration ceases at some time during the consonant in 15 to 35 percent of such fricatives (Haggard, 1978; K. N. Stevens et al., 1992).

Acoustic data for a voiced fricative in intervocalic position are given in figure 8.76. The figure shows a spectrogram (the utterance is *a zip*), together with spectra sampled at selected points within the utterance, and plots of the amplitude of the first harmonic, the amplitude of the frication noise at high frequencies, the time course of $F1$, the difference $H1 - H2$ between the amplitudes of the first and second harmonics, and the fundamental frequency. To permit a direct comparison of the voiced fricative with the voiceless cognate, data for the utterance *a sip* are displayed in figure 8.77. The spectrogram is shown, as well as the same five parameters that are plotted in figure 8.76.

In the voiced fricative (see figure 8.76), the first formant falls to about 200 Hz at the VC boundary, and rises from this frequency at the release. The rate of movement of $F1$ is somewhat slower than it is at the implosion or release of a voiced stop consonant. (The rate of change of A_c in figure 8.2 at the edges of the fricative is much slower than the rate of change of about 50 cm^2/s assumed in chapter 7 for alveolar stops. This rate of change of constriction size is a determining factor for the rate of movement of $F1$.) For the voiceless fricative (third panel in the left column of figure 8.77) the first formant decreases very little at the implosion, and begins relatively high at the release, as has been seen in section 8.1. Glottal vibration ends earlier and begins later, and consequently the decreased $F1$ associated with formation of the constriction is not evident in the sound.

The amplitude of the first harmonic ($H1$) in figure 8.76 shows a slight increase as the fricative is approached during the first vowel, presumably as a consequence of a decreasing first-formant frequency. There is then a decrease in $H1$ as the constriction is formed (signaled by the drop in $F1$), and $H1$ continues to decrease throughout the fricative. In this utterance, $H1$ decreases by 10 dB in about 50 ms following the formation of the constriction. This decrease is not inconsistent with a decrease of about 50 percent in transglottal pressure (assuming the amplitude of the glottal pulses is proportional to $\Delta P^{1.5}$), as suggested by the top left panel and the bottom right panel of figure 8.75. The first-harmonic amplitude continues to decrease to the point where glottal vibration is no longer visible in the waveform. In the case of the voiceless fricative, $H1$ remains constant until glottal vibration ends, and it begins at full amplitude at the onset of glottal vibration.

The noise amplitude in the voiced fricative (defined here as the peak spectrum amplitude in the frequency range of 3.5 to 5.0 kHz) increases gradually during the initial 50 ms of the fricative, and then reaches a relatively stable value over the last part of the fricative. This increased noise amplitude later in the constricted interval is presumably a consequence of the increased pressure across the constriction as the transglottal pressure decreases. The noise amplitude begins to decrease just prior to the onset of the full glottal amplitude in the following vowel. In the voiceless fricative (second panel under the spectrogram in figure 8.77) the noise amplitude remains relatively constant, with a slight dip in the middle of the consonantal interval.

Near the end of the vowel preceding the fricative, the harmonic difference $H1 - H2$ increases for both the voiced and the voiceless consonants, indicating some abduction of the glottis in preparation for the fricative. The increase at the end of the vowel is greater, however, for the voiceless fricative, reflecting the greater glottal abduction in anticipation of the voiceless interval. For the voiced fricative, this harmonic difference drops rather abruptly at the onset of vocal fold vibration, suggesting that the glottal

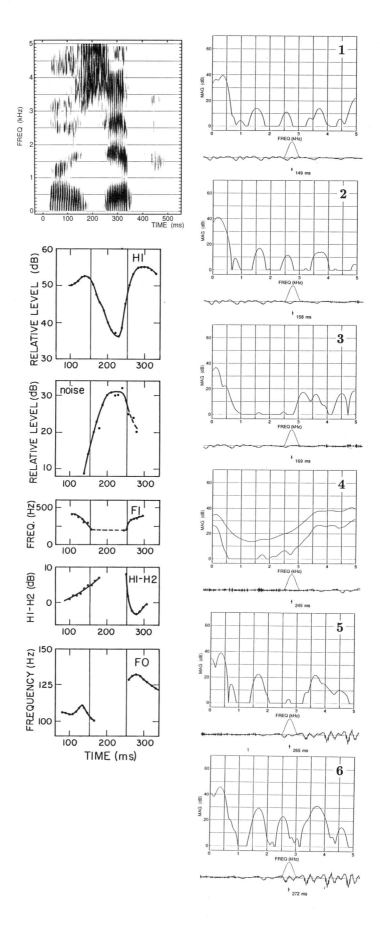

opening returns to a more adducted configuration rather rapidly following release of the constriction, similar to the estimate of A_g in figure 8.75. The fundamental frequency near the beginning of the second vowel shows a rise in the case of the voiced consonant, similar to that observed for the voiced stop. The $F0$ parameter starts high following the voiceless consonant, suggesting that there is a stiffening of the vocal folds during the voiceless interval, as discussed in connection with figure 8.70 for voiceless stop consonants.

8.4.4 Summary of Characteristics of Voiced Obstruent Consonants

During the closure or constricted interval for an obstruent consonant, there is a pressure buildup behind the constriction, and consequently a reduced pressure drop across the glottis. The increased supraglottal pressure creates an outward force on the walls of the vocal tract as well as on the surfaces of the glottis. To produce a voiced obstruent, the speaker can facilitate vocal fold vibration during the consonantal interval by decreasing the stiffness of the vocal tract walls and of the vocal folds. Decreasing the stiffness of the walls allows the vocal tract volume to expand more readily, and therefore delays the buildup of pressure behind the consonantal constriction. There is a delay, then, in the decrease in transglottal pressure, with the result that the vocal folds can continue to vibrate. When the vocal folds are slackened, vibration is possible at a reduced transglottal pressure. The maintenance of a transglottal pressure is also enhanced by active expansion of the vocal tract volume, in part by lowering the larynx. Lowering the larynx has the further effect of tilting the cricoid cartilage in relation to the thyroid cartilage, thereby decreasing the vocal fold stiffness. Thus several factors can combine to facilitate vocal fold vibration during voiced obstruents. To generate a voiceless obstruent, a speaker can inhibit glottal vibration during the consonantal interval by increasing the stiffness of the vocal tract walls and of the vocal folds, and by actively preventing the vocal tract volume from expanding. These maneuvers will cause the intraoral pressure to increase rapidly, and the consequent reduction in transglottal pressure will lead to cessation of vocal fold vibration. This inhibition of glottal vibration can be enhanced

Figure 8.76 Samples of acoustic data for the intervocalic voiced fricative consonant /z/ in the utterance *a zip*. The spectrogram of the utterance is shown at the top left, and below this are: $H1$, the amplitude of the first harmonic, measured as in figure 8.71; "noise," the amplitude of the frication noise, taken to be the peak spectrum amplitude (6.4-ms window) in the frequency range of 3.5 to 5 kHz; $F1$, the first formant frequency, measured as in figure 8.71; the difference $H1 - H2$ between the amplitudes (in decibels) of the first and second harmonics; and $F0$, the fundamental frequency. The vertical lines are estimates of the points where intraoral pressure begins to build up and where the pressure begins to decrease, based on examination of the acoustic record. Spectra at selected points near the left and right boundaries of the fricative are displayed at the right, together with waveforms and time windows (6.4-ms duration). The noise spectrum (panel 4) was obtained by averaging spectra over a 55-ms time interval. All other spectra were calculated with a single time window.

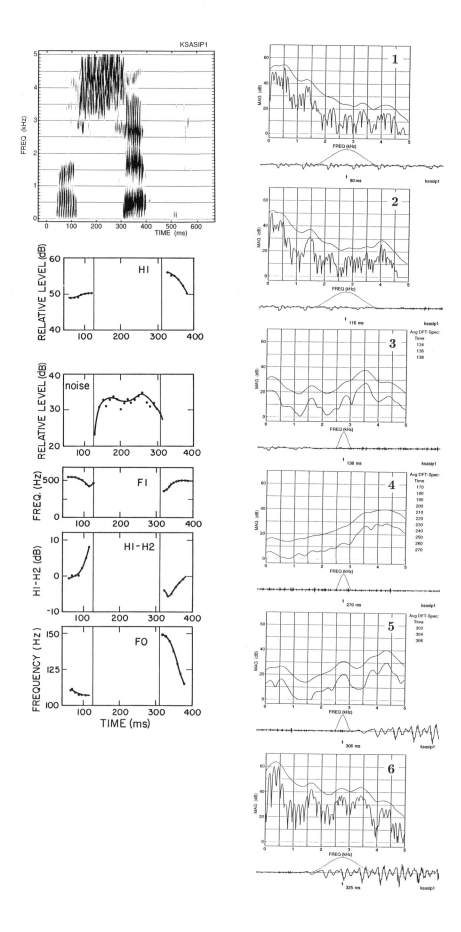

by actively spreading the glottis (and also by actively constricting the glottis). The increase or decrease in vocal fold stiffness that is implemented for a voiceless or voiced obstruent is reflected in an increase or decrease in the frequency of glottal vibration in the first few tens of milliseconds of the vowel following the obstruent.

Models of the production of voiced and voiceless obstruent consonants incorporate parameters to account for all of these factors: active changes in the stiffness of the vocal tract walls and of the vocal folds, and active modification of the vocal tract volume, including raising and lowering of the larynx with consequent modification of vocal fold stiffness. The models proposed in this section have attempted to quantify these parameters.

Figure 8.77 Samples of acoustic data for the intervocalic voiceless fricative /s/ in the utterance *a sip*, for comparison with the voiced fricative in figure 8.76. The same adult male speaker produced both utterances. The various plots in the left column of this figure parallel the plots given in figure 8.76. Spectra 1, 2, and 6 were calculated with a time window of 26 ms to show the relative amplitudes of the harmonics immediately before the offset of glottal vibration and immediately following the onset of voicing. Panels 3, 4, and 5 show spectra averaged over a time interval near the onset of frication (spectrum 3), in the middle of the fricative (spectrum 4), and near the end of the fricative (spectrum 5). Peaks corresponding to *F2* and *F3* are evident at the edges of the fricative.

9 Sonorant Consonants

9.1 NASAL CONSONANTS

9.1.1 Articulatory Description

Like the stop consonants described in chapter 7, nasal consonants are produced by forming a complete closure at some point along the length of the oral region of the vocal tract. Thus the changes in the cross-sectional area of the supraglottal constriction and in other aspects of the supraglottal configuration such as the tongue body follow trajectories similar to those shown in figure 7.1 for stop consonants. The principal difference, however, is that for a nasal consonant the velopharyngeal port is open during the time there is a supraglottal closure, and there is no pressure increase behind the constriction. In figure 9.1 the location of the velopharyngeal port is shown in the midsagittal configuration of the vocal tract for labial and alveolar nasal consonants. The context in which each consonant is produced is given in the figure legend.

The time course of the cross-sectional area of the velopharyngeal opening in relation to the supraglottal closure for an intervocalic nasal consonant is shown schematically in figure 9.2. The peak value of 0.2 cm^2 shown for the velopharyngeal area is an estimate, since there appear to be no quantitative data on the value of this area for nasal consonants. The value is based on inferences from acoustic data and from measurements showing only a very small increase in intraoral pressure relative to atmospheric pressure (less than 1 cm H$_2$O) for a nasal consonant. The total time from the beginning to the end of the lowering-raising movement of the soft palate is expected to be 200 to 250 ms, as discussed in section 1.3.3. The time that the velopharyngeal port is actually open would be somewhat less than this. This time is taken to be about 200 ms in figure 9.2. The schematization of the time course of the velopharyngeal opening in figure 9.2 is based on what is known about the timing of this gesture in a typical utterance in English, although the times of opening and closing depend to some extent on the syllable affiliation of the nasal consonant (Krakow, 1993). Different timing of the velopharyngeal area in relation to the consonant closure and release

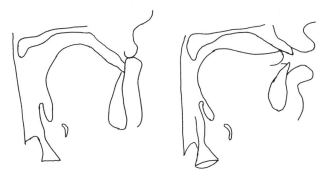

Figure 9.1 Midsagittal sections through the vocal tract during the production of nasal consonants produced by closing the lips (left) and raising the tongue tip to the alveolar ridge (right). For the labial consonant, the context is "*Mets tes beaux habits,*" and for the alveolar consonant the context is "*Une réponse ....*" (Adapted from Bothorel et al., 1986.)

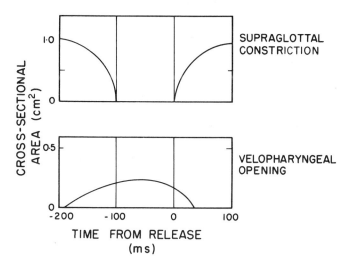

Figure 9.2 Schematization of the time course of the cross-sectional area of the oral constriction (upper panel) and of the velopharyngeal opening (lower panel) during production of a nasal consonant in intervocalic position. The detailed shapes of these trajectories depend on the place of articulation for the consonant and for the adjacent sounds.

might be expected in other languages, and some variability in the timing will certainly occur among speakers of a given language. Since the average pressure above the glottis remains near atmospheric pressure, and if the vocal folds remain in a configuration for modal voicing during the time when there is closure in the oral cavity, the folds will continue to vibrate in a normal manner during this interval. This time in which there is closure of the oral cavity with continuing vocal fold vibration is called the nasal murmur.

As in the case of stop-consonant production, the rate of closure and of release of the constriction will tend to be different depending on whether the closure is formed with the lips or the tongue tip, or by raising the dorsum of the tongue to make contact with the hard or soft palate. The rates of closure for these various nasal consonants are expected to be about the same as for the cognate stop consonants. There may be some difference in the trajectories of the release, however, since in the case of the nasal consonant there is no intraoral pressure to create extra abducting forces on the articulatory structure that forms the constriction (cf. Fujimura, 1961). The difference will be especially marked for the velar nasal consonant, since the intraoral pressure plays an important role in determining the trajectory of the release for a velar stop consonant, as has been seen in figure 7.6.

9.1.2 Low-Frequency Sound Output

During the nasal murmur, the sound is radiated from the nose, and there is a complete closure of the oral cavity. The spectrum of the volume velocity at the nose is the product of the spectrum of the glottal volume velocity and the transfer function from the glottal source to the nose output. As we have seen in section 3.6.2, the lowest pole of this transfer function is in the range of 250 to 300 Hz for an adult (Båvegård et al., 1993). To a first approximation, this pole is a Helmholtz resonance between the acoustic compliance of the vocal tract volume and the acoustic mass of the nasal passages, including the velopharyngeal opening. However, the volume of the sinuses, as well as the impedance of the walls, also plays a role in determining the frequency of this lowest resonance. The bandwidth of this pole is expected to be somewhat greater than the $F1$ bandwidth for a high vowel because of additional losses at the walls of the nasal passages, and is estimated to be about 100 Hz. At the fundamental frequency (100 to 200 Hz, on average), therefore, the magnitude of the transfer function is slightly greater than its zero-frequency value of 0 dB—probably in the range of 1.5 to 4.0 dB.

Immediately preceding and following the nasal murmur, the output is a combination of the volume velocity from the nose and the mouth, with the mouth output being dominant when the area of the oral constriction exceeds the area of the velopharyngeal opening (assumed here to be about 0.2 cm^2). The transfer function from the glottal source to the combined output for this nasalized configuration has a lowest pole that is in the range of 300 to 900 Hz depending on the vowel configuration and the gender of the speaker. Again the transfer function in the frequency range of the fundamental is only slightly greater than 0 dB. Since we expect little change in the amplitude and spectrum of the glottal source during the interval from the preceding vowel through the murmur into the following vowel, then there will be essentially no change in the amplitude of the first harmonic throughout this time interval. This property of continuity or lack of change in the low-frequency spectrum amplitude occurs for any voiced consonant that is produced with negligible increase in the pressure above the glottis, that is, for any sonorant consonant.

As shown in section 3.6.2, the second pole of the transfer function during the nasal murmur is in the range of 750 to 1000 Hz (neglecting the effects of pole-zero pairs resulting from coupling to the sinuses). The amplitude of the spectral peak corresponding to this pole tends to be weak, since the relatively low frequency of the first resonance reduces the amplitudes of higher peaks in the transfer function. The amplitude of the spectrum in this frequency range around 1000 Hz is somewhat variable, however, and can be influenced by a zero in the transfer function, whose frequency depends on the place of articulation of the consonant, as will be discussed in section 9.1.3 below.

As figure 9.2 shows, there is coupling to the nasal cavity during the interval of a few tens of milliseconds prior to the closure for the nasal consonant, and (usually) for a briefer interval following the release. During these times, then, the sound that is radiated from the mouth (and from the nose) is characteristic of a nasal vowel. When the cross-sectional area of the oral constriction exceeds that of the velopharyngeal opening (usually within 10 ms of the closure or release, particularly for the rates of movement characteristic of labial and alveolar places of articulation), the output is primarily from the mouth opening. Typically, the transfer function from glottal volume velocity to mouth volume velocity in the low-frequency range encompassed by the first-formant frequency is characterized by two poles and a zero, neglecting additional pole-zero pairs due to coupling to the sinuses. That is, the single pole corresponding to the first formant for the corresponding non-nasal transfer function is replaced by the pole-zero-pole triplet, as has been shown in section 6.9. The lower of these poles is generally in the frequency range of 300 to 900 Hz (as noted above), the higher one is in the range of 600 to 1200 Hz, and the zero is either between the two poles or is higher than both. (See, e.g., figure 6.36.) If there is an interval in which the vowel is non-nasal preceding the closure or following the release (times less than -180 ms and greater than $+30$ ms in figure 9.2), one of the poles merges with the zero, leaving a single pole that is the first formant of the non-nasal vowel. The frequency at which the pole-zero pair merges is the natural frequency of the nasal cavity with a closed velopharyngeal port, which we take here to be 500 Hz.

Trajectories of the lower poles and zero for a typical sequence with a nasal consonant between two vowels with a non-nasal $F1 = 500$ Hz are schematized in figure 9.3a. Also shown (figure 9.3b) are estimated spectra in the low-frequency range, sampled at several points in this sequence. These points are identified during the closing phase, but a similar sequence will occur during the release, except that at the release the points will be more closely spaced. When there is no nasal coupling, before time -180 ms and after time $+30$ ms in this example, the low-frequency pole and zero cancel, and a single low-frequency prominence remains as the first formant, as indicated by spectrum 1 in figure 9.3b. During the nasal murmur, there is a low-frequency prominence around 250 Hz, and a second resonance in the vicinity of 1 kHz (spectrum 4). The lowest zero in the nasal murmur is 1 kHz or higher, depending on the place of closure, and this is not shown in the figure. There is an abrupt change in the frequency of the zero near the closure and the

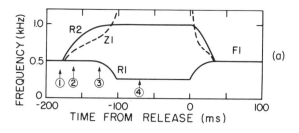

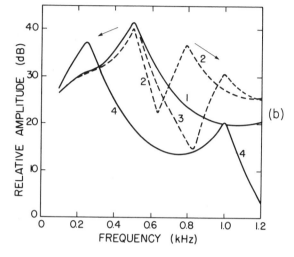

Figure 9.3 (a) Approximate trajectories of the components of the low-frequency pole-zero-pole combination during production of a nasal consonant in intervocalic position. The two resonances are labeled R1 and R2, and the trajectory of the zero Z1 is indicated by a dashed line. Times of implosion and release of the consonant are −100 and 0 ms, respectively. The frequency of the zero during the nasal murmur depends on the place of articulation, and is usually above 1000 Hz. During the time intervals when Z1 and R1 cancel each other, the remaining low-frequency pole becomes the first formant F1, as indicated. The estimated spectra at the points labeled 1 through 4 are displayed in (b). The arrows show the directions of movement of the spectral peaks as the articulators move from the vowel to the consonant configuration.

release, as will be discussed in the following sections. When the amount of nasal coupling is small, the nasal pole and zero converge toward the natural frequency of the nasal cavity with a closed posterior termination. Spectrum 2 is sampled at a point where the nasal coupling is minimal. In the transition region the pole R2 and the zero Z1 separate as the nasal coupling increases, and the pole R1 moves toward 250 Hz as the zero increases in frequency,[1] as shown by spectra 3 and 4.

Some of the details of the changes in the spectrum in figure 9.3b are quite variable, and depend on the vowel environment and on the rates of change of the area of the oral constriction and of the velopharyngeal opening. The general picture can, however, be summarized as follows: (1) The spectrum at frequencies below the lowest spectral prominence shows very little change in amplitude as the supraglottal constriction is closed and then released. (2)

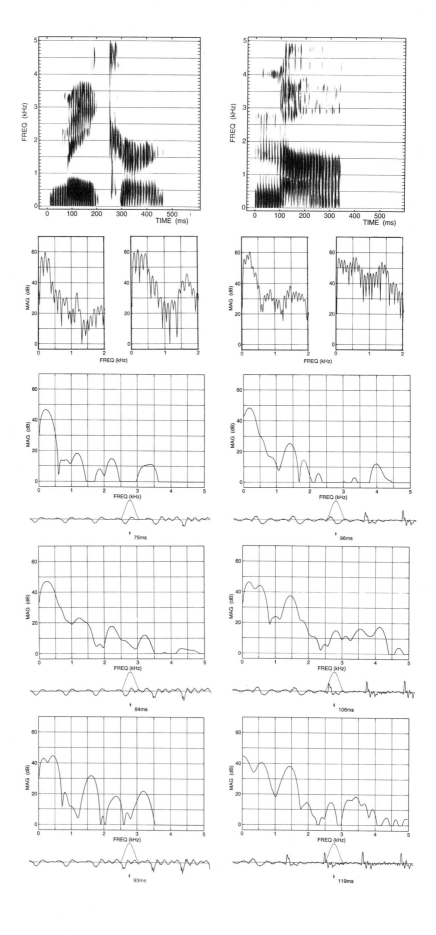

An extra peak appears above the first formant frequency immediately before the closure, and a similar peak appears briefly immediately following the release. When the first formant frequency of the vowel is high, the extra peak might appear below the first formant. (3) During the murmur, the low-frequency spectrum is dominated by the peak at about 250 Hz, and there are no other spectral peaks in the vicinity of this prominence. A second resonance appears in the spectrum in the vicinity of 1000 Hz, and this peak is continuous with the extra prominence that occurs in the vowel spectrum preceding and following the nasal murmur. (4) There is a rather rapid change in the frequency of the low-frequency prominence at the closure and at the release. If the first formant of the adjacent vowel is below about 500 Hz (e.g., if the vowel is a high vowel), then the merging of the pole $R2$ with the zero $Z1$ occurs above the first-formant frequency rather than below it. (In figure 9.3a, $R2$ and $Z1$ merge at about the frequency $F1$ of the first formant.)

Examples of these lower-frequency acoustic characteristics in an utterance of a nasal consonant are shown in figure 9.4. Spectra are sampled at several times immediately preceding and following the release of the nasal consonant /m/ in the word *maker* and following the /n/ release in the syllable /nɑ/. Immediately below each spectrogram there are two narrow-band spectra which are sampled just before and just after the nasal consonant release. These low-frequency spectra show that there is little change in the amplitude of the first harmonic between these spectra (3 dB increase in one case, and 0 dB in the other). The narrow-band spectrum for /m/ shows evidence for a broad spectral peak around 750 Hz (corresponding to $R2$ in figure 9.3a, and for /n/ this peak is more prominent at about 850 Hz. The wide-band spectra (three lowest panels in figure 9.4) show that the low-frequency peak dominates the spectrum during the murmur in both utterances, and its frequency is about 200 Hz. The second peak in the murmur appears at about 750 Hz in /m/ and 850 Hz in /n/, the latter peak appearing as a shoulder on the curve above the lowest prominence. Immediately following the release (which is at about 82 ms and 104 ms on the time scales on the spectrograms, and between the first and third spectrum in each utterance) the first formant appears at about 450 Hz in one case and 550 Hz in the other (bottom spectra in the figure). This abrupt appearance of $F1$ occurs within a time interval of 10 to 20 ms, as suggested by the calculations in figure 9.3 showing the shift between spectrum 3 (sampled during the transition) and spectrum 4 (sampled in the murmur). Evidence for the nasal resonance $R2$ has almost disappeared in the bottom spectra of figure 9.4.

Figure 9.4 Spectrograms of the word *maker* (left) and the syllable /nɑ/ (right) produced by two different male speakers are shown at the top. The two low-frequency spectra immediately below each spectrogram (time window = 26 ms) are sampled in the nasal murmur (left spectrum) and soon after the consonant release (right spectrum). The bottom three spectra in each column were sampled with a time window of 6.4 ms (as shown on the waveform in each case) as centered on three successive glottal periods immediately before the consonant release and just after the release. See text.

9.1.3 High-Frequency Sound Output

At the implosion and at the release of the closure in the oral cavity for a nasal consonant, there is usually a rapid change in the spectrum of the radiated sound. This change is a consequence of two factors: (1) the rapid change in the configuration of the vocal tract (and of the velopharyngeal opening), leading to shifts in the natural frequencies of the combined nasal and vocal tract (i.e., in the poles of the transfer function from glottis to output), and (2) the switch in the output from the nose to the combined output of nose and mouth, leading to a rapid change in the zeros of the transfer function, particularly the lowest zero. The time course of the spectrum change depends on the place in the oral cavity where the closure is made and on the details of the constriction shape and its rate of change. In the case of nasal consonants which are produced with an oral closure that is not at the lips, an additional contribution to the spectrum change at the release (or implosion) is the abrupt introduction (or extinction) of the resonance of the cavity anterior to the constriction, since this resonance is not excited during the murmur.

9.1.3.1 Labial Nasal Consonants
When the closure is formed at the lips or with the tongue blade, the transfer function from the volume velocity at the glottis to that at the nose during the closure interval is characterized by a number of poles, with the lowest being at 250 to 300 Hz, as we have observed. There are zeros in the transfer function at frequencies for which the impedance looking into the mouth cavity from the location of the velopharyngeal port is zero. In the case of a labial closure, the length of this mouth cavity is about one-half of the total length of the vocal tract, and hence the lowest zero is at a frequency of about 1000 to 1200 Hz for an adult. A second zero is expected at about three times this frequency. The average spacing of the poles during the nasal murmur is in the range of 650 to 750 Hz for an adult. This average spacing corresponds to a total length of oral plus nasal tract of 25 to 28 cm: about 14 to 17 cm for the oral tract, and about 11 cm for the nasal tract, as described in section 1.1.3.

A few milliseconds following the release of the closure, the mouth opening becomes greater than the velopharyngeal opening, and the principal output from the system shifts from the nose to the mouth. Within this brief time interval, the zeros shift to new positions appropriate for a nasalized vowel. Most of the poles shift upward rather quickly as the acoustic mass of the labial constriction decreases, except that there is a slower downward shift in the poles that are associated with the nasal cavity as the area of the velopharyngeal opening decreases. (See, e.g., resonance $R2$ in figure 9.3a.) A similar pattern but in the reverse direction occurs at the implosion.

The pattern of change of the poles and the lowest zero of the transfer function is schematized in figure 9.5, for changes in the configuration depicted in figure 9.2. In order to simplify the analysis, we omit consideration of the zeros above the first zero $Z1$. The higher zeros have a smaller effect on the

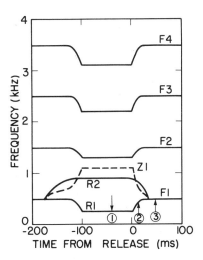

Figure 9.5 Schematization of trajectories of poles and zeros of the transfer function of the vocal tract for a labial nasal consonant in intervocalic position. The transfer function is the ratio of the total volume velocity from the nose and mouth to the volume velocity at the glottis. The labial closure occurs between 0 and −100 ms on the abscissa. The lowest zero is labeled as Z1, and is shown as a dashed line. Zeros above Z1 are not shown. Poles are indicated by solid lines, including the two low-frequency poles R1 and R2 that replace the first formant during the interval when the velopharyngeal port is open. For times remote from the closure, poles and zeros due to acoustic coupling to the nasal cavity are canceled, and only the natural frequencies of the oral cavity remain, labeled F1 through F4. The vowel configuration is taken to have a uniform cross-sectional area. The points labeled 1, 2, and 3 indicate times at which the spectrum envelopes in figure 9.6 are calculated.

overall transfer function than does the lowest zero, and their changes are expected to be somewhat less consistent. We also omit in our analysis higher poles that become paired with the highest zeros. During the nasal murmur there is a series of free poles (i.e., omitting poles that can be paired with zeros) with an average spacing of about 900 Hz, corresponding to an overall length of the pharyngeal and nasal cavities of about 19.6 cm, with a zero at about 1100 Hz. The frequencies of the poles associated primarily with the vocal tract (excluding the nasal cavity) show abrupt changes near closure and release, similar to stop consonants (cf. figures 7.14 and 7.15), while the poles associated primarily with the nasal cavity increase and decrease more slowly as the area of the velopharyngeal port increases and decreases. (The assignment of poles exclusively to the oral and pharyngeal tract and to the nasal cavity is, of course, only an approximation, except when the velopharyngeal opening is small. However, this view of the sound-generating process captures the main attributes of the changes in the spectrum near the implosion and the release.) When the velopharyngeal port is closed (less than −180 ms and greater than 30 ms in figure 9.5), the zero Z1 merges with a pole (shown as R2 in the figure) as coupling to the nasal cavity is reduced, and we are left with the formants of the non-nasal vowel (labeled F1 through F4 in the figure).

The zero, shown as a dashed line in figure 9.5, undergoes an abrupt decrease in frequency as the principal acoustic output shifts from the nose to the mouth at the consonant release. As noted above, this lowest zero (the one that is at about 1100 Hz during the nasal murmur in figure 9.5) undergoes initial movement to a frequency appropriate for a nasal vowel, that is, from 1100 Hz to about 600 to 800 Hz, with a continuing downward movement to 500 Hz. The initial rapid shift occurs in a time interval of about 10 ms or less if we assume a rate of increase of the area of the lip opening to be 100 cm^2/s. In 10 ms, this area has reached 1.0 cm^2, which is well in excess of the assumed velopharyngeal area of 0.2 cm^2, indicating that the predominant output is from the mouth opening, with a first zero in the region of 600 to 800 Hz.

This abrupt shift of the first zero $Z1$ has a large effect on the spectrum of the sound, and is expected to account for a significant change in spectrum amplitude in the vicinity of the boundary, particularly in the region of the second formant. The spectral change is illustrated in figure 9.6, where we show spectrum envelopes calculated at three different times: (1) during the nasal murmur (which, for simplicity, is assumed to remain constant throughout the murmur); (2) 10 ms following the release; and (3) after the effect of nasalization has gone away (after about 30 ms in this case). (The reverse sequence of spectra would occur at the implosion, with a somewhat different timing.) In calculating these spectral envelopes, we have omitted consideration of the pole-zero pairs above 1500 Hz, on the assumption that they have only a small effect on the spectrum. One significant attribute of the sequence of spectra is the abrupt increase in spectrum amplitude in the vicinity of the frequency of the second formant. This is the frequency region in which the zero is present in the nasal murmur, and which is abruptly vacated by the zero at the instant of release. This frequency is below the second-formant frequency for the adjacent vowel. The calculations indicate that the jump in spectrum amplitude in the $F2$ range in the initial 30 ms is about 20 dB. Of this increase in spectrum amplitude, about 9 dB is due to the abrupt decrease in $Z1$ and its merging with the nasal pole, whereas about 12 dB is due to the rise in the lowest resonance $R1$ from 250 to 500 Hz. For frequencies above the $F2$ range, there is also an abrupt increase in spectrum amplitude in the 30-ms interval following the release. Much of the increase in spectrum amplitude in the $F2$ range and at higher frequencies occurs in the initial 10 ms following the release, since there are significant movements of the lowest resonance $R1$ and of $Z1$ during this brief time interval.

During the 10- to 20-ms interval immediately following the release, the second formant ($F2$) rises rapidly, similar to the movement of $F2$ for other labial consonants such as stops. The amount of this rise is relatively small in figure 9.5, where $F2$ for the adjacent vowel is at 1500 Hz. The rise would be considerably greater if the following vowel were a front vowel with a higher $F2$, as has been shown in section 7.4.2. The onset of this $F2$ movement is marked, as we have seen, by an abrupt increase in amplitude of the $F2$ spectral peak. Immediately prior to the implosion, there is a downward move-

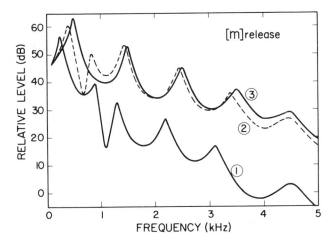

Figure 9.6 Spectrum envelopes calculated at three times in the vicinity of the point where the release of the labial closure occurs for a nasal consonant. The three points are identified on the pole-zero plot in figure 9.5. A similar sequence of spectra, but in the reverse order, would occur in the vicinity of the implosion. Since some of the zeros and poles move very rapidly in the vicinity of the release and the implosions, some smoothing of these spectra and spectrum changes would be observed in measured spectra at these points.

ment of $F2$, followed by an abrupt decrease in the amplitude of the $F2$ peak in the spectrum. If the adjacent vowel is a back vowel, the change in the frequency of $F2$ immediately preceding and following the closure is usually small.

Other changes in the spectrum occur at higher frequencies, but these are not expected to be as consistent or as abrupt as the change in the second-formant range. Thus, for example, at frequencies well above the second formant in figure 9.6, the spectrum amplitude continues to rise after the initial 10 ms, whereas the amplitude of the $F2$ peak shows little further increase after the initial 10 ms. That is, the amplitude at the lower frequencies ($F2$ range) increases more abruptly than it does at higher frequencies. This pattern has been predicted previously for labial stops (see figure 7.16).

The frequencies of $R2$, $Z1$, and $F2$ will depend somewhat on the adjacent vowel, with $Z1$ being lower for back vowels than for front vowels. The pattern of amplitude change of the $F2$ prominence and of higher-frequency prominences is expected, then, to be different depending on the vowel that is adjacent to the nasal consonant.

The various acoustic attributes of the implosion and release of a labial nasal consonant in the utterance *a mill* are illustrated in figures 9.7 and 9.8. Figure 9.7 shows a spectrogram at the top, and spectra sampled at selected times in the sound, with waveforms displayed below the spectra. Most of the spectra (numbered 1 to 10) are calculated pitch-synchronously with a relatively short time window of 6.4 ms, in order to capture the rapid spectrum changes that occur at the implosion and at the release. The three spectra at the bottom of figure 9.7 (labeled A to C) were calculated with a longer time window, to show more clearly the frequency of the zero and the nearby

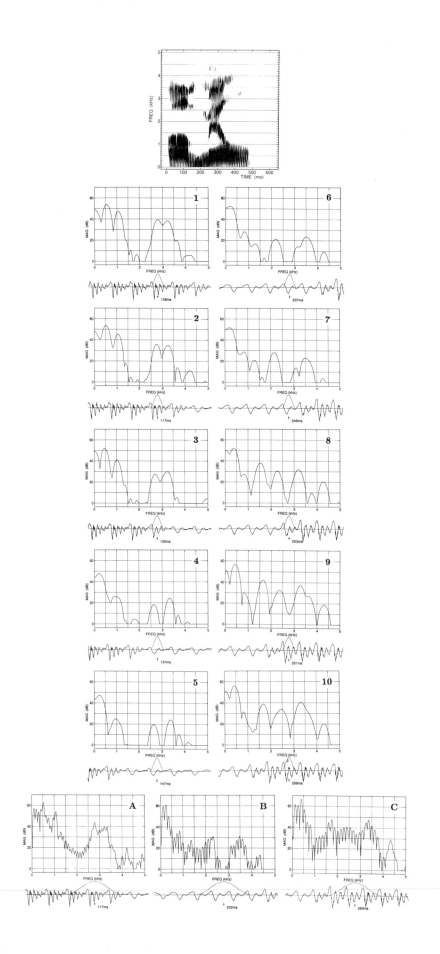

pole immediately prior to the implosion, during the nasal murmur, and immediately following the release. The curves in figure 9.8 show the amplitudes of the different formant peaks as a function of time, as measured from the short-time spectra.

Examining first the sequence of spectra and the amplitude changes at the release, we observe the abrupt increase of about 17 dB in amplitude $A2$ of the spectral peak corresponding to $F2$ at about 1500 Hz in frames 7 and 8 (246 to 253 ms in figure 9.8). The frequency of this peak rises by about 200 Hz over the 15-ms time interval from frames 8 to 10, as the front-vowel configuration is reached. The higher frequency peaks corresponding to $F3$ and $F4$ also exhibit an increase in amplitude, but this increase is less abrupt and extends over a longer time interval than the increase in $A2$, as shown in figure 9.8. A similar pattern of change in the amplitude of these peaks but in the reverse sequence is evident at the implosion of the consonant. In the few glottal periods in the reduced vowel prior to the implosion, the frequency of $F2$ remains low (about 1 kHz), and does not show a further decrease as the instant of closure is reached. The amplitude of this $F2$ prominence undergoes an abrupt decrease of about 15 dB from frame 3 to frame 4 (from 128 to 137 ms in figure 9.8).

The spectra with greater frequency resolution (time window of 30 ms) at the bottom of figure 9.7 show the zero in the nasal murmur (panel B) at about 1100 Hz, that is, at about the same frequency as that in the calculations with a neutral adjacent vowel (see figures 9.5 and 9.6). Prior to the implosion and immediately following the release, some effects of nasal coupling can be seen in these spectra. There is essentially no change in the amplitude of the first harmonic from the murmur into the following vowel, as noted earlier.

9.1.3.2 Alveolar Nasal Consonants When the closure for a nasal consonant is formed with the tongue blade, as shown in the right of figure 9.1, the length of the mouth cavity from the velopharyngeal port to the point of closure is somewhat less than it is for a labial consonant—about 5 to 6 cm for an alveolar closure compared with about 7 to 8 cm for a labial closure. The lowest zero in the nasal murmur for an adult vocal tract is usually in the range of 1600 to 1900 Hz, and a second zero is expected at about three times this frequency. (This second zero is not well defined, however, because of the finite width of the side branch in the nasopharyngeal airway.) The lowest of these zeros is shown in figure 9.9 as a dashed line labeled Z1 in the

Figure 9.7 Acoustic data obtained from a labial nasal consonant /m/ in the utterance *a mill*. A spectrogram of the utterance is shown at the top, and the panels under the spectrogram are spectra sampled at the points indicated on the waveforms below the spectra. The numbered spectra in the two columns in the middle of the figure are discrete Fourier transforms calculated with a Hamming window of duration 6.4 ms. Spectra 1 to 5 in the left column are sampled at successive glottal periods near the consonant implosion, and spectra 6 to 10 in the right column are sampled near the consonant release. The three spectra at the bottom are calculated with a Hamming window of duration 30 ms. These spectra are sampled (A) just prior to consonant closure, (B) in the nasal murmur, and (C) just after consonant release.

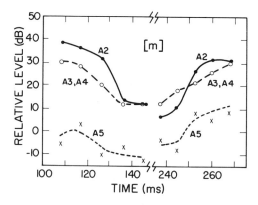

Figure 9.8 Amplitudes of spectral peaks corresponding to the formants *F2* through *F5* for portions of the utterance *a mill* shown in figure 9.7. The curves labeled *A3, A4* give the maximum amplitude in the third- and fourth-formant region. The amplitudes are obtained from short-time spectra of the type given in figure 9.7, sampled pitch-synchronously. The time scale is the same as the time scales on the spectrogram and waveforms in figure 9.7.

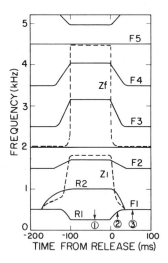

Figure 9.9 Estimated trajectories of poles and zeros of the transfer function of the vocal tract for an alveolar nasal consonant in intervocalic position. Poles and zeros are labeled as in figure 9.5. The zero *Zf* accounts for acoustic coupling to the front cavity during the nasal murmur, as discussed in the text. The points labeled 1, 2, and 3 indicate times at which the spectrum envelopes in figure 9.10 are calculated.

murmur portion of the estimated pattern of poles and zeros for an intervocalic alveolar nasal consonant.

The movement of *F2* near the implosion and the release in figure 9.9 is similar to the *F2* change discussed in chapter 7 for an alveolar stop consonant (cf. figure 7.22). We also show movements of *F3* and *F4* in these regions. The pattern of movements of the various poles and zeros in the figure is schematic, but it is intended to capture the essential attributes that are responsible for the spectral changes near the implosion and the release.

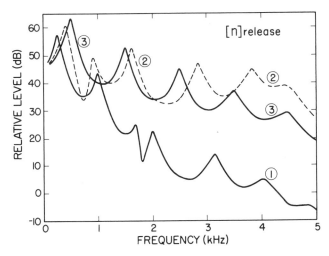

Figure 9.10 Same as figure 9.6, except that the calculated spectra correspond to points in the vicinity of the release for an alveolar nasal consonant. The higher zero Zf is assumed to be canceled by a nearby pole, so that it does not give rise to a dip in the spectrum.

As we have seen in our discussion of stop consonants, there is an acoustic cavity anterior to the closure for an alveolar consonant, and a typical value for the lowest natural frequency of this front cavity is 4500 Hz for a male vocal tract. During the nasal murmur, this front cavity resonance is not excited. We can account for the front cavity by including a pole in the transfer function at a frequency of 4500 Hz during the nasal consonant configuration. However, during the nasal murmur we must include a zero at the same frequency in order to cancel the pole, indicating no acoustic coupling to this resonance. This pole-zero pair is labeled with $F5$ and Zf in figure 9.9. Immediately preceding and following the interval of oral closure, the zero undergoes an abrupt change in frequency, leaving the pole $F5$ to be manifested as a spectral peak in the sound. The trajectory of Zf is shown in figure 9.9, where it is falling abruptly and merges with a pole that forms one of the resonances during the nasal murmur (at 2000 Hz in this case).

Within a few milliseconds of the release of the alveolar closure (or a few milliseconds prior to the implosion), the cross-sectional area of the alveolar constriction becomes greater than the velopharyngeal opening. As we have seen for the labial release, the principal output from the system shifts from the nose to the mouth within this interval, and the zeros shift to new positions appropriate for a nasalized vowel. There are also shifts in the poles as the tongue body moves toward a configuration for the following vowel, similar to the movements at the release of an alveolar stop consonant. At the implosion there is a similar pattern of movement of the zeros and poles but in the reverse direction. (The velopharyngeal opening at the implosion might be greater, however, than it is at the release.) The rapid change of the zeros, particularly the lowest zero $Z1$, has a significant effect on the spectrum, particularly the amplitude of the spectral peak corresponding to $F2$.

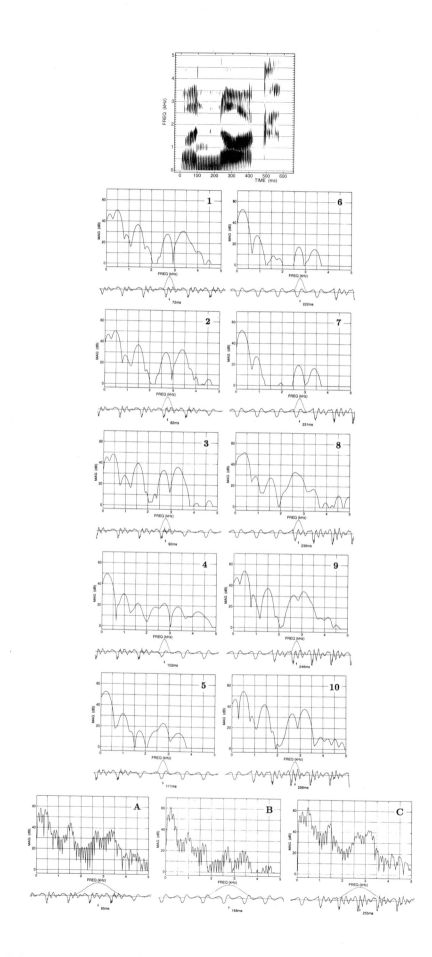

This effect is diminished somewhat by the appearance of the zero Zf at about 2 kHz in figure 9.9.

Calculated spectra at three points in the vicinity of the release are shown in figure 9.10. (A similar sequence of spectra will occur near the implosion, but in the reverse order.) These estimated spectra are in the murmur, about 10 ms after the release, and in the vowel after the velopharyngeal port has been closed, so that there is no acoustic coupling to the nasal cavity. As in the calculations for the labial nasal consonant, we have neglected the effects on the spectrum of the zeros above $Z1$ and the poles with which they are associated, except for the zero Zf that accounts for the cavity anterior to the constriction. Within about 10 ms following the release, we observe an abrupt rise in spectrum amplitude in the vicinity of the frequency of the second formant (about 1650 Hz in this case). The second-formant frequency then undergoes a downward movement. The increase in spectrum amplitude of the $F2$ prominence over the 30-odd milliseconds of the transition is about 26 dB. Around 1000 Hz the amplitude increase at the release is small compared with the amplitude increase in the same frequency range for the labial release (see figure 9.6). There is a significant increase in spectrum amplitude of 20 dB or more for all spectral peaks higher than $F2$ during the 10-ms interval following the release. At high frequencies (4000 Hz and above) the calculations show an *overshoot* in the spectrum amplitude immediately following the release, as a consequence of the abrupt downward movement of Zf, which causes the appearance of an extra peak at high frequencies, and a subsequent downward shift in the frequencies of the higher formants $F2$ to $F4$.

An example of an alveolar nasal consonant is given in figures 9.11 and 9.12. The utterance is *a knock*, and figure 9.11 shows a spectrogram, short-time spectra (6.4-ms window) sampled at several points in the vicinity of the implosion and the release (labeled 1 to 10), and portions of the waveform near the implosion and release of the /n/. Also shown in this figure are three spectra (A to C), with a longer time window of 30 ms, sampled just prior to the implosion, in the nasal murmur, and just after the release. At the release, we observe an abrupt jump in spectrum amplitude in the mid- and high-frequency ranges, from frame 7 to frame 9. These changes in amplitude are shown graphically at the right side of figure 9.12. For example, the amplitude increase over a time interval of one glottal period is more than 20 dB in the $F2$ range, and similar increases are evident in the $F3$ range and near 4500 Hz. The increases in $A2$ through $A4$ continue through the second period following the release. The fall in the second-formant frequency is also evident in the spectra in figure 9.11 over the few periods following the release. Over

Figure 9.11 Acoustic data obtained from an alveolar nasal consonant /n/ in the utterance *a knock*. A spectrogram of the utterance is shown at the top, and the panels below the spectrogram are spectra sampled at several points and with different time windows. The sampling times and windows are as described in the legend for figure 9.7.

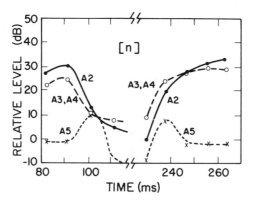

Figure 9.12 Amplitudes of spectral peaks corresponding to formants *F2* through *F5* for portions of the utterance *a knock*, shown in figure 9.11. The amplitudes are obtained from spectra of the type given in figure 9.11, sampled pitch-synchronously. The time scale is the same as the time scales on the spectrogram and waveforms in figure 9.11.

this time interval, spectra 6 to 10 show that there is little change in spectrum amplitude in the vicinity of 1000 Hz, in contrast to the release for a labial nasal consonant, where the increase in spectrum amplitude in this frequency range is relatively large. The difference is presumably due to the fact that for the labial murmur there is a zero in the transfer function in the vicinity of 1000 Hz, and the abrupt movement of this zero at the release causes a rise in the spectrum amplitude in this frequency range. In the case of the alveolar, the frequency of the lowest zero in the murmur is higher, and as the zero shifts from this higher frequency to a frequency lower than 1000 Hz, the influence on the spectrum amplitude around 1000 Hz is not as great. Some evidence of an increase in spectrum amplitude in the frequency range of 4 to 5 kHz at the release can be seen in frame 8, as well as in figure 9.12. This increase can presumably be attributed to the sudden introduction of the cavity anterior to the constriction at the instant of release, as we have seen.

Similar sequences of events, but in the reverse order, can be observed in the spectra in the vicinity of the implosion. There is a relatively abrupt decrease in spectrum amplitude at high frequencies (*F2* and above) at the implosion (spectra 3 to 5 in figure 9.11 and times 90 to 110 ms in figure 9.12), of at least 20 dB. Again, the change in spectrum amplitude around 1000 Hz is much less. A rise in *F2* is evident as movement occurs into the implosion of the consonant.

The spectra in figure 9.11 with the finer frequency resolution show more detail concerning the low-frequency pole-zero patterns. During the nasal murmur for /n/, the zero is evident at about 1900 Hz. The effects of nasalization can be seen in the spectra immediately preceding the implosion and following the release, with an extra spectral peak around 800 to 900 Hz.

The changes in spectrum amplitude at the implosion and at the release for a labial and an alveolar are illustrated further in figure 9.13. This figure shows data on the amplitude changes at these boundaries for a number of

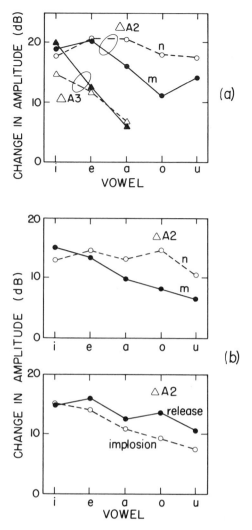

Figure 9.13 Changes in spectrum amplitude of the second-formant prominence at the implosion and release of nasal consonants /m,n/ in the environment of several vowels, as indicated on the abscissa. Average data for one male and one female speaker. (a) The changes $\Delta A2$ and $\Delta A3$ in $F2$ and $F3$ amplitudes when the spectrum amplitude is measured with a time window of 30 ms, and the two spectra are centered about 20 ms on either side of the implosion or the release. The curves give average values for implosion and release. (b) Measured values of $\Delta A2$ when the spectra are measured pitch-synchronously with a time window of 6.4 ms. The spectra are sampled one glottal period apart (about 8 ms) for the male speaker and two glottal periods apart (about 11 ms) for the female speaker. The upper part of (b) gives averages over implosion and release; the lower part shows data for the implosion and the release separately, averaged over the two consonants /m/ and /n/.

utterances of the form /VNV/, where V is one of the vowels /i e ɑ o u/ and N is one of /m n/. Two speakers (one female and one male) produced two repetitions of these ten utterances. Two kinds of measurements of spectrum change were made near the consonant implosion and release: (1) A 30-ms window was positioned on either side of the discontinuity, and the amplitudes of spectral peaks corresponding to F2 and F3 were made on the resulting spectra. The spacing between the spectra was 30 to 40 ms. (2) A 6.4-ms window was positioned on a glottal pulse on either side of the discontinuity, and similar measures of peak amplitudes were made. In the case of the male speaker, two adjacent glottal pulses were selected around a point where the spectrum was changing most rapidly, whereas for the female speaker the relevant spectra were separated by two glottal periods. The spacing between the spectra was about the same for the two speakers: 7 to 11 ms.

The data on amplitude changes for the longer time window, averaged over the two speakers and over implosion and release, are shown in the top panel of figure 9.13. The measured change in the amplitude of the F2 prominence ($\Delta A2$) for /n/ is 18 to 20 dB and does not vary much with vowel environment. This result is presumably a consequence of the fact that the articulatory configuration for /n/ is not strongly influenced by the adjacent vowel. For /m/ the amplitude change is similar to that for /n/ before front vowels, but there is a decrease in $\Delta A2$ for back vowels, reflecting the influence of the adjacent vowel on the articulatory configuration for /m/. This top panel of the figure also shows that the change in amplitude in the F2 region is greater than that in the F3 region. (No data are given for non-low back vowels, for which the amplitudes of formants above F2 are relatively weak.) The movement of the zero appears to cause a greater change in the second-formant amplitude, since the zero in the murmur is close to F2, as shown in figures 9.5 and 9.9. The measured data are in general consistent with the theoretical analyses given above.

In the high-frequency region around F5, the analysis in connection with figure 9.9 suggests that there should be a rather abrupt change in the spectrum amplitude at the vowel-consonant (VC) and consonant-vowel (CV) boundaries for the consonant /n/, because the short cavity in front of the constriction (with a natural frequency corresponding roughly to F5) is excited immediately before the implosion or after the release, but is not excited during the nasal murmur. This condition does not occur when the consonant is /m/. Indeed, measurements (for the male speaker whose utterances contributed to the data in figure 9.13) indicate an abrupt change in spectrum amplitude in the F5 region of about 20 dB at a boundary with /n/ and about 8 dB at a boundary with /m/ for the front vowels /i/ and /e/. For back vowels with weaker high-frequency spectrum amplitude, the difference is not as marked. For the female speaker, however, for whom F5 was at somewhat higher frequencies, consistent differences in amplitude change in the F5 region between /m/ and /n/ were not obtained.

The changes in amplitude at the frequency of the $F2$ peak over a 7- to 11-ms interval, using a short time window, are given in the second and third panels of figure 9.13. The second panel, comparing /m/ and /n/, but averaged over implosion and release, shows that 60 to 70 percent of the amplitude change (in decibels) usually occurs over this relatively short time interval.

At the bottom of the figure, the data on amplitude change, averaged over the two consonants, are shown separately for the consonantal implosion and release. Evidently the amplitude change is somewhat more abrupt for the release than for the implosion. This difference may be a reflection of different rates of change of the velopharyngeal opening at the two boundaries of the consonant.

9.1.3.3 Velar Nasal Consonants

We consider next articulatory and acoustic events at the implosion and the release of nasal consonants produced by raising the tongue body to make contact with the soft palate. During the nasal murmur, the length of the cavity between the velopharyngeal opening and the oral closure is very short, and there is no zero in the transfer function, U_n/U_s (where U_n = volume velocity at the nose output and U_s = glottal volume velocity), at least in the frequency region below 3 kHz. This transfer function is an all-pole transfer function, and the lowest resonance is about 250 Hz for an adult, as it is for nasal murmurs with other places of articulation.

The movement of the tongue body from a preceding vowel configuration toward a velar closure or from the closure toward a following vowel gives rise to a rate of change of cross-sectional area that is considerably slower than that for an alveolar or labial closure. We have estimated this rate of change in the vicinity of the implosion or release to be about 25 cm²/s for a velar stop consonant, and we assume the same rate for velar nasal consonants.

Immediately prior to the release of the closure for a velar nasal consonant (or immediately following the implosion), the oral cavity in front of the constriction is isolated from the remainder of the system, and there is no acoustic excitation of this cavity. The length of this cavity for an adult speaker is in the range of 3 to 7 cm depending on whether the closure is made in the more anterior region of the hard palate or in the vicinity of the soft palate. The lowest natural frequency of this front cavity would be in the range of 1200 to 3000 Hz. (The lower end of this range could be still lower if the lips were rounded, causing a narrowing of the lip opening.) One way of characterizing the transfer function U_n/U_s from glottal source to nose output during the nasal murmur is to say that there are pole-zero pairs at the frequencies of the front-cavity resonances, and the poles and the zeros exactly cancel as long as the closure is maintained and the output is from the nose. When the constriction is released, this front cavity becomes coupled to the system, the zero begins to separate from the pole corresponding to one of these resonances, and a peak corresponding to this natural frequency appears in the spectrum of the output.

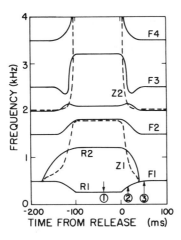

Figure 9.14 Estimated trajectories of poles and zeros of the transfer function of the vocal tract for a velar nasal consonant in intervocalic position. Poles and zeros are labeled as in figure 9.5. In this case Z1 and Z2 account for acoustic coupling to the cavity anterior to the velar constriction, and these zeros are canceled by poles during the nasal murmur, as discussed in the text. The points labeled 1,2, and 3 indicate times at which the spectrum envelopes in figure 9.15 are calculated.

In figure 9.14 we show the estimated movement of the poles and zeros in the transfer function of the system when a velar nasal consonant occurs in intervocalic position between two neutral vowels. During the murmur there is a pole-zero pair at the lowest natural frequency of the front cavity (1800 Hz in this case) and another pair at a higher frequency (beyond the range of the figure). Otherwise, the transfer function during the nasal murmur contains only poles—at 250, 1200, 2100, and 3200 Hz in the figure.

Immediately following the release (and also preceding the implosion), there is an output U_m from the mouth opening as well as from the nose. The nasal output continues to dominate, however, until the acoustic mass of the oral cavity exceeds the acoustic mass of the path through the nasal cavity. For the estimated rate of increase of cross-sectional area given above, the time at which this crossover occurs is probably in the range of 10 to 15 ms. This time is considerably longer than the corresponding time for a labial or alveolar nasal consonant.

When the size of the constriction exceeds this critical value and most of the output is from the mouth opening, the transfer function U_m/U_s is characterized by poles and zeros as for a nasal vowel. The lowest of the zeros drops below 1000 Hz, and becomes about 500 Hz when the velopharyngeal port is closed, as we have seen in section 3.6.1, and the next highest zero becomes roughly 2000 Hz. Thus when the closure is in the more posterior position, there will be a relatively rapid downward movement of the frequency of the zero from about 1800 Hz to 1000 Hz and lower. A principal acoustic consequence of this movement is that immediately following the

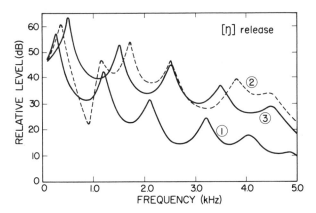

Figure 9.15 Same as figure 9.6, except that the calculated spectra correspond to points in the vicinity of the release for a velar nasal consonant. The second zero Z2 is assumed to be canceled by a nearby pole in these spectra, and hence does not give rise to a dip in the spectrum at point 2.

release the resonance at 1800 Hz appears as a prominent peak in the spectrum, since it is no longer obscured or canceled by the zero.

Sketched in figure 9.15 are the calculated spectra during the nasal murmur (spectrum 1) and at a point after the mouth output becomes dominant (spectrum 2). Also shown (spectrum 3) is the spectrum envelope after the steady-state position for the vowel is achieved, and the velopharyngeal port is closed. We observe in spectrum 2 the appearance of the peak corresponding to $F2$ (at about 1650 Hz) during the 20-ms interval after the release. This $F2$ spectrum peak appears at a frequency where there was no peak in the spectrum during the murmur. There is also a significant increase in spectrum amplitude at high frequencies above $F3$ (about 20 dB) during this time interval. As we proceed from spectrum 2 to spectrum 3, the frequency of the $F2$ spectrum peak decreases.

In figure 9.16 we show acoustic data in the vicinity of the implosion and release for the velar nasal consonant in the utterance *sung it*. As in the examples of labial and alveolar nasal consonants, we display the spectrogram and several spectra sampled near the consonantal implosion and release. A series of ten spectra sampled pitch-synchronously with short time windows are given, together with three spectra calculated with longer windows. The latter spectra are sampled just prior to the implosion, during the nasal murmur, and following the release. Shown in figure 9.17 are plots of the trajectories of $F1$, $F2$, and $F3$ (and of other prominences) during the few glottal periods prior to and following the closure, and graphs of the time course of the amplitudes of the spectral peaks.

Examination of the short-time spectra in figure 9.16 shows a rapid decrease in amplitude of the $F2$ peak (at about 1.5 kHz) at the implosion between frames 3 and 5, and an abrupt reappearance of that peak (at about 1.8 kHz) at the release between frames 6 and 8. The abrupt change in this amplitude $A2$ is evident in figure 9.17, and $A2$ is quite weak (and sometimes

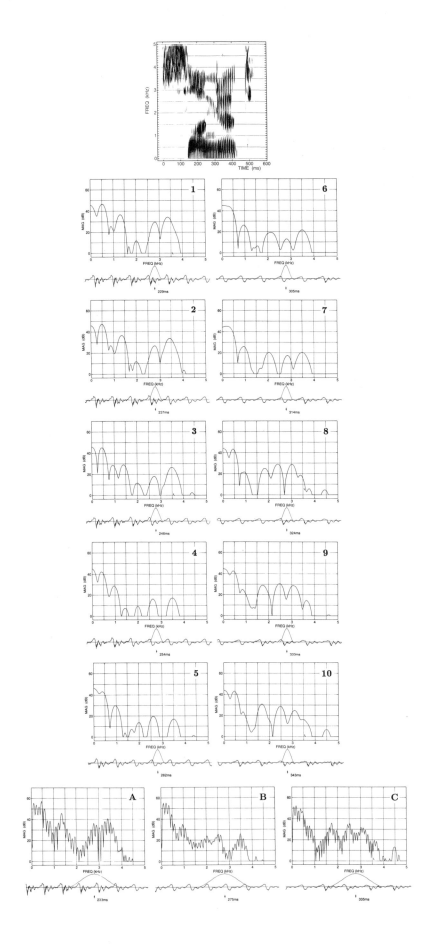

not observable) during the consonant interval. An abrupt change in $A3$ is also evident, although the change is not as great as in $A2$. The first-formant amplitude shows little change between the vowel and the consonant. An extra peak Fn can be observed in the spectra in the murmur and also preceding the implosion and following the release, and is in the expected frequency range. This extra peak becomes weaker in the preceding and following vowels as it becomes cancelled by a zero in the transfer function. The tendency of $F2$ and $F3$ to move closer together for the velar configuration is apparent in figure 9.17. The spectra during the murmur in figure 9.16 (panels 3 to 7) show a peak at about 2 kHz, as predicted from the schematized trajectories in figure 9.14. The lack of a zero in the spectrum of the nasal murmur below $F3$ is evident in the narrow-band spectrum B at the bottom of figure 9.16. The relatively large change in the amplitude of the $F2$ spectral prominence from spectrum A to B and from B to C can also be seen.

An example of a velar nasal consonant in the environment of a high front vowel is shown in figure 9.18. The utterance is *sing easy*. Immediately preceding the consonant implosion, there is some nasalization in the vowel, as evidenced by a broad shoulder or peak in the spectrum in the vicinity of 750 Hz, in panels 1 to 3. The second and third formants come together at the implosion, indicating a velar constriction at a place where the natural frequencies of the cavities anterior and posterior to the constriction are about equal, at about 2500 Hz. The point at which closure is made is thus about 3.5 cm posterior to the mouth opening. At the implosion, the spectrum amplitude of the $F2$–$F3$ peak decreases by about 20 dB over a time interval of 13 ms (spectra 3 to 5 in figure 9.18), as one of the poles in the transfer function is essentially annihilated by a zero. The decrease in spectrum amplitude in the $F4$ region is less abrupt. Through the murmur, the position of the constriction appears to move forward, and the natural frequency of the front cavity shifts upward to about 3100 Hz, as evidenced by the prominence that is manifested as a shoulder in the spectrum adjacent to the $F4$ peak in spectra 9 and 10, following the consonant release. The proximity of $F3$ and $F4$ at the release is evident in the spectrogram and in the spectra sampled immediately following the release. Within the murmur, there is evidence of a zero around 3 kHz (spectrum B at the bottom of the figure), and this zero shifts downward slightly throughout the murmur. The presence of this zero indicates that the posterior end of the palatovelar constriction is roughly 3 cm forward of the velopharyngeal opening. At the release, the spectral peak at 3500 Hz increases in amplitude by about 20 dB in a 15-ms interval (spectra 7 to 9), whereas the increase in amplitude of the peak at 2500 Hz is less abrupt. Some nasalization remains in the vowel during this interval.

Figure 9.16 Acoustic data obtained from a velar nasal consonant /ŋ/ in the utterance *sung it*. A spectrogram of the utterance is shown at the top, and the panels under the spectrogram are spectra sampled at several points and with different time windows. See legend for figure 9.7.

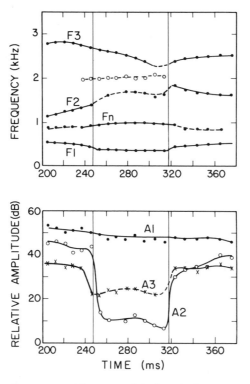

Figure 9.17 The top panel displays the frequencies of the first, second, and third formants (*F1*, *F2*, and *F3*) for portions of the utterance *sung it* shown in figure 9.16, together with an additional peak *Fn* that is a consequence of nasalization. The dashed portions of the curves are regions where the spectra do not show clear prominences. The open circles show the frequency of an additional spectral prominence during the nasal murmur. The bottom panel shows the amplitudes of spectral peaks corresponding to *F1*, *F2*, and *F3*. The amplitudes and frequencies are obtained from spectra of the type given in figure 9.16, sampled pitch-synchronously. The time scale is the same as the time scales on the spectrogram and waveforms in figure 9.16.

9.1.4 Summary of Acoustic Characteristics of Nasal Consonants

During the murmur of a nasal consonant, the spectrum has a low-frequency prominence at about 250 Hz, and there is also a weaker prominence in the vicinity of 1000 Hz. The latter is a resonance that is associated with the nasal cavity with an opening of the velopharyngeal port at its posterior end. In addition, there are spectral peaks in the murmur that are dependent on whether the consonantal closure is made with the lips, the tongue blade, or the tongue body. The spectrum of the murmur is also influenced by a zero in the transfer function from glottal to nose volume velocity. The frequency of this zero is a consequence of the side branch between the velopharyngeal opening and the point of closure in the oral cavity. It is lowest (vicinity of 1000 Hz) for a labial, higher for an alveolar, and usually much higher for a velar.

When a nasal consonant is released into a following vowel, there is an abrupt change in the spectrum, particularly in some frequency regions. A principal attribute of this change is an increase of 15 to 20 dB in spectrum amplitude in the vicinity of the second or third formant of the following vowel, depending on the articulator producing the consonant. An appreciable part of this spectrum change is due to a rapid downward movement of the lowest zero as the output shifts from the nose to the mouth. The transitions of the second and third formants following the release of a nasal consonant depend on the following vowel, and are similar to those of a stop consonant produced with the same articulator. The spectral changes at the implosion of a postvocalic nasal consonant are similar to those at the consonant release, except in the reverse order, and possibly with some diminution in the rapidity of spectral change.

9.2 GLIDES

We consider now the glides—a class of consonants produced with a constriction that is not sufficiently narrow to cause a significant average pressure drop across the constriction during normal voicing. Turbulence noise is not generated in the vicinity of the constriction and the vocal folds continue to vibrate in more or less the same manner during the constricted interval as they do in the adjacent vocalic intervals. In this sense, these consonants are similar to nasal consonants, which are also produced with little or no pressure drop in the airways above the glottis. The difference, however, is that for the nasals the oral cavity is closed, and there is a bypass for the air through the nasal cavities, whereas for the glides the air flows past a constriction in the vocal tract.

We examine first the aerodynamic aspects of the glides, and the low-frequency properties of the sound that is produced when the vocal tract is constricted in this manner. We then consider the nature of the spectrum when the constriction is located at different places in the vocal tract, as well as the time variations that occur in the sound immediately preceding and following this interval when the consonant is in intervocalic position. Our discussion here is restricted to consonants that are produced with a narrowing in the front part of the vocal tract, that is, between the velar region and the lips. The discussion of /h/, which is often also considered as a glide, has been given in section 8.3.

9.2.1 Low-Frequency Characteristics of Glides

The minimum cross-sectional area that can be achieved without creating a significant pressure drop across the constriction during the glottal cycle can be calculated approximately using the relations discussed in sections 1.2.2 and 2.1.7. The pressure P_m in the mouth when there is a glottal constriction of area A_g and a supraglottal constriction of area A_c is given approximately by

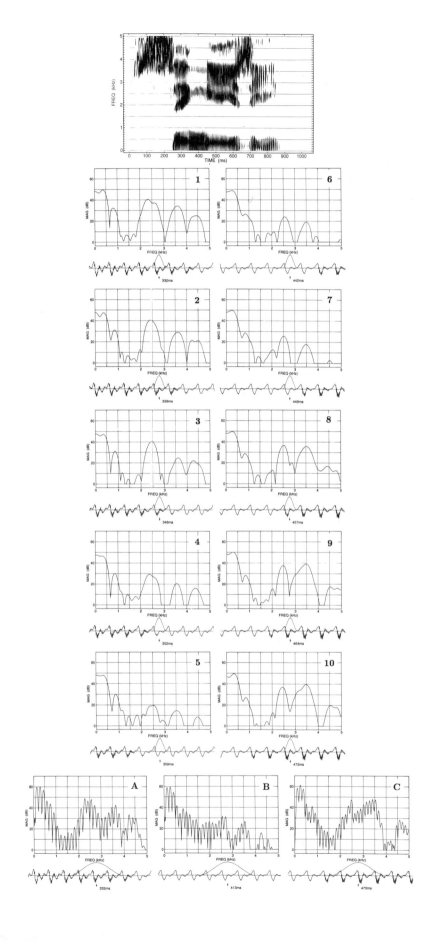

$$P_m = \frac{1}{1 + \left(\dfrac{A_c}{A_g}\right)^2} P_s, \tag{9.1}$$

where P_s = subglottal pressure (cf. equation [2.17]). Thus if P_m is to be less than about one-fourth of P_s, then A_c should be about 1.7 times A_g. If we take the average glottal area during the open portion of the glottal cycle for an adult speaker to be about 0.1 cm^2, and if we assume $P_s = 8$ cm H$_2$O, then A_c should be greater than about 0.17 cm^2 if P_m is not to exceed 2 cm H$_2$O. We shall take the minimum cross-sectional area A_c for a glide, therefore, to be 0.17 cm^2.

As has been shown in section 3.4.2, the frequency of the first formant for these constricted configurations is given approximately by

$$F1 = \sqrt{F1_c^2 + (F1')^2}, \tag{9.2}$$

where $F1_c$ is a constant equal to about 180 Hz for an adult, and $F1'$ is the first-formant frequency if the walls of the vocal tract are assumed to be hard. The term $F1_c$ arises because the vocal tract walls have a finite acoustic mass. When the vocal tract can be approximated as a resonator with volume V, with a neck of area A_c and length ℓ_c, then

$$F1' = \frac{c}{2\pi\sqrt{\dfrac{V\ell_c}{A_c}}}, \tag{9.3}$$

where c = velocity of sound. The first-formant frequency is lower if the constriction is farther forward in the vocal tract (thus making V larger), and if the constriction is longer and has a smaller cross-sectional area.

As a consequence of the amplitude relationships discussed in section 3.2, a decrease in $F1$ causes a reduction in the spectrum amplitude of the sound, both in the amplitude of the $F1$ peak in the spectrum and in the amplitudes of the higher-frequency spectral peaks. A low $F1$ resulting from the formation of a narrow constriction thus tends to reduce the amplitude of the sound during the constricted interval and accentuate the contrast in loudness between the nonsyllabic region of the glide and the nucleus of an adjacent vowel.

Given that the cross-sectional area A_c in the expression for $F1'$ is at the minimum value of about 0.17 cm^2, the first-formant frequency will achieve as low a value as possible if the volume V and the constriction length ℓ_c are as large as possible. There are two configurations that satisfy these conditions: (1) a configuration for which a relatively long constriction in the palatal region is formed with the tongue blade by raising and fronting the tongue

Figure 9.18 Acoustic data obtained from a velar nasal consonant /ŋ/ in the utterance *sing easy*. A spectrogram is shown at the top, and the panels under the spectrogram are spectra sampled at several points and with different time windows. See legend for figure 9.7.

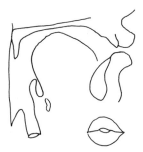

Figure 9.19 Midsagittal sections when the vocal tract reaches its most constricted configuration for the glides /w/ (left) and /j/ (right). In the case of /w/, the frontal lip contour is also shown, to illustrate the lip rounding. (Adapted from Bothorel et al., 1986.)

body into a position like the vowel /i/ but with a narrower constriction, and (2) a configuration produced by forming a narrow lip opening with rounding of the lips, similar to the vowel /u/ but again with a narrower constriction. The vocal tract configurations that are achieved when these two glides reach their maximally constricted positions are shown in figure 9.19. In the case of the rounded configuration, the tongue body is placed in a raised and backed position, and consequently this glide can be considered to be velar as well as rounded or labial. For the configuration with the high front tongue body position the lips are not rounded, but may be spread. The reasons for these secondary adjustments are discussed below. For both configurations, the tongue root is advanced to maximize the volume in the pharyngeal region, as well as to push the tongue body upward to form a narrow constriction near the hard or soft palate.

If the glide is produced in intervocalic position, the relevant articulatory parameters that control the position of the tongue body, lip protrusion, and tongue root advancing must be manipulated from values appropriate for the vowel to values for the glide and back again. As we have seen in section 1.3.3, the total time taken to perform these maneuvers is in the range of 200 to 250 ms. The rates of change of the cross-sectional area preceding and following the time of maximum constriction are expected to be slower than those for stop consonants.

In the case of the palatal configuration, the volume behind the constriction (for an adult male vocal tract) is about 50 cm^3, and the constriction has an effective length of about 3.0 cm if the cross-sectional area is taken to be 0.17 cm^2. (The acoustic mass of the constriction is approximated as the sum of a narrow section of area 0.17 cm^2 and length 1.0 cm and a somewhat wider section of area 0.4 cm^2 and length 4.7 cm. This constriction has the same acoustic mass as a constriction of area 0.17 cm^2 and length 3.0 cm.) The Helmholtz resonance for this configuration, assuming a hard-walled vocal tract, is about 190 Hz. When the effect of the walls is included, the calculated $F1$ is $\sqrt{180^2 + 190^2} = 260$ Hz. This value is appropriate for an adult male, and may be slightly higher for an adult female, whose vocal tract dimensions

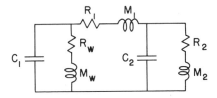

Figure 9.20 Low-frequency equivalent circuit for the labial glide configuration /w/ in figure 9.19, including the resistances R_1 and R_2 at the velar and labial constrictions, and the impedance of the walls R_w and M_w.

are smaller. We note, however, that the wall effects reduce the sensitivity of $F1$ to differences in vocal tract dimensions.

For the rounded velar configuration, the first-formant frequency can be calculated from the equivalent circuit shown in figure 9.20. The dimensions are assumed to be the following:

Volume behind velar constriction	35 cm³
Volume between velar and labial constrictions	15 cm³
Cross-sectional area of velar constriction	0.2 cm²
Cross-sectional area of labial constriction	0.17 cm²
Effective length of velar constriction	3.5 cm
Effective length of labial constriction	0.8 cm

The lowest natural frequency of this configuration, assuming hard walls (i.e., with M_w and R_w removed in figure 9.20), is about 200 Hz. Application of the wall correction gives about 270 Hz, that is, approximately the same as for the palatal glide. It may be noted that both the velar and the labial constriction contribute to the lowering of $F1$. If only one of these constrictions were formed, $F1$ would be higher (290 Hz for the velar constriction alone, and 410 Hz for the labial constriction alone).

These calculations of $F1$ for the two constricted vocal tract shapes in figure 9.19, together with the estimates of the minimum cross-sectional area based on aerodynamic considerations, indicate that the minimum $F1$ expected for a glide is about 260 Hz. A lower value can be achieved only if some pressure is built up in the vocal tract behind the constriction, with the possibility of turbulence noise generation at the constriction.

Precise measurements of $F1$ for glides are difficult to make because of the proximity of $F1$ to the fundamental frequency. Average data for a number of utterances of the form /ə'GVt/ and /ə'GVp/, where $G = $ /w j/, and $V = $ /i ɪ ɛ æ ɑ ʌ ʊ u/, were obtained from a female and a male speaker. Average values of $F1$ across all vowel environments are given in the first two columns of table 9.1. The differences between the two speakers are negligible, and the measurements are consistent with the theoretical analysis given above. The $F1$ values at the minimum point in the glide did, however, show a dependence on the following vowel, as columns 3 and 4 of the table indi-

Table 9.1 Low-frequency acoustic characteristics of the glides /w/ and /j/ produced by a female and a male speaker

	F1 (Hz)		Average before high vowels	Average before non-high vowels	Average reduction of A1 before high vowels (dB)	Average reduction of A1 before non-high vowels (dB)
	w	j				
Female	280	253	245	291	12.2	6.9
Male	298	250	255	293	9.1	5.1

Note: Data are averages from utterances of the form /ə'wV/ and /ə'jV/, with eight different vowels and two repetitions of each sequence. Each entry is an average of data from sixteen utterances. See text.

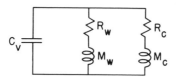

Figure 9.21 Low-frequency equivalent circuit for the palatal glide configuration /j/ in figure 9.19.

cate. When /w/ and /j/ precede a high vowel, F1 is about 40 Hz lower than for a following non-high vowel. One might speculate that a more constricted glide is produced when the adjacent vowel is a high vowel in order to enhance the contrast between the glide and the following syllabic nucleus. Without this enhancement, the change in F1 from the glide to the vowel would be minimal. Such enhancement is not needed for a following non-high vowel, for which F1 is significantly higher than it is in the glide.

The airflow through the narrow constriction or constrictions contributes an acoustic resistance due to the kinetic pressure drop, and the resulting additional acoustic losses cause an increase in the bandwidth of the first formant, relative to its bandwidth for a less constricted vocal tract. Since F1 is relatively low, wall losses also contribute to the bandwidth of F1. The low-frequency equivalent circuit for the palatal glide, including the effect of losses, is given in figure 9.21. The acoustic compliance C_v represents the vocal tract volume, and the two parallel paths represent the walls (M_w and R_w) and the constriction (M_c and R_c). Values of M_w and R_w, from section 1.1.3.7, are 0.015 gm/cm^4 and 7.5 dyne-s/cm^5, respectively, assuming a surface area of about 100 cm^2. For the palatal constriction, $M_c = 0.020$ gm/cm^4, and $R_c = \rho U/A_c^2$ for a constriction of area A_c and airflow U. We take the average U to be 150 cm^3/s, and $A_c = 0.17$ cm^2, giving a resistance of 5.9 dyne-s/cm^5. The bandwidth of the resonance for the circuit in figure 9.21 is calculated to be 60 Hz. When this bandwidth is added to the contribution from other sources of loss, particularly at the glottis, the overall bandwidth

Figure 9.22 The solid line shows the typical shape of a pulse of glottal volume velocity for an open vowel. The dashed line indicates schematically the modification of this pulse for a glide which is produced with a relatively narrow constriction in the vocal tract.

of $F1$ is expected to be in the range of 100 to 150 Hz, that is, somewhat greater than the bandwidth normally observed for most vowels. A similar $F1$ bandwidth is calculated for the labiovelar glide.

Another consequence of the narrowed vocal tract constriction for a glide is to modify the shape of the pulses of volume velocity at the glottis, as has been discussed in section 2.1.7. The airflow U through the constriction during the changing glottal volume flow causes a pressure drop across the constriction. This pressure drop is given by

$$\Delta P_c = M_c \frac{dU}{dt} + \frac{\rho U^2}{2A_c^2}, \tag{9.4}$$

where U is the volume flow and M_c is the acoustic mass of the constriction. For a "normal" glottal pulse, dU/dt during the opening phase is roughly 250,000 cm³/s², and the maximum U is about 400 cm³/s. Each of the terms in equation (9.4), therefore, can reach a maximum of about 3 to 5 cm H_2O. The result is a reduced transglottal pressure during the rising phase of the glottal flow, leading to a modified pulse of the form shown schematically in figure 9.22. The overall effect is to reduce somewhat the amplitude of the glottal pulses and hence to reduce the spectrum amplitude at low frequencies.

Estimates of the change in the glottal source have been made from acoustic measurements of the spectrum in the constricted interval and in the following vowel for utterances containing /w/ and /j/ (Bickley and Stevens, 1987). Average data for six speakers show that the amplitude of the first harmonic of the glottal source decreases by 2 to 3 dB during the constricted interval, whereas the spectrum amplitude of the source at frequencies in the $F2$ range for /j/ can decrease by about 9 dB. Electroglottographic data indicate an increased open time of the glottal area of about 10 percent during the constricted interval for /w/ and /j/ (Bickley and Stevens, 1987). The dashed waveform in figure 9.22 has been drawn to be consistent with these observations.

In summary, the formation of a narrow vocal tract constriction for a glide has several acoustic consequences at low frequencies: a lowering of the first-formant frequency, a modest increase in the bandwidth of $F1$, and a reduction in the amplitude of the glottal pulse. Each of these factors contributes to a reduction in the spectrum amplitude of the first-formant peak. The contribution of the bandwidth increase, on average, is probably in the range 2 to

5 dB, and that due to the change in the glottal pulse is expected to be 2 to 3 dB. Measured reductions in the amplitude $A1$ of the first-formant prominence due to these factors have been shown to be in the range 5 to 10 dB for /w/ and /j/ (Bickley and Stevens, 1987; see also Espy-Wilson, 1992). Some examples of the reduction in $A1$ during glides have been given in figure 5.2.

The amplitude $A1$ of the first-formant peak was measured in the glide and in the following vowel in the utterances for which the data in table 9.1 were obtained. The amplitude differences $\Delta A1$ showed considerable variability, particularly across vowel contexts, and were in the range of 2 to 16 dB. However, these differences depended on whether the following vowel was a high vowel or a non-high vowel. The data are given in the last two columns of table 9.1. When the glide precedes a high vowel, the $F1$ amplitude increase from the glide to the vowel is about 4 dB greater than in the context of a non-high vowel. This result is consistent with a hypothesis that the glide is more narrowly constricted before a high vowel. This more extreme constriction not only lowers $F1$ but also reacts back on the glottal source to reduce its amplitude at low frequencies, resulting in further enhancement of the acoustic contrast between the glide and the adjacent high vowel.

The above discussion has suggested that there is a minimum constriction size that is consistent with the production of a glide with no significant increase in intraoral pressure. It should be noted, however, that there is not a requirement for this minimum constriction size to be achieved each time a glide is produced. This kind of precision is not needed, since the principal requirement for a glide (which always occurs immediately preceding a vowel, at least in English) appears to be that there is a sufficiently reduced low-frequency amplitude relative to the vowel.

The low-frequency acoustic characteristics we have been discussing are intended to apply to the moment in time when the vocal tract is in its most constricted position during the production of a glide. When a glide is in intervocalic position, the size of the vocal tract constriction formed by the tongue body or the lips becomes smaller near the end of the first vowel, remains in the constricted configuration for a few tens of milliseconds, and then increases as the articulatory structures move toward the following vowel. Direct observations of the time course of the constriction size are difficult to make. The trajectory of $F1$ vs. time provides an indication of the change in the cross-sectional area of the constriction, since when $F1$ is relatively low it is a Helmholtz resonance (corrected for the effect of the yielding walls). If we assume a simple model with a volume V, with A_c = area of the constriction and ℓ_c = length of the constriction, and with a natural frequency of the closed vocal tract equal to 180 Hz, then we can write

$$F1 = \sqrt{\left(\frac{c}{2\pi}\right)^2 \cdot \frac{A_c}{V\ell_c} + 180^2} \tag{9.5}$$

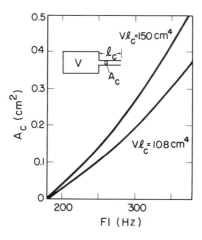

Figure 9.23 Calculated relation between the constriction area A_c and the lowest natural frequency $F1$ for the model shown in the inset. Model configurations corresponding to two values of the product $V\ell_c$ are considered: $V\ell_c = 150$ cm^4 is appropriate for a male palatal glide ($V = 50$ cm^3, $\ell_c = 3$ cm), and $V\ell_c = 108$ cm^4 is appropriate for a female palatal glide ($V = 40$ cm^3, $\ell_c = 2.7$ cm). The effect of yielding walls is included, so that $F1 = 180$ Hz when $A_c = 0$.

or

$$A_c = \left(\frac{2\pi}{c}\right)^2 V\ell_c(F1^2 - 180^2). \tag{9.6}$$

Typical values for V and ℓ_c for a palatal constriction might be 50 cm^3 and 3.0 cm ($V\ell_c = 150$ cm^4) for a male vocal tract, and 40 cm^3 and 2.7 cm ($V\ell_c = 108$ cm^4) for a female vocal tract. The graph given in figure 9.23 shows the relation between A_c and $F1$ for each of these cases.

Spectrograms of two utterances /ə'jɑt/ and /ə'wɪt/ produced by a male and a female speaker are shown in figure 9.24, together with estimates of the $F1$ trajectories superimposed on the spectrograms. For the male speaker the minimum value of $F1$ is lower than that for this female speaker in the utterance /ə'jɑt/ (about 260 Hz for the male and 320 Hz for the female). Consequently the minimum cross-sectional area as determined from figure 9.23 is about the same for the male and the female models (about 0.2 cm^2). The low-frequency model for the labial glide is somewhat more complex than that for the palatal glide, but a similar minimum cross-sectional area is expected for the labial.

The $F1$ trajectories in figure 9.24 indicate that $F1$ shows a broad minimum, and increases on either side of this minimum by about 100 Hz over a time interval of about 50 ms. If we approximate the $F1$ contour over this 100-ms interval by a symmetrical parabola, then, using equation (9.6), we can obtain a rough estimate of how the cross-sectional area of the vocal tract changes with time over this region. The results of this calculation for the female and the male speaker are given in figure 9.25. The curves rise slowly and then more steeply from the minimum around 0.2 cm^2. The maximum rate of change of cross-sectional area in this time interval is at the edges (± 50 ms)

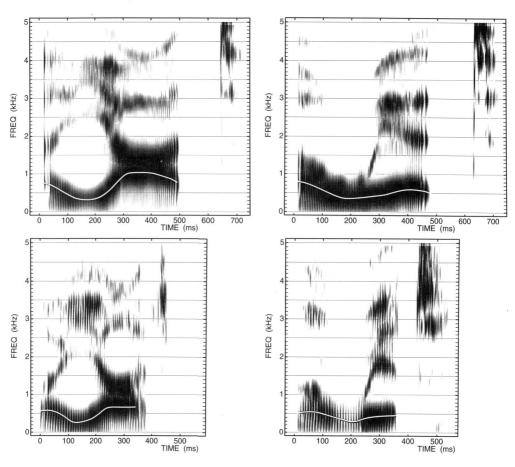

Figure 9.24 Spectrograms of the utterances /ə'jɑt/ and /ə'wɪt/ produced by a female speaker (top) and a male speaker (bottom). Measured $F1$ trajectories are superimposed on the spectrograms.

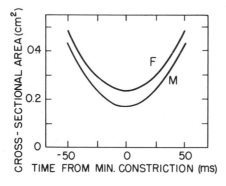

Figure 9.25 Estimated time course of the cross-sectional area formed by the constriction for a glide, derived from calculations based on $F1$ trajectories of the type shown in figure 9.24. The $F1$ trajectories are approximated by parabolas, as described in the text. Equation (9.6) and figure 9.23 were used to calculate the areas. Calculations are based on average formant trajectories for several glides produced by a male (M) and a female (F) speaker.

and is about 10 cm²/s. This rate of change of area can be compared with that estimated at the implosion and release of labial and alveolar stops (100 and 50 cm²/s, respectively) and velar stops (25 cm²/s).

9.2.2 High-Frequency Characteristics of Glides

As we have seen, both the palatal glide and the labial glide are produced with constrictions that are long and narrow, and give rise to a first-formant frequency that must not decrease below a value that is consistent with the lack of a significant average pressure drop across the constriction. The two types of constrictions—palatal in one case and labial combined with velar in the other—result in sound outputs with very different spectral shapes above the frequency of the first formant. We turn now to examine these contrasting spectral shapes.

9.2.2.1 Labial Glide When the lip opening is narrowed, there is a decrease in the second- and higher-formant frequencies, as well as a lowering of $F1$, as expected on the basis of the analysis in section 3.3. Raising of the tongue body in the velar region produces a secondary constriction near the middle of the vocal tract, as shown in figure 9.19. The effect of this secondary constriction near the middle of a tube that is narrowed at both ends is to lower $F2$ still further, since the distribution of volume velocity within the vocal tract for this configuration at this frequency has a maximum in the velar region. (This relation between the distribution of volume velocity in a tube for a particular mode and the shift in frequency of that mode when a perturbation is made in the shape of the tube has been discussed in section 3.3.5.) The secondary constriction also has the effect of raising $F3$ slightly, so that the net effect is for $F3$ to change little relative to its average frequency for vowels. The frequency of the third formant for this configuration, however, has little relevance for perception since the lowered $F1$ and $F2$ cause a greatly reduced amplitude of the $F3$ spectral peak.

An approximation to $F2$ can be obtained from the lumped circuit for the labial glide configuration, given in figure 9.20. Since $F2$ is relatively low, the wavelength is sufficiently long that the lumped circuit is reasonably valid. The second natural frequency for that circuit, given the element values listed in section 9.2.1, is about 700 Hz.

If the narrowing produced by the lip rounding and the raised tongue body for the labial glide is severe, as it is for the dimensions assumed in connection with figure 9.20, the kinetic resistances at the constrictions in the presence of airflow will cause a significant increase in the bandwidth of $F2$. The principal contributor to the losses is the constriction at the lips, since the acoustic mass of the labial constriction is smaller than that of the constriction produced with the tongue body. (See equation [3.55].) If we again assume an average airflow of 150 cm³/s, the resistances R_1 and R_2 in figure 9.20 are, respectively, 4.3 and 5.9 dyne-s/cm⁵, and the contribution of these resistances to the bandwidth of $F2$ is about 150 Hz. If other sources of loss are included, an $F2$ bandwidth in excess of 200 Hz is expected.

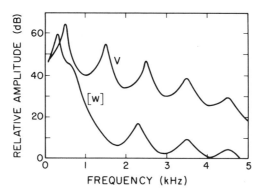

Figure 9.26 The lower curve gives the calculated spectrum envelope for the constricted interval in the glide /w/. The upper curve is the estimated spectrum of a neutral vowel V, assuming the same glottal volume velocity waveform. Additional modifications are expected in the spectrum of the glide due to the effects of the supraglottal constrictions on the glottal source, as discussed in the text.

The calculated spectrum envelope for this labial glide when it is maximally constricted is shown in figure 9.26. This spectrum is calculated assuming a somewhat widened bandwidth of $F1$ (100 Hz) and an $F2$ bandwidth of 200 Hz. Displayed for comparison is the spectrum envelope for a neutral vowel with equally spaced formant frequencies. The amplitude and spectrum of the glottal volume velocity waveform are the same for the glide and for the vowel. The spectrum of the glide shows a reduced amplitude of the $F1$ spectral peak in relation to the vowel (about a 5-dB difference), the suppressed $F2$ peak due to its increased bandwidth, and the weak spectrum amplitude at high frequencies as a consequence of the lowered frequencies of the first and second formants. Some additional decrease in amplitude of the glide of 2 to 3 dB is expected since there will be a reduced amplitude of the glottal pulses due to the increased acoustic impedance of the constricted vocal tract. If this additional decrease is included, the reduction in $F1$ amplitude in the glide relative to the vowel is consistent with the data in table 9.1 for non-high vowels. Except for the spectral prominence at $F1$, the spectrum of the labial glide has no peaks that are important perceptually. The $F2$ prominence is flattened by increased acoustic losses, and the $F3$ and higher prominences are at least 30 dB lower in level than the $F1$ peak, and are obscured by the upward spread of masking from $F1$ (cf. section 4.2.6).

When the labial glide is in intervocalic position, the first and second formants tend to move downward into the glide and upward following the release of the glide. The spectral peak corresponding to $F2$ is more prominent in the transition into and out of the constricted configuration than it is at the time when the constriction is narrowest, and the amplitudes of higher-frequency spectral peaks become greater.

Examples of spectra sampled in utterances of /ə'wɪt/ by a female and a male talker are shown in figure 9.27. Spectra are calculated in the middle of the glide, and in the preceding and following vowels. The utterances are the

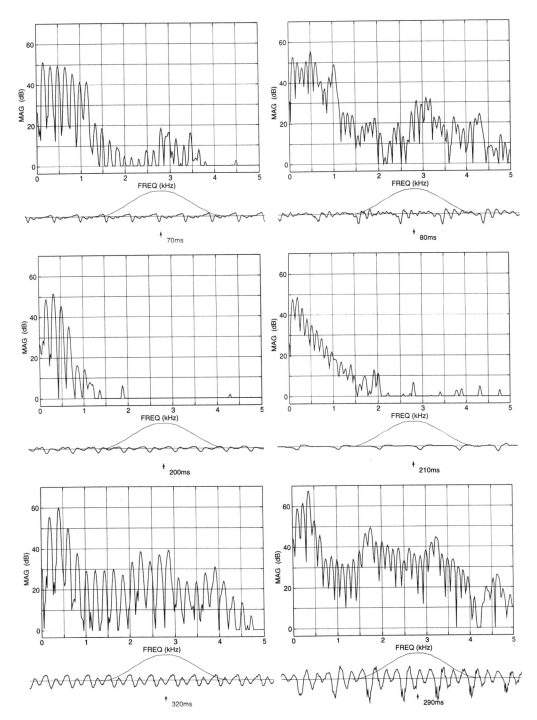

Figure 9.27 Spectra sampled at several points through the utterance /ə'wɪt/, produced by a female speaker (left) and a male speaker (right). In each case, the spectrum in the middle is sampled near the point of maximum constriction, and the spectra on the top and bottom are sampled in the preceding unstressed vowel and the following stressed vowel, respectively. Waveforms and time windows (30 ms) are shown below the spectra.

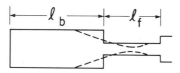

Figure 9.28 The configuration of tubes given by the solid lines is a first approximation to the vocal tract shape for the palatal glide. The dashed lines represent a modification that is a somewhat better approximation for estimating the frequencies of F2 and F3. The lengths of the back (ℓ_b) and front (ℓ_f) cavities are labeled.

same as those for which spectrograms are given in figure 9.24. The change in amplitude of the *F1* peak from the glide to the stressed vowel is 9 to 17 dB in these examples—somewhat greater than the difference predicted from the calculated spectra in figure 9.26. Presumably there is some reduction in the amplitude of the glottal waveform during the glide as a consequence of the loading by the constricted vocal tract, and this reduction may in some cases be more than the 2 to 3 dB estimated above, particularly before a high vowel, as observed in table 9.1. This interpretation is supported by the observation that the amplitude of the first harmonic is somewhat lower in the glide than it is in the following vowel (6 dB lower for the female speaker and 10 dB lower for the male speaker).

The spectra also show that the second formant is sufficiently wide and close to *F1* during the glide that it is not evident as a separate prominence, as expected from the calculated spectrum in figure 9.26. Finally, the spectral peak corresponding to *F3* in the glide is more than 30 dB below that in the adjacent vowel. This difference is somewhat greater than the calculation in figure 9.26 would predict, presumably because the loading on the glottis has an influence on the glottal spectrum.

9.2.2.2 Palatal Glide Whereas the sound produced with a labial and tongue body constriction has a maximally low *F2*, the glide produced with the tongue blade against the palate (shown in figure 9.19) gives rise to a second-formant frequency that is high and is close to *F3* and *F4*. The formant pattern can be estimated roughly from the simple resonator shape given by the solid lines in figure 9.28, that is, the shape that has been used to approximate the configuration for the vowel /i/. The first-formant frequency, as we have seen, is a Helmholtz resonance (with a correction for the acoustic mass of the walls).

A rough approximation to the second-, third-, and fourth-formant frequencies is obtained by estimating the uncoupled natural frequencies of the back and front sections, whose lengths are ℓ_b and ℓ_f, respectively. If we select $\ell_b = 10$ cm and $\ell_f = 6$ cm, we obtain $F2 = c/2\ell_b = 1770$ Hz, $F3 = c/2\ell_f = 2950$ Hz, and $F4 = c/\ell_b = 3540$ Hz. Modification of the shape to be somewhat more realistic, as shown by the dashed lines in figure 9.28, could lead to a raising of *F2* from this calculated value. The increase in *F2* is a consequence of the narrowing over the anterior region of the back cavity.

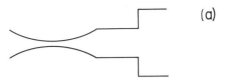

(a)

(b)

Figure 9.29 (a) Model of front cavity used to estimate the frequency and bandwidth of the front-cavity resonance for a palatal glide. (b) Circuit representation of model in (a), consisting of a transmission line with a termination at each end. The elements R_c and M_c represent the impedance at the narrowest point in (a). The transmission line has a characteristic impedance that changes along its length.

The change in shape of the narrow front cavity of length ℓ_f can also lead to a change in F3. If the narrowing is in the middle of this cavity, where there is a maximum in the sound pressure distribution, F3 will increase and will become close to F4. On the other hand, if the narrowing is toward the posterior end of the cavity, F3 will not change or will be displaced downward, and be close to F2. The natural frequencies corresponding to F2 and F4 are resonances of the back cavity, which has a relatively large volume, and their bandwidths are not greatly influenced by radiation effects or by the kinetic resistance at the constriction. The third formant, however, is a resonance of the small front cavity, and its bandwidth is strongly influenced by the radiation resistance and by the kinetic resistance of the constriction.

An estimate of the frequency and bandwidth of F3 can be made from the model of the front cavity given in figure 9.29a, with a narrow opening at the posterior end of the cavity. A transmission-line representation is given in figure 9.29b, including the radiation impedance Z_R. The transmission line is an approximation to the tube in front of the narrowest point. We take the effective cross-sectional area and length of the narrow constriction at the posterior end to be 0.17 cm^2 and 0.5 cm, respectively. The area and length of the main tube are taken to be 0.4 cm^2 and 4.8 cm. This configuration gives a natural frequency of about 3000 Hz. If we assume an average airflow of 150 cm^3/s, the acoustic resistance R_c of the constriction is $\rho \times 150/(0.17)^2 = 5.9$ acoustic ohms. This resistance is in series with an acoustic mass M_c of $\rho \times 0.5/0.17 = 0.0034$ gm/cm^4. The reactance of this acoustic mass, $2\pi f M_c$, dominates the acoustic impedance of the constriction at 3000 Hz. If the maximum acoustic volume velocity at the open end is U_m, then the acoustic volume velocity U_c at the narrow constriction at a frequency of 3000 Hz (for which the wavelength $\lambda = 11.8$ cm) is

$$U_c = \left| U_m \cos\left(\frac{2\pi \times 4.8}{11.8} \right) \right| = 0.83 U_m. \tag{9.7}$$

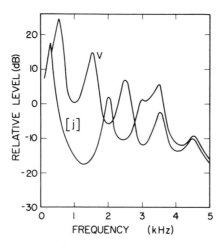

Figure 9.30 The curve with the lower first formant gives the calculated spectrum envelope for the constricted interval in the glide /j/. The curve labeled V is the estimated spectrum of a neutral vowel, assuming the same glottal volume velocity waveform. Additional modifications are expected in the spectrum of the glide due to the effects of the supraglottal constriction on the glottal source. See text.

To calculate the approximate contribution of the resistance R_c to the bandwidth, we use equation (3.40). In this equation the power dissipated in R_c is $(1/2)U_c^2R_c$, and the average energy stored is $1/4\ U_m^2\ \ell_{eff}\cdot\rho/A$, where ℓ_{eff} is the equivalent length of the cavity (equal to $\lambda/2 = 5.9$ cm) and A is the cross-sectional area (0.4 cm^2 in this case). From equation (3.40) the bandwidth contribution is

$$B_c = \frac{R_c}{\pi\cdot\dfrac{\rho\ell}{A}}\left(\frac{U_c}{U_m}\right)^2 \cong 80\,Hz. \tag{9.8}$$

This component of the bandwidth is quite sensitive to the cross-sectional area of the constriction. Adding the bandwidth due to the radiation loss (about 100 Hz, taking into account the widened mouth opening, as described in section 3.4.1), and from other sources such as viscosity and heat conduction, yields a total bandwidth of $F3$ in the range of 200 to 300 Hz.

The calculated spectrum envelope for this palatal glide when it is in the maximally constricted configuration is shown in figure 9.30. This spectrum does not include a possible reduction in the amplitude of the glottal pulses as a consequence of loading by the constricted vocal tract. We again contrast this spectrum envelope with that of a neutral vowel. The attribute of interest for the glide is the broad energy concentration in the frequency range of 3 to 4 kHz. This energy concentration is dominated by the $F4$ peak at 3.5 kHz, which is relatively narrow, and which is accentuated by the proximity of $F3$ at 3.0 kHz. The third formant is not manifested as a separate spectral prominence but rather as a shoulder on the low-frequency side of the $F4$ peak. The $F3$–$F4$ peak dominates the $F2$ prominence, which is well separated from $F3$ in this case. The amplitude of the $F4$ peak in the calculated spectrum is slightly stronger in the glide than in the vowel. That is, the high-frequency amplitude reduction that is to be expected as a consequence of the lowered $F1$ is compensated by the enhanced high-frequency prominence due to the raising of $F2$ and $F3$ to bring these formants into closer proximity to $F4$. However, there will be an additional reduction in the high-frequency spectrum amplitude in the glide due to the effect of the narrowed vocal tract shape on the glottal waveform (Bickley and Stevens, 1987).

While the details of the calculations given above are subject to individual variation, the general form of the spectrum for the palatal glide seems clear. In the mid- and high-frequency range, there is an upward-sloping spectrum dominated by a broad peak in the $F4$ range. This domination of the $F4$ peak over the $F2$ peak is accentuated if one takes into account the greater sensitivity of the ear in that frequency range due primarily to the resonance of the ear canal. The higher-frequency dominance is achieved because $F3$ is adjusted to be high and close to $F4$ (or, in some cases, lower and close to $F2$) and because there are significant acoustic losses for this formant from both the radiation and the kinetic resistance.

When the palatal glide is adjacent to a vowel, the formant frequencies undergo transitions between the glide and the vowel. The second- and third-formant frequencies tend to be lower in the vowel than in the glide. These formants (particularly $F3$) are manifested in the vowel as individual spectral prominences, whereas in the glide they contribute to the overall shape of the spectrum but do not necessarily appear as well-defined prominences.

When the vowel adjacent to a palatal glide is a back vowel there is sometimes a change in cavity affiliation of $F2$ and $F3$ during the movement from the vowel to the glide. For example, in the case of the configuration for /ɑ/, $F3$ is often associated with the back cavity and $F2$ with the front cavity. During the motion from the /ɑ/ configuration to the configuration for a palatal glide, $F2$ increases and $F3$ decreases initially. Ultimately, the resonance of the front cavity becomes associated with $F3$, and $F2$ becomes a back-cavity resonance. The movements of the "back-cavity" and "front-cavity" resonances during the maneuver from the vowel to the palatal glide and back again are shown schematically as dashed lines in figure 9.31. The two uncoupled resonances intersect. The actual resonances, of course, never intersect, and follow trajectories as indicated by the solid lines. In particular, we observe that $F3$ undergoes a reversal of direction of motion during the movement into and out of the glide. Both $F2$ and $F3$ reach a maximum at the midpoint of the glide. The initial downward movement of $F3$ and upward movement of $F2$ can also be explained in terms of perturbation theory, if we assume that the initial movement toward the /j/ configuration from a neutral vowel configuration involves a perturbation of the type shown in figure 9.32. This narrowing of the tube is centered on a minimum in the volume velocity pattern for $F2$ and is near a maximum in the pattern for $F3$ (as displayed in figures 3.9 and 3.19), and therefore leads to an upward movement of $F2$ and a downward movement of $F3$.

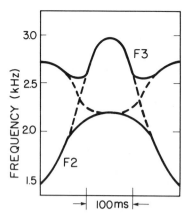

Figure 9.31 Schematized representation of formant trajectories and resonances associated with front and back cavities for a palatal glide /j/ between two vowels /ɑ/. The front-cavity resonance rises and falls, and intersects with the back-cavity resonance, which falls and rises. The actual formant frequencies for the coupled system are given by the solid lines. The scales are approximate only.

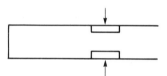

Figure 9.32 Schematized representation of initial perturbation of uniform vocal tract during movement to /j/ configuration. This perturbation leads to an upward movement of F2 and a downward movement of F3.

Figure 9.33 gives examples of spectra sampled in the utterances of /ə'jɑt/ shown earlier in figure 9.24. Again, the spectra are sampled near the most constricted point in the glide and in the adjacent vowels. As in the case of the labial glide (see figure 9.27), the amplitude of the first harmonic is slightly less in the glide than in the following vowel, indicating some reduction in the amplitude of the glottal pulses during the more constricted interval. The proximity of F3 and F4 is evident in the glide, although in these examples the F3 peak is more prominent than the calculated spectrum in figure 9.30 would suggest. The spectrum amplitude of the glide in the F3–F4 region is slightly higher than that in the preceding unstressed vowel, but is less than the amplitude in that region for the following stressed vowel. As noted above, the high-frequency amplitude of the glottal spectrum in the glide may be weaker than that in the vowel, because of the influence of the narrow constriction for the glide.

9.2.3 Summary of Characteristics of Glides

The glides /w/ and /j/ are produced with a narrowing in the oral cavity that is more constricted than for a high vowel. This configuration leads to a rela-

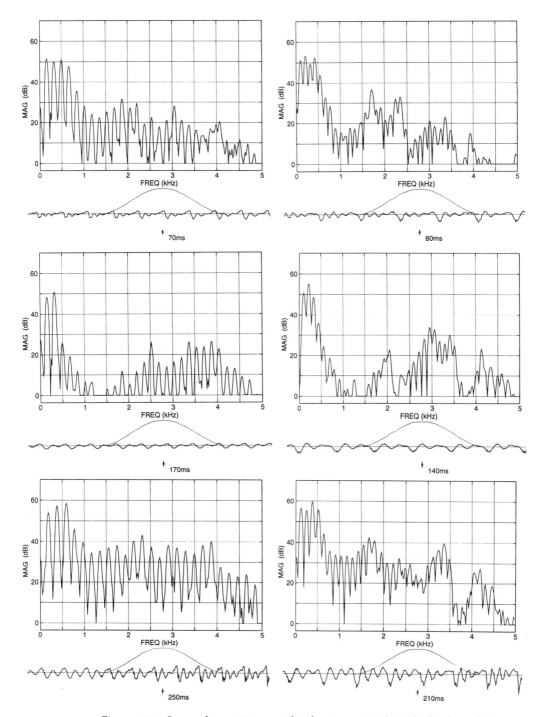

Figure 9.33 Same as figure 9.27, except that the utterance is /ə'jɑt/. The female speaker is represented in the left panels and the male speaker in the right panels.

tively low first-formant frequency in the range of 250 to 300 Hz. The constriction size is not sufficiently small that it produces turbulence noise at the constriction. It can, however, have an influence on the glottal source, causing a reduction in spectrum amplitude during the time when the vocal tract is most constricted, particularly at high frequencies. The low $F1$ and the source modification result in a reduced low-frequency amplitude for a glide in relation to an adjacent vowel, so that there is an enhanced contrast between the vowel and the glide. The duration of the movements of the formants from the minimum constriction point for a glide into a vowel is 100 ms or more, and the rate of increase of the constriction area is considerably slower than that for a stop consonant.

For the labial glide, the tongue body and lip constrictions lead to an $F2$ well below 1 kHz, and to a relatively wide bandwidth of $F2$. As a consequence, $F2$ shows only a weak prominence adjacent to the dominant $F1$ peak in the spectrum. The relatively long palatal constriction for the glide /j/ gives rise to a high-frequency $F2$ and $F3$, with $F3$ being close to $F4$. The $F3$ bandwidth is relatively large due to radiation losses and losses at the palatal constriction, whereas the bandwidths of $F2$ and $F4$ are generally smaller. Changes in cavity affiliations of the formants as the vocal tract moves from a palatal glide to a vowel (particularly a back vowel) can lead to a reversal in the direction of movement of $F3$ during the transition from the glide to the vowel configuration.

9.3 LIQUIDS

We turn next to another class of consonants for which the constriction is not sufficiently narrow to cause a significant pressure drop due to the glottal airflow, or to cause turbulence noise to be generated in the vicinity of the constriction. The consonants to be described in this section are called liquids.[2] They differ from the glides in that the constriction is much shorter than that produced with the tongue blade or with the tongue body and rounded lips for the glides. Another significant difference between liquids and glides, or between liquids and vowels, is that the airway between the glottis and the lips for liquids cannot be approximated as a simple tube in which one-dimensional waves propagate. Rather, the tongue in the oral cavity is shaped in such a way that there is a split or bifurcation of the airway. This splitting of the airway has certain acoustic consequences in the middle and higher frequencies that differentiate the spectra of liquids from those of glides and vowels. We restrict our consideration here to two liquids that are produced by raising the tongue blade so that the edges of the blade near the tongue tip are close to the hard palate. A constriction is formed between the hard palate and the edge of the tongue blade or the apex of the tongue, and the length of this constriction is relatively short. The two liquids we will examine in detail are the ones that occur in American English—a lateral, which is relatively common in languages (Maddieson, 1984), and a retroflex approxi-

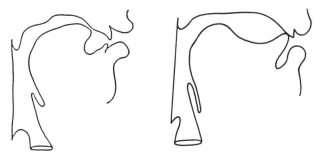

Figure 9.34 Midsagittal sections of the vocal tract for the liquid consonants /r/ (left) and /l/ (right). The midsagittal sections do not reflect the fact that in each case there is an acoustic path around the lateral edges of the tongue blade. The representation of /l/ is adapted from Narayanan et al. (1995b).

mant, which is somewhat less common. Midsagittal sections of the vocal tract for typical productions of these consonants are shown in figure 9.34. These midsagittal sections do not, of course, show the presence of an acoustic path around the edges of the tongue blade.

The discussion here is concerned for the most part with liquid consonants in prevocalic position.

9.3.1 Low-Frequency Characteristics of Liquids

In common with the glides described above in section 9.2, and with the nasal consonants, the sonorant liquids have the distinguishing attribute that airflow through the constriction can occur with little or no pressure drop. Consequently the vocal folds continue to vibrate to produce approximately the same volume velocity waveform through the time interval in which the consonantal constriction is maintained. Thus there is little change in the amplitude of the fundamental component of the sound as the vocal tract moves from a vowel configuration through the consonantal configuration and back to a more open vowel configuration. As we have seen, this condition requires that the cross-sectional area of the constriction during the consonant should be no less than about 0.17 cm^2.

The fact that the constriction is shorter for the liquids than for the glides results in a higher first-formant frequency for the liquids. If we assume a constriction length of 1.0 cm and a volume of 40 cm^3 behind the constriction, and we include the effect of the yielding walls (as discussed above in section 9.2, and in section 3.4.2), then the calculated lowest natural frequency of the resonator for a liquid is about 400 Hz. This is slightly higher than the frequency of $F1$ for a high vowel. Measurements of average values of $F1$ for liquid consonants in prestressed position are in the range of 350 to 480 Hz for female speakers and 330 to 430 Hz for male speakers (Espy-Wilson, 1987, 1992; K. N. Stevens and Blumstein, 1994; Westbury et al., 1995; Hagiwara, 1995).

As in the case of the glides, the narrow constriction for the liquids introduces acoustic losses that increase the bandwidth of the first formant. Calculations of the acoustic losses due to the vocal tract walls and the kinetic resistance at the constriction, assuming an average airflow of 150 cm^3/s, show an increase in F1 bandwidth of about 80 Hz, over and above the expected bandwidth of about 60 Hz due to other sources of loss. This increase in the bandwidth of F1 during the constricted interval for the liquid will tend to broaden the low-frequency spectral peak and to reduce the spectrum amplitude at the peak, and hence reduce the overall amplitude. In addition, the narrow constriction can have an effect on the glottal vibration pattern, leading to a further decrease in the low-frequency amplitude, as discussed in section 2.1.7. The reduced amplitude will help to contrast a nonsyllabic liquid with the amplitude peak in the adjacent syllabic nucleus, even though the first-formant frequency in an adjacent vowel might be lower than that in the liquid if the adjacent vowel is a high vowel. For example, if F1 for an adjacent vowel is 500 Hz, with a bandwidth of, say, 80 Hz, then the expected amplitude of the F1 spectral peak for a liquid will be at least 7 dB below that for the following vowel—about 2 dB because of the lowered frequency of F1 and about 5 dB because of the increased bandwidth of F1, with a possible additional decrease in the source amplitude.

Measurements have been made of the amplitude of the F1 prominence for the two liquids /r/ and /l/ in prestressed position before a variety of vowels in English. The words with initial liquids were in a sentence frame, preceded by an unstressed vowel. Average data for two speakers (one female, one male) show that this level is an average of about 10 dB below the level of the F1 prominence in the vowel, measured 50 ms after the consonant release. The standard deviation across vowel environments for a given consonant and speaker ranges from 2 to 5 dB. Similar data are reported in Bickley and Stevens (1987) and in Espy-Wilson (1992). This measured change is a few decibels greater than the expected change due to the greater F1 bandwidth in the liquid and due to the average change in the frequency of F1 between the liquid and the vowel, and provides evidence that there is an additional reduction due to a decrease in the amplitude of the glottal source during the time when the vocal tract is constricted for the liquid. The change in amplitude of the F1 peak is expected to be less than 10 dB when the liquid is adjacent to a reduced vowel (K. N. Stevens and Blumstein, 1994), since the degree of constriction for the consonant is probably less in this context.

Spectrograms of examples of /r/ and /l/ in an intervocalic prestressed environment are shown in figure 9.35. The contour of F1 vs. time is superimposed on each spectrogram. The minimum value of F1 during the liquids is about 400 Hz. The change in F1 at the release of the lateral is more abrupt than the movement in F1 for the retroflex consonant, presumably reflecting a more rapid change in cross-sectional area of the constriction at the lateral release. The time over which the F1 trajectory undergoes the fall and rise between the two vowels appears to be somewhat shorter for the liquids than

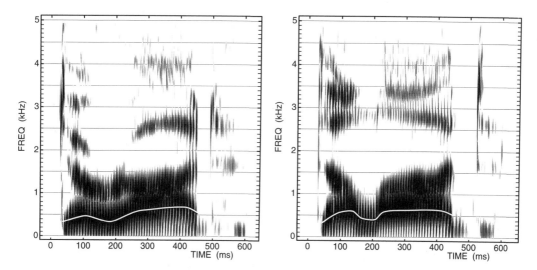

Figure 9.35 Spectrograms of the utterances /dəˈrɑd/ (left) and /dəˈlɑd/ (right) produced by a male speaker. The time course of the first-formant frequency during the liquid consonant is overlaid on the spectrogram.

for the glides, possibly as a consequence of the fact that the shorter constriction for the liquids begins to have a significant effect on $F1$ only when a more narrowed configuration is reached. As will be observed later (and as can be seen in the spectrograms at higher frequencies), the acoustic effects of the movements toward and away from the retroflex or lateral configurations extend over a time that is considerably longer than the interval in which there is a significant effect on $F1$.

9.3.2 High-Frequency Characteristics of Liquids

While the low-frequency spectrum during the constricted interval for liquids has the common attribute of an $F1$ that is not as low as that for a glide, together with a widened $F1$ bandwidth, significant spectral differences at higher frequencies can be achieved by adjusting the way the tongue blade is configured to form the constriction. We will consider two contrasting configurations of the tongue blade that will lead to a high-frequency spectrum characterized either by a front-cavity resonance that is lowered and positioned close to $F2$, or by a raised front-cavity resonance that is close to $F4$. Both configurations are realized by adjusting the tongue blade in a way that introduces an additional acoustic side branch in the airway between the glottis and the lips.

9.3.2.1 Retroflex Liquid Consonant
We consider first a configuration that lowers the front-cavity resonance and positions it close to $F2$. We shall identify this front-cavity natural frequency as F_R. The basic approach here is to locate the constriction formed by the tongue blade such that the natural

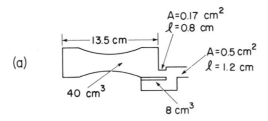

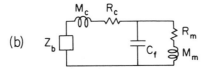

Figure 9.36 (a) Schematized model of the vocal tract used for estimating the acoustic characteristics of a retroflex consonant. The side branch representing the space under the tongue is shown, together with the constrictions formed by the tongue blade and the lips. (b) Equivalent circuit used to obtain the approximate frequency of the front-cavity resonance of the configuration in (a). The volume of the front cavity is represented by C_f, and the constrictions posterior and anterior to the cavity are represented by R_c, M_c, R_m, and M_m. Z_b is the impedance of the cavity behind the constriction.

frequency of the portion of the vocal tract in front of the constriction is about equal to the natural frequency of the portion behind the constriction (excluding $F1$, which can be approximated as a Helmholtz resonance). This condition is achieved by raising the apex of the tongue above the floor of the oral cavity, creating a space on the underside of the tongue, as shown in the midsagittal configuration in figure 9.34a. This configuration indicates that there is some rounding of the lips, presumably to extend the length of the front cavity and thereby to enhance the lowering of its natural frequency.

A model of the vocal tract configuration for /r/ in figure 9.34, given in figure 9.36a, can be used to estimate the frequencies of $F2$ and F_R. The dimensions of this model are appropriate for an adult male vocal tract. The Helmholtz resonance for this configuration is about 380 Hz, taking into account the labial constriction as well as the constriction for the tongue blade, and correcting for the effect of the vocal tract walls. This is approximately the $F1$ value calculated above in section 9.3.1. The back cavity, of length 13.5 cm and cross-sectional area 3.0 cm², would have a lowest natural frequency of about 1310 Hz if its cross-sectional area were uniform. This frequency is not influenced much by the constriction and by coupling to the front cavity. However, the backing of the tongue body that can be seen in figure 9.34 causes a narrowing in the back cavity, as shown in the model of figure 9.36a, and this narrowing will lower the back-cavity resonance slightly. A second resonance of the back cavity will occur at roughly twice the frequency of the first resonance, that is, around 2600 Hz.

The front cavity is represented by a volume of about 8 cm³, including the space under the tongue blade, and by a narrowed lip opening. The calculated natural frequency for this cavity, assuming no acoustic coupling through the constriction, is about 1290 Hz. This frequency is shifted upward, however, by the impedance looking back into the constriction and the rear cavity. An equivalent circuit for the front cavity, showing the impedance of the constriction (depicted by R_c and M_c) and the impedance Z_b of the back cavity, is given in figure 9.36b. The front-cavity resonance is calculated to be about 1660 Hz when coupling to the back cavity is taken into account. The overall configuration of figure 9.36a, then, gives rise to an F_R that is considerably lower than $F3$ for a vowel, and $F2$ and F_R are rather close together.

The acoustic losses at the constriction add very little to the bandwidth of the back-cavity resonance because the impedance looking forward into the constriction from the back cavity is very high compared with the characteristic impedance of the back cavity. The bandwidth of $F2$ arises, then, from other sources, particularly the glottis, and is expected to be about 100 Hz. On the other hand, losses at the constriction cause a substantial bandwidth increase for the front-cavity resonance, which has a higher impedance level than the back cavity. The contribution of the constriction to the bandwidth of F_R can be calculated from the equivalent circuit in figure 9.36b. We assume, as before, an average airflow U through the constriction of 150 cm^3/s, giving a kinetic resistance, $R_c = \rho \times 150/(0.17)^2 = 5.9$ acoustic ohms. The acoustic impedance in series with this resistance is

$$j\omega M_c - j\frac{\rho c}{A_b} \cot \frac{\omega \ell_b}{c} = jX, \tag{9.9}$$

where $M_c = \rho \times 0.8/0.17$ gm/cm^4 = acoustic mass of the constriction, and A_b and ℓ_b are the area and length of the back cavity, as in figure 9.36a. If we set $jX = j\omega M_{eq}$, then the contribution of R_c to the bandwidth of F_R is approximately[3]

$$\Delta B_R \cong \frac{R_c}{2\pi M_{eq}} \times \left(\frac{M_m}{M_{eq}}\right)^2, \tag{9.10}$$

where M_m is the acoustic mass of the mouth opening, as shown in figure 9.36b. This bandwidth contribution is calculated to be approximately 100 Hz. If the bandwidth due to radiation loss and other sources is added, the overall bandwidth of the front-cavity resonance is about 200 Hz.

For the midsagittal configuration of /r/ in figure 9.34, the acoustic path from glottis to lips has, in effect, a side branch that is formed by the space under the tongue blade, as represented schematically in the model in figure 9.36a. This side branch introduces a zero in the transfer function from the glottis to the lips, as well as contributing to the low value of F_R. If the length of this side branch is ℓ, and if its cross section is assumed to be uniform, then this zero (which we shall call Z_R) is at a frequency of $c/4\ell$. In this case, ℓ is estimated to be about 4 cm, so that the zero in the transfer function is in the range of 3 kHz. This zero can be displaced upward or downward, however, depending on the exact configuration of the cavity under the tongue blade. The acoustic effect of this zero is to weaken the spectrum in the frequency

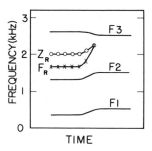

Figure 9.37 Schematized time course of first three formant frequencies ($F1$, $F2$, and $F3$) and additional pole and zero (F_R and Z_R) when a retroflex consonant is released into a vowel.

range above the spectral prominence formed by $F2$ and F_R. The frequency of the zero will always be higher than the natural frequency F_R of the front cavity.

When the retroflex consonant /r/ is released into a vowel, the tongue blade is displaced downward from its raised position, and within a few tens of milliseconds the space under the tongue blade is shortened and finally obliterated. The sequence of acoustic events can be interpreted by examining the changes in the natural frequencies of the system and in the zero that is caused by the side branch under the tongue blade. The trajectories of these frequencies during the consonant release are schematized in figure 9.37. We represent as F_R and Z_R the additional pole and zero that are a consequence of the sublingual cavity. At some point during the release, the pole and zero annihilate each other, and only the original third formant remains, at a frequency of about 2500 Hz in this case. The exact trajectories of F_R and Z_R, including the point at which they cancel, are expected to show considerable variability. For example, spectrum analysis for a retroflex consonant can show a zero as low as 2 kHz.

This analysis suggests that it is convenient to describe the spectrum of the retroflex consonant during the constricted interval as an all-pole spectrum ($F1, F2$, and $F3$ in figure 9.37, together with higher formants) modified by a pole-zero pair (F_R and Z_R in figure 9.37).

The calculated spectrum envelope for the /r/ configuration in figure 9.34, as modeled in figure 9.36a and modified by a zero at 2 kHz, is given in figure 9.38. In order to show the effect of F_R and Z_R we display the components contributing to the spectrum envelope: the all-pole spectrum derived from $F1, F2, F3$, and so on, and the contribution of the pole-zero pair. The significant spectral prominence at about 1300 Hz is evident. The greater bandwidth of F_R is manifested in the spectrum as a "shoulder" on the high-frequency side of the prominence, and not as a separate spectral peak. There is a lack of spectral energy above 2 kHz because of the low $F1$ and $F2$. This attribute is enhanced by the zero in the transfer function, as shown in the middle panel of figure 9.38.

One consequence of the contribution of the pole-zero pair to the spectrum is a weakening of the amplitudes of the spectral peaks corresponding to $F3$ and to higher formants. When the tongue blade is displaced downward at

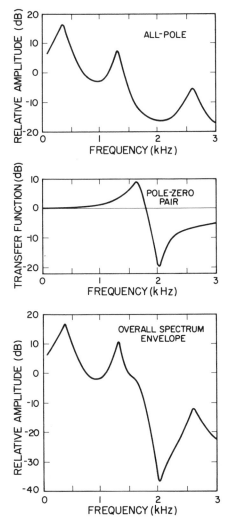

Figure 9.38 Construction of the spectrum envelope for a retroflex consonant. The calculated spectrum envelope is given at the bottom. The top two panels show that the spectrum envelope can be considered as the sum (in decibels) of the spectrum envelope corresponding to an all-pole system with no side branch and the transfer function for a pole-zero pair representing the presence of a side branch.

the release of the retroflex consonant, the resulting merging of Z_R and F_R causes a rather abrupt increase in the amplitudes of these higher formant peaks. This increase in high-frequency spectrum amplitude from the merging of the pole-zero pair is in addition to the amplitude change that is a consequence of any increase that may occur in $F1$ and $F2$ following the consonantal release.

The spectral prominence or shoulder corresponding to F_R is sometimes interpreted as a low-frequency third formant $F3$. This is not an unreasonable interpretation, since, as figures 9.37 and 9.38 show, F_R comes close to merging with $F3$ after release of the consonant, and the spectral peak corresponding to $F3$ during the constricted interval may be very weak.

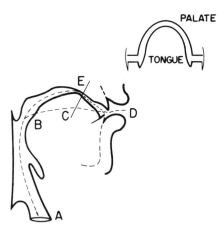

Figure 9.39 Estimate of midsagittal configuration of the vocal tract for producing a "bunched" /r/. The dashed lines indicate the acoustic paths along the midline of the vocal tract and around the sides of the bunched tongue in the palatal region. An estimate of the cross-sectional shape in the palatal region is shown.

It is generally considered that there are two alternative ways of producing the consonant /r/ in American English: one with a raised tongue blade as shown in figure 9.34 and the other with the tongue bunched in the palatal region and with the tongue tip lowered (Delattre and Freeman, 1968; Espy-Wilson et al., 1997). A possible conception of the articulatory shape for this "bunched" /r/ is schematized in figure 9.39. The midline of the tongue is raised to make a narrow constriction in the palatal region, but the sides of the tongue blade are drawn inward, as shown by the sketch of the cross section in this region. Thus there is an acoustic path around the sides of the tongue blade as well as along the midline over the dorsal surface of the tongue. These two paths are indicated by dashed lines in the figure.

A detailed analysis of the acoustic behavior of this configuration has not been worked out. However, an approximate analysis can give the general properties of the transfer function for this vocal tract shape. A tentative analysis is to regard the acoustic path around the sides of the tongue (ABCD in figure 9.39) to be the main path, and to consider the path along the midline, with a narrow constriction formed by the tongue blade, to form a side branch to the principal airway (BE in the figure). The length of this side branch BE is estimated to be about 4 cm, leading to a zero in the vocal tract transfer function at about 2.2 kHz. The natural frequency of the front cavity ED is probably about 1500 Hz, and the main acoustic path could have a natural frequency of about 1200 Hz, leading to a pole-zero pattern not unlike that shown in figure 9.37 for the retroflex consonant. That is, the consonant /r/ produced with a bunched tongue could have acoustic characteristics similar to those for the retroflex configuration.

Both methods of producing /r/—raising the tongue blade and creating a space under it, or keeping the tongue tip low and bunching the tongue— have the effect of introducing an extra resonance in the frequency range

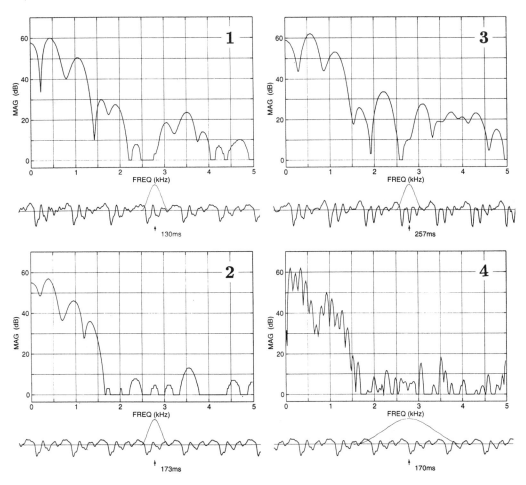

Figure 9.40 Spectra sampled at several points in the utterance /də′rɑd/, for which a spectrogram is shown in figure 9.35. Spectra 1, 2, and 3 are calculated using a short (6.4 ms) time window, whereas spectrum 4 uses a longer (30 ms)time window. Spectra 2 and 4 are sampled near the most constricted part of the consonant /r/, and show the close proximity of F2 and F_R, at about 950 and 1350 Hz, with evidence of a weak F3 peak at 2300 Hz and a zero just below 2000 Hz. Spectra 1 and 3 are sampled during the initial movement from the initial vowel and the final movement toward the final vowel, respectively. These spectra show a double peak corresponding to F_R and F3 in the frequency range 1.5 to 2.5 kHz.

normally occupied by F2. The characteristic acoustic pattern is a pair of spectral peaks in this F2 range.[4]

An example of a spectrogram of a retroflex consonant in intervocalic position (for the utterance /dərɑd/) has been shown previously in figure 9.35. In figure 9.40, we display spectra sampled at various times in the vicinity of the point of maximum constriction. Shown in figure 9.41 are plots of F1, F2, F_R, and F3 vs. time, together with the amplitudes of the spectral prominences corresponding to these resonances and to F4, which remains at a frequency of about 3 kHz. Evidence for movements of the tongue blade and tongue body associated with the retroflex consonant can be seen in the second and

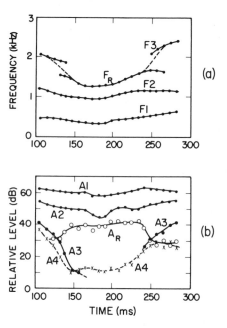

Figure 9.41 (a) Measured frequencies of the spectral peaks corresponding to $F1$, $F2$, $F3$, and F_R in the vicinity of /r/ in the utterance /dəˈrad/. A double peak appears in the spectrum around 130 and 260 ms, as shown in the spectra in figure 9.40, and these two peaks are labeled as F_R and $F3$. In the vicinity of these times dashed lines are drawn to indicate the frequency of an "equivalent" prominence. (b) Amplitudes of the spectral prominences $A1$, $A2$, A_R, $A3$, and $A4$ corresponding to the various formants and to the additional resonance F_R. The prominence corresponding to $F3$ between 150 and 240 ms is too weak to see, and points are not plotted for $F3$ and $A3$ in this time interval.

third formants and in F_R over a time interval of about 170 ms (from about 110 to 280 ms in figure 9.41). The tongue blade raising for retroflexion has an influence on the high-frequency spectrum before there is a substantial effect on $F1$. The spectra and the plots of the frequencies show that at about 130 ms and 250 ms the third formant essentially splits into two peaks. The $F3$ peak becomes weak and is replaced by the F_R peak at about 130 ms, and the reverse happens as the consonant is released.

The proximity of $F2$ and F_R is evident in the spectra and in the frequency plots at the point of maximum constriction in figures 9.40 (panels 2 and 4) and 9.41. Some additional reduction in the high-frequency spectrum amplitude in these examples is probably caused by a modification of the glottal spectrum during the constricted interval. A weak prominence corresponding to $F3$ is evident in the spectra of the consonant in the frequency range 2.0 to 2.5 kHz. This $F3$ prominence is not visible consistently in the spectrum, and is not displayed in the middle of the consonant region in figure 9.41.

The amplitude plots in figure 9.41 show the relatively low amplitude of the $F3$ prominence during the constricted interval. There is a rapid rise in $A3$ (and, to a lesser extent, $A4$) during the movement from the consonant to the vowel. This amplitude increase is 10 to 15 dB over a time interval of 40 ms.

This increase is in part a consequence of the rise in $F1$, $F2$, and F_R (which eventually merges with Z_R). These changes in the lower formant frequencies do not account for all of the increase in the high-frequency spectrum amplitude, and calculations show that 5 to 10 dB of the increase must be a consequence of the change in the spectrum of the glottal output as the consonant constriction is released (cf. Bickley and Stevens, 1987).

Additional examples of prevocalic /r/ are given in figure 9.42. The spectrograms in the figure are obtained from utterances of the word *rug* by a female and a male speaker. The frequencies and amplitudes of the various spectral prominences in these utterances are also plotted in the figure. There are substantial individual differences in the details of the frequency and amplitude plots in figures 9.41 and 9.42, particularly in the way in which the two spectral peaks corresponding to F_R and $F3$ merge into a single peak in the transition from the retroflex to the vowel. The common attributes for all cases, however, are the low F_R close to $F2$ during the constricted interval, and the rapid rise in spectrum amplitude in the $F3$ and $F4$ regions. The maximum rate of increase at the release appears to be in the range 10 to 20 dB over a 20-ms time interval.

Measurements of the formant frequencies of prestressed /r/ have been reported by several investigators (Espy-Wilson, 1987; Hagiwara, 1995; Westbury et al., 1995). These data show considerable variability across speakers and across vowel environments. The ranges of average values given in these reports are summarized in table 9.2.

9.3.2.2 Laterals We turn next to the class of liquids that are produced with an $F3$ that is as high as possible, and well separated from $F2$. The constriction is produced with the tongue blade in contact with the alveolar ridge on the midline, as shown in the midsagittal section of the vocal tract during production of a lateral, in figure 9.34. The lateral has the special characteristic that contact between the hard palate and the lateral edges of the tongue is usually made only along one of these lateral edges and not on the other. In some cases, contact with the hard palate is only on the midline, with the apex of the tongue, and there is no contact along either of the lateral edges of the tongue blade. We restrict our consideration here to configurations for which contact is made along one lateral edge. Another attribute of the lateral consonant in English is a backed and somewhat lowered tongue body position, as shown in figure 9.34 (Sproat and Fujimura, 1993; Narayanan et al., 1995b).

The acoustic behavior of the vocal tract when it is in the configuration of a lateral consonant can be modeled only approximately by an interconnection of resonators in which one-dimensional waves propagate with no side branches. An analysis based on a more complex distribution of sound pressure in the vocal tract is required if a more quantitative prediction of the radiated sound is desired. In order to sketch out the broad features of the radiated sound, however, we base our analysis on an approximate representation in terms of coupled resonators.

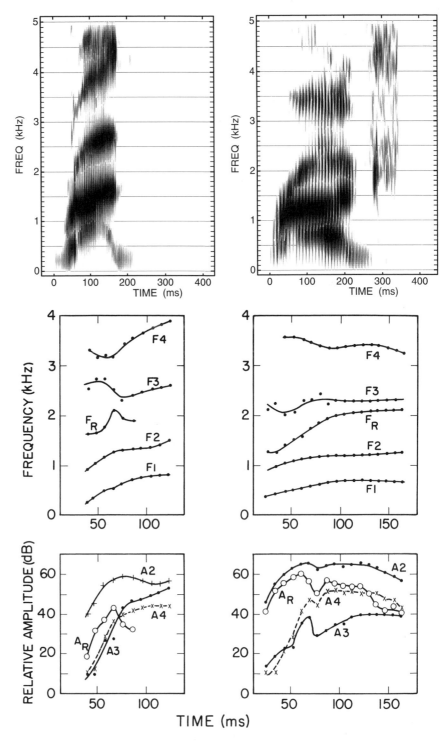

Figure 9.42 At the top are spectrograms of the utterance *rug* produced by a female speaker (left) and a male speaker (right). Below the spectrograms are the frequencies and amplitudes of the various spectral peaks, measured from spectra of the type shown in figure 9.40. For the female speaker, the extra resonance F_R is observable over only part of the time interval shown, whereas it is evident throughout the time interval for the male speaker.

Table 9.2 Ranges of average values of frequencies (in hertz) of first three resonances of prevocalic /r/ as reported by Espy-Wilson (1987), Hagiwara (1995), and Westbury (1995)

	F1	F2	F_R
Female speakers	360–480	1030–1240	1800–2050
Male speakers	330–430	880–1200	1380–1610

Note: The different studies used different numbers of speakers and contexts.

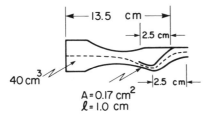

Figure 9.43 Schematization of the vocal tract shape for purposes of calculating the acoustic characteristics of a lateral consonant. Approximate dimensions are shown for the back cavity, the side branch formed by the tongue blade, and the cavity in front of the constriction. The dashed line indicates the midline of the acoustic path from glottis to lips.

The lateral edge of the tongue blade that is not in contact with the palate forms the major constriction in the airway between the glottis and the lips. As with other liquids and glides, we shall assume the minimum cross-sectional area of this constriction to be 0.17 cm², although the area might not always reach this minimum value. As figure 9.34 shows, the tongue body is in a somewhat backed position for the lateral configuration we are considering here (although, of course, laterals with other tongue body configurations are possible), and hence there is a narrowing of the back cavity in a region 4 to 7 cm from its posterior end. The model in figure 9.43 is an approximation to the resonator configuration for a lateral, and shows the main features of the back cavity shape.

The volume of air within the space enclosed by the palate, the closed lateral edge of the tongue blade, and the upper surface of the tongue blade form a side branch in the main acoustic path from the glottis to the lips (Fant, 1960). The model in figure 9.43 shows the principal acoustic path as a dashed line, and the cavity forming a side branch to this path is evident. It is difficult to estimate the effective length of this side branch, since data on the cavity shapes are not available. In the model in figure 9.43, the length of this side branch is estimated to be about 2.5 cm, and the volume of this partially enclosed space is probably about 2 or 3 cm³. A somewhat longer and larger side branch has been estimated by Fant (1960). The model shows that this cavity is coupled to the system at a point immediately anterior to the constriction. The side branch only provides an approximation to the acoustic behavior of the system at high frequencies (above about 1500 Hz). Based on estimates of the possible tongue shapes for laterals, and on acoustic data (to be described below), it is assumed that the effective length of the side branch can be in the range of 2 to 4 cm, depending on the speaker and on the vowel adjacent to the lateral consonant.

As we have seen earlier, in section 9.3.1, the first-formant frequency can be calculated assuming a simple Helmholtz resonator. For the model of figure 9.43, we obtain $F1 \cong 360$ Hz, after correcting for the effects of the finite wall impedance. Losses at the constriction contribute about 80 Hz to the bandwidth of $F1$, as we have observed.

The resonance of the back cavity, which is assumed to be about 13.5 cm long, would give a second-formant frequency of about 1310 Hz if the tube were uniform. The effect of tongue body backing will lower this frequency, and we will take $F2$ to be about 1100 Hz. Acoustic losses at the constriction contribute to the bandwidth of the back-cavity resonance, and this contribution is calculated to be about 40 Hz, as tabulated in section 3.4.5. This amount is added to the $F2$ bandwidth of about 100 Hz from other sources of loss. Higher-frequency modes of the back cavity also play a role in shaping the properties of the sound for the lateral configuration. A uniform tube of length 13.5 cm would give natural frequencies of about 2620 Hz and 3930 Hz. The lower of these two frequencies will be shifted up somewhat because of the narrowing near the midpoint of the back cavity and the higher one may be shifted down slightly. We assume these frequencies to be about 2800 and 3900 Hz for purposes of estimating the spectrum for the lateral.

One consequence of the side branch in figure 9.43 is to add a zero in the vocal tract transfer function. The zero is at a frequency for which the impedance looking into the side branch becomes zero. For the dimensions given in the figure (a length of 2.5 cm for the side branch, with some tapering at the anterior end), this frequency is in the range of 3500 to 4000 Hz. Based on the estimated range for this length given above (2 to 4 cm), the lowest zero resulting from the side branch can be in the frequency range of 2200 to 4400 Hz.

The configuration in figure 9.43 also has a natural frequency associated with the cavity in front of the constriction. If we assume, as in the model, that the effective length of this cavity is about 2.5 cm, then its natural frequency is roughly 3500 Hz. With the combination of radiation loss and losses at the constriction, we take the bandwidth of this resonance to be relatively large, at about 1 kHz.

In the high-frequency range of 1500 to 4000 Hz, then, the lateral configuration is expected to exhibit a cluster of three poles and one zero. The exact frequencies of the components of this cluster depend on the shape of the back cavity, particularly the tongue body position, and on the detailed shape of the anterior portion of the vocal tract. Even though the values of these critical frequencies may be variable, it is evident that the capability exists for adjusting the configuration of the tongue blade to produce such a cluster that leads to a particular high-frequency gross spectrum shape in relation to an adjacent vowel. Acoustic analysis of lateral consonants (discussed below) shows the presence of the broad, multipeaked, high-frequency prominence resulting from this cluster of three poles and a zero, and indicates that the frequency of the lowest peak in this cluster is usually raised somewhat relative to the average position of F3 for a vowel. For the model in figure 9.43, we have estimated that F3 is 2800 Hz—somewhat higher than the average F3 of about 2500 Hz for a male speaker. Some variability is expected in the frequencies of the poles and zero for the lateral configuration depending on the vowel environment and on the individual speaker. Small changes in the frequency of the zero can give rise to large changes in the amplitudes of the spectral peaks corresponding to the poles in this higher-frequency region. Consequently, when the vocal tract is in the lateral configuration, considerable variability can be expected in the spectral shape in the frequency range of 2500 to 4000 Hz.

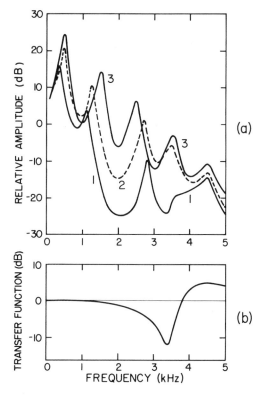

Figure 9.44 The upper panel shows the calculated spectrum envelope at three points in time during the release of a lateral consonant into a neutral vowel. Spectrum 1 is the estimated spectrum during the lateral configuration. The poles (and their bandwidths), in hertz, used to calculate this spectrum are: 360 (160), 1100 (140), 2800 (150), 3500 (300), 3900 (1000), and 4500 (400). There is a zero at 3400 (300). Spectrum 3 is the estimated spectrum envelope for a neutral vowel. Spectrum 2 (dashed line) is the estimated spectrum envelope about 10 ms following the lateral release. The three points in time corresponding to these three spectra are shown on the pole-zero time plots in figure 9.45. The lower panel shows the component of the vocal tract transfer function corresponding to the zero at 3400 Hz and the pole at 3900 Hz. As shown in figure 9.45, the zero moves upward to extinguish the pole immediately following the lateral release.

The calculated spectrum for a lateral configuration like the one modeled in figure 9.43 is shown as spectrum 1 in figure 9.44, together with the spectrum (curve 3) for a neutral vowel. The frequencies and bandwidths of the poles and zero that were used in the calculation are summarized in the figure legend. The lower amplitudes of the $F1$ and $F2$ spectral peaks in the lateral in relation to those in the vowel, due to their lower frequencies and increased bandwidths, are evident, as well as the broad irregular high-frequency spectral prominence. In this example, the zero has been placed at about 3.4 kHz, so that the peak associated with the pole at 3.5 kHz is suppressed. The contribution of the pole-zero pair to the overall spectrum for the lateral configuration is displayed below the spectrum envelope, in figure 9.44b.

During the few tens of milliseconds following the release of a lateral consonant into a vowel, the rate of release of the apex of the tongue is expected to be similar to that for an alveolar stop consonant, but the downward movement of the lateral edges may be slower. Consequently, the overall rate of increase of the cross-sectional area of the constriction is probably slower than it is for an alveolar stop or nasal consonant. Possible time courses for the various formants and for the high-frequency pole-zero pair when a lateral consonant is released into a neutral vowel are sketched in figure 9.45. A small decrease in $F3$ is shown in the figure, on the assumption that there will be a forward movement of the tongue body following the release, resulting in a decrease in the natural frequency of the back cavity. To simplify the picture, we have assumed $F4$ and $F5$ to remain constant across the release. Considerable variety is expected in this pattern in the middle and high frequencies, depending on the speaker and on the vowel context of the lateral consonant. A common attribute, however, is some irregularity in the spec-

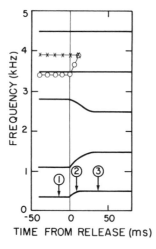

Figure 9.45 Schematization of a possible time course of the various natural frequencies and the zero as a lateral consonant is released into a following neutral vowel. The pole-zero pair that becomes annihilated is represented by x's and o's. The points labeled 1, 2, and 3 indicate times where the spectra in figure 9.44 are calculated.

trum of the lateral in this frequency range, with at least one additional spectral prominence over and above those normally expected for a vowel. The increase in area of the constriction results in a rapid increase in $F1$ and a somewhat slower increase in $F2$, and the decrease in the kinetic acoustic resistance at the constriction will result in a rapid decrease in the bandwidths to values more appropriate for a vowel.

As the apex of the tongue lowers, and as the lateral edges of the tongue blade fall, the side branch disappears, and the zero in the vocal tract transfer function is eliminated. The annihilation of the zero occurs by merging with a pole—in this case the pole at 3900 Hz. Thus the perturbation caused by the zero at 3.4 kHz and the pole at 3.9 kHz, shown in figure 9.44, disappears. The effect of the pole-zero pair on the transfer function is mostly confined to frequencies near the pole and the zero. The general effect, however, is to modify the shape of the spectrum in this high-frequency range.

The effects of the changes in the frequency and bandwidth of $F1$ and $F2$, as well as the rapid shift of the high-frequency zero, are illustrated by the calculated spectrum corresponding to curve 2 in figure 9.44. The rapid rise in the frequencies $F1$ and $F2$ causes an abrupt rise in the amplitude of the cluster of formant peaks in the high-frequency range. The annihilation of the zero causes an additional abrupt rise in amplitude of the spectrum in the vicinity of 3.5 kHz, giving a total rise of about 13 dB from spectrum 1 to spectrum 2.

Not considered in figure 9.44 is the possibility that the spectrum of the glottal source may be modified during the constricted interval because of the acoustic and aerodynamic effect of the constriction (Bickley and Stevens, 1987). This modification would reduce the amplitude of spectrum 1 by a few decibels at high frequencies, and the increase in spectrum amplitude at high frequencies following the release would be greater than the increase shown in figure 9.44.

Experimental data (to be described below) indicate that much of this modification of the higher-frequency spectrum shape occurs within 10 to 20 ms following the release. Thus the movement of the zero following the release is rapid, as shown in figure 9.45.

If a lateral consonant is produced in intervocalic or postvocalic position, spectral changes of the same kind can occur at the consonant implosion. However, the sequence of movements of the tongue blade and tongue body is often not simply the reverse of the movements that occur at the release. The movements of several structures from configurations appropriate for the preceding vowel must be coordinated to achieve the lateral configuration. The tongue body must be maneuvered to a backed position, the apex of the tongue must make contact with the hard palate, one of the edges of the tongue must make contact with the palate along some portion of its length, and the other edge must be positioned to leave a narrow constriction. The timing of contact of the tongue tip in relation to the positioning of the edges of the tongue can have a significant effect on the way the acoustic spectrum changes during the interval when the closure is being formed.

When the lateral consonant is in intervocalic position, there appears to be considerable asymmetry in the acoustic pattern, with the implosion of the consonant showing less discontinuity and the $F2$ transition prior to the transition extending over a longer time interval than at the release. The principal source of this asymmetry is uncertain, but it is likely that the requirement for backness of the tongue body, coupled with the need to position and to shape the tongue blade with some precision, causes a reduction in the rates of movement of these structures.

Acoustic data for the lateral consonant in the utterance /dəlad/ are given in figures 9.46 and 9.47. Spectra sampled during the constricted interval and immediately preceding and following the constricted interval for the lateral are shown, together with plots of the amplitudes and frequencies of various spectral peaks. The utterance is the same as that shown earlier in figure 9.35b.

The spectra and the spectrogram (right side of figure 9.35) show the changes in the formant frequencies and the amplitudes of the spectral peaks, particularly at the time of release, which is at about 210 ms. The changes in amplitudes are displayed more clearly in the amplitude plots in figure 9.47b. The amplitudes change more rapidly at the release than at the implosion (at about 150 ms), and the increase in $A4$ is especially abrupt (compare the short-time spectra 4 and 5 at 217 and 233 ms). The movements of the second formant and the changes in the amplitudes of the spectral peaks extend well beyond the implosion and release of the lateral consonant. Near the beginning of the constricted interval, the third formant prominence splits into two spectral peaks (spectrum 2 at 157 ms), and both are plotted in figure 9.47a. Apparently the acoustic path near the tongue blade splits into two channels, leading to a replacement of the pole in the vocal tract transfer function at about 2800 Hz by a pole-zero-pole cluster.

Frequencies of $F1$ and $F2$ for prestressed lateral consonants, measured 10 ms before the consonant release, are shown in the first two columns of table 9.3. Average data (and standard deviations) are given for a female and a male speaker producing words containing /l/ preceded by nine to eleven different vowels (K. N. Stevens and Blumstein, 1994). The frequency of the spectral prominence in the vicinity of $F3$ was variable, and is not given. The ranges of values of $F1$ and $F2$ are consistent with data reported by Espy-Wilson (1987). The variability of the formant frequencies was not entirely random. Values of $F2$ tended to be higher than average before front vowels and lower than average before back vowels; $F1$ was lower when the lateral was before a high vowel than before a low vowel.

Patterns of spectral change at the lateral closure for postvocalic laterals and at the lateral release for syllable-initial laterals have been measured for the same utterances (K. N. Stevens and Blumstein, 1994). Spectra similar to the 6.4-ms spectra in figure 9.46 were sampled at times 10 ms on either side of the estimated points of closure and release. Changes in the amplitudes and frequencies of the first two spectral prominences (corresponding to $F1$ and

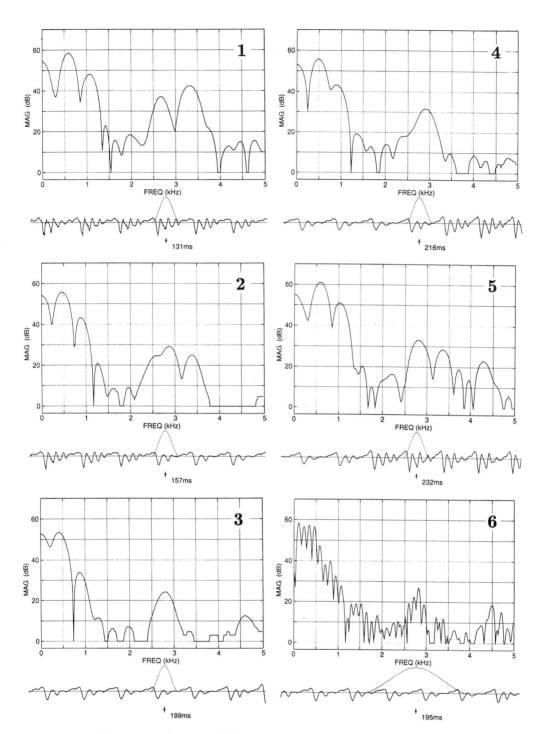

Figure 9.46 Spectra sampled at several points within the utterance /dəˈlɑd/, a spectrogram of which is shown in figure 9.35. Spectra 1 to 5 are obtained with a time window of 6.4 ms, centered on individual glottal pulses. At time 157 ms (spectrum 2), there is evidence of a double peak in the F3 range, apparently resulting from two slightly asymmetrical acoustic paths around the tongue blade. The increase in spectrum amplitude of the F4 peak (around 3400 Hz) is especially abrupt from 217 to 233 ms (spectra 4 and 5). Spectrum 6 is obtained with a 30-ms time window centered at a time immediately prior to the release (about the same time as spectrum 3). The peak at 1400 Hz is assumed to be a tracheal resonance.

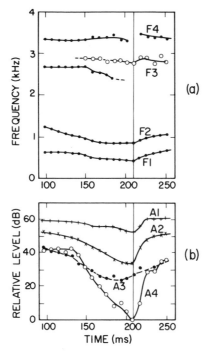

Figure 9.47 (a) Measured frequencies of the spectral peaks corresponding to $F1$ through $F4$ in the vicinity of /l/ in the utterance /dəˈlɑd/. A double peak appears in the spectrum in the region of 150 to 180 ms, labeled $F3$ in this figure and shown in spectrum 2 in figure 9.46. (b) Amplitudes of the spectral prominences corresponding to the first four formants. At around time 208 ms, the $F4$ prominence is too weak to be visible on the spectrum, presumably because it is obscured by a zero in the transfer function. The abrupt increase in $A4$ at the release is apparent, as are the somewhat gentler increases in $A2$ and $A1$.

Table 9.3 Measurements of formant frequencies and changes in formant frequencies and formant amplitudes at the release (prestressed) and closure (poststressed) of lateral consonants, for two speakers

		$F1$ (Hz)	$F2$ (Hz)	$\Delta F1$ (Hz)	$\Delta F2$ (Hz)	$\Delta A1$ (dB)	$\Delta A2$ (dB)	$\Delta A3$ (dB)
Prestressed	Female	350 (67)	1180 (84)	190 (66)	280 (190)	6 (3.1)	13 (2.6)	14 (4.0)
	Male	360 (43)	900 (120)	150 (42)	220 (113)	9 (2.2)	13 (2.4)	12 (4.8)
Poststressed	Female			20 (75)	100 (75)	2 (1.5)	5 (2.0)	3 (3.3)
	Male			60 (53)	150 (91)	1 (1.4)	5 (3.0)	3 (3.2)

Note: Columns 1 and 2 give measurements of $F1$ and $F2$ (and standard deviations) in lateral consonants preceding a number of different vowels, for two speakers. Columns 3–7 list measurements of changes in formant frequencies $\Delta F1$ and $\Delta F2$, and in formant amplitudes ($\Delta A1$, $\Delta A2$, $\Delta A3$) over a 20-ms interval around the points of closure and release for lateral consonants. These different data are averages (and standard deviations) for utterances with nine to eleven different vowel environments, for two syllable positions as shown.
Data from K. N. Stevens and Blumstein, 1994

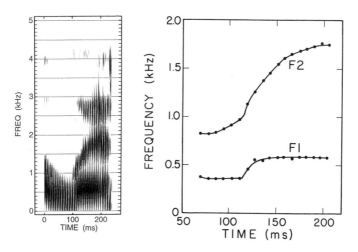

Figure 9.48 Left, Spectrogram of the utterance *a let*. Right, Frequencies of first two formants preceding and following the release of /l/, with points given at each glottal period.

*F*2) over this time interval were measured and averaged over the vowel environments for each speaker. The maximum amplitude of the high-frequency spectral prominence corresponding to *F*3 and *F*4 was also measured in each spectrum and the change in this amplitude (called $\Delta A3$) over the 20-ms interval was calculated. These various amplitude and frequency differences are summarized in columns 3 to 7 in table 9.3. They provide a measure of the "strength" of the spectral discontinuity that occurs at the times of closure and release of lateral consonants. The data show a clear difference between prestressed and postvocalic laterals, with the discontinuities in amplitudes and frequencies being much smaller and more variable for the postvocalic consonants. In postvocalic position, the /l/ is often similar to the offglide of a diphthong. Values of *F*1 and *F*2 in postvocalic position are not given because they were quite variable.

The formant movements over the 50 to 100 ms preceding the discontinuity for a postvocalic lateral or following the discontinuity for a prevocalic lateral reflect the fact that the tongue body is in a backed position during the constricted interval. If the vowel following a lateral is a back vowel, the upward movement of *F*2 after the initial abrupt change is relatively small, whereas for a following front vowel the *F*2 movement is extensive. An example, for the utterance *a let*, is given in figure 9.48. A spectrogram is shown, together with measurements of *F*1 and *F*2. As the figure shows, the upward movement of *F*2 begins before the tongue tip release, indicating that the forward movement of the tongue body in anticipation of the front vowel begins before the release. The time taken for *F*2 to attain a value close to that of the vowel is about 110 ms. There is an initial rapid rise of *F*1 and *F*2 as the tongue blade is released, followed by a slower movement of *F*2 as the tongue body moves forward.

The pattern of spectral change at the release of a lateral consonant has some similarities to the release of a nasal consonant, in that both show a relatively abrupt rise in amplitude for some spectral peaks. There are, however, significant differences. The frequency of the lowest resonance tends to be higher for the lateral than for the nasal consonant. Furthermore, in the transition from the nasal murmur to the following vowel, a resonance at about 1000 Hz becomes annihilated by merging with a zero (see figures 9.5 and 9.9), whereas for the lateral, $F2$ at about the same frequency shows continuity with $F2$ of the following vowel.

9.3.3 Summary of Characteristics of Liquids

The liquids /r/ and /l/ considered in this section are produced by raising the tongue blade to form a narrowing of the airway in the region of the hard palate. In common with glides, these liquids are produced with little or no pressure increase behind the constriction and with continuous glottal vibration. The amplitude and spectrum of the glottal source may decrease slightly due to the influence of the constriction. The frequency of the first formant for liquids is higher than that for glides. The spectrum amplitude of this lowest spectral prominence is generally lower than that of following vowels as a consequence of a greater $F1$ bandwidth and a reduced amplitude of the glottal source. The liquids /r/ and /l/ in English are usually produced with a somewhat backed tongue body configuration. The second formant for both liquids is primarily a resonance of the cavity posterior to the main constriction in the oral cavity, and is generally in the frequency range of 900 to 1200 Hz. A further difference between liquids and glides is that the acoustic path in the oral cavity for liquids contains a side branch or more than one parallel path, leading to the presence of additional poles and zeros in the vocal tract transfer function in the frequency range above 1500 Hz. In intervocalic position, the acoustic influence of liquid consonants in the mid- and high-frequency range extends over a time interval of 200 to 250 ms, and the liquids are similar to glides in this respect.

In the case of the retroflex /r/, the space under the raised tongue blade (or possibly an additional parallel path when the tongue is bunched) gives rise to an additional resonance in the frequency range of 1500 to 2000 Hz, together with a zero at a higher frequency that depresses the spectrum amplitude above this frequency range. This additional resonance F_R has a relatively wide bandwidth due to constriction losses, and appears in the spectrum as a weak prominence just above the more prominent second formant peak during the most constricted part of the /r/.

The vocal tract configuration for /l/ has a complete midline closure of the tongue blade. The blade is shaped so that the main airway passes around its lateral edge (or edges), and a side branch to this airway is formed on the midline. The acoustic effect of this configuration is to introduce an additional pole and zero in the vocal tract transfer function in the frequency range above about 2 kHz. The resonance of the cavity in front of the constriction formed by the tongue blade is usually somewhat higher (by roughly 300 Hz) than the average $F3$ for the speaker. The net result is a relatively wide gap between $F2$ and $F3$, and a cluster of three poles and a zero forming a broad spectral prominence in the frequency range normally occupied by $F3$ and $F4$. At the release of a lateral consonant into a vowel there are some abrupt changes in the frequencies and amplitudes of the spectral prominences.

10 Some Influences of Context on Speech Sound Production

In chapters 6 through 9 we examined the acoustics of the production of vowels and consonants when these sounds occur in relatively simple contexts, usually in consonant-vowel (CV) or vowel-consonant-vowel (VCV) utterances. By limiting the context, it was possible to specify rather precisely the articulatory aspects of the utterances and to develop models for estimating the acoustic patterns from the articulation. For consonants, the main concern was the articulatory and acoustic properties in the vicinity of the landmark at the consonant release, when the consonant was followed by a vowel. In the case of vowels, the discussion in chapter 6 was, for the most part, concerned with steady-state vowels, or at least the aspects of vowels that are minimally influenced by adjacent consonants. When the segments occur in other contexts, particularly in more complex sequences within a syllable or in sentences that are produced in a conversational or casual style, their articulatory and acoustic attributes may be modified. In this chapter examples of several types of modifications in different contexts and speaking styles are described.

10.1 CONSONANT SEQUENCES AT SYLLABLE ONSET

One important source of variability in the implementation of the distinctive features for a segment is the position of the segment in a syllable. When a consonant is in a CV syllable, there is an opportunity to represent in the sound a number of cues for the consonant features. These cues can reside in the sound near the instant of release, immediately prior to the release, or in the few tens of milliseconds following the release. When there is a sequence of two consonants at the beginning or end of a syllable, however, the cues for the features of the consonants may have a different form. The initial consonant, for example, is released into another consonant rather than into a vowel, and consequently the formant transitions that signal the consonant place of articulation are not present in their usual form.

Figure 10.1 shows spectrograms of the two words *spot* and *scot* produced by a female speaker. The initial consonant /s/ in these two words is modified slightly by the following voiceless consonant, which is a labial in one case and a velar in the other.

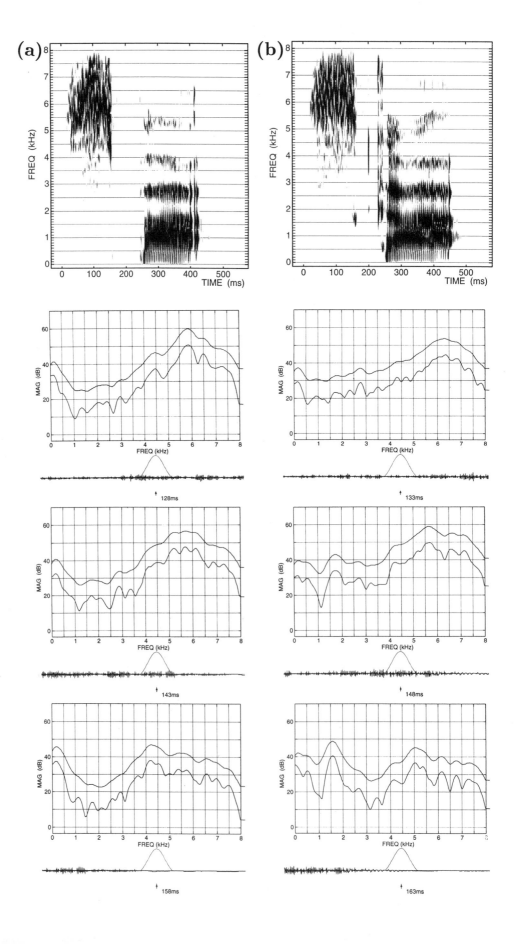

During the fricative consonant in the initial cluster /sp/, the glottis is relatively open, and the constriction is formed by the tongue blade, as described in section 8.1, with a short front cavity having a length of about 1.5 cm. This leads to a front-cavity resonance of about 5.9 kHz, probably corresponding to the sixth formant for this speaker. When the lips are closed to form the labial stop consonant, the natural frequency of this front cavity decreases. The rate of decrease of the lip area is expected to be about 50 cm²/s, so that the time taken for the lips to close is about 20 ms, assuming an initial area of about 1.0 cm² and assuming the velocity to be constant. The total time is probably somewhat longer than 20 ms because time is needed to accelerate the lip movement from its static position for the /s/. The cross-sectional area of the tongue blade constriction is 0.1 to 0.2 cm², with a length of about 0.5 cm. The natural frequency when the lips are closed is a Helmholtz resonance, and is calculated to be in the range of 2.5 to 3.5 kHz for a female speaker. Thus the frequency of the front-cavity resonance is calculated to decrease rapidly as the lip area becomes smaller. This rapid fall of the spectral peak for the noise, with a final frequency of about 2.5 to 3.5 kHz, is consistent with measurements of the frication noise for /s/ in sequences like /sp/ and /sm/ for a female speaker. The front cavity is somewhat longer for a male speaker, and the final frequency is estimated to be in the range of 2 to 3 kHz.

The smoothly changing frequency of the front-cavity resonance is not reflected directly in a continuous decrease in a peak in the spectrum. In fact the high-frequency spectral peak for /s/ may begin as F5 (or F6), and then become F4 and possibly F3, and these changes will occur in jumps rather than being continuous. Below the spectrogram of *spot* in figure 10.1a, three spectra are shown, sampled at 15-ms intervals close to the time of the /p/ closure. In the first of these spectra, the major peak at about 5900 Hz corresponds to the front-cavity resonance for /s/, probably the sixth formant. At a time 15 ms later a peak at 5200 Hz also appears (probably F5). In the third spectrum the major peak is at 4200 Hz, corresponding to F4, and there is a sharp reduction in amplitude at higher frequencies.

When /s/ is followed by /k/, the formation of the velar constriction with the tongue body causes turbulence noise to be generated at that constriction. This noise source excites the cavity anterior to the velar constriction, which in the case of the utterance in figure 10.1b has a natural frequency of about 1.6 kHz. If we assume a rate of decrease of area of the velar constriction to be about 25 cm²/s, as noted in sections 1.3.3 and 7.4.4, then the time interval over which the velar cross-sectional area is less than 0.2 cm² is about 8 ms. If

Figure 10.1 The top panels are spectrograms of the words *spot* (left) and *scot* (right) spoken by a female talker. The spectra below each spectrogram are sampled at three times 15 ms apart near the end of the frication noise for /s/, and show the changes in the spectrum as the closure is made for the /p/ or /k/. The spectra are obtained by averaging a sequence of 6.4-ms spectra over a 10-ms time interval. The upper curve in each panel is a smoothed version of the measured spectrum.

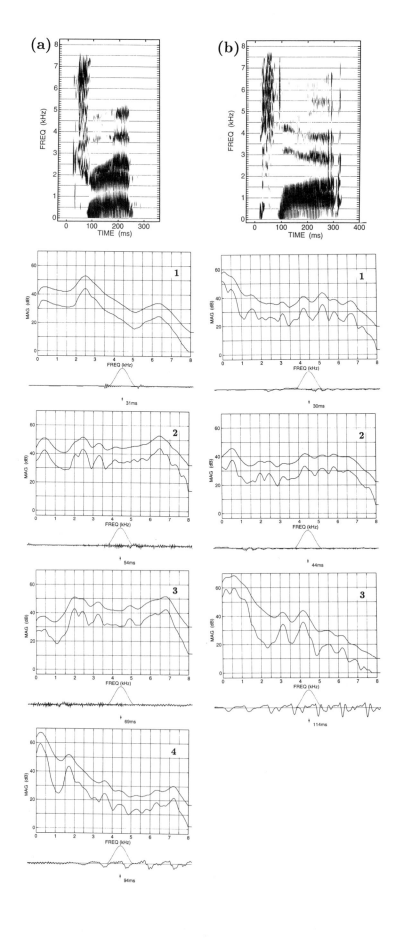

we take the cross-sectional area of the alveolar constriction for /s/ to be about 0.2 cm², then this time interval of 8 ms is the time over which the pressure drop across the velar constriction is significant, and the airflow is sufficient for the generation of turbulence noise at that constriction. The result is the generation of a brief burst of noise with a spectral prominence at the frequency of the front-cavity resonance. This burst of frication noise occurs, then, at the termination of the frication noise generated at the alveolar constriction, the tongue tip constriction being released at the time the velar constriction is formed.

The sequence of acoustic events near the end of the fricative is shown by the three spectra below the spectrogram of *scot* in figure 10.1b. There is a transition from the fricative, with a major spectrum prominence at about 6.4 kHz in the first spectrum, to the velar burst, with two prominences at 1.6 and 5.0 kHz in the third spectrum. The prominence at 5.0 kHz is presumably a second resonance of the cavity anterior to the velar constriction. At the time of release of the /k/ into the following /ɑ/, the frequency of the spectral peak in the burst is about 2.0 kHz. The increase of the front-cavity resonance from 1.6 to 2.0 kHz occurs because of the increased area of the tongue blade constriction during the time interval from the velar closure to the release.

The two examples in figure 10.1 show that the place of articulation of a stop consonant that follows /s/ in a consonant cluster can be signaled by perturbations in the noise spectrum for /s/ as the consonant closure is made. Cues for the stop-consonant place of articulation are also carried in the burst spectrum and in the formant movements following the consonant release.

Syllable-initial consonant clusters consisting of a stop consonant followed by a liquid or glide are shown in figure 10.2. The words are *drip* and *plot*. In the case of the word *drip* in figure 10.2a, the spectrogram shows that there is an interval of about 50 ms from the release of the stop consonant to the onset of glottal vibration. This is significantly longer than the burst duration of about 10 ms that is observed when a syllable-initial voiced stop consonant is followed by a vowel. (See section 8.4.) In the sequence /dr/ the constriction formed by the tongue blade for /r/ is in place at the time of release of the /d/. The cross-sectional area of this constriction is probably about 0.17 cm², and remains at this value for 50 ms or more following the release. The airflow through this constriction following the release comes from the recoil of the vocal tract walls and from the flow through the glottis. The pressure drop at the constriction due to this airflow is sufficient to maintain an intraoral pressure during this initial 50-odd milliseconds, and hence there is a delay before the transglottal pressure becomes sufficiently large to initiate glottal vibration.

Figure 10.2 The top panels are spectrograms of the words *drip* (left) and *plot* (right) produced by a female talker. The spectra below each spectrogram are sampled near the consonant release (top spectra), just after onset of glottal vibration (bottom spectra), and at intermediate points. Spectra are measured as in figure 10.1.

Acoustic events following the stop-consonant release are illustrated by the sequence of spectra below the spectrogram. There is an initial transient with spectral prominences at about 2.5 and 6.5 kHz (spectrum 1), indicating a front cavity with a length of about 3.4 cm. The frequency of the lower prominence is considerably lower than that for an alveolar release into a vowel, and reflects a more posterior position for the tongue tip when the consonant precedes an /r/. During the 20 ms following the release, this prominence remains at about 2.5 kHz, as the tongue tip is displaced downward. After this time, other prominences appear in the spectrum (spectra 2 and 3), suggesting that a turbulence noise source is being generated at a more posterior position, possibly at a constriction formed by the tongue surface in the oral or pharyngeal region. The persistence of a prominence at about 6.5 kHz, the frequency of the second resonance of the front cavity, is evidence that turbulence noise continues to be generated at the widening constriction formed by the tongue blade. Following the onset of glottal vibration (spectrum 4) the spectrum shows the expected $F1$ and $F2$ peaks and a wideband resonance at about 2.2 kHz corresponding to a front-cavity resonance for /r/, as described in section 9.3.

The spectrogram for *plot*, in figure 10.2b, shows a delay of about 80 ms from the release to the onset of glottal vibration. At the time of the labial release, the glottis is presumably spread, as it is for any prestressed voiceless stop consonant, and the glottis gradually closes until it is in a configuration that permits vocal fold vibration.

The sequence of articulatory events can be inferred from the series of spectra below the spectrogram in figure 10.2b. At the instant of release (spectrum 1) there is a brief transient, and this transient excites the various resonances of the vocal tract behind the lips. The tongue blade is apparently not in contact with the hard palate at this moment of release since there is excitation of several resonances. The strong low-frequency amplitude suggests a monopole source at the glottis. After about 15 ms, the tongue blade makes contact with the hard palate, and a lateral constriction is in place (spectrum 2). The major turbulence noise source appears to be at the lips, however, presumably due to airflow impinging on the lip surface. There is a broad peak in the noise spectrum at high frequencies (4 to 6 kHz), with a reduced amplitude at lower frequencies due to a zero in the transfer function. At a time in the noise portion (at about 70 ms) there is a reduction in the noise. This reduction probably occurs as a result of a narrowing of the lateral tongue blade constriction, causing a reduced airflow and an increased pressure behind the constriction. When there is a release of the tongue blade constriction, a brief high-frequency burst appears (at about 90 ms), and the consequent reduction in intraoral pressure creates a condition that results in initiation of glottal vibration. The spectrum about 20 ms after this voicing onset (spectrum 3) shows the expected two low-frequency formants for the lateral, $F2$ having a wider bandwidth, together with a relatively high $F3$, as described in section 9.3.

Substantial individual differences are expected in this sequence of events at the release of this /pl/ cluster, particularly in the timing of the tongue blade closure and in the sequencing of the sources at the lips, glottis, and tongue blade. An example of a somewhat different acoustic pattern for the /pl/ cluster is given in figure 10.3, which shows a spectrogram and spectrum for the word *plod* produced by an adult male speaker. Again there is a delay of about 80 ms from the release of the labial consonant to the onset of glottal vibration. The spectrum of the initial transient and burst (spectrum 1) shows the expected falling shape with no major spectral prominences, although there are minor prominences corresponding to resonances posterior to the labial constriction. As the lips open, the turbulence noise source appears to shift from the lips to the lateral tongue blade constriction, leading to spectral peaks at 2400 Hz (probably a front-cavity resonance) and at 3200 Hz (probably a resonance of the cavity posterior to the tongue blade constriction), as in spectrum 2. The peak at 2.7 to 3.0 kHz in spectrum 3 and, later, in spectrum 4 after glottal vibration begins is presumably the front-cavity resonance. The tongue blade release occurs at about 270 ms, as can be seen in the spectrogram. This utterance in figure 10.3 differs from that in figure 10.2b in that in figure 10.3 turbulence noise is generated at the tongue blade constriction soon after the labial release, whereas in figure 10.2b turbulence noise continues to be generated in the vicinity of the lips.

A syllable-initial consonant cluster that requires timing of the velopharyngeal opening in relation to the oral articulators is illustrated in figure 10.4. The word is *small*, and, like the initial /sp/ cluster in figure 10.1, is produced by superimposing a labial closure on the fricative consonant /s/. In the example of figure 10.4, the labial closure causes a lowering of the frequency of the short front-cavity resonance, and this decrease in the resonance is evident in the spectrogram (figure 10.4a) over a time interval of 10 to 20 ms just prior to the /m/ closure. At the time of the /m/ closure, the velopharyngeal port is closed, and there is an increased pressure in the oral cavity. About 10 to 20 ms after the labial closure, the velopharyngeal port opens, and the intraoral pressure drops as air flows through this opening. The pressure release is marked by a brief, weak transient in the sound (evident only if the waveform is amplified), as the flow into the nasal cavity increases abruptly. The spectrum of this transient, in panel 2 of figure 10.4b, shows prominences at about 600 and 2100 Hz, corresponding to the first two resonances of the nasal cavity. (The additional prominence at 1450 Hz is probably a vocal tract resonance.) These are roughly equal to the resonances that are assumed in sections 6.9 and 9.1, where the acoustic attributes of nasal vowels and nasal consonants are described. The cross-sectional area of the velopharyngeal port increases, as shown schematically in figure 10.4c, and coupling to the nasal cavity continues until shortly after the release of the labial consonant, at about 350 ms. The glottal opening follows a trajectory similar to that in the initial cluster /sp/. There is a widened glottis during the /s/, and the glottal area decreases following the labial closure until the glottal

Some Influences of Context on Speech Sound Production

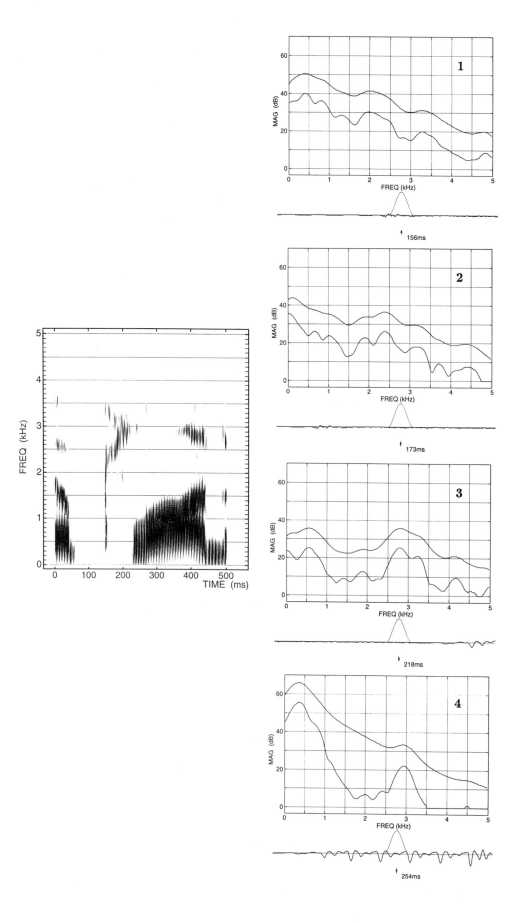

spacing is sufficiently small to result in glottal vibration (at 320 ms). During the time interval from the opening of the velopharyngeal port to the onset of glottal vibration, turbulence noise is generated at the glottis or at the velopharyngeal opening. The spectrum sampled in this brief time interval is given in panel 3 of figure 10.4b. For comparison, panels 1 and 4 show the spectrum during /s/ and in the nasal murmur preceding the labial release. Figure 10.4c also shows the estimated time course of the openings formed by the tongue blade and the lips during the sequence of movements for this consonant cluster. In effect, the sequence of articulatory events for the /sm/ cluster is the same as that for /sp/ except that the velopharyngeal port is timed to open just after the labial closure and to close just after the labial release. The time between the opening of the velopharyngeal port and the labial release is relatively short, leading to a brief duration for the nasal murmur.

10.2 CONSONANT SEQUENCES ACROSS SYLLABLE BOUNDARIES

The articulatory and acoustic patterns of consonants can take a variety of shapes when they occur in syllable-final position, particularly when there is a sequence of two or more consonants at a syllable boundary. Some examples can be seen in the spectrogram of figure 10.5, which is the sentence *I can't go up to Sweden*.

We examine first the acoustic pattern for the consonant sequence joining the words *can't go* and the sequence /pt/ in *up to*. In the latter sequence, the expected downward movement of F2 and F3 can be observed as the closure for the labial /p/ is formed. There is, however, no acoustic evidence for the labial release, presumably because the alveolar closure is formed before the labial release occurs, so that there is no airflow at the labial release and hence no generation of sound. The release of the syllable-initial /t/ has the expected acoustic attributes, with aspiration following the release. The absence of a release burst for the initial consonant in a two-stop sequence across a syllable boundary is common. The place of articulation for the first consonant is signaled by the formant transitions at the closure, and acoustic events at the release provide cues for the second consonant. The time between closure and release for the two-consonant sequence is greater than the time for a singleton consonant in intervocalic position.

A more complex sequence of events occurs for the consonants in *can't go*. Here the release of the syllable-initial /g/ has the expected burst and formant transitions. In syllable-final position, the voiceless consonant /t/ is often produced with adduction of the vocal folds. This adduction maneuver can lead to glottalization, which is manifested in the sound by low-frequency irregular

Figure 10.3 The spectrogram is the utterance *a plod* produced by a male talker. The spectra (from top to bottom) are sampled as in figure 10.2b. Comparison with figure 10.2b illustrates differences between speakers in producing the consonant cluster /pl/.

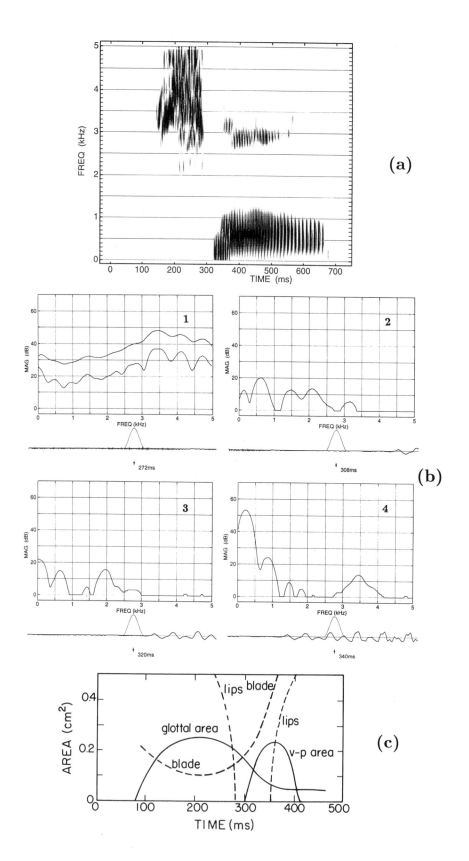

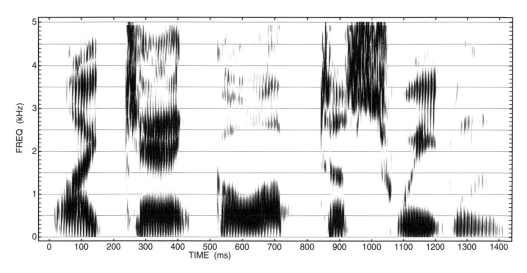

Figure 10.5 Spectrogram of the sentence *I can't go up to Sweden* (male speaker), illustrating modifications of consonants when they occur in a sequence of two or more consonants. The text discusses the sequences /nt#g/ (400 to 550 ms), /p#t/ (700 to 850 ms), /sw/ (1000 to 1150 ms), and /dn̩/ (1200 to 1270 ms).

glottal pulses. This glottalization is evident in the spectrogram in the vicinity of 420 ms. However, it is common for implementation of the tongue blade closure for a syllable-final alveolar stop consonant to be omitted when it is followed by a syllable-initial velar consonant, leaving only the glottalization as evidence for the presence of the alveolar stop consonant. With no specification of an articulator to form a closure for this consonant, the tongue body articulator for the following velar consonant becomes the articulator for the preceding underlying alveolar consonant. Following the usual nasal assimilation rule for English, the preceding nasal consonant takes the place of articulation of the following stop consonant. The result is a velar nasal consonant that is terminated by glottalization. The formant transitions immediately preceding the closure (at about 410 ms in figure 10.5) are consistent with a tongue body closure.

Two other consonants or consonant sequences in figure 10.5 illustrate additional forms of variability depending on the context. In the /sw/ cluster in the word *Sweden*, the labiovelar glide following /s/ causes a decrease in the front-cavity resonance within the fricative from about 3.5 to 2.5 kHz. This rounded portion of the fricative is followed by turbulence noise generation at the velar constriction, giving rise to excitation of the second for-

Figure 10.4 (a) Spectrogram of the word *small* (male speaker). (b) Spectra sampled at several times between the end of /s/ (spectrum 1) and the onset of glottal vibration (spectrum 4). Spectra are measured as in figure 10.1. (c) Schematized estimates of the time course of the cross-sectional areas of four orifices as this utterance is produced: area of constriction formed by the tongue blade; area of the glottal opening; area of constriction formed by the lips; and area of the velopharyngeal port (v-p area).

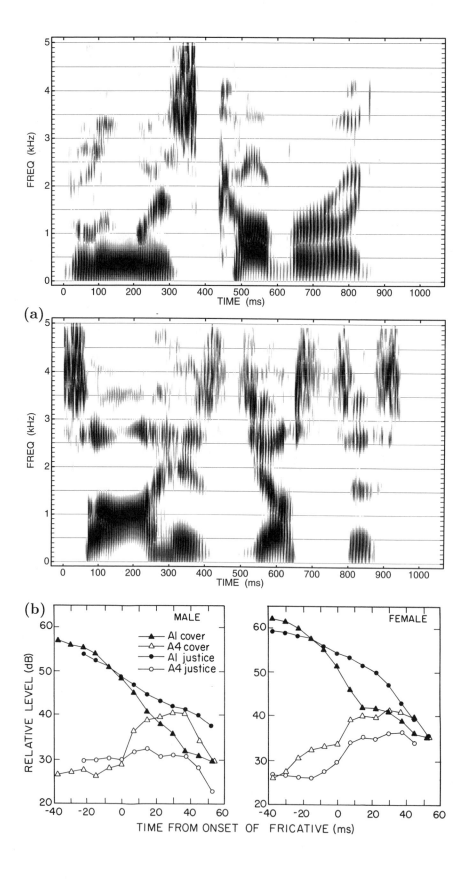

(a)

(b)

mant. The glottis remains spread during this time interval. In this utterance the labial constriction becomes sufficiently narrow that the turbulence noise weakens significantly. At about 1080 ms the vocal folds become more approximated and the labial opening increases, creating conditions that permit glottal vibration to begin.

The nucleus of the final syllable in the word *Sweden* is produced as a syllabic [n̩]. The closure for the alveolar consonant is made at about 1200 ms, and glottal vibration continues after the closure, with a reduced amplitude because of the increased intraoral pressure. At about 1260 ms, the velopharyngeal port opens and the pressure is released. The tongue blade remains in the alveolar position, however, so that the syllabic [n̩] terminates the utterance.

The consonant sequences in *can't go* and *up to* illustrate situations where there is a modification of the gesture of a major articulator (the tongue blade in *can't go*) or an overlap of the closure of one major articulator and the release of another (closure for /t/ and release of /p/ in *up to*). We consider now examples of the modifications that can occur in the voicing characteristics of a sequence of two obstruent consonants when one segment is voiced and the other is voiceless. This sequence is compared with a sequence of two obstruents both of which are voiced. In particular, we examine the sequences /z # k/ in the utterance *his cover* and /z # ǰ/ in *his justice*; the first element is a voiced fricative and the second is either a voiceless aspirated stop or a voiced affricate. Spectrograms of these utterances (excerpted from sentences) are displayed in figure 10.6a.

As described in section 8.4, a voiced fricative is normally produced with some spreading of the glottis (in order to cause sufficient pressure drop across the supraglottal constriction), together with slackening of the vocal tract walls (particularly in the pharyngeal region) and of the vocal folds as the larynx is displaced downward. The voiceless aspirated stop is produced with some stiffening of the vocal tract walls and the vocal folds, and with a spreading of the glottis which reaches a maximum around the time of release of the consonant. In the second example (*his justice*) the glottis is somewhat abducted for the voiced affricate, and with vocal tract and vocal fold slackening similar to that for a voiced fricative. Since the laryngeal and pharyngeal adjustments for the syllable-initial consonants /k/ and /ǰ/ are quite different, it is expected that these gestures will influence the corresponding adjustments for the preceding /z/.

Figure 10.6 (a) Spectrograms of utterances (male speaker) "... blew his cover again" (top) and "... saw his justice done" (bottom). The text discusses the sequences *his cover* (200 to 750 ms), and *his justice* (280 to 950 ms). (b) Measurements of spectrum amplitude in the two versions of the word *his* at low frequencies (solid dots) and at high frequencies (open dots) as a function of time. The amplitude measures are $A1$, the amplitude of the first-formant spectrum prominence, and $A4$, the amplitude of the largest spectrum prominence in the $F4$–$F6$ region. Average data from three repetitions for a male speaker (left) and a female speaker (right). See text.

Some Influences of Context on Speech Sound Production

Some estimate of this influence can be made from acoustic analysis of the vowel-consonant (VC) sequence in the two utterances of *his* in figure 10.6a (200 to 370 ms in the upper spectrogram and 300 to 460 ms in the lower spectrogram). Two measurements were made on spectra sampled at 7.5-ms intervals from the middle of the vowel to the end of frication for /z/. One measurement is the amplitude $A1$ of the first-formant spectral prominence. During the fricative, this prominence is at a low frequency around 200 Hz, and is a measure of the amplitude of the residual glottal vibration. The other measurement is the amplitude $A4$ of the largest spectrum peak in the $F4-F6$ region. During the fricative, this peak represents the relative amplitude of the frication noise source as it excites the short front-cavity resonance.

Figure 10.6b shows the time course of these measurements for the two utterances as produced by a male and a female speaker. (The data are averages over three repetitions for each speaker.) For both speakers, the voicing characteristics of the following consonant have an influence that extends back to the onset of the fricative. When the following consonant is voiced, significant amplitude of glottal vibration is maintained through the fricative. The following voiceless consonant, on the other hand, causes an additional reduction in the glottal amplitude of about 10 dB, so that there is essentially no residual glottal vibration at the end of the fricative. The amplitude of the noise component is substantially reduced in the voiced environment relative to its value in the voiceless environment, the difference being in the range 5 to 10 dB.

It is evident from these data that the relevant laryngeal and pharyngeal adjustments for the following voiceless stop consonant are initiated near the beginning of the fricative consonant. The time from the beginning of the fricative to the voiceless stop release is about 120 ms. The glottis returns to a modal configuration 20 to 30 ms after onset of glottal vibration for /k/, which in turn is about 50 to 60 ms after the release. Thus the total time over which the glottal opening-closing movement occurs is somewhat greater than 200 ms. This time interval is consistent with the movement times for the glottis given in section 1.3.3, which estimates a duration of 200 to 250 ms for a complete movement cycle from a modal configuration to abduction and back to modal.

One can surmise, then, that the laryngeal and pharyngeal states for these utterances change with time in the manner schematized in figure 10.7. In each panel there are two curves—one for the sequence in *his cover* (solid lines) and the other for the sequence in *his justice* (dashed lines). The upper panel is a representation of the glottal area, and shows greater glottal spreading when the following consonant is a voiceless aspirated stop. This greater spreading begins early in the frication for /z/, shortly after time 0 in the figure. The middle panel is a schematic representation of a generalized parameter ranging from stiff to slack, and is intended to depict a combination of the stiffnesses of the supraglottal surfaces and the vocal folds. The voice-

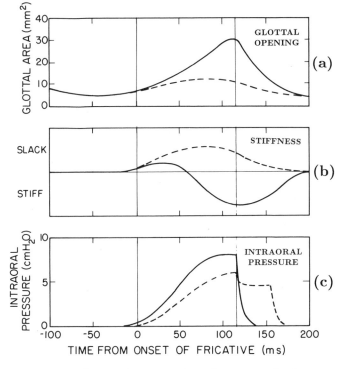

Figure 10.7 Schematized estimates of articulatory events for the two versions of *his* in figure 10.6a. (a) Estimates of the glottal opening. (b) Schematization of variation of stiffness or slackness of vocal folds and of vocal tract walls. (c) Intraoral pressure. Vertical lines indicate onset of fricative in *his* and release of following stop consonant /k/ or /ʒ/. Solid lines are for the utterance *his cover*, and dashed lines for *his justice*.

less stop induces stiffening which overrides the initial slackening for the voiced fricative. When the following consonant is voiced, the slackening continues throughout the consonantal interval in which there is increased intraoral pressure. The estimated variation in intraoral pressure is displayed in the bottom panel. The pressure builds up to the full subglottal pressure P_s (taken here to be 8 cm H_2O) for the voiceless stop, but falls short of P_s when there is a following voiced consonant. The result is a reduced amplitude of frication noise in /z/ when it is followed by the voiced affricate. The pressure traces begin to diverge near the beginning of the syllable-final voiced fricative.

The examples in figures 10.6 and 10.7 illustrate how the acoustic attributes of two adjacent obstruent consonants can be modified depending on the underlying voicing characteristics of the consonants. This modification comes about in part because the stiffening or slackening and glottal abduction or adduction gestures that are involved in implementing the voicing features can extend over time intervals of 200 to 250 ms, leading to substantial interaction between the gestures for the individual consonants.

10.3   SOME EFFECTS OF CONTEXT ON VOWEL PRODUCTION

As noted in chapter 6, the principal articulator that is manipulated to produce distinctions for vowels is the tongue body. Rounding of the lips can also play a role, particularly for non-low back vowels, and other articulators can be involved in some languages. The production of some consonants also places constraints on the tongue body. For example, consonants for which a constriction is formed by the tongue blade require that the tongue body be positioned in such a way that the blade can make contact in the appropriate region of the palate or the alveolar ridge. In particular, the tongue body is fronted for alveolar consonants, as observed in section 7.4.3. The production of a velar consonant requires raising of the tongue body, and formation of a labial constriction or closure also places some constraints on the positioning of the tongue body.

We have also seen in section 1.3 that there are limitations on the rate at which articulatory structures like the tongue body can move from one position to another. For example, the time taken for the tongue body to move from a backed to a fronted position is about 100 ms, and the time for a complete movement cycle from back to front to back is in the range of 200 to 300 ms. Thus if a consonant requires a fronted tongue body but the following vowel is a back vowel, a time of at least 100 ms after consonant release is required before a tongue body position appropriate for the vowel is reached. A similar time is required for the tongue body to move from the vowel position to the position for the following consonant, and additional time is needed for the tongue body to reverse direction. Consequently one might expect that if the time from the release of an initial consonant to the closure for a postvocalic consonant is less than 200 to 300 ms, the consonants could have some effect on the vowel throughout its length. In rapid speech, vowel durations are often shorter than 200 ms, and hence a vowel can be influenced significantly by the adjacent consonants.

Examples of the effects of consonants on the formant frequencies of vowels are given in figure 10.8 (K. N. Stevens and House, 1963). This figure shows the first- and second-formant frequencies measured at the midpoints of vowels produced in isolated consonant-vowel-consonant syllables, with the same initial and final consonants. Data for eight vowels are given, and the contexts are organized into classes according to consonantal place of articulation. The points representing a "null" context are for utterances of isolated vowels or vowels in the context /h-d/. The average durations of the vowels are in the range of 150 to 350 ms, with the lax vowels /ɪ ɛ ʌ ʊ/ being at the lower end of this range (House, 1961). As the data show, there is substantial undershoot of $F2$, particularly for some consonant contexts and for some vowels. For example, when the lax vowel /ɪ/ is surrounded by consonants produced with the tongue blade, $F2$ in the middle of the vowel is about 200 Hz lower (on average) than its value when the vowel is in a context where negligible consonantal effects are expected.

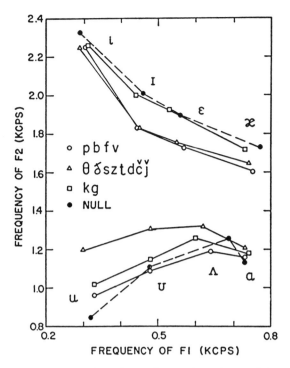

Figure 10.8 Values of *F1* and *F2* at the midpoint of the vowel for eight vowels, plotted to demonstrate the effect of place of articulation of the consonantal context. The contexs are divided into three groups: velars (open squares); postdentals (open triangles); labials (open circles). Values for vowels in the null environment (averages of formant frequencies for vowels in isolation and in context /h-d/) are included for comparison (black dots). Points represent average values for three talkers. (From K. N. Stevens and House, 1963.)

The influence of consonant context on the formant frequencies of a vowel is evident in the spectrograms in figure 10.6a, which show the vowel /ʌ/ in the words *cover* and *justice*. In the former word, the second-formant frequency in the vowel (centered at about 530 ms) remains low because the tongue body is in a backed position in both the initial velar stop and the final labial fricative. In the word *justice*, the surrounding /ǰ/ and /s/ constrain the tongue body to be fronted, and, as a consequence, *F2* in the vowel (centered at about 590 ms) is higher than in the word *cover*. Average measurements of the formant frequencies in the middle of each of these vowels for three repetitions of the words (in a sentence context) by a female and a male speaker are given in table 10.1. There is a difference of 200 to 300 Hz in the *F2* values for the two words. There is also a difference in *F1*, particularly for the female speaker. This "undershoot" in *F1* for /ʌ/ in *justice* is probably due to the constraint that /ǰ/ places on the tongue body height. (The anomaly of a high *F3* in *justice* for the female speaker is probably a consequence of a spectral modification due to the introduction of an additional path in the vocal tract when the tongue blade is raised.)

The degree to which a vowel undergoes modification because of the influence of an adjacent segment depends on several factors. One contributing

Table 10.1 Measurements of formant frequencies (in hertz) at the midpoint of the vowel /ʌ/ in the words *cover* and *justice* embedded in a sentence

	Female			Male		
	F1	*F2*	*F3*	*F1*	*F2*	*F3*
cover	750	1320	2810	600	1050	2530
justice	630	1550	3540	560	1310	2560

Note: Average data for three repetitions from a female and a male speaker.

factor is the presence in the language of a contrasting vowel that differs minimally from the target vowel, so that the formant frequencies of this vowel are close to those of the target vowel. The allowed influence of context on the target vowel can be greater if the adjacent vowel is distant, but must be smaller if the shift in the formant pattern due to context can lead to misinterpretation of the vowel. Thus it is expected that the contextual modifications of vowels in a given language are different depending on the inventory of vowels in the language. (See, e.g., Manuel, 1990.)

Other factors that determine the influence of context are the rate of speaking and the clarity of the speech. As has been noted above, the influence of a consonant on the formant frequencies of a vowel can extend over a time interval of 100 to 150 ms, and consequently this influence will encompass a greater region of a vowel when the vowel is relatively short. Slower speech tends to have longer vowels and hence the effect of adjacent consonants is reduced, particularly near the centers of the vowels. There is some evidence that a speaker has control of clarity of speaking, somewhat independently of rate of speaking (Krause, 1995). That is, the speaker can adopt a strategy that reduces the influence of context, either through greater effort that shortens the 100-odd milliseconds time to move from one tongue body position to another, or by adopting a different strategy that brings other compensating articulator movements into play.

10.4 REDUCED VOWELS

Reduced vowels in English, sometimes called schwa vowels, are usually not specified for the feature [back]. That is, reduced vowels do not contrast in this feature. The vowels in many function words in English are produced as schwa, as well as certain vowels in content words with two or more syllables. Since the tongue body position for these vowels is not constrained for backness, it is expected that the formant frequencies (particularly *F2*) will be strongly influenced by adjacent vowels or consonants that require particular tongue body positions. This relative malleability of reduced vowels has been examined by Koopmans-van Beinum (1980), by Magen (1989), and by others. The fact that significant contextual modification of reduced vowels is permitted suggests that these vowels can be relatively short, that is, signifi-

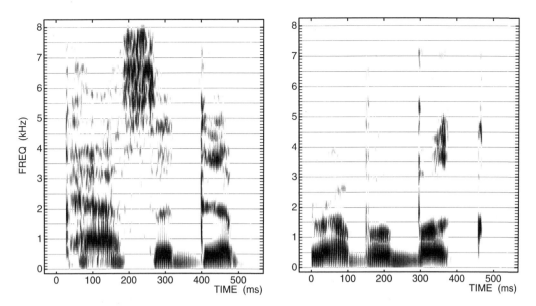

Figure 10.9 Spectrograms of the sequences *pass a dip* (left) and *rub a book* (right) extracted from sentences produced by a female talker, illustrating modification of schwa vowel by context.

Table 10.2 Formant frequencies (in hertz) in the middle of the schwa vowel for the utterances *pass a dip* and *rub a book*, as spoken in a sentence context

	Female			Male		
	F1	F2	F3	F1	F2	F3
pass a dip	494	1785	3513	423	1491	2624
rub a book	410	1071	2908	488	912	2474

Note: Data are averages for three repetitions by a female and a male speaker.

cantly shorter than the 100-odd milliseconds normally required to complete a movement of an articulator from one configuration to another.

An example of the effect of context on reduced vowels is given in figure 10.9. This figure shows spectrograms of portions of two sentences; one sentence contains the sequence *pass a dip*, and the other contains *rub a book*. The vowels of interest are the schwa vowels, which in these examples have a duration of about 50 ms. In the first phrase, the schwa (centered at 290 ms) is preceded and followed by alveolar consonants that constrain the tongue body to be in a fronted position, and the vowels in the adjacent syllables are front vowels. The consonant context in the second phrase (with the schwa centered at 185 ms) is labial, which imposes minimal constraints on tongue body backness, and the adjacent syllable nuclei are back vowels. It is evident that F2 for the schwa is much lower in the second phrase than in the first. Average formant frequencies in midvowel for three repetitions of this utterance (in a sentence context) by a female and a male speaker are given in table

10.2. The strong effect of context on $F2$ is apparent, but there is not a consistent influence on the tongue body height, as indicated by $F1$.

The reduced vowels in the example in figure 10.9 were preceded and followed by consonants with the same articulator—the tongue blade in *pass a dip* and the lips in *rub a book*. For these sequences, production of the schwa requires that the consonantal articulator be released and then returned to the closed (or constricted) position. The time required to perform this opening-closing maneuver in these utterances is substantially less than the time of 200 to 250 ms needed to perform a full opening-closing gesture that has the goal of achieving a particular target configuration in the open (vocalic) position. In the case of these two utterances, the only requirement for the schwa vowel is that an oral opening be created for the vowel, either by the tongue blade or by the lips. Given that $F1$ in the vowel is about 450 Hz, the maximum cross-sectional area formed within the vowel by the lips or tongue blade is estimated to be about 0.3 cm^2, assuming a uniform tube behind the constriction and an effective constriction length of about 0.7 cm. The duration of the opening-closing movement of the articulator that forms this small opening can be substantially less than the 200 to 250 ms required for the larger, goal-directed movement. If the movement of the articulator begins in the middle of the preceding consonant and ends in the middle of the following consonant, the duration is about 130 to 140 ms in the examples in figure 10.9, although the length of the reduced vowel occupies only a portion of this total (about 50 ms).

If the consonants preceding and following a schwa vowel are produced with different articulators, the duration of the vowel can be considerably shorter than 50 ms. The release of one articulator for the initial consonant can be immediately followed by the closure of the second articulator that forms the final consonant. Examples are the first vowel and the third vowel in the word *monopoly* and the middle vowel in the word *classical*. Spectrograms of these two words, excerpted from the middle of sentences, are displayed in figure 10.10. The duration of the first vowel in *monopoly* is 50 ms and the duration of the third vowel (from /p/ release to /l/ closure) is 30 ms. In the word *classical*, there is just one glottal pulse for the middle vowel. In utterances that are even more rapid or casual, the release of the consonant preceding the schwa can overlap with the closure of the following consonant, and essentially remove any evidence of a vocalic opening of the oral cavity.

The short duration of reduced vowels makes them susceptible to contextual influences other than tongue body position in adjacent vowels and consonants. For example, the first vowel in the word *monopoly* in figure 10.10 is surrounded by nasal consonants. Not unexpectedly, acoustic analysis shows that the reduced vowel is strongly nasalized. This nasalization is evident in the vowel as a widened first formant, leading to a reduced overall amplitude of the vowel. If the consonants preceding and following the schwa vowel are produced with a spread glottis, then the glottal spreading gesture of the ini-

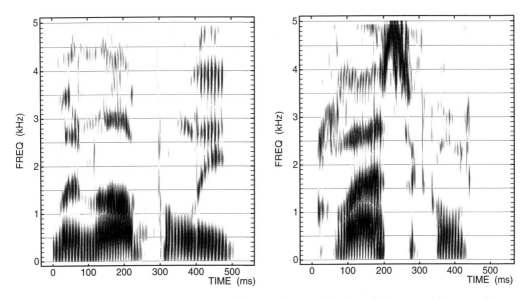

Figure 10.10 Spectrograms of the words *monopoly* (left) and *classical* (right) extracted from sentences produced by a male talker, giving examples of brief reduced vowels. In *monopoly* the reduced vowels are at 50 and 320 ms; in *classical* it is at 280 ms.

tial consonant may overlap with the similar gesture for the following consonant. The result is that the glottis does not return to a modal configuration in the vowel. If the vowel is sufficiently short, the glottis may not achieve an opening that is sufficiently small to allow glottal vibration, and the vowel is produced with an aspiration source. An example is the middle vowel in the word *classical* in figure 10.10. This schwa vowel is preceded and followed by voiceless obstruents. There is only brief glottal vibration in this case between the release of /s/ and the closure for /k/. The timing of the acoustic events in the vicinity of this reduced vowel can be observed in the waveform of a portion of the word *classical*, displayed in figure 10.11. The single glottal pulse for the vowel has an opening phase beginning at 277 ms, with a closing excitation phase at 282 ms. Preceding this pulse, the spectrogram and the waveform show a brief interval in which the high-frequency frication noise weakens, and the primary acoustic source is aspiration noise.

Articulatory movements are estimated, at least in schematic form, from these acoustic data in figure 10.12. A subglottal pressure of 8 cm H_2O is assumed. Displayed in figure 10.12a is an estimate of the area of the glottal opening as it varies with time. The solid line is the estimate of the actual glottal cross-sectional area, and the dashed line is the area that would exist if there were no passive abducting force resulting from increases in the supraglottal pressure. The figure shows that the hypothesized active glottal opening (dashed line) increases to a maximum for the voiceless fricative and then decreases to an area of about 0.04 cm², corresponding roughly to the average area for a modal configuration. The actual glottal area is, however,

Some Influences of Context on Speech Sound Production

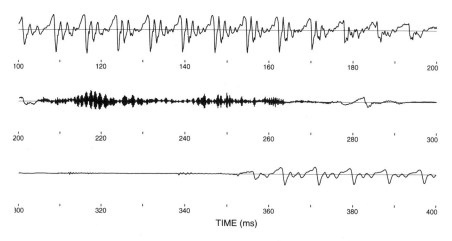

Figure 10.11 Sound pressure waveform of a portion of the word *classical*, for which the spectrogram is shown in figure 10.10. Of particular interest is the reduced vowel at time 280 ms.

modified by the time-varying supraglottal pressure as an oral constriction is made, first with the tongue blade for /s/ and then with the tongue body for /k/. The time variations of the areas of these two constrictions are shown in figure 10.12b. These changes are similar to those considered for fricatives and velar stops in sections 8.1.1 and 7.4.4, respectively. If a subglottal pressure of 8 cm H_2O is assumed, the intraoral pressure and the modified glottal area can be calculated, following the methods described in section 8.1.1. The intraoral pressure is given in figure 10.12c, and the calculated glottal area is in figure 10.12a (solid line). It is noted that the maximum opening in the oral cavity for the brief reduced vowel is estimated to be about 0.2 cm². This relatively narrow opening, formed by the tongue body, leads to a calculated first-formant frequency of about 330 Hz (based on the Helmholtz formula, assuming an effective constriction length of 2 cm and a volume of 40 cm³, with a correction for yielding walls). This is approximately equal to the measured $F1$ for this vowel. The $F1$ bandwidth is expected to be large, given the appreciable glottal opening. Figure 10.12a shows that the calculated glottal opening has a maximum in both consonants, but this double peak is a consequence of glottal movements resulting from changes in the supraglottal pressure.

The examples of reduced vowels illustrated in figures 10.9 to 10.12 show that the acoustic and articulatory properties of these vowels are highly sensitive to their context. The front-back tongue body position is determined by the adjacent vowels and consonants, the maximum opening of the oral cavity during a reduced vowel can be less than 0.3 cm², and the glottal or velopharyngeal characteristics of an adjacent consonant can spread throughout the vowel. The last two of these attributes can lead to a reduction in the overall amplitude of the reduced vowel.

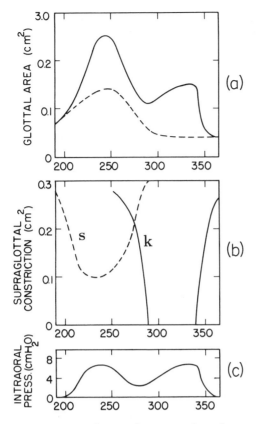

Figure 10.12 Schematized estimates of articulatory events over a portion of the word *classical* (in figures 10.10 and 10.11) centered around the middle reduced vowel. (a) Estimated cross-sectional area of the glottal opening. The dashed line is the area that would exist if there were no abducting forces due to the increased supraglottal pressure. The solid line is the estimated actual glottal area, including the effects of the subglottal pressure. (b) Estimated cross-sectional area of constriction formed by the tongue blade for /s/ (dashed line) and by the tongue body for /k/ (solid line). (c) Estimated supraglottal pressure. A subglottal pressure of 8 cm H_2O is assumed.

10.5 SUMMARY AND DISCUSSION

In this chapter we have given examples of several kinds of modifications that occur in the acoustic and articulatory manifestations of phonetic segments when they are produced in different contexts within words and sentences. These modifications can be of two kinds. The context can influence the acoustic representation of one or more features of a segment, but without removing entirely the acoustic evidence for the features. Or, the modification is such that one or more features in the canonical representation of the segment (of the type listed in tables 5.1, 5.3, and 5.4) are modified. In the latter case, there is no evidence in the sound that particular feature values in the underlying lexical representation have been implemented.

Some Influences of Context on Speech Sound Production

Several examples have been given to illustrate modifications of the acoustic cues for particular features while maintaining intact some evidence for the features. The modifications are described by comparison with the expected canonical acoustic attributes for the segments as they occur in simple CV or VC syllables. For a given consonantal segment, these modifications often arise because the acoustic representation of the adjacent segment cannot carry the transitions that are normally observed when that segment is a vowel. In the case of a vowel segment, there can be modifications of formant frequencies or of attributes related to the glottal or velopharyngeal configurations due to the influence of adjacent consonants or nearby vowels, particularly if the vowel is relatively short.

Examples of consonantal modifications discussed in this chapter include the consonant sequences /sp/ and /sk/ (figure 10.1), /pl/ and /dr/ (figures 10.2 and 10.3), /sm/ (figure 10.4), /sw/ (figure 10.5), /p#t/ (as in *up to*, figure 10.5), and /z#k/ and /z#ǰ/ (figures 10.6 and 10.7). In some of these examples, the interaction between the adjacent consonants occurs with the primary articulators (e.g., the influence of the labial closure on /s/ in /sp/), whereas in others the interaction occurs at the level of the glottal configuration (e.g., /z#k/ and /z#ǰ/) or the velopharyngeal configuration (e.g., the delayed onset of glottal vibration following /s/ in the cluster /sm/, leading to a short nasal murmur). Contextual effects on vowels include the influence of consonants on stressed vowels, as in figure 10.8, and, in the case of reduced vowels, the influence of the consonantal context on formant frequencies (see figure 10.9), on nasalization (as in *monopoly*, in figure 10.10), and on the glottal configuration (as in *classical*, in figures 10.10 and 10.11).

Two examples of unequivocal feature changes in a segment due to an adjacent segment have been given in this chapter. Both are illustrated in figure 10.5. One is the consonant sequence in *can't go*, where there is a change of the consonant articulator for /nt/ from tongue blade to tongue body. Another example, in the same figure, is the reduction of the sequence /ən/ in *Sweden* to syllabic /n̩/.[1]

In the examples given here, the context-conditioned modifications occur in the articulator-bound features, as opposed to articulator-free features. Sequences in which changes in articulator-free features can occur include words containing the stop consonant /g/ followed by an unstressed vowel (as in the word *legal*), where the velar consonant can be produced as [+continuant]. Other examples are the sequence *win that race*, where /ð/ can be implemented as [+sonorant, +nasal] rather than as [−sonorant] (Manuel, 1995), and the word *wrestling*, where the [+vocalic] syllabic nucleus /l̩/ is sometimes produced as a [+consonantal] segment, and the word is then realized with two rather than with three syllables.

Several general observations can be made from the examples of phonetic modifications given in this chapter. One is that the detailed acoustic attributes of vowel and consonant segments depend on the environment in which the segments occur. In much of this book we have focused on the articulatory and acoustic properties of segments in stressed CV and VC syllables, but other contexts can lead to significantly different properties, particularly in the acoustic representation. A second observation is that, as long as the articulatory gestures associated with the various features of a segment are implemented, there are usually acoustic consequences of these gestures that permit the features to be recovered from the sound. These acoustic consequences and their representation in the peripheral auditory system can be predicted from articulatory-acoustic-auditory relations of the type described in chapters 1 through 4. Finally, although it can be argued that words are stored in memory in terms of segments and features, a speaker may modify some of these features in casual speech. However, there are strong constraints on the types of feature modifications that are allowed. A listener must resort to knowledge of the language at levels above the segment and feature to recover the words from such casually produced utterances.

Notes

Chapter 1

1. The acoustic relevance of this parameter derives from the expression for the acoustic mass of a short tube, $M_A = \rho \ell / A$, where $\rho = $ density of air, $\ell = $ length of tube, and $A = $ cross-sectional area of tube.

2. The meaning of *modal voicing* is discussed in more detail in section 2.1.

3. The estimations of the glottal opening for voiced and voiceless fricative consonants are based on several kinds of indirect evidence. Simultaneous records of subglottal pressure and intraoral pressure during fricative consonant production (Ladefoged, 1963) show that the intraoral pressure is slightly less than the subglottal pressure, indicating a small pressure drop at the glottal constriction. Furthermore, the more extensive data on intraoral pressure in the absence of subglottal pressure records (Hixon, 1966; Arkebauer et al., 1967) always indicate that the intraoral pressure is somewhat below the subglottal pressure that is normally used in speech.

4. It has been observed by Peter Ladefoged (personal communication, 1997) that in a language such as Pirahã, a sequence of three consecutive vowels can have alternating tones in which the time between high tone peaks is usually about 150 ms (e.g., the word àbáàátí, to make a path), suggesting that the minimum times given above could be revised downward.

Chapter 2

1. The effective mechanical compliance of the lower mass when the upper mass forms a complete closure is given by $C_1' = C_1 C_c / (C_1 + C_c)$, where C_1 and C_c are the mechanical compliance of the lower mass and the coupling compliance between the two masses, respectively, as shown in figure 2.2.

2. The factor of 2 takes into account the contribution of positive and negative frequencies.

Chapter 3

1. When the cross-sectional area changes abruptly over some portion of the length of the vocal tract, the wavefronts can deviate from plane waves, indicating the presence of higher modes of propagation over a limited region of the vocal tract. These higher modes can modify slightly the analysis that is based on simple plane wave propagation, but the modification is usually small.

2. Sometimes the use of *formant* is restricted to natural frequencies of the vocal tract proper when there is no coupling to the nasal cavities. In order to avoid confusion, we will not use the term in reference to the natural frequency of a configuration with nasal coupling.

3. In order to focus on the effects of formant frequency changes on the shape of the spectrum, the formant bandwidths in figure 3.5 have been set at a constant value of 80 Hz. As will be shown in section 3.4, several factors cause the bandwidth to change, depending on the formant frequencies and the vocal tract shape.

4. Strictly speaking, the criterion that must be satisfied if the large tube is to have little effect on the natural frequencies of the narrow tube is that the magnitude of its reactance, which is $|(\rho c/A_2)\tan k\ell_2|$, be small compared to that of the narrow tube, which is $|(\rho c/A_1)\cot k\ell_1|$. At most frequencies, this criterion is satisfied if $A_2 \gg A_1$.

5. These results were derived in section 3.3.1 only for the uniform tube configuration, but they can be shown for the more general case.

6. This bandwidth is calculated by determining the radiation impedance at the 2-cm² mouth opening, calculating the impedance 2 cm behind this opening, and using this impedance for the load that terminates the narrow 0.6-cm² section. The length of this narrow section is adjusted so as to maintain a natural frequency of 2950 Hz.

7. The calculations on which this graph is based assume that the first formant is a Helmholtz resonance. A more precise calculation for higher values of $F1$ would show the effect of the walls to be even less than the figure indicates.

8. Equation (3.58) for the bandwidth assumes that the impedance terminating the posterior end of the vocal tract is simply the impedance of the glottal slit. This impedance is in fact in series with the impedance looking into the subglottal system. The subglottal impedance also has a resistive component, and hence the resistive component of the total impedance is greater than the value used in deriving equation (3.58). Consequently equation (3.58) gives bandwidth values that may be somewhat high, and provides approximate upper limits to the bandwidth contribution due to glottal and subglottal losses.

9. These calculations neglect the effect of the subglottal impedance, which may have an influence on the formant frequency, particularly for larger glottal openings. See note 8.

10. For certain consonants, such as /s/ or /š/, the lower teeth form an obstacle that is partially in the airstream, and is close to the constriction, and a small negative correction should be applied to the spectrum amplitude of the source. See discussion of fricative consonants in section 8.1.

11. The assumption of no interaction is only an approximation, and is made here simply to illustrate the nature of the transfer function expected for this configuration.

Chapter 5

1. For a discussion of some principles governing the constraints on consonant sequences, see Clements (1990) and references cited therein.

2. For a more complete discussion of the organization of features in a treelike structure, see Clements (1985) and Keyser and Stevens (1994).

3. These conventions for omitting feature specifications are not adhered to rigidly in tables 5.3 and 5.4. For example, the features [spread glottis] and [constricted glottis] are not distinctive in English, but they are nevertheless often specified in tables of this kind. The question of under-specification of features is a large and controversial one, and will not be discussed here.

Chapter 8

1. We neglect here any active increase that may occur in vocal fold stiffness for a voiceless obstruent. This increased stiffness can contribute to inhibition of vocal fold vibration during the

consonant. The role of changes in vocal fold stiffness to facilitate or inhibit glottal vibration for obstruents is discussed in section 8.4.

2. Data for Polish are reported in Halle and Stevens (1991b).

3. The model of figure 8.39, in which the glottal end is closed, gives only an approximate estimate of the dipole component of the aspiration noise source. A more accurate model should include the impedance of the constricted glottis. If this impedance were included in the model, the lowest zero would not be at zero frequency but would be at a higher frequency. For example, this frequency would be at about 1400 Hz for the source at 2.5 cm. This refinement of the model would influence the estimation of the dipole component at lower frequencies. However, in the frequency range below about 2 kHz, the monopole source is the dominant source. That source spectrum is not influenced by the glottal opening. Consequently, although use of the model of figure 8.39 may give a poor approximation to the effective dipole source at low frequencies, the error in the overall source spectrum in figure 8.40 is probably small.

4. The maximum will occur slightly later because there is a small delay (of about 0.5 ms) as the air flows from the glottis to the epiglottis where the high-frequency noise is generated.

Chapter 9

1. Strictly speaking, two poles such as $R1$ and $R2$ cannot intersect, as figure 9.3a shows. Since at the point of intersection the acoustic coupling to the nasal cavity is small, these two poles can become very close.

2. In some languages there are liquid consonants for which turbulence noise is produced at the constriction formed by the tongue blade (cf. Catford, 1977; Maddieson, 1984). In this section we consider only liquids that are sonorant.

3. The method for calculating the bandwidth increase due to the resistance of the constriction is similar to that used in section 9.2.2 for the glide /j/.

4. Using an x-ray microbeam system, Westbury et al. (1995) have shown that different speakers use a wide range of tongue shapes to produce /r/. Their acoustic analysis of these productions of /r/ shows little relation between the different tongue shapes and the resulting formant patterns.

Chapter 10

1. In this example, it could be argued that the features in the segments /ə/ and /n/ are merged into one segment, and that all the features are accounted for in the sound, albeit in modified form. In this view, reduction to syllabic /n̩/ would not be considered a feature change.

References

Abry, C., and L.-J. Boë (1986). "Laws" for lips. *Speech Communication, 5,* 97–104.

Adams, S. G., G. Weismer, and R. D. Kent (1993). Speaking rate and speech movement velocity profiles. *Journal of Speech and Hearing Research, 36,* 41–54.

Adler, R. B., L. J. Chu, and R. M. Fano (1960). *Electromagnetic energy transmission and radiation.* New York: Wiley.

Alipour-Haghighi, F., and I. R. Titze (1991). Elastic models of vocal-fold tissues. *Journal of the Acoustical Society of America, 90,* 1326–1331.

Allen, J. B., and S. T. Neely (1992). Micromechanical models of the cochlea. *Physics Today,* July, 40–47.

Ananthapadmanabha, T. V., and G. Fant (1982). Calculation of the true glottal flow and its components. *Speech Transmission Laboratory, Quarterly Progress and Status Report 1,* Royal Institute of Technology, Stockholm, 1–30; also in *Speech Communication, 1,* (1982), 167–184.

Arkebauer, H. J., T. J. Hixon, and J. C. Hardy (1967). Peak intraoral air pressures during speech. *Journal of Speech and Hearing Research, 10,* 196–208.

Atkinson, J. E. (1973). *Aspects of intonation in speech: Implications from an experimental study of fundamental frequency.* Ph.D. dissertation, University of Connecticut, Storrs.

Atkinson, J. E. (1978). Correlation analysis of the physiological factors controlling fundamental voice frequency. *Journal of the Acoustical Society of America, 63,* 211–222.

Badin, P. (1989). Acoustics of voiceless fricatives: Production theory and data. *Speech Transmission Laboratory Quarterly Progress and Status Report 3,* Royal Institute of Technology, Stockholm, 33–55.

Baer, T. (1975). *Investigation of phonation using excised larynxes.* Unpublished Ph.D. thesis, Massachusetts Institute of Technology, Cambridge, MA.

Baer, T., P. J. Alfonso, and K. Honda (1988). Electromyography of the tongue muscles during vowels in /əpVp/ environment. *Annual Bulletin of the Research Institute of Logopedics and Phoniatrics, No. 22,* University of Tokyo, 7–18.

Baer, T., G. C. Gore, L. C. Gracco, and P. W. Nye (1991). Analysis of vocal tract shape and dimensions using magnetic resonance imaging: Vowels. *Journal of the Acoustical Society of America, 90,* 799–828.

Båvegård, M., G. Fant, J. Gauffin, and J. Liljencrants (1993). Vocal tract sweeptone data and model simulations of vowels, laterals and nasals. *Speech Transmission Laboratory Quarterly Progress and Status Report 4,* Royal Institute of Technology, Stockholm, 43–76.

Beckman, M. E., and J. Edwards (1993). Articulatory evidence for differentiating stress categories. In P. A. Keating (ed.), *Phonological structure and phonetic form: Papers in laboratory phonology III*. Cambridge, U.K.: Cambridge University Press, 7–33.

Békésy, G. von (1960). *Experiments in hearing*. New York: McGraw-Hill.

Békésy, G. von, and W. A. Rosenblith (1951). The mechanical properties of the ear. In S. S. Stevens (ed.), *Handbook of experimental psychology*. New York: Wiley, 1075–1115.

Benguerel, A.-P., and T. K. Bhatia (1980). Hindi stop consonants: An acoustic and fiberscopic study. *Phonetica, 37*, 134–148.

Benguerel, A.-P., H. Hirose, M. Sawashima, and T. Usijima (1976). Laryngeal control in French stops: A fiberoptic, acoustic, and electromyographic study. *Research Institute of Logopedics and Phoniatrics Annual Bulletin No. 10*, University of Tokyo, 81–100.

Beranek, L. L. (1954). *Acoustics*. New York: Wiley.

Berlin, C. I. (1994). Scientific substrates of hearing. In F. D. Minifie (ed.), *Introduction to communication sciences and disorders*. San Diego: Singular, 561–601.

Bickley, C. A., and K. N. Stevens (1986). Effects of a vocal tract constriction on the glottal source: Experimental and modelling studies. *Journal of Phonetics, 14*, 373–382.

Bickley, C. A., and K. N. Stevens (1987). Effects of a vocal tract constriction on the glottal source: Data from voiced consonants. In T. Baer, C. Sasaki, and K. Harris (eds.), *Laryngeal function in phonation and respiration*. San Diego: College Hill Press, 239–253.

Binh, N., and J. Gauffin (1983). Aerodynamic measurements in an enlarged static laryngeal model. *Speech Transmission Laboratory Quarterly Progress and Status Report 2-3*, Royal Institute of Technology, Stockholm, 36–60.

Bjuggren, G., and G. Fant (1964). The nasal cavity structures. *Speech Transmission Laboratory Quarterly Progress and Status Report 4*, Royal Institute of Technology, Stockholm, 5–7.

Bothorel, A., P. Simon, F. Wioland, and J.-P. Zerling (1986). *Cinéradiographie des voyelles et consonnes du français*. Institut de Phonetique de Strasbourg, France.

Bouhuys, A., J. Mead, D. F. Proctor, and K. N. Stevens (1968). Pressure-flow events during singing. *Annals of the New York Academy of Sciences, 55*, 165–176.

Briscoe, W. A., and A. B. Dubois (1958). The relationship between airway conductance and lung volume in subjects of different age and body size. *Journal of Clinical Investigation, 37*, 1279–1285.

Broadbent, B. H., Sr., B. H. Broadbent, Jr., and W. H. Golden (1975). *Bolton standards of dentofacial developmental growth*. St. Louis: Mosby.

Carlson, R., B. Granström, and G. Fant (1970). Some studies concerning perception of isolated vowels. *Speech Transmission Laboratory Quarterly Progress and Status Report 2-3*, Royal Institute of Technology, Stockholm, 19–35.

Carney, L. H., and C. D. Geisler (1986). A temporal analysis of auditory-nerve fiber responses to spoken stop consonant-vowel syllables. *Journal of the Acoustical Society of America, 79*, 1896–1914.

Catford, J. C. (1977). *Fundamental problems in phonetics*. Bloomington: Indiana University Press.

Chen, M. Y. (1995). Acoustic parameters of nasalized vowels in hearing-impaired and normal-hearing speakers. *Journal of the Acoustical Society of America 98*, 2443–2453.

Chiba, T., and M. Kajiyama (1941). *The vowel: Its nature and structure*. Tokyo: Tokyo-Kaiseikan.

Chistovich, L. A. (1985). Central auditory processing of peripheral vowel spectra. *Journal of the Acoustical Society of America, 77*, 789–805.

Chistovich, L. A., and V. V. Lublinskaya (1979). The "center of gravity" effect in vowel spectra and critical distance between the formants: Psychoacoustical study of the perception of vowel-like stimuli. *Hearing Research, 1,* 185–195.

Chistovich, L. A., R. L. Sheikin, and V. V. Lublinskaya (1979). "Centers of gravity" and spectral peaks as the determinants of vowel quality. In B. Lindblom and S. Ohman (eds.), *Frontiers of speech communication research.* London: Academic Press, 143–157.

Chomsky, N., and M. Halle (1968). *The sound pattern of English.* New York: Harper & Row.

Clements, G. N. (1985). The geometry of phonological features. *Phonology Yearbook, 2,* 223–250.

Clements, G. N. (1990). The role of the sonority cycle in core syllabification. In J. Kingston and M. E. Beckman (eds.), *Papers in laboratory phonology: Between the grammar and physics of speech.* Cambridge: Cambridge University Press, 283–333.

Conrad, W. A. (1980). A new model of the vocal cords based on a collapsible tube analogy. *Medical Research Engineering, 13,* 7–10.

Conrad, W. A. (1983). Collapsible tube model of the larynx. In I. R. Titze and R. C. Scherer (eds.), *Vocal fold physiology: Biomechanics, acoustics, and phonatory control.* Denver: Denver Center for the Performing Arts, 328–348.

Cranen, B., and L. Boves (1987). On subglottal formant analysis. *Journal of the Acoustical Society of America, 81,* 734–746.

Creelman, C. D. (1962). Human discrimination of auditory duration. *Journal of the Acoustical Society of America, 34,* 582–593.

Crystal, T. H. and A. S. House (1990). Articulation rate and the duration of syllables and stress groups in connected speech. *Journal of the Acoustical Society of America, 88,* 101–112.

Cutler, A., and D. M. Carter (1987). The predominance of strong initial syllables in the English vocabulary. *Computer Speech and Language, 2,* 133–142.

Dang, J., K. Honda, and H. Suzuki (1994). Morphological and acoustical analysis of the nasal and the paranasal cavities. *Journal of the Acoustical Society of America, 96,* 2088–2100.

Daniloff, R. G. and K. L. Moll (1968). Coarticulation of lip rounding. *Journal of Speech and Hearing Research, 11,* 707–721.

Daniloff, R. G., K. Wilcox, and M. J. Stephens (1980). An acoustic-articulatory description of children's defective /s/ productions. *Journal of Communication Disorders, 13,* 347–363.

Davis, H. (1951). Psychophysiology of hearing and deafness. In S. S. Stevens (ed.), *Handbook of experimental psychology.* New York: Wiley, 1116–1180.

Delattre, P. (1954). Les attributs acoustiques de la nasalit'e vocalique et consonantique. *Studia Linguistica, 8,* 103–109.

Delattre, P. (1965). La nasalité vocalique en français et en anglais. *French Review, 39,* 92–109.

Delattre, P., and D. Freeman (1968). A dialect study of American /r/'s by x-ray motion picture. *Language, 44,* 26–68.

Delgutte, B. (1980). Representation of speech-like sounds in the discharge patterns of auditory-nerve fibers. *Journal of the Acoustical Society of America, 68,* 843–857.

Delgutte, B. (1984a). Codage de la parole dans le nerf auditif. Sc.D. thesis, l'Université Pierre et Marie Curie, Paris.

Delgutte, B. (1984b). Speech coding in the auditory nerve II: Processing schemes for vowel-like sounds. *Journal of the Acoustical Society of America, 75,* 879–886.

Delgutte, B., and N. Y. S. Kiang (1984a). Speech coding in the auditory nerve I: Vowel-like sounds. *Journal of the Acoustical Society of America, 75,* 866–878.

Delgutte, B., and N. Y. S. Kiang (1984b). Speech coding in the auditory nerve: III. Voiceless fricative consonants. *Journal of the Acoustical Society of America, 75,* 887–896.

Delgutte, B., and N. Y. S. Kiang (1984c). Speech coding in the auditory nerve: IV. Sounds with consonant-like dynamic characteristics. *Journal of the Acoustical Society of America, 75,* 897–907.

Deng, L., and C. D. Geisler (1987). Responses of auditory-nerve fibers to nasal consonant-vowel syllables. *Journal of the Acoustical Society of America, 82,* 1977–1988.

Dickson, D. R., and W. Maue-Dickson (1982). *Anatomical and physiological bases of speech.* Boston: Little, Brown.

Dixit, R. P. (1975). *Neuromuscular aspects of laryngeal control, with special reference to Hindi.* Ph.D. dissertation, University of Texas, Austin.

Dubois, A. B. (1964). Resistance to breathing. In W. O. Fenn and H. Rahn (eds.), *Handbook of Physiology: Respiration,* Vol. 1. Washington, DC: American Physiological Society, 451–462.

Dunn, H. K. (1961). Methods of measuring vowel formant bandwidths. *Journal of the Acoustical Society of America, 33,* 1737–1746.

Erickson, D. (1993). Laryngeal muscle activity in connection with Thai tones. *Annual Bulletin No. 27, Research Institute of Logopedics and Phoniatrics,* University of Tokyo, 135–149.

Espy-Wilson, C. Y. (1987). *An acoustic-phonetic approach to speech recognition: Application to the semivowels.* Ph.D. thesis, Massachusetts Institute of Technology, Cambridge, MA.

Espy-Wilson, C. Y. (1992). Acoustic measures for linguistic features distinguishing the semivowels /w j r l/ in English. *Journal of the Acoustical Society of America, 92,* 736–751.

Espy-Wilson, C. Y., S. Narayanan, S. E. Boyce, and A. Alwan (1997). Acoustic modelling of American English /r/. *Proceedings of Eurospeech,* Rhodes, Greece, Vol. 1, 1239–1242.

Ewan, W. G., and R. Krones (1974). Measuring larynx movement using the thyroumbrometer. *Journal of Phonetics, 2,* 327–335.

Fant, G. (1956). On the predictability of formant levels and spectrum envelopes from formant frequencies. In *For Roman Jakobson.* The Hague, Netherlands: Mouton, 109–120.

Fant, G. (1960). *Acoustic theory of speech production.* The Hague, Netherlands: Mouton.

Fant, G. (1962). Formant bandwidth data. *Speech Transmission Laboratory Quarterly Progress and Status Report 1,* Royal Institute of Technology, Stockholm, 1–3.

Fant, G. (1972). Vocal tract wall effects, losses, and resonance bandwidths. *Speech Transmission Laboratory Quarterly Progress and Status Report 2-3,* Royal Institute of Technology, Stockholm, 28–52.

Fant, G. (1973a). *Speech sounds and features.* Cambridge, MA: MIT Press.

Fant, G. (1973b). Stops in CV-syllables. In G. Fant, *Speech sounds and features.* Cambridge, MA: MIT Press, 110–139.

Fant, G. (1979). Glottal source and excitation analysis. *Speech Transmission Laboratory Quarterly Progress and Status Report 1,* Royal Institute of Technology, Stockholm, 85–107.

Fant, G. (1980). The relations between area functions and the acoustic signal. *Phonetica,* 55–86.

Fant, G. (1982a). Preliminaries to analysis of the human voice source. *Speech Transmission Laboratory Quarterly Progress and Status Report 4,* Royal Institute of Technology, Stockholm, 1–27.

Fant, G. (1982b). The voice source—Acoustic modeling. *Speech Transmission Laboratory Quarterly Progress and Status Report 4*, Royal Institute of Technology, Stockholm, 28–48.

Fant, G., K. Ishizaka, J. Lindqvist, and J. Sundberg (1972). Subglottal formants. *Speech Transmission Laboratory Quarterly Progress Report 1*, Royal Institute of Technology, Stockholm, 1–12.

Fant, G., and A. Kruckenberg (1989). Preliminaries to the study of Swedish prose reading and reading style. *Speech Transmission Laboratory Quarterly Progress and Status Report 2*, Royal Institute of Technology, Stockholm.

Fant, G., and J. Liljencrants (1979). Perception of vowels with truncated intraperiod decay envelopes. *Speech Transmission Laboratory Quarterly Progress and Status Report 1*, Royal Institute of Technology, Stockholm, 79–84.

Fant, G., J. Liljencrants, and Q. G. Lin (1985). A four-parameter model of glottal flow. *Speech Transmission Laboratory Quarterly Progress and Status Report 4*, Royal Institute of Technology, Stockholm, 1–13.

Fant, G., and Q. Lin (1987). Glottal source—Vocal tract acoustic interaction. *Speech Transmission Laboratory Quarterly Progress and Status Report 1*, Royal Institute of Technology, Stockholm, 13–27.

Fant, G., L. Nord, and P. Branderud (1976). A note on the vocal tract wall impedance. *Speech Transmission Laboratory Quarterly Progress and Status Report 4*, Royal Institute of Technology, Stockholm, 13–20.

Feldtkeller, R., and E. Zwicker (1956). *Das Ohr als Nachrichtenempfänger*. Stuttgart: S. Hirzel Verlag.

Fink, B. R. (1975). *The human larynx: A functional study*. New York: Raven Press.

Fink, B. R., and R. J. Demarest (1978). *Laryngeal biomechanics*. Cambridge MA: Harvard University Press.

Finkelhor, B. K., I. R. Titze, and P. Durham (1987). The effect of viscosity changes in the vocal folds on the range of oscillation. *Journal of Voice*, 1, 320–325.

Flanagan, J. L. (1955). Difference limen for formant amplitude. *Journal of Speech and Hearing Disorders*, 22, 205–212.

Flanagan, J. L. (1957). A difference limen for vowel formant frequency. *Journal of the Acoustical Society of America*, 27, 613–617.

Flanagan, J. L. (1958). Some properties of the glottal sound source. *Journal of Speech and Hearing Research*, 1, 99–116.

Flanagan, J. L. (1972). *Speech analysis, synthesis, and perception*. Berlin: Springer-Verlag.

Fletcher, H. (1940). Auditory patterns. *Reviews of Modern Physics*, 12, 47–65.

Fletcher, H. (1953). *Speech and hearing in communication*. New York: Van Nostrand.

Folkins, J. W. (1981). Muscle activity for jaw closing during speech. *Journal of Speech and Hearing Research*, 24, 601–615.

Fromkin, V. (1964). Lip positions in American English vowels. *Language and Speech*, 7, 215–225.

Fujimura, O. (1961). Bilabial stop and nasal consonants: A motion picture study and its acoustical implications. *Journal of Speech and Hearing Research*, 4, 233–246.

Fujimura, O., and Y. Kakita (1978). Remarks on quantitative description of the lingual articulation. In B. Lindblom and S. Ohman (eds.), *Frontiers of speech communication research*. London: Academic Press, 17–24.

591   References

Fujimura, O., and J. Lindqvist (1971). Sweep-tone measurements of vocal-tract characteristics. *Journal of the Acoustical Society of America, 49*, 541–558.

Fujisaki, H. (1992). Modeling the process of fundamental frequency contour generation. In Y. Tohkura, E. Vatikiotis-Bateson, and Y. Sagisaka (eds.), *Speech perception, production and linguistic structure*. Amsterdam: IOS Press, 313–326.

Furst, M., and J. L. Goldstein (1982). A cochlear nonlinear transmission-line model compatible with combination tone psychophysics. *Journal of the Acoustical Society of America, 72*, 717–726.

Gauffin, J., and J. Sundberg (1978). Pharyngeal constrictions. *Phonetica, 35*, 157–168.

Geisler, C. D., and S. M. Silkes (1991). Responses of "lower-spontaneous-rate" auditory-nerve fibers to speech syllables presented in noise. II: Glottal-pulse periodicities. *Journal of the Acoustical Society of America, 90*, 3140–3148.

Gobl, C. (1989). A preliminary study of acoustic voice quality correlates. *Speech Transmission Laboratory Quarterly Progress and Status Report 4*, Royal Institute of Technology, Stockholm, 9–22.

Goldstein, M. E. (1976). *Aeroacoustics*. New York: McGraw-Hill.

Goldstein, U. G. (1980). *An articulatory model for the vocal tracts of growing children*. Ph.D. dissertation, Massachusetts Institute of Technology, Cambridge, MA.

Green, D. M. (1976). *An introduction to hearing*. New York: Erlbaum.

Green, D. M., C. R. Mason, and G. Kidd, Jr. (1984). Profile analysis: Critical bands and duration. *Journal of the Acoustical Society of America, 75*, 1163–1167.

Greenwood, D. D. (1961a). Auditory masking and the critical band. *Journal of the Acoustical Society of America, 33*, 484–502.

Greenwood, D. D. (1961b). Critical bandwidth and the frequency coordinates of the basilar membrane. *Journal of the Acoustical Society of America, 33*, 1344–1356.

Guinan, J. J., Jr. (1988). Physiology of the olivocochlear efferents. In J. Syka and R. B. Masterton (eds.), *Auditory pathway, structure and function*. New York: Plenum Press, 253–267.

Haggard, M. (1978). The devoicing of voiced fricatives. *Journal of Phonetics, 6*, 95–102.

Hagiwara, R. (1995). Acoustic realizations of American /r/ as produced by women and men. *Working Papers in Phonetics, No. 90*, University of California at Los Angeles.

Hall, J. L. (1974). Two-tone distortion products in a nonlinear model of the basilar membrane. *Journal of the Acoustical Society of America, 56*, 1818–1828.

Halle, M. (1990). Features. In W. Bright (ed.), *Oxford international encyclopedia of linguistics*. New York: Oxford University Press.

Halle M., and K. N. Stevens (1969). On the feature "advanced tongue root." *MIT Research Laboratory of Electronics Quarterly Progress Report 94*, 209–215.

Halle M., and K. N. Stevens (1971). A note on laryngeal features. *MIT Research Laboratory of Electronics Quarterly Progress Report 101*, 198–213.

Halle, M., and K. N. Stevens (1991a). Knowledge of language and the sounds of speech. In J. Sundberg, L. Nord, and R. Carlson (eds.), *Music, language, speech and brain*. London: Macmillan, 1–19.

Halle, M., and K. N. Stevens (1991b). The postalveolar fricatives of Polish. *Speech Communication Group Working Papers 7*, Research Laboratory of Electronics, Massachusetts Institute of Technology, Cambridge MA, 77–94; also in S. Kiritani, H. Hirose, and H. Fujisaki (eds.), *Speech production and language: In honor of Osamu Fujimura* (1996), Berlin: Mouton de Gruyter, 177–193.

Hanson, H. M. (1995). *Glottal characteristics of female speakers.* Ph. D. dissertation, Harvard University, Cambridge MA.

Hanson, H. M. (1997). Glottal characteristics of female speakers: Acoustic correlates. *Journal of the Acoustical Society of America, 101,* 466–481.

Hattori, S., K. Yamamoto, and O. Fujimura (1958). Nasalization of vowels in relation to nasals. *Journal of the Acoustical Society of America, 30,* 267–274.

Hawkins, J. E., Jr., and S. S. Stevens (1950). The masking of pure tones and of speech by white noise. *Journal of the Acoustical Society of America, 22,* 6–13.

Heinz, J. M. (1956). Fricative consonants. *Acoustics Laboratory Quarterly Report,* October–December, Massachusetts Institute of Technology, Cambridge, MA, 5–7.

Heinz, J. M., and Stevens, K. N. (1965). On the relations between lateral cineradiographs, area functions, and acoustics of speech, In *Proceedings of the Fourth International Congress on Acoustics,* Stuttgart, Vol. 1a, A44.

Hillenbrand, J., L. A. Getty, M. J. Clark, and K. Wheeler (1995). Acoustic characteristics of American English vowels. *Journal of the Acoustical Society of America, 97,* 3099–3111.

Hirano, M. (1975). Phonosurgery: Basic and clinical investigations. *Otologia, 21,* 239–440.

Hirano, M., S. Kurita, and T. Nakashima (1981). The structure of the vocal folds. In K. N. Stevens and M. Hirano (eds.), *Vocal fold physiology.* Tokyo: University of Tokyo Press, 33–41.

Hirano, M., S. Kurita, and T. Nakashima (1983). Growth, development and aging of human vocal folds. In D. M. Bless and J. H. Abbs (eds.), *Vocal fold physiology: Contemporary research and clinical issues.* San Diego: College-Hill Press, 22–43.

Hirsh, I. J. (1959). Auditory perception of temporal order. *Journal of the Acoustical Society of America, 31,* 759–767.

Hixon, T. J. (1966). Turbulent noise sources for speech. *Folia Phoniatrica, 18,* 168–182.

Hixon, T. J. (1987). Respiratory function in speech. In T. J. Hixon (ed.), *Respiratory function in speech and song.* Boston: College-Hill Press, 1–54.

Hixon, T. J., M. D. Goldman, and J. Mead (1973). Kinematics of the chest wall during speech production: Volume displacements of the rib cage, abdomen, and lung. *Journal of Speech and Hearing Research, 16,* 78–115.

Hixon, T. J., J. Mead, and M. D. Goldman (1976). Dynamics of the chest wall during speech production: Function of the thorax, rib cage, diaphragm, and abdomen. *Journal of Speech and Hearing Research, 19,* 297–356.

Hixon, T. J., F. D. Minifie, and C. A. Tait (1967). Correlates of turbulence noise production for speech. *Journal of Speech and Hearing Research, 10,* 133–140.

Hoemeke, K. A., and R. L. Diehl (1994). Perception of vowel height: The role of $F1$–$F0$ distance. *Journal of the Acoustical Society of America, 96,* 661–674.

Hollein, H. (1983). In search of vocal frequency control mechanisms. In D. M. Bless and J. H. Abbs (eds.), *Vocal fold physiology: Contemporary research and clinical issues.* San Diego: College-Hill Press, 361–367.

Holmberg, E. B., R. E. Hillman, and J. S. Perkell (1988). Glottal airflow and transglottal air pressure measurements for male and female speakers in soft, normal, and loud voice. *Journal of the Acoustical Society of America, 84,* 511–529.

Holmberg, E. B., R. E. Hillman, J. S. Perkell, P. C. Guiod, and S. L. Goldman (1995). Comparisons among aerodynamic, electroglottographic, and acoustic spectral measures of female voice. *Journal of Speech and Hearing Research, 38,* 1212–1223.

Honda, K., and O. Fujimura (1991). Intrinsic vowel F0 and phrase-final F0 lowering: Phonological vs. biological explanations. In J. Gauffin and B. Hammarberg (eds.), *Vocal fold physiology Acoustic, perceptual, and physiological aspects of voice mechanisms.* San Diego: Singular, 149–157.

Honda, K., H. Hirai, and N. Kusakawa (1993). Modeling vocal tract organs based on MRI and EMG observations and its implication on brain function. *Annual Bulletin No. 27, Research Institute of Logopedics and Phoniatrics,* University of Tokyo, 37–49.

House, A. S. (1961). On vowel duration in English. *Journal of the Acoustical Society of America, 33,* 1174–1178.

House, A. S., and G. Fairbanks (1953). The influence of consonantal environment upon the secondary acoustical characteristics of vowels. *Journal of the Acoustical Society of America, 25,* 105–113.

House, A. S., and K. N. Stevens (1958). Estimation of formant bandwidths from measurements of transient response of the vocal tract. *Journal of Speech and Hearing Research, 1,* 309–315.

Hudspeth, A. J., and V. S. Markin (1994). The ear's gears: Mechanoelectrical transduction by hair cells. *Physics Today 47,* No. 2, 22–28.

Ishizaka, K., and J. L. Flanagan (1972). Synthesis of voiced sounds from a two-mass model. *Bell System Technical Journal, 51,* 1233–1268.

Ishizaka, K., J. C. French, and J. L. Flanagan (1975). Direct determination of vocal tract wall impedance. *IEEE Transactions on Acoustics, Speech, and Signal Processing, ASSP-23,* 370–373.

Ishizaka, K., and M. Matsudaira (1968). What makes the vocal cords vibrate? In *Proceedings of Sixth International Congress of Acoustics,* Tokyo, B1–3.

Ishizaka, K., and M. Matsudaira (1972). Fluid mechanical considerations of vocal cord vibration. *SCRL Monograph 8,* Speech Communication Research Laboratory, Santa Barbara, CA.

Ishizaka, K., M. Matsudaira, and T. Kaneko (1976). Input acoustic-impedance measurement of the subglottal system. *Journal of the Acoustical Society of America, 60,* 190–197.

Isshiki, N. (1964). Regulatory mechanism of voice intensity variation. *Journal of Speech and Hearing Research, 7,* 17–29.

Isshiki, N., and R. Ringel (1964). Air flow during the production of selected consonants. *Journal of Speech and Hearing Research, 7,* 233–244.

Jakobson, R., C. G. M. Fant, and M. Halle (1952). Preliminaries to speech analysis: The distinctive features and their correlates. *Acoustics Laboratory Technical Report 13,* Massachusetts Institute of Technology, Cambridge MA; reprinted by MIT Press, Cambridge MA, 1967.

Johansson, C., J. Sundberg, H. Wilbrand, and C. Ytterbergh (1983). From sagittal distance to area: A study of transverse, cross-sectional area in the pharynx by means of computer tomography. *Speech Transmission Laboratory Quarterly Progress and Status Report 4,* Royal Institute of Technology, Stockholm, 39–49.

Johnson, D. H. (1980). The relationship between spike rate and synchrony in responses of auditory-nerve fibers to single tones. *Journal of the Acoustical Society of America, 68,* 1115–1122.

Kakita, Y., M. Hirano, and K. Ohmaru (1981). Physical properties of the vocal fold tissue: Measurement on excised larynges. In K. N. Stevens and M. Hirano (eds.), *Vocal fold physiology.* Tokyo: University of Tokyo Press, 377–397.

Kaneko, T., T. Masuda, A. Shimada, H. Suzuki, K. Hayasaki, and K. Komatsu (1987). Resonance characteristics of the human vocal fold in vivo and in vitro by impulse excitation. In T. Baer, C. Sasaki, and K. Harris (eds.), *Laryngeal function in phonation and respiration,* Boston: College-Hill Press, 349–365.

Kent, R. D., and K. L. Moll (1972). Cinefluorographic analyses of selected lingual consonants. *Journal of Speech and Hearing Research, 15,* 453–473.

Kewley-Port, D., and C. S. Watson (1994). Formant-frequency discrimination for isolated English vowels. *Journal of the Acoustical Society of America, 95,* 485–496.

Keyser, S. K., and K. N. Stevens (1994). Feature geometry and the vocal tract. *Phonology, 11,* 207–236.

Kiang, N. Y.-S., and E. C. Moxon (1972). Physiological considerations in artificial stimulation of the inner ear. *Annals of Otology, Rhinology, and Laryngology, 81,* 714–730.

Kiang, N. Y.-S., and E. C. Moxon (1974). Tails on tuning curves of auditory-nerve fibers. *Journal of the Acoustical Society of America, 55,* 620–630.

Kiang, N. Y.-S., T. Watanabe, E. C. Thomas, and L. F. Clark (1965). *Discharge patterns of single fibers in the cat's auditory nerve.* Cambridge, MA: MIT Press.

Kingston, J., and R. L. Diehl (1994). Phonetic knowledge. *Language, 70,* 419–453.

Klatt, D. H., and L. C. Klatt (1990). Analysis, synthesis, and perception of voice quality variations among female and male talkers. *Journal of the Acoustical Society of America, 87,* 820–857.

Klatt, D. H., K. N. Stevens, and J. Mead (1968). Studies of articulatory activity and airflow during speech. *Annals of the New York Academy of Sciences, 155,* 42–55.

Koopmans-van Beinum, F. J. (1980). *Vowel contrast reduction: An acoustic and perceptual study of Dutch vowels in various speech conditions.* Ph.D. dissertation, University of Amsterdam.

Krakow, R. A. (1993). Nonsegmental influences on velum movement patterns: Syllables, sentences, stress, and speaking rate. In M. K. Huffman and R. A. Krakow (eds.), *Phonetics and phonology*, vol. 5: *Nasals, nasalization, and the velum.* San Diego: Academic Press, 87–116.

Krause, J. C. (1995). *The effects of speaking rate and speaking mode on intelligibility.* Unpublished SM thesis, Massachusetts Institute of Technology, Cambridge, MA.

Kringlebotn, M., and T. Gundersen (1985). Frequency characteristics of the middle ear. *Journal of the Acoustical Society of America, 77,* 159–164.

Kuehn, D. P., and K. L. Moll (1976). A cineradiographic study of VC and CV articulatory velocities. *Journal of Phonetics, 4,* 303–320.

Kurita, S., K. Nagata, and M. Hirano (1983). A comparative study of the larger structure of the vocal fold. In D. M. Bless and J. H. Abbs (eds.), *Vocal fold physiology: Contemporary research and clinical issues.* San Diego: College-Hill Press, 1–21.

Ladefoged, P. (1962). Subglottal activity during speech. In *Proceedings of the Fourth International Congress of Phonetic Sciences.* The Hague, Netherlands: Mouton: 73–91.

Ladefoged, P. (1963). Some physiological parameters in speech. *Language and Speech, 6,* 109–119.

Ladefoged, P. (1968). Linguistic aspects of respiratory phenomena. *Annals of the New York Academy of Sciences, 155,* 141–151.

Ladefoged, P., and I. Maddieson (1996). *The sounds of the world's languages.* Cambridge MA: Blackwell.

Ladefoged, P., and A. Traill (1994). Clicks and their accompaniments. *Journal of Phonetics, 22,* 33–64.

Landahl, M. T. (1975). Wave mechanics of boundary layer turbulence and noise. *Journal of the Acoustical Society of America, 57,* 824–831.

Lee, R. C., E. H. Frank, A. J. Grodzinsky, and D. K. Roylance, (1981). Oscillatory compressional behavior of articular cartilage and its associated electromechanical properties. *Journal of Biomechanical Engineering, 103,* 280–292.

Liberman, M. C. (1978). Auditory-nerve responses from cats raised in a low-noise chamber. *Journal of the Acoustical Society of America, 63,* 442–455.

Liljencrants, J. (1985). *Speech synthesis with a reflection-type line analog.* D.Sc. thesis, Royal Institute of Technology, Stockholm.

Liljencrants, J. (1991). A translating and rotating mass model of the vocal folds. *Speech Transmission Laboratory Quarterly Progress and Status Report 1,* Royal Institute of Technology, Stockholm, 1–18.

Liljencrants, J. (1994). Control of voice quality in a glottal model. In O. Fujimura and M. Hirano (eds.), *Vocal fold physiology: Voice quality control.* San Diego: Singular, 97–112.

Liljencrants, J., and B. Lindblom (1972). Numerical simulation of vowel quality systems: The role of perceptual contrast. *Language, 48,* 839–862.

Lin, Q. (1987). Nonlinear interaction in voice production. *Speech Transmission Laboratory Quarterly Progress Status Report 1,* Royal Institute of Technology, Stockholm, 1–12.

Lin, Q. (1990). *Speech production theory and articulatory speech synthesis.* Ph.D. thesis, Department of Speech Communication and Music Acoustics, Royal Institute of Technology, Stockholm.

Lindau, M. (1979). The feature expanded. *Journal of Phonetics, 7,* 163–176.

Lindqvist, J., and J. Sundberg (1972). Acoustic properties of the nasal tract. *Speech Transmission Laboratory Quarterly Progress and Status Report 1,* Royal Institute of Technology, Stockholm, 13–17.

Lindsay, P. H., and D. A. Norman (1972). *Human information processing: An introduction to psychology.* New York: Academic Press.

Löfqvist, A., T. Baer, N. S. McGarr, and R. S. Story (1989). The cricothyroid muscle in voicing control. *Journal of the Acoustical Society of America, 85,* 1314–1321.

Maddieson, I. (1984). *Patterns of sounds.* Cambridge, U.K.: Cambridge University Press.

Maeda, S. (1982a). Acoustic cues for vowel nasalization: A simulation study. *Journal of the Acoustical Society of America, 72,* Suppl. 1, 102.

Maeda, S. (1982b). The role of the sinus cavities in the production of nasal vowels. In *Proceedings of ICASSP-82,* Paris, 911–914.

Maeda, S. (1987). On the generation of sound in stop consonants. *Speech Communication Group Working Papers 5,* Massachusetts Institute of Technology, Cambridge MA, 1–14.

Magen, H. S. (1989). *An acoustic study of vowel-to-vowel coarticulation in English.* Ph.D. dissertation, Yale University, New Haven, CT.

Malme, C. I. (1959). Detectability of small irregularities in a broadband noise spectrum. *Research Laboratory of Electronic Quarterly Progress Report 52,* Massachusetts Institute of Technology, Cambridge MA, 139–142.

Manuel, S. Y. (1990). The role of contrast in limiting vowel-to-vowel coarticulation in different languages. *Journal of the Acoustical Society of America, 88,* 1286–1298.

Manuel, S. Y. (1995). Speakers nasalize /ð/ after /n/, but listeners still hear /ð/. *Journal of Phonetics, 23,* 453–476.

Manuel, S. Y., and K. N. Stevens (1989). Acoustic properties of /h/. *Journal of the Acoustical Society of America, 86,* Suppl. 1, S49.

Manuel, S. Y., and K. N. Stevens (1995). Formant transitions: Teasing apart consonant and vowel contributions. In *Proceedings of the ICPHS 95*, Stockholm, Vol. 4, 436–439.

Mårtensson, A. (1968). The functional organization of the intrinsic laryngeal muscles. *Annals of the New York Academy of Sciences, 155*, 91–97.

Mårtensson, A., and C. R. Skoglund (1964). Contraction properties of intrinsic laryngeal muscles. *Acta Physiologica Scandinavica, 60*, 318–336.

Massey, N. S. (1994). *Transients at stop-consonant releases.* Unpublished SM thesis, Massachusetts Institute of Technology, Cambridge, MA.

Maue, W. (1971). *Cartilages, ligaments, and articulations of the adult human larynx.* Ph.D. dissertation, University of Pittsburgh, PA.

McGowan, R. S. (1992). Tongue-tip trills and vocal-tract wall compliance. *Journal of the Acoustical Society of America, 91*, 2903–2910.

Miller, G. A. (1947). Sensitivity to changes in the intensity of white noise and its relation to masking and loudness. *Journal of the Acoustical Society of America, 19*, 609–619.

Miller, G. A. (1948). The perception of short bursts of noise. *Journal of the Acoustical Society of America, 20*, 160–170.

Miller, J. D., C. C. Wier, R. E. Pastore, W. J. Kelly, and R. J. Dooling (1976). Discrimination and labeling of noise-buzz sequences with varying noise-lead times. *Journal of the Acoustical Society of America, 60*, 410–417.

Moll, K. L. (1960). Cinefluorographic techniques in speech research. *Journal of Speech and Hearing Research, 3*, 227–241.

Moll, K. L., and R. G. Daniloff (1971). Investigation of the timing of velar movements during speech. *Journal of the Acoustical Society of America, 50*, 678–684.

Moore, B. C. J. (1978). Psychological tuning curves measured in simultaneous and forward masking. *Journal of the Acoustical Society of America, 63*, 524–532.

Mooshammer, C., P. Hoole, and B. Kühnert (1995). On loops. *Journal of Phonetics, 23*, 3–21.

Morse, P. M. (1948). *Vibration and sound.* New York: McGraw-Hill.

Morse, P. M., and H. Feshbach (1953). *Methods of theoretical physics.* New York: McGraw-Hill.

Mow, V. C., M. H. Holmes, and W. M. Lai, (1984). Fluid transport and mechanical properties of articular cartilage: A review. *Journal of Biomechanics, 17*, 377–394.

Mrayati, M., R. Carré, and B. Guerin (1988). Distinctive regions and modes: A new theory of speech production. *Speech Communication, 7*, 257–286.

Narayanan, S. S., A. A. Alwan, and K. Haker (1995a). An articulatory study of fricative consonants through magnetic resonance imaging. *Journal of the Acoustical Society of America, 98*, 1325–1347.

Narayanan, S. S., A. Alwan, and K. Haker (1995b). An articulatory study of liquid approximants in American English. In *Proceedings of the ICPhS 95*, Stockholm, Vol. 3, 576–579.

Nelson, W. L., J. S. Perkell, and J. R. Westbury (1984). Mandible movements during increasingly rapid articulations of single syllables: Preliminary observations. *Journal of the Acoustical Society of America, 75*, 945–951.

Ohala, J., and P. Ladefoged (1970). Further investigation of pitch regulation in speech. *UCLA Working Papers in Phonetics, 14*, 12–24.

Ohala, J. J., and C. J. Riordan (1980). Passive vocal tract enlargement during voiced stops. *Report of the Phonology Laboratory No. 5*, University of California at Berkeley, 78–88.

Ohde, R. N. (1984). Fundamental frequency as an acoustic correlate of stop consonant voicing. *Journal of the Acoustical Society of America, 75*, 224–230.

Ohman, S. E. G. (1967). Numerical model of coarticulation. *Journal of the Acoustical Society of America, 41*, 310–320.

Painter, C. (1973). Cineradiographic data on the feature "covered" in Twi vowel harmony. *Phonetica 28*, 97–120.

Pastel, L. (1987). *Turbulent noise sources in vocal tract models.* Unpublished SM thesis, Massachusetts Institute of Technology, Cambridge, MA.

Perkell, J. S. (1969). *Physiology of speech production: Results and implications of a quantitative cineradiographic study. Research monograph No. 53.* Cambridge, MA: M.I.T. Press.

Perkell, J. S. (1971). Physiology of speech production: A preliminary study of two suggested revisions of the features specifying vowels. *Research Laboratory of Electronics Quarterly Progress Report No. 102*, Massachusetts Institute of Technology, Cambridge MA, 123–138.

Perkell, J. S., and C.-M. Chiang (1986). Preliminary support for a 'hybrid' model of anticipatory coarticulation. In *Proceedings of the Twelfth International Congress of Acoustics*, Toronto, A3–6.

Perkell, J. S., R. E. Hillman, and E. B. Holmberg (1994). Group differences in measures of voice production and revised values of maximum airflow declination rate. *Journal of the Acoustical Society of America, 96*, 695–698.

Perkell, J. S., and M. L. Matthies (1992). Temporal measures of anticipatory labial coarticulation for the vowel /u/: Within- and cross-subject variability. *Journal of the Acoustical Society of America, 91*, 2911–2925.

Perkell, J. S., M. L. Matthies, M. A. Svirsky, and M. I. Jordan (1995). Goal-based speech motor control: A theoretical framework and some preliminary data. *Journal of Phonetics, 23*, 23–35.

Perkell, J. S., and W. L. Nelson (1982). Articulatory targets and speech motor control: A study of vowel production. In S. Grillner, B. Lindblom, J. Lubker, A. Persson (eds.), *Speech motor control.* New York: Pergamon Press, 187–204.

Perrier, P., L.-J. Boë, and R. Sock (1992). Vocal tract area function estimation from midsagittal dimensions with CT scans and a vocal tract cast: Modeling of the transition with two sets of coefficients. *Journal of Speech and Hearing Research, 35*, 53–67.

Peterson, G. E., and H. Barney (1952). Control methods used in a study of the vowels. *Journal of the Acoustical Society of America, 24*, 175–184.

Peterson, L. C., and B. P. Bogert (1950). A dynamical theory of the cochlea. *Journal of the Acoustical Society of America, 22*, 369–381.

Pickett, J. M. (1980). *The sounds of speech communication.* Baltimore: University Park Press.

Pisoni, D. B. (1977). Identification and discrimination of the relative onset time of two component tones: Implications for voicing perception in stops. *Journal of the Acoustical Society of America, 61*, 1352–1361.

Poort, K. L. (1994). Underlying control strategies for the production of stop consonants. *Journal of the Acoustical Society of America, 95*, No. 5, Pt.2, 2818.

Poort, K. L. (1995). *Stop consonant production: An articulation and acoustic study.* Unpublished SM thesis, Massachusetts Institute of Technology, Cambridge, MA.

Prame, E. (1994). Measurements of the vibrato rate of ten singers. *Journal of the Acoustical Society of America, 96*, 1979–1984.

Proctor, D. F. (1968). The physiological basis of voice training. *Annals of the New York Academy of Sciences, 155*, 208–228.

Rabinowitz, W. M. (1977). *Acoustic-reflex effects on the input admittance and transfer characteristics of the human ear.* Ph.D. dissertation, Massachusetts Institute of Technology, Cambridge, MA.

Rice, D. H., and S. D. Schaefer (1993). *Endoscopic paranasal sinus surgery,* 2nd ed. New York: Raven Press.

Riesz, R. R. (1928). Differential intensity sensitivity of the ear for pure tones. *Physical Review 31,* 867–875.

Rosenberg, A. (1971). Effect of glottal pulse shape on the quality of natural vowels. *Journal of the Acoustical Society of America, 49,* 583–590.

Rothenberg, M. (1968). The breath stream dynamics of simple-released-plosive production.* *Bibliotheca Phonetica No. 6,* Basel: S. Karger.

Rothenberg, M. (1973). A new inverse-filtering technique for deriving the glottal air flow waveform during voicing. *Journal of the Acoustical Society of America, 53,* 1632–1645.

Rothenberg, M. (1981). Acoustic interaction between the glottal source and the vocal tract. In K. N. Stevens and M. Hirano (eds.), *Vocal fold physiology.* Tokyo: University of Tokyo Press, 305–323.

Sachs, M. B., and P. Abbas (1974). Rate vs. level functions for auditory nerve fibers in cats: tone-burst stimuli. *Journal of the Acoustical Society of America, 56,* 1835–1847.

Sachs, M. B., and N. Y. S. Kiang (1968). Two-tone inhibition in auditory-nerve fibers. *Journal of the Acoustical Society of America, 43,* 1120–1128.

Sachs, M. B., and E. D. Young (1979). Encoding of steady-state vowels in the auditory nerve: Representation in terms of discharge rate. *Journal of the Acoustical Society of America, 66,* 470–479.

Sachs, M. B., and E. D. Young (1980). Effects of nonlinearities on speech encoding in the auditory nerve. *Journal of the Acoustical Society of America, 68,* 858–875.

Sagey, E. (1986). *The representation of features and relations in nonlinear phonology.* Ph.D. dissertation, Massachusetts Institute of Technology, Cambridge, MA.

Scharf, B. (1978). Loudness. In E. C. Carterette and M. P. Friedman (eds.), *Handbook of perception*: Vol. 4, *Hearing.,* New York: Academic Press, 187–242.

Scherer, R., and I. R. Titze (1983). Pressure-flow relationships in a model of the laryngeal airway with a diverging glottis. In D. M. Bless and J. H. Abbs (eds.), *Vocal fold physiology: Contemporary research and clinical issues.* San Diego: College-Hill Press, 179–193.

Schroeder, M. R. (1967). Determination of the geometry of the human vocal tract by acoustic measurements. *Journal of the Acoustical Society of America, 41,* 1002–1010.

Schroeder, M. R. (1973). An integrable model for the basilar membrane. *Journal of the Acoustical Society of America, 53,* 429–434.

Scully, C., E. Castelli, E. Brearley, and M. Shirt (1992). Analysis and simulation of a speaker's aerodynamic and acoustic patterns for fricatives. *Journal of Phonetics, 20,* 39–51.

Shadle, C. (1985a). The acoustics of fricative consonants. *RLE Technical Report 506,* Massachusetts Institute of Technology, Cambridge, MA.

Shadle, C. H. (1985b). Intrinsic fundamental frequency of vowels in sentence context. *Journal of the Acoustical Society of America, 78,* 1562–1567.

Shaw, E. (1974). The external ear. In W. Keidel and D. Neff (eds.), *Handbook of sensory physiology. Auditory system,* Vol. 1. Berlin: Springer Verlag, 455–490.

Silkes, S. M., and C. D. Geisler (1991). Responses of "lower-spontaneous-rate" auditory-nerve fibers to speech syllables presented in noise. I: General characteristics. *Journal of the Acoustical Society of America, 90*, 3122–3139.

Sinex, D. G., and L. P. McDonald (1988). Average discharge rate representation of voice onset time in the chinchilla auditory nerve. *Journal of the Acoustical Society of America, 83*, 1817–1827.

Smith, B. L., and A. McLean-Muse (1986). Articulatory movement characteristics of labial consonant productions by children and adults. *Journal of the Acoustical Society of America, 80*, 1321–1328.

Södersten, M., and P. A. Lindestad (1990). Glottal closure and perceived breathiness during phonation in normally speaking subjects. *Journal of Speech and Hearing Research, 33*, 601–611.

Sonninen, A. (1968). The external frame function in the control of pitch in the human voice. *Annals of the New York Academy of Sciences, 155*, 68–89.

Sproat, R., and O. Fujimura (1993). Allophonic variation in English /l/ and its implications for phonetic implementation. *Journal of Phonetics, 21*, 291–311.

Srulovicz, P., and J. L. Goldstein (1983). A central spectrum model: A synthesis of auditory-nerve timing and place cues in nonaural communication of frequency spectrum. *Journal of the Acoustical Society of America, 73*, 1266–1276.

Staelin, D. H., A. W. Morgenthaler, and J. A. Kong (1994). *Electromagnetic waves.* Englewood Cliffs, NJ: Prentice-Hall.

Stevens, K. N. (1952). *The perception of sounds shaped by resonant circuits.* Sc.D. dissertation, Massachusetts Institute of Technology, Cambridge, MA.

Stevens, K. N. (1971). Airflow and turbulence noise for fricative and stop consonants: Static considerations. *Journal of the Acoustical Society of America, 50*, 1180–1192.

Stevens, K. N. (1972). The quantal nature of speech: Evidence from articulatory-acoustic data. In P. B. Denes and E. E. David Jr. (eds.), *Human communication: A unified view.* New York: McGraw Hill, 51–66.

Stevens, K. N. (1977). Physics of laryngeal behavior and larynx models. *Phonetica, 34*, 264–279.

Stevens, K. N. (1985). Evidence for role of acoustic boundaries in the perception of speech sounds. In V. Fromkin (ed.), *Phonetic linguistics.* New York: Academic Press, 243–255.

Stevens, K. N. (1989). On the quantal nature of speech. *Journal of Phonetics, 17*, 3–46.

Stevens, K. N. (1993a). Modelling affricate consonants. *Speech Communication, 13*, 33–43.

Stevens, K. N. (1993b). Models for the production and acoustics of stop consonants. *Speech Communication, 13*, 367–375.

Stevens, K. N., and S. E. Blumstein (1994). Attributes of lateral consonants. *Journal of the Acoustical Society of America, 95*, 2875.

Stevens, K. N., S. E. Blumstein, L. Glicksman, M. Burton, and K. Kurowski (1992). Acoustic and perceptual characteristics of voicing in fricatives and fricative clusters. *Journal of the Acoustical Society of America 91*, 2979–3000.

Stevens, K. N., and H. M. Hanson (1995). Classification of glottal vibration from acoustic measurements. In O. Fujimura and M. Hirano (eds.), *Vocal fold physiology: Voice quality control.* San Diego: Singular, 147–170.

Stevens, K. N., and A. S. House (1963). Perturbation of vowel articulations by consonantal context: An acoustical study. *Journal of Speech and Hearing Research, 6*, 111–128.

Stevens, S. S. (1936). A scale for the measurement of a psychological magnitude: Loudness. *Psychological Review, 43*, 405–416.

Stevens, S. S., and M. Guirao (1967). Loudness functions under inhibition. *Perception and Psychophysics, 2*, 459–465.

Stevens, S. S., and J. Volkmann (1940). The relation of pitch to frequency: A revised scale. *American Journal of Psychology, 53*, 329–353.

Stewart, J. (1967). Tongue root position in Akan vowel harmony. *Phonetica, 16*, 185–204.

Streeter, V. L. (1962). *Fluid mechanics.* New York: McGraw-Hill.

Subtelny, J. D., J. H. Worth, and M. Sakuda (1966). Intraoral pressure and rate of flow during speech. *Journal of Speech and Hearing Research, 9*, 498–518.

Sundberg, J. (1994). Acoustic and psychoacoustic aspects of vocal vibrato. *Speech Transmission Laboratory Quarterly Progress and Status Report 2-3*, Royal Institute of Technology, Stockholm, 45–67.

Sussman, H. M., P. F. MacNeilage, and R. J. Hanson (1973). Labial and mandibular dynamics during the production of bilabial consonants: Preliminary observations. *Journal of Speech and Hearing Research, 16*, 385–396.

Svirsky, M. A., K. N. Stevens, M. L. Matthies, J. Manzella, J. S. Perkell, and R. Wilhelms-Tricarico (1997). Tongue surface displacement during obstruent stop consonants. *Journal of the Acoustical Society of America, 102*, 562–571.

Syrdal, A. K., and H. S. Gopal (1986). A perceptual model of vowel recognition based on the auditory representation of American English vowels. *Journal of the Acoustical Society of America, 79*, 1086–1100.

Tarnoczy, T. von (1971). Das durchschnittliche Energie-Spektrum der Sprache (für sechs Sprachen). *Acustica, 24*, 57–74.

Titze, I. R. (1988). The physics of small-amplitude oscillation of the vocal folds. *Journal of the Acoustical Society of America, 83*, 1536–1552.

Titze, I. (1989). Physiologic and acoustic differences between male and female voices. *Journal of the Acoustical Society of America, 85*, 1699–1707.

Titze, I. R. (1992). Phonation threshold pressure: A missing link in glottal aerodynamics. *Journal of the Acoustical Society of America, 91*, 2926–2935.

Traill, A. (1985). Phonetic and phonological studies of !Xóõ Bushman. *Quellen zur Khoisan-Forschung, 1*, Hamburg: Helmut Buske.

Traill, A. (1994). The perception of clicks in !Xóõ. *Journal of African Languages, 15*, 161–174.

Traunmüller, H. (1981). Perceptual dimensions of openness in vowels. *Journal of the Acoustical Society of America, 69*, 1465–1475.

Upshaw, B. (1992). *Timing of syllables sequences in speech.* Unpublished SB thesis, Massachusetts Institute of Technology, Cambridge, MA.

Van den Berg, J. (1960). An electrical analogue of the trachea, lungs and tissues. *Acta Physiologica et Pharmacologica Néerlandica, 9*, 361–385.

Van den Berg, J., J. T. Zantema, and P. Doornenbal, Jr. (1957). On the air resistance and the Bernoulli effect of the human larynx. *Journal of the Acoustical Society of America, 29*, 626–631.

Verdolini-Marston, K., I. R. Titze, and D. Drucker (1990). Changes in phonation threshold pressure with induced conditions of hydration. *Journal of Voice, 4*, 142–151.

Vogten, L. L. M. (1974). Pure-tone masking; a new result from a new method. In E. Zwicker and E. Terhardt (eds.), *Facts and models in hearing*. New York: Springer Verlag, 142–155.

Vogten, L. L. M. (1978a). Low-level pure-tone masking: A comparison of "tuning curves" obtained with simultaneous and forward masking. *Journal of the Acoustical Society of America, 63*, 1520–1527.

Vogten, L. L. M. (1978b). Simultaneous pure-tone masking: The dependence of masking asymmetries on intensity. *Journal of the Acoustical Society of America, 63*, 1509–1519.

Wegel, R. L., and C. E. Lane (1924). The auditory masking of one pure tone by another and its possible relation to the dynamics of the inner ear. *Physical Review, 23*, 266–285.

Westbury, J. R. (1983). Enlargement of the supraglottal cavity and its relation to stop consonant voicing. *Journal of the Acoustical Society of America, 73*, 1322–1336.

Westbury, J. R., and J. Dembowski (1993). Articulatory kinematics of normal diadochokinetic performance. *Annual Bulletin No. 27, Research Institute of Logopedics and Phoniatrics*, University of Tokyo, 13–36.

Westbury, J. R., M. Hashi, and M. J. Lindstrom (1995). Differences among speakers in articulation of American English /r/: An x-ray microbeam study. In *Proceedings of the ICPhS95*, Stockholm, Vol. 4, 50–57.

Wilde, L. F. (1995). *Analysis and synthesis of fricative consonants*. Ph. D. dissertation, Massachusetts Institute of Technology, Cambridge, MA.

Wodicka, G. R., A. M. Lam and V. Bhargara (1993). Acoustic impedance of the maternal abdomen. *Journal of the Acoustical Society of America, 94*, 13–18.

Wood, S. (1979). A radiographic analysis of constriction locations for vowels. *Journal of Phonetics 7*, 25–43.

Yost, W. A., and D. W. Nielson (1977). *Fundamentals of hearing: An introduction*. New York: Holt, Rinehart & Winston.

Young, E. D., and M. B. Sachs (1979). Representation of steady-state vowels in the temporal aspects of the discharge patterns of populations of auditory-nerve fibers. *Journal of the Acoustical Society of America, 66*, 1381–1403.

Zemlin, W. R. (1988). *Speech and hearing science: Anatomy and physiology*, 3rd ed. Englewood Cliffs NJ: Prentice-Hall.

Zwicker, E. (1975). Scaling. In W. Keidel and D. Neff (eds.), *Handbook of sensory physiology. Auditory system*, Vol. 3, Berlin: Springer Verlag, 401–448.

Zwicker, E., G. Flottorp, and S. S. Stevens (1957). Critical bandwidth in loudness summation. *Journal of the Acoustical Society of America, 29*, 548–557.

Zwicker, E., and E. Terhardt (1980). Analytical expressions for critical-band rate and critical bandwidth as a function of frequency. *Journal of the Acoustical Society of America, 68*, 1523–1525.

Zwislocki, J. (1950). Theory of the acoustical action of cochlea. *Journal of the Acoustical Society of America, 22*, 778–784.

Zwislocki, J. (1965). Analysis of some auditory characteristics. In R. D. Luce, R. R. Bush, and E. Galanter (eds.), *Handbook of mathematical psychology*, Vol. 3, New York: Wiley, 1–97.

Zwislocki, J. (1981). Sound analysis in the ear: A history of discoveries. *American Scientist, 69*, 184–192.

Index

Quantal theory, 148

Radiation characteristic, 67, 127–128, 199–200
  directional characteristic, 199–200
  from vocal tract walls, 200–202
Radiation impedance, 153
Resonators, excitation of
  by glottal noise source, 171–175
  by periodic glottal source, 168–170
  principles, 167–168
  by sources above the glottis, 175–187
  by transients, 184–187
Respiration, 1–5
  dynamics of, 49–51
  equivalent circuit, 4, 49
  kinematics of, 40, 41
Retroflex liquid consonants, 535–543. *See also* Liquids
  bunched tongue blade, 540
  examples, 535, 541–544
  formant frequencies, 544
  model for, 536
  spectrum shape, 537–539
Reynolds number, 28, 29, 34, 35
Rounding. *See* Lips

Sinuses, nasal, 19–20, 189, 315
Source-filter theory, 128–130
Standing waves, 139–140
Stop consonants, unaspirated. *See also* Labial stop consonants; Alveolar stop consonants; Velar stop consonants
  acoustic models, 146–148
  aerodynamic models, 51–53, 113–115, 324–326, 331
  airflows and pressures, 331–334
  auditory nerve responses, 223
  first-formant transitions, 334–340
  release mechanisms, 118, 329
  release rates, 44–48, 326
Stop consonants, voiceless aspirated, 451–465. *See also* Aspiration
  aerodynamic model, 452–453
  airflow, 453–456
  examples, 461–464
  noise sources, 457–460
  noise spectra, 460–461
  voicing onset, 455–458
Subglottal cavities
  acoustic properties, 165n, 196–197, 438–440
  effect on aspirated consonants, 437–440

effect on vowels, 196–198, 299–303
  model of, 66, 91–92, 197, 438
Subglottal pressure, range for speech, 35, 71
Suction. *See* Clicks
Supraglottal airways
  aerodynamic model, 51–53, 326, 331, 453
  anatomy, 15–27
Syllabic nasal, 569, 580n

Thorax, 3
Thyroid cartilage, 6
Tongue, 21
  kinematics, 42–43, 47–48
  volume, 24
Tongue blade, movements, 46–47, 326
Tongue body
  features, 250–252
  movements, 43, 236
  position for vowels, 261, 269, 271
Tongue root, 15, 269, 468
  advanced, 251, 295
  constricted, 251
  movements, 42–43
Trachea, 1. *See also* Subglottal cavities
Transfer function of vocal tract
  all-pole form for vowels, 130–135
  effects of multiple paths, 195–196
  effects of side branch, 194–195
  general form, 130
Transient sources, 117–121
  model for, 117
  spectrum of, 120
  for stop consonants, 348
Turbulence noise sources. *See also* Aspiration
  dependence on flow, dimensions, 103
  dipole source, 102–104
  at glottis, 102, 108–109, 115–116, 171–175, 347–348, 428–436, 442–450, 457–460, 477, 577
  model of, 102
  monopole source, 106–107
  noise bursts for stop consonants, 112–115, 347–348
  simultaneous with glottal vibration, 115–116
  sources at two constrictions, 108–112
  spectrum of source, 104, 107
Tympanic membrane, 204–205

Uvula, 21

Velar stop consonants, 365–377
  examples, 372–375